T0230241

Lecture Notes in Computer Science 1169

Edited by G. Goos, J. Hartmanis and J. van Leeuwen

Advisory Board: W. Brauer D. Gries J. Stoer

Springer
Berlin
Heidelberg
New York
Barcelona
Budapest
Hong Kong
London
Milan
Paris
Santa Clara
Singapore
Tokyo

Manfred Broy Stephan Merz
Katharina Spies (Eds.)

Formal
Systems Specification

The RPC-Memory Specification
Case Study

Springer

Series Editors

Gerhard Goos, Karlsruhe University, Germany

Juris Hartmanis, Cornell University, NY, USA

Jan van Leeuwen, Utrecht University, The Netherlands

Volume Editors

Manfred Broy
Stephan Merz
Katharina Spies
Technische Universität München, Institut für Informatik
Arcisstr. 21, D-80290 München, Germany
E-mail: {broy/merz/spies}@informatik.tu-muenchen.de

Cataloging-in-Publication data applied for

Die Deutsche Bibliothek - CIP-Einheitsaufnahme

Formal systems specification : the RPC-memory specification case study / Manfred Broy ...
(ed.). - Berlin ; Heidelberg ; New York ; Barcelona ; Budapest ; Hong Kong ; London ; Milan ;
Paris ; Santa Clara ; Singapore ; Tokyo : Springer, 1996
(Lecture notes in computer science ; Vol. 1169)
ISBN 3-540-61984-4
NE: Broy, Manfred [Hrsg.]; GT

CR Subject Classification (1991): C.2.4, D.2.1, D.2.4, D.2.10, F.3.1

ISSN 0302-9743
ISBN 3-540-61984-4 Springer-Verlag Berlin Heidelberg New York

Typesetting: Camera-ready by author
SPIN 10549153   06/3142 – 5 4 3 2 1 0   Printed on acid-free paper

Preface

The growing interest in a scientifically based method for the specification, refinement, implementation, and verification of distributed, concurrent, interacting systems is caused by the wide areas of their applications. These include operating systems, computer networks, telecommunications, wide-area nets, such as the Internet or the World Wide Web, and all kinds of reactive systems embedded in technical devices such as in the automotive and avionics industries. Other typical applications are business applications and hardware/software codesign. New applications are emerging rapidly. As it turned out in the 1970's, providing good methods, techniques, models, and notations for system development is not a trivial task at all. Therefore the area of the formal foundation of the development of concurrent interacting systems has attracted many researchers since the stimulating work by Edsger Dijkstra, Tony Hoare, and others.

The subject of distributed interactive systems also leads to intricate theoretical problems, which have stimulating relationships to many areas of mathematics, logics, and electrical engineering. Not surprisingly, some of the work in these areas became more and more focused on isolated problems rather separated from the original motivation, namely to provide a scientifically well-founded and practically applicable development method that includes specification, refinement, and verification. A second problem is that over the years a large and confusing variety of different approaches have been developed. This richness, reflecting the large amount of creativity and new ideas of researchers, provides us with an overwhelming variety of aspects for the design and the analysis of systems. On one hand, this is good, since it gives a richer source of material on which practical techniques could be based. Unfortunately, this can be confusing for practical engineers who are interested in improving their methods by providing formal foundations. Even for the more research-oriented engineers in that area, it is not easy to keep track of all the different approaches and to understand their advantages and disadvantages.

Case studies can provide a basis for comparing, relating, and evaluating various approaches. There have been several actions in the past to provide case studies and to compare different methods on the basis of these case studies. Some of them provided a variety of different cases for the application. As a result, for every case study only a small number of approaches were applied. Therefore the comparison between a large number of methods was not supported. In another experiment, the case study was rather large, so not too many solutions were presented due to the overhead needed to work out the case study.

But even in these cases, it became clear that case studies provide a very valuable opportunity to improve our possibilities to compare and further develop our methods. First of all, they provide a real basis to evaluate approaches. And, more than the examples presented by the various methods by themselves, they really test how far a method is able to adapt to particular requirements and methodological needs. More important, there is another remarkable effect. The test cases guide the attention of the researchers in the applicability of their methods. As a result of several case studies, researchers had to admit that in their current form their methods were actually not applicable and were forced to extend and modify their theories, notations, and techniques. This way, an interesting feedback was set up between the attempt to provide a solution to a case study and the further development of the methods. Obviously, case studies help to focus the attention of the researchers onto the critical issues in the development task.

Based on these considerations I suggested to Leslie Lamport in fall 1993 that we again do an experiment by providing a further case study. For a fair comparison, of course, case studies should be sufficiently large to meet the actual requirements of practical applications. Moreover a variety of case studies is needed since the different approaches may be better suited for different areas of applications and therefore a comparison on the basis of only one specific case study is certainly not fair. After several meetings and discussions, Leslie and I decided to provide just one case study and to choose its size to be not too large, however, to make sure that several steps of development were part of the exercise. The reason was that we were interested in looking not only at the pure specification task but also at refinement and verification.

Finally, we decided to choose an example that is typical for the area of operating systems and hardware applications, at least on the logical level of hardware architecture, and to include in this example a number of typically important issues such as failures, fairness, and real time. Leslie wrote a first version of the problem description and, after a few iterations, the problem statement was sent out together with the invitations to a workshop in Dagstuhl.

The workshop, which took place in September 1994, was very stimulating. Originally, we were afraid that after two days the participants would be completely fed up with the problem. As it turned out, this was not the case at all. On the contrary, new aspects of the problem were discovered and discussed. Striking was the fact that for many of the presented solutions, the ideas on modeling the problem and solution proved more important than the chosen methods and notations. Correspondingly, the individual methods were often just used as a representation vehicle and did not govern the basic specification, refinement, and verification ideas. This showed to a large extent that the notation and theoretical basis should not be over-emphasized and that the methods and techniques to find good ideas for modeling, representing, and refining systems should also attract enough attention.

After the workshop, we went through several iterations to collect written versions of the presented solutions. We went through two stages of a careful cross-refereeing process and finally came to the text presented here.

After many discussions on the issue of providing a careful comparison and evaluation of the written solutions we very modestly decided to include only a short synopsis paper in this volume in which the approaches were roughly explained and related. Clearly much more work can and needs to be done here. However, being involved in some of the solutions ourselves, it would not have been fair for us to draw too far-reaching conclusions. So we leave it to the reader and to future activities to provide a more careful analysis and comparison of the results of our experiment.

Looking back at the whole activity, I consider this experiment a success and a helpful contribution to the research community as well as to the engineering community for those interested in experimenting with formally based approaches to the design of systems.

It is a pleasure to thank the people who helped put this experiment forward. My thanks go to Leslie Lamport for an effective and stimulating cooperation, to Schloss Dagstuhl for providing an excellent place for the workshop, to Stephan Merz who helped a lot in organizing the workshop and carefully read the contributions in the refereeing process, and to Katharina Spies who helped in many ways in correspondence with the authors and who showed an admirable patience with all the little problems and difficulties that arose in the refereeing process. Finally my thanks go to Springer-Verlag who helped in a very gentle and efficient way to publish this experiment as a volume in the Lecture Notes in Computer Science.

Munich, July 1996   Manfred Broy

Acknowledgement

There is no book without authors. This is especially true for this collection of articles since we misused authors as reviewers for the contributions. We did this move since we considered the authors of articles as the best experts of the specified problem. Moreover, we were interested in an interaction between the proponents of the quite different methods. For all these reasons, we decided to establish a cross-refereeing process.

It is our pleasure to thank all the reviewers

M. Abadi,
E. Astesiano,
D. Barnard,
E. Best,
J. Cuéllar,
R. Gotzhein,
J. Hooman,
H. Hungar,
B. Jonsson,
J.N. Kok,
R. Kurki-Suonio,
L. Lamport,
K. Larsen,
S. Merz,
O. Müller,
M. Nielsen,
G. Reggio,
M. Rinderspacher,
B. Steffen,
K. Stølen,
K. Sunesen,
C. Weise

for their prompt and precise work in the last few months. Only because of their readiness for fruitful and mostly peaceful discussions and cooperation with the authors we can present contributions of selected quality in this collection. We are especially grateful for the cross-refereeing efforts to prepare assessments of the articles which were very helpful in the preparation of the synopsis you find in this volume.

Table of Contents

Manfred Broy, Leslie Lamport:
The RPC-Memory Specification Problem – Problem Statement   1

1 The Procedure Interface 1

2 A Memory Component 1

3 Implementing the Memory 2
   3.1 The RPC Component 2
   3.2 The Implementation 3

4 Implementing the RPC Component 3
   4.1 A Lossy RPC 3
   4.2 The RPC Implementation 4

Manfred Broy, Stephan Merz, Katharina Spies:
The RPC-Memory Case Study: A Synopsis 5

1 About this Book 5

2 The Problem 6

3 The Solutions 8
   3.1 Criteria for Classification 8
   3.2 Reviews of Individual Contributions 11

4 Conclusion 19

Martín Abadi, Leslie Lamport, Stephan Merz:
A TLA Solution to the RPC-Memory Specification Problem . 21

Introduction 21

1 The Procedure Interface 22
   1.1 The Module and its Parameters 23
   1.2 State Functions, State Predicates, and Actions 24
   1.3 Temporal Formulas 25

2 A Memory Component 27
   2.1 The Parameters 27
   2.2 The Memory Specification 28
   2.3 Solution to Problem 1 34

3 Implementing the Memory 36
   3.1 The RPC Component 36
       The Parameters Module 37
       Problem 2: The RPC Component's Specification 39
   3.2 The Implementation 41

The Memory Clerk 41
The Implementation Proof 42

4 Implementing the RPC Component 52
4.1 A Lossy RPC 53
4.2 The RPC Implementation 54
The RPC Clerk 54
The Implementation Proof 56

References 63

Index 65

Egidio Astesiano, Gianna Reggio:

A Dynamic Specification of the RPC-Memory Problem 67

1 Introduction 67

2 Dynamic Specifications (DSPECs) 69
2.1 The formal model for dynamic systems 69
2.2 Dynamic structures 70
2.3 A logic for DSPECs 71
2.4 Dynamic specifications 74

3 A Development Process for Dynamic Systems 75
3.1 Development process 75
3.2 How to write a DSPEC 76
Simple dynamic system 77
Concurrent dynamic system 78
3.3 Specification presentation 79

4 MC Requirement Specification (PHASE 1) 79
Natural description 79
Border determination 79
Basic data structures 79
Interactions 81
States 81
Activity 82
Shadow spots 84

5 The Reusable Specification of RPC 85
The acceptable actual parameters 85
Interactions 86
States 87
Activity 87

6 MC Development (First Step of PHASE 2) 89
Natural description 89
Basic data structures 90
Components of MC 93

The reliable memory component RMC 93

The remote procedure caller RPC 93

The clerk CLERK 94

Interactions 94

States 95

Activity 95

Interactions (of MC) 98

States (of MC) 98

Activity (of MC) 99

Correctness justification 102

7 Discussing our Solution 104

Eike Best:
**A Memory Module Specification Using Composable
High-Level Petri Nets** 109

1 Introduction 109

2 The M-net Model 110

2.1 Definition of M-nets 110

2.2 Transition rule and unfolding 112

2.3 Composition operations 114

3 Behavioural Notions 117

3.1 Occurrence sequences and permutations 117

3.2 Collapsing transitions 119

3.3 Implementation relation 120

4 Memory Specification 123

4.1 Notation 123

4.2 Reliable and unreliable memory 124

5 Memory Implementation 130

5.1 The *RPC* module 131

5.2 The implementation 133

5.3 Main result 135

5.4 Progress and fairness 137

6 A Lossy Remote Procedure Call Component 139

6.1 Time M-nets 140

6.2 Lossy *RPC* module 140

7 Discussion 143

7.1 In retrospect 143

7.2 Answers to [6] 145

7.3 Safety and liveness specifications 146

A Proofs 148

Johan Blom, Bengt Jonsson:
  Constraint Oriented Temporal Logic Specification 161

  1 Introduction 161

  2 Temporal Logic 163
    2.1 Syntax and Informal Semantics 163

  3 Semantics 164

  4 Using LTL to Specify Concurrent Systems 165
    4.1 Specification of State Changes 165
    4.2 State transition diagrams 166
    4.3 Specifying Components 167
    4.4 Combining components 168

  5 Overall Structure of the Specification 168

  6 The Memory Cells 169

  7 The Memory Interface 171
    7.1 Unreliable Memory Interface 171
    7.2 Reliable Memory Interface 174
    7.3 Solution to Problem 1 174

  8 Problem 2 – The RPC Component 176
    8.1 Solution to Problem 2 177

  9 Problem 3 – The Clerk Component 177
    9.1 Solution to Problem 3 180

Manfred Broy:
  **A Functional Solution to the RPC-Memory Specification
  Problem** 183

  1 Introduction 183

  2 The Basic System Model 184

  3 Basic Message Sets Involved 186

  4 The Unreliable and the Reliable Memory Component 187

  5 The Remote Procedure Call Component 191

  6 Implementation with the Help of a Clerk 193

  7 The Composed System 194

  8 Specification of the Lossy RPC Component 195

  9 A Clerk for the Lossy RPC Component 196

  10 Composing the Clerk and the Lossy RPC Component 197

  11 Conclusion 197

A Mathematical Basis 198

B State Transition Specification of the Memory Component . . 200

C A Trace Solution to the Memory Specification Problem . . . 202

D Proof of the Verification Conditions 204

Jorge Cuéllar, Dieter Barnard, Martin Huber:
A Solution Relying on the Model Checking of Boolean
Transition Systems 213

0 Introduction 213

1 The Procedure Interface 215
   1.1 Data types 215
   1.2 Interfaces in TLT 216

2 A Memory Component 220
   2.1 The Memory Specification 222
   2.2 The Server Specification 223
   2.3 Result and UserConnector Modules 225
   2.4 Conjunction of Modules 226
   2.5 Solution to Problem 1(a)(i): 228
   2.6 The Reliable Server Specification 228
   2.7 The Refinement of Server 229

3 A RPC Component 229
   3.1 The RPC Specification 230
   3.2 The RPC Implementation 232
   3.3 The Refinement of Server 234

4 A Lossy RPC Component 235
   4.1 Timed Instructions 235
   4.2 The Lossy RPC Specification 237
   4.3 The Supervising Clerk 240
   4.4 Proof of the Real-time Property in Problem 5(b) 241

5 Conclusion 242

A An Introduction to TLT 244
   A.1 Concrete States and Transitions 244
   A.2 Boolean Algebras 244
   A.3 Boolean Transition Systems 245
   A.4 Conjunction of Boolean Transition Systems 245
   A.5 Parameterization of Boolean Transition Systems 247
   A.6 Translating the Program Notation 250

Reinhard Gotzhein:

**Applying a Temporal Logic to the RPC-Memory
Specification Problem** 253

1 Introduction 253

2 The Formalism 254
    2.1 Elementary concepts 254
    2.2 System architecture 255
    2.3 System behaviour 256
    2.4 System 262
    2.5 System refinement 262

3 The Memory Component 263
    3.1 A temporal logic 264
    3.2 Specification of the unreliable memory component 265
    3.3 Refinements of the unreliable memory component 269

4 Are Architectural Requirements Important? 271

5 Conclusion 272

Jozef Hooman:

**Using PVS for an Assertional Verification of the
RPC-Memory Specification Problem** 275

0 Introduction 275
    0.1 Formal Background 276
    0.2 Basic PVS Framework 277

1 The Procedure Interface 282

2 A Memory Component 284
    2.1 Basic Properties of Memory 284
    2.2 Inner Memory 285
    Equivalent Formulation of the Inner Memory 286
    2.3 Memory 288
    2.4 Simplifying the Memory Specification 290
    2.5 Reliable Memory 292
    Correctness of Reliable Memory 293
    2.6 Failing Memory 293
    Correctness of Failing Memory 293

3 Implementing the Memory 294
    3.1 The RPC Component 294
    3.2 The Implementation 296
    Correctness of the Implementation 298

4 Implementing the RPC Component 299
    4.1 A Lossy RPC 299

4.2 The RPC Implementation 300
    Correctness of the RPC Implementation 302

5 Concluding Remarks 303

Hardi Hungar:
**Specification and Verification Using a Visual Formalism on
Top of Temporal Logic** 305

1 Specifics of this Solution 305
  1.1 Methodology 305
  1.2 Problem Coverage 306

2 The Implementation Language 308
  2.1 Processes and Programs 308
  2.2 The Semantics of Programs 309

3 The Specification Language 312
  3.1 The Logic 312
  3.2 Symbolic Timing Diagrams 313

4 Specification of the Memory Component 316
  4.1 The Protocol of Calls and Replies 316
  4.2 Specification of the Functional Behavior 318
  4.3 Reliability 321

5 Implementing the Memory 322
  5.1 Specification and Verification of the Protocol 322
  5.2 Specification and Verification of the Functional Behavior 324

6 Verifying an Implementation 328
  6.1 Practical Experiments 335

7 Observations 336
  7.1 Timing Diagrams Versus Temporal Logic 336
  7.2 Adequateness of Temporal Logic 336

8 Conclusion 337

Nils Klarlund, Mogens Nielsen, Kim Sunesen:
A Case Study in Verification Based on Trace Abstractions . . . 341

1 Introduction 341

2 Monadic Second-Order Logic on Strings 345
  2.1 FIDO 347
  2.2 Automated translation and validity checking 349

3 Systems 350
  3.1 Composition 351
  3.2 Implementation 353

4 Relational Trace Abstractions 354
   4.1 Decomposition 355

5 The RPC-Memory Specification Problem 356
   5.1 The procedure interface 356
   5.2 A memory component 357
   Problem 1 362

6 Implementing the Memory 362
   6.1 The RPC component 363
   Problem 2 367
   6.2 The implementation 367
   Problem 3 369

7 Verifying the Implementation 369

Reino Kurki-Suonio:
Incremental Specification with Joint Actions:
The RPC-Memory Specification Problem 375

1 Introduction 375

2 Foundations in TLA 376
   2.1 Correspondence to Canonical TLA Expressions 376
   2.2 Objects and Actions 377
   2.3 Refinement by Superposition 378
   2.4 Combination of Specifications 379
   2.5 Modeling vs. Specification 380

3 Components and Processes 381
   3.1 Component and Process Classes 381
   3.2 Computational Steps by Processes 381

4 Procedure Calls 382
   4.1 Interface Processes 382
   4.2 Calls and Returns 383
   4.3 Notes on the Formalism 386
   4.4 Safety Properties 387
   4.5 Reliable Procedure Calls 387
   4.6 Call Structures 388

5 Memory Components 388
   5.1 Memory Class 388
   5.2 Memory Actions 389
   5.3 Liveness Properties 390
   5.4 Reliable Memory 390
   5.5 Simplified Memory 391

6 The RPC Component 391
   6.1 RPC Component Class 391

6.2 RPC Actions 392

7 Implementing the Memory 393
7.1 RPC-Memory Classes 393
7.2 RPC-Memory Actions 393
7.3 Correctness of the Implementation 394

8 Lossy RPC Component 397
8.1 Superposing Real-Time Properties 397
8.2 Zeno Behaviors 397
8.3 Classes for Lossy RPC 398
8.4 Actions for Lossy RPC 398

9 RPC Implementation 399
9.1 Classes for RPC Implementation 399
9.2 Actions for RPC Implementation 400
9.3 Receivers with Bounded Response Times 401
9.4 Correctness of the Implementation 401

10 Concluding Remarks 402

Kim G. Larsen, Bernhard Steffen, Carsten Weise:
The Methodology of Modal Constraints 405

1 Introduction 405

2 Modal Transition Systems 407

3 Actions, Design Patterns and Projective Views 410
3.1 Abstract Actions 410
3.2 Projective Views 411
3.3 Generalizations 413
3.4 Sufficient Proof Condition 414

4 Specification of the Untimed Problem 415
4.1 Specification of the Memory Component 415
4.2 Specification of the RPC Mechanism 420
4.3 The Clerk 423

5 Applying the Method 425
5.1 Formal Specification of the Implementation 425
5.2 Proof of Correctness 426
Step 1: Application of the Sufficient Proof Condition 426
Step 2: Skolemization 427
Step 3(a): Abstraction by Refinement 427
Step 3(b): Abstraction by Factorization 427

6 Timed Modal Specification 429

7 Specification of the Timed Problem 430

8 Applying the Method 431

9 Conclusion and Future Work 433

Judi Romijn:
Tackling the RPC-Memory Specification Problem with
I/O Automata 437

1 Introduction 437
   1.1 Notes on the problem specification 438
      Ambiguities 438
      Observable versus internal behaviour 438
      Fairness and real time 438
   1.2 Notes on the I/O automata model 438
      Benefits 438
      Imperfections 439
      What we added to the classic model 439
   1.3 Further remarks 440
      Acknowledgements 440

2 Preliminaries 440
   2.1 Fair I/O automata 440
   2.2 Details on fair I/O automata 440
      Specification 440
      Presentation 441
      Proofs 441

3 Specifications and Verifications for Problem 1 441
   3.1 Problem 1(a): Specification of two Memory Components 441
      Data types 442
      The Memory component 442
      Liveness 443
      The Reliable Memory component 445
      Liveness 445
   3.2 Problem 1(b): *RelMemory* implements *Memory* 445
      Safety 445
      Deadlock freeness 446
      Implementation 446
   3.3 Problem 1(c): Nothing but *MEM_FAILURE*$_P$ actions? 446

4 Specifications and Verifications for Problem 2 447
   4.1 Problem 2: Specification of the RPC component 447
      Data types 447
      Specification 447
      Liveness 448

5 Specifications and Verifications for Problem 3 448
   5.1 Problem 3: Specification of the composition 448

Data types 448
A front end for the RPC component 449
Liveness 449
Renaming component *RelMemory* 449
Liveness 451
The implementation 451
Liveness 451
5.2 Set-up for the verification 453
An intermediate automaton 453
Liveness 453
5.3 Problem 3: *MemoryImp* implements *Memory* 453
*Memory** implements *Memory* 453
MemoryImp implements *Memory** 456
Invariants 456
Safety 458
Deadlock freeness 459
The main result 460

6 Specifications for Problem 4 460
6.1 Problem 4: Specification of a lossy RPC 460
Data types 461

7 Specifications and Verifications for Problem 5 461
7.1 Problem 5(a): The RPC implementation *RPCImp* 461
Data types 461
Specification 461
The composition 463
7.2 Problem 5(b): *RPCImp* implements *RPC* 463
A new implementation and specification 465
Admissible trace inclusion 466
Weak refinement 467
Fairness is preserved 468

A Safe and Fair I/O Automata 471
A.1 Safe I/O automata 471
Enabling of actions 471
Executions 471
Traces 471
A.2 Fair I/O automata 472
Enabling of sets 472
Fair executions 472
Fair traces 472
Implementation relation 472
Fairness as a liveness condition 472

B Timed and Fair Timed I/O Automata 473
B.1 Timed I/O automata 473
Timed Traces 473

B.2 Fair timed I/O automata 474
    Enabling of sets 474
    Fair executions 475
    Fair timed traces 475
    Implementation relation 475

Ketil Stølen:
Using Relations on Streams to Solve the RPC-Memory
Specification Problem 477

1 Introduction 477

2 Streams and Operators on Streams 478

3 Problem I: The Memory Component 479
  3.1 Basic Definitions 480
  3.2 The Sequential Memory Component 481
  3.3 The Concurrent Memory Component 482
  3.4 The Repetitive Memory Component 483
  3.5 Timed Streams and Operators on Timed Streams 485
  3.6 The Reliable Memory Component 486
  3.7 The Unreliable Memory Component 488
  3.8 Implementation 490

4 Problem II: The RPC Component 490
  4.1 Basic Definitions 490
  4.2 The Sequential RPC Component 491
  4.3 The RPC Component 494

5 Problem III: Implementing the Unreliable Memory
   Component 495
  5.1 Basic Assumptions 495
  5.2 The Sequential Clerk Component 496
  5.3 The Clerk Component 497
  5.4 The Implementation 497
  5.5 Verification 498

6 Problem IV: The Lossy RPC Component 506
  6.1 The Sequential Lossy RPC Component 506

7 Problem V: Implementing the RPC Component 508
  7.1 The Sequential RPC Clerk Component 508
  7.2 The Implementation 510
  7.3 Verification 510

8 Conclusions 514

9 Acknowledgements 515

A Specifying the Hand-Shake Protocol 515

Rob T. Udink, Joost N. Kok:

**The RPC-Memory Specification Problem: UNITY +
Refinement Calculus** 521

1 Introduction 521

2 The ImpUNITY Programming Language 522

3 The ImpUNITY Logic 525

4 Program Refinement 527

5 The RPC-Memory Specification Problem 529
    5.1 Implementing the RPC Component 533

6 Refinement Steps for The Memory Component 533

7 Conclusions 539

List of Authors 541

The RPC-Memory Specification Problem
Problem Statement

Manfred Broy
Leslie Lamport

1 The Procedure Interface

The problem calls for the specification and verification of a series of *components*. Components interact with one another using a procedure-calling interface. One component issues a *call* to another, and the second component responds by issuing a *return*. A call is an indivisible (atomic) action that communicates a procedure name and a list of *arguments* to the called component. A return is an atomic action issued in response to a call. There are two kinds of returns, *normal* and *exceptional*. A normal call returns a *value* (which could be a list). An exceptional return also returns a value, usually indicating some error condition. An exceptional return of a value *e* is called *raising exception e*. A return is issued only in response to a call. There may be "syntactic" restrictions on the types of arguments and return values.

   A component may contain multiple *processes* that can concurrently issue procedure calls. More precisely, after one process issues a call, other processes can issue calls to the same component before the component issues a return from the first call. A return action communicates to the calling component the identity of the process that issued the corresponding call.

2 A Memory Component

The component to be specified is a memory that maintains the contents of a set MemLocs of locations. The contents of a location is an element of a set MemVals. This component has two procedures, described informally below. Note that being an element of MemLocs or MemVals is a "semantic" restriction, and cannot be imposed solely by syntactic restrictions on the types of arguments.

Name	Read
Arguments	loc : an element of MemLocs
Return Value	an element of MemVals
Exceptions	BadArg : argument loc is not an element of MemLocs.
	MemFailure : the memory cannot be read.
Description	Returns the value stored in address loc.
Name	Write
Arguments	loc : an element of MemLocs
	val : an element of MemVals
Return Value	some fixed value

Exceptions	BadArg : argument loc is not an element of MemLocs, or argument val is not an element of MemVals.
	MemFailure : the write *might* not have succeeded.
Description	Stores the value val in address loc.

The memory must eventually issue a return for every Read and Write call.

Define an *operation* to consist of a procedure call and the corresponding return. The operation is said to be *successful* iff it has a normal (nonexceptional) return. The memory behaves as if it maintains an array of atomically read and written locations that initially all contain the value InitVal, such that:

- An operation that raises a BadArg exception has no effect on the memory.
- Each successful Read(l) operation performs a single atomic read to location l at some time between the call and return.
- Each successful Write(l, v) operation performs a sequence of one or more atomic writes of value v to location l at some time between the call and return.
- Each unsuccessful Write(l, v) operation performs a sequence of zero or more atomic writes of value v to location l at some time between the call and return.

A variant of the Memory Component is the Reliable Memory Component, in which no MemFailure exceptions can be raised.

Problem 1 (a) Write a formal specification of the Memory component and of the Reliable Memory component.

(b) Either prove that a Reliable Memory component is a correct implementation of a Memory component, or explain why it should not be.

(c) If your specification of the Memory component allows an implementation that does nothing but raise MemFailure exceptions, explain why this is reasonable.

3 Implementing the Memory

3.1 The RPC Component

The RPC component interfaces with two environment components, a *sender* and a *receiver*. It relays procedure calls from the sender to the receiver, and relays the return values back to the sender. Parameters of the component are a set Procs of procedure names and a mapping ArgNum, where ArgNum(p) is the number of arguments of each procedure p. The RPC component contains a single procedure:

Name	RemoteCall
Arguments	proc : name of a procedure
	args : list of arguments
Return Value	any value that can be returned by a call to proc

Exceptions   RPCFailure : the call failed
            BadCall : proc is not a valid name or args is not a
                syntactically correct list of arguments for proc.
            Raises any exception raised by a call to proc
Description   Calls procedure proc with arguments args

A call of RemoteCall(proc, args) causes the RPC component to do one of the following:

- Raise a BadCall exception if args is not a list of ArgNum(proc) arguments.
- Issue one call to procedure proc with arguments args, wait for the corresponding return (which the RPC component assumes will occur) and either (a) return the value (normal or exceptional) returned by that call, or (b) raise the RPCFailure exception.
- Issue no procedure call, and raise the RPCFailure exception.

The component accepts concurrent calls of RemoteCall from the sender, and can have multiple outstanding calls to the receiver.

Problem 2 Write a formal specification of the RPC component.

3.2 The Implementation

A Memory component is implemented by combining an RPC component with a Reliable Memory component as follows. A Read or Write call is forwarded to the Reliable Memory by issuing the appropriate call to the RPC component. If this call returns without raising an RPCFailure exception, the value returned is returned to the caller. (An exceptional return causes an exception to be raised.) If the call raises an RPCFailure exception, then the implementation may either reissue the call to the RPC component or raise a MemFailure exception. The RPC call can be retried arbitrarily many times because of RPCFailure exceptions, but a return from the Read or Write call must eventually be issued.

Problem 3 Write a formal specification of the implementation, and prove that it correctly implements the specification of the Memory component of Problem 1.

4   Implementing the RPC Component

4.1   A Lossy RPC

The Lossy RPC component is the same as the RPC component except for the following differences, where δ is a parameter.

- The RPCFailure exception is never raised. Instead of raising this exception, the RemoteCall procedure never returns.
- If a call to RemoteCall raises a BadCall exception, then that exception will be raised within δ seconds of the call.

- If a RemoteCall(p, a) call results in a call of procedure p, then that call of p will occur within δ seconds of the call of RemoteCall.
- If a RemoteCall(p, a) call returns other than by raising a BadCall exception, then that return will occur within δ seconds of the return from the call to procedure p.

Problem 3 Write a formal specification of the Lossy RPC component.

4.2 The RPC Implementation

The RPC component is implemented with a Lossy RPC component by passing the RemoteCall call through to the Lossy RPC, passing the return back to the caller, and raising an exception if the corresponding return has not been issued after $2\delta + \epsilon$ seconds.

Problem 4 (a) Write a formal specification of this implementation.

(b) Prove that, if every call to a procedure in Procs returns within ϵ seconds, then the implementation satisfies the specification of the RPC component in Problem 2.

The RPC-Memory Case Study: A Synopsis *

Manfred Broy, Stephan Merz, and Katharina Spies

Institut für Informatik, Technische Universität München
Arcisstr. 21, 80290 München, Germany

1 About this Book

The RPC-Memory specification problem was proposed by Broy and Lamport as a case study in the formal design of distributed and concurrent systems. The idea was to use it as a basis for comparing various approaches to formal specification, refinement, and verification. Various preliminary solutions were presented and discussed during a workshop at Schloss Dagstuhl, Germany, in September 1994. Authors were then given the opportunity to revise their specifications to reflect the discussions at the seminar. An extensive refereeing process ensured and authors were encouraged to discuss their solutions with the referees.

This volume contains fifteen solutions to the RPC-Memory problem that resulted from this process. The formalisms that underly the specifications reflect different schools of system specification, including Petri nets, temporal and higher-order logics, various formats of transition systems or automata, and stream-based approaches, supporting various degrees of formalized or computer-assisted verification. The contributors were free to solve only those aspects of the problem that they considered particularly important or omit aspects that could not be adequately represented in the chosen formalism.

Section 2 of this introductory overview reviews the specification problem, discussing its structure and the problems posed to the participants. In section 3 we attempt to classify the solutions contained in this volume. We indicate which parts of the problem have been addressed and what we believe to be the key points of each solution. This would have been impossible without the help of the referees who supplied us with excellent overviews and appraisals. In fact, this section contains literal quotes from the referee reports, and we would like to think of our contribution as mostly redactorial, trying to ensure a common format and uniform criteria of classification. In order to maintain the anonymity of the individual referees, we do not attribute the quotes we make. A list of all referees involved in the edition of this volume is included separately. We conclude in section 4 with a summary of some of the lessons that we have learned from this case study.

This article does not attempt to provide an in-depth analysis of the solutions to the case study: because we have contributed solutions ourselves it would have been difficult to ensure a truly impartial assessment of the other contributions. Besides, such an analysis would have taken more time and energy than

---

* This work was partially sponsored by the Sonderforschungsbereich 342 "Werkzeuge und Methoden für die Nutzung paralleler Rechnerarchitekturen"

we were prepared to expend. Nevertheless, we hope that our classification can be helpful to researchers and even practicing software engineers who try to apply formal methods to concrete problems, and can perhaps even indicate links between formal methods developed from different theoretical backgrounds. On the other hand, we are aware that our subjective backgrounds and predilections have influenced the presentation of the contributions in this overview. Any misrepresentations are entirely our fault.

2   The Problem

This section reviews the specification problem, reproduced on pages 1–4 of this volume, and highlights key issues that the contributions were expected to address.

The problem calls for the specification of a series of components. The problem statement begins with a description of the procedure interface employed by all components. Each component is required to accept concurrent calls from different client processes, although there can be at most one outstanding call per process to facilitate identification of return values. Specification methods that emphasize modularity could be expected to give a separate specification of the interface behavior and reuse that specification in subsequent component specifications.

Next, the problem statement describes the individual components and poses five specific problems:

1. The first problem calls for the specification of a memory component that accepts Read and Write calls with appropriate parameters. The problem requires the memory to behave as if it consisted of an array of memory cells for which atomic read and write operations are defined. These atomic operations may fail and may be retried by the memory, hence a call to the memory may lead to the execution of several atomic read and write operations. Alternatively, the memory may raise the exception MemFailure, indicating that the operation may not have succeeded. (An unsuccessful Write operation may still have caused a successful atomic write to the memory.) Most contributors understood the wording of the informal description as a description of the externally visible memory behavior (as suggested by the phrase "as if"), not the actual memory operation. Specifically, the informal description explicitly stated the possibility of retries only for Write calls: whereas an external observer may be able to tell that a Write call has ben retried if there are concurrent Read calls for the same location, an observer will only be able to witness the effect of the last atomic read in response to a Read call. This issue has nevertheless caused some controversy, because the memory implementation (problem 3) describes an explicit mechanism for retries that allows several atomic reads in response to a Read call of the memory component. The solutions by Best, Romijn, and Hooman include a formal proof of the (observational) equivalence of the "single-atomic-read" and the

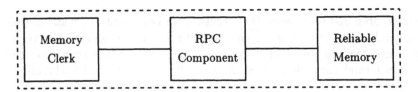

Fig. 1. Implementation of the memory component

"multiple-atomic-read" behaviors, whereas Larsen, Steffen, and Weise consider the problem statement to be flawed in this respect.

The first problem also introduces two variants of the memory component:
- the reliable memory component, which never returns a failure exception
- the ever-failing memory component, which always fails.

Participants were asked whether these variants are a valid implementation of the original memory component, and, if so, why this is a reasonable assumption. The solutions are unanimous in their answers: all regard both variants as a valid implementation. The rationale to consider the ever-failing memory an (unavoidable) implementation is that the specification cannot rule out a catastrophic failure of the memory. Several authors remark that probabilistic approaches could be employed to distinguish a memory that never works from one that fails only temporarily.

2. The second problem requires the specification of an RPC (remote procedure call) component. It offers a single RemoteCall procedure whose arguments are a procedure name and a list of arguments to be passed on to a server. If these arguments are "syntactically" correct, the RemoteCall is translated to an appropriate call of the server. When the server replies, the result is passed back to the client. However, there may also be failures, in which case the RPC component issues an RPCFailure exception.

3. The third problem asks for a formal proof of implementation of a memory component by the configuration of components shown in figure 1: A reliable memory is combined with an RPC component. The memory clerk component (that is only implicitly described in the problem statement) translates Read and Write calls to appropriate calls of the RPC's RemoteCall procedure and translates RPCFailure exceptions to MemFailure exceptions, ensuring that the implementation has the same interface as the memory component. The clerk may also retry calls for which the RPC has signalled an RPCFailure exception.

It was assumed that any formalism designed for the specification of reactive systems would support the implementation of a single component by three components as indicated in figure 1. An important criterion was whether a rigorous, possibly computer-assisted, proof could be provided in the chosen framework.

4. The fourth problem describes a "lossy RPC" component, whose functional behavior is similar to the RPC component, but that guarantees a certain timing behavior. Specifically, it will both forward client calls to the server

and transmit results back to the client within δ seconds from when it has received the call or result. If the server does not respond, the lossy RPC component may fail to return a result to the client.

5. Finally, the fifth problem asks to prove that the original RPC component is implemented by a lossy RPC component and an auxiliary component (called the RPC clerk in most solutions) that raises an RPCFailure exception when more than $2\delta + \epsilon$ seconds have elapsed since the RemoteCall was received from the client, assuming that the server always responds within ϵ seconds. This assumption is necessary because the RPC implementation is allowed to return both an exceptional and a normal result if the server is too slow. Abadi, Lamport, and Merz explain that the informal description of the lossy RPC component and its clerk is problematic because it allows situations where a client process sends a second request before the lossy RPC has answered the first one. They suggest that it would have been sensible to replace the handshaking protocol imposed by the procedure interface by a protocol where a sender process can issue a new call after a certain timeout period. Cuellar, Barnard, and Huber introduce a timeout action that causes the lossy RPC component to forget a pending call.

3 The Solutions

3.1 Criteria for Classification

In tables 1 to 3 we have classified the solutions to the RPC memory specification problem according to a number of criteria that we explain now. Thereafter we give a short review for each solution.

Coverage This entry describes which subproblems have been addressed in the solution.

Means of presentation Most formalisms rely on a textual presentation of specifications as programs or formulas, sometimes even in machine-readable formats. Some formalisms additionally or exclusively provide a graphical notation for specifications, which may have a formal semantics or be purely illustrative.

Modularity We call a specification modular if it is subdivided into meaningful parts that can be understood independently and can be reused in different contexts.

Properties vs. operational We indicate whether the formalism emphasizes abstract, property-oriented descriptions of the interface or models specifications more operationally, for example using a programming notation. Typically, logic-based formalisms would fall under the first category, and process algebra or transition systems would represent the second one. In fact, the distinction is seldom clear-cut: firstly, many formalisms support both forms of specification, secondly, even formalisms that are more oriented towards operational specifications often require sophisticated liveness or fairness constraints. We indicate which specification style has been used in the solution of the RPC memory problem.

Solution: authors (number)	Coverage	Means of presentation	Modularity	Properties vs. operational
Abadi, Lamport, Merz (1)	1–5	TLA formulas, diagrams	yes	operational
Astesiano, Reggio (2)	1–3	structured nat. lang., algebraic spec.	yes	rather operational
Best (3)	1–5	annotated (timed) Petri nets	yes	operational
Blom, Jonsson (4)	1–3 (no proofs)	LTL formulas, diagrams	yes	mainly operational
Broy (5)	1–5 (no proof for 5)	predicates on streams	yes	property-oriented
Cuellar, Barnard, Huber (6)	1–5	Unity-like notation, temporal logic	yes	operational
Gotzhein (7)	1, short discussion of 2,3	temporal logic formulas	little (spec. of architecture)	property-oriented
Hooman (8)	1–5	PVS theories	yes	property-oriented
Hungar (9)	1–3 (incomplete specification)	timing diagrams, TL formulas, CSP	little	property-oriented
Klarlund, Nielsen, Sunesen (10)	1–3	logic on strings, Fido system descriptions	no	property-oriented
Kurki-Suonio (11)	1–5	TLA formulas, diagrams	yes	operational
Larsen, Steffen, Weise (12)	1–5	transition systems, diagrams	little (spec. patterns)	mainly operational
Romijn (13)	1–5	I/O automata	yes	operational
Stølen (14)	1–5	predicates on streams	yes	property-oriented
Udink, Kok (15)	1–3	Unity-like programs	yes	operational

Table 1. Classification of solutions

Hiding Formalisms that (mostly) rely on building an operational model of the specified system require a way to hide state components that are only introduced as auxiliary constructs to describe the model in order to avoid overspecification. This category indicates the presence of a hiding operator in the specification language. It does not apply to property-oriented specification formats.

Environment vs. component Some formalisms advocate a separation of environment and component specifications, for example to obtain an open-system specification. Other formalisms specify the overall behavior of the system together with its environment.

Stepwise refinement A few solutions indicate how the implementations described in the problem statement could have been derived from the abstract specification in a succession of refinement steps, sometimes presented as a succession of classes in an object-oriented development style. Although step-

Solution: authors (number)	Hiding	Environment vs. component	Stepwise refinement	Decomposition
Abadi, Lamport, Merz (1)	existential quantification	separate	no	yes (but not finite-state)
Astesiano, Reggio (2)	no (but "implementation function")	mixed	yes	no
Best (3)	restriction operator	no environment assumptions	yes	no
Blom, Jonsson (4)	existential quantification	mixed	no	yes (but not finite-state)
Broy (5)	not applicable	separate (ass.-commitment style)	partly	no
Cuellar, Barnard, Huber (6)	visibility annotations	separate	no	yes (finite state)
Gotzhein (7)	not applicable	mixed	only high-level specification	no
Hooman (8)	not applicable	separate	no	no
Hungar (9)	not applicable	separate (ass.-commitment style)	no	yes
Klarlund, Nielsen, Sunesen (10)	"hand-coded" in the proof	mixed	no	yes
Kurki-Suonio (11)	no	no	object-oriented reuse	no
Larsen, Steffen, Weise (12)	restriction operator	mixed	specification patterns	yes (finite-state)
Romijn (13)	external vs. internal actions	syntactic distinction	no	yes (but not finite-state)
Stølen (14)	yes (existentially quantified oracles)	input, output streams	yes	no
Udink, Kok (15)	local variables	mixed	yes	no

Table 2. Classification of solutions (continued)

wise refinement was not required in the RPC memory case study, we include this feature in the table.

Decomposition We indicate whether the component specifications have been further decomposed into several "lightweight" and largely independent processes. For example, the memory can be described as an array of memory cells that function uniformly. Similarly, all client processes may be treated in the same way by the components. Decomposition may help in the refinement proofs; it is a necessary prerequisite for those approaches that rely on model-checking a finite-state abstraction of the system.

Style of proof Proofs can be presented in various degrees of formalization. Informal, textbook-style proofs typically contain arguments about the operational behavior of a system. More rigorous proofs rely on "mathematical" (semantic) style of reasoning or are performed in a system of formal logic. Finally, in the case of machine-checked proofs, we distinguish between the

Solution: authors (number)	Style of proof	Related solutions
Abadi, Lamport, Merz (1)	formal	4, 11, 13, 6
Astesiano, Reggio (2)	outline	
Best (3)	informal	
Blom, Jonsson (4)	no proofs	1, 13
Broy (5)	mathematical	14, 10
Cuellar, Barnard, Huber (6)	model-checking	12, 9, 1
Gotzhein (7)	no proofs	
Hooman (8)	interactive	
Hungar (9)	model-checking	6, 12, 7
Klarlund, Nielsen, Sunesen (10)	decision procedure	6, 9, 12
Kurki-Suonio (11)	informal outline	1, 15
Larsen, Steffen, Weise (12)	model-checking, formal abstraction	6, 10, 3
Romijn (13)	mathematical	1
Stølen (14)	mathematical	5
Udink, Kok (15)	outline	6, 11

Table 3. Classification of solutions (end)

use of automatic decision procedures such as model checking and interactive theorem provers. Because all components are infinite-state systems, model checking can only be applied after building finite-state abstractions of the components.

Related solutions For each solution we indicate what we believe to be the most closely related solutions.

3.2   Reviews of Individual Contributions

We list the individual solutions in alphabetical order. For each solution we give a short summary and indicate what we believe are the most relevant issues raised in the contributions. These sections are largely based on the referees' comments. We are grateful for the permission to reprint excerpts from their evaluations.

Contribution 1 M. ABADI, L. LAMPORT, S. MERZ: A TLA SOLUTION
The contribution presents a complete solution to the RPC-Memory specification problem. The specifications are presented as modules in the specification language TLA$^+$, which is based on the Temporal Logic of Actions (TLA). The concepts of TLA and TLA$^+$ required to understand the solution are explained as they are used. Several aspects of the solution are illustrated with the help of predicate-action diagrams, a graphical formalism whose semantics is given in terms of TLA formulas. The modules of TLA$^+$ allow for reuse of specifications, for example of the procedure interface specification or of basic "data types" such as sequences.

The logic TLA supports an operational style of specification, but also provides temporal logic operators to express standard invariant and liveness properties. Syntactic restrictions on well-formed TLA formulas ensure that all formulas are invariant under stuttering, hence the implementation relation can be expressed as logical implication. Existential quantification over state variables corresponds to hiding of internal state components. The authors give separate specifications of the environment and the components and indicate how one would write assumption-guarantee specifications. A non-interleaving style of specification helps to decompose the specifications into pieces of manageable complexity, which simplifies the verification tasks. The proofs are formal, based on the logical rules of TLA. Refinement mappings and history variables are used in the proofs of existentially quantified formulas. Proof outlines appear in the paper, the complete proofs are available separately. No machine assistance has been used in verification.

Related solutions include the DisCo approach presented in solution 11 by R. Kurki-Suonio, whose semantics is based on TLA. The TLT formalism of solution 6 by J. Cuellar, D. Barnard, and M. Huber has some similarity with TLA. Solution 4 by J. Blom and B. Jonsson, although based on standard linear-time temporal logic, uses a very similar structure of the specification, as does solution 13 by J. Romijn, which is based on I/O automata.

Contribution 2 E. ASTESIANO, G. REGGIO: A DYNAMIC SPECIFICATION OF THE RPC-MEMORY PROBLEM
The contribution covers problems 1 to 3 of the RPC-Memory problem. The main interest of the authors has been to suggest a methodology for the transition from a natural language description to a formal specification, using an intermediate, structured, informal specification. In particular, the component to be developed has to be delimited from its environment. The formal specifications are expressed as a combination of algebraic specifications, labelled transition systems (also presented in an algebraic way), and formulas of a CTL-like branching time temporal logic. The composition of separate components does not rely on predefined operators but is also specified explicitly in an algebraic style. Every specification is accompanied by an informal part written in structured natural language that explains the formal specification, discusses its requirements, and lists "shadow spots", which represent inconsistencies or ambiguities in the informal document.

Refinement steps may produce so-called design specifications that contain only Horn clauses (and, in particular, no temporal logic formulas) and can be simulated using a rapid-prototyping tool. The implementation of the memory component by a system composed of a reliable memory, an RPC component, and a memory clerk is presented as a single refinement step. The paper contains an outline of an implementation proof, the full proof is available as a technical report.

The paper is unique in this volume in its emphasis on making the transition from informal to formal specifications an explicit part of formal system development. The authors emphasize the importance of validating an implementation with the help of rapid prototyping. On the other hand, formal verification appears to be less of a concern to the authors.

The formal basis of the approach is comparable to other contributions based on transition systems such as contributions 13 by Romijn or 12 by Steffen, Larsen, and Weise.

Contribution 3 E. Best: A Memory Module Specification using Composable High-level Petri Nets
This contribution covers all subproblems of the RPC-Memory specification problem. Specifications are expressed in a formalism called M-nets that combines annonated, high-level Petri nets with CCS-like composition operators such as parallel composition, restriction, and synchronous events. A real-time extension of M-nets is used for subproblems 4 and 5. The formalism and its use are explained in the paper. The implementation relation is defined as the inclusion of observable traces. The use of a common formalism for both specifications and implementations facilitates stepwise refinement as is illustrated in the paper: the memory specification is obtained by a series of refinements that either add requirements or allow additional behavior.

The formalism is largely based on graphical notation and employs operational concepts that are rather intuitive. Decomposition into concurrent subsystems is very natural with Petri nets, it also gives rise to an independence relation that aids in proving an implementation correct. Annotations at places and transitions are used to formulate constraints that cannot be conveniently expressed as a Petri net. The paper indicates the verification conditions necessary to prove the implementation relation. Textbook-style, informal refinement proofs are given in the appendix.

Contribution 4 J. Blom, B. Jonsson: Constraint oriented temporal logic specification
The contribution presents solutions to problems 1 to 3 of the RPC memory case study, excluding proofs. The authors use standard temporal logic of linear time (LTL) to specify the memory as a conjunction of constraints, each of which captures some aspect of the component's behavior and is of manageable complexity. This style of decomposition is facilitated by a non-interleaving model of the system, at the cost of introducing some non-obvious fairness requirements. The structure of the specification suggests a particular system architecture where different components interact via synchronous events (similar to process algebra) represented as flexible predicates. Each constraint is specified in a largely operational style, essentially as a transition system. Hiding of internal state components is achieved by flexible quantification of flexible variables. Parts of the specifications are explained with the help of diagrams that provide a graphical syntax for LTL formulas. The paper contains an outline of the topmost level of a refinement proof, but does not discuss its details.

Both the structure of the specification and the formalism are quite similar to contribution 1 by Abadi, Lamport, and Merz. Solution 13 by Romijn, which is based on I/O automata instead of temporal logic, uses a similar structure.

Contribution 5 M. BROY: A FUNCTIONAL SOLUTION TO THE RPC-MEMORY SPECIFICATION PROBLEM

The contribution presents assumption-commitment specifications of all subproblems in the RPC-Memory case study. The specifications use a "black-box" perspective, describing the allowed input-output behavior of each component as a relation on timed streams with the internal structure of components hidden. It is shown that a complex specification can be made understood with the help of appropriately defined auxiliary symbols and predicates: each informal requirement of the specification problem is matched with a clause in the formal, stream-based specification. The paper contains a short introduction to the formalism, a more detailed exposé is given in the appendix together with an alternative, trace-based specification of the memory component.

The contribution emphasizes modularity of specifications: each requirement can be understood independently from the others. This is possible because the specification expresses a relation between streams (i.e., values) rather than variables or events (i.e., names). Modularity helps in verifying that the implementation is a refinement of the high-level specification. The necessary proofs concerning problem 3 of the case study are given in the appendix.

The most closely related contribution is that by Stølen (14). The contribution 10 by Klarlund, Nielsen, and Sunesen is also based on a stream model, but its internal structure is quite different, motivated by the use of a formal (monadic second-order) logic and the emphasis of associated decision procedures.

Contribution 6 J. CUELLAR, D. BARNARD, M. HUBER: A SOLUTION RELYING ON THE MODEL CHECKING OF BOOLEAN TRANSITION SYSTEMS

This contribution addresses all parts of the RPC-Memory case study. Specifications are expressed in the language TLT (temporal logic of transitions), which combines a Unity-like programming notation with a temporal logic that bears some resemblance to TLA. The formalism supports communication via shared variables as well as synchronous communication, modelled as joint actions of the environment and the component. Visibility annotations in variable declarations serve to distinguish between state components of the environment and the component. Assumptions about the behavior of the environment may be stated in a special section of TLT modules; they give rise to verification conditions when modules are composed. The module system helps to break specifications into manageable pieces, but has a rather complicated, non-compositional semantics.

The main emphasis in this solution is on abstraction and decomposition. It is shown how a factorization technique can be used to reduce the implementation proof to a finite-state problem, which has reportedly been handled by the TLT model checker. However, the paper is a little vague about the details of the actual verification. It is not clear whether the real-time implementation proof has been handled by the model checker or not.

Contribution 12 by Steffen, Larsen, Weise and contributionand 9 by Hungar rely on similar abstraction techniques in the context of modal transition systems and branching-time temporal logic. Also related is the paper 10 by Klarlund, Nielsen, and Sunesen in its use of automatic decision procedures in verification.

Udink and Kok (solution 15) base their contribution on a somewhat similar variant of Unity, while the temporal logics used in solutions 1 by Abadi, Lamport, Merz and 4 by Blom and Jonsson are related to the temporal logic part of TLT.

Contribution 7 R. GOTZHEIN: APPLYING A TEMPORAL LOGIC
The paper presents a solution to problem 1 of the RPC-Memory case study and discusses how the implementation of the memory (problems 2 and 3) could be described and verified. The author advocates an approach where behavior and system architecture are specified together and demonstrates how such a formalism could be defined. The architecture is given as a network of agents, connected through interaction points. The approach involves a notion of refinement that allows both agents and interaction points to be refined into more detailed networks. The functional specification of an agent is expressed as a property-oriented description of its behavior at the interface level, expressed as a list of temporal logic formulas.

Rather than giving a fixed temporal logic, the author suggests to choose a logic that is sufficiently expressive for the specification problem at hand. For the RPC-Memory problem he chooses a many-sorted first-order branching time logic with operators to refer to the future, to the past, to actions, to the number of actions, and to intervals. The specification is expressed as one page of formulas of this logic. The semantic definitions necessary to understand the specification are given in the paper.

Because it does not define the memory implementation, the paper does not include any proofs, although refinement is discussed at a general level. The expressiveness of the logic leaves some doubts whether formal verification would actually be feasible. The memory specification is already of worrisome complexity, maybe indicating that a purely behavioral approach is not very well suited for this kind of specification problem.

Contribution 8 J. HOOMAN: USING PVS FOR AN ASSERTIONAL VERIFICATION OF THE RPC-MEMORY SPECIFICATION PROBLEM
This contribution presents a complete solution of the RPC-Memory problem carried out in an assertional framework developed over several years by the author. All specifications and verification conditions have been checked mechanically with the help of the interactive theorem prover PVS (Prototype Verification System). The author uses the higher-order logic of PVS to express properties that are more conventionally expressed in some kind of temporal logic. The framework and its support by PVS are explained in the article.

In this approach, specifications are expressed as assumption-commitment pairs that define a formal theory of the component's behavior in a well-behaved environment. For the RPC-Memory problem, however, environment and component are modelled as a single system, hence all environment assumptions are trivial. The formalism is property-oriented, constraining the acceptable behaviors (sequences of events) at the interface level. The contribution shows that machine-checked (although not automatic) verification of the RPC-Memory system is possible even without decomposition of the component specifications into "lightweight" processes.

The contribution is unique both in the theoretical underpinnings of the assertional approach it uses and in the use of an interactive theorem prover as a tool to write specifications and prove theorems about them.

Contribution 9 H. HUNGAR: SPECIFICATION AND VERIFICATION USING A VISUAL FORMALISM ON TOP OF TEMPORAL LOGIC
This contribution covers problems 1 to 3 of the RPC-Memory case study. Technically, specifications are expressed in an assumption-commitment variant of the branching-time temporal logic CTL, using a property-oriented specification style. The specifications are expressed with the help of symbolic timing diagrams (STDs), whose formal semantics is given by a translation to CTL. However, with some practice, STDs can be understood intuitively. Both the logic and the diagrams are introduced in the paper to the extent necessary to be able to read the specifications. The author has, in his own words, mainly been concerned with "the formal verification of key properties of a design, [...] less emphasis [has been] put on issues like completeness of the specification". In fact, he gives an example of a run that satisfies the specification, but does not conform to the informal memory specification. He argues that such behaviors are too pathological to occur in any realistic implementation.

The paper also includes CSP-like programs for the memory, RPC, and memory clerk components and explains techniques such as decomposition, abstraction, and model checking to verify such programs against CTL specifications. Part of the verifications required for the RPC-Memory problem has reportedly been performed with the help of automatic tools developed at the University of Oldenburg, although no details of the verification are given in the paper.

The use of abstraction and model-checking is similar to the frameworks used in contribution 6 by Cuellar, Barnard, and Huber and contribution 12 by Larsen, Steffen, and Weise. Contribution 7 by Gotzhein is another solution that relies on property-oriented temporal-logic specifications.

Contribution 10 N. KLARLUND, M. NIELSEN, K. SUNESEN: A CASE STUDY IN VERIFICATION BASED ON TRACE ABSTRACTIONS
The paper addresses problems 1 to 3 of the RPC-Memory specification problem using behavioral component specifications expressed in a monadic second-order logic over finite strings, which allows to specify the safety part of the specifications. The system description language Fido provides a high-level notation that can be translated into formulas of the target logic. The verification part is carried out with the help of an automatic decision procedure called MONA.

The emphasis in this solution is on the availability of an automatic decision procedure for the considered logic. In particular, all theorems have been checked by the MONA tool. However, the correctness of the underlying abstractions to finite-state systems is left implicit in the paper (strictly speaking, only a finite-state instance of the problem has actually been verified). The implementation relation is defined as inclusion of observable traces, where the notion of observability is defined by the user as appropriate for the problem at hand. For the present case study, the authors notice that atomic reads should not be made observable unless a Read call to the memory may induce several atomic reads.

The paper is related to the solutions 6 by Cuellar, Barnard, and Huber, 9 by Hungar, and 12 by Larsen, Steffen, and Weise in its use of finite-state abstractions to perform automatic verification. The semantic model is related to the stream model used in the solutions 5 by Broy and 14 by Stølen, but is restricted to safety properties.

Contribution 11 R. KURKI-SUONIO: INCREMENTAL SPECIFICATION WITH JOINT ACTIONS: THE RPC-MEMORY SPECIFICATION PROBLEM
The contribution covers all aspects of the RPC-Memory case study. The solution is developed in an object-oriented fashion that emphasizes the reuse of subcomponents and basic patterns of interactions. The computational model is based on the synchronization of environment and component via joint actions. The semantic basis for the formalism is Lamport's Temporal Logic of Actions (TLA), with some additional ideas from Back's refinement calculus. The method is supported by prototyping tools that animate specifications. However, the aspect of tool support is not discussed in this paper.

The specifications are presented as a succession of class and action definitions, presented as TLA formulas. Several diagrams, including state charts, provide additional explanation, although they are not given a semantics of their own. The emphasis in this approach is on modularity: Certain restrictions on the allowed modifications of an action in a subclass ensure that safety properties of a class are inherited by subclasses, at least for the untimed part. Each class definition can be understood as defining an automaton that is further refined in subclasses. The lack of distinction between external and internal state components and between environment assumptions and component commitments is justified by the emphasis on producing models rather than abstract specifications. The method does however provide the vehicle of "ghost variables" that allows state variables of a superclass to be eliminated in a subclass when they are no longer needed. The approach favors the development of an implementation by stepwise refinement where correctness (at least for safety properties) is guaranteed by construction. For the present case study, the implementation consists of components that have been developed separately, so there is a need for separate correctness proofs. The paper includes informal arguments why the implementation is correct and shows how these could be turned into formal TLA proofs of implementation.

Solution 1 by Abadi, Lamport, and Merz is related in its use of TLA as its semantic basis. The specification language contains ideas similar to those underlying Unity and TLT (see contributions 15 by Udink and Kok and 6 by Cuellar, Barnard, and Huber).

Contribution 12 K. LARSEN, B. STEFFEN, C. WEISE: THE METHODOLOGY OF MODAL CONSTRAINTS
The contribution addresses all subproblems of the case study, except that no liveness properties are specified. The specifications are written as modal transition systems, which add a distinction between "may" and "must" transitions and a form of conjunction to constructs from process algebras such as CCS, resulting in an interesting mix of operational and property-oriented specification

styles. The underlying theory is explained to the extent necessary to understand the solution.

The individual specifications are expressed in the form of transition diagrams that reuse a number of basic patterns. The specification is decomposed into fine-grained specifications that concern individual memory locations, client processes, and memory values. This decomposition together with an abstraction step allows for the use of a model checker for verification, which has reportedly been performed using the TAV tool developed by the authors. The price to pay is a highly complex structure of the specification. It was not clear to the referees whether the specification actually conforms to the informal description or not. In particular, modelling the dependency between write and read actions turned out to be non-trivial and resulted in a complex transition system.

The paper is related to solution 6 by Cuellar, Barnard, and Huber, solution 9 by Hungar, and solution 10 by Klarlund, Nielsen, and Sunesen in its use of finite-state abstractions and model checking.

Contribution 13 J. ROMIJN: TACKLING THE RPC-MEMORY SPECIFICATION PROBLEM WITH I/O AUTOMATA

Romijn's contribution gives solutions for all subproblems of the RPC-Memory case study. The specifications are expressed in the framework of I/O automata with fairness constraints. The timed part of the specification problem required an extension of the model of fair I/O automata. The distinction between internal, external, and environment events is built into the semantics of I/O automata, although it is noted in the paper that this "syntactic" distinction is not enough, for example, to express the assumption that certain environment actions happen within a specified time bound.

Each component specification is given as the composition of one I/O automaton per client process. The paper includes a statement of all verification conditions necessary to prove refinement and sketches their proofs, including a proof that a memory component that allows multiple atomic reads per **Read** request cannot be distinguished from one that allows at most one atomic read. An addendum to the contribution, which is available separately, contains the complete proofs for all theorems in mathematical and partly formal (predicate logic) style.

The structure of the specifications is similar to that of contributions 1 by Abadi, Lamport, and Merz and 4 by Blom and Jonsson, although the semantic basis is different.

Contribution 14 K. STØLEN: USING RELATIONS ON STREAMS TO SOLVE THE RPC-MEMORY SPECIFICATION PROBLEM

The paper addresses all subproblems of the RPC-Memory case study. Component specifications are expressed as relations between input and output streams, which model communication histories of input and output channels. Composition of specifications corresponds to the conjunction of the input-output relations. A specification refines another specification if any input-output behavior of the former is also an input-output behavior of the latter. Thus, refinement corresponds to logical implication. The paper distinguishes between time-independent and time-dependent specifications. A time-independent specification is based on untimed streams. A time-dependent specification employs timed streams and can express timing constraints and causalities.

The paper deviates from the problem statement in that the handshake protocol is not imposed. This means for example that the user may send a new call before the memory component issues a reply to the previous call by the same user. An appendix shows how handshake communication can be introduced as a refinement.

The specifications are developed in several steps, starting from an unfailing memory for one client process. The paper emphasizes the use of oracles to describe the time-independent nondeterministic behavior in a structured way. Essentially, an oracle represents the nondeterministic choices made by the component; it can be viewed as an additional, hidden input stream to the specification describing the functional component behavior. Constraints on oracles impose fairness or compatibility requirements. The paper gives conventional mathematical proofs for the correctness of the implementation.

The contribution is related to solution 5 by Broy.

Contribution 15 R. UDINK, J. N. KOK: THE RPC-MEMORY SPECIFICATION PROBLEM: UNITY + REFINEMENT CALCULUS
The contribution covers subproblems 1 to 3 of the RPC-Memory case study. The authors have extended the Unity specification language with a module system that provides local and global variables. On the logical level, they have added concepts from the refinement calculus developed by Back and Kurki-Suonio. The individual specifications are given as modules in this Unity-like language.

The specification style is operational, internal and external variables are distinguished by the module system. The method provides transformation rules that preserve all temporal properties of programs, even when applied to a module in isolation. The paper contains an outline of the necessary steps in the refinement proof for the memory component. The method is currently not supported by interactive or automatic proof checkers.

The contribution is related to the solution 6 by Cuellar, Barnard, and Huber in its use of a Unity-like framework, and to solution 11 by Kurki-Suonio in its emphasis on transformational derivation and its foundation in the action systems formalism.

4 Conclusion

Although we do not want to and cannot come to a final judgement, it is helpful to draw some conclusions. Which of the contributions as solutions to the RPC case study a reader may prefer, depends very much on taste and style. The idea of the whole experiment was never to have Olympic Games in specification, refinement, and verification. However, it is worthwhile to draw some final conclusions.

First of all, it was very interesting to see how the choice of the individual methods that were used to tackle the problem was often less important for the quality of the final solutions than the modeling ideas of the specifiers. Certainly, the creativity and expertise, and of course also the routine of the person applying a method, are more important for the result than the particular notation and model used. Of course, there are methods and models which do not provide certain helpful concepts and, therefore, make the life of the specifier a little harder. However, even plain predicate logic is a very powerful tool, and if a method comprises first-order predicate logic or at least a sufficient fragment of it, many ideas can be expressed, maybe less explicitly, but nevertheless they can be made to work. This is certainly not surprising. It is like it is for programming languages: a good programmer can write good quality programs even in a bad programming language, and a bad programmer can write bad programs even in a good programming language.

As a consequence of the observations we made above, it was interesting to see how over the time working on the case study the authors of the contributions were concentrating more and more on aspects of how to apply their methods, such that theoretical questions became less and less important. This was certainly what we expected and what we intended with the case study. The idea was to stimulate researchers in that area to concentrate more on application issues and less on maybe not so important theoretical aspects. This worked out perfectly.

Another thing which worked out very convincingly was the cross-refereeing process. It showed that a very fruitful discussion was possible between proponents of quite different methods. Also here, the case study was a major contribution to improving the understanding of researchers working in the field of different methods. And this is, finally, what we would really like to achieve: to make sure that researchers in that area look over the fence, respect the advantages of other approaches, learn enough about them to be able to combine them in such a way that it finally leads to a comprehensive understanding of the field and of how the methods can work together, such that we come step by step closer to a practical application.

An aspect, very important for practical considerations, is the economy of a method. How long does it take to learn it, how long does it take to use it for a particular problem. Here our little experiment does not provide much input. We think most of the methods around and also those used in this volume are not at a stage where these questions can be tackled successfully.

Acknowledgements We gratefully acknowledge helpful comments by M. Abadi, E. Best, L. Lamport, and K. Stølen on previous versions of this paper.

A TLA Solution to the RPC-Memory Specification Problem

Martín Abadi[1], Leslie Lamport[1], and Stephan Merz[2]

[1] Systems Research Center, Digital Equipment Corporation
[2] Institut für Informatik, Technische Universität München

Abstract. We present a complete solution to the Broy-Lamport specification problem. Our specifications are written in TLA$^+$, a formal language based on TLA. We give the high levels of structured proofs and sketch the lower levels, which will appear in full elsewhere.

Introduction

Broy and Lamport have proposed a specification and verification problem [5]. It calls for specifying simple memory and RPC (remote procedure call) components, and proving the correctness of two simple implementations. We present a complete solution to this problem using TLA, the temporal logic of actions [12]. We assume the reader is familiar with Broy and Lamport's problem statement.

Since the problem is so much simpler than the ones encountered in real applications, any approach that claims to be both practical and formal should allow a completely formal solution. Our specifications are written in TLA$^+$, a formal language based on TLA. Our proofs are completely formal, except that some names are abbreviated for readability. We use a hierarchical proof method [10] that is the most reliable way we know of to write hand proofs. Here, we present only the higher levels of the proofs. Proofs carried down to the level where each justification involves instantiation of proof rules and simple predicate logic will be available on a Web page [4]. Although our proofs are careful and detailed, neither they nor the specifications have been checked mechanically; minor errors undoubtedly remain.

Rigor entails a certain degree of tedium. A complete programming language requires boring details like variable declarations that can be omitted in informal pseudo-code. Writing specifications is harder with a formal language than with an informal approach—even one based on a formalism. Formal proofs that are detailed enough to be easy to check are long and boring. However, rigor has its advantages. Informal specifications can be ambiguous. The short, interesting proofs favored by mathematicians are notoriously error prone. Our specifications and proofs are rigorous, hence somewhat laborious.

We assume no prior knowledge of TLA or TLA$^+$. Concepts and notations are explained as they are introduced; the index on page 65 can help the reader find those explanations. TLA is described in detail in [12], and there are several published examples of TLA$^+$ specifications [11, 14]. Further information about TLA and TLA$^+$ can be found on the Web [9].

The problem is not very challenging for TLA, TLA⁺, or our proof style. With our experience, it was possible to grind out the requisite specifications and proofs without much thought. More difficult was choosing from among the many possible ways of writing the specifications. We tried to make the specifications as clear as possible without unduly complicating the correctness proofs. We benefited from studying the many preliminary solutions presented at a Dagstuhl workshop on the specification problem. In particular, we emulated some of these solutions by writing our specifications as the composition of individual process specifications. We also benefited from comments by Ketil Stølen.

We found no significant ambiguities in the problem statement, perhaps because we had first-hand knowledge of the authors' intent. However, we did discover some anomalies in the lossy-RPC specification, which we discuss in Section 4. Our presentation parallels Broy and Lamport's problem statement. In particular, our section numbering corresponds to theirs, with the addition of lower-level sections.

1 The Procedure Interface

A TLA specification is a temporal-logic formula. It expresses a predicate on behaviors, where a behavior is an infinite sequence of states and a state is an assignment of values to variables. TLA⁺ is a formal language for writing TLA specifications. It introduces precise conventions for definitions and a module system with name scoping that is modeled after those of programming languages. In this paper, we describe TLA and TLA⁺ as they are used.

TLA does not have any built-in communication primitives such as message passing or data streams. One can use TLA to define such primitives.[3] We begin by specifying a procedure-calling interface in which a multiprocess caller component interacts with a multiprocess returner component. In this section, we present a module named *ProcedureInterface* that is meant to help specify systems that use the procedure-calling interface. As we explain below, a system may have several such interfaces, described by different "copies" of the module.

We describe a rather arbitrary, abstract procedure-calling interface. One might want a specification that describes an actual procedure-calling software standard, complete with register-usage conventions. One might also want a different high-level abstraction. We can convert our specifications into ones with a different interface abstraction by using an *interface refinement*, as described in [3, page 518] and [7].

Our specification makes precise one important detail that is not quite stated in the informal specification. We interpret the requirement:

[A]fter one process issues a call, other processes can issue calls to the

---

[3] Like most logics, TLA uses variables. One could therefore say that TLA formulas use shared variables as a communication primitive. In the same sense, one could say that the equations $x + y = 7$ and $x - y = 1$ communicate via the shared variables x and y.

same component before the component issues a return from the first call.

to imply that the same process cannot issue another call until the first one returns.

1.1 The Module and its Parameters

Module *ProcedureInterface* is given in Figure 1 on this page. The module first declares some parameters, which are the free symbols that may appear in the expressions defined by the module. By replacing defined symbols with their definitions, all expressions defined in the module can be reduced to ones containing only the parameters and the primitives of TLA$^+$. The parameter ch is the vari-

---

module *ProcedureInterface*

parameters
  $PrIds, Args$: CONSTANT
  ch : VARIABLE

$caller(p) \triangleq \langle ch[p].arg, ch[p].cbit \rangle$
$rtrner(p) \triangleq \langle ch[p].res, ch[p].rbit \rangle$
$Calling(p) \triangleq ch[p].cbit \neq ch[p].rbit$
$Call(p, v) \triangleq \wedge \neg Calling(p)$
$\qquad\qquad\quad \wedge ch[p].cbit' \neq ch[p].rbit$
$\qquad\qquad\quad \wedge ch[p].arg' = v$
$Return(p, v) \triangleq \wedge Calling(p)$
$\qquad\qquad\qquad \wedge ch[p].rbit' = ch[p].cbit$
$\qquad\qquad\qquad \wedge ch[p].res' = v$

$LegalCaller \triangleq \forall p \in PrIds : \neg Calling(p) \wedge \Box[\exists a \in Args : Call(p, a)]_{caller(p)}$
$LegalReturner \triangleq \forall p \in PrIds : \Box[\exists v : Return(p, v)]_{rtrner(p)}$

Fig. 1. Module *ProcedureInterface*.

able representing the interface. A VARIABLE parameter can have a different value in different states of a behavior. TLA is an untyped logic, so there are no type constraints on the values a variable can have. A CONSTANT parameter is one that has the same value in every state of a behavior. The constant parameter *PrIds* is the set of all process identifiers; for each p in *PrIds*, process p of the caller component issues calls to the corresponding process p of the returner component. The parameter *Args* is the set of all "syntactically correct" procedure arguments.

Suppose some module M has a set P of process identifiers and two procedure-calling interfaces, represented by the variables x and y, with syntactically correct argument values in sets S_x and S_y, respectively. Module M will include all the definitions from module *ProcedureInterface* twice, with the following substitutions for its parameters:

$$ch \leftarrow x, \quad PrIds \leftarrow P, \quad Args \leftarrow S_x$$
$$ch \leftarrow y, \quad PrIds \leftarrow P, \quad Args \leftarrow S_y$$

It is conventional to follow the parameter declarations with a horizontal bar. These bars have no semantic significance.

1.2 State Functions, State Predicates, and Actions

To model the procedure-calling interface, we let $ch[p]$ be a "channel" over which process p of the caller component interacts with process p of the returner component. Our model uses a standard two-phase handshake protocol [16] illustrated in Figure 2 on this page. Channel $ch[p]$ contains two "wires" controlled by the

	initial state	call $Read(23)$	return .333	call $Write(14, 3.5)$	
$ch[p].cbit$:	0	1	1	0	$\dots$
$ch[p].arg$:	—	$\langle$ "Read", 23 $\rangle$	$\langle$ "Read", 23 $\rangle$	$\langle$ "Write", 14, 3.5 $\rangle$	$\dots$
$ch[p].rbit$:	0	0	1	1	$\dots$
$ch[p].res$:	—	—	.333	.333	$\dots$

Fig. 2. The two-phase handshake protocol for the channel $ch[p]$.

caller—a signaling wire $ch[p].cbit$ and an argument-passing wire $ch[p].arg$—and two wires controlled by the returner—a signaling wire $ch[p].rbit$ and a result-returning wire $ch[p].res$.

In the standard two-phase handshake protocol shown in Figure 2, the signaling values $ch[p].cbit$ and $ch[p].rbit$ are bits. For simplicity, we allow them to assume arbitrary values, since all that matters is whether or not they equal one another.

The *ProcedureInterface* module defines the state function $caller(p)$ to be the pair $\langle ch[p].arg, ch[p].cbit \rangle$ composed of the process p caller's wires. A state function is an expression that may contain variables and constants. It is interpreted semantically as a mapping from states to values. For example, $ch[p].arg$ is the state function that assigns to any state the arg record component of the pth array element of the value that the state assigns to the variable ch.[4] The state

---

[4] This value is unspecified if the value assigned to ch by the state is not an array whose pth element is a record with an arg component.

function *rtrner*(p) is similarly defined to be the pair composed of the returner's wires.

The module defines the state predicate *Calling*(p) to equal TRUE iff (if and only if) the values on the two signaling wires are unequal. A state predicate is a boolean-valued expression that may contain variables and constants; it is interpreted semantically as a mapping from states to booleans. For the handshake protocol, *Calling*(p) equals TRUE iff process p is in the middle of a procedure call (the caller has issued a call and the returner has not yet returned).

Next comes the definition of the action *Call*(p, v). An action is a boolean-valued expression that may contain variables and constants, and the operator ' (prime), which may not be nested. Semantically, it is interpreted as a boolean-valued function on steps, where a step is a pair of states. Unprimed expressions refer to the first (old) state, and primed expressions refer to the second (new) state. For example, the action $(x + 1)' = y$ is true of a step iff 1 plus the value assigned to x by the new state equals the value assigned to y by the old state. Action *Call*(p, v) describes the issuing of a call with argument v by the process p caller. More precisely, a step represents this event iff it is a *Call*(p, v) step (one for which *Call*(p, v) equals TRUE). The first conjunct[5] in the definition asserts that a call on channel $ch[p]$ is not in progress. The second conjunct asserts that the new value of $ch[p].cbit$ is different from the old value of $ch[p].rbit$. The final conjunct asserts that the new value of $ch[p].arg$ equals v. Readers familiar with conventional programming languages or state-transition systems can think of *Call*(p, v) as an atomic statement or transition that is enabled when ¬*Calling*(p, v) is true, that nondeterministically sets $ch[p].rbit$ to any value different from $ch[p].cbit$, and that sets $ch[p].arg$ to v.

Action *Return*(p, v) represents the issuing of a return with result v by the process p returner. We do not distinguish in the interface description between normal and exceptional returns—the distinction will be encoded in the result v.

1.3   Temporal Formulas

Module *ProcedureInterface* concludes by defining the two temporal formulas *LegalCaller* and *LegalReturner*. Formula *LegalCaller* is defined in terms of formulas of the form $I \wedge \Box[N]_v$ where I is a state predicate, N is an action (called the *next-state action*), and v is a state function. A temporal formula is true or false on a behavior (an infinite sequence of states). Viewed as a temporal formula, a predicate I is true on a behavior iff I is true in the first state. The formula $\Box[N]_v$ is true of a behavior iff the action $[N]_v$, which is defined to equal $N \vee (v' = v)$, is true for every step (successive pair of states) in the behavior. Thus, $I \wedge \Box[N]_v$ asserts of a behavior that I is true in the first state and every step is an N step or leaves the value of v unchanged. Formula *LegalCaller* therefore asserts that, for every p in *PrIds*:

---

[5] We let a list of formulas bulleted with ∧ or ∨ denote the conjunction or disjunction of the formulas, using indentation to eliminate parentheses. We also let ⇒ have lower precedence than the other Boolean operators.

- The predicate $\neg Calling(p)$ is true in the initial state. In other words, initially there is no call in progress on channel $ch[p]$.

- Every step is either a $Call(p, a)$ step, for some a in $Args$, or else leaves $caller(p)$ unchanged. In other words, every step that changes the caller's part of the interface $ch[p]$ is a $Call(p, a)$ step with a legal argument a.

Formula $LegalCaller$ specifies what it means for a caller to obey the two-phase handshake protocol. It specifies the values of $caller(p)$, for p in $PrIds$. More precisely, $LegalCaller$ is a temporal formula whose semantic meaning is a predicate on behaviors that depends only on the values assigned by the states of a behavior to the state functions $caller(p)$ and $ch[p].rbit$. We interpret it as describing the possible values of $caller(p)$ as a function of the values of $ch[p].rbit$. Since we consider $caller(p)$ to represent the part of an interface controlled by the caller component, we consider $LegalCaller$ to be the specification of a caller. However, the reader should not confuse this intuitive interpretation of $LegalCaller$ with its formal semantics as a predicate on behaviors.

Formula $LegalReturner$ is similar to $LegalCaller$. It asserts that, for every process p, every change to the returner's part of the interface $ch[p]$ is a $Return(p, v)$ step for some value v. It is our specification of what it means for a returner component to obey the handshake protocol. Formula $LegalReturner$ has no initial predicate because we have arbitrarily assigned the initial condition on the channel to the caller's specification.[6] Unlike $LegalCaller$, which requires that the arguments be elements of $Args$, formula $LegalReturner$ does not place any restriction on the results returned. This asymmetry arises because the specification problem involves syntactic restrictions on arguments, but not on results. A more realistic general-purpose interface specification would include as an additional parameter the set of legal results and would define $LegalReturner$ to assert that results are in this set.

Composing a caller component and a returner component produces a system in which the two components interact according to the protocol. In TLA, composition is conjunction [3]. A simple calculation, using predicate logic and the fact that $\Box$ distributes over $\wedge$ and $\forall$, shows that $LegalCaller \wedge LegalReturner$ is equivalent to

$$\forall p \in PrIds : \wedge \neg Calling(p)$$
$$\wedge \Box \begin{bmatrix} \vee \wedge \exists a \in Args : Call(p, a) \\ \wedge rtrner(p)' = rtrner(p) \\ \vee \wedge \exists v : Return(p, v) \\ \wedge caller(p)' = caller(p) \end{bmatrix}_{\langle caller(p), rtrner(p) \rangle}$$

This formula asserts that, for each process p, initially p is not processing a procedure call, and every step is either[7] (i) a $Call(p, a)$ step, for a legal argument

---

[6] Each component's specification would have had an initial condition on its signaling wire had we constrained the values of those wires—for example, by requiring signaling values to be 0 or 1.

[7] For any actions A and B, an $A \vee B$ step is an A step or a B step.

a, that leaves *rtrner*(*p*) unchanged, (ii) a *Return*(*p*, *v*) step that leaves *caller*(*p*) unchanged, or (iii) a step that leaves both *caller*(*p*) and *rtrner*(*p*) unchanged. The conjunction of the specifications of the two components therefore expresses what we would expect to be the specification of the complete handshake protocol. (The conjunction represents two components communicating over the same channel because the specifications have the same free variable *ch*.)

We are using a noninterleaving representation [3], in which a single step can represent operations performed by several processes. This approach seems more convenient for this specification problem than the more traditional interleaving representation, in which each step represents an operation of at most one process. TLA is not inherently biased towards either specification style.

2 A Memory Component

In this section we give two specifications of the memory component described in the problem statement. In both specifications, the memory component supports read and write operations. The two specifications differ on whether the memory component is reliable; the unreliable version can return memory-failure exceptions, while the reliable version cannot.

2.1 The Parameters

For expository reasons, we split the specifications into two modules. The first module, *MemoryParameters*, is given in Figure 3 on this page. It declares the parameters of the memory specification. The **export** statement is explained below.

The **parameters** section declares the following parameters.

―――――――――― **module** *MemoryParameters* ――――――――――

export *MemoryParameters*, *E*

parameters
    MemLocs, *MemVals*, *InitVal*, *Vals*, *PrIds* : CONSTANT
    memCh : VARIABLE

---

assumption
    ParamAssump $\triangleq$ $\land$ *MemLocs* $\cup$ *MemVals* $\subseteq$ *Vals*
                       $\land$ { "BadArg", "MemFailure" } $\cap$ *MemVals* = { }
                       $\land$ *InitVal* $\in$ *MemVals*

LegalArgs $\triangleq$ ({ "Read" } $\times$ *Vals*) $\cup$ ({ "Write" } $\times$ *Vals* $\times$ *Vals*)

include *ProcedureInterface* **as** *E* **with** *ch* $\leftarrow$ *memCh*, *Args* $\leftarrow$ *LegalArgs*

Fig. 3. Module *MemoryParameters*.

memCh This variable represents the procedure-calling interface to the memory.

MemLocs, *MemVals*, *InitVal* As in the problem statement, *MemLocs* is a set of memory locations, *MemVals* is a set of values that can be stored in those locations, and *InitVal* is the initial value of all locations.

Vals This is the set of syntactically legal argument values mentioned in the problem statement. In particular, we assume that the procedure-calling mechanism allows only read and write calls with arguments in *Vals*.

PrIds The same as for the *ProcedureInterface* module.

The module next asserts assumption *ParamAssump* about the constant parameters. The assumption's first conjunct states that *MemLocs* and *MemVals* are subsets of *Vals*, so every semantically legal argument is also syntactically legal. The second conjunct states that the strings "BadArg" and "MemFailure" are not elements of *MemVals*. These strings are used to represent the corresponding exceptions in the problem statement. For convenience, we let a successful read operation return a memory value and represent an exception by returning one of these strings. A successful write operation returns the string "OK". The third conjunct of *ParamAssump* asserts that *InitVal* is an element of *MemVals*, a condition implied by the problem statement.

The module defines *LegalArgs* to be the set of syntactically legal arguments of procedure calls to the memory.

Finally, the **include** statement includes a copy of the *ProcedureInterface* module, with each defined symbol X renamed as $E.X$, with *memCh* substituted for the parameter *ch*, with *LegalArgs* substituted for the parameter *Args*, and with *PrIds* (which is a parameter of the current module) implicitly substituted for the parameter *PrIds*. For example, this statement includes the definitions:

$$E.caller(p) \triangleq \langle memCh[p].arg, memCh[p].cbit \rangle$$
$$E.LegalCaller \triangleq \forall p \in PrIds :$$
$$\wedge \neg E.Calling(p)$$
$$\wedge \Box[\exists a \in LegalArgs : E.Call(p, a)]_{E.caller(p)}$$

The E in the **export** statement asserts that all these included definitions are exported. Exported symbols are the ones obtained by any other module that includes the *MemoryParameters* module. The *MemoryParameters* in the **export** statement asserts that the symbols defined in the module itself—in this case, *ParamAssump* and *LegalArgs*—are exported. Omitting an **export** statement in a module M is equivalent to adding the statement **export** M.

2.2 The Memory Specification

The specifications of the reliable and unreliable memories are contained in module *Memory* of Figure 4 on the next page and Figure 5 on page 30. The module begins by importing the *MemoryParameters* module. The **import** statement is

────────── **module** *Memory* ──────────

import *MemoryParameters*
export *Memory*, *E*

────────── **module** *Inner* ──────────

parameters
   mem, *result* : VARIABLE

$NotAResult \triangleq$ CHOOSE v :
                    $v \notin \{$ "OK", "BadArg", "MemFailure" $\} \cup MemVals$

$MInit(l) \triangleq mem[l] = InitVal$

$PInit(p) \triangleq result[p] = NotAResult$

$Read(p) \triangleq \exists l : \wedge E.Calling(p)$
                   $\wedge memCh[p].arg = \langle$ "Read", $l \rangle$
                   $\wedge result'[p] = $ **if** $l \in MemLocs$ **then** $mem[l]$
                                        else "BadArg"
              $\wedge$ UNCHANGED $E.rtrner(p)$

$Write(p, l) \triangleq \exists v : \wedge E.Calling(p)$
                       $\wedge memCh[p].arg = \langle$ "Write", $l, v \rangle$
                       $\wedge \vee \wedge (l \in MemLocs) \wedge (v \in MemVals)$
                           $\wedge mem'[l] = v$
                           $\wedge result'[p] = $ "OK"
                       $\vee \wedge \neg((l \in MemLocs) \wedge (v \in MemVals))$
                           $\wedge result'[p] = $ "BadArg"
                           $\wedge$ UNCHANGED $mem[l]$
                       $\wedge$ UNCHANGED $E.rtrner(p)$

$Fail(p) \triangleq \wedge E.Calling(p)$
              $\wedge result'[p] = $ "MemFailure"
              $\wedge$ UNCHANGED $E.rtrner(p)$

$Return(p) \triangleq \wedge result[p] \neq NotAResult$
                $\wedge result'[p] = NotAResult$
                $\wedge E.Return(p, result[p])$

$RNext(p) \triangleq Read(p) \vee (\exists l : Write(p, l)) \vee Return(p)$

$UNext(p) \triangleq RNext(p) \vee Fail(p)$

$pvars(p) \triangleq \langle E.rtrner(p), result[p] \rangle$

$RPSpec(p) \triangleq \wedge PInit(p)$
                 $\wedge \Box[RNext(p)]_{pvars(p)}$
                 $\wedge \text{WF}_{pvars(p)}(RNext(p)) \wedge \text{WF}_{pvars(p)}(Return(p))$

Fig. 4. First part of module *Memory*.

$$
\begin{aligned}
UPSpec(p) \ \triangleq \ & \wedge \ PInit(p) \\
& \wedge \ \Box[UNext(p)]_{pvars(p)} \\
& \wedge \ \mathrm{WF}_{pvars(p)}(RNext(p)) \ \wedge \ \mathrm{WF}_{pvars(p)}(Return(p))
\end{aligned}
$$

$$
MSpec(l) \ \triangleq \ MInit(l) \ \wedge \ \Box[\exists\, p \in PrIds : Write(p,l)]_{mem[l]}
$$

$$
IRSpec \ \triangleq \ (\forall\, p \in PrIds : RPSpec(p)) \ \wedge \ (\forall\, l \in MemLocs : MSpec(l))
$$

$$
IUSpec \ \triangleq \ (\forall\, p \in PrIds : UPSpec(p)) \ \wedge \ (\forall\, l \in MemLocs : MSpec(l))
$$

$$
RSpec \ \triangleq \ \exists\, mem, result : Inner.IRSpec
$$

$$
USpec \ \triangleq \ \exists\, mem, result : Inner.IUSpec
$$

Fig. 5. Second part of module *Memory*.

equivalent to simply copying the entire *Memory* module—its parameter declarations, assumption, and definitions—into the current module. (However, imported definitions are not automatically exported.) The **export** statement is needed because we want to use formula *E.LegalCaller* in asserting the correctness of an implementation.

The reader should note the distinction between **import** and **include**. Importing a module imports its definitions and parameters. Including a module includes its definitions (with renaming), but its parameters are instantiated, not included.

We now explain our specification in a top-down fashion, starting with the final definition. Our specifications of the reliable and unreliable memory components are the formulas *RSpec* and *USpec* defined in Figure 5, at the end of the module. The two specifications are almost identical, so we now discuss only *RSpec*, the reliable-memory specification. Afterwards, we explain how *USpec* differs from it.

Formula *RSpec* is defined to equal $\exists\, mem, result : Inner.IRSpec$. Intuitively, it asserts of a behavior that there exist assignments of values for the variables *mem* and *result*—possibly assigning different values in each state of the behavior—for which the behavior satisfies *Inner.IRSpec*. Formula $\exists\, mem, result : Inner.IRSpec$ asserts nothing about the actual values of the variables *mem* and *result*; it is the specification obtained by "hiding" *mem* and *result* in the specification *Inner.IRSpec*.

Since *mem* and *result* are not free variables of the specification, they should not be parameters of module *Memory*. We therefore introduce a submodule named *Inner* having these variables as its parameters.[8] The symbol *IRSpec* defined in submodule *Inner* is named *Inner.IRSpec* when used outside the submodule. The symbol *Inner.IRSpec* can appear only in a context in which *mem* and *result* are declared—for example, in the scope of the quantifier $\exists\, mem, result$.

---

[8] Instead of introducing a submodule, we could have made *mem* and *result* explicit parameters of all the definitions in which they now occur free.

The bound variable *mem* represents the current contents of memory; $mem[l]$ equals the contents of memory location l. The bound variable *result* records the activity of the memory component processes. For each process p, $result[p]$ initially equals *NotAResult*, which is a value different from any that a procedure call can return.[9] When process p is ready to return a result, that result is $result[p]$. (Even though it is ready to return, the process can "change its mind" and choose a different result before actually returning.)

Formula *IRSpec* is the conjunction of two formulas, which describe two components that constitute the memory component. The first component is responsible for communicating on the channel *memCh* and managing the variable *result*; the second component manages the variable *mem*.

The second conjunct is itself the conjunction[10] of formulas $MSpec(l)$, for each memory location l. We view $MSpec(l)$ as the specification of a separate process that manages $mem[l]$. Formula $MSpec(l)$ has the familiar form $I \wedge \Box[N]_v$. It asserts that $MInit(l)$ holds in the initial state, and that every step is either a $Write(p, l)$ step for some process p, or else leaves $mem[l]$ unchanged. The initial predicate $MInit(l)$ asserts that $mem[l]$ equals *InitVal*, the initial memory value. Action $Write(p, l)$, which we discuss below, is enabled only when the memory component is processing a procedure call by process p to write some value v to location l; a $Write(p, l)$ step sets the new value of $mem[l]$ to this v.

The first conjunct of *IRSpec* is the conjunction of formulas $RPSpec(p)$ for each process p in *PrIds*. We view $RPSpec(p)$ as the specification of a process that manages the returner's part of the channel $memCh[p]$ and the variable $result[p]$. Formula $RPSpec(p)$ has the form $I \wedge \Box[N]_v \wedge F$. A formula $\Box[N]_v$ asserts that every step that changes v is an N step, but it does not require any such steps to occur. It allows a behavior in which v never changes. We require that certain changes do occur by conjoining an additional condition F, which constrains what must eventually happen but does not disallow any individual step. We call $I \wedge \Box[N]_v$ the *safety* condition of the specification and F its *fairness* or *liveness* condition. We now examine the safety condition of $RPSpec(p)$; its fairness condition is considered below.

A formula $I \wedge \Box[N]_v$ describes how the state function v may change. For $RPSpec(p)$, the subscript v is the state function $pvars(p)$, which is defined to be the pair $\langle E.rtrner(p), result[p] \rangle$. A pair changes iff one of its elements changes, so $RPSpec(p)$ describes changes to $E.rtrner(p)$, the returner's part of the communication channel $memCh[p]$, and to $result[p]$.

We explain $RPSpec(p)$ with the help of the predicate-action diagram [13] of Figure 6 on the next page. This diagram has the following meaning.

– The small arrow indicates that initially, $result[p]$ equals *NotAResult*.

---

[9] The definition of *NotAResult* in submodule *Inner* uses the operator CHOOSE, which is the TLA$^+$ name for Hilbert's ε [15]. We can define *NotAResult* in this way because the axioms of set theory imply that, for every set S, there exists a value not in S.

[10] Informally, we often think of $\forall x \in S : F(x)$ as the conjunction of the formulas $F(x)$ for all x in S.

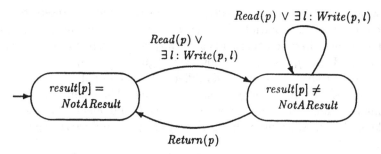

Fig. 6. A predicate-action diagram of $pvars(p)$ for formula $RPSpec(p)$ of the *Memory* module.

- When $result[p]$ equals *NotAResult*, the pair $pvars(p)$ can be changed only by a $Read(p)$ step or a $Write(p, l)$ step, for some l. Such a step sets $result[p]$ unequal to *NotAResult*.

- When $result[p]$ is not equal to *NotAResult*, the pair $pvars(p)$ can be changed only by a $Read(p)$ step, some $Write(p, l)$ step, or a $Return(p)$ step. A $Read(p)$ or $Write(p, l)$ step leaves $result[p]$ unequal to *NotAResult*, while a $Return(p)$ step sets it to *NotAResult*.

Predicate-action diagrams are defined formally in [13] to represent TLA formulas. The assertion that Figure 6 is a diagram for $RPSpec(p)$ means that $RPSpec(p)$ implies the formula represented by the diagram. In general, one can draw many different diagrams for the same formula. Proving that a diagram is a predicate-action diagram for a specification helps confirm our understanding of the specification. The proof for Figure 6 is trivial. This diagram is actually equivalent to the safety part of $RPSpec(p)$.

To complete our understanding of the safety part of $RPSpec(p)$, we must examine what steps are allowed by the actions $Read(p)$, $Write(p, l)$, and $Return(p)$. Action $Read(p)$ is enabled when $E.Calling(p)$ is true and $memCh[p].arg$ equals ⟨ "Read", l⟩ for some l, so the process p caller has called the read procedure with argument l and the process p returner has not yet returned a result. If l is a legal memory address, then a $Read(p)$ step sets $result[p]$ to $mem[l]$; otherwise it sets $result[p]$ to the string "BadArg". The step leaves $E.rtrner$ unchanged. (The TLA$^+$ action UNCHANGED v is defined to equal $v' = v$, for any state function v.) Action $Write(p, l)$ is similar. It is enabled when there is a pending request to write some value v in memory location l; it sets $result[p]$ to the appropriate result and sets $mem[l]$ to v iff the request is valid.

Action $Return(p)$ issues the return of $result[p]$ and resets $result[p]$ to equal *NotAResult*. The action is enabled iff $result[p]$ is unequal to *NotAResult* and action $E.Return(p)$ is enabled, which is the case iff $E.Calling(p)$ equals TRUE.

Looking at Figure 6 again, we now see that returner process p goes through the following cycle. It waits (with $result[p]$ equal to *NotAResult*) until a procedure call occurs. It then does one or more internal $Read(p)$ or $Write(p, l)$

steps, which choose $result[p]$. Finally, it returns $result[p]$ and resets $result[p]$ to $NotAResult$. Allowing multiple $Write(p, l)$ steps is important because $mem[l]$ could be changed between those steps by $Write(q, l)$ steps for some q different from p. Such $Write(q, l)$ steps are allowed by Figure 6 (and by $RPSpec(p)$) if they do not change $pvars(p)$. It makes no difference to the final specification $RSpec$ whether or not multiple $Read(p)$ steps are allowed. The changes to $memCh$ are the same as if only the last one were performed, and $memCh$ is the only free variable of $RSpec$. Allowing multiple $Read(p)$ steps simplifies the specification a bit.

This completes our explanation of the safety condition of $RPSpec(p)$. We now consider the fairness condition. The safety condition of $RPSpec(p)$ implies that the steps described by Figure 6 are the only ones that are allowed to happen. We want the fairness condition to assert that they must happen. In particular, we want to assert the following two requirements: (L1) after a procedure call has been issued, the transition out of the $result[p] = NotAResult$ state eventually occurs, and (L2) the transition back to that state eventually occurs.

These requirements are expressed with *weak fairness* formulas of the form $WF_v(A)$. Such a formula asserts that if the action $A \wedge (v' \neq v)$ remains continually enabled, then an $A \wedge (v' \neq v)$ step must occur. In other words, if it remains possible to take an A step that changes v, then such a step must eventually be taken.

Condition L1 is implied by $WF_{pvars(p)}(RNext(p))$. To see this, suppose that $result[p]$ equals $NotAResult$ and a read or write call is issued. Then $Read(p)$ or some $Write(p, l)$ action is enabled, so $RNext(p)$ is enabled. Assuming that the caller obeys the handshake protocol, action $RNext(p)$ will remain enabled until a $Read(p)$ or $Write(p, l)$ step occurs. Formula $WF_{pvars(p)}(RNext(p))$ therefore implies that a $RNext(p)$ step does occur, and that step can only be the desired $Read(p)$ or $Write(p, l)$ step.

Formula $WF_{pvars(p)}(RNext(p))$ implies that, while $result[p] \neq NotAResult$ remains true, $RNext(p)$ steps must keep occurring. However, those steps could be $Read(p)$ or $Write(p, l)$ steps. ($Read(p)$ steps can change $pvars(p)$ if intervening steps by other processes keep changing $mem[l]$.) Formula $WF_{pvars(p)}(Return(p))$, the second conjunct of $RPSpec(p)$'s fairness condition, asserts that a $Return(p)$ step must eventually occur when $result[p] \neq NotAResult$ holds.

There are other possible fairness conditions for $RPSpec(p)$. Two other obvious choices are obtained by replacing $WF_{pvars(p)}(RNext(p))$ with one of the following:

$$WF_{pvars(p)}(Read(p)) \ \wedge \ WF_{pvars(p)}(\exists l : Write(p, l))$$

$$WF_{pvars(p)}(Read(p)) \ \wedge \ (\forall l : WF_{pvars(p)}(Write(p, l)))$$

It is not hard to check that the conjunction of $E.LegalCaller$ (the specification that the caller obeys the handshake protocol) and the safety condition of $RPSpec(p)$ implies that both formulas are equivalent to $WF_{pvars(p)}(RNext(p))$, for any p in $PrIds$. We care what the memory component does only when the caller obeys the protocol. Hence, any of these three choices of fairness conditions for *RPSpec(p)* yield essentially the same specification. (The three fairness conditions need not be equivalent on a behavior in which *memCh[p].arg* changes while the memory is processing a procedure call by process *p*.)

Weak fairness is a standard concept of concurrency [6, 17]. The reader who is not already familiar with it may find fairness conditions difficult to understand. Fairness can be subtle, and it is not obvious why we express it in TLA with WF formulas. For example, it might seem easier to express L1 by writing the temporal-logic formula

$$(result[p] = NotAResult) \wedge E.Calling(p) \leadsto (result[p] \neq NotAResult)$$

which asserts that if *result[p]* ever equals *NotAResult* when *E.Calling(p)* is true, then it must eventually become unequal to *NotAResult*. We have found that the use of arbitrary temporal-logic formulas makes it easy to write incorrect specifications, and using WF formulas helps us avoid errors.

Finally, let us consider the specification *USpec* of the unreliable memory component. It is identical to *RSpec* except it has action *UNext(p)* instead of *RNext(p)* as its next-state action. Action *UNext(p)* differs from *RNext(p)* by also allowing internal *Fail(p)* steps, which set *result[p]* to "MemFailure". Such steps can occur instead of, before, after, or between *Read(p)* or *Write(p,l)* steps. We could have replaced *RNext(p)* with *UNext(p)* in the fairness condition; *LegalCaller* implies that the two definitions of *USpec* are equivalent. However, it might seem odd to require the eventual occurrence of a step that may be a failure step.

2.3   Solution to Problem 1

(a) Formulas *RSpec* and *USpec* are what we call *component specifications*. They describe a system containing a properly operating (reliable or unreliable) memory component. Whether they constitute the specifications of a memory depends on what the specifications are for.

Component specifications can be used to describe a complete system in which all the components function properly, allowing us to prove properties of the system. The simplest such complete-system specification of a system containing a reliable memory component is *RSpec ∧ E.LegalCaller*, which asserts that the memory component behaves properly and the rest of the system follows the handshake protocol.

Another possible use of a memory specification is to serve as a contract between the user of the memory and its implementor. Such a specification should be satisfied by precisely those behaviors that represent physical histories in which the memory fulfills its obligations. Formula *RSpec* cannot serve as such a specification because it says nothing about the memory's environment. A real memory that uses the two-phase handshake protocol will display completely unpredictable behavior if its environment does not correctly follow the protocol. To be implementable, the specification must assert only that *RSpec* is satisfied if the memory's environment satisfies the caller's part of the handshake protocol—in other words, if $E.LegalCaller$ is satisfied. We might therefore expect the specification of a reliable memory to be $E.LegalCaller \Rightarrow RSpec$. However, for reasons explained in [3], we instead write this specification as the formula $E.LegalCaller \xrightarrow{+} RSpec$. This formula means roughly that $RSpec$ remains true as long as $E.LegalCaller$ does. Such a formula is called an *assumption/guarantee specification* [8]; the memory guarantees to satisfy its component-specification $RSpec$ as long as the environment assumption $E.LegalCaller$ is satisfied.

When we present a component specification as a solution to one of the specification problems, we indicate its environment assumption. Writing the corresponding assumption/guarantee specification is then trivial.

When we write a component specification, we think of steps satisfying the specification's next-state action as representing operations performed by that component. We could make this an explicit assumption by formally attributing every step to either the component or its environment, as described in [3]. However, whether the component or its environment actually performs an operation is a question of physical reality, and the connection between a mathematical specification and reality can never be made completely formal.

The assumption $ParamAssump$ about the parameters is not part of our memory component specifications, since the formulas $RSpec$ and $USpec$ are not defined in terms of $ParamAssump$. We could weaken the specifications by adding $ParamAssump$ as an assumption and writing, for example, $ParamAssump \Rightarrow RSpec$. We do not need to do so; as we will see below, putting the assumption $ParamAssump$ into the $Memory$ module allows us to use it when proving the correctness of an implementation of the memory component.

(b) In TLA, implementation is implication. To prove that a reliable memory implements an unreliable one, it suffices to prove the theorem $RSpec \Rightarrow USpec$. The proof is easy; expanding the definitions shows that it suffices to prove $\Box[RNext(p)]_{pvars(p)} \Rightarrow \Box[UNext(p)]_{pvars(p)}$, which is trivial since $RNext(p)$ obviously implies $UNext(p)$.

In general, we would not expect such an implication to be valid. For example, it would not have been valid had we written $\mathrm{WF}_{pvars(p)}(UNext(p))$ instead of $\mathrm{WF}_{pvars(p)}(RNext(p))$ in the fairness condition of $UPSpec(p)$. Component specifications like $RSpec$ and $USpec$ describe how the component should behave when its environment behaves properly. They do not constrain the environment's behavior, and they may allow bizarre behaviors when the environment behaves improperly. A priori, there is no reason why the particular bizarre behaviors allowed by $RSpec$ as the result of an incorrectly functioning environment should also be allowed by $USpec$. Hence, we would expect $RSpec \Rightarrow USpec$ to be true only for those behaviors satisfying the memory's environment specification, $E.LegalCaller$. We would therefore expect to prove only $E.LegalCaller \Rightarrow (RSpec \Rightarrow USpec)$, which is equivalent to

$$E.LegalCaller \wedge RSpec \Rightarrow USpec \qquad (1)$$

We can also phrase implementation in terms of assumption/guarantee specifications. Such specifications are satisfied by precisely those behaviors in which the memory meets its obligation. We would expect the assumption/guarantee specification of the reliable memory to imply that of the unreliable memory:

$$(E.LegalCaller \overset{+}{\Rightarrow} RSpec) \Rightarrow (E.LegalCaller \overset{+}{\Rightarrow} USpec) \qquad (2)$$

The relation between the two forms of implementation conditions exemplified by (1) and (2) is investigated in [3]. Because our two memory-component specifications are so similar, we can prove $RSpec \Rightarrow USpec$, which implies (1) and (2).

(c) If the memory is implemented with unreliable components that can fail forever, then there is no way to guarantee that anything but "MemFailure" exceptions will ever occur. (For example, this will be the case if it is implemented with an RPC component that always returns "RPCFailure" exceptions.)

We can easily define a memory that guarantees eventual success. We do so by requiring that if enough calls of some particular kind are issued, then one of them eventually succeeds. Different conditions are obtained by different choices of the kind of calls—for example, calls to a particular memory location, or reads by a particular process. Such conditions can be expressed using *strong fairness* formulas of the form $SF_v(A)$. This formula asserts that if $A \wedge (v' \neq v)$ is enabled often enough, then an $A \wedge (v' \neq v)$ step must occur. (Strong fairness is stronger than weak fairness because it requires a step to occur if the action is enabled often enough, even if the action does not remain continuously enabled.) For example, to strengthen the specification to require that, if process p keeps issuing calls, then it will eventually receive a result other than "MemFailure", we simply replace the fairness condition of $UPSpec(p)$ by:

$$\wedge \; SF_{pvars(p)}(Read(p) \vee (\exists\, l \,:\, Write(p, l)))$$
$$\wedge \; SF_{pvars(p)}(Return(p) \wedge (result[p] \neq \text{"MemFailure"}))$$

To solve Problem 3 (proving the correctness of a memory implementation), we would then need to add a corresponding liveness condition to the RPC component.

3 Implementing the Memory

The memory implementation is obtained by composing a memory clerk component, an RPC component, and a reliable memory component. The memory clerk translates memory calls into RPC calls, and optionally retries RPC calls when they result in RPC failures. In this section we describe the RPC and the memory clerk components, and then prove the correctness of the implementation.

3.1 The RPC Component

The RPC component connects a sender to a receiver. As with the memory component, we split its specification into two modules.

The Parameters Module The specification of the RPC component begins with module *RPCParameters* in Figure 7 on this page; the module declares parameters and both makes and includes some definitions. The *RPCParameters*

───────── **module** *RPCParameters* ─────────

export *RPCParameters, Snd, Rcv*
import *Naturals, Sequences*

parameters *sndCh, rcvCh* : VARIABLE
                Procs, ArgNum, Vals, PrIds : CONSTANT

---

assumption *ParamAssump* $\triangleq$ *ArgNum* $\in$ [*Procs* $\rightarrow$ *Nat*]

LegalSndArgs $\triangleq$ {"RemoteCall"} $\times$ STRING $\times$ *Seq*(*Vals*)

LegalRcvArgs $\triangleq$
{$s \in$ *Seq*(*Procs* $\cup$ *Vals*) : $\wedge$ *Len*(*s*) > 0
                         $\wedge$ *Head*(*s*) $\in$ *Procs*
                         $\wedge$ *Tail*(*s*) $\in$ *Seq*(*Vals*)
                         $\wedge$ *Len*(*s*) $= 1 + ArgNum[Head(s)]$ }

include *ProcedureInterface* **as** *Snd* **with** *ch* $\leftarrow$ *sndCh*, *Args* $\leftarrow$ *LegalSndArgs*
include *ProcedureInterface* **as** *Rcv* **with** *ch* $\leftarrow$ *rcvCh*, *Args* $\leftarrow$ *LegalRcvArgs*

Fig. 7. Module *RPCParameters*.

module imports the module *Naturals*, a predefined module that defines the natural numbers and the usual operators on them. It then imports the *Sequences* module, which defines operators on finite sequences. In TLA$^+$, an *n*-tuple $\langle v_1, \ldots, v_n \rangle$ is a function whose domain is the set $\{1, \ldots, n\}$ of natural numbers, where $\langle v_1, \ldots, v_n \rangle[i]$ equals v_i, for $1 \leq i \leq n$.[11] The *Sequences* module represents sequences as tuples. The module appeared in [14] (without the definition of *Seq*, which was not needed there) and is given without further explanation in Figure 8 on the next page. It defines the usual operators *Head*, *Tail*, $\circ$ (concatenation), and *Len* (length) on sequences, as well as the operator *Seq*, where *Seq*(*S*) is the set of sequences of elements in *S*. (The values of *Head*(*s*) and *Tail*(*s*) are not constrained when *s* is the empty sequence.)

The parameters declared in module *RPCParameters* have the following interpretations:

sndCh The procedure-calling interface between the sender and the RPC component.

---

[11] TLA$^+$ uses square brackets to denote function application. An "array variable" is just a variable whose value is a function.

rcvCh The procedure-calling interface between the RPC component and the receiver.

Procs, ArgNum As in the problem statement, *Procs* is a set of legal procedure names and *ArgNum* is a function that assigns to each legal procedure name its number of arguments.

Vals The set of all possible syntactically valid arguments.

PrIds The same as for the *ProcedureInterface* module.

Assumption *ParamAssump* asserts that *ArgNum* is a function with domain *Procs* and range a subset of the set *Nat* of natural numbers. (The definition of *Nat* comes from the *Naturals* module.)

The module next defines *LegalSndArgs* to be the set of syntactically valid arguments with which the RPC component can be called. Calls to the RPC component take two arguments, the first of which is an element of STRING, the set of all strings, and the second of which is a sequence of elements in *Vals*. We use the same convention as in the memory specification, that the argument of a procedure call is a tuple consisting of the procedure name followed by its arguments. The RPC component has a single procedure, whose name is "RemoteCall".

The module defines *LegalRcvArgs* to be the set of syntactically valid arguments with which the RPC component can call the receiver. These consist of all tuples of the form $\langle p, v_1, \ldots, v_n \rangle$ with p in *Procs*, the v_i in *Vals*, and n equal to *ArgNum[p]*.

Finally, the module includes two copies of the *ProcedureInterface* module, one for each of the interfaces, with the appropriate instantiations. The **export** statement (at the beginning of the module) exports these included definitions.

──────────────── **module** *Sequences* ────────────────

import *Naturals*

$$OneTo(n) \triangleq \{i \in Nat : (1 \le i) \wedge (i \le n)\}$$
$$Seq(S) \triangleq \text{UNION } \{[OneTo(n) \to S] : n \in Nat\}$$
$$Len(s) \triangleq \text{CHOOSE } n : (n \in Nat) \wedge ((\text{DOMAIN } s) = OneTo(n))$$
$$Head(s) \triangleq s[1]$$
$$Tail(s) \triangleq [i \in OneTo(Len(s) - 1) \mapsto s[i + 1]]$$
$$(s) \circ (t) \triangleq [i \in OneTo(Len(s) + Len(t)) \mapsto \textbf{if } i \le Len(s)$$
$$\textbf{then } s[i]$$
$$\textbf{else } t[i - Len(s)]]$$

Fig. 8. Module *Sequences*.

Problem 2: The RPC Component's Specification The specification of the RPC component appears in module *RPC* of Figure 10 on page 40. It is the formula $\exists\, rstate : Inner.ISpec$, where *ISpec* is defined in a submodule named *Inner*.

We explain the specification *ISpec* with the aid of the diagram of Figure 9 on this page. This is a predicate-action diagram for *ISpec* of all changes to

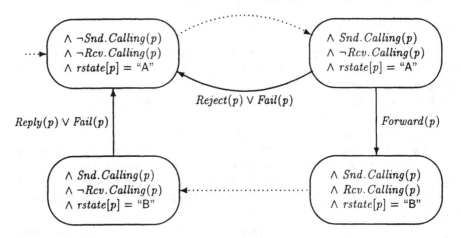

Fig. 9. A predicate-action diagram of *vars*(p) for formula *ISpec* of module *RPC*, where p is an element of *PrIds*. (The dotted arrows are not formally part of the diagram.)

vars(p), where p is any element of *PrIds*. The state function *vars*(p) is the triple $\langle rstate[p], Snd.rtrner(p), Rcv.caller(p)\rangle$ that forms the state of the RPC component's process p. The dotted arrows are not formally part of the diagram. The initial-condition arrow indicates obligations of both the RPC component and its environment; the other dotted arrows represent state changes caused by the environment that do not change the RPC component's state. (Recall that ...*Calling*(p) can be changed by either the caller changing ...*caller*(p) or the returner changing ...*rtrner*(p).) The top dotted arrow represents the sender's action of calling the RPC component, which makes *Snd.Calling*(p) true. The bottom dotted arrow represents the receiver's return action, which makes *Rcv.Calling* false.

The solid arrows (the real arrows of the predicate-action diagram) represent steps of process p of the RPC component. The *Forward*(p) action relays the call to the receiver, making *Rcv.Calling*(p) true. The *Fail*(p) action returns "RPCFailure". The *Reject*(p) action returns "BadCall" without relaying the request. The *Reply*(p) action returns to the sender the result returned by the receiver. The variable *rstate* is needed to distinguish the upper right and lower-left states. The values "A" and "B" are arbitrary; any two values can be used.

The specification *Spec* of the RPC component appears in module *RPC* of

Figure 10 on this page. It is similar enough to the memory specification that it

---

──────────── **module** *RPC* ────────────

import *RPCParameters, Naturals, Sequences*
export *RPC, Snd, Rcv*

──────────── **module** *Inner* ────────────

parameters
  rstate : VARIABLE

$Init(p) \triangleq (rstate[p] = \text{``A''}) \wedge \neg Rcv.Calling(p)$

$RelayArg(p) \triangleq \langle sndCh[p].arg[2] \rangle \circ sndCh[p].arg[3]$

$Forward(p) \triangleq \wedge\; Snd.Calling(p) \wedge (rstate[p] = \text{``A''})$
$\qquad\qquad\quad \wedge\; RelayArg(p) \in LegalRcvArgs$
$\qquad\qquad\quad \wedge\; Rcv.Call(p, RelayArg(p))$
$\qquad\qquad\quad \wedge\; rstate'[p] = \text{``B''}$
$\qquad\qquad\quad \wedge\; \text{UNCHANGED } Snd.rtrner(p)$

$Reject(p) \triangleq \wedge\; rstate[p] = \text{``A''}$
$\qquad\qquad\quad \wedge\; RelayArg(p) \notin LegalRcvArgs$
$\qquad\qquad\quad \wedge\; Snd.Return(p, \text{``BadCall''})$
$\qquad\qquad\quad \wedge\; \text{UNCHANGED } \langle rstate[p], Rcv.caller(p) \rangle$

$Fail(p) \triangleq \wedge\; \neg Rcv.Calling(p)$
$\qquad\qquad\; \wedge\; Snd.Return(p, \text{``RPCFailure''})$
$\qquad\qquad\; \wedge\; rstate'[p] = \text{``A''}$
$\qquad\qquad\; \wedge\; \text{UNCHANGED } Rcv.caller(p)$

$Reply(p) \triangleq \wedge\; \neg Rcv.Calling(p) \wedge (rstate[p] = \text{``B''})$
$\qquad\qquad\quad \wedge\; Snd.Return(p, rcvCh[p].res)$
$\qquad\qquad\quad \wedge\; rstate'[p] = \text{``A''}$
$\qquad\qquad\quad \wedge\; \text{UNCHANGED } Rcv.caller(p)$

$Next(p) \triangleq Forward(p) \vee Reject(p) \vee Fail(p) \vee Reply(p)$

$vars(p) \triangleq \langle rstate[p], Snd.rtrner(p), Rcv.caller(p) \rangle$

$ISpec \triangleq \forall\, p \in PrIds : Init(p) \wedge \Box[Next(p)]_{vars(p)} \wedge \text{WF}_{vars(p)}(Next(p))$

$Spec \triangleq \exists\, rstate : Inner.ISpec$

Fig. 10. The specification of the RPC component.

should require little additional explanation. The definition of *RelayArg* makes use
of the way sequences are represented as tuples, and it may seem a little obscure.
When the sender's process p has called the RPC component, $RelayArg(p)$ is the
argument with which the RPC component should call the receiver. For example,

if the RPC component is called with argument $\langle$ "RemoteCall", "Write", $\langle 17, \sqrt{2} \rangle \rangle$, then $RelayArg(p)$ equals $\langle$ "Write", $17, \sqrt{2} \rangle$. In the definitions of the actions, we have eliminated some redundant instances of the conjuncts $Snd.Calling(p)$ and $\neg Rcv.Calling(p)$ that appear in the predicate-action diagram; $Snd.Calling(p)$ is implied by $Snd.Return(p,\ldots)$, and the diagram shows that $\neg Rcv.Calling(p)$ is implied by $rstate[p] =$ "A" in every reachable state.

Formula $Spec$ of the RPC module is the component specification of the RPC component. The component's environment specification is $Snd.LegalCaller \wedge Rcv.LegalReturner$. As described above, the conjunction of these two formulas is the specification of a complete system consisting of an RPC component and a sender and receiver that obey the handshake protocol; combining the formulas with the $\stackrel{+}{\rhd}$ operator yields an assumption/guarantee specification of the RPC component.

3.2 The Implementation

The Memory Clerk We now present the specification of the memory clerk, which is quite similar to that of the RPC component. It begins with module *MemClerkParameters* of Figure 11 on this page. The module declares the following parameters:

sndCh, *rcvCh* The procedure-calling interfaces between the clerk and the memory's caller, and between the clerk and the RPC component.

Vals, *PrIds* The same as for the *MemoryParameters* and *ProcedureInterface* modules, respectively.

The definitions of *LegalSndArgs* and *LegalRcvArgs* and the inclusion of two copies of the *ProcedureInterface* module serve the same purpose as they do in the *RPCParameters* module.

─────────────── **module** *MemClerkParameters* ───────────────

export *MemClerkParameters*, *Snd*, *Rcv*

parameters *sndCh*, *rcvCh* : VARIABLE
PrIds, *Vals* : CONSTANT

$LegalSndArgs \triangleq (\{$ "Read" $\} \times Vals) \cup (\{$ "Write" $\} \times Vals \times Vals)$

$LegalRcvArgs \triangleq \{$ "RemoteCall" $\} \times \{$ "Read", "Write" $\} \times Seq(Vals)$

include *ProcedureInterface* **as** *Snd* **with** $ch \leftarrow sndCh, Args \leftarrow LegalSndArgs$
include *ProcedureInterface* **as** *Rcv* **with** $ch \leftarrow rcvCh, Args \leftarrow LegalRcvArgs$

Fig. 11. Module *MemClerkParameters*.

The specification of the memory clerk is a formula $\exists\, cstate : Inner.ISpec$. The formula $ISpec$ is described by the predicate-action diagram of Figure 12 on this page, which is similar to that of Figure 9 (page 39). The $Reply(p)$ and

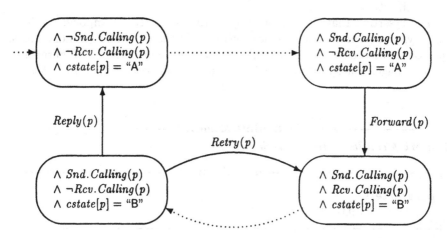

Fig. 12. A predicate-action diagram of $vars(p)$ for formula $ISpec$ of module $MemClerk$, where p is an element of $PrIds$. (The dotted arrows are not formally part of the diagram.)

$Forward(p)$ actions play the same role as in the RPC component's specification. Action $Retry(p)$ retries an RPC call that has yielded an RPC failure.

The clerk's specification $Spec$ appears in Module $MemClerk$ of Figure 13 on the next page. The safety part can be deduced from the predicate-action diagram as we did for the RPC component. The liveness part is a bit trickier. We want to require that the clerk eventually returns from a call, assuming the RPC component eventually returns from each call. Weak fairness on the $Forward(p)$ action ensures progress from the upper-right to the lower-right state of the predicate-action diagram. Strong fairness of $Reply(p)$ is required to ensure eventual progress from the lower-left to the upper-left state; weak fairness would allow behaviors in which the clerk keeps performing $Retry(p)$ steps without ever performing a $Reply(p)$ step.

The Implementation Proof We now formally assert that the composition of a memory clerk, an RPC component, and a reliable memory implements an unreliable memory; and we describe the proof of that assertion.

Since implementation is implication, the assertion that every behavior allowed by an implementation Imp satisfies a specification $Spec$ is expressed by the formula $Imp \Rightarrow Spec$. However, as discussed in Section 2.3, we expect to prove the correctness of an implementation only under the assumption that the environment behaves correctly. If *Env* is the environment's specification, then we expect *Imp* ⇒ *Spec* to be satisfied only by behaviors that satisfy *Env*. Thus, correctness of the implementation means that *Env* ∧ *Imp* ⇒ *Spec* is valid. Composition is conjunction, so validity of this formula asserts that every behavior allowed by the composition of the environment and the implementation satisfies the specification.

The assertion that the composition of the clerk, RPC component, reliable memory, and environment specifications implies the unreliable memory's specification is theorem *Impl* of module *MemoryImplementation* in Figure 14 on the next page. The specification of the unreliable memory's environment is for-

---

──────────────── module *MemClerk* ────────────────

import *MemClerkParameters, Sequences*

──────────────── module *Inner* ────────────────

parameters
    cstate : VARIABLE

$Init(p) \triangleq (cstate[p] = \text{``A''}) \wedge \neg Rcv.Calling(p)$

$RelayArg(p) \triangleq \langle \text{``RemoteCall''}, Head(sndCh[p].arg), Tail(sndCh[p].arg)\rangle$

$ReplyVal(p) \triangleq$ **if** $rcvCh[p].res = \text{``RPCFailure''}$ **then** "MemFailure"
                                                                    else $rcvCh[p].res$

$Forward(p) \triangleq \wedge Snd.Calling(p) \wedge (cstate[p] = \text{``A''})$
                $\wedge Rcv.Call(p, RelayArg(p))$
                $\wedge cstate'[p] = \text{``B''}$
                $\wedge$ UNCHANGED $Snd.rtrner(p)$

$Retry(p) \triangleq \wedge (cstate[p] = \text{``B''}) \wedge (rcvCh[p].res = \text{``RPCFailure''})$
                $\wedge Rcv.Call(p, RelayArg(p))$
                $\wedge$ UNCHANGED $\langle cstate[p], Snd.rtrner(p)\rangle$

$Reply(p) \triangleq \wedge \neg Rcv.Calling(p) \wedge (cstate[p] = \text{``B''})$
                $\wedge Snd.Return(p, ReplyVal(p))$
                $\wedge cstate'[p] = \text{``A''}$
                $\wedge$ UNCHANGED $Rcv.caller(p)$

$Next(p) \triangleq Forward(p) \vee Retry(p) \vee Reply(p)$

$vars(p) \triangleq \langle cstate[p], Snd.rtrner(p), Rcv.caller(p)\rangle$

$ISpec \triangleq \forall p \in PrIds :$
                $\wedge Init(p) \wedge \Box[Next(p)]_{vars(p)}$
                $\wedge \text{WF}_{vars(p)}(Forward(p)) \wedge \text{SF}_{vars(p)}(Reply(p))$

$Spec \triangleq \exists cstate : Inner.ISpec$

Fig. 13. The component specification of the memory clerk.

——— module *MemoryImplementation* ———

import *MemoryParameters, Memory*

parameters
   crCh, rmCh : VARIABLE

---

assumption
   FailureNotAValue $\triangleq$ "RPCFailure" $\notin$ *MemVals*

Procs $\triangleq$ {"Read", "Write"}
ArgNum $\triangleq$ [$i \in Procs \mapsto$ **case** (i = "Read") $\to 1$, (i = "Write") $\to 2$]

include *RPC* **as** *R* **with** *sndCh* $\leftarrow$ *crCh*, *rcvCh* $\leftarrow$ *rmCh*

include *MemClerk* **as** *C* **with** *sndCh* $\leftarrow$ *memCh*, *rcvCh* $\leftarrow$ *crCh*

include *Memory* **as** *M* **with** *memCh* $\leftarrow$ *rmCh*

theorem
   Impl $\triangleq$ *E.LegalCaller* $\land$ *C.Spec* $\land$ *R.Spec* $\land$ *M.RSpec* $\Rightarrow$ *USpec*

Fig. 14. Module *MemoryImplementation*.

mula *E.LegalCaller*, included from module *ProcedureInterface* by the imported module *Memory*. The composition is described schematically by the following picture.

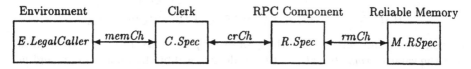

When composing two components by conjoining their specifications, the components are "connected" by instantiating their corresponding interface variable parameters with the same variable. The implementing module's specifications have been included with renaming; the specification *USpec* of the memory is imported from the *Memory* module.

The **theorem** statement asserts that the formula named *Impl* is a consequence of the assumptions *FailureNotAValue*[12] and *ParamAssump* (imported from module *MemoryParameters*), and the laws of TLA.

For convenience, we have gathered many of the definitions imported and included by module *MemoryImplementation* in Figure 15 on page 46. In this figure and in our proof, we use the following naming conventions: (i) we eliminate the "*Inner.*" from symbol names—for example, writing *C.Retry(p)* instead of *C.Inner.Retry(p)*, and (ii) if *X* is the name of a formula of the form $\forall p \in PrIds$:

---

[12] We believe the theorem to be correct without assumption *FailureNotAValue*, but our proof uses the assumption.

Y, then we let $X(p)$ denote the formula Y—as in $R.ISpec(p)$. The figure also defines the following additional symbols: pv, m, e, c, r, and $E.Next$.[13]

Theorem *Impl* has the form $H \Rightarrow \exists\, mem, result : G$. In predicate logic, one proves a formula $\exists\, y : P(y) \Rightarrow \exists\, x : Q(x)$ by proving $P(y) \Rightarrow Q(\overline{x})$ for a suitable instantiation $\overline{x}$ of x. In temporal logic, the instantiation is called a *refinement mapping* [1]. To prove *Impl*, we define a pair of state functions $\overline{mem}$ and $\overline{result}$ and prove $F \Rightarrow \overline{G}$, where F is the formula obtained by removing the existential quantifiers from H, and $\overline{G}$ is the formula obtained by substituting $\overline{mem}$ and $\overline{result}$ for *mem* and *result* in G.

For our proof, we let $\overline{mem}$ equal *mem* (which comes from $M.RSpec$). To define $\overline{result}$, we must introduce a *history variable* [1]. Intuitively, a history variable a is one that is added to remember what happened in the past. Formally, proving $F \Rightarrow \overline{G}$ by "adding a history variable a" means choosing a variable a that does not appear in F and $\overline{G}$, finding a formula *Hist* of a particular form that guarantees that $\exists\, a : Hist$ is valid, and proving $F \wedge Hist \Rightarrow \overline{G}$. Our history variable *rmhist* is defined so that, for each p in *PrIds*, the value of $rmhist[p]$ is initially equal to "A". It is set to "B" when process p of the reliable memory component returns to the RPC component or when process p of the RPC component issues a failure return to the clerk. It is reset to "A" when process p of the clerk returns to the caller. Formally, we define:

$$
\begin{aligned}
h &\;\triangleq\; rmhist[p] \\
HNext(p) &\;\triangleq\; h' = \textbf{if } M.Return(p) \vee R.Fail(p) \\
&\qquad\qquad \textbf{then } \text{``B''} \\
&\qquad\qquad \textbf{else if } C.Reply(p) \textbf{ then } \text{``A''} \\
&\qquad\qquad\qquad\qquad\quad \textbf{else } h \\
Hist &\;\triangleq\; \forall\, p \in PrIds : (h = \text{``A''}) \wedge \Box[HNext(p)]_{\langle c,r,m,h \rangle}
\end{aligned}
$$

It should be intuitively obvious that, for every p in *PrIds*, formula *Hist* implies that the value of $rmhist[p]$ at any time is determined by the values of c, r, and m up to that time. A general theorem of TLA proves the validity of $\exists\, rmhist : Hist$.

The High-Level Proof We describe a structured proof of theorem *Impl*, in the style of [10]. We first present the high-level proof. It uses the state function $\overline{result}$, which we define later (the high-level proof is independent of its definition), and the temporal formula:

$$
\begin{aligned}
IPImp(p) \;\triangleq\; &E.LegalCaller(p) \wedge C.ISpec(p) \wedge R.ISpec(p) \\
&\wedge M.RPSpec(p) \wedge (\forall\, l \in MemLocs : M.MSpec(l)) \wedge Hist(p)
\end{aligned}
$$

For any formula F, we let $\overline{F}$ be the formula obtained by substituting $\overline{result}$ for *result* in F. Note that all formulas in the proof are interpreted in the con-

---

[13] We define a number of operators with implicit parameters that are not parameters of module *MemoryImplementation*—for example, the parameters p and $result[p]$ that appear in the definition of m. If we were being truly formal, such definitions would occur in modules that made the parameters explicit, and these modules would then be included in the proof in contexts where the parameters are declared.

The Specification

Unreliable Memory Component   (imported from *Memory*)

$pv \triangleq pvars(p)$

$UNext(p) \triangleq Read(p) \vee (\exists\, l : Write(p,l)) \vee Return(p) \vee Fail(p)$

$UPSpec(p) \triangleq \wedge\, PInit(p) \wedge \Box[UNext(p)]_{pv}$
$\qquad\qquad\quad \wedge\, \mathrm{WF}_{pv}(RNext(p)) \wedge \mathrm{WF}_{pv}(Return(p))$

$MSpec(l) \triangleq MInit(l) \wedge \Box[\exists\, p \in PrIds : Write(p,l)]_{mem[l]}$

$IUSpec \triangleq \wedge\, \forall\, p \in PrIds : UPSpec(p)$
$\qquad\qquad \wedge\, \forall\, l \in MemLocs : MSpec(l)$

$USpec \triangleq \exists\, mem, result : IUSpec$

The Implementation

The Environment   (included from *ProcedureInterface* via import of *Memory*)

$e \triangleq E.caller(p)$

$E.Next(p) \triangleq \exists\, a \in LegalArgs : E.Call(p,a)$

$E.LegalCaller \triangleq \forall\, p \in PrIds : \neg E.Calling(p) \wedge \Box[E.Next(p)]_e$

Clerk   (included from *MemClerk*)

$c \triangleq C.vars(p)$

$C.Next(p) \triangleq C.Forward(p) \vee C.Retry(p) \vee C.Reply(p)$

$C.ISpec(p) \triangleq \wedge\, C.Init(p) \wedge \Box[C.Next(p)]_c$
$\qquad\qquad\quad \wedge\, \mathrm{WF}_c(C.Forward(p)) \wedge \mathrm{SF}_c(C.Reply(p))$

$C.Spec \triangleq \exists\, cstate : \forall\, p \in PrIds : C.ISpec(p)$

RPC Component   (included from *RPC*)

$r \triangleq R.vars(p)$

$R.Next(p) \triangleq R.Forward(p) \vee R.Reject(p) \vee R.Fail(p) \vee R.Reply(p)$

$R.ISpec(p) \triangleq R.Init(p) \wedge \Box[R.Next(p)]_r \wedge \mathrm{WF}_r(R.Next(p))$

$R.Spec \triangleq \exists\, rstate : \forall\, p \in PrIds : R.ISpec(p)$

Reliable Memory Component   (included from *Memory*)

$m \triangleq M.pvars(p)$

$M.RNext(p) \triangleq M.Read(p) \vee (\exists\, l : M.Write(p,l)) \vee M.Return(p)$

$M.RPSpec(p) \triangleq \wedge\, M.PInit(p) \wedge \Box[M.RNext(p)]_m$
$\qquad\qquad\qquad \wedge\, \mathrm{WF}_m(M.RNext(p)) \wedge \mathrm{WF}_m(M.Return(p))$

$M.MSpec(l) \triangleq M.MInit(l) \wedge \Box[\exists\, p \in PrIds : M.Write(p,l)]_{mem[l]}$

$M.IRSpec \triangleq \wedge\, \forall\, p \in PrIds : M.RPSpec(p)$
$\qquad\qquad\quad \wedge\, \forall\, l \in MemLocs : M.MSpec(l)$

$M.RSpec \triangleq \exists\, mem, result : M.IRSpec$

Fig. 15. Formulas defined in module *MemoryImplementation*, plus a few extra definitions.

text of the *MemoryImplementation* module. The variable declarations in the ASSUME (including the implicit declaration of p in the assumption $p \in PrIds$) are necessary, otherwise the formulas in the PROVE part would contain undeclared variables. The following high-level proof is a simple exercise in predicate-logic reasoning with the operators $\forall$ and $\exists$, since these operators (applied to temporal-logic formulas) obey the usual rules of first-order logic.

1. ASSUME: 1. *cstate, rstate, mem, result, rmhist* : VARIABLE
   2. $p \in PrIds$ _____
   PROVE: $IPImp(p) \Rightarrow \overline{UPSpec(p)}$
   PROOF: Proved below.

2. ASSUME: 1. *cstate, rstate, mem, result, rmhist* : VARIABLE
   2. $l \in MemLocs$
   PROVE: $(\forall q \in PrIds : IPImp(q)) \Rightarrow \overline{MSpec(l)}$
   PROOF: Proved below.

3. ASSUME: *cstate, rstate, mem, result, rmhist* : VARIABLE
   PROVE: $E.LegalCaller \wedge C.ISpec \wedge R.ISpec \wedge M.IRSpec \wedge Hist \Rightarrow \overline{IUSpec}$
   PROOF: By steps 1 and 2, since $\forall$ distributes over $\wedge$, barring (which is just substitution) distributes over $\forall$ and $\wedge$, and we can deduce $(\forall u \in U : P(u)) \Rightarrow (\forall u \in U : Q(u))$ by proving $P(u) \Rightarrow Q(u)$ for any u in U.

4. ASSUME: *cstate, rstate, mem, result, rmhist* : VARIABLE
   PROVE: $E.LegalCaller \wedge C.ISpec \wedge R.ISpec \wedge M.IRSpec \wedge Hist \Rightarrow USpec$
   PROOF: By step 3, since we can deduce $F \Rightarrow \exists x : G(x)$ by proving $F \Rightarrow G(\overline{x})$, for some state function $\overline{x}$.

5. Q.E.D.
   PROOF: By step 4 and the validity of $\exists\, rmhist : Hist$, since we can deduce $(\exists x : F(x)) \Rightarrow G$ by proving $F(x) \Rightarrow G$, assuming x does not occur in G, and we can deduce the equivalence of $\exists x, y : F(x) \wedge G(y)$ and $(\exists x : F(x)) \wedge (\exists y : G(y))$, assuming x does not occur in $G(y)$ and y does not occur in $F(x)$.

The Lower-Level Proof At the heart of our argument lie the proofs of steps 1 and 2. They are based on the predicate-action diagram of Figure 16 on the next page. We introduce the abbreviations T and F for TRUE and FALSE, and UC for UNCHANGED. The operator S is defined to assert that

- For each of the three channels *memCh*, *crCh*, and *rmCh*, there is a call in progress on that channel iff the corresponding one of the first three arguments equals T.

- The values of *cstate[p]*, *rstate[p]*, and *rmhist[p]* equal the last three arguments, where "AB" indicates a value of either "A" or "B".

- Certain relations hold among the other variables—for example, if the first argument is T, then *memCh[p].arg* is an element of *LegalArgs*.

- *mem[l]* is an element of *MemVals*, for all l in *MemLocs*.

The formal definition of S appears in Figure 17 on page 49. It may help in

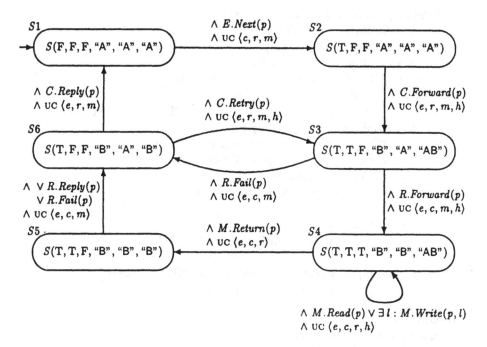

Fig. 16. A predicate-action diagram of $\langle e, c, r, m, h\rangle$ for $IPImp(p)$, where p is an element of $PrIds$.

understanding this definition to observe that:

$$E.Calling(p) \equiv C.Snd.Calling(p)$$
$$C.Rcv.Calling(p) \equiv R.Snd.Calling(p)$$
$$R.Rcv.Calling(p) \equiv M.E.Calling(p)$$

We have labeled the state predicates in the predicate-action diagram $S1, \ldots,$ $S6$. We define those labels to be synonymous with their respective predicates, so $S2$ equals $S(T, F, F, "A", "A", "A")$. We define the state function $\overline{result}$ so that $\overline{result}[p]$ has the value given in Figure 17, for each p in $PrIds$.

The Proof of Step 1 Intuitively, the proof of step 1 is as follows.

1.1. The implementation's initial condition implies the initial condition $S1$ of the predicate-action diagram.

1.2. The implementation's next-state action implies that the diagram describes all possible state transitions. There are six conditions, one for each state predicate in the diagram.

1.3. The initial condition $S1$ of the predicate-action diagram implies the initial condition $\overline{PInit(p)}$ of $\overline{UPSpec(p)}$.

1.4. Each of the actions allowed by the predicate-action diagram implements (implies) some disjunct of the next-state action $\overline{UNext(p)}$ of $\overline{UPSpec(p)}$, or else leaves $\overline{pv}$ unchanged.

$S(ECalling, CCalling, RCalling, cs, rs, rh) \triangleq$
$\quad \wedge \wedge ECalling \equiv E.Calling(p)$
$\quad\quad \wedge ECalling \Rightarrow (memCh[p].arg \in LegalArgs)$
$\quad \wedge \wedge CCalling \equiv R.Snd.Calling(p)$
$\quad\quad \wedge CCalling \Rightarrow (crCh[p].arg = C.RelayArg(p))$
$\quad\quad \wedge \neg CCalling \wedge (cstate[p] = \text{"B"}) \Rightarrow$
$\quad\quad\quad crCh[p].res \in MemVals \cup \{\text{"OK"}, \text{"BadArg"}, \text{"RPCFailure"}\}$
$\quad \wedge \wedge RCalling \equiv M.E.Calling(p)$
$\quad\quad \wedge RCalling \Rightarrow (rmCh[p].arg = R.RelayArg(p))$
$\quad\quad \wedge \neg RCalling \Rightarrow (result[p] = NotAResult)$
$\quad\quad \wedge \neg RCalling \wedge (rstate[p] = \text{"B"}) \Rightarrow$
$\quad\quad\quad rmCh[p].res \in MemVals \cup \{\text{"OK"}, \text{"BadArg"}\}$
$\quad \wedge\ cs = cstate[p]$
$\quad \wedge\ rs = rstate[p]$
$\quad \wedge\ rmhist[p] \in$ **if** $rh = \text{"AB"}$ **then** $\{\text{"A"}, \text{"B"}\}$
$\quad\quad\quad\quad\quad\quad\quad\quad\quad$ **else** $\{rh\}$
$\quad \wedge\ result[p] \in MemVals \cup \{NotAResult, \text{"OK"}, \text{"BadArg"}\}$
$\quad \wedge\ \forall l \in MemLocs\ :\ mem[l] \in MemVals$

$\overline{result}[p]\ =$
$\quad$ **case** $S1 \vee S2\ \rightarrow\ result[p]$,
$\quad\quad\quad S3\ \rightarrow$ **if** $h = \text{"A"}$ **then** $result[p]$
$\quad\quad\quad\quad\quad\quad\quad\quad\quad$ **else** "MemFailure" ,
$\quad\quad\quad S4\ \rightarrow$ **if** $(h = \text{"B"}) \wedge (result[p] = NotAResult)$
$\quad\quad\quad\quad\quad$ **then** "MemFailure"
$\quad\quad\quad\quad\quad$ **else** $result[p]$,
$\quad\quad\quad S5\ \rightarrow\ rmCh[p].res$,
$\quad\quad\quad S6\ \rightarrow$ **if** $crCh[p].res = \text{"RPCFailure"}$ **then** "MemFailure"
$\quad\quad\quad\quad\quad\quad\quad\quad\quad\quad\quad\quad$ **else** $crCh[p].res$

Fig. 17. The formal definitions of S and $\overline{result}[p]$, for p in $PrIds$.

1.5. All the temporal reasoning, including the proof of the fairness properties, is left for the final Q.E.D. step.

The formal proof is as follows.

1.1. $\neg E.Calling(p) \wedge C.Init(p) \wedge R.Init(p) \wedge M.PInit(p)$
$\quad \wedge (\forall l \in MemLocs : M.MInit(l)) \wedge (h = \text{"A"}) \Rightarrow S1$

1.2. ASSUME: 1. $\wedge [E.Next(p)]_e$
$\quad\quad\quad\quad \wedge [C.Next(p)]_c \wedge [R.Next(p)]_r \wedge [M.RNext(p)]_m$
$\quad\quad\quad\quad \wedge \forall l \in MemLocs : [\exists q \in PrIds : M.Write(q, l)]_{mem[l]}$
$\quad\quad\quad\quad \wedge [HNext(p)]_{\langle c,r,m,h \rangle}$
$\quad\quad\quad\quad 2.\ \neg$UNCHANGED $\langle e, c, r, m, h \rangle$
$\quad$ PROVE: 1. $S1 \Rightarrow S2' \wedge E.Next(p) \wedge$ UC $\langle c, r, m \rangle$
$\quad\quad\quad\quad 2.\ S2 \Rightarrow S3' \wedge C.Forward(p) \wedge$ UC $\langle e, r, m, h \rangle$

3. $S3 \Rightarrow \lor S4' \land R.Forward(p) \land \text{UC} \langle e, c, m, h \rangle$
   $\lor S6' \land R.Fail(p) \land \text{UC} \langle e, c, m \rangle$
4. $S4 \Rightarrow \lor S4' \land (M.Read(p) \lor \exists l : M.Write(p, l))$
   $\land \text{UC} \langle e, c, r, h \rangle$
   $\lor S5' \land M.Return(p) \land \text{UC} \langle e, c, r \rangle$
5. $S5 \Rightarrow S6' \land (R.Reply(p) \lor R.Fail(p)) \land \text{UC} \langle e, c, m \rangle$
6. $S6 \Rightarrow \lor S1' \land C.Reply(p) \land \text{UC} \langle e, r, m \rangle$
   $\lor S3' \land C.Retry(p) \land \text{UC} \langle e, r, m, h \rangle$

1.3. $S1 \Rightarrow \overline{PInit(p)}$

1.4. 1. $S1 \land S2' \land E.Next(p) \land \text{UC} \langle c, r, m \rangle \Rightarrow \text{UC} \, \overline{pv}$
   2. $S2 \land S3' \land C.Forward(p) \land \text{UC} \langle e, r, m, h \rangle \Rightarrow \text{UC} \, \overline{pv}$
   3. a. $S3 \land S4' \land R.Forward(p) \land \text{UC} \langle e, c, m, h \rangle \Rightarrow \text{UC} \, \overline{pv}$
      b. $S3 \land S6' \land R.Fail(p) \land \text{UC} \langle e, c, m \rangle \Rightarrow \overline{Fail(p)}$
   4. a. $S4 \land S4' \land M.Read(p) \land \text{UC} \langle e, c, r, h \rangle \Rightarrow \overline{Read(p)}$
      b. ASSUME: l : CONSTANT
         PROVE: $S4 \land S4' \land M.Write(p, l) \land \text{UC} \langle e, c, r, h \rangle \Rightarrow \overline{Write(p, l)}$
      c. $S4 \land S5' \land M.Return(p) \land \text{UC} \langle e, c, r \rangle \Rightarrow \text{UC} \, \overline{pv}$
   5. a. $S5 \land S6' \land R.Reply(p) \land \text{UC} \langle e, c, m \rangle \Rightarrow \text{UC} \, \overline{pv}$
      b. $S5 \land S6' \land R.Fail(p) \land \text{UC} \langle e, c, m \rangle \Rightarrow \overline{Fail(p)}$
   6. a. $S6 \land S1' \land C.Reply(p) \land \text{UC} \langle e, r, m \rangle \Rightarrow \overline{Return(p)}$
      b. $S6 \land S3' \land C.Retry(p) \land \text{UC} \langle e, r, m, h \rangle \Rightarrow \overline{Fail(p)}$
   7. $\text{UC} \langle e, c, r, m, h \rangle \Rightarrow \text{UC} \, \overline{pv}$

1.5. Q.E.D.

The proofs of 1.1–1.4 are straightforward, tedious exercises. The part of the proof that shows that the Clerk and RPC components relay their arguments properly requires a bit of simple reasoning about sequences—for example, to prove

$$(memCh[p].arg \in LegalArgs) \Rightarrow (C.RelayArg(p) \in C.LegalRcvArgs)$$

The rest of the proof involves a fairly mindless expanding of definitions and application of first-order logic.

The Proof of Step 1.5 We now give the high-level proof of step 1.5, which is the only part of the proof of step 1 that involves temporal logic.

LET: $Inv(p) \triangleq S1 \lor S2 \lor S3 \lor S4 \lor S5 \lor S6$

1.5.1. $IPImp(p) \Rightarrow \Box Inv(p)$
   PROOF: By 1.1, 1.2, and the laws of TLA, which allow us in general to deduce $P \land (\forall u \in U : \Box[N(u)]_{v(u)}) \Rightarrow \Box I$ from $P \Rightarrow I$ together with $I \land (\forall u \in U : [N(u)]_{v(u)}) \Rightarrow I'$. (Take U to be $\{u_1, u_2, u_3\} \cup MemLocs$, let $N(u_1)$ be $E.Next(p)$, etc.)

1.5.2. $IPImp(p) \land \Box Inv(p) \Rightarrow \overline{PInit(p)} \land \Box[\overline{UNext(p)}]_{\overline{pv}}$
   PROOF: 1.1–1.4 show that $IPImp(p)$ implies $\overline{PInit(p)}$ and that
   $Inv(p) \land [E.Next(p)]_e \land [C.Next(p)]_c \land [R.Next(p)]_r \land [M.RNext(p)]_m$
   $\land (\forall l \in MemLocs : [\exists q \in PrIds : M.Write(q, l)]_{mem[l]})$
   $\land [HNext(p)]_{\langle c, r, m, h \rangle}$

implies $\overline{[UNext(p)]_{\overline{pv}}}$. The result is now obtained from the laws of TLA, which allow us in general to infer $\Box I \wedge (\forall u \in U : \Box[N(u)]_{v(u)}) \Rightarrow \Box[M]_w$ from $I \wedge I' \wedge (\forall u \in U : [N(u)]_{v(u)}) \Rightarrow [M]_w$.

1.5.3. $IPImp(p) \wedge \Box Inv(p) \Rightarrow \overline{WF_{pv}(RNext(p))} \wedge \overline{WF_{pv}(Return(p))}$

PROOF: Described below.

1.5.4. Q.E.D.

PROOF: Step 1.5 (which asserts step 1) follows from 1.5.1–1.5.3 by propositional logic.

The Proof of Step 1.5.3 To complete the proof of step 1, we must prove 1.5.3, which shows that the specification's fairness properties are satisfied. We give an intuitive sketch of the proof. To prove $\overline{WF_{pv}(RNext(p))}$, we must show that if $\overline{RNext(p)}$ is continuously enabled, then a $\overline{RNext(p)}$ step must eventually occur. To prove $\overline{WF_{pv}(Return(p))}$, we must show that if $\overline{Return(p)}$ is continuously enabled, then a $\overline{Return(p)}$ step must eventually occur. The two actions are disabled in state $S1$. Therefore, to prove the two fairness properties, it suffices to show that, if any of $S2$–$S6$ ever holds, then $S1$ must eventually hold. It is clear from the diagram that this follows from the two conditions: (i) none of the predicates $S2$–$S5$ can hold forever and (ii) if $S6$ holds repeatedly, then $S1$ must eventually hold. The following implementation fairness properties imply condition (i):

- $WF_c(C.Forward(p))$ implies that $S2$ cannot hold forever.

- $WF_r(R.Next(p))$ implies that $S3$ cannot hold forever.

- $WF_m(M.RNext(p))$ implies that if $S4 \wedge (result[p] = NotAResult)$ holds, then $S4 \wedge (result[p] \neq NotAResult)$ eventually holds, and $WF_m(M.Return(p))$ then implies that $S5$ eventually holds.

- $WF_r(R.Next(p))$ implies that $S5$ cannot hold forever.

Condition (ii) follows from $SF_c(C.Reply(p))$, which implies that if $S6$ holds repeatedly, then $S1$ eventually holds. The proof rules of TLA have been designed expressly to formalize this style of informal reasoning. We omit the formal proof.

The Proof of Step 2 Finally, we must prove step 2. We now confess that, to simplify the exposition, we have structured the proof incorrectly. The proof of 2 requires steps 1.1–1.4 and step 1.5.1, for an arbitrary p in $PrIds$. Those steps should be brought out either as a separate lemma, or as level-1 steps. Here, we violate the rules of structured proofs and use those steps directly in the proof of 2.

2.1. $(\forall q \in PrIds : IPImp(q) \wedge \Box Inv(q)) \Rightarrow \overline{MInit}(l)$

PROOF: By the assumption that $l \in MemLocs$, since $M.MInit(l)$ trivially implies $\overline{MInit}(l)$ (the two formulas are the same).

2.2. $\wedge\, [E.Next(p)]_e$
 $\wedge\, [C.Next(p)]_c \wedge [R.Next(p)]_r \wedge [M.RNext(p)]_m$
 $\wedge\, \forall\, l1 \in MemLocs\; :\; [\exists\, q1 \in PrIds : M.Write(q1, l1)]_{mem[l1]}$
 $\wedge\, [HNext(p)]_{\langle c,r,m,h \rangle}$
 $\wedge\, Inv(p) \wedge Inv(p)'$
 $\wedge\, [M.Write(q, l)]_{mem[l]}$
 $\Rightarrow\, [\overline{Write(q, l)}]_{\overline{mem[l]}}$

PROOF: $Inv(p) \wedge M.Write(p, l)$ implies $S4$, for any p. We consider two cases. (i) If $\neg$UNCHANGED $\langle e, c, r, m, h \rangle$ holds, then the result follows from part 4 of 1.2 and part 4b of 1.4. (ii) If UNCHANGED $\langle e, c, r, m, h \rangle$ holds, then $S4$ and $Inv(p)'$ imply $S4'$, and the result follows from part 4b of 1.4.

2.3. Q.E.D.
 PROOF: 2.1, 2.2, and the laws of TLA show that
$$(\forall\, q \in PrIds\; :\; IPImp(q) \wedge \Box Inv(q)) \Rightarrow \overline{MSpec(l)}$$
The result then follows from 1.5.1.

4   Implementing the RPC Component

The problem statement introduces a lossy RPC component, which resembles the RPC component but does not raise "RPCFailure" exceptions and may fail to return. Much as with the memory implementation of Section 3, we specify the lossy RPC and an RPC clerk, and prove that their composition implements the RPC specification.

The problem statement's informal description of the lossy RPC component is problematic for reasons we now explain. The RPC component of Problem 2, specified in module *RPC*, is just as lossy as the "lossy" one—neither will return to the sender if the receiver fails to return. The additional timing constraints on the lossy RPC component, together with the description of the RPC implementation, suggest that a sender process should be able to issue a new call if a previous one has not returned. However, issuing a second call without waiting for a return violates the handshake protocol of the procedure-calling interface.

A physical component cannot act correctly without some form of synchronization with its environment. If we eliminate the handshake protocol's requirement that the environment must wait for a return before issuing the next call, we must introduce some other form of synchronization. The problem suggests a new protocol in which a sender process can issue a call when either (a) there is no outstanding call, or (b) some time ρ has elapsed since the previous call. For such an interface to be useful, the sender needs to know for which call a result is being returned. This requires either tagging the calls and returns or, more conventionally, specifying that the lossy RPC component never reply to a call more than time ρ after it was issued.

Although replacing the handshake protocol with a timed protocol would produce a more sophisticated example, it is a departure from the problem statement. A literal reading of that statement requires the lossy RPC component to obey the procedure-calling protocol, which forbids more than one outstanding call per process. We therefore adopt this requirement in the specification of the lossy RPC component in Section 4.1 below. This requirement affects our solution to Problem 5, the implementation of an RPC component by composing an RPC clerk with a lossy RPC component. If the lossy RPC component never returns a call by process p and the clerk has returned an RPC failure for that call, then the clerk must always return RPC failures to later calls by p.

4.1 A Lossy RPC

The only novelty in the specification of the lossy RPC component is its use of real-time constraints. We express these constraints as in [2], by introducing a variable parameter *now*, whose value represents the current time, and defining five temporal operators RT, $VTimer$, $MaxTimer$, $MinTimer$, and $NonZeno$ (called NZ in [2]). We briefly review these operators.

- The temporal formula $RT(v)$ asserts that (a) *now* is a monotonically non-decreasing real number and (b) steps that change *now* leave v unchanged. Typically, v is a tuple of relevant variables other than *now*, so (b) essentially means that changes to these variables are considered to be instantaneous.

- If A is an action and v a state function such that any A step changes v, and if t is a variable that does not occur in A or v, then the temporal formula $VTimer(t, A, \delta, v) \land MaxTimer(t)$ asserts that A cannot be enabled for more than δ time units before the next A step occurs.

- If A is an action and v a state function such that any A step changes v, and if t is a variable that does not occur in A or v, then the temporal formula $VTimer(t, A, \delta, v) \land MinTimer(t, A, v)$ asserts that A must be continuously enabled for at least δ time units before the next A step occurs.

- The temporal formula $NonZeno$ asserts that *now* keeps increasing without bound, so time marches on.

We define these operators in module *RealTime* of Figure 18 on the next page. This module has appeared before [11, 14], except that earlier versions did not include *NonZeno*. It imports module *Reals*, which defines the set *Real* of real numbers and some of the usual operators on them such as $>$.

The specification of the lossy RPC component is given in module *LossyRPC* of Figure 19 on page 55. The structure of this specification is familiar.[14] This specification is based on that of the RPC component. The initial condition and next-state action are the same as for the ordinary RPC component, except for the use of timing constraints and the absence of $Fail(p)$ steps. The timing constraint $MaxProcess(s, p)$ asserts that a $Forward(p)$ or a $Reject(p)$ step must occur within

---

[14] We have not bothered to introduce a separate module containing the parameter declarations. Names prefixed by "*Inner.*" are defined in submodule *Inner* of the imported *RPC* module. Module *LossyRPC*'s submodule is called *LInner* to avoid name conflicts with the imported submodule.

---
module *RealTime*
---

import *Reals*

parameters *now* : VARIABLE
∞ : CONSTANT

---

assumption *InfinityUnReal* $\triangleq$ $\infty \notin Real$

$RT(v) \triangleq \land now \in Real$
$\qquad \land \Box[(now' \in \{r \in Real : now < r\}) \land (v' = v)]_{now}$
$VTimer(x, A, \delta, v) \triangleq$
$\quad \land x = $ **if** ENABLED $\langle A \rangle_v$ **then** $now + \delta$
$\qquad\qquad\qquad\qquad\quad$ **else** ∞
$\quad \land \Box[x' = $ **if** (ENABLED $\langle A \rangle_v)'$
$\qquad\qquad\qquad$ **then if** $\langle A \rangle_v \lor \neg$ENABLED $\langle A \rangle_v$ **then** $now' + \delta$
$\qquad\qquad\qquad\qquad\qquad\qquad\qquad\qquad\qquad$ **else** x
$\qquad\qquad$ **else** ∞ $]_{\langle x,v \rangle}$
$MaxTimer(x) \triangleq \Box[(x \neq \infty) \Rightarrow (now' \leq x)]_{now}$
$MinTimer(x, A, v) \triangleq \Box[A \Rightarrow (now \geq x)]_v$
$NonZeno \triangleq \forall t \in Real : \Diamond(now > t)$

Fig. 18. Module *RealTime*.

δ seconds[15] of when it becomes enabled; the timing constraint $MaxReturn(s, p)$ asserts that a $Return(p)$ step must occur within δ seconds of when it becomes enabled.

4.2 The RPC Implementation

The RPC Clerk The RPC clerk passes requests to the lossy RPC component. According to the problem statement:

> The RPC component is implemented with a Lossy RPC component by passing the *RemoteCall* call through to the Lossy RPC, passing the return back to the caller, and raising an exception if the corresponding return has not been issued after $2\delta + \epsilon$ seconds.

Read literally, this requirement implies that, if the lossy RPC component returns more than $2\delta + \epsilon$ seconds after it is called, then the clerk must raise an exception. For example, if the RPC component returns a result $3\delta + \epsilon$ seconds after it is

---

[15] Strictly speaking, it asserts that the step must occur before *now* increases by more than δ; we interpret such an increase to represent the passing of δ seconds—rather than the passing of δ years or δ kilometers.

─────────────── **module** *LossyRPC* ───────────────

import *RPC, RealTime, Reals*

parameters δ : CONSTANT

---

assumption

    $DeltaAssump \triangleq (\delta \in Real) \wedge (\delta > 0)$

─────────────── **module** *LInner* ───────────────

  parameters

    rstate : VARIABLE

  $LNext(p) \triangleq Inner.Forward(p) \vee Inner.Reject(p) \vee Inner.Reply(p)$

  $MaxProcess(s, p) \triangleq$

      $\wedge \ VTimer(s, Inner.Forward(p) \vee Inner.Reject(p), \delta,$

             $\langle Inner.vars(p), Snd.caller(p) \rangle)$

      $\wedge \ MaxTimer(s)$

  $MaxReturn(s, p) \triangleq$

      $\wedge \ VTimer(s, Inner.Reply(p), \delta, \langle Inner.vars(p), Rcv.rtrner(p) \rangle)$

      $\wedge \ MaxTimer(s)$

  $LISpec \triangleq$

      $\forall p \in PrIds : \wedge \ Inner.Init(p) \wedge \Box[LNext(p)]_{Inner.vars(p)}$

                  $\wedge \ RT(Inner.vars(p))$

                  $\wedge \ \exists s : MaxProcess(s, p)$

                  $\wedge \ \exists s : MaxReturn(s, p)$

$Spec \triangleq \exists rstate : LInner.LISpec$

Fig. 19. Module *LossyRPC*.

called and the clerk has not yet raised an exception, then the clerk cannot return the result; it must raise an exception. We find it convenient to adopt the more sensible requirement that the clerk returns an exception only if it has not yet received a result. Thus, if the RPC component returns a result $3\delta + \epsilon$ seconds after it is called, and the clerk has not yet raised an exception, then the clerk will return the result.

There is another aspect of the problem statement that is bizarre. In light of the timing assumptions on the environment, one would expect the clerk to have to return either a result or an exception within some fixed length of time. However, the problem statement makes no such requirement, implying only that the clerk must eventually return. We follow the problem statement in this respect; the resulting mix of eventuality and real-time requirements yields a more interesting example.

Our RPC clerk is specified in module *RPCClerk* of Figure 20 on the next page. The specification is similar to that of the memory clerk. The major differences are that there are no *Retry(p)* steps, and that there is a *Fail(p)* timeout action, which cannot be executed until it has been enabled for at least τ seconds. Correctness of the *RPC* component's implementation is proved under the assumption that τ is greater than $2\delta + \epsilon$.

The Implementation Proof The correctness of the RPC implementation is asserted in Module *RPCImplementation* in Figure 21 on page 58. The four components of the implementation are pictured below, where the sender and receiver form the environment.

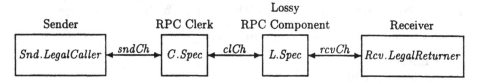

Formula *RcvTiming* asserts the requirement that the receiver always return within ϵ seconds of when it is called. Theorem *Impl* asserts that the composition of the components' specifications, together with condition *RcvTiming* and the assumption *NonZeno* that time keeps advancing, implies the specification of the *RPC* component.

The proof of theorem *Impl* has a structure similar to that of the proof of the memory implementation in Section 3.2. As in that proof, we eliminate the prefixes "*Inner.*" and "*LInner.*" from symbol names. Definitions from module *RPCImplementation* along with some additional definitions appear in Figure 22 on page 59. We have overloaded symbols such as *C.ISpec*, using the convention that $X(a_1, \ldots, a_n)$ is defined to be X with quantification over $a_1, \ldots, a_n$ removed. The "timing" definitions give names to actions and predicates that occur in the *RealTime* module.

To define the refinement mapping $\overline{rstate}$, we must again introduce a history variable *lrhist*, where *lrhist[p]* equals "A" iff the lossy RPC component has performed a *Reject(p)* action, but the RPC clerk component has not yet returned the result to the sender. The formal definition is as follows:

$$h \triangleq lrhist[p]$$
$$HNext(p) \triangleq h' = \textbf{if } L.Reject(p) \textbf{ then } \text{``A''}$$
$$\textbf{else if } C.Reply(p) \textbf{ then } \text{``B''}$$
$$\textbf{else } h$$
$$Hist \triangleq \forall p \in PrIds : (h = \text{``B''}) \land \Box[HNext(p)]_{\langle c,l,h \rangle}$$

The validity of $\exists \, lrhist : Hist$ is again asserted by a general TLA theorem.

```
┌──────────────────────── module RPCClerk ────────────────────────┐
│ import Sequences, Reals                                          │
│ parameters sndCh, rcvCh : VARIABLE                               │
│            PrIds, Vals, τ : CONSTANT                             │
├──────────────────────────────────────────────────────────────────┤
```

assumption
$$TauAssump \triangleq (\tau \in Real) \land (\tau > 0)$$

$$LegalArgs \triangleq \{\text{"RemoteCall"}\} \times \text{STRING} \times Seq(Vals)$$

include *ProcedureInterface* **as** *Snd* **with** $ch \leftarrow sndCh$, $Args \leftarrow LegalArgs$
include *ProcedureInterface* **as** *Rcv* **with** $ch \leftarrow rcvCh$, $Args \leftarrow LegalArgs$

```
┌──────────────────────── module Inner ────────────────────────┐
```

parameters
  cstate : VARIABLE

$$Init(p) \triangleq (cstate[p] = \text{"A"}) \land \neg Rcv.Calling(p)$$

$$
\begin{aligned}
Forward(p) \triangleq \;& \land\; Snd.Calling(p) \land (cstate[p] = \text{"A"}) \\
& \land\; Rcv.Call(p, sndCh[p].arg) \\
& \land\; cstate'[p] = \text{"B"} \\
& \land\; \text{UNCHANGED } Snd.rtrner(p)
\end{aligned}
$$

$$
\begin{aligned}
Fail(p) \triangleq \;& \land\; Rcv.Calling(p) \land (cstate[p] = \text{"B"}) \\
& \land\; Snd.Return(p, \text{"RPCFailure"}) \\
& \land\; cstate'[p] = \text{"A"} \\
& \land\; \text{UNCHANGED } Rcv.caller(p)
\end{aligned}
$$

$$
\begin{aligned}
Reply(p) \triangleq \;& \land\; \neg Rcv.Calling(p) \land (cstate[p] = \text{"B"}) \\
& \land\; Snd.Return(p, rcvCh[p].res) \\
& \land\; cstate'[p] = \text{"A"} \\
& \land\; \text{UNCHANGED } Rcv.caller(p)
\end{aligned}
$$

$$Next(p) \triangleq Forward(p) \lor Fail(p) \lor Reply(p)$$

$$vars(p) \triangleq \langle cstate[p], Snd.rtrner(p), Rcv.caller(p) \rangle$$

$$
\begin{aligned}
MinFail(s, p) \triangleq \;& \land\; VTimer(s, Fail(p), \tau, vars(p)) \\
& \land\; MinTimer(s, Fail(p), vars(p))
\end{aligned}
$$

$$
\begin{aligned}
ISpec \triangleq \forall p \in PrIds : \;& \land\; Init(p) \land \Box[Next(p)]_{vars(p)} \\
& \land\; RT(vars(p)) \land \exists s : MinFail(s, p) \\
& \land\; WF_{vars(p)}(Next(p))
\end{aligned}
$$

$$Spec \triangleq \exists cstate : Inner.ISpec$$

Fig. 20. The component specification of the RPC clerk.

The High-Level Proof The high-level proof uses the state function $\overline{rstate}$ and the temporal formula

$$IImp(p, et, ct, pt, rt) \triangleq$$
$$Snd.LegalCaller(p) \wedge Rcv.LegalReturner(p) \wedge RcvT(p, et)$$
$$\wedge \; C.ISpec(p, ct) \wedge L.LISpec(p, pt, rt) \wedge Hist(p) \wedge NonZeno$$

We define $\overline{rstate}$ later; the only property we use in the high-level proof is that the timers et, ct, pt, and rt do not occur in its definition.

1. ASSUME: 1. $cstate, rstate, et, ct, pt, rt, lrhist$: VARIABLE
   2. $p \in PrIds$
   PROVE: $IImp(p, et, ct, pt, rt) \Rightarrow \overline{ISpec(p)}$
   PROOF: Proved below.
2. ASSUME: 1. $cstate, rstate, lrhist$: VARIABLE
   2. $p \in PrIds$
   PROVE: $(\exists\, et, ct, pt, rt : Snd.LegalCaller(p) \wedge Rcv.LegalReturner(p)$
   $\wedge \; RcvT(p, et) \wedge \overline{C.ISpec(p, ct)} \wedge L.LISpec(p, pt, rt)$
   $\wedge \; Hist(p)) \;\Rightarrow\; \overline{ISpec(p)}$
   PROOF: By step 1 and TLA quantifier rules, because et, ct, pt, and rt do not occur in the definition of $IPSpec(p)$ or $\overline{rstate}$, so they do not occur in $\overline{ISpec(p)}$.

──────── module *RPCImplementation* ────────

import *RPC, RPCParameters, Reals, RealTime*

parameters
   τ, δ, ϵ : CONSTANT
   $clCh$: VARIABLE

---

assumption
   $TDEAssump \triangleq \wedge \{\tau, \delta, \epsilon\} \subseteq \{r \in Real : r > 0\}$
   $\wedge\; \tau > 2 * \delta + \epsilon$

$RcvTiming \triangleq \forall\, p \in PrIds :$
   $\exists\, s : \wedge RT(Rcv.rtrner(p))$
   $\wedge \; VTimer(s, \exists\, v : Rcv.Return(p, v), \epsilon, rcvCh[p])$
   $\wedge \; MaxTimer(s)$
include *LossyRPC* **as** *L* **with** $sndCh \leftarrow clCh, rcvCh \leftarrow rcvCh$
include *RPCClerk* **as** *C* **with** $sndCh \leftarrow sndCh, rcvCh \leftarrow clCh$

theorem
   $Impl \triangleq Snd.LegalCaller \wedge Rcv.LegalReturner \wedge RcvTiming$
   $\wedge \; C.Spec \wedge L.Spec \wedge NonZeno \;\Rightarrow\; Spec$

Fig. 21. Module *RPCImplementation*.

The Specification

RPC Component (imported from *RPC*)

$v \stackrel{\Delta}{=} vars(p)$

$Init(p) \stackrel{\Delta}{=} (rstate[p] = \text{"A"}) \wedge \neg Rcv.Calling(p)$

$Next(p) \stackrel{\Delta}{=} Forward(p) \vee Reject(p) \vee Fail(p) \vee Reply(p)$

$ISpec(p) \stackrel{\Delta}{=} Init(p) \wedge \Box[Next(p)]_v \wedge \text{WF}_v(Next(p))$

$Spec \stackrel{\Delta}{=} \exists\, rstate : \forall\, p \in PrIds : ISpec(p)$

The Implementation

The Sender (imported from *RPC*)

$s \stackrel{\Delta}{=} Snd.caller(p)$

$Snd.Next(p) \stackrel{\Delta}{=} \exists\, a \in LegalSndArgs : Snd.Call(p, a)$

$Snd.LegalCaller \stackrel{\Delta}{=} \forall\, p \in PrIds : \neg Snd.Calling(p) \wedge \Box[Snd.Next(p)]_s$

The Receiver (imported from *RPC*)

$r \stackrel{\Delta}{=} Rcv.rtrner(p)$

$Rcv.Next(p) \stackrel{\Delta}{=} \exists\, v : Rcv.Return(p, v)$

$Rcv.LegalReturner \stackrel{\Delta}{=} \forall\, p \in PrIds : \Box[Rcv.Next(p)]_r$

$RcvT(p, et) \stackrel{\Delta}{=} \wedge\, RT(r) \wedge VTimer(et, Rcv.Next(p), \epsilon, rcvCh[p])$
$\qquad\qquad\qquad \wedge\, MaxTimer(et)$

RPC Clerk (included from *RPCClerk*)

$c \stackrel{\Delta}{=} C.vars(p)$

$C.ISpec(p, ct) \stackrel{\Delta}{=} \wedge\, C.Init(p) \wedge \Box[C.Next(p)]_c \wedge WF_c(C.Next(p))$
$\qquad\qquad\qquad\quad \wedge\, RT(c) \wedge C.MinFail(ct, p)$

$C.Spec \stackrel{\Delta}{=} \exists\, cstate : \forall\, p \in PrIds : C.ISpec(p)$

Lossy RPC (included from *LossyRPC*)

$l \stackrel{\Delta}{=} L.vars(p)$

$L.LISpec(p, pt, rt) \stackrel{\Delta}{=} \wedge\, L.Init(p) \wedge \Box[L.LNext(p)]_l$
$\qquad\qquad\qquad\qquad\quad \wedge\, RT(l) \wedge L.MaxProcess(pt, p) \wedge L.MaxReturn(rt, p)$

$L.Spec \stackrel{\Delta}{=} \exists\, rstate : \forall\, p \in PrIds : L.LISpec(p)$

Timing

$TNext(x) \stackrel{\Delta}{=} (now' \in \{r \in Real : now < r\}) \wedge (x' = x)$

$VInit(t, A, \delta, x) \stackrel{\Delta}{=} t = \text{if } \text{ENABLED } \langle A \rangle_x \text{ then } now + \delta \text{ else } \infty$

$VNext(t, A, \delta, x) \stackrel{\Delta}{=} t' = \text{if } (\text{ENABLED } \langle A \rangle_x)'$
$\qquad\qquad\qquad\qquad\qquad \text{then if } \langle A \rangle_x \vee \neg\text{ENABLED } \langle A \rangle_x \text{ then } now' + \delta$
$\qquad\qquad\qquad\qquad\qquad\qquad\qquad\qquad\qquad \text{else } t$
$\qquad\qquad\qquad\qquad\qquad \text{else } \infty$

$MaxNext(t) \stackrel{\Delta}{=} (t \neq \infty) \Rightarrow (now' \leq t)$

$MinNext(t, A) \stackrel{\Delta}{=} A \Rightarrow (now \geq t)$

Fig. 22. Definitions from module *RPCImplementation*, plus a few more.

3. ASSUME: *cstate, rstate, lrhist* : VARIABLE
   PROVE: *Snd.LegalCaller* ∧ *Rcv.LegalReturner* ∧ *RcvTiming*
   $\qquad$ ∧ *C.ISpec* ∧ *L.LISpec* ∧ *Hist* ⇒ *Spec*
   PROOF: By step 2 and TLA quantifier rules.
4. Q.E.D.
   PROOF: By step 3, the validity of ∃ *lrhist* : *Hist*, and TLA quantifier rules.

The Proof of Step 1 The proof of step 1 is based on the predicate-action diagram of Figure 23 on this page. In this diagram and in the rest of the proof, we assume that ≥ is defined so that $r \geq s$ is false unless both r and s are elements of the set *Real* of real numbers. We use notation similar to that in the proof of the

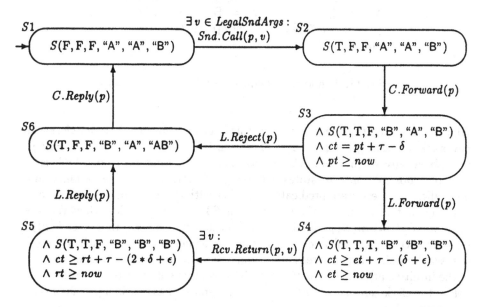

Fig. 23. A predicate-action diagram of ⟨*s, r, c, l, h*⟩ for *IImp(p, et, ct, pt, rt)*.

memory implementation. The formal definition of S appears in Figure 24 on the next page. Again, we define the labels $S1, \ldots, S6$ that appear in the predicate-action diagram of Figure 23 to be synonymous with their respective predicates. We define the state function $\overline{rstate}$ so that:

$$\overline{rstate}[p] \;=\; \textbf{case} \; \begin{array}{ll} S1 \lor S2 \lor S3 & \to \; \text{``A''}, \\ S4 \lor S5 & \to \; \text{``B''}, \\ S6 & \to \; lrhist[p] \end{array}$$

Because we require that the timer variables not occur in $\overline{rstate}$, we must replace $S3$, $S4$, and $S5$ by just their S conjuncts in the actual definition of $\overline{rstate}[p]$.

The proof of the safety part of the RPC component's specification involves proving that Figure 23 is a correct predicate-action diagram for the formula

$$S(ECalling, CCalling, LCalling, cs, rs, lh) \triangleq$$
$$\wedge \wedge Snd.Calling(p) \equiv ECalling$$
$$\wedge ECalling \Rightarrow (sndCh[p].arg \in LegalSndArgs)$$
$$\wedge \wedge C.Rcv.Calling(p) \equiv CCalling$$
$$\wedge CCalling \Rightarrow (clCh[p].arg = sndCh[p].arg)$$
$$\wedge L.Rcv.Calling(p) \equiv LCalling$$
$$\wedge cstate[p] = cs$$
$$\wedge rstate[p] = rs$$
$$\wedge \wedge lrhist[p] \in \text{if } lh = \text{``AB''} \text{ then } \{\text{``A''}, \text{``B''}\}$$
$$\text{else } \{lh\}$$
$$\wedge (lrhist[p] = \text{``A''}) \Rightarrow \wedge L.RelayArg(p) \notin L.LegalRcvArgs$$
$$\wedge clCh[p].res = \text{``BadCall''}$$
$$\wedge (lrhist[p] = \text{``B''}) \wedge (cs = \text{``B''}) \wedge \neg CCalling$$
$$\Rightarrow (clCh[p].res = rcvCh[p].res)$$
$$\wedge now \in Real$$

Fig. 24. The formal definition of S, for p in $PrIds$.

IImp(p, et, ct, pt, rt). The key step in this proof is showing that the clerk can never take a $C.Fail(p)$ step. The proof is essentially as follows. Because $C.Fail(p)$ is enabled only when $C.Rcv.Calling(p)$ is true and $cstate[p]$ equals "B", such a step is possible only in states satisfying $S3$, $S4$, or $S5$. The equality and inequalities in these state predicates, together with the assumptions on τ, δ, and ϵ, imply that ct is greater than now when $S3$, $S4$, or $S5$ holds. However, the conjunct $C.MinFail(ct, p)$ in the clerk's specification asserts that a $C.Fail(p)$ step can occur only when ct is less than or equal to now, so such a step is impossible. This invariance reasoning about timer values is a direct formalization of the intuitive argument that the lossy RPC component must return from a call before the clerk can take a $Fail(p)$ step. It is typical of assertional proofs of real-time properties.

The formal proof of step 1 is analogous to the proof of step 1 of the memory implementation. Steps 1.1 and 1.2 assert that the predicate-action diagram describes the initial state and transitions of formula $IImp(p, et, ct, pt, rt)$; steps 1.3 and 1.4 assert that the system described by the predicate-action implements the initial condition and next-state relation of $\overline{ISpec(p)}$; and step 1.5 completes the proof.

1.1. $\neg Snd.Calling(p) \wedge C.Init(p) \wedge L.Init(p) \wedge (h = \text{``B''}) \wedge (now \in Real)$
$\Rightarrow S1$

1.2. ASSUME: $\wedge\, [Snd.Next(p)]_s \wedge [Rcv.Next(p)]_r$
$\wedge\, [C.Next(p)]_c \wedge [L.LNext(p)]_l \wedge [HNext(p)]_{\langle c,l,h\rangle}$
$\wedge\, [TNext(r)]_{now} \wedge [TNext(c)]_{now} \wedge [TNext(l)]_{now}$
$\wedge\, [VNext(et, Rcv.Next(p), \epsilon, rcvCh[p])]_{\langle et, rcvCh[p]\rangle}$
$\wedge\, [MaxNext(et)]_{now}$
$\wedge\, [VNext(ct, C.Fail(p), \tau, c)]_{\langle ct,c\rangle}$
$\wedge\, [MinNext(ct, C.Fail(p))]_c$
$\wedge\, [VNext(pt, L.Forward(p) \vee L.Reject(p), \delta,$
$\quad\quad \langle l, C.Rcv.caller(p)\rangle)]_{\langle pt, \langle l, C.Rcv.caller(p)\rangle\rangle}$
$\wedge\, [MaxNext(pt)]_{now}$
$\wedge\, [VNext(rt, L.Reply(p), \delta,$
$\quad\quad \langle l, Rcv.rtrner(p)\rangle)]_{\langle rt, \langle l, Rcv.rtrner(p)\rangle\rangle}$
$\wedge\, [MaxNext(rt)]_{now}$

PROVE: 1. $S1 \Rightarrow \vee\ S1' \wedge \mathrm{UC}\ \langle s,r,c,l,h\rangle$
$\vee\ S2' \wedge Snd.Next(p) \wedge \mathrm{UC}\ \langle r,c,l\rangle$

2. $S2 \Rightarrow \vee\ S2' \wedge \mathrm{UC}\ \langle s,r,c,l,h\rangle$
$\vee\ S3' \wedge C.Forward(p) \wedge \mathrm{UC}\ \langle s,r,l\rangle$

3. $S3 \Rightarrow \vee\ S3' \wedge \mathrm{UC}\ \langle s,r,c,l,h\rangle$
$\vee\ S4' \wedge L.Forward(p) \wedge \mathrm{UC}\ \langle s,r,c\rangle$
$\vee\ S6' \wedge L.Reject(p) \wedge (h' = \text{``A''}) \wedge \mathrm{UC}\ \langle s,r,c\rangle$

4. $S4 \Rightarrow \vee\ S4' \wedge \mathrm{UC}\ \langle s,r,c,l,h\rangle$
$\vee\ S5' \wedge Rcv.Next(p) \wedge \mathrm{UC}\ \langle s,c,l\rangle$

5. $S5 \Rightarrow \vee\ S5' \wedge \mathrm{UC}\ \langle s,r,c,l,h\rangle$
$\vee\ S6' \wedge L.Reply(p) \wedge \mathrm{UC}\ \langle s,r,c,h\rangle$

6. $S6 \Rightarrow \vee\ S6' \wedge \mathrm{UC}\ \langle s,r,c,l,h\rangle$
$\vee\ S1' \wedge C.Reply(p) \wedge \mathrm{UC}\ \langle s,r,l\rangle$

1.3. $S1 \Rightarrow \overline{Init(p)}$

1.4.   1. $S1 \wedge S2' \wedge Snd.Next(p) \wedge \mathrm{UC}\ \langle r,c,l\rangle \Rightarrow \mathrm{UC}\ \overline{v}$
2. $S2 \wedge S3' \wedge C.Forward(p) \wedge \mathrm{UC}\ \langle s,r,l\rangle \Rightarrow \mathrm{UC}\ \overline{v}$
3. $S3 \wedge S4' \wedge L.Forward(p) \wedge \mathrm{UC}\ \langle s,r,c\rangle \Rightarrow \overline{Forward(p)}$
4. $S3 \wedge S6' \wedge L.Reject(p) \wedge (h' = \text{``A''}) \wedge \mathrm{UC}\ \langle s,r,c\rangle \Rightarrow \mathrm{UC}\ \overline{v}$
5. $S4 \wedge S5' \wedge Rcv.Next(p) \wedge \mathrm{UC}\ \langle s,c,l\rangle \Rightarrow \mathrm{UC}\ \overline{v}$
6. $S5 \wedge S6' \wedge L.Reply(p) \wedge \mathrm{UC}\ \langle s,r,c,h\rangle \Rightarrow \mathrm{UC}\ \overline{v}$
7. $S6 \wedge S1' \wedge C.Reply(p) \wedge \mathrm{UC}\ \langle s,r,l\rangle \Rightarrow \overline{Reply(p)} \vee \overline{Reject(p)}$
8. $\mathrm{UC}\ \langle s,r,c,l,h\rangle \Rightarrow \mathrm{UC}\ \overline{v}$

1.5. Q.E.D.

The proofs of steps 1.1–1.4 use simple properties of real numbers and predicate logic. They are omitted.

The Proof of Step 1.5 The high-level proof of step 1.5 is analogous to the proof of step 1.5 of the memory implementation in Section 3.2.

LET: $Inv(p) \triangleq S1 \vee S2 \vee S3 \vee S4 \vee S5 \vee S6$
1.5.1. $IImp(p, et, ct, pt, rt) \Rightarrow \Box Inv(p)$

PROOF: This follows from 1.1 and 1.2, using exactly the same reasoning as in the corresponding step of the memory implementation proof.

1.5.2. $IImp(p, et, ct, pt, rt) \wedge \Box Inv(p) \Rightarrow \overline{Init(p)} \wedge \Box[\overline{Next(p)}]_{\overline{v}}$

PROOF: From 1.1, 1.3, and 1.4, using the TLA proof rules explained in the memory implementation proof.

1.5.3. $IImp(p, et, ct, pt, rt) \wedge \Box Inv(p) \Rightarrow \overline{WF_v(Next(p))}$

PROOF: Described below.

1.5.4. Q.E.D.

PROOF: Step 1 follows from 1.5.1–1.5.3 by propositional logic.

The Proof of Step 1.5.3 It remains to prove step 1.5.3, which asserts that the fairness property of the RPC specification is satisfied. We sketch the argument intuitively. To prove $\overline{WF_v(Next(p))}$, it is enough to show that $\overline{Next(p)}$ cannot be continuously enabled. The action is disabled in state $S1$. Therefore, it suffices to show that, if any of $S2$–$S6$ ever holds, then $S1$ must eventually hold. It is clear from the predicate-action diagram of Figure 23 that this follows if we can prove that none of the predicates $S2$–$S6$ can hold forever, which is established as follows:

- The implementation fairness property $WF_c(C.Next(p))$ implies that neither $S2$ nor $S6$ can hold forever.

- To show that $S3$ cannot hold forever, observe that pt remains unchanged while $S3$ holds. Since $S3$ asserts that pt is greater than or equal to *now*, and *NonZeno* implies that *now* increases without bound, $S3$ must eventually become false. Similar reasoning shows that neither $S4$ nor $S5$ can hold forever.

Observe how *NonZeno* allows us to deduce eventual progress from invariance properties. The RT, $VTimer$, $MinTimer$, and $MaxTimer$ formulas used to specify real-time system requirements are all safety properties. We infer liveness properties from them by using the *NonZeno* assumption.

References

1. Martín Abadi and Leslie Lamport. The existence of refinement mappings. *Theoretical Computer Science*, 82(2):253–284, May 1991.

2. Martín Abadi and Leslie Lamport. An old-fashioned recipe for real time. *ACM Transactions on Programming Languages and Systems*, 16(5):1543–1571, September 1994.

3. Martín Abadi and Leslie Lamport. Conjoining specifications. *ACM Transactions on Programming Languages and Systems*, 17(3):507–534, May 1995.

4. Martín Abadi, Leslie Lamport, and Stephan Merz. The Dagstuhl example—a TLA solution. World Wide Web page at http://www.research.digital.com/SRC /dagstuhl/dagstuhl.html. It can also be found by searching the Web for the 26-letter string formed by concatenating uid and lamportdagstuhlspecprob.

5. Manfred Broy and Leslie Lamport. The RPC-memory specification problem. In this volume. Also available on [4].

6. Nissim Francez. *Fairness*. Texts and Monographs in Computer Science. Springer-Verlag, New York, Berlin, Heidelberg, Tokyo, 1986.

7. Rob Gerth, Ruurd Kuiper, and John Segers. Interface refinement in reactive systems. In W. R. Cleaveland, editor, *3rd International Conference on Concurrency Theory*, volume 630 of *Lecture Notes in Computer Science*, pages 77–93, Berlin, Heidelberg, 1992. Springer-Verlag.

8. Cliff B. Jones. Specification and design of (parallel) programs. In R. E. A. Mason, editor, *Information Processing 83: Proceedings of the IFIP 9th World Congress*, pages 321–332, Amsterdam, September 1983. IFIP, North-Holland.

9. Leslie Lamport. TLA—temporal logic of actions. At URL http://www.research.digital.com/SRC/tla/ on the World Wide Web. It can also be found by searching the Web for the 21-letter string formed by concatenating uid and lamporttlahomepage.

10. Leslie Lamport. How to write a proof. *American Mathematical Monthly*, 102(7):600–608, August-September 1993.

11. Leslie Lamport. Hybrid systems in TLA$^+$. In Robert L. Grossman, Anil Nerode, Anders P. Ravn, and Hans Rischel, editors, *Hybrid Systems*, volume 736 of *Lecture Notes in Computer Science*, pages 77–102, Berlin, Heidelberg, 1993. Springer-Verlag.

12. Leslie Lamport. The temporal logic of actions. *ACM Transactions on Programming Languages and Systems*, 16(3):872–923, May 1994.

13. Leslie Lamport. TLA in pictures. *IEEE Transactions on Software Engineering*, 21(9):768–775, September 1995.

14. Leslie Lamport and Stephan Merz. Specifying and verifying fault-tolerant systems. In H. Langmaack, W.-P. de Roever, and J. Vytopil, editors, *Formal Techniques in Real-Time and Fault-Tolerant Systems*, volume 863 of *Lecture Notes in Computer Science*, pages 41–76. Springer-Verlag, September 1994.

15. A. C. Leisenring. *Mathematical Logic and Hilbert's ε-Symbol*. Gordon and Breach, New York, 1969.

16. Carver Mead and Lynn Conway. *Introduction to VLSI Systems*, chapter 7. Addison-Wesley, Reading, Massachusetts, 1980.

17. Amir Pnueli. The temporal semantics of concurrent programs. In Gilles Kahn, editor, *Semantics of Concurrent Computation*, volume 70 of *Lecture Notes in Computer Science*, pages 1–20. Springer-Verlag, July 1979.

Index

├────────┤ (horizontal bar), 24
$\langle v_1, \ldots, v_n \rangle$ (tuple or sequence), 37
$'$ (prime), 25
$[N]_v$, 25
□, 25
∃, 30
⇒ (implication), precedence of, 25
$\overset{+}{\Rightarrow}$, 35
∧ and ∨, lists of, 25

action, 25
    next-state, 25
arg component of channel, 24
Args, 23
array, 37
assumption, of a module, 28
assumption/guarantee, 35

behavior, 22

caller, 22
caller(p), 24
Calling(p), 25
ch, 24
channel, 24
CHOOSE, 31
component specification, 34
composition is conjunction, 26
CONSTANT parameter, 23

export, 28

F (FALSE), 47
fairness, 31
function, 37

handshake protocol, 24
hiding, 30
history variable, 45

implementation is implication, 35
import, 28
include, 28

LegalCaller, 26
LegalReturner, 26
liveness, 31
LossyRPC module, 55

MaxProcess, 53
MaxReturn, 54
MaxTimer, 53
MemClerk module, 43
MemClerkParameters module, 41
Memory module, 29, 30
MemoryImplementation module, 44
MemoryParameters module, 27
MinTimer, 53

Naturals module, 37
next-state action, 25
NonZeno, 53
NotAResult, 31
now, 53

parameter, of a module, 23
predicate-action diagram, 31
PrIds, 23
prime, 25
ProcedureInterface module, 23

Real, 53
Reals module, 53
RealTime module, 54
refinement mapping, 45
res component of channel, 24
returner, 22
RPC module, 40
RPCClerk module, 57
RPCImplementation module, 58
RPCParameters module, 37
rtrner(p), 25

safety, 31
sequence, 37
Sequences module, 38
SF (strong fairness), 36

state, 22
state predicate, 25
step, 25
STRING, 38
Stølen, Ketil, 22
submodule, 30

T (TRUE), 47
temporal formula, 25
theorem, 44
TLA^+, 22
tuple, 37
types, absence of, 23

UC (UNCHANGED), 47
UNCHANGED, 32

VARIABLE parameter, 23
VTimer, 53

WF (weak fairness), 33

A Dynamic Specification of the RPC-Memory Problem*

Egidio Astesiano – Gianna Reggio

Dipartimento di Informatica e Scienze dell'Informazione
Università di Genova, Italy
Viale Dodecaneso, 35 – Genova 16146, Italy
{ astes,reggio } @ disi.unige.it

1 Introduction

To handle the RPC-Memory Specification Problem we have used the SMoLCS method for the formal specification of dynamic systems developed by our group in the last ten years. SMoLCS consists of integrated logic specification formalisms at different levels of abstraction, from very abstract requirements till detailed designs, with methodological guidelines for supporting the development of a specification (see e.g. [2, 4, 7], for the theoretical and technical foundations and [11] for the methodological aspects).

We present in this paper the treatment of two parts of the RPC-Memory Specification Problem, corresponding to Sect. 1, 2 and 3 of [6].

The RPC-Memory Specification Problem (see [6]) could be seen as the development of a memory component (shortly denoted by MC from now on) starting with the initial requirements, corresponding to Sect. 1 and 2 of [6], later refined by a high-level implementation, whose main features are given in Sect. 3 of [6].

MC requirements We have interpreted Sect. 1 and 2 of [6] as a description of requirements, since there the activity of MC is not completely determined; e.g.: for all $n \geq 1$ the MC that receives n calls and then satisfies them in the reception order and so on, is an admissible realization.

First development step Here we have a refinement of the requirements given before; indeed Sect. 3 of [6] describes in a more precise way MC by saying to realize it using a RPC component, a reliable MC (RMC) and, as suggested afterwards also a CLERK. Moreover following the suggestion of [6] we have considered RPC apart by giving for it a reusable parameterized specification, and then we have used here a particular instantion.

Now we briefly list the main problems posed by tackling the RPC-Memory Specification Problem and how they are handled in our formalism.

The components are open dynamic systems, i.e. systems evolving along the time and interacting with the external (w.r.t. them) environment by receiving procedure calls and returning results; the idea is to model dynamic systems with

---

* This work has been partially supported by HCM-MEDICIS, HCM-EXPRESS and MURST 40%.

labelled transition systems. Moreover we have also to handle data structures (locations, memory values, list of arguments, ...); they are modelled by many-sorted first-order structures. The two models are integrated in the so called dynamic structures: just many-sorted first-order structures, also providing for the fact that we have to model different dynamic systems (MC, RMC, RPC, ...) characterized by different behaviours.

Then we need specifications using such models for two different purposes:

- *requirement* for expressing the starting and intermediate requirements on a dynamic system; they should determine a class of dynamic structures, all those formally and abstractly modelling systems having such requirements;
- *design* for expressing the abstract architectural design of a dynamic system; they should determine one dynamic structure, the one formally and abstractly modelling the designed system.

As for the usual logic specifications of abstract data types, a dynamic specification is a pair $(D\Sigma, AX)$, where $D\Sigma$ is a dynamic signature (a particular many-sorted signature with transition predicates) and AX is a set of axioms on $D\Sigma$.

Dynamic specifications with loose semantics (i.e. whose semantics is the class of all $D\Sigma$-dynamic structures satisfying AX) are meant for requirement. Now, first-order logic is adequate for expressing requirements on the data structures as "InitValue cannot be a location", but cannot be used to express the requirements on the MC behaviour, for example liveness properties, like "MC must eventually issue a return for each call". Thus we have extended first-order logic with combinators of the branching-time temporal logic for expressing properties on the behaviour of the dynamic systems (see [7, 8]).

To express design specifications we need to identify essentially just one model; to this end we adopt the well-known algebraic approach of the so-called "initial semantics" (if AX is a set of positive conditional formulae, then there exists the initial model of a dynamic specification characterized by "minimal truth", i.e. a ground atomic formula holds on it iff it is a logical consequence of the axioms in AX).

The notion of implementation between classic specifications of abstract data types (see [13]) can be naturally extended to dynamic specifications and, e.g., we can formally define, and then prove, that the specification given in the first development step is a correct implementation of that of the MC requirements.

Unfortunately such proofs have to be done by hand, since at the moment there are no tools for helping the verification, except some methodological guidelines; neither automatic tools (e.g. a model checker, a theorem prover) nor theoretical ones (e.g. a sound and/or complete deductive system, a refinement calculus). We have only a software rapid prototyper for design specifications, which helps us to gain confidence in the designed system and to detect several errors, just by examining the behaviour of the specified system (see [1]).

The results of the first two steps are presented in Sect. 4 and 6 and the reusable specification for RPC is presented in Sect. 5. The basis of our specification framework, dynamic specifications, are reported in Sect. 2 and the associated development method for dynamic system is briefly sketched in Sect. 3. Finally in Sect. 7 we discuss our solution.

2 Dynamic Specifications (DSPECs)

Dynamic specifications, shortly DSPECs, extend the logic (algebraic) specification of abstract data types, see [13], to the specification of types of dynamic systems. In this paper, with the term *dynamic system* we generically denote systems that are able to modify their own state during time, so processes and concurrent/reactive/distributed systems are typical examples.

2.1 The formal model for dynamic systems

In the DSPEC approach a dynamic system is modelled by a *labelled transition tree* defined by means of a *labelled transition system*.

Definition 1. A *labelled transition system* (shortly *lts*) is a triple
$(STATE, LAB, \rightarrow)$,
where $STATE$ and LAB are two sets whose elements are, respectively, the *states* and the *labels* of the system, while $\rightarrow \subseteq STATE \times LAB \times STATE$ represents the *transition relation*. A triple (st, l, st') belonging to $\rightarrow$ is called a *transition* and is usually written as $st \xrightarrow{l} st'$. □

A dynamic system D can be modelled by an lts $(STATE, LAB, \rightarrow)$ and an initial state $st_0 \in STATE$.

The elements in $STATE$ that can be reached starting from st_0 are the intermediate interesting states in the life of D, while the transition relation $\rightarrow$ describes the capabilities of D to pass from one intermediate state to another one. So a transition $st \xrightarrow{l} st'$ has the following meaning: D in the state st *is able* to pass to the state st' by performing a transition whose interaction with the external world is described by the label l; thus l provides information both on the conditions on the external world making effective this capability and on the changes in the external world caused by this transition.

Given an lts, we can associate with each $st_0 \in STATE$ a *transition tree* that is a labelled tree whose root is decorated by st_0, whose nodes are decorated by states and whose edges by labels; the structure of the tree is given by means of the following rule: between two nodes decorated, respectively, by st and st' there exists an edge labelled by l iff $st \xrightarrow{l} st'$. In a transition tree the order of the edges is not meaningful and two subtrees decorated in the same way and with the same root are identified.

Concurrent dynamic systems, i.e. dynamic systems having cooperating components that are in turn other dynamic systems, can be modelled through particular ltss obtained by composing other ltss describing such components.

2.2 Dynamic structures

First, we briefly report the main definitions about first-order structures.

A *(many-sorted, first-order) signature* is a triple $\Sigma = (S, OP, PR)$, where
- S is a set (the set of the *sorts*);
- OP is a family of sets: $\{OP_{w,s}\}_{w \in S^*, s \in S}$ (*operation symbols*);
- PR is a family of sets: $\{PR_w\}_{w \in S^+}$ (*predicate symbols*).

A Σ *first-order structure* is a triple $A = (\{A_s\}_{s \in S}, \{Op^A\}_{Op \in OP}, \{Pr^A\}_{Pr \in PR})$ consisting of the *carriers*, the *interpretation of the operation symbols* and the *interpretation of the predicate symbols*. More precisely:
- if $s \in S$, then A_s is a set;
- if $Op: s_1 \times \ldots \times s_n \to s$, then $Op^A: A_{s_1} \times \ldots \times A_{s_n} \to A_s$ is a function;
- if $Pr: s_1 \times \ldots \times s_n$, then $Pr^A \subseteq A_{s_1} \times \ldots \times A_{s_n}$.

Usually we write $Pr^A(a_1, \ldots, a_n)$ instead of $(a_1, \ldots, a_n) \in Pr^A$.

Given a signature Σ with set of sorts S, a *sort assignment* on Σ is an S-indexed family of sets $X = \{X_s\}_{s \in S}$.

Given a sort assignment X, the *term structure* $T_\Sigma(X)$ is the Σ-structure defined as follows, using T to denote $T_\Sigma(X)$:
- $x \in X_s$ implies $x \in T_s$;
- $Op \in OP_{\Lambda, s}$ implies $Op \in T_s$;
- $t_i \in T_{s_i}$ for $i = 1, \ldots, n$ and $Op \in OP_{s_1 \ldots s_n, s}$ imply $Op(t_1, \ldots, t_n) \in T_s$;
- $Op^T(t_1, \ldots, t_n) = Op(t_1, \ldots, t_n)$ for all $Op \in OP$;
- $Pr^T = \emptyset$ for all $Pr \in PR$.

If $X_s = \emptyset$ for all $s \in S$, then $T_\Sigma(X)$ is simply written T_Σ and its elements are called *ground terms*.

In this paper we assume that structures have *nonempty carriers*.

An lts can be represented by a first-order structure A on a signature with two sorts, *state* and *label*, whose elements correspond to states and labels of the system, and a predicate $\to$: *state* $\times$ *label* $\times$ *state* representing the transition relation. The triple $(A_{state}, A_{label}, \to^A)$ is the corresponding lts. Obviously we can have ltss whose states are built by states of other ltss (for modelling concurrent dynamic systems); in such a case we use structures with different sorts corresponding to states and labels and with different predicates corresponding to transition relations.

In a formal model for dynamic systems we may need to consider data too (for example, the data manipulated by the dynamic systems such as natural numbers); to handle these cases our structures may have also sorts that just correspond to data and not to states or labels of ltss.

The first-order structures corresponding to ltss are called *dynamic structures* and are formally defined as follows.

Definition 2.

- A *dynamic signature* $D\Sigma$ is a pair (Σ, DS), where:
  - $\Sigma = (STATE, OP, PR)$ is a signature;
  - $DS \subseteq STATE$ is the set of the *dynamic sorts*, i.e. sorts corresponding to dynamic systems (states of ltss);

· for all $ds \in DS$ there exist a sort $lab\_ds \in STATE - DS$ (the sort of the labels) and a predicate $\_ \overset{\_}{\rightarrow} \_: ds \times lab\_ds \times ds \in PR$ (the transition predicate).

– A *dynamic structure* on $D\Sigma$ (shortly a $D\Sigma$-dynamic structure) is just a Σ-first-order structure; the term structure $T_{D\Sigma}(X)$ is just $T_\Sigma(X)$, where X is a sort assignment on $D\Sigma$. □

2.3   A logic for DSPECs

Having defined dynamic structures as our models for dynamic systems, we now introduce an appropriate logical formalism for expressing properties about them.

The properties can be subdivided in two classes: properties of the static data, including the data used for defining states and labels, that we briefly name "static properties"; and properties on the activity of the dynamic systems, such as liveness or safety requirements, that we briefly name "dynamic properties". While first-order logic is sufficient for static properties, for the dynamic ones we enrich it with the combinators of the past branching-time temporal logic with edge formulae, see [7, 8]. Moreover, since dynamic structures are classified depending on their signature also the formulae of the logic will be given below depending on a signature.

We give now some technical definitions on dynamic structures that will be used in the following. Let D be a $D\Sigma$-dynamic structure and ds a dynamic sort of $D\Sigma$.

$PATH(D, ds)$ denotes the set of the *paths* for the dynamic systems of sort ds, i.e. the set of all sequences of transitions having form either (1) or ... or (4) below:

(1) $\ldots d_{-2}\ l_{-2}\ d_{-1}\ l_{-1}\ d_0\ l_0\ d_1\ l_1\ d_2\ l_2\ \ldots$

(2) $d_0\ l_0\ d_1\ l_1\ d_2\ l_2\ \ldots$

(3) $\ldots d_{-2}\ l_{-2}\ d_{-1}\ l_{-1}\ d_0$

(4) $d_0\ l_0\ d_1\ l_1\ d_2\ l_2\ \ldots\ d_n$ $n \geq 0$

where for all integers i, $d_i \in D_{ds}$, $l_i \in D_{lab\_ds}$ and $(d_i, l_i, d_{i+1}) \in \rightarrow^D$. Notice that both a single state d and a single transition $d\ l\ d'$ may be a path.

If σ has form either (3) or (4) is said *right-bounded*, while if it has form either (2) or (4) is said *left-bounded*.

If σ is right-bounded, then $LastS(\sigma)$ denotes the *last state* of σ; analogously if σ is left-bounded, $FirstS(\sigma)$ denotes the *first state* of σ; while if σ is left-bounded, then $FirstL(\sigma)$ denotes the *first label* of σ, if exists, i.e. if σ is not just a state.

$\sigma \in PATH(D, ds)$ is *right-maximal* (*left-maximal*) iff either σ is not right-bounded (left-bounded) or there do not exist l, d' s.t. $(LastS(\sigma), l, d') \in \rightarrow^D$ $((d', l, FirstS(\sigma)) \in \rightarrow^D)$.

A *composition operation* is defined on paths: $\sigma \cdot \sigma' =_{def}$ if $\sigma = \ldots d_{n-1}\ l_{n-1}\ d_n$ and $\sigma' = d_n\ l_n\ d_{n+1}\ l_{n+1}\ldots$ then
      $\ldots d_{n-1}\ l_{n-1}\ d_n\ l_n\ d_{n+1}\ l_{n+1}\ \ldots$ else undefined.

A *pointed path* is a pair $\langle \sigma_p, \sigma_f \rangle$ s.t. σ_p is left-maximal and right-bounded, σ_f is right-maximal and left-bounded and $LastS(\sigma_p) = FirstS(\sigma_f)$; it represents a complete behaviour for the dynamic system in the state $LastS(\sigma_p)$ coinciding with $FirstS(\sigma_f)$, σ_p is the past part and σ_f the future part.

Definition (Formulae)

The set of formulae, denoted by $F(D\Sigma, X)$, and the family of the sets of path formulae, denoted by $\{PF(D\Sigma, X)_{ds}\}_{ds \in DS}$, on $D\Sigma = ((S, OP, PR), DS)$ and a sort assignment X are defined by multiple induction as follows. For each $s \in S$ and $ds \in DS$:

formulae

- $Pr(t_1, \ldots, t_n) \in F(D\Sigma, X)$ $Pr: s_1 \times \ldots \times s_n \in PR,\ t_i \in T_{D\Sigma}(X)_{s_i}, i = 1 \ldots n$
- $t_1 = t_2 \in F(D\Sigma, X)$ $t_1, t_2 \in T_{D\Sigma}(X)_s$
- $\neg\, \phi_1, \phi_1 \supset \phi_2, \forall\, x\,.\,\phi_1 \in F(D\Sigma, X)$ $\phi_1, \phi_2 \in F(D\Sigma, X), x \in X$
- $\Delta(t, \pi) \in F(D\Sigma, X)$ $t \in T_{D\Sigma}(X)_{ds}, \pi \in PF(D\Sigma, X)_{ds}$

path formulae

- $[\lambda x\,.\,\phi] \in PF(D\Sigma, X)_{ds}$ $x \in X_{ds},\ \phi \in F(D\Sigma, X)$
- $\langle \lambda x\,.\,\phi \rangle \in PF(D\Sigma, X)_{ds}$ $x \in X_{lab\_ds},\ \phi \in F(D\Sigma, X)$
- $\pi_1\,\mathcal{U}\,\pi_2, \pi_1\,\mathcal{S}\,\pi_2 \in PF(D\Sigma, X)_{ds}$ $\pi_1, \pi_2 \in PF(D\Sigma, X)_{ds}$
- $\bigcirc\, \pi \in PF(D\Sigma, X)_{ds}$ $\pi \in PF(D\Sigma, X)_{ds}$
- $\neg\, \pi_1, \pi_1 \supset \pi_2, \forall\, x\,.\,\pi_1 \in PF(D\Sigma, X)_{ds}$ $\pi_1, \pi_2 \in PF(D\Sigma, X)_{ds}, x \in X_s$ $\square$

The formulae of our logic include the usual ones of many-sorted first-order logic with equality; if $D\Sigma$ contains dynamic sorts, they include also formulae built with the transition predicates. Notice that path formulae are just an ingredient, though an important one, for building the temporal formulae.

The formula $\Delta(t, \pi)$ can be read as "for every path $\langle \sigma_p, \sigma_f \rangle$ pointed in the state denoted by t, the path formula π holds on $\langle \sigma_p, \sigma_f \rangle$". We anchor these formulae to states, following the ideas in [9]. The difference is that we do not model a single system but, in general, a type of systems, so there is not a single initial state but several of them, hence the need for an explicit reference to states (through terms) in the formulae built with Δ.

The formula $[\lambda x\,.\,\phi]$ holds on the pointed path $\langle \sigma_p, \sigma_f \rangle$ whenever ϕ holds at the first state of σ_f, which is also the last state of σ_p; while the formula $\langle \lambda x\,.\,\phi \rangle$ holds on the pointed path $\langle \sigma_p, \sigma_f \rangle$ if σ_f is not just a single state and ϕ holds at the first label of σ_f.

Finally, $\bigcirc$, $\mathcal{U}$ and $\mathcal{S}$ are the so called next, (future) until and (past) since combinators.

If A is a Σ-structure, a *variable evaluation* $V: X \to$ A is a sort-respecting assignment of values in A to *all* the variables in X. If $t \in T_\Sigma(X)$, the *interpretation of* t *in* A w.r.t. V is denoted by $t^{A,V}$ and given as follows:

- $x^{A,V} = V(x)$
- $Op(t_1, \ldots, t_n)^{A,V} = Op^A(t_1^{A,V}, \ldots, t_n^{A,V})$.

Definition (Semantics of formulae) *Let* D *be a* $D\Sigma$-*dynamic structure and* V *a variable evaluation of* X *in* D; *then we define by multiple induction:*

- *the validity of a formula* ϕ *in* D *w.r.t.* V *(written* $D, V \models \phi$*),*
- *the validity of a path formula* π *on a pointed path* $\langle \sigma_p, \sigma_f \rangle$ *in* D *w.r.t.* V *(written* $D, V, \langle \sigma_p, \sigma_f \rangle \models \pi$*),*

as follows:

formulae

- $D, V \models Pr(t_1, \ldots, t_n)$ *iff* $(t_1^{D,V}, \ldots, t_n^{D,V}) \in Pr^D$
- $D, V \models t_1 = t_2$ *iff* $t_1^{D,V} = t_2^{D,V}$
- $D, V \models \neg \phi$ *iff* $D, V \not\models \phi$
- $D, V \models \phi_1 \supset \phi_2$ *iff either* $D, V \not\models \phi_1$ *or* $D, V \models \phi_2$
- $D, V \models \forall x . \phi$ *iff for each* $v \in D_s$, *with* s *sort of* x, $D, V[v/x] \models \phi$
- $D, V \models \Delta(t, \pi)$ *iff*
  for each $\langle \sigma_p, \sigma_f \rangle$ *s.t.* $FirstS(\sigma_f) = t^{D,V}$, $D, V, \langle \sigma_p, \sigma_f \rangle \models \pi$

path formulae

- $D, V, \langle \sigma_p, \sigma_f \rangle \models [\lambda x . \phi]$ *iff* $D, V[FirstS(\sigma_f)/x] \models \phi$
- $D, V, \langle \sigma_p, \sigma_f \rangle \models \langle \lambda x . \phi \rangle$ *iff* $FirstL(\sigma_f)$ *is defined and* $D, V[FirstL(\sigma_f)/x] \models \phi$.
- $D, V, \langle \sigma_p, \sigma_f \rangle \models \pi_1 \, \mathcal{U} \, \pi_2$ *iff*
  there exist σ_1, σ_2 *s.t.* $\sigma_f = \sigma_1 \cdot \sigma_2$, $D, V, \langle \sigma_p \cdot \sigma_1, \sigma_2 \rangle \models \pi_2$ *and*
  for each σ_1', σ_1'' *s.t.* $\sigma_1 = \sigma_1' \cdot \sigma_1''$ *and* $\sigma_1' \neq \sigma_1$, $D, V, \langle \sigma_p \cdot \sigma_1', \sigma_1'' \cdot \sigma_2 \rangle \models \pi_1$
- $D, V, \langle \sigma_p, \sigma_f \rangle \models \pi_1 \, \mathcal{S} \, \pi_2$ *iff*
  there exist σ_1, σ_2 *s.t.* $\sigma_p = \sigma_1 \cdot \sigma_2$, $D, V, \langle \sigma_1, \sigma_2 \cdot \sigma_f \rangle \models \pi_2$ *and*
  for each σ_2', σ_2'' *s.t.* $\sigma_2 = \sigma_2' \cdot \sigma_2''$ *and* $\sigma_2'' \neq \sigma_2$, $D, V, \langle \sigma_1 \cdot \sigma_2', \sigma_2'' \cdot \sigma_f \rangle \models \pi_1$
- $D, V, \langle \sigma_p, \sigma_f \rangle \models \bigcirc \pi$ *iff* $\sigma_f = st \, l \, \sigma'$ *and* $D, V, \langle \sigma_p \cdot (st \, l \, FirstS(\sigma')), \sigma' \rangle \models \pi$
- $D, V, \langle \sigma_p, \sigma_f \rangle \models \neg \pi$ *iff* $D, V, \langle \sigma_p, \sigma_f \rangle \not\models \pi$
- $D, V, \langle \sigma_p, \sigma_f \rangle \models \pi_1 \supset \pi_2$ *iff either* $D, V, \langle \sigma_p, \sigma_f \rangle \not\models \pi_1$ *or* $D, V, \langle \sigma_p, \sigma_f \rangle \models \pi_2$
- $D, V, \langle \sigma_p, \sigma_f \rangle \models \forall x . \pi$ *iff for each* $v \in D_{ds}, D, V[v/x], \langle \sigma_p, \sigma_f \rangle \models \pi$

ϕ *is* valid *in* D *(written* $D \models \phi$*) iff* $D, V \models \phi$ *for all evaluations* V. $\square$

In the above definitions we have used a minimal set of combinators; in practice, however, it is convenient to use other, derived, combinators; we list below those that we shall use in this paper, together with their semantics.

- **true**, **false**, $\vee$, $\wedge$, $\exists$ and $\equiv$, defined in the usual way
- $\Diamond \, \pi =_{\text{def}}$ **true** $\mathcal{U} \, \pi$ (eventually in the future π)
  $D, V, \langle \sigma_p, \sigma_f \rangle \models \Diamond \, \pi$ iff
  there exist σ_1, σ_2 s.t. $\sigma_f = \sigma_1 \cdot \sigma_2$, and $D, V, \langle \sigma_p \cdot \sigma_1, \sigma_2 \rangle \models \pi$
- $\Diamond \mathbf{P} \, \pi =_{\text{def}}$ **true** $\mathcal{S} \, \pi$ (some time in the past π)
  $D, V, \langle \sigma_p, \sigma_f \rangle \models \Diamond \mathbf{P} \, \pi$ iff
  there exist σ_1, σ_2 s.t. $\sigma_p = \sigma_1 \cdot \sigma_2$, $D, V, \langle \sigma_1, \sigma_2 \cdot \sigma_f \rangle \models \pi$
- $\nabla(t, \pi) =_{\text{def}} \neg \, \Delta(t, \neg \pi)$ (in one case)
  $D, V \models \nabla(t, \pi)$ iff
  there exists $\langle \sigma_p, \sigma_f \rangle$ s.t. $FirstS(\sigma_f) = t^{D,V}$ and $D, V, \langle \sigma_p, \sigma_f \rangle \models \pi$

Whenever in ϕ there are no free variables of dynamic sort except x: $[\lambda x . \phi]$ is abbreviated to $[\phi]$, moreover $[s = t]$ is abbreviated to $[t]$; analogously $\langle \lambda x . \phi \rangle$ and $\langle l = t \rangle$ are abbreviated respectively to $\langle \phi \rangle$ and $\langle t \rangle$.

2.4 Dynamic specifications

Definition 3. A *DSPEC (dynamic specification)* is a pair $SP = (D\Sigma, AX)$ where $D\Sigma$ is a dynamic signature and $AX \subseteq F(D\Sigma, X)$.

The *models* of SP, $Mod(SP)$, are the $D\Sigma$-dynamic structures D s.t. the formulae in AX are valid in D. $\square$

We need to consider two different kinds of DSPECs:

requirement for expressing the starting and intermediate requirements of a dynamic system; a requirement DSPEC should determine a class of dynamic structures, all those formally and abstractly modelling systems having such requirements; technically the semantics of a requirement DSPEC is the class of its models (loose semantics);

design for expressing the abstract design of a dynamic system, i.e. to abstractly and formally define the way we intend to design the system; a design DSPEC should determine one dynamic structure, the one formally and abstractly modelling the designed system; technically the semantics of a design DSPEC is the initial element in the class of its models, if any (recall that the initial element is unique up to isomorphism).

A DSPEC may not have an initial model, since it might contain an axiom like $t_1 = t_2 \lor t_1 = t_3$; so we have to restrict the form of the axioms used in design specifications, by considering only *conditional* axioms having the following form: $\alpha_1 \land \ldots \land \alpha_n \supset \alpha$, where α_i and α are atoms i.e. either $Pr(t_1, \ldots, t_n)$ or $t = t'$.

Proposition 4. *Given a DSPEC $SP = (D\Sigma, AX)$ where AX is a set of conditional axioms, then there exists (unique up to isomorphism) I_{SP} initial in $Mod(SP)$ characterized by*

- *for all $t_1, t_2 \in T_{D\Sigma}$ of the same sort* $I_{SP} \models t_1 = t_2$ *iff* $AX \vdash t_1 = t_2$;
- *for all $Pr \in PR$ and all $t_1, \ldots, t_n \in T_{D\Sigma}$ of appropriate sorts* $I_{SP} \models Pr(t_1, \ldots, t_n)$ *iff* $AX \vdash Pr(t_1, \ldots, t_n)$;

where $\vdash$ denotes provability in the Birkhoff sound and complete deductive system for conditional axioms, whose rules are:

$$t = t \qquad \frac{t = t'}{t' = t} \qquad \frac{t = t' \quad t' = t''}{t = t''}$$

$$\frac{t_i = t_i' \quad i = 1, \ldots, n}{Op(t_1, \ldots, t_n) = Op(t_1', \ldots, t_n')} \qquad \frac{t_i = t_i' \quad i = 1, \ldots, n \quad Pr(t_1, \ldots, t_n)}{Pr(t_1', \ldots, t_n')}$$

$$\frac{\alpha_1 \land \ldots \land \alpha_n \supset \alpha \qquad \alpha_i \quad i = 1, \ldots, n}{\alpha}$$

$$\frac{F}{\overline{V}(F)} \quad V\colon X \to \mathrm{T}_\Sigma(X)$$

$\overline{V}(F)$ *is F where each occurrence of a variable, say x, has been replaced by $V(x)$.*
□

A notion of "correct implementation" between DSPECs has been given (see [4]) as follows: a requirement SP is *implemented* by SP' with respect to $\mathcal{F}$, a function from specifications into specifications, iff $Mod(\mathcal{F}(SP')) \subseteq Mod(SP)$. The function $\mathcal{F}$ describes how the parts of SP are realized in SP' (implementation as realization); while implementation as refinement is obtained by requiring inclusion of the classes of models. Notice that this definition applies whatever the kind of SP' (either requirement or design); in the latter case the class of it models just contains the initial one and those isomorphic to it.

3   A Development Process for Dynamic Systems

3.1   Development process

The development process supported by DSPEC consists of different phases from the presentation of the informal idea of what we have to realize till the coding of the dynamic system in a programming language. ¿From a phase it is possible to go back to the previous phases either because some part has been modified or because an error has been found.

Each phase of the development process is characterized by the production of a document, having a particular structure, which guides and documents the activities of the phase.

The development process starts from what we call *natural description*, i.e. a document, given by the client, describing the system to be realized using some natural language.

PHASE 1 During this phase we analyse the dynamic system trying to determine its essential requirements and after to specifiy them by a requirement DSPEC.

The analysis starts from the natural description; but it may be that in the natural description there are ambiguities, inconsistencies, or parts whose only possible interpretation is not sensible; these points, called *shadow spots*, should be reported in a document together with possible choices; if the shadow spots are too many or too relevant preventing to determine the requirements, the natural description should be returned to the client to be modified.

The *border determination* is another part of document of this phase; it gives the motivations for deciding which parts of the dynamic system have been included in the specification. That is relevant, because within DSPECs it is not possible to give requirements on the environment of the specified dynamic system; thus where to place the border of the dynamic system, i.e.

which parts of the outside environment to specify, depends on the relevance of the requirements about such parts.

Summarizing, during **PHASE 1** we have to produce a document consisting of: the natural description, the border determination, the shadow spots description and the specification of the requirements, just a requirement DSPEC.

PHASE 2 The requirement DSPEC given in **PHASE 1** is developed through an appropriate number of (development) steps; in each step we make more detailed the features of the system to realize until its complete definition.

A development step is further split in:

- an *analysis step*, in which we either refine the requirement on the system or design some of its parts; the result of the analysis is formalized by a DSPEC, which may be either of kind requirement (when the requirements have been refined), or design (when each part of the system has been designed), or mixed, i.e. a combination of subspecifications of kind design with other of kind requirement (when only some parts of the system have been designed).

- a *correctness verification step* which verifies that the specification given at this step is a correct implementation of the previous one (for the first step of this phase, of the requirement specification of **PHASE 1**). Clearly, it may happen that the current specification is wrong (i.e. cannot be a correct implementation), in such cases we have either to redo the current step, or if instead the error is in the previous steps or in the requirements, to go back to modify them appropriately.

Summarizing, during a development step of **PHASE 2** we have to produce a document consisting of: a natural description saying which choices have been done in the step, a DSPEC of the appropriate kind and a *justification of the correctness of the step*.

PHASE 2 ends with a step producing a design DSPEC.

PHASE 3 If the specification given in the last development step of **PHASE 2** is prototypable, then we can perform tests on it using the prototyping tool (see [1]) for verifying the consistency between the starting idea of the system (in the natural description) and the produced design. The rapid prototyper given a design specification of a dynamic system and a state of such system generates in an interactive way (parts of) the labelled transition tree starting from such state, and so allows to analyse the behaviour of the system starting from such state.

If the result of such tests is not satisfactory, we have go back to modify the previous steps.

PHASE 4 If the result of the tests of **PHASE 3** is satisfactory, the dynamic system is coded using a programming language following the usual criteria of efficiency and correctness.

3.2 How to write a DSPEC

The development process presented in the previous subsection requires to write down several DSPECs; here we present some guidelines for writing a DSPEC of a dynamic system.

First, the dynamic system should be classified in *simple* or *concurrent*; concurrent systems are those whose activity is determined by the activity of several components, which are in turn dynamic systems (either simple or concurrent), also of different types. Thus the guidelines below distinguish between the two cases. Clearly the classification in simple and concurrent of a system is relative to a step and a simple system may be refined by a concurrent one in the next step.

Simple dynamic system

Basic data structures Determine and specify the data structures used by the dynamic system.

States Determine and specify the intermediate relevant situations in the life of the dynamic system (i.e. the states of the lts modelling it) as a data structure, with a main sort corresponding to such states. Then the main sort is made dynamic.

Interactions Determine and specify the interactions of the dynamic system with the external world (i.e. the labels of the lts modelling it) as a data structure, whose main sort will be the sort of label associated with the dynamic sort given in the previous point, and having an operation for each *kind* of interactions; these operations may have several arguments describing the information exchanged between the system and the external world during each interaction of such kind.

Activity Determine and specify the activity of the dynamic system (i.e. the transitions of the lts modelling it) represented by the arrow predicate associated with the dynamic sort given before.

> **requirement** We have to give the relevant properties on the transitions, which are usually grouped depending on the kind of the performed interaction.
>
> Let $L: s_1 \times \ldots \times s_n \to lab\_ds$ be an operation representing the interactions of a certain kind; these properties may express:
>
> – *necessary conditions* on the initial/final state of a capability with interaction of " kind L" (which reactions we expect from the system after its execution and what must have happened before):
> $$st \xrightarrow{L(t_1,\ldots,t_n)} st' \supset \phi(st,t_1,\ldots,t_n,st') \wedge \Delta(st',\pi_f) \wedge \Delta(st,\pi_p)$$
> where $t_1, \ldots, t_n$ are terms of sort $s_1, \ldots, s_n$ respectively, and st, st' are terms of sort ds, π_f is a path formula built with the future temporal combinators and π_p with the past ones.
>
> – *sufficient conditions* for the system to have a transition capability with interaction of "kind L"; these properties are very important in the specification of a reactive system, since they express that the system in some cases eventually must be able to accept a certain external stimulation. These properties may have various forms:

- $\phi(st) \supset \triangledown(st, \langle L(t_1, \ldots, t_n) \rangle)$
  (the system has (immediately) a capability to do such interaction)
- $\phi(st) \supset \triangle(st, \diamond \langle L(t_1, \ldots, t_n) \rangle)$
  (in any case the system will eventually perform such interaction)
- $\phi(st) \supset \triangle(st, \diamond [\lambda x . \triangledown (x, \langle L(t_1, \ldots, t_n) \rangle)])$
  (in any case the system will eventually have the capability to do such interaction)

where $t_1, \ldots, t_n$ are terms of sort $s_1, \ldots, s_n$ respectively, and st is a term of sort ds.

Whole behaviour properties i.e. properties that are not related to the occurrence of particular interactions but refer to a whole behaviour. Their structure is simply $\triangle(st, \pi)$, where st is a term of dynamic sort; e.g. π may express a *responsiveness* property, i.e. has form $(\square \diamond \pi_1) \supset (\square \diamond \pi_2)$.

design We have to define the system transitions by giving a set of conditional axioms of the form: $cond(st, l, st') \supset st \xrightarrow{l} st'$, where st, st', l are terms of sort ds and lab_ds respectively, and $cond(st, l, st')$ is a conjunction of atoms; recall that the only transitions of the specified system are those which can be proved by the given axioms by using the deductive system of Prop. 4.

Concurrent dynamic system

Basic data structures As in the simple case.

Components Determine and specify following these same guidelines the components of the concurrent system, which are in turn dynamic systems.

States As in the simple case, but now they are defined by putting together the states of the components.

Interactions As in the simple case.

Activity Determine and specify the activity of the dynamic system, the transitions, by considering also the activities (transitions) of its components.

requirement As for the simple case, the only difference is that not only the system can perform transitions, but also its components.

design We have to define the system transitions by giving a set of conditional axioms of the form:
$$\phi(l, l_1, \ldots, l_n) \wedge c_1 \xrightarrow{l_1} c'_1 \wedge \ldots c_n \xrightarrow{l_n} c'_n \supset$$
$$st(c_1, \ldots, c_n) \xrightarrow{l} st'(c'_1, \ldots, c'_n),$$
where $l_1, \ldots, l_n, l$, are terms of label sorts, $c_1, \ldots, c_n, c'_1, \ldots, c'_n$ are variables of sort states of the components and $st(c_1, \ldots, c_n)$ ($st'(c'_1, \ldots, c'_n)$) is a term denoting a state of the concurrent system where the components are in the states $c_1, \ldots, c_n$ respectively. Notice that the above constraints on the form of axioms ensure that only the interactions of the component transitions are relevant for the composition, and so that interactions really represent the transition interfaces.

3.3 Specification presentation

To be able to present in a sensible way the specifications produced during the development process, a specification language for DSPEC, METAL see [10], has been developed with a precise "friendly" syntax (e.g. no esoteric symbols but mnemonic keywords) and with facilities for helping to write down complex and large specifications. The constructs of METAL will be briefly explained when used in the specifications of the RPC-Memory Specification Problem, by comments enclosed by [and].

Furthermore, each formal DSPEC is accompanied by a strictly correspondent informal specification (natural language text following a particular structure). In this paper these informal specifications are presented as line-by-line comments of the formal ones, but it is also possible to give as first those informal specifications, present and discuss them with the client and after derive from them the formal counterpart, see [3]. Notice the strict correspondence between the informal text and the corresponding formal part.

It is also possible to associate a graphical presentation, both with the formal and the informal specifications, to improve their readability; to give the flavour we report some of the diagrams associated with RPC-Memory Specification Problem, see e.g. Fig. 1.

4 MC Requirement Specification (PHASE 1)

To give the requirements on MC corresponds to PHASE 1 of the development process associated with DSPECs (see Sect. 3), and means to determine which are all processes described by Sect. 1 and 2 of [6]; i.e. to define the class of all dynamic structures modelling such processes by using a requirement DSPEC.

Below we report the documents produced during this phase together with some comments. The formal specifications are written using the specification language METAL, see [10], while the corresponding informal specifications are reported as line-by-line comments and typed using the *italic font*.

Natural description Sect. 1 and 2 of [6].

Border determination The universe of MC consists of MC itself and of the other components; moreover within a component there are several processes in parallel calling the MC's procedures. In the natural description there is a requirement on such processes: they cannot start a new procedure call before to have terminated any previous ones (by receiving a result). Since this property will be used to define MC, the border of the specified dynamic system should enclose all components; however in this report to save space we consider it to enclose exactly MC.

Basic data structures The basic data structures part contains the specifications of those data structures used by the dynamic system.

Universe of the values [METAL offers a textual notation for all signature items (sorts, operations, predicates and axioms) plus a special notation for constants (**cn**), which are the zero-ary operations; "if ... then ..." is just the syntax for the conditional logic combinator.]

UNIVERSE =
universe of the values either arguments or return values of the MC *procedures*
requirement
sort universe

cn Init_Value: universe   *value initially contained in the locations*
cn Write_End: universe   *value returned by a successful Write call*
cn BadArg, MemFailure: universe   *exceptional values*

BadArg and MemFailure are different
ax not BadArg = MemFailure

checks whether a universe element is a memory value/a location
pr Is_MemVal, Is_Loc: universe

a universe element cannot be both a memory value and a location
ax not (Is_MemVal(u) and Is_Loc(u))

Init_Value is a memory value while Write_End is not so
ax Is_MemVal(Init_Value) and not Is_MemVal(Write_End)

BadArg and MemFailure are neither memory values nor locations
ax not (Is_MemVal(BadArg) or Is_MemVal(MemFailure))
ax not (Is_Loc(BadArg) or Is_Loc(MemFailure))
end

Process identifier

PID =
identifiers of the processes (in some other components) originally issuing the calls
requirement sort pid **end**

Calls ["**use**" is the METAL construct for modularly building specifications; below **use** UNIVERSE means that the CALL specification has all sorts, operations and predicates of UNIVERSE with the properties expressed in UNIVERSE.]

CALL =   *calls of the* MC *procedures*
design
use UNIVERSE
sort call

takes two universe elements and returns a Write call
op Write: universe universe -> call
takes a universe element and returns a Read call
op Read: universe -> call

pr Correct: call   *checks if a call is correct*
if the first argument is a location and the second a memory value, then a Write
call is correct
ax if Is_Loc(u) and Is_MemVal(u') then Correct(Write(u,u'))
if the argument is a location, then a Read call is correct
ax if Is_Loc(u) then Correct(Read(u))
end

Interactions

MC_INTERACT =
requirement
use CALL, PID

to receive a call and a process identifier (of the process in some other component
that has originally issued the call)
op RECEIVE: call pid -> lab_mc

to return a result and a process identifier (of the process in some other component
that finally will get the result)
op RETURN: universe pid -> lab_mc

auxiliary predicate
checks if an interaction does not concern a given process identifier
pr No_Concern: lab_mc pid
ax No_Concern(RECEIVE(c,pi),pi') iff not pi = pi'
ax No_Concern(RETURN(u,pi),pi') iff not pi = pi'
end

Notice that here we have used a requirement DSPEC for the MC interactions,
since we only know that MC has at least the above interactions, but we do not
know completely such interactions.

States [The METAL construct "**dsort** mc: _ - _ -> _" declares "mc" to be
a dynamic sort and implicitly also the associated sort of labels ("lab_mc") and
transition predicate "**pr** _ - _ -> _: mc lab_mc mc".]

MC_STATE =
requirement
use UNIVERSE
dsort mc: _ – _ –> _

returns the content of a location in a given state
op Cont: mc universe -> universe
the content of a location is a memory value
ax if Is_Loc(u) then Is_MemVal(Cont(mc,u))
end

Activity [Below "...in any case ...", "until", "since" and "next" are the METAL syntaxes for the combinators of the temporal logic $\triangle(\ldots,\ldots)$, $\mathcal{U}$, $\mathcal{S}$ and $\bigcirc$, introduced in Sect. 2.3.]

MC =
requirement
use MC_INTERACT, MC_STATE

** 1 **
if MC *receives a non-correct call and pi, then*
ax if not Correct(c) and mc – RECEIVE(c,pi) –> mc′ then
        in any case it will perform interactions non-concerning pi until
        mc′ in any case < No_Concern(y,pi) > until
            will return either BadArg or MemFailure and pi
            (u = BadArg or u = MemFailure) and < RETURN(u,pi) >

** 2 **
if MC *receives a correct call Read(u) and pi, then*
ax if mc – RECEIVE(Read(u),pi) –> mc′ and Correct(Read(u)) then
        in any case it will perform interactions non-concerning pi until
        mc′ in any case < No_Concern(y,pi) > until
            either will return the content of u and pi
            ((exists u′: [Cont(x,u) = u′] and next < RETURN(u′,pi) >)
            or will return MemFailure and pi
            or < RETURN(MemFailure,pi) >)

** *3* **

if MC *receives a correct call Write(u,u′) and pi, then*

ax if mc – RECEIVE(Write(u,u′),pi) -> mc′ and Correct(Write(u,u′)) then
          in any case it will perform interactions non-concerning pi until
        mc′ in any case < No_Concern(y,pi) > until
              either will change the content of u to u′ and after
              ([Cont(x,u) ≑ u′] and next
                  will perform interactions non-concerning pi until
                  (< No_Concern(y,pi) > until
                      will return Write_End and pi
                      < RETURN(Write_End,pi) >))
              or will return MemFailure and pi
              or < RETURN(MemFailure,pi) >

** *4* **

if MC *returns BadArg and pi, then*

ax if mc – RETURN(BadArg,pi) -> mc′ then
          in any case it has performed interactions non-concerning pi since
        mc′ in any case < No_Concern(y,pi) > since
              has received a non-correct call and pi
              < exists c: not Correct(c) and y = RECEIVE(c,pi) >

** *5* **

if MC *returns MemFailure and pi, then*

ax if mc – RETURN(MemFailure,pi) -> mc′ then
          in any case it has performed interactions non-concerning pi since
        mc′ in any case < No_Concern(y,pi) > since
              has received a call and pi
              < exists c: y = RECEIVE(c,pi) >

** *6* **

if MC *returns Write_End and pi, then*

ax if mc – RETURN(Write_End,pi) -> mc′ then
          in any case it has performed interactions non-concerning pi since
        mc′ in any case < No_Concern(y,pi) > since
              has received a correct write call and pi
              < exists u, u′: Correct(Write(u,u′)) and >
              y = RECEIVE(Write(u,u′),pi)

*** 7 ***

if MC *returns a memory value and pi, then*

ax   if mc – RETURN(u,pi) –> mc' and Is_MemVal(u) then
       in any case it has performed interactions non-concerning pi since
      mc' in any case < No_Concern(y,pi) > since
         has received a correct read call and pi
         < exists u': Correct(Read(u)) and y = RECEIVE(Read(u),pi) >

*** 8 ***

if MC *changes the content of a location u to u', then*

ax   if mc – y –> mc' and (not Cont(mc,u) = u') and Cont(mc',u) = u' then
      in any case for some pi
      mc' in any case exists pi:
         it has performed interactions non-concerning pi since
         (< No_Concern(y,pi) > since
            has received a correct call Write(u,u') and pi
            < y = RECEIVE(Write(u,u'),pi) and Correct(Write(u,u')) >)

end

For MC and any other dynamic system appearing in the RPC-Memory Specification Problem, together with the obvious properties about reacting to stimuli, as 1, 2 and 3, we have considered also a set of properties which may be termed "no unsolicited reactions", as 4, ..., 8 (i.e. properties requiring that some activities of a system can be present only as reactions to previously received stimuli).

Shadow spots The points listed below are not very clear in the natural description of MC; for each of them we report also how we have settled it.

- Which are the available locations in a memory component? We have chosen that all locations are available.
- Are properties 4, ..., 7 necessary? We have opted for yes.
- Are the locations subject to failures?, i.e. can they change their content by themselves? We have opted for no (property 8).
- Can MemFailure be returned as result of a non-correct call? We have opted for yes.

The structure of the specification of the MC requirements is graphically reported in Fig. 1; there square boxes correspond to specifications of data structures and rounded boxes to dynamic systems; enclosure of boxes corresponds to the fact that a specification uses another specification. The small letters enclosed by parenthesis near data structure names are used to denote generic elements of such structures. Finally the arrows leaving the MC box correspond to the MC interactions; "..." means that MC may have other interactions.

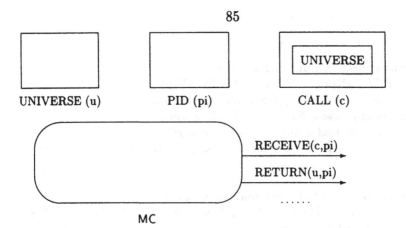

Fig. 1. The requirement specification of MC

5 The Reusable Specification of RPC

In this section we give the specification of the parametric simple system corresponding to RPC, to be (re)used in the specification of the implementation of MC. From Sect. 3 of [6] we have that the parameter is a data structure corresponding to the procedure names; for simplicity, in the following we take instead as parameter a data structure corresponding to the universe of values, the process identifiers, the calls and the remote calls.

The acceptable actual parameters Clearly not any data structure may be used to instantiate RPC; the properties on the acceptable ones are given by the following specification. An actual parameter is acceptable iff its signature contains all items of the signature of PAR with the properties expressed by the axioms of PAR.

PAR =   *the essential properties of the* RPC *parameter*
requirement
use NAT
universe of the values either arguments or results of the RPC *procedures*
sort universe

sort exception   *exceptional values*
cn BadCall, RPCFailure: exception

sort proc   *procedure names*
given a procedure name returns the number of its arguments
op ArgNum: proc -> nat

an exception and a procedure name are universe values
op E: exception -> universe
op P: proc -> universe

check if a universe element is a list of length n
pr   Is_List: universe nat

if a universe element is a list with length n and with length m, then n is equal to m
ax   if Is_List(u,n) and Is_List(u,m) then n = m

exceptions and procedure names are not list
ax   not Is_List(E(e),n) and not Is_List(P(p),n)

identifiers of the processes (in some other components) originally issuing the calls
sort pid

sort rcall   *remote calls received by* RPC

the remote calls are made by two universe elements (the procedure name and the list of the arguments)
op   < _ ; _ >: universe universe -> rcall
ax   exists u, u': rc = < u ; u' >
ax   if < u ; u' > = < u1 ; u1' > then u = u1 and u' = u1'

checks if a remote call is correct
pr   Remote_Correct: rcall

a remote call is correct iff
ax   Remote_Correct(u,u') iff
u is a procedure name p and u' a list whose length is the number of arguments of p
exists p: u = P(p) and Is_List(u', ArgNum(p))

sort call   *calls of the* MC *procedures*

transforms a remote call into the corresponding call
op   Call: rcall -> call
end

Interactions The interactions of the reusable RPC are given by a parametric specification. [**generic** is the keyword for introducing the formal parameter X (a specification), while PAR expresses which are the correct actual ones.]

RPC_P_INTERACT =
generic X: PAR
design
use X, PID

*to receive (from the sender) a remote call and an identifier (of the process in some
other component that has originally issued the call)*
op RECEIVE_REM: rcall pid -> lab_rpc

*to return (to the sender) a result (of a remote call) and an identifier (of the
process in some other component that finally will get the result)*
op RETURN_REM: universe pid -> lab_rpc

*to send a call (to the receiver) and an identifier (of the process in some other
component that has originally issued the call)*
op SEND: call pid -> lab_rpc

*to receive a (call) result (from the receiver) and an identifier (of the process in
some other component that finally will get the result)*
op RECEIVE_CALL_RES: universe pid -> lab_rpc
end

States We have no requirements on the states of the reusable RPC.

RPC_P_STATE = **requirement dsort** rpc: _ – _ –> _ **end**

Activity In this case we have also a kind of properties, that may be termed "acceptance vitality", as R7 and R8 (i.e. properties requiring that the system must surely, at certain points, have the capabilities to receive stimuli; these properties e.g. avoids that the forever stopped system is a correct implementation.
[Below "eventually" is the METAL syntax for the combinator of the temporal logic $\Diamond$, introduced in Sect. 2.3.]

RPC_P =
generic X: PAR
design
use RPC_P_INTERACT(X), RPC_P_STATE

** *R1* **
if RPC receives a correct remote call rc and pi, then
ax if rpc – RECEIVE_REM(rc,pi) -> rpc' and Remote_Correct(rc) then
in any case it will eventually
ax rpc' in any case eventually
   either send the call corresponding to rc and pi or return RPCFailure and pi
   (< SEND(Call(rc),pi) > or < RETURN_REM(E(RPCFailure),pi) >)

** R2 **

if RPC receives a non-correct remote call rc and pi, then
ax   if rpc – RECEIVE_REM(rc,pi) -> rpc' and not Remote_Correct(rc) then
         in any case it will eventually return BadCall and pi
         rpc' in any case eventually < RETURN_REM(E(BadCall),pi) >

** R3 **

if RPC receives a result u and pi, then
ax   if rpc – RECEIVE_CALL_RES(u,pi) -> rpc' then
         in any case it will eventually
         rpc' in any case eventually
             return either u or RPCFailure and pi
             ((u' = u or u' = E(RPCFailure)) and < RETURN_REM(u',pi) >)

** R4 **

if RPC sends a call c and pi, then
ax   if rpc – SEND(c,pi) -> rpc' then
         in any case it
         rpc' in any case
             has not sent any other calls with pi since
             < not exists c': y = SEND(c',pi) > since
                 has received a remote call corresponding to c and pi
                 < exists rc: c = Call(rc) and y = RECEIVE_REM(rc,pi) >

** R5 **

if RPC returns a result u different from RPCFailure and pi, then
ax   if rpc – RETURN_REM(u,pi) -> rpc' and not(u = RPCFailure) then
         in any case it
         rpc' in any case
             has not returned any other results with pi since
             < not exists u': y = RETURN_REM(u',pi) > since
                 has received u and pi
                 < RECEIVE_CALL_RES(u,pi) >

** R6 **

if RPC returns RPCFailure and pi, then
ax   if rpc – RETURN_REM(RPCFailure,pi) -> rpc' then
         in any case it
         rpc' in any case
             has not returned any other results with pi since
             < not exists u': y = RETURN_REM(u',pi) > since
                 (either has received some result and pi
                 (< exists u': y = RECEIVE_CALL_RES(u',pi) >
                 or has received some remote call and pi)
                 or < exists rc: y = RECEIVE_REM(rc,pi) >)

** R7 **

in any case RPC *will eventually*

ax rpc in any case eventually

   reach a state where may receive any remote call

   [forall rc, pi: exists rpc': x – RECEIVE_REM(rc,pi) -> rpc']

** R8 **

in any case RPC *will eventually*

ax rpc in any case eventually

   reach a state where may receive any result

   [forall u, pi: exists rpc': x – RECEIVE_CALL_RES(u,pi) -> rpc']

end

6   MC Development (First Step of PHASE 2)

Here we consider a refinement of the requirements on MC, given in Sect. 4, following what said in Sect. 3 of [6]; there MC is implemented by using a RPC component, a reliable MC (RMC) and, as suggested afterwards, also a CLERK. Moreover, always following [6], the RPC component is given by instantiating a reusable process, whose parameterized specification has been given apart in Sect. 5. Notice that in this development step a simple system has been refined into a concurrent one.

As said in Sect. 3 a development step should produce, other than a specification, a natural description of the performed development and a justification of the correctness of such step; furthermore the specification should be structured following the system structure, as graphically reported in Fig. 2. There the components are represented by enclosing the rounded boxes corresponding to them into that of the whole system.

Natural description

 Sect. 3 of [6] plus the following assumptions on which are the processes composing the implementing system.

 The implementation consists of three processes: RMC, RPC and CLERK handling the communication with outside MC. CLERK receives from outside the calls of the MC procedures and after forwards them to RPC. Furthermore it receives the results of the calls from RPC; if such results are different from RPCFailure, then after it will return them outside MC, otherwise either it retries to send to RPC the call that has originated the result or it will return a MemFailure exception; surely for each call it will return a result eventually.

 The assumption on the activity of the processes calling the MC procedures "they cannot start a new procedure call before to have terminated any previous ones (by receiving a result)" is used to give this implementation of MC, since it implies that it is not possible to have two outstanding calls issued by the same process; so it allows to use the process identifier to uniquely identify the

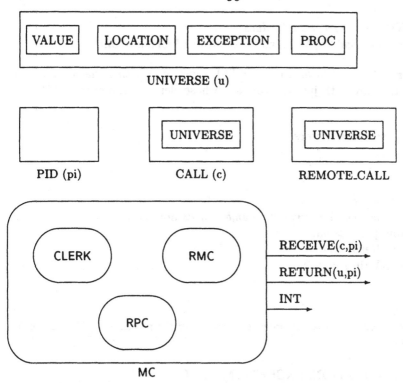

Fig. 2. The requirement specification of MC (First Step of PHASE 2)

outstanding calls (there is at most one outstanding call originally issued by a process).

Basic data structures
The data structure defined in this part will be available to all components of the system.

Universe of the values
Here, the universe values are of different kinds, as memory values, locations, exceptions, procedure names, which are given by separate specifications as follows.

VALUE =   *memory values*
requirement
sort value
cn Init_Value: value   *value initially contained in the locations*
end

LOCATION =   *locations*
requirement sort location **end**

EXCEPTION = *exceptional values*
enum exception: BadArg MemFailure BadCall RPCFailure **end**

[**enum** srt: Id1 ... Idn **end** is a METAL shortcut denoting the specification
of a data structure with just the sort srt, whose elements are exactly Id1, ...,
Idn.]

PROC = *procedure names*
design
use NAT
sort proc
cn Write, Read: proc
given a procedure name returns the number of its arguments
op ArgNum: proc -> nat
ax ArgNum(Read) = 1
ax ArgNum(Write) = 2
end

UNIVERSE =
universe of the values either arguments or results of the procedures of MC *or of its
components*
design
use VALUE, LOCATION, EXCEPTION, PROC
sort universe

a memory value, a location, an exception and a procedure name are universe values
op V: value -> universe
op L: location -> universe
op E: exception -> universe
op P: proc -> universe

cn Write_End: universe   *value returned by a successful Write call*

sort list   *lists of values*

cn Empty_List: list   *empty list*
op _ _: universe list -> list   *adds a value to a list*

op Length: list -> nat   *given a list returns its length*
ax Length(Empty_List) = 0
ax Length(u ls) = Length(ls) + 1

a list of values is a value
op LS: list -> universe

check whether a universe element is a list of a given length
pr Is_List: universe nat
ax if n = Length(ls) then Is_List(LS(ls), n)

check whether a universe element is not RPCFailure
pr Is_Not_RPCFailure: universe
ax Is_Not_RPCFailure(L(l))
ax Is_Not_RPCFailure(V(v))
ax Is_Not_RPCFailure(P(p))
ax Is_Not_RPCFailure(LS(ls))
ax Is_Not_RPCFailure(E(BadArg))
ax Is_Not_RPCFailure(E(MemFailure))
ax Is_Not_RPCFailure(E(BadCall))
end

Process identifier

PID =
identifiers of the processes (in some other components) originally issuing the calls
requirement sort pid **end**

Calls

CALL =   *calls of the MC procedures*
design
use UNIVERSE
sort call
op Write: universe universe -> call
op Read: universe -> call
end

Remote calls

REMOTE_CALL =   *remote calls received by RPC*
design
use UNIVERSE

sort rcall
the remote calls are made by two universe elements (the procedure name and the list of the arguments)
op < _ ; _ >: universe universe -> rcall

pr Remote_Correct: rcall   *checks if a remote call is correct*
if u is a list whose length is the number of arguments of p, then
a remote call consisting of p and u is correct
ax if Is_List(u, ArgNum(p)) then Remote_Correct(P(p),u)
end

Components of MC

MC is a concurrent system with three components, which in turn are other dynamic systems: CLERK, RMC and RPC.

The reliable memory component RMC

MC' is a specification of the memory component defined as in Sect. 4, except that now the basic data structures universe of values and calls are those specified in this development step; clearly the axioms have to be slightly changed to use the new data; e.g. axiom 1 becomes

ax if not Correct(c) and mc – RECEIVE(c,pi) –> mc' then
    mc' in any case < No_Concern(y,pi) > until
        (< RETURN(E(BadArg),pi) > or < RETURN(E(MemFailure),pi) >)

RMC =
requirement
use rename sort mc to rmc in MC'

** RM1 **
RMC *cannot return MemFailure*
ax not rmc – RETURN(E(MemFailure),pi) –> rmc'

** RM2 **
in any case RMC *will eventually*
ax rmc in any case eventually
        reach a state where may receive any call
        [(forall c, pi: exists x': x – RECEIVE(c,pi) –> x')
end

Axiom RM1 requires the reliability; while axiom RM2, an acceptance vitality property, is needed to use RMC to build the implementation of MC; indeed it avoids that a process which will be never able to receive a call may be chosen to realize RMC.

The remote procedure caller RPC Also in this case the structure of the specification is graphically reported in Fig. 3; there the square boxes enclosed in the rounded box corresponding to RPC represent the basic static structures of MC used by RPC.

The actual parameter

The specification APAR, used to instantiate the parametric specification RPC_P to get the specification of RPC, defines the data used by such process, precisely the universes of values, the process identifiers, the calls and the remote calls.

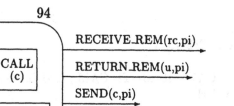

Fig. 3. The specification of RPC

APAR =
design
use UNIVERSE, PID, CALL, REMOTE_CALL
transforms a remote call into the corresponding call
op Call: rcall -> call
ax Call(< P(Read) ; LS(u Empty_List) >) = Read(u)
ax Call(< P(Write) ; LS(u u' Empty_List) >) = Write(u,u')
end

RPC = RPC_P(APAR)   *the* RPC *used for implementing* MC

The above specification is correct, since APAR is a correct parameter for RPC_P, i.e. its signature includes that of PAR and the axioms of PAR hold in APAR.

The clerk CLERK Also in this case the structure of the specification is graphically reported in Fig. 4.

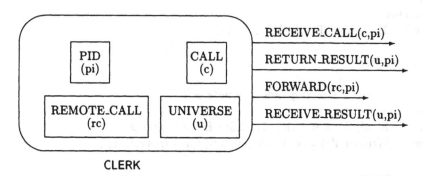

Fig. 4. The specification of CLERK

Interactions We precisely know the interactions of CLERK with its external world, and so we use a design specification for them.

CLERK_INTERACT =
design
use PID, CALL, REMOTE_CALL, UNIVERSE
sort lab_clerk

to receive (from outside MC) a call and an identifier (of the process in some other component that has originally issued the call)
op RECEIVE_CALL: call pid -> lab_clerk

to return (outside MC) a result and an identifier (of the process in some other component that finally will get the result)
op RETURN_RESULT: universe pid -> lab_clerk

to forward (to RPC) a remote call and an identifier (of the process in some other component that has originally issued the call)
op FORWARD: rcall pid -> lab_clerk

to receive (from RPC) a result (of a remote call) and an identifier (of the process in some other component that finally will get the result)
op RECEIVE_RESULT: universe pid -> lab_clerk
end

States

CLERK_STATE = **requirement dsort** clerk: _ – _ -> _ **end**

Activity

CLERK =
requirement
use CLERK_INTERACT, CLERK_STATE

auxiliary operation

given a call returns the corresponding remote call
op Remote: call -> rcall
ax Remote(Read(u)) = < P(Read) ; LS(u Empty_List) >
ax Remote(Write(u,u')) = < P(Write) ; LS(u u' Empty_List) >

auxiliary predicate

given a clerk state cl, a process identifier pi and a call c, checks if c is the last call received with pi in cl (notice that it is also the only outstanding one concerning pi)
pr Is_Last_Call: clerk call pid

ax Is_Last_Call(cl,c,pi) iff
> *in any case cl*
> cl in any case
>> *has not received another call and pi since*
>> < not exists c′: y = RECEIVE_CALL(c′,pi) > since
>>> *has received c and pi*
>>> < RECEIVE_CALL(c,pi) >

** *C1* **

if CLERK *receives a call c and pi, then*
ax if cl – RECEIVE_CALL(c,pi) –> cl′ then
> *in any case it will eventually*
> cl′ in any case eventually
>> *forward the remote call corresponding to c and pi*
>> < FORWARD(Remote(c),pi) >

** *C2* **

if u is not RPCFailure and CLERK *receives u and pi, then*
ax if Is_Not_RPCFailure(u) and cl – RECEIVE_RESULT(u,pi) –> cl′ then
> *in any case it will eventually return result u and pi*
> cl′ in any case eventually < RETURN_RESULT(u,pi) >

** *C3* **

if CLERK *receives RPCFailure and pi, then*
ax if cl – RECEIVE_RESULT(RPCFailure,pi) –> cl′ then
> *in any case it will eventually*
> cl′ in any case eventually
>> *either forward the remote call corresponding to*
>> (< exists c: y = FORWARD(Remote(c),pi) and
>>> *the last call received with pi and pi*
>>> Is_Last_Call(cl′,c,pi) >
>> *or return result MemFailure and pi*
>> or < RETURN_RESULT(E(MemFailure),pi) >)

** *C4* **

if CLERK *forwards a remote call rc and pi, then*

ax   if cl – FORWARD(rc,pi) –> cl′ then

   there exists a call c s.t. rc is its corresponding remote call and
   exists c: rc = Remote(c) and
      in any case it
      cl′ in any case
         has not forwarded any remote call with pi since
         (< not exists rc′: FORWARD(rc′,pi) > since
            either has received c and pi
            (< RECEIVE_CALL(c,pi) >
            or has received RPCFailure and pi and
            or (< RECEIVE_RESULT(RPCFailure,pi) > and
               c is last call received with pi
               Is_Last_Call(cl′,c,pi))))

** *C5* **

if CLERK *returns a result u different from MemFailure and pi, then*

ax   if cl – RETURN_RESULT(u,pi) –> cl′ and not(u = MemFailure) then
      in any case it
      cl′ in any case
         has not returned any result with pi since
         (< not exists u′: y = RETURN_RESULT(u′,pi) > since
            it has received a call and pi and
            < exists c: y = RECEIVE_CALL(c,pi) >) and
         has not received any other result and pi since
         (< not exists u′: y = RECEIVE_RESULT(u′,pi) > since
            it has received u and pi
            < RECEIVE_RESULT(u,pi) >)

** *C6* **

if CLERK *returns the result MemFailure and pi, then*

ax   if cl – RETURN_RESULT(MemFailure,pi) –> cl′ then
      in any case it
      cl′ in any case
         has not returned any result with pi since
         (< not exists u′: y = RETURN_RESULT(u′,pi) > since
            it has received a call with pi and
            < exists c: y = RECEIVE_CALL(c,pi) >) and
         has not received any other result with pi since
         (< not exists u′: y = RECEIVE_RESULT(u′,pi) > since
            it has received RPCFailure and pi
            < RECEIVE_RESULT(RPCFailure,pi) >)

** *C7* **
if CLERK *receives a call c and pi, then*
ax   if cl – RECEIVE_CALL(c,pi) -> cl' then
        in any case it will eventually return a result
        cl' in any case eventually < exists u: y = RETURN_RESULT(u,pi) >

** *C8* **
in any case CLERK *will eventually*
ax   cl in any case eventually
        reach a state where may receive any result
        [forall u, pi: exists cl': x – RECEIVE_RESULT(u,pi) -> cl']
end

Interactions (of MC)

In this development step we precisely fix the interactions of MC with its external world, and so we use a design specification for them; notice that now MC has one interaction not present in the requirement specification (INT).

MC_INTERACT =
design
use CALL, PID
sort lab_mc
to receive a call and a process identifier (of the process in some other component that has originally issued the call)
op   RECEIVE: call pid -> lab_mc
to return a result and a process identifier (of the process in some other component that finally will get the result)
op   RETURN: universe pid -> lab_mc
to perform an internal action
cn   INT: lab_mc
end

States (of MC)

In this development step we also precisely fix the intermediate states of MC; they are just given by the states of its three components, and so we use a design specification for them.

MC_STATE =
design
use RPC, CLERK, RMC
dsort mc: _ – _ -> _
op   _ | _ | _: rmc rpc clerk -> mc
end

Activity (of MC)

The requirements on the activity of MC in this development step are different from those on its components; indeed here we have to express properties on the activity of a concurrent dynamic system, relating the fact that a component perform an action with the fact that another component performs another action

(e.g. saying that if CLERK forwards a remote call, such call must be received by RPC). Thus we need a kind of "distributed" temporal logic, with combinators for saying e.g. that a component of a concurrent system will eventually perform some action. Since we know the distributed structure of MC (it has three components) we can use the logic presented in Sect. 2.3; indeed the following path formula

exists rmc, rpc, cl, rmc', rpc', cl':

[x = rmc | rpc | cl] and next [x = rmc' | rpc' | cl' and rpc – lp –> rpc']

holds on a path of MC whenever in the first transition of such path the component RPC has performed a transition labelled by lp; in the following such formula will be simply written as < RPC: lp >. Clearly, we have to assume that the formula

if rpc – lp –> rpc' and rpc – lp' –> rpc' then lp = lp'

is satisfied by the RPC specification; but this requirement is not problematic, because any specification of a dynamic system without this property may be transformed into another one with such property and behaving equivalently.

Analogous abbreviations can be defined for the RMC and CLERK components, written < RMC: lm > and < CLERK: lc > respectively.

[Below "some time" is the METAL syntax for the combinator of the temporal logic $\Diamond \mathbf{P}$, introduced in Sect. 2.3.]

MC =
requirement
use MC_STATE, MC_INTERACT

The activity of MC is fully determined by those of its components

** *1'* **
in any case if MC *performs an action, then*
ax mc in any case if < 1 > then
          at least one of the components performs an action
          (exists lc: < CLERK: lc >) or
          (exists lp: < RPC: lp >) or
          (exists lm: < RMC: lm >)

MC *cannot stop its components forever*

** *2'* **
if CLERK *can perform some action, then*
ax if exists cl', lc: cl – lc –> cl' then
             in any case it will eventually perform some action
             cl | rpc | rmc in any case eventually exists lc": < CLERK: lc" >

*** 3' ***

if RPC *can perform some action, then*
ax   if exists rpc', lp: rpc – lp –> rpc' then
        in any case it will eventually perform some action
        cl | rpc | rmc in any case eventually exists lp'': < RPC: lp'' >

*** 4' ***

if RMC *can perform some action, then*
ax   if exists rmc', lm: rmc – lm –> rmc' then
        in any case it will eventually perform some action
        cl | rpc | rmc in any case eventually exists lm'': < RMC: lm'' >

CLERK *takes care of the interactions of* MC *with the external world*

*** 5' ***

in any case
ax   mc in any case
        if MC *receives a call and pi, then* CLERK *receives them*
        if < RECEIVE(c,pi) > then < CLERK: RECEIVE_CALL(c,pi) >

*** 6' ***

in any case
ax   mc in any case
        if CLERK *receives a call and pi, then* MC *receives them*
        if < CLERK: RECEIVE_CALL(c,pi) > then < RECEIVE(c,pi) >

*** 7' ***

in any case
ax   mc in any case
        if MC *returns a result and pi, then* CLERK *returns them*
        if < RETURN(u,pi) > then < CLERK: RETURN_RESULT(u,pi) >

*** 8' ***

in any case
ax   mc in any case
        if CLERK *returns a result and pi, then* MC *returns them*
        if < CLERK: RETURN_RESULT(u,pi) > then < RETURN(u,pi) >

** *9'* *****

in any case

ax mc in any case
        if MC *performs an internal action, then*
        if < INT > then
            CLERK *neither returns a result nor receives a call*
            ((not exists u, pi: < CLERK: RETURN_RESULT(u,pi) >) and
               (not exists c, pi: < CLERK: RECEIVE_CALL(c,pi) >))

Cooperation between CLERK *and* RPC

** *10'* ******

in any case

ax mc in any case
        if CLERK *forwards a remote call and pi, then*
        if < CLERK: FORWARD(rc,pi) > then
        RPC *will eventually receive them*
        eventually < RPC: RECEIVE_REM(rc,pi) >

** *11'* ******

in any case

ax mc in any case
        if RPC *receives a remote call and pi, then*
        if < RPC: RECEIVE_REM(rc,pi) > then
        some time CLERK *has forwarded them*
        some time < CLERK: FORWARD(rc,pi) >

** *12'* ******

in any case

ax mc in any case
        if RPC *returns a result and pi, then*
        if < RPC: RETURN_REM(u,pi) > then
        CLERK *will eventually receive them*
        eventually < CLERK: RECEIVE_RESULT(u,pi) >

** *13'* ******

in any case

ax mc in any case
        if CLERK *receives a result and pi, then*
        if < CLERK: RECEIVE_RESULT(u,pi) > then
        some time RPC *has returned them*
        some time < RPC: RETURN_REM(u,pi) >

Cooperation between RPC *and* RMC

**** *14'* ****
in any case
ax mc in any case
       if RPC *sends a call and pi, then*
      if < RPC: SEND(c,pi) > then
         RMC *will eventually receive them*
         eventually < RMC: RECEIVE(c,pi) >

**** *15'* ****
in any case
ax mc in any case
       if RMC *receives a call and pi, then*
      if < RMC: RECEIVE(c,pi) > then
         some time RPC *has sent them*
         some time < RPC: SEND(c,pi) >

**** *16'* ****
in any case
ax mc in any case
       if RMC *returns a result and pi, then*
      if < RMC: RETURN(u,pi) > then
         RPC *will eventually receive them*
         eventually < RPC: RECEIVE_CALL_RES(u,pi) >

**** *17'* ****
in any case
ax mc in any case
       if RPC *receives a result and pi, then*
      if < RPC: RECEIVE_CALL_RES(u,pi) > then
         some time RMC *has sent them*
         some time < RMC: SEND(c,pi) >
end

Notice that property 10' implicitly requires also that RPC will eventually have the capability to receive a remote call; but that is already ensured by the RPC properties (axiom R7), so the specification of MC is "conservative" w.r.t. that of RPC. Similarly, the properties 12', 14' and 16' require that some component must have some action capabilities, but such capabilities are already ensured by axioms C8, RM2 and R8.

Correctness justification
The check of the correctness of the development step follows the specification structure, so first we consider the basic data structures, then states, interactions and finally the properties on the activity. To improve the readability in the

following we will add the suffix either 1 or 2 to the names of the specifications to distinguish those defined in the requirement phase (Sect. 4) and those in this development step.

Basic data Structures

The signatures of UNIVERSE1 and of UNIVERSE2 are different; thus we have to add to UNIVERSE2

cn Init_Value: universe
cn BadArg, MemFailure: universe
pr Is_MemVal, Is_Loc: universe

defined by the axioms

ax Init_Value = V(Init_Value)
ax BadArg = E(BadArg)
ax MemFailure = E(MemFailure)
ax Is_MemVal(V(v))
ax Is_Loc(L(lc))

and to hide all symbols not present in UNIVERSE1.

This modification of UNIVERSE2 can be expressed as a function from specifications into specifications, see at the end of Sect. 2.4. Then it is very easy to verify that all axioms of UNIVERSE1 hold in the modified version of UNIVERSE2.

Similarly we can see that CALL2 is a correct implementation of CALL1. In this case we have to add to CALL2 the predicate

pr Correct: call

defined by the axioms

ax Correct(Write(L(lc),V(v)))
ax Correct(Read(L(lc))).

PID2 coincides with PID1.

States

To see that MC_STATE2 is a correct implementation of MC_STATE1 we have to add to MC_STATE2 the operation

op Cont: mc universe -> universe

defined by

ax Cont(cl | rpc | rmc) = Cont(rmc)

and to hide the operation _ | _ | _.

Interactions

To see that MC_INTER2 is a correct implementation of MC_INTER1 we have to add to MC_INTER2 the constant **cn** INT: lab_mc.

Activity

For lack of room we only report the proof that axiom 1 holds in MC2; those for the other axioms are analogous.

By axiom 5', if **MC2** performs RECEIVE(c,pi) with c non correct, then CLERK performs RECEIVE_CALL(c,pi).

By axioms C1, 2' and 1', **CLERK** will eventually perform FORWARD(Remote(c),pi).
By axiom 10', **RPC** will eventually perform RECEIVE_REM(Remote(c),pi).
Since Remote(c) is correct as remote call, by axioms 3', 2' and R1 we have two possible cases:

1. **RPC** will eventually perform SEND(c,pi).
   By axiom 14', **RMC** will eventually perform RECEIVE(c,pi).
   Since c is not correct, by axiom 1 **RMC** will eventually perform
   RETURN(u,pi), with u either equal to E(BadArg) or to E(MemFailure).
   By axiom 16', **RPC** will eventually perform RECEIVE_CALL_RES(u,pi).
   By axioms R3 and 3', we have two possible cases:
   (a) **RPC** will eventually perform RETURN_REM(u,pi).
       By axiom 12', **CLERK** will eventually perform RECEIVE_RESULT(u,pi).
       By axiom C2 and 2',
       CLERK will eventually perform RETURN_RESULT(u,pi).
       By axiom 8', **MC2** will perform RETURN(u,pi).
       OK
   (b) **RPC** will eventually perform RETURN_REM(E(RPCFailure),pi)
       By axiom 12', **CLERK** will eventually perform
       RECEIVE_RESULT(E(RPCFailure),pi).
       By axiom C3 we have two cases:
       i. **CLERK** will eventually perform
          RETURN_RESULT(E(MemFailure),pi).
          By axiom 8', **MC2** will perform RETURN(E(MemFailure),pi).
          OK
       ii. **CLERK** will eventually perform FORWARD(Remote(c),pi).
           Then the proof goes on as from the beginning; axiom C7 prevents the
           case in which forever the second alternative is taken; thus a result
           will be returned eventually.
           OK
2. **RPC** will eventually perform RETURN_REM(E(RPCFailure),pi).
   As in 1b.
   OK

We have still to prove that before returning the right result MC2 does not perform any other interaction concerning pid; that follows from the properties of the various components prohibiting "unsolicited reactions" as R4, R5, C4 and C5 and by property 1' ensuring that all transitions of MC2 are due to transitions of its components.

7 Discussing our Solution

Here we try to present the main features of our solution of RPC-Memory Specification Problem, highlighting the positive and negative aspects.

Structured/modular specification The specifications presented in this paper are structured and modular, moreover their structures correspond to the structures of the specified systems; that allows also the possibility of reusing specification parts (see, e.g. the parameterized RPC component).

Uniform treatment of specifications at different levels The specifications of the system at different levels of abstraction, in our terminology requirement and design specifications, have the same structure and the specification language treats similarly the common parts (the only difference is in the form of the axioms and in the intended semantics of the specifications).

Adequacy to the RPC-Memory Specification Problem One of the relevant feature of our solution is that it takes into account all parts and aspects of the RPC-Memory Specification Problem (Sect. 1, 2, and 3 of [6]); so we have formalized *exactly* RPC-Memory Specification Problem, except for the "shadow spots" and without having to extend/modify the method. For example:

- MC is seen as an "open" system interacting with its external environment;
- the non-concurrent aspects, as those about the data used by the components, have been considered;
- reusable (parameterized) parts, as the RPC, may be specified including the properties on the parameters;
- concurrent/distributed systems, as the first refinement of [6], are explicitly handled.

In [6] further development steps were considered (see Sect. 4); but there (real) time aspects were involved and so we have not considered them. Indeed, in SMoLCS there are no special features for handling the (real) time aspects, so the specification about this part is not standard. It can be done under the assumption that the duration of all atomic actions of all components is given using a common discrete time unit. If this assumption is sensible, then SMoLCS specifications may handle the timed features (see, e.g. [12], which presents the specification of a controller of a system performing various checks each 5, 30, ... minutes).

Instead, also in order to show how our method works at the later stages of the development, in [5] we have worked out, making some particular choices, two further development steps.

Second development step We start to design the system specified in Sect. 6 by assuming that its components cooperate by synchronous message exchange and that perform their activities in a free independent way (i.e. there are no overall constraints on them).

Third and last development step We fully design the three components of the system specified above, CLERK, RPC and RMC, and so we get a complete design, i.e. a complete definition, of the MC that we have worked out.

Prototyping of the developed system The MC determined above has been tested by using the prototyping tools, see [1].

No overspecification Our specification expresses only what is contained in the RPC-Memory Specification Problem text in [6]; no need to embed in the specification other features, like particular kind of message exchange between the components of a system and particular kinds of scheduling of the activity of such components. On the contrary, the features that one usually forgets to mention when describing a system, since they seem obvious but are not guaranteed by default, are explicitly expressed by our specification (e.g. the point that the memory cells may or may not fail). Moreover each feature is directly expressed in the specification, and not by means of either a coding or a low level implementation.

Readability We think that our solution is rather readable due to the two-rail approach (informal and formal specifications), to the structuring of the specification, and to the syntactic richness and friendliness of the metalanguage METAL (e.g. distributed infix syntax, absence of "esoteric" symbols).

Long specification text Our specification, to have the advantages listed in the previous points, is long, and in some sense also complex (that is due mainly to the presence of some overhead, as the typed nature of the metalanguage, which requires an explicit declaration of all used symbols). Such unpleasantness may be overcome by using interactive editors/browers, and using the specification structure as a basis for giving a hypertext version of the documents produced during the development; so to be able, e.g. to drop the informal comments/formulae just by a click of the mouse.

About "correctness", "validation", ... Our method is still much unfinished and lacking in this respect, since we do not have a standard proof assistant. We have plans for establishing a friendly connection with some general tool for associated proofs, like PVS.

Here we briefly summarize what we have done for what concerns the general problem of correctness/validation using the supports (e.g. software tools) offered by the SMoLCS methodology to help this task.

We have a parser and a type checker for the SMoLCS specification language METAL; and so we have first controlled the static correctness of our specifications detecting some errors concerning a conceptual confusion between "calls" and "remote calls". We have fixed them, by introducing two distinct data structures for calls and for remote calls.

After we have tried to see if our design specification given in PHASE 2 was correct w.r.t. the requirements given in PHASE 1, i.e. to give the "correctness justification part". The methodology does not offer either software tools (as theorem provers and model checkers) or theoretical ones (as sound and complete deductive systems for the used logics and refinement calculi). The proof has to be done by hand and presented using the natural language, as it usually done for proving a theorem of analysis. We have done this proof, which is briefly reported in Sect. 6, detecting some errors.

Our specification of MC (see Sect. 4) allows that the memory component may refuse to receive calls forever; but such kind of component cannot work as part of the implementation. This point has been solved by adding property RM2 to the specification of RMC, see Sect. 6.

Another error found during the proof is the following. The first version of the MC specification required that in case of incorrect calls the exception RPCFailure cannot be returned, while the implementation may return RPCFailure for any call. We have simply fixed it by changing the requirements on MC.

Harder has been to prove the correctness of the further development steps, but in such case we have heavily used the rapid prototyper to analyze the behaviour of the design system. We have immediately found that there were several problems in earlier versions, mainly deadlocks, due to RPC and to CLERK.

Has the use of SMoLCS really worked? That means, have we got any benefits by using SMoLCS to develop MC? Also in this case SMoLCS presents the benefits already found in previous applications:

- it obliges the client to clarify a lot its idea of the system to be developed. In this case all shadow spots are questions for the client; e.g. it is relevant the point about the failures. Furthermore these questions may be discussed with the client using only the informal part of the specification.
- it helps to validate the implementation; we have found several errors in a first version of the implementation, also without tools for automatizing the proof.

Acknowledgement We warmly thank Stefano Ferrua for helping to prove the correctness of the implementation.

References

1. E. Astesiano, F. Morando, and G. Reggio. The SMoLCS Toolset. In Mosses P.D., Nielsen M., and Schwartzbach M.I., editors, *Proc. of TAPSOFT '95*, number 915 in LNCS, pages 810–801. Springer Verlag, Berlin, 1995.
2. E. Astesiano and G. Reggio. SMoLCS-Driven Concurrent Calculi. In H. Ehrig, R. Kowalski, G. Levi, and U. Montanari, editors, *Proc. TAPSOFT'87, Vol. 1*, number 249 in LNCS, pages 169–201. Springer Verlag, Berlin, 1987.
3. E. Astesiano and G. Reggio. Formally-Driven Friendly Specifications of Concurrent Systems: A Two-Rail Approach. Technical Report DISI–TR–94–20, DISI – Università di Genova, Italy, 1994. Presented at ICSE'17-Workshop on Formal Methods, Seattle April 1995.
4. E. Astesiano and G. Reggio. Algebraic Dynamic Specifications: An Outline. Technical Report DISI–TR–95–08, DISI – Università di Genova, Italy, 1995.
5. E. Astesiano and G. Reggio. A Dynamic Specification of the Complete Development of the RPC-Memory. Technical Report DISI–TR–96–02, DISI – Università di Genova, Italy, 1996.
6. M. Broy and L. Lamport. The RPC-Memory Specification Problem. In this volume.

7. G. Costa and G. Reggio. Abstract Dynamic Data Types: a Temporal Logic Approach. In A. Tarlecki, editor, *Proc. MFCS'91*, number 520 in LNCS, pages 103–112. Springer Verlag, Berlin, 1991.

8. G. Costa and G. Reggio. Specification of Abstract Dynamic DataTypes: A Temporal Logic Approach. *T.C.S.*, 1996. To appear.

9. Z. Manna and A. Pnueli. The Anchored Version of the Temporal Framework. In J.W. de Bakker, W.-P. de Roever, and G. Rozemberg, editors, *Linear Time, Branching Time and Partial Order in Logics and Models for Concurrency*, number 354 in LNCS. Springer Verlag, Berlin, 1989.

10. F. Parodi and G. Reggio. METAL: a Metalanguage for SMoLCS. Technical Report DISI–TR–94–13, DISI – Università di Genova, Italy, 1994.

11. G. Reggio, D. Bertello, and A. Morgavi. The Reference Manual for the SMoLCS Methodology. Technical Report DISI–TR–94–12, DISI – Università di Genova, Italy, 1994.

12. G. Reggio and E. Crivelli. Specification of a Hydroelectric Power Station: Revised Tool-Checked Version. Technical Report DISI–TR–94–17, DISI – Università di Genova, Italy, 1994.

13. M. Wirsing. Algebraic Specifications. In J. van Leeuwen, editor, *Handbook of Theoret. Comput. Sci.*, volume B, pages 675–788. Elsevier, 1990.

A Memory Module Specification
Using Composable High-Level Petri Nets

Eike Best

Institut für Informatik, Universität Hildesheim,
Marienburger Platz 22, D-31141 Hildesheim,
e.best@informatik.uni-hildesheim.de

Abstract. This paper describes a solution of the RPC-memory specification problem defined by M. Broy and L. Lamport on the occasion of a Dagstuhl seminar in 1994. The approach is based on a recently developed model of composable high-level Petri nets called M-nets, on which CCS-like composition operations such as parallel composition, restriction and transition synchronisation are defined. Correctness proofs are given in terms of interface transition trace inclusion.

1   Introduction

The high-level Petri net model devised by H.J. Genrich, K. Jensen [8, 11] and others can be viewed as a means of abstracting and abbreviating large elementary nets. A standard operation defined on a high-level net is its unfolding into an elementary net. In the M-net model proposed in [4], a class of high-level nets is enriched with CCS-like composition operations [16] such as choice, parallel composition, transition synchronisation and restriction. Synchronisation and restriction are driven by parametrised actions generalising the action algebra of CCS. It is shown in [4, 12] that all operations are coherent with respect to unfolding, in the sense that unfolding a composed net amounts to composing the individual unfoldings.

This paper presents an M-net solution of the RPC-memory specification problem defined in [6]. The problem asks for the modelling of a set of components to access remote memory. A remote user can request a service by issuing an RPC (remote procedure call) with parameters *read* or *write* and further parameters specifying a location and (in case of a *write*) a value. This interface calls other components performing the corresponding local *read* or *write* actions. Parametrised M-net actions can be used directly to model such procedure interfaces.

The paper is structured as follows. Section 2 introduces M-nets and a small set of operations needed for solving the RPC-memory specification problem. In section 3 a relation of implementation between two M-nets is defined. Section 4 describes a multi-level M-net specification of the memory system. Section 5 presents its implementation in terms of an RPC-module and states its correctness in terms of the notion of implementation defined in section 3. In section 6 it is shown how the RPC-module can be implemented by a timed lossy module. Section 7 contains some discussion. Proofs can be found in the appendix.

2 The M-net Model

Section 2.1 defines structure and markings of an M-net. Section 2.2 defines transition rule and unfolding of M-nets. Section 2.3 describes some composition operations on M-nets.

2.1 Definition of M-nets

Let $a, b, c, \ldots$ be variables and let $v, w, \ldots$ be values. An *M-net* is a structure $N = (S, T, \iota)$ where, as usual [20], S is the set of *places* and T is the set of *transitions* (satisfying $S \cap T = \emptyset$). In the following, we use letters $s, \ldots$ to denote places and $t, \ldots$ to denote transitions. The *inscription* function ι associates:

- With every place $s \in S$, a *label* $\lambda(s)$ (as described below) and a nonempty set of values (also called its *color* [11] or *type*) $\alpha(s)$. We use the pair notation $\iota(s) = (\lambda(s)|\alpha(s))$ to separate label from type.
- With every pair (s, t) and (t, s) (for $s \in S$ and $t \in T$), a multiset of variables or values.
- With every transition t, a pair $\iota(t) = (\lambda(t)|\alpha(t))$ where $\lambda(t)$ is its *label* (as described below) and $\alpha(t)$ is a predicate (also called the *guard* of t).

For a transition t, the set $Var(t)$ is defined as the union of all variables occurring in multisets $\iota(s, t)$ and $\iota(t, s')$ (for all $s, s' \in S$) or occurring freely in $\iota(t)$. We show later that, without loss of generality, it may be assumed that ι satisfies

$$(s \neq s' \Rightarrow \alpha(s) \cap \alpha(s') = \emptyset) \quad \text{and} \quad (t \neq t' \Rightarrow Var(t) \cap Var(t') = \emptyset). \tag{1}$$

However, for succinctness, we will not enforce this property in our examples.

The label $\lambda(s)$ is, by definition, an element of $\{e, i, x\}$. If $\lambda(s) = e$ then s is *initial*, if $\lambda(s) = i$ then s is *internal*, and if $\lambda(s) = x$ then s is *final*. $\lambda(s)$ drives place-based composition operations. For instance, composing two nets sequentially means that the final places of the first are combined with the initial places of the second and become internal places in the combined net [3, 17]. A typical place inscription is $\iota(s) = (i \mid \{0, 1, 2\})$. This means that s is internal and may hold tokens 0, 1 or 2.

The label $\lambda(t)$ is, by definition, a multiset of *parametrised actions*. If $\lambda(t) \neq \emptyset$ then t is called *external*, or an *interface transition*, otherwise it is called *internal*. We distinguish interface transitions by representing them pictorially by the double-square symbol ▢, reserving the single-square symbol □ for internal transitions. A parametrised action is a term of the form $A(a_1, \ldots, a_m)$ where A is an *action symbol* and $a_1, \ldots, a_m$ are either values or variables. We assume that there is a sufficiently large supply of action symbols and that every one of them has an arity ar (such as m for A above). Furthermore we assume that there exists a bijection $^-$ called *conjugation* from action symbols to action symbols satisfying

$$\forall A: (\overline{A} \neq A) \wedge (\overline{\overline{A}} = A) \wedge (ar(\overline{A}) = ar(A)).$$

For example, if $m=2$ then $A(a,a)$, $\overline{A}(b,2)$ and $\overline{A}(2,3)$ are parametrised actions. A parametrised action is *constant* (or a *ground action*) if all of its parameters are values. The action algebra of CCS [16] is a special case of the above with all arities being zero. In the sequel we use upper-case letters, or words containing upper-case letters, to denote action symbols. $\lambda(t)$ drives transition-based composition operations. For instance, as in CCS, transition synchronisation is driven by conjugate action symbols in the labels of two transitions. A typical transition inscription is $\iota(t) = (\,\{A(a,b),\overline{B}(b,a)\} \mid a{=}5 \wedge b{\geq}0\,)$. This indicates that for the enabling of t, a binding of variables in $Var(t)$ has to be found. Under such a binding, the label and the guard of t evaluate to a multiset of ground actions and a truth value, respectively. For example, under the binding $a \mapsto 1, b \mapsto 2$, the above inscription evaluates to $(\,\{A(1,2),\overline{B}(2,1)\} \mid \mathbf{false}\,)$.

A *marking* M of N is a function associating with every place s a finite multiset $M(s)$ over $\alpha(s)$. When an initially marked M-net $\Sigma = (S,T,\iota,M^0)$ is given we refer to the set of its transitions by $T_\Sigma{=}T$ and to its initial marking by $M^0_\Sigma{=}M^0$. Figure 1 shows three marked M-nets. For instance, the net Σ_3 on the right-hand side is $(\{s_1,s_2\},\{t_3\},\iota,M^0_3)$ with

$$
\begin{array}{ll}
\lambda(s_1) = \mathbf{e} & \alpha(s_1) = \{\bullet\} \\
\lambda(s_2) = \mathbf{x} & \alpha(s_2) = \{\bullet\} \\
\lambda(t_3) = \{X(c,d)\} & \alpha(t_3) = (d{=}1{-}c) \\
\iota(s_1,t_3) = \{a\} & \iota(t_3,s_1) = \emptyset \\
\iota(s_2,t_3) = \emptyset & \iota(t_3,s_2) = \{b\} \\
M^0_3(s_1) = \{\bullet\} & M^0_3(s_2) = \emptyset.
\end{array}
$$

We also have $Var(t_1){=}\{a,b\}$, $Var(t_2){=}\{a,b,c,d,e,f\}$ and $Var(t_3){=}\{a,b,c,d\}$.

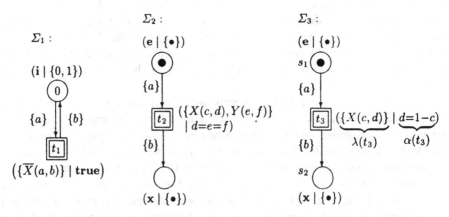

Fig. 1. Three marked M-nets Σ_1 (left), Σ_2 (middle) and Σ_3 (right)

2.2 Transition rule and unfolding

A *binding of* t, where t is a transition, is a function σ associating a value with every variable in $Var(t)$.[1] A binding of t is *legal* if variables get assigned values from the types of the places they correspond to, i.e. if b is a variable occurring in $\iota(s,t)$ then $\sigma(b) \in \iota(s)$ and if a is a variable occurring in $\iota(t, s')$ then $\sigma(a) \in \iota(s')$. In what follows we will tacitly assume all bindings to be legal, unless specified otherwise. A binding σ of t is *enabling (for t)* if the predicate $\iota(t)$ evaluates to **true** under σ. A marking M *activates t under σ (or 'in mode σ')* if σ enables t and, moreover, for all places s, the multiset of values $\iota(s,t)[\sigma]$ (i.e. σ applied to every individual element of $\iota(s,t)$) is a sub-multiset of $M(s)$. If M activates t in mode σ then t may *occur in mode* σ yielding a successor marking M' which is calculated as follows (using multiset difference $-$ and multiset sum $+$):

$$M'(s) \quad = \quad (M(s) - (\iota(s,t)[\sigma])) + (\iota(t,s)[\sigma])$$

for every place s. In this formula, $\iota(s,t)[\sigma]$ and $\iota(t,s)[\sigma]$ denote the tokens *consumed* and *produced*, respectively, on place s. We also write $M \xrightarrow{t:\sigma} M'$ if M activates t in mode σ and M and M' are related as above.

To illustrate these definitions, consider figure 1 and three bindings for transition t_3 of Σ_3 (recall that $Var(t_3) = \{a, b, c, d\}$):

$$\sigma_1 : a \mapsto \bullet, b \mapsto 0, c \mapsto 1, d \mapsto 0$$
$$\sigma_2 : a \mapsto \bullet, b \mapsto \bullet, c \mapsto 1, d \mapsto 1$$
$$\sigma_3 : a \mapsto \bullet, b \mapsto \bullet, c \mapsto 1, d \mapsto 0.$$

The first binding σ_1 is not legal because the value of b is not in the type of the corresponding place s_2. The second binding is legal but not enabling for t_3 because predicate $\alpha(t_3)$ does not evaluate to **true**. The third binding σ_3 is legal and enabling for t_3, and, moreover, the initial marking M_3^0 of Σ_3 activates t_3 in mode σ_3. After the occurrence of t_3 in mode σ_3, M_3^0 is changed into the marking M_3^1 defined by $M_3^1(s_1) = \emptyset$ and $M_3^1(s_2) = \{\bullet\}$. Note that σ_3 is still legal and enabling for t_3, but M_3^1 does not activate t_3 in mode σ_3 (due to there being insufficiently many tokens $\bullet$ on place s_1).

As another example, in the net Σ_2 shown in the middle of figure 1,

$$a \mapsto \bullet, b \mapsto \bullet, c \mapsto 0, d \mapsto 1, e \mapsto 1, f \mapsto 1$$

is a binding activating t_2 at marking $M_{\Sigma_2}^0$. If t_2 occurs under this binding, then the effect is to remove a token $\bullet$ from its input place and to add a token $\bullet$ to its output place. By contrast, the binding

$$a \mapsto \bullet, b \mapsto \bullet, c \mapsto 0, d \mapsto 1, e \mapsto 1, f \mapsto 0$$

does not enable t_2 because it makes the guard $d = e = f$ false. In Σ_1, the binding $a \mapsto 1, b \mapsto 1$ is legal and enabling for t_1 but does not activate t_1 under the shown marking, because there is no 1 token on the input place of t_1.

---

[1] In the following, we use standard notation relating to bindings: if $\mathcal{O}$ is some object then $\mathcal{O}[\sigma]$ denotes $\mathcal{O}$ where σ is applied (elementwise) to $\mathcal{O}$.

Note that whether or not a binding activates a transition t depends only on $Var(t)$. This implies that any consistent renaming of variables within $Var(t)$ (and in the inscriptions of t and its surrounding arcs) does not affect the semantics of the M-net. In particular, we may – as was said above – assume without loss of generality that $t \neq t'$ implies $Var(t) \cap Var(t') = \emptyset$.

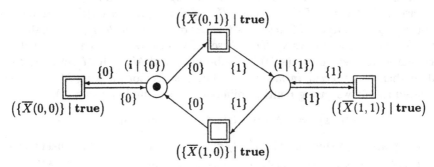

Fig. 2. Unfolding $U(\Sigma_1)$ of net Σ_1 on the left-hand side of figure 1

Note also that the transition rule depends only on the types $\alpha(s)$ of places and the guards $\alpha(t)$ of transitions. In particular, it is independent of their labels λ. The same is true for unfolding, which turns an arbitrary M-net into an elementary net, where an M-net is called *elementary* (E-net for short) iff:

- Place types are singletons.
- Arc inscriptions are finite multisets over the types of the corresponding place.
- All transitions t satisfy $Var(t) = \emptyset$ and $\alpha(t) = $ **true**.

E-nets and arc-weighted P/T-nets [20] carrying place labels from the set $\{e, i, x\}$ and transition labels from the set of multisets over ground actions are in 1–1 correspondence with each other. To transform a labelled arc-weighted P/T-net into an elementary M-net, attach to every place an arbitrary singleton value set (e.g. $\iota(s) = \{s\}$ where s is its name) and to every transition a guard **true**. For arcs (s, t), add a multiset containing the only element of $\iota(s)$ as many times as specified by its weight, and do the same for arcs (t, s'). The labels remain the same. To obtain a labelled arc-weighted P/T-net from an elementary M-net, apply the converse construction, simply forgetting all value sets and replacing them by the singleton set $\{\bullet\}$ and replacing all arc inscriptions by their cardinalities.

Let $\Sigma = (S, T, \iota, M)$ be a marked M-net. Its *unfolding* $U(\Sigma) = (S_U, T_U, \iota_U, M_u)$ is defined as follows:

- $S_U = \{s_v \mid s \in S$ and $v \in \alpha(s)\}$,
  where for each $s_v \in S_U$: $\lambda(s_v) = \lambda(s)$ and $\alpha(s_v) = \{v\}$.
- $T_U = \{t_\sigma \mid t \in T$ and σ is an enabling binding of $t\}$,
  where for each $t_\sigma \in T_U$: $\lambda(t_\sigma) = (\lambda(t))[\sigma]$ and $\alpha(t_\sigma) = (\alpha(t))[\sigma]$.

– $\iota_U(s_v, t_\sigma) = (\iota(s,t)[\sigma])\lceil_v$ and $\iota_U(t_\sigma, s_v) = (\iota(t,s)[\sigma])\lceil_v.$[2]
– For every place $s_v \in S_U$, $M_U(s_v) = M(s)\lceil_v$.

Clearly, $U(\Sigma)$ is an elementary M-net. Moreover, Σ and $U(\Sigma)$ are behaviourally equivalent in the sense that $M \xrightarrow{t:\sigma} M'$ in Σ iff $M_U \xrightarrow{t_\sigma:id} M'_U$ in $U(\Sigma)$.

For example, figure 2 shows the E-net $U(\Sigma_1)$ associated with the M-net Σ_1 on the left-hand side of figure 1. The two places of the unfolded net correspond to the two possible tokens on the place of Σ_1, namely 0 on the left and 1 on the right. The four transitions correspond to the four enabling bindings of transition t_1 in figure 1. The place corresponding to value 0 has a (single) initial token because the place in Σ_1 carries a (single) token 0.

On elementary M-nets, there exists a canonical notion of isomorphism: two (marked) E-nets are called *isomorphic* iff there exists an arc-preserving, label-preserving and marking-preserving bijection between their places and transitions. If Σ is elementary then Σ and $U(\Sigma)$ are isomorphic. Two M-nets Σ and Σ' are called *unfolding-equivalent* (in symbols: $\Sigma \equiv \Sigma'$) iff their unfoldings are isomorphic. Unfolding-equivalence can be characterised graph theoretically [9, 13] and linear algebraically [5]. To all intents and purposes, unfolding-equivalent M-nets Σ and Σ' describe the same system. For instance, consider figure 3 where Σ_1 and Σ_2 are unfolding-equivalent. Σ_3 shows their common unfolding (which is thus also unfolding-equivalent with both Σ_1 and Σ_2) and Σ_4 shows the equivalent labelled place/transition-net.

The operation of renaming variables consistently within $Var(t)$ is unfolding-preserving, and so is the operation of exchanging a value set $\alpha(s)$ with an isomorphic set $\alpha(s)'$ (modifying types and operations as necessary). Hence every M-net can be transformed into an unfolding-equivalent one satisfying (1).

2.3 Composition operations

In this section we describe three composition operations on M-nets: (disjoint) parallel composition, restriction and transition synchronisation. Two nets are combined by *disjoint parallel composition* by forming their disjoint union.[3] This operation (obviously) commutes with unfolding in the following sense:

$$U(\Sigma_1 \| \Sigma_2) \equiv U(\Sigma_1) \| U(\Sigma_2).$$

We define *restriction* to be a mixed operation $\Sigma \, \mathrm{rs} \, A$ accepting an M-net Σ and an action symbol A and returning a net in which all transitions (together with their surrounding arcs) whose labels contain at least one action term $A(a_1, \ldots, a_m)$ or $\overline{A}(a_1, \ldots, a_m)$ are deleted. We also need *transition synchronisation* which adds, rather than deletes, transitions to a net Σ. Following [3], synchronisation is defined as a sort of 'converse' of restriction. By definition, $\Sigma \, \mathrm{sy} \, A$ is the smallest net satisfying the following:

---

[2] Where, by definition, $\mu\lceil_v$ is the multiset containing v as many times as μ and all other elements zero times.

[3] Suitably renaming places and transitions if necessary.

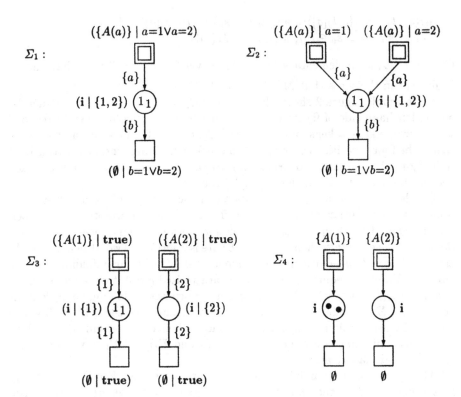

Fig. 3. Illustration of the notion of unfolding-equivalence

- The sets of places of Σ and Σ **sy** A are the same.
- Every transition of Σ is also a transition of Σ **sy** A.
- If t, t' are transitions of Σ **sy** A and t'' arises from t and t' by a basic synchronisation step entailed by $(A, \overline{A})$, then t'' is a transition of Σ **sy** A.

The heart of this definition is that of a basic synchronisation step [4]. We explain this definition first and illustrate it on an example later. Define t'' to arise from t and t' by a *basic synchronisation step* (entailed by $(A, \overline{A})$) if (without loss of generality) $Var(t) \cap Var(t') = \emptyset$ and, moreover,

(a) The label of t contains a term $A(\dots)$ and the label of t' contains a conjugate term $\overline{A}(\dots)$.
(b) Variables and constants in the parameter lists of $A(\dots)$ and $\overline{A}(\dots)$ are unified and renamed consistently throughout $Var(t)$ and $Var(t')$.
(c) The label of t'' equals the multiset sum of the labels of t and t', minus the two terms mentioned in (a), modulo the renamings (b).
(d) The arcs surrounding t'' are the multiset sum of the arcs surrounding t and t', modulo renamings (b).

(e) The guard of t'' is the logical conjunction of the guards of t and t', modulo renamings (b).

Intuitively speaking, this operation may be characterised as CCS-like synchronisation extended to action terms of arbitrary arity (viz. (a)). It involves *unification* (of the parameter lists of the two participating actions, viz. (b)), *multiset sum* (of labels, (c), and arcs, (d)) and *conjunction* (of guards, (e)).

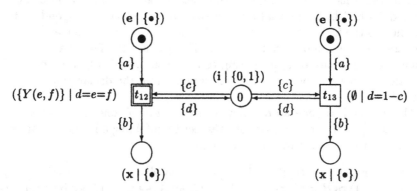

Fig. 4. Synchronisation and restriction of the nets in figure 1 over X

As an example, figure 4 shows the net $((\Sigma_1\|\Sigma_2\|\Sigma_3)\ \mathbf{sy}\ X)\ \mathbf{rs}\ X$ where Σ_1, Σ_2 and Σ_3 are as in figure 1. Transition t_{12} of figure 4 arises by basic synchronisation from transitions t_1 and t_2 of $\Sigma_1\|\Sigma_2\|\Sigma_3$ as follows: t_1 and t_2 contain conjugate action terms $\overline{X}(a,b)$ and $X(c,d)$. To synchronise them by the operator $\mathbf{sy}\ X$, the variables in $Var(t_1)$ and $Var(t_2)$ are first made disjoint by a first renaming, and then the parameter lists of $\overline{X}(a,b)$ and $X(c,d)$ are considered equal by a second renaming. The effect is that a is considered the same variable as c and b is considered the same variable as d in the vicinities of t_1 and t_2 (but there are other suitable identifications – in general, introduction of fresh variables is necessary). Modulo these identifications, t_{12} is the multiset sum of t_1 and t_2 except that its guard is the logical conjunction of the guards of t_1 and t_2 and the two action terms $\overline{X}(a,b)$ and $X(c,d)$ which have effected the synchronisation are subtracted from the resulting label. Transition t_{13} of figure 4 is a synchronisation of transitions t_1 and t_3 of figure 1 according to the same principle. Note that it is internal.

Suppose that $X(v,w)$ and $Y(v',w')$ represent, respectively, a value change of variable X from v to w and of variable Y from v' to w'. Then the above example can be viewed as a high-level net representation of the program fragment

$$\cdots\ \mathbf{begin}\ \mathbf{var}\ X{:}\{0,1\}\ (\mathbf{init}\ 0);\ \langle X := Y\rangle\ \|\ \langle X := 1{-}X\rangle\ \mathbf{end}\ \cdots$$

which specifies a block with a local variable X of type $\{0,1\}$ and a global variable Y which is assumed to be declared of type $\{0,1\}$ in some outer block. Nets Σ_1, Σ_2 and Σ_3 of figure 1 correspond, in that order, to the declaration

var $X{:}\{0,1\}$, the atomic action $\langle X{:}{=}Y\rangle$ and the atomic action $\langle X{:}{=}1{-}X\rangle$. The label $\{X(c,d),Y(e,f)\}$ and the guard $d{=}e{=}f$ in Σ_2 indicate that the value of Y remains the same $(e{=}f)$ while the value of X changes from whatever it was previously (c) to the value of Y $(d{=}e)$. Thus, t_2 is a translation of $\langle X{:}{=}Y\rangle$. Similarly, t_3 is a translation of $\langle X{:}{=}1{-}X\rangle$. Transition t_1 represents all possible value changes of X.

The synchronisation and restriction $(\Sigma_1\|\Sigma_2\|\Sigma_3)$ **sy** X **rs** X describes the block in the sense that in the resulting net of figure 4, any value changes of X are described by appropriate connections to the place corresponding to X. This models the fact that X is local to the block. Any value changes of Y, however, are described implicitly by a label. This models the fact that Y is global to the block. Transition t_{12} is waiting to be synchronised with a corresponding transition carrying a conjugate label $\overline{Y}$ coming from the declaration of Y in an outer block.

The **sy** and **rs** operators enjoy a uniform set of coherence and algebraic properties [4]; both are coherent with respect to unfolding and commutative and idempotent with respect to action symbols:

$$
\begin{aligned}
U(\Sigma\text{ rs }A) &= U(\Sigma)\text{ rs }A & U(\Sigma\text{ sy }A) &= U(\Sigma)\text{ sy }A \\
(\Sigma\text{ rs }A)\text{ rs }B &= (\Sigma\text{ rs }B)\text{ rs }A & (\Sigma\text{ sy }A)\text{ sy }B &= (\Sigma\text{ sy }B)\text{ sy }A \\
(\Sigma\text{ rs }A)\text{ rs }A &= \Sigma\text{ rs }A & (\Sigma\text{ sy }A)\text{ sy }A &= \Sigma\text{ sy }A.
\end{aligned}
$$

As a consequence, Σ **rs** $\mathcal{A}$ and Σ **sy** $\mathcal{A}$ are well-defined for any finite set $\mathcal{A}$ of action names. Furthermore, all operations are stable with respect to unfolding-equivalence. That is, if $\Sigma \equiv \Sigma'$ and $\Sigma_i \equiv \Sigma_i'$ $(i{=}1,2)$ then $\Sigma_1\|\Sigma_2 \equiv \Sigma_1'\|\Sigma_2'$ as well as Σ **rs** $A \equiv \Sigma'$ **rs** A and Σ **sy** $A \equiv \Sigma'$ **sy** A.

3 Behavioural Notions

In section 3.1, occurrence sequences – i.e. interleavings – of M-nets are defined. Section 3.2 introduces a way of describing the collapsing of two sets of sequential transitions into single ones. Section 3.3 defines a notion of implementation between two (initially marked) M-nets and describes some examples.

3.1 Occurrence sequences and permutations

Consider an M-net Σ with initial marking $M^0{=}M_\Sigma^0$. An *occurrence sequence* of Σ starting with an arbitrary marking M_0 is defined as a (finite or infinite) alternating sequence

$$
\tau = M_0(t_1,\sigma_1)M_1(t_2,\sigma_2)M_2\ldots
$$

such that $(M_{j-1} \xrightarrow{t_j:\sigma_j} M_j)$ for $j{\geq}1$. A marking M is called *reachable* in Σ if there is an occurrence sequence from the initial marking M^0 to M.

We now define an equivalence on occurrence sequences with respect to per-mutations of independent transitions in the style of [2, 14]. For a transition t of Σ

let $^\bullet t$ and $t^\bullet$ denote the sets of places $\{s|\iota(s,t)\neq\emptyset\}$ and $\{s|\iota(t,s)\neq\emptyset\}$, respectively. The transition sets $^\bullet s$ and $s^\bullet$ (for $s\in S$) are defined similarly.

Let t and t' be transitions of Σ (which could be the same ones) and let M be a marking of Σ. We define (t,t') to be *enabled concurrently* under a pair of bindings (σ,σ') of $Var(t)$ and $Var(t')$, respectively, if for all places s, the multiset of values $(\iota(s,t)[\sigma]+\iota(s,t')[\sigma'])$ is a sub-multiset of $M(s)$. If M enables t and t' concurrently under σ and σ', then M enables both t under σ and t' under σ'. However, the converse need not be true, because (t,σ) and (t',σ') may be in conflict under M. A sufficient condition for them to be concurrently enabled is that they are both enabled and $^\bullet t\cap{}^\bullet t'=\emptyset$.

Let τ and τ' be two occurrence sequences of Σ. We define $\tau\equiv_0\tau'$ if τ and τ' can be decomposed as follows:

$$\tau = \tau_1\underbrace{(t,\sigma)M(t',\sigma')}\tau_2 \quad\text{and}\quad \tau' = \tau_1'\underbrace{(t',\sigma')M'(t,\sigma)}\tau_2'$$
$$\quad\quad\quad (1) \quad\quad\quad\quad\quad\quad\quad\quad (2)$$

such that $\tau_1=\tau_1'$, $\tau_2=\tau_2'$ and the last marking of τ_1 (which is also the last marking of τ_1') enables (t,σ) and (t',σ') concurrently. Note that not necessarily $M=M'$. For example, in figure 5 we have

$$M^0(t,\sigma_1)M^1(u,\sigma_2)M^2(t',\sigma_3)M^3 \equiv_0 M^0(t,\sigma_1)M^1(t',\sigma_3)M^{2'}(u,\sigma_2)M^3$$

with $\sigma_1 : a\mapsto 1, b\mapsto 1, d\mapsto 1$, $\sigma_2 : a\mapsto 1, b\mapsto 1, c\mapsto 0, d\mapsto 0$ and $\sigma_3 : a\mapsto 1$.

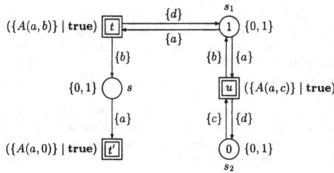

Fig. 5. Illustration of $\equiv_0$ and of collapsing

For finite τ and τ' we define $\tau\equiv\tau'$ iff $\tau\equiv_0^*\tau'$.[4] For a sequence τ, $[\tau]_\equiv$ denotes its equivalence class with respect to $\equiv$. Two $\equiv$-equivalent sequences can be viewed as expressing the same behaviour of Σ modulo commutativity of concurrently enabled transitions.

The consideration of $\equiv$-equivalence is necessary because, for example, a transition on the specification level may be split into two successive transitions on

---

[4] This definition can be generalised to infinite sequences by a more elaborate construction of forming the reflexive transitive closure; consult [2].

the implementation level, an opening one and a closing one (such as t and t' in figure 5). In an interleaving behaviour, an instance of an opening transition may occur much earlier than a corresponding instance of the closing transition. By $\equiv$-permutations they may be brought into neighbouring positions. This is described in the next section.

3.2   Collapsing transitions

Two nonempty disjoint sets of transition $T \subseteq T_\Sigma$ and $T' \subseteq T_\Sigma$ are called *in sequence* (in Σ) if there exists a place $s_{TT'}$ such that

- $M_\Sigma^0(s_{TT'})=\emptyset$,
- $\forall t' \in T': {}^\bullet t'=\{s_{TT'}\}$ or $\forall t \in T: t^\bullet=\{s_{TT'}\}$,
- for all $t \in T$ and $t' \in T': |\iota(t, s_{TT'})|=1=|\iota(s_{TT'}, t')|$.

The idea is that place $s_{TT'}$ sequentialises every transition in T with every transition in T'. This ensures – in a sense to be made precise – that when $t \in T$ is combined with $t' \in T'$, behavioural properties remain unchanged. For example, $\{t\}$ and $\{t'\}$ are in sequence in figure 5. Their sequentialising place is $s_{\{t\}\{t'\}}=s$.

A relation $\delta \subseteq 2^{T_\Sigma} \times 2^{T_\Sigma}$ is called a *collapsing* if (a) whenever $(T,T') \in \delta$ then (T,T') are in sequence, and (b) the elements of δ are mutually disjoint, i.e., if $(T,T') \in \delta$ and $(U,U') \in \delta$, then $T \cap U=T \cap U'=T' \cap U=T' \cap U'=\emptyset$.[5] For instance, in figure 5, $\delta=\{(\{t\}, \{t'\})\}$ is a collapsing.

Let a collapsing δ be given. An occurrence sequence τ is called δ-*complete* if, for every $(T,T') \in \delta$, whenever, in τ, some 'opening' instance of $t \in T$ puts some token m on place $s_{TT'}$ then there exists a subsequent 'closing' instance of some transition $t' \in T'$ which takes m away from $s_{TT'}$. For instance, in figure 5 with the δ defined above, $\tau_0=M^0(t, \sigma_1)M^1(u, \sigma_2)M^2$ is not δ-complete, but $\tau_1=M^0(t, \sigma_1)M^1(u, \sigma_2)M^2(t', \sigma_3)M^3$ is.

If τ is finite and δ-complete then, for any $(T,T') \in \delta$, $M(s_{TT'})=\emptyset$ in the marking M reached after τ. If $\delta=\emptyset$ then every occurrence sequence is δ-complete. By suitable $\equiv$-transformations, any δ-complete sequence can be brought into a canonical form: call τ δ-*respectful* if, whenever $(T,T') \in \delta$, every opening instance of $t \in T$ in τ, putting some token m on $s_{TT'}$, is immediately followed by a closing instance of some transition $t' \in T'$, removing this same token m from $s_{TT'}$.

Claim 1   Let τ be δ-complete. Then there exists a sequence $\tau' \in [\tau]_\equiv$ such that τ' is δ-respectful.   ∎1

The proof of this claim (which is given in the appendix) shows that there may be more than one candidates for τ'. We may pick any one of them and call it the canonical δ-respectful derivative, τ^δ, of τ, because all subsequent considerations are independent of this choice. If $\delta=\emptyset$ then $\tau^\delta=\tau$. For example, for the δ and τ_1 defined above (figure 5), we may choose $\tau_1^\delta=M^0(t, \sigma_1)M^1(t', \sigma_3)M^{2'}(u, \sigma_2)M^3$.

---

[5] That $T \cap T'=\emptyset$ and $U \cap U'=\emptyset$ already follows from their being in sequence.

In the last part of this section we consider a marked M-net Σ, a collapsing δ on Σ, and a δ-respectful occurrence sequence τ of Σ. Our aim is to define an abstraction of τ called the δ-trace $\epsilon(\tau)$, by which we mean a sequence of (valuated) labels of transitions of τ. Intuitively, $\epsilon(\tau)$ describes the 'externally visible' behaviour generated by τ. We wish to consider neighbouring δ-related pairs of transitions as single entities; their combined label arises as the union of the two participating labels. We define $\epsilon(\tau)$ inductively. Suppose τ is of the form

$$\underbrace{\ldots \; M_{i-1}(t_i, \sigma_i) M_i(t_{i+1}, \sigma_{i+1}) M_{i+1}(t_{i+2}, \sigma_{i+2})}_{(1)} \; \ldots$$

and suppose that $\epsilon(\tau)$ has already been constructed for the prefix up to and including (1). There are two possibilities for t_i: either t_i is in no set $T \in dom(\delta)$, or t_i is in some such set.

Consider the first possibility. Then we extend $\epsilon(\tau)$ by the multiset $\lambda(t_i)[\sigma_i]$, i.e. the multiset of action terms $\lambda(t_i)$ subjected to the binding σ_i (i.e. a multiset of ground action terms). If $\lambda(t_i)[\sigma_i]$ is empty then, by definition, this has the same effect as appending the empty word to $\epsilon(\tau)$, i.e. $\epsilon(\tau)$ is simply left as it was. The construction of $\epsilon(\tau)$ is then continued, starting with (t_{i+1}, σ_{i+1}).

Now consider the second possibility. Then there is a pair $(T, T') \in \delta$ such that $t_i \in T$ and $t_{i+1} \in T'$. Valuation σ_i assigns values to $Var(t_i)$ including the (only) variable, say b, in $\iota(t_i, s_{TT'})$. Valuation σ_{i+1} assigns values to $Var(t_{i+1})$, including variable a in $\iota(s_{TT'}, t_{i+1})$. Note that the value of b under σ_i equals the value of a under σ_{i+1} (since this is exactly the token put on place $s_{TT'}$ by t_i and removed from place $s_{TT'}$ by t_{i+1}). Without loss of generality, we may assume that the variables of t_i and t_{i+1} are disjoint. Then define $\sigma_i \cup \sigma_{i+1}$ as the binding of $Var(t_i) \uplus Var(t_{i+1})$ determined by σ_i and σ_{i+1}, and note that this is well-defined. Then, we extend $\epsilon(\tau)$ by the multiset $(\lambda(t_i) + \lambda(t_{i+1}))[\sigma_i \cup \sigma_{i+1}]$ of ground actions, and the construction of $\epsilon(\tau)$ is continued starting with (t_{i+2}, σ_{i+2}). For example, for τ_1^δ (figure 5) we have $\epsilon(\tau_1^\delta) = \{A(1,1), A(1,0)\}\{A(1,0)\}$.

Note that, in general, $\epsilon(\tau)$ is a sequence over the alphabet $\mathcal{G}(\Sigma, \delta)$ (the *valuated action symbols*), which is defined as follows: $\mathcal{G}(\Sigma, \delta) = \mathcal{G}^a \cup \mathcal{G}^b$, where $\mathcal{G}^a$ is the set of all $\lambda(t)[\sigma]$, with t being a transition of Σ *not* in some $T \cup T'$ with $(T, T') \in \delta$ and σ is a binding of $Var(t)$, and $\mathcal{G}^b$ is the set of all $(\lambda(t) + \lambda(t'))[\sigma \cup \sigma']$, where $t \in T$ and $t' \in T'$ with $(T, T') \in \delta$, σ and σ' are, respectively, bindings of $Var(t)$ and $Var(t')$, and $\sigma \cup \sigma'$ is as above.

3.3   Implementation relation

Let two marked M-nets Σ_1 and Σ_2, a collapsing δ_1 on Σ_1 and a collapsing δ_2 on Σ_2 be given. Let $\mathcal{G}_1 = \mathcal{G}(\Sigma_1, \delta_1)$ and $\mathcal{G}_2 = \mathcal{G}(\Sigma_2, \delta_2)$. Our aim here is to define under which circumstances Σ_1 may be called an 'implementation' of Σ_2. More precisely, we wish to capture the idea that every externally visible (δ_1-complete) behaviour of Σ_1 has a corresponding externally visible behaviour of Σ_2 (while the latter may have more behaviours which are not captured by the implementation).[6]

---

[6] In terms of CCS this would mean, for instance, that a implements $a + b$.

Since there is no *a priori* relationship between the transition interfaces $\mathcal{G}_1$ and $\mathcal{G}_2$ of Σ_1 and Σ_2, this notion of implementation must be given with respect to a (partial) identification of those interfaces.

In this observational view, an *identification between Σ_1 and Σ_2* is a relation

$$\rho \subseteq \mathcal{G}_1 \times \mathcal{G}_2.$$

Relation ρ can be extended to a relation between sequences over $\mathcal{G}_1$ and sequences over $\mathcal{G}_2$: inductively, for finite sequences, ρ is the smallest relation such that $(\emptyset, \emptyset) \in \rho$ (as $\emptyset$ plays the role of empty sequence) and $(\epsilon_1, \epsilon_2) \in \rho$ for $\epsilon_1 \neq \emptyset \neq \epsilon_2$ iff

$$\exists \epsilon_1' \preceq \epsilon_1, \epsilon_2' \preceq \epsilon_2, g_1 \in \mathcal{G}_1, g_2 \in \mathcal{G}_2 : (\epsilon_1' g_1 = \epsilon_1) \wedge (\epsilon_2' g_2 = \epsilon_2) \wedge (\epsilon_1', \epsilon_2') \in \rho \wedge (g_1, g_2) \in \rho,$$

where $\preceq$ denotes the prefix relation; this definition can be extended canonically to infinite sequences.

In particular, for every abstracted sequence $\epsilon(\tau)$ of Σ_1 there may be a number of corresponding sequences ϵ' over $\mathcal{G}_2$ with $(\epsilon(\tau), \epsilon') \in \rho$. In general, such an ϵ' does not have to correspond to any occurrence sequence of Σ_2. If it always does, then we define Σ_1 to implement Σ_2. More precisely, let τ_1 be a δ_1-respectful occurrence sequence of Σ_1 and let τ_2 be a δ_2-respectful occurrence sequence of Σ_2. We define τ_1 and τ_2 to be *$\delta\rho$-related* if $(\epsilon(\tau_1), \epsilon(\tau_2)) \in \rho$. Moreover, Σ_1 is defined to *implement Σ_2 directly*, in symbols $\Sigma_1 \sqsubseteq_\rho^{\delta_1\delta_2} \Sigma_2$, iff for every δ_1-complete behaviour τ_1 of Σ_1 there exists a δ_2-complete behaviour τ_2 of Σ_2 such that $\tau_1^{\delta_1}$ and $\tau_2^{\delta_2}$ are $\delta\rho$-related.

In the remainder of this paper we always have $\delta_2 = \emptyset$, and in the remainder of this section we abbreviate $\delta = \delta_1$ and $\sqsubseteq_\rho^\delta = \sqsubseteq_\rho^{\delta\emptyset}$.

Observe some special cases:

Claim 2   Assume Σ_2 is obtained from Σ_1 by omitting a place and its surrounding arcs, let $\delta = \emptyset$ and ρ identity. Then $\Sigma_1 \sqsubseteq_\rho^\delta \Sigma_2$.

Proof: Omitting a place at most adds, but does not restrict, behaviour.
∎2

Claim 3   Assume Σ_1 is obtained from Σ_2 by omitting a transition and its surrounding arcs, let $\delta = \emptyset$ and ρ the inclusion relation. Then $\Sigma_1 \sqsubseteq_\rho^\delta \Sigma_2$.

Proof: Omitting a transition at most restricts, but does not add, behaviour.
∎3

Moreover, let ρ be the identification between an M-net Σ and its unfolding $U(\Sigma)$, i.e. identity on valuated labels. Then $\Sigma \sqsubseteq_\rho^\emptyset U(\Sigma)$ and $U(\Sigma) \sqsubseteq_{\rho^{-1}}^\emptyset \Sigma$. Note also that $\sqsubseteq_\rho^\delta$ is stable over unfolding-preserving transformations, i.e. if $\Sigma_1' \equiv \Sigma_1$, $\Sigma_1 \sqsubseteq_\rho^\delta \Sigma_2$ and $\Sigma_2 \equiv \Sigma_2'$, then $\Sigma_1' \sqsubseteq_{\rho'}^{\delta'} \Sigma_2'$ where ρ' and δ' are the same as ρ and δ except for the obvious identifications between Σ_1, Σ_1' and Σ_2, Σ_2'.

Note that $\sqsubseteq_\rho^\delta$ is a relation of 'direct implementation' which is not, in general, transitive, because collapsing a transition may be nested. Thus it is convenient to define its transitive closure. Let Σ_1 and Σ_2 (with their respective initial markings) and a relation ρ as above be given. Then Σ_1 is called an *implementation of*

Σ_2 (with respect to ρ), in symbols $\Sigma_1 \sqsubseteq_\rho \Sigma_2$, if there are initially marked nets $\Sigma^0, \ldots, \Sigma^m$ and relations $\delta^1, \ldots, \delta^m$ as well as relations $\rho^1, \ldots, \rho^m$ such that

$$\Sigma_1 = \Sigma^0 \, , \; \Sigma^m = \Sigma_2 \, , \; \Sigma^{j-1} \sqsubseteq_{\rho^j}^{\delta^j} \Sigma^j \text{ for } 1 \le j \le m \text{ and } \rho = \rho^1 \circ \ldots \circ \rho^m.$$

This relation is obviously transitive.

The notion of implementation defined above is weak in the sense that, for instance, a net with an empty set of external traces would be called an implementation of any other net. In section 7.3 we discuss strengthening it.

Next in this section, we identify a class of pairs of M-nets of which the first implements the second. The idea is that whenever $t \in T$ and $t' \in T'$ for some $(T, T') \in \delta$ then, essentially, t and t' may be replaced by a single transition. We need this technique for the case that either: $t \in T$ is fixed and combined with every $t' \in T'$; or: every $t \in T$ is combined with a fixed $t' \in T'$; or: every $t \in T$ is combined with every $t' \in T'$.

Let Σ_1 be an initially marked M-net, let δ be a collapsing and let $(T, T') \in \delta$ with sequentialising place $s = s_{TT'}$. Moreover let $t_0 \in T$. Let Σ_2 be the same net as Σ_1 except that: (a), for every pair (t_0, t') such that $t' \in T'$, a new transition, say $t_0 t'$ (or $[t_0, t']$ to emphasise the fact that this new transition has been derived by collapsing from two old ones), with connections and inscription as defined below, is introduced; (b), transition t_0 is omitted from the net. We claim that Σ_1 implements Σ_2, and that in Σ_2, $T \setminus \{t_0\}$ and T' are in sequence.

The connections of $t_0 t'$ (i.e. its surrounding arcs) are the same as those of t_0 and t', minus the one that leads from t_0 to s and the one that leads from s to t'. Suppose the former has label $\{b\}$ and the latter has label $\{a\}$ in Σ_1 and suppose $Var(t_0) \cap Var(t') = \emptyset$. The guard of $t_0 t'$ is defined as $(\alpha(t_0)[b \leftarrow x] \wedge \alpha(t')[a \leftarrow x])$ where x is a fresh variable and $\alpha[y \leftarrow x]$ means α with y substituted by x. Finally, the label of $t_0 t'$ is defined as $(\lambda(t_0)[b \leftarrow x] + \lambda(t')[a \leftarrow x])$.

This construction is symmetric in the sense that every transition $t \in T$ could be paired with a fixed transition $t'_0 \in T'$, or every $t \in T$ could be paired with every $t' \in T'$, by exactly the same definition. Figure 6 shows an example of this transformation. The left-hand side shows a net Σ_1 with four transitions such that $\{t_1, t_2\}$ and $\{t'_1, t'_2\}$ are in sequence with a sequentialising place s. The right-hand side of the figure shows the net Σ_2 which results when both t_1 and t_2 are paired with transition t'_2.

Claim 4 Using the above notation (pairing a fixed $t \in T$ with all $t' \in T'$) let δ be $\{(\{t\}, T')\}$ and ρ be identity. Then $\Sigma_1 \sqsubseteq_\rho^\delta \Sigma_2$. ∎4

To end this section, we appeal to claim 4 to show that certain 'null loops' can be eliminated. To this end, consider figure 7. The M-net on its North-Western (NW) corner contains two places with the same value sets and a loop between them which shifts the value 1 from one place to the other. We show that these two places can, in effect, be combined into one place. The NE-net of figure 7 arises from the NW-net when place s is considered as a sequentialising place of its participating transitions.

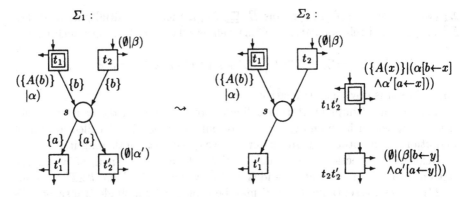

Fig. 6. Example of (partial) collapsing of transitions

The NW-net implements the NE-net (with the collapsing $\delta_1 = \{(\{z, w\}, \{y, u\})\}$ and identity $\rho_1 = \{(A, A)\}$) by claim 4. Furthermore, the NE-net implements the SW-net of figure 7 by a direct proof: every sequence of the former can be transformed into an equivalent sequence of the latter simply by omitting all instances of transition $[z, y]$ and one of the surrounding markings (which are equal because $[z, y]$ leaves markings invariant). Finally, the SW-net is unfolding-equivalent with the SE-net of figure 7 since transitions $[w, u]$ and $[w, y]$ have a **false** guard and can never be activated.

4 Memory Specification

In this section we consider the specification problem defined in [6]. After giving some introductory definitions in section 4.1, we develop a specification *Spec* of the memory module by means of a sequence of increasingly complex M-nets in section 4.2 which capture the requirements of [6] one by one.

4.1 Notation

We use the following naming conventions:

$v, w \in Val$	(Values)
$l, l_0, \ldots \in Loc$	(Locations)
$p, p_0, \ldots \in Pcss$	(Processes)
$a, b, c, d, \ldots$	(Arc variables)
$ReadCall, WriteCall, \ldots$	(Action symbols).

We use arc variables in such a way that $\{a\}$ and $\{c\}$ always label arcs from places to transitions and $\{b\}$ and $\{d\}$ always label arcs from transitions to places. The RPC-memory specification problem calls for modules to be composed at the interfaces provided by their transitions. In the following we may therefore assume that all places are internal, i.e. have label i. We will simply omit these labels. Quotes from [6] will be reproduced in italic quotation style.

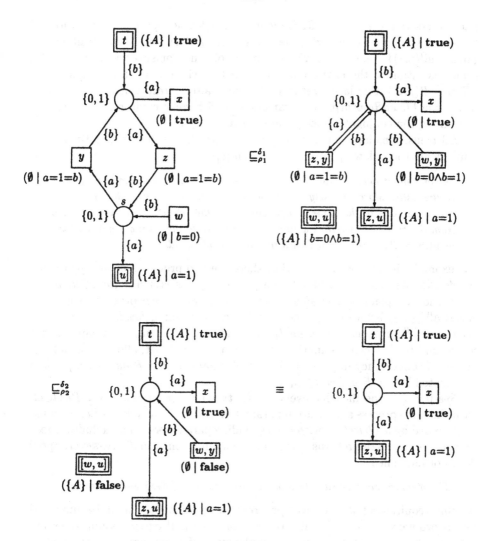

Fig. 7. Illustration of the collapsing of 'null loops'

4.2 Reliable and unreliable memory

In this section we describe a series of specifications, $Spec0$–$Spec3$, such that $Spec0$ incorporates only the minimal requirements of a memory module while $Spec3$ incorporates the full set of requirements. For each of the specifications $Speci$, we also define two variants, $Speci'$ and $Speciu$ ($i=0, 1, 2, 3$) which incorporate one type of exception and two types of exceptions, respectively: $Speci'$ is $Speci$ plus $BadArg$ exceptions and $Speciu$ is $Speci'$ plus $MemFail$ exceptions. Eventually, we will be interested in $Spec3'$ (which is 'reliable memory' according to [6]) and $Spec3u$ (which is 'unreliable memory' according to [6]).

A basic component, $Spec0$, is shown in figure 8. Procedure names and their parameters referring to the RPC-memory specification problem are expressed by action symbols and arc variables, respectively. The idea is that 'calling' the $\{ReadCall(p,l)\}$ transition of $Spec0$ consists of synchronising transition t_1 with some transition of the environment of $Spec0$ which contains a conjugate label $\{\overline{ReadCall}(p,l)\}$. Similarly, 'returning' a value after a $read$ consists of synchronising the $\{ReadReturn(p,l,v)\}$ transition t_2 with some environment transition containing the conjugate label $\{\overline{ReadReturn}(p,l,v)\}$.

All transitions have a parameter $p \in Pcss$, which is a process identifier. This implements the following requirement from [6]:

'A component may contain multiple processes that can concurrently issue procedure calls. More precisely, after one process issues a call, other processes can issue calls to the same component before the component issues a return from the first call. A return action communicates to the calling component the identity of the process that issued the corresponding call'.

For example, it may be the case that there are two processes p_1 and p_2 issuing $ReadCalls$ one after the other. When process p_1 has issued a $ReadCall(p_1, l_1)$ to location l_1, place s^0 contains a token (p_1, l_1) and when process p_2 issues a $ReadCall(p_2, l_2)$ before p_1 has accepted the corresponding $ReadReturn(p_1, l_1, .)$, then place s^0 contains two tokens (p_1, l_1) and (p_2, l_2). It may even happen that $p_1 = p_2$ and $l_1 = l_2$ (then the marking on s^0 is a true multiset, allowing for a large degree of concurrency in general); it may also happen that $ReadReturn(p_2, l_2, .)$ is executed before $ReadReturn(p_1, l_1, .)$.

$Spec0$ merely specifies that every $ReadReturn$ must be preceded by a $ReadCall$ with the same process and location parameters and that every $WriteReturn$ must be preceded by a $WriteCall$ with corresponding parameters. This excludes 'spontaneous' read or write returns – a requirement left implicit in [6]. However, $Spec0$ does not implement

'The memory must eventually issue a return for every Read *and* Write *call'.*

As this requirement is a typical progress assumption, it cannot be modelled by an ordinary net (nor by an ordinary program). Progress assumptions are captured by the consideration of completeness of executions as described in section 5.4. Note that in $Spec0$, reading and writing are oblique with respect to their parameter v. $Spec0$ imposes no restriction on value correctness. For instance, a value 5 may be written to a location l, followed immediately by a read of 3 from the same location l.

Before adding value correctness, we show how the left-hand side of $Spec0$ can be modified to yield two versions of 'less reliable' memory interface specification, $Spec0'$ and $Spec0u$, which allow exceptions as defined in [6] to happen. To express the requirement

*'*BadArg:*argument* loc *is not an element of* MemLocs *'*,

the existence of a set of non-locations called $NonLoc$ is assumed. A $BadArg_r$ exception (transition v_1 in figure 9) is raised in case $l \in NonLoc$. The $MemFail$ exception (transition v_2 in figure 9) models

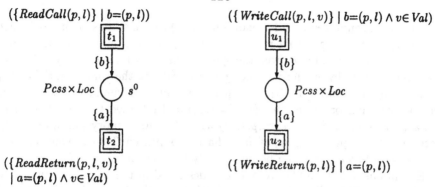

Fig. 8. Specification *Spec0*

'MemFailure:*the memory cannot be read*'.

Figure 9 shows the *read* part of *Spec0u*. We do not show the *write* part since it is analogous (it is not entirely symmetrical but easy to derive, and it will be shown later explicitly for *Spec3u*). We define *Spec0'* as *Spec0u* minus transition v_2 and the corresponding *MemFail* transition in the *write* part (such that *Spec0'* is the same as *Spec0* plus *BadArg* exceptions).

Figure 9 illustrates a general pattern for adding exceptions to specifications. They are simply described as additional behavioral possibilities at the control flow places at which the exception may occur.

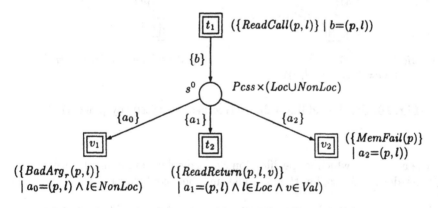

Fig. 9. *Spec0u* – adding exceptions to *Spec0* (only the *read* part)

Adding value correctness to *Spec0* is done in *Spec1* (figure 10) whose central place *s* models memory. The initial marking ⊗ of *s* is defined to be the set of pairs $\{(l, v_l^0) | l \in Loc\}$, where v_l^0 denotes the initial value at location *l*. This models

'*The memory behaves as if it maintains an array of atomically read and written locations that initially all contain the value* InitVal '.

Note that s is connected by side conditions (only) to transitions t_2 and u_1 (which are the ones involving actual memory accesses). Transition u_1 specifies that a *WriteCall* fetches a value w from the specified memory location l (by $c=(l,w)$), and overwrites it by v, the parameter of the call, at the same location l (by $d=(l,v)$); by a *ReadReturn* (transition t_2), a value v is similarly fetched from the specified memory location l (by $c=(l,v)$) and returned to the caller (since v is a parameter of $ReadReturn(p,l,v)$) as well as to memory (since $d=(l,v)$). Note that the conjuncts $v \in Val$ of *Spec0* have disappeared. They are now implicit because variables c and d can be bound only to tuples in $Loc \times Val$.

Exceptions may be added to *Spec1* as described in the transformation from *Spec0* into *Spec0'* (adding *BadArg*) and further into *Spec0u* (adding *BadArg* and *MemFail*). The new transitions have no connection to place s, which models

'*An operation that raises a* BadArg *exception has no effect on the memory*',

and (for the time being) also that *MemFail* exceptions have no effect on the memory. Specifications *Spec1'* and *Spec1u* are not shown pictorially.

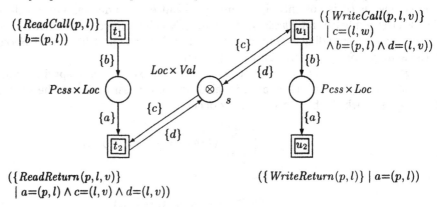

Fig. 10. *Spec1* – adding value correctness to *Spec0* (by place s)

In the next step, which is specification *Spec2* displayed in figure 11, we model read/write-detachedness, i.e. the 'at some time between' clauses of

'*Each successful* Read(l) *operation performs . . . an atomic read to location* l *at some time between the call and return. Each successful* Write(l, v) *operation performs . . . atomic writes of value* v *to location* l *at some time between the call and return*',

by separating actual reading from *ReadReturn* and actual writing from *WriteCall*. In *Spec2* the *ReadReturn* and *WriteCall* transitions, t_2 and u_1, of *Spec1* are, therefore, split into two successive transitions, t_2', t_2'' and u_1', u_1''. Actual memory accesses are now internal rather than external. They cannot be invoked from the outside (i.e. cannot be synchronised with any matching conjugate transitions).

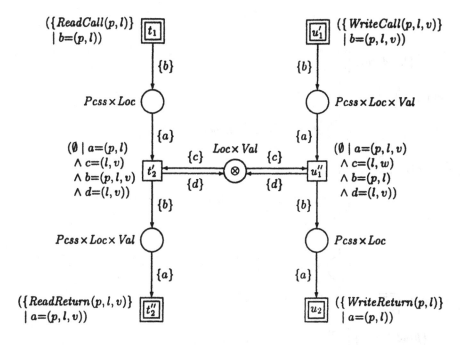

Fig. 11. *Spec2* – adding detachedness to *Spec1* (splitting t_2 and u_1)

Figure 12 shows an unreliable version, *Spec2u*, of *Spec2*. We show only the general pattern of this specification because of its analogy to *Spec0u* shown in figure 9. Note that as required [6], the *BadArg$_r$* exception gets detected straight away before an actual read while *MemFail* can occur at any time. This models

'An operation that raises a BadArg *exception has no effect on the memory'.*

A *MemFail* exception may now have an effect on the memory if it is raised between a memory access and the corresponding (*write*) return.

In the final step of the specification we add the requirement that writes may be repeated [6]. This models the emphasised part of the sentence

'Each successful Write(*l, v*) *operation performs a sequence of one or more atomic writes of value v to location l at some time between the call and return.'*

Again there are three versions of this specification: *Spec3* (without exceptions), *Spec3'* (with *BadArg* but no *MemFail* exceptions) and *Spec3u* (with *BadArg* and *MemFail* exceptions). This time we do not show *Spec3*, but we show *Spec3'* (in figure 13) and *Spec3u* (in figure 17),[7] because they correspond, respectively, to

'reliable memory' and *'unreliable memory'*.

---

[7] This figure has been given a place rather later in the paper in order to enable a direct comparison between *Spec3u* and a net defined at a later point, *Impl*.

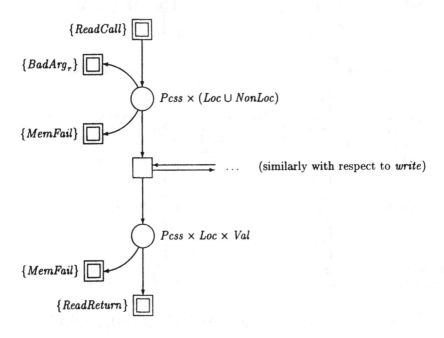

Fig. 12. *Spec2u* – adding exceptions to *Spec2* (pattern)

Spec3′ contains one additional transition, $\widetilde{u_1''}$, with respect to *Spec2′*, but note that in order to enable the repeated write, the place s' just below 'actual write' needs to have type $Pcss \times Loc \times Val$ instead of $Pcss \times Loc$ as in *Spec2′*. This allows transitions 'actual write' and 'repeated actual write' to put the value v with which they are called not only on s but also on s', which is necessary because when writes are repeated, the value which is to be written must still be known. Note that the inscription of the new transition is the same as that of the 'actual write'. The specification of unreliable memory with repeated writes, *Spec3u*, which is shown below in figure 17, can be obtained from *Spec3′* in the same way as *Speciu* is obtained from *Speci′* (i=0,1,2), i.e. by adding *MemFail*.

For the purpose of the next claim let ρ be the inclusion relation and let $\sqsubseteq$ denote $\sqsubseteq_\rho^\emptyset$. Note that the identifications expressed by this choice of ρ are not freely invented but are part of the motivation behind the series of specifications.

Claim 5 $Spec0 \sqsupseteq Spec1 \sqsupseteq Spec2 \sqsubseteq Spec3$
$\quad\quad\quad\quad \sqcap \quad\quad\ \sqcap \quad\quad\ \sqcap \quad\quad\ \sqcap$
$\quad\quad\quad Spec0' \sqsupseteq Spec1' \sqsupseteq Spec2' \sqsubseteq Spec3'$
$\quad\quad\quad\quad \sqcap \quad\quad\ \sqcap \quad\quad\ \sqcap \quad\quad\ \sqcap$
$\quad\quad\quad Spec0u \sqsupseteq Spec1u \sqsupseteq Spec2u \sqsubseteq Spec3u.$ ∎5

Note that the series of specifications defined in this section does not provide

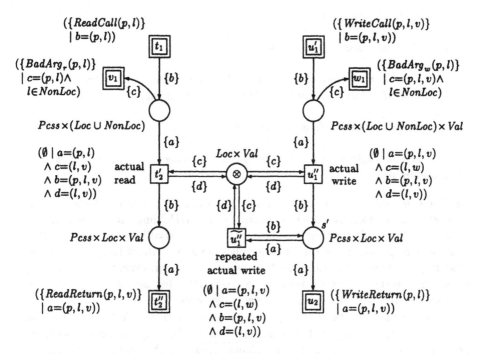

Fig. 13. Reliable memory: $Spec3'$ – adding repeated write to $Spec2'$

a strictly increasing sequence of implementations. This lies in the nature of the problem: while value correctness restricts behaviour and detachedness leaves behaviour invariant modulo transition splitting, repeated write adds behaviour. Moreover, $Spec3u$ does not implement $Spec3'$ with respect to the choice of ρ, because $Spec3u$ has an execution $M^0\{ReadCall\}M^1\{MemFail\}M^2$ for which no corresponding execution exists in $Spec3'$. We select $Spec=Spec3u$, i.e. unreliable remote memory with repeated writes, to be our specification of interest. An implementation of $Spec$, using a remote procedure call interface and reliable memory $Spec3'$, is described in the next section.

5   Memory Implementation

In section 5.1 we specify a Remote Procedure Call (RPC) interface, by means of which a user may issue remote calls and receive remote returns using the specific parametric 'procedure constants' *read* and *write*. Section 5.2 describes an implementation of $Spec$ using an RPC interface with access to reliable memory as specified by $Spec3'$. Section 5.3 describes the main result. Finally, section 5.4 investigates progress and fairness properties of the solution.

5.1 The *RPC* module

We introduce new naming conventions:

$$r \in \{read, write\} \subseteq ProcPar \quad \text{(Procedure parameters)}$$
$$arglist = [arg_1, \ldots, arg_k] \in Args \quad \text{(Argument lists)}$$

with $|arglist|=k$, $ArgNum(read)=1$ and $ArgNum(write)=2$. This models

> '... *mapping* ArgNum, *where* ArgNum(p) *is the number of arguments of each procedure p*'

for the two procedure constants, *read* and *write*, which are relevant in our context.[8] Figure 14 shows the specification of the *RPC* interface. When *RPC* is called in mode *read*, it either has parameter list $arglist=[l]$ (with a location l) or raises an exception, and when *RPC* is called in mode *write*, it has parameter list $arglist=[l, v]$ (with a location l and value v) or raises an exception. Conversely, when *RPC* returns in mode *read*, it has parameter list $arglist=[l, v]$ and when it returns in mode *write*, it has parameter list $arglist=[l]$.

By its transitions tu_1 and tu_2, the *RPC* interface interacts with any user (a 'sender' [6]) who is capable of issuing $\overline{RemoteCall}(\ldots)$ commands with appropriate parameter lists and using $\overline{RemoteReturn}(\ldots)$ commands to wait for the results of previous calls. By its transitions y_1, z'_1, y''_2, z_2, q_1 and q_2, the *RPC* module interacts with any of the specifications *Speci*, *Speci'* or *Speciu* ($i=0, 1, 2, 3$) defined in the previous section (the 'receivers' [6]). With respect to *Speci*, *Speci'* and *Speciu*, the *RPC* interface plays the role of a caller (made explicit by overbarring action names) while *Speci*, *Speci'* or *Speciu* play the role of callees. More precisely, depending on the parameter r with which it is called, the *RPC* module invokes either *ReadCall* or *WriteCall* and waits for the subsequent *Returns* or *BadArg* exceptions. This models

> '*The RPC component interfaces with two environment components, a* sender *and a* receiver. *It relays procedure calls from the sender to the receiver, and relays the return values back to the sender*'.

RPC may also raise *BadCall* and *RPCFailure* exceptions (cf. transitions t_B, t'_F and t_F) to the sender. Moreover, *RPC* has a retry transition t_R which is simply a differently labelled copy of the *RemoteCall* transition tu_1. This allows t_R to be synchronised without tu_1 being synchronised at the same time.

It is not exactly clear from [6] under which circumstances exception *BadCall* should be raised. The two relevant sentences are

> 'BadCall:proc *is not a valid name or* args *is not a syntactically correct list of arguments for* proc';
> '*Raise a* BadCall *exception if* args *is not a list of* ArgNum(proc) *arguments*'.

---

[8] What has been called p in [6] has generally been called r in this paper.

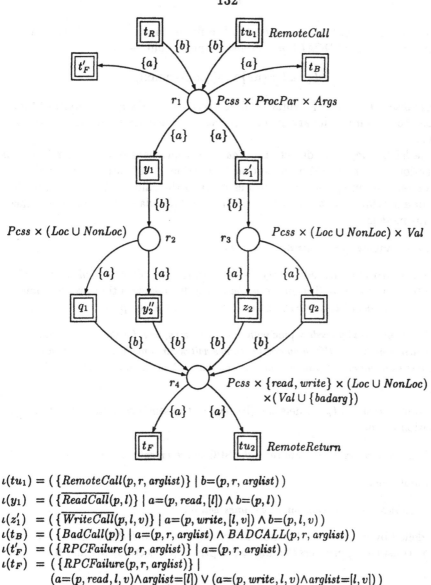

$\iota(tu_1) = (\{RemoteCall(p, r, arglist)\} \mid b=(p, r, arglist))$

$\iota(y_1) = (\{\overline{ReadCall}(p, l)\} \mid a=(p, read, [l]) \wedge b=(p, l))$

$\iota(z'_1) = (\{\overline{WriteCall}(p, l, v)\} \mid a=(p, write, [l, v]) \wedge b=(p, l, v))$

$\iota(t_B) = (\{BadCall(p)\} \mid a=(p, r, arglist) \wedge BADCALL(p, r, arglist))$

$\iota(t'_F) = (\{RPCFailure(p, r, arglist)\} \mid a=(p, r, arglist))$

$\iota(t_F) = (\{RPCFailure(p, r, arglist)\} \mid$
$\qquad (a=(p, read, l, v) \wedge arglist=[l]) \vee (a=(p, write, l, v) \wedge arglist=[l, v]))$

$\iota(t_R) = (\{RPCRetry(p, r, arglist)\} \mid b=(p, r, arglist))$

$\iota(y''_2) = (\{\overline{ReadReturn}(p, l, v)\} \mid a=(p, l) \wedge b=(p, read, l, v))$

$\iota(z_2) = (\{\overline{WriteReturn}(p, l)\} \mid a=(p, l, v) \wedge b=(p, write, l, v))$

$\iota(tu_2) = (\{RemoteReturn(p, r, arglist)\} \mid a=(p, r, l, v) \wedge$
$\qquad ((v \in Val \wedge r=read \wedge arglist=[l, v]) \vee (v \in Val \wedge r=write \wedge arglist=[l])$
$\qquad \vee (v=badarg \wedge arglist=[l, badarg])))$

$\iota(q_1) = (\{\overline{BadArg_r}(p, l)\} \mid a=(p, l) \wedge b=(p, read, l, badarg) \wedge l \in NonLoc)$

$\iota(q_2) = (\{\overline{BadArg_w}(p, l)\} \mid a=(p, l, v) \wedge b=(p, write, l, badarg) \wedge l \in NonLoc)$.

Fig. 14. Specification of the RPC component

Hence the transition t_B labelled *BadCall* in figure 14, which models this, has a parametric guard $BADCALL(p, r, arglist)$, which could be either

$$r \notin \{read, write\} \lor \lnot(\text{good-syntax}),$$

to formalise the notion of 'syntactically correct', or $|arglist| \neq ArgNum(r)$ to formalise the notion of 'the argument list does not have the right number of elements'.

The *RPC* component detects any *BadArg* exceptions raised by either *ReadCall* (transition q_1 in figure 14) or *WriteCall* (transition q_2 in figure 14). Upon detection of such an exception, *RPC* passes it on to the calling environment in the form of a special value $badarg \notin Val$ which is accommodated in the type of place r_4. This models

'*Raises any exception raised by a call to* proc'.

Normal return is indicated by tu_2 being executed in mode $r=read$ or $r=write$, while tu_2 being executed in mode $v=badarg$ indicates exception propagation of *BadArg* to the sender. Transition tu_2 thus models the (a) part of

'*Issue one call to procedure* proc *with arguments* args, *wait for the corresponding return (which the RPC component assumes will occur) and either* (a) *return the value (normal or exceptional) returned by that call, or* (b) *raise the* RPCFailure *exception*',

Moreover, transition t_F models the (b) part of the sentence quoted above, while transition t'_F models

'*Issue no procedure call, and raise the* RPCFailure *exception*'.

The requirement

'*... (which the RPC component assumes will occur) ...*',

is modelled by places r_2 and r_3 not having any attached *RPCFailure* exceptions and by considering progress/timing assumptions (cf. sections 5.4 and 6).

5.2   The implementation

Before putting *RPC* and reliable memory *Spec3'* in parallel and synchronising them, the requirement

'*If the call (to RPC) raises an* RPCFailure *exception, then the implementation may either reissue the call to the RPC component or raise a* MemFailure *exception*'

needs to be dealt with. This specifies a retry facility which, besides invoking a fresh *RemoteCall* after an *RPCFailure*, may result in a memory failure *RPCMemFail* at the *RPC* module level.

For this purpose, the *RPC* module needs to have the further interface transition t_R. Even after a successful *WriteReturn*, the *RPC* module cannot afford to ignore the value v of an attempted *write*, unless a corresponding *RemoteReturn* has actually been executed. This is because in case of an *RPCFailure*, the retry module must be aware of the value that should have been written. Thus, tokens on place r_4 of figure 14 have to carry a value even if they correspond to a past *write*. The value v of such a *write* is dropped only when a normal return happens, i.e. through the annotation of transition *RemoteReturn*.

The retry behaviour specified above is modelled by the *Retry* module shown in figure 15. Note how the overbarring in figure 15 provides for the interaction of this module with its environment: overbarred transitions labelled $\overline{RPCFailure}$ and $\overline{RPCRetry}$ (i.e. t'_R) denote interactions between *Retry* and transitions t'_F, t_F and t_R of *RPC* (figure 14), while non-overbarred transition t_M (*RPCMemFail*) signals an exception to the environment at the same level as the *RemoteCall*, *BadCall* and *RemoteReturn* transitions of *RPC*.

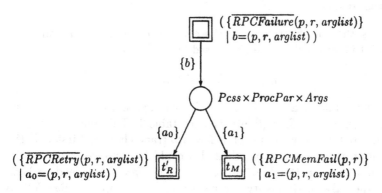

Fig. 15. The *Retry* module

We may now put together the *RPC* module, the *Retry* module and reliable memory *Spec3'* as follows:

$$Impl \equiv (\,(Retry \parallel RPC \parallel Spec3')$$
$$\mathbf{sy}\ \{\ ReadCall, ReadReturn, WriteCall, WriteReturn,$$
$$RPCFailure, RPCRetry, BadArg_r, BadArg_w\ \}$$
$$\mathbf{rs}\ \{\ ReadCall, ReadReturn, WriteCall, WriteReturn,$$
$$RPCFailure, RPCRetry, BadArg_r, BadArg_w\ \}\,).$$

Note that according to section 2.3, this is a well-defined M-net. It is shown in figure 16. We briefly explain the origins of the transitions of *Impl*. The internal transition t_R comes from a synchronisation of transitions t_R of figure 14 and t'_R of figure 15 over the pair $\{RPCRetry, \overline{RPCRetry}\}$ of conjugate action symbols.[9]

---

[9] We strive to use names for transitions and places consistently. However, sometimes it is convenient to re-use already used names, such as t_R in figures 14 and 16.

Transition y_1 comes from synchronising transitions labelled $\overline{ReadCall}$ (in RPC, figure 14) and $ReadCall$ (in $Spec3'$, figure 13). Transitions y_2'', z_1' and z_2 arise from similar synchronisations. Transition t_B signals the $BadCall$ exception of the RPC component to its environment (at the same level as the $RPCMemFail$ exception t_M). Transition q stems from synchronising the $RPCFailure$ transition t_F' of RPC (figure 14) with the $\overline{RPCFailure}$ transition of $Retry$. Transition t_F comes similarly from synchronising the $RPCFailure$ transition t_F of RPC with the $\overline{RPCFailure}$ transition of $Retry$. Transition q_1 comes from synchronising the $BadArg_r$ transition of $Spec3'$ with the $\overline{BadArg_r}$ transition q_1 of RPC; it describes the detection of the $BadArg$ exception after a $ReadCall$. Transition q_2 describes similarly the detection of a $BadArg$ exception after a $WriteCall$. Note that q, t_F, q_1 and q_2 are internal to the implementation. The detection of $BadArg$ exceptions is passed to the environment by creating the special token $badarg$ on place s_6, which is a copy of r_4.

5.3 Main result

Figure 17 shows the specification $Spec=Spec3u$. To compare $Impl$ and $Spec$, problem-inherent identifications are formalised by a relation

$$\rho_{Impl} \subseteq \mathcal{G}_1 \times \mathcal{G}_2,$$

where $\mathcal{G}_1$ are the valuated action symbols of $Impl$ (figure 16) and $\mathcal{G}_2$ are the valuated action symbols of $Spec$ (figure 17); see table 1. This relation is given implicitly in [6], but there is room for a few arbitrary choices. Firstly, if the $BadCall$ exception is raised in $Impl$, then this could be mapped either to the $MemFail$ exceptions or to the $BadArg$ exceptions of $Spec$ (or indeed to both of them). For the sake of simplicity, we have chosen to map any $BadCall$ to $MemFail$. This justifies lines (e) and (f) of table 1. Secondly, if a $RemoteCall$ is executed with a syntactically incorrect parameter list, then this must eventually yield a $BadCall$ exception in $Impl$ and is modelled by a $MemFail$ exception in $Spec$, but before the latter, a $ReadCall$ or a $WriteCall$ must occur (depending on the mode in which $RemoteCall$ was executed). To enable such a call, we need to assume that both Loc and Val are nonempty sets, so that we may pick arbitrary (but fixed) elements $l_0 \in Loc$ and $v_0 \in Val$. This justifies lines (c) and (d) of table 1, where it is assumed that $arglist_0 \neq [l]$ and $arglist_0' \neq [l, v]$. All other elements of ρ_{Impl} are determined by the problem statement.

To understand table 1, consider, for instance, line (i). Check figure 16 to see that in mode $read$, the parameter list of tu_2 is $(p, read, [l, v])$, and check figure 17 to see that the parameter list of t_2'' is (p, l, v). Consider a binding with $p=p_1$ (a concrete procedure p_1), $l=l_1$ (a concrete location l_1) and $v=5$ (a concrete value). Line (i) of table 1 means that the valuated label $\{RemoteReturn(p_1, read, [l_1, 5])\}$ of $Impl$ is, by definition, related to the valuated label $\{ReadReturn(p_1, l_1, 5)\}$ of $Spec$, i.e. $(\{RemoteReturn(p_1, read, [l_1, 5])\}, \{ReadReturn(p_1, l_1, 5)\}) \in \rho_{Impl}$.

The other lines of table 1 have similar meaning, and the main result is Claim 6.

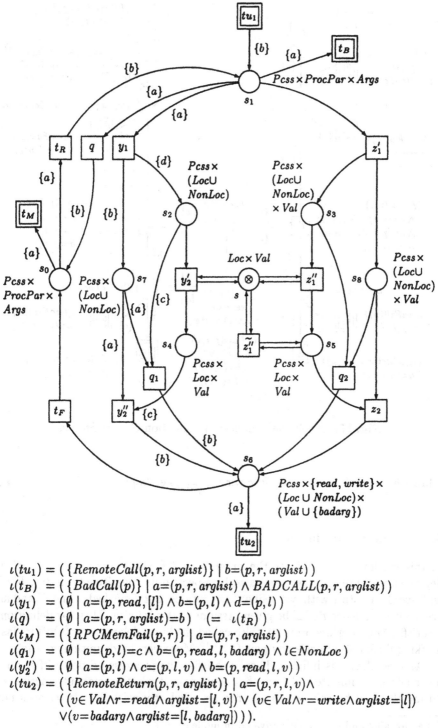

$\iota(tu_1) = (\{RemoteCall(p, r, arglist)\} \mid b=(p, r, arglist))$

$\iota(t_B) = (\{BadCall(p)\} \mid a=(p, r, arglist) \wedge BADCALL(p, r, arglist))$

$\iota(y_1) = (\emptyset \mid a=(p, read, [l]) \wedge b=(p, l) \wedge d=(p, l))$

$\iota(q) = (\emptyset \mid a=(p, r, arglist)=b)$ $(= \iota(t_R))$

$\iota(t_M) = (\{RPCMemFail(p, r)\} \mid a=(p, r, arglist))$

$\iota(q_1) = (\emptyset \mid a=(p, l)=c \wedge b=(p, read, l, badarg) \wedge l \in NonLoc)$

$\iota(y_2'') = (\emptyset \mid a=(p, l) \wedge c=(p, l, v) \wedge b=(p, read, l, v))$

$\iota(tu_2) = (\{RemoteReturn(p, r, arglist)\} \mid a=(p, r, l, v) \wedge$
$((v \in Val \wedge r=read \wedge arglist=[l, v]) \vee (v \in Val \wedge r=write \wedge arglist=[l])$
$\vee (v=badarg \wedge arglist=[l, badarg]))).$

Fig. 16. Implementation *Impl* and some of its inscriptions

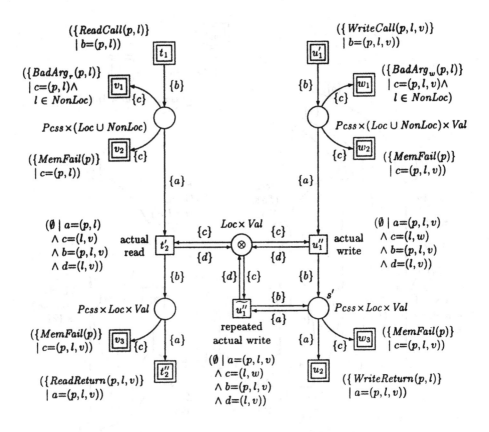

Fig. 17. Unreliable memory: Specification $Spec = Spec3u$

Claim 6 *Impl* implements *Spec* w.r.t. ρ_{Impl}, i.e. $Impl \sqsubseteq_{\rho_{Impl}} Spec$. ■6

5.4 Progress and fairness

In this section we investigate the progress and fairness properties of *Impl* in dependence of the same properties with respect to its constituents, *Retry*, *RPC* and *Spec3'*. To start with, we define these notions. Let a marked M-net Σ and an occurrence sequence τ of Σ be given. Assume that τ is finite. Then, by definition, τ satisfies the progress property (also called the finite delay property) iff its last marking does not activate any pair (t, σ).[10] Moreover, by definition, τ is fair.

Assume that τ is infinite. Then τ satisfies the progress property iff it does not contain an infinite tail such that some pair (t, σ) is permanently activated during this tail by tokens that do not get used otherwise, but (t, σ) does not

---

[10] I.e., for all t and σ, t is not activated in mode σ.

	In *Impl*:		In *Spec*:
(a)	$(tu_1:)$ $RemoteCall(p, read, [l])$	$(t_1:)$	$ReadCall(p, l)$
(b)	$(tu_1:)$ $RemoteCall(p, write, [l, v])$	$(u_1':)$	$WriteCall(p, l, v)$
(c)	$(tu_1:)$ $RemoteCall(p, read, arglist_0)$	$(t_1:)$	$ReadCall(p, l_0)$
(d)	$(tu_1:)$ $RemoteCall(p, write, arglist_0')$	$(u_1':)$	$WriteCall(p, l_0, v_0)$
(e)	$(t_B:)$ $BadCall(p)$	$(v_2:)$	$MemFail(p)$
(f)	$(t_B:)$ $BadCall(p)$	$(w_2:)$	$MemFail(p)$
(g)	$(t_M:)$ $RPCMemFail(p, read)$	$(v_3:)$	$MemFail(p)$
(h)	$(t_M:)$ $RPCMemFail(p, write)$	$(w_3:)$	$MemFail(p)$
(i)	$(tu_2:)$ $RemoteReturn(p, read, [l, v])$	$(t_2'':)$	$ReadReturn(p, l, v)$
(j)	$(tu_2:)$ $RemoteReturn(p, write, [l])$	$(u_2:)$	$WriteReturn(p, l)$
(k)	$(tu_2:)$ $RemoteReturn(p, read, [l, badarg])$	$(v_1:)$	$BadArg_r(p, l)$
(l)	$(tu_2:)$ $RemoteReturn(p, write, [l, badarg])$	$(w_1:)$	$BadArg_w(p, l)$.

Table 1. Identification ρ_{Impl} between *Impl* and *Spec*

occur in the tail. Moreover, τ is strongly fair towards some pair (t, σ) iff it has no infinite tail activating (t, σ) infinitely often but not containing (t, σ), and weakly fair towards (t, σ) if it has no infinite tail activating (t, σ) permanently but not containing it.

Figure 18 explains the differences between these notions in terms of elementary nets. In Σ_1, the sequence $uuu \ldots$ does not satisfy the progress property (nor is it weakly or strongly fair). In Σ_2, the sequence $uuu \ldots$ satisfies the progress property but is (in both senses) unfair towards t. In Σ_3, the sequence $uu'uu' \ldots$ is weakly but not strongly fair towards t.

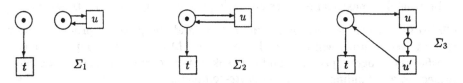

Fig. 18. Explanation of progress and fairness

The difference between progress and fairness is related to maximality in partial order semantics. For example, figure 19 shows partial order executions σ_1 and π_2 such that π_1 is non-maximal for Σ_1 (because a t-event can be added) while π_2 is maximal for Σ_2, even though both of them are infinite and have the same transition interleavings.

Claim 7 If *Retry*, *RPC* and *Spec3'* satisfy the progress property then *Impl* does so, too. More precisely, if τ is an occurrence sequence violating the progress

Fig. 19. Two partial order executions π_1 (π_2) of Σ_1 (resp. Σ_2) of figure 18

property with respect to *Impl*, then at least one of the three projections of τ onto the subsystems *Retry*, *RPC* or *Spec3'* violates progress with respect to the corresponding subsystem. ■7

Next, consider the M-net *Impl* in figure 16. We say that an infinite occurrence sequence τ is *read*-complete iff it has no infinite tail which contains an instance of tu_1 with label $\{RemoteCall(p_1, read, [l_1])\}$ but no subsequent instance of tu_2 with label $\{RemoteReturn(p_1, read, [l_1, v])\}$ (with any value v) or instance of t_M with label $\{RPCMemFail(p_1, read)\}$. The notion of τ being *write*-complete is defined analogously. The next property states that when progress is assumed and certain conflict resolutions are assured to be fair, then it is guaranteed that every *read* request will eventually either be served, or an *RPCMemFail* exception be signalled.

Claim 8 Fairness towards transitions y_1 and tu_2 (figure 16) and the progress property imply that 'A *read* return will eventually be issued'. More precisely, suppose that τ satisfies the progress property and is (weakly) fair towards y_1 and tu_2 (with respect to any binding). Then τ is *read*-complete. ■8

Note that fairness towards t_M is not needed. Claim 8 gives conditions for

'The RPC call can be retried arbitrarily many times because of RPCFailure *exceptions, but a return from the* Read *or* Write *call must eventually be issued'*

to be true. The next claim states an analogous property for *write* requests.

Claim 9 Fairness towards z_1', tu_2 and z_2 and the progress property imply that 'A *write* return will eventually be issued'. More precisely, suppose that τ satisfies the progress property and is (weakly) fair towards z_1', tu_2 and z_2 (with respect to any binding). Then τ is *write*-complete. ■9

6 A Lossy Remote Procedure Call Component

In this section we describe an implementation of the *RPC*-module shown in figure 14 by means of a timed lossy module *LRPC*. The latter may exhibit adverse behaviour, in the sense that tokens may get lost in its interior. However, under certain assumptions about its temporal properties, it can be shown that *LRPC* still implements *RPC*. In designing *LRPC*, we make use of the multilabel feature of M-nets.

Section 6.1 describes the enriched temporal model we need. Section 6.2 presents the lossy *RPC* module.

6.1 Time M-nets

We use *time nets* [1, 7, 15, 18] where transitions are given time intervals $[\gamma_1, \gamma_2]$ with numbers γ_1 and γ_2 satisfying $0 \leq \gamma_1 \leq \gamma_2 \leq \infty$. Their semantics can be understood informally as follows. Suppose t is a transition with attached time interval $[\gamma_1, \gamma_2]$. Suppose further that $S_t = {}^\bullet t$ is the set of input places of t. Suppose that a collection of tokens with identity μ on S_t enables t in mode σ. We may imagine that exactly in the moment this enabling starts to exist, a small stopwatch $W(\mu, t)$ appears; this stopwatch refers to μ and to t.[11] $W(\mu, t)$ starts counting time from 0 upwards and disappears as soon as the conditions for its existence cease to be true, i.e. as soon as either t or some other transition take away some token(s) from μ (even if such token(s) are immediately returned to S_t, in which case a new stopwatch appears). For definiteness we assume that time is counted in seconds, and thus γ_1 and γ_2 are either natural numbers or ∞. The rule for the occurrence of t is that

- If $W(\mu, t)$ ceases to exist before it has shown time γ_1 (exclusively) then this must be due to some pair $(t', \sigma') \neq (t, \sigma)$ (note that we may have $t' = t$, but it may not be the identical μ and t);
- $W(\mu, t)$ may not exist after time γ_2 (exclusively). Thus, in particular, if γ_2 is not ∞ then $W(\mu, t)$ must disappear between 0 and time γ_2 (inclusively), be it through occurrence of t in mode σ during $[\gamma_1, \gamma_2]$ or through some other (t', σ') using tokens from μ during $[0, \gamma_2]$.

More informally, this means that 't may not occur through μ before γ_1, and not be enabled by μ after γ_2'. In particular, if $\gamma_1 = \gamma_2$ then t *must* occur at time γ_1 with μ, unless some (other) transition makes $W(\mu, t)$ disappear between time 0 and time γ_1 (inclusively). If $\gamma_1 = \gamma_2 = 0$ then this means that t occurs with μ in the same instant as it is enabled by μ, unless some (other) transition takes μ-tokens away at the same instant. We may also have $\gamma_1 = 0$ and $\gamma_2 = \infty$. This means that no timing constraints are imposed on t. In this way, non-time M-nets are special cases of time M-nets with all intervals being $[0, \infty]$. It may even be the case that $\gamma_1 = \gamma_2 = \infty$, which specifies t as dead. For a more formal definition of time Petri nets, the reader may consult [1, 7, 18, 21, 22].

6.2 Lossy *RPC* module

A specification of the lossy *RPC* interface, *LRPC*, is given in figure 20. For the sake of brevity, we do not give the parameters of action symbols, nor do we specify transition guards; they can (hopefully) be inserted by analogy from previously given ones. The interior interface of *LRPC*, comprising transitions y_1, z_1', q_1, y_2'', z_2 and q_2, is the same as the interior interface of *RPC*. This models

'The Lossy RPC component is the same as the RPC component except for the following differences, where δ is a parameter'.

---

[11] If t is also enabled by a different collection μ' of tokens on S_t then there is a different stopwatch for μ' and t, which may show a different time than $W(\mu, t)$.

Instead of the *RPCFailure* and *RPCRetry* transitions of *RPC*, there are now two internal transitions t^2 and t^3 representing the potential loss of tokens. The timing constraints are such that 'loss' transitions t^2 and t^3 can occur at any time if they are enabled. The loss of tokens models

> 'The RPCFailure *exception is never raised. Instead of raising this exception, the* RemoteCall *procedure never returns'.*

The timing constraint $[0, \delta]$ of t^1 models

> '*If a call to* RemoteCall *raises a* BadCall *exception, then that exception will be raised within δ seconds of the call'.*

The timing constraints $[0, \delta]$ of y_1 and z_1' model

> '*If a* RemoteCall(p, a) *call results in a call of procedure p, then that call of p will occur within δ seconds of the call of* RemoteCall*'.*

Finally, the timing constraint $[0, \delta]$ of t^4 models

> '*If a* RemoteCall(p, a) *call returns other than by raising a* BadCall *exception, then that return will occur within δ seconds of the return from the call to procedure p'.*

Note that the interval $[0, \infty]$ attached to t^2 and t^3 may not be replaced by $[0, \delta]$ because the transitions in conflict with t^2 and t^3 are external, and in a larger net they may not be enabled at the same time as t^2 or t^3; thus, replacing the interval $[0, \infty]$ at t^2 (or t^3) by a smaller one would mean imposing a restriction on the problem which is not implied by its specification.

The task is to implement *RPC* using a mechanism of passing remote calls through to the *LRPC* component, and returning normally or raising exceptions:

> '*The* RPC *component is implemented with a Lossy RPC component by passing the* RemoteCall *call through to the Lossy RPC, passing the return back to the caller, and raising an exception if the corresponding return has not been issued after $2\cdot\delta+\epsilon$ seconds'.*

We realise this – using multilabels – by the passing-through-module P shown in figure 21. Transition u^3, which must occur exactly at time $2\cdot\delta+\epsilon+1$ after its enabling, unless some other transition (which in this case could only be u^4, since u^2 is not yet enabled at time $2\cdot\delta+\epsilon$) takes away the enabling token, functions as a timeout for transition u^4. Each occurrence of u^3 takes away one of the enabling tokens of u^4. Then, only u^2 remains enabled, and its time constraint implies that it must occur at some time point strictly after $2\cdot\delta+\epsilon$ (or not at all). Thus, P has the effect of requiring that, if u^4 misses its chance of occurring between time 0 and time $2\cdot\delta+\epsilon$, it becomes disabled and u^2 may get executed instead. This models the second part of the above specification.

Observe that u^0 in figure 21 has a label consisting of two action symbols, namely $\{RemoteCall, \overline{LossyCall}\}$. Therefore, u^0 can be synchronised with transition t^0 of *LRPC*, yielding an external transition having only one action symbol

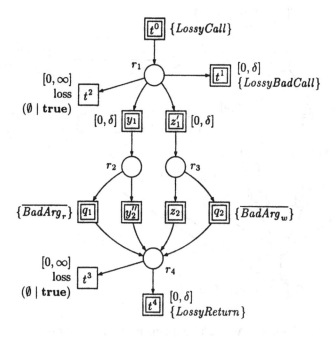

Fig. 20. Specification *LRPC* of Lossy *RPC* (compare with figure 14)

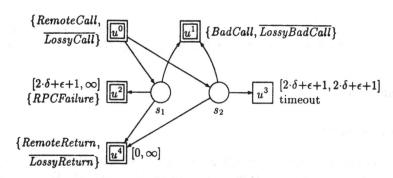

Fig. 21. The 'passing through' module *P*

RemoteCall in its label, and thus serving the same purpose as transition tu_1 of *RPC*. Similarly, transition u^1 can be synchronised with transition t^1 of *LRPC* and transition u^4 can be synchronised with transition t^4 of *LRPC*, which realises the first part of the above specification. In all, we have:

$$RPCImpl \equiv ((P \parallel LRPC) \textbf{ sy } \{LossyCall, LossyBadCall, LossyReturn\}$$
$$\textbf{rs } \{LossyCall, LossyBadCall, LossyReturn\}).$$

The resulting net is shown in figure 22. Note that the interval of *RemoteReturn* is the intersection of the two intervals of its constituent transitions.

Finally, let $\rho_{RPCImpl}$ be the obvious inclusion of *RPCImpl* into *RPC*.

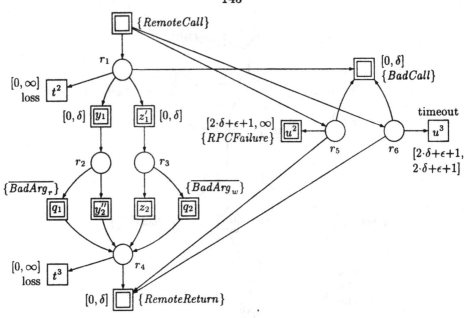

Fig. 22. An *RPC* implementation *RPCImpl*

Claim 10 If every *ReadCall* and every *WriteCall* returns within ϵ seconds, either normally or exceptionally, then $RPCImpl \sqsubseteq_{\rho_{RPCImpl}} RPC$. ■10

7 Discussion

7.1 In retrospect

A solution of the RPC-memory specification problem by Broy/Lamport [6] was given in terms of high-level Petri nets, more precisely, M-nets [4]. For the construction of the implementation, composition operations defined on M-nets – in particular, parallel composition, synchronisation and restriction – were used. The construction consisted of a succession of increasingly detailed specifications, which arise by adding the requirements defined in [6] one by one. For the proof that the implementation meets its specification, several simple proof techniques were isolated. In particular, techniques of unfolding-preserving transformations [9, 13], place/transition omission (claims 2 and 3) and a technique for transition collapsing (claim 4) were identified as relevant. The proof consists of repeated applications of these techniques, and only in its last part (showing that $Impl^{(v)}$ implements *Spec*) has a problem-specific argument been used.

What is perhaps nice in this approach is that both the construction of the solution and the proof can be done in small steps which correspond in a meaningful way to aspects and decompositions of the problem. In this way, it is possible to understand each step of the development by itself. I also like to have the specifications and implementations represented as marked nets because their behaviour can readily be visualised and understood.[12]

What is not so nice, perhaps, is that the repetitive parts of the proof do not (yet) seem to be easily automisable. What was also not so nice is that I had to spend quite some time on developing the necessary theory in sections 3.2 and 3.3, even though I did not have to invent an ad-hoc extension of any existing net model, as I had originally feared when first seeing the document [6].

In the development and proof of the solution, there has been no mention of deadlock properties. The reader may have noticed that our notion of collapsing is critical in this respect. Figure 23 shows a pattern of unsafe and safe splittings of transition a. If a is split into an internal action followed by a, as in the left-hand side of the figure, new deadlocks may be introduced in some environments.[13] However, if the split involves a feedback loop (whose pattern is described by transition t_f on the right-hand side of figure 23) then no new deadlocks are introduced. The reader may scan the proof of claim 6 below and check that any critical splitting is done under the premise that feedbacks such as t_f are available. Thus, it may be expected that in any environment, our implementation *Impl* is deadlock-free if and only if its specification *Spec* is, although we give no proof of this.

We have also investigated the fairness properties of our solution, emphasising on examining which conditions on its constituent parts are necessary to guarantee some measure of desired service (full service is not guaranteed since there may be a variety of exceptions). It turns out that with a few fair conflict resolutions, it can be guaranteed that requests will eventually be served. (In practice, instead of implementing fair conflict resolutions involving an exception, one may think of spending an extra effort to avoid exceptions altogether.)

An idea for future work could be to translate all proofs into the language of partial order semantics [2, 10]. This could be beneficial because in our existing proofs, the finger is sometimes pointed at specific tokens m on specific places s, and on a transition t putting m on s and a transition t' removing the very same m from s. While in interleaving semantics this could appear to be a slightly fuzzy notion (particularly since two same elements of a multiset are indistinguishable), it becomes a perfectly clear notion in partial order process (as opposed to trace or pomset [14, 19]) semantics, since m is then represented as a place between two events representing t and t', respectively.

Another idea for future work could be the investigation of congruences regarding the implementation relation $\sqsubseteq_\rho$. For example, it is fairly clear that $\Sigma_1 \sqsubseteq_\rho \Sigma_2$ implies $(\Sigma_1 \| \Sigma) \sqsubseteq_\rho (\Sigma_2 \| \Sigma)$. It is less clear whether or not similar properties hold for **rs** and **sy** . Such properties are needed, for instance, in order to deduce from claims 6 and 10 that if *RPC* is replaced by *RPCImpl* in the definition of *Impl*, then claim 6 continues to hold.

---

[12] But I agree that such an argument is highly training and experience dependent.

[13] This is analogous to transforming a CCS term $(a+b)$ into the term $((\tau.a)+b)$.

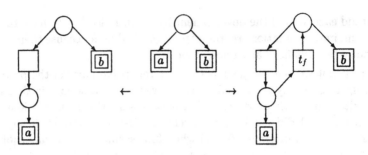

Fig. 23. Unsafe (left) and safe (right) splitting of a

7.2 Answers to [6]

'*Write a formal specification of the Memory component and of the Reliable Memory component*'.

See $Spec=Spec3u$ (figure 17) and $Spec3'$ (figure 13), respectively.

'*Either prove that a Reliable Memory component is a correct implementation of a Memory component, or explain why it should not be*'.

See claim 5; viz., the 'either' case.

'*If your specification of the Memory component allows an implementation that does nothing but raise* MemFailure *exceptions, explain why this is reasonable*'.

It does. This is due not to the specification, but to the notion of implementation we have defined (i.e. the notion of a relation between two specifications, one of which may then be called an implementation of the other). As discussed above, this notion covers a minimum to be reasonably required of an implementation. A discussion of how it can be strengthened is deferred to section 7.3.

'*Write a formal specification of the RPC component*'.

See RPC in figure 14.

'*Write a formal specification of the implementation, and prove that it correctly implements the specification of the Memory component*'.

See $Impl$ (figure 16) and claim 6.

'*Write a formal specification of the Lossy RPC component*'.

See $LRPC$ in figure 20.

'*Write a formal specification of this implementation*'.

See $RPCImpl$ in figure 22.

'*Prove that, if every call to a procedure in* Procs *returns within ϵ seconds, then the implementation satisfies the specification of the RPC component*'.

See claim 10.

7.3 Safety and liveness specifications

As was mentioned in section 3.3, the implementation relation is weak in the sense that, for instance, a net with the empty set of visible traces implements any other net. However, if it is desired to strengthen the notion of implementation to express, say, that some implementation exhibits not just adequate but also desired behaviour, then this can be achieved by using the very same definition in the other direction.

For instance, consider $Spec3'$ which implements $Spec3u$. The latter has additional behaviour which cannot be found in $Spec3'$. Suppose we wish to express that $Spec3'$ covers a certain subset – say, the nonexceptional subset – of the behaviours of $Spec3u$. To express this formally in our example, it is possible to erase the exceptional subset from $Spec3u$, obtaining $Spec3$. To show that $Spec3'$ indeed covers the nonexceptional behaviour of $Spec3u$, it needs to be shown that $Spec3$ implements $Spec3'$. As this is true, it proves that $Spec3'$ allows all nonexceptional behaviour of $Spec3u$ (in addition to proving, as was done in the paper, that $Spec3'$ does not allow behaviour disallowed by $Spec3u$).

Generalising this observation, if a specification S can be divided into two parts: S_{live}, which specifies behaviour that must necessarily be found in an implementation, and S_{safe}, which specifies behaviour which an implementation must necessarily adhere to, then for some system I to be an implementation satisfying both S_{live} and S_{safe}, it must be shown that

$$S_{live} \sqsubseteq I \sqsubseteq S_{safe}.$$

For instance, with $S_{live}=Spec3$ and $S_{safe}=Spec3u$, $I=Spec3'$ satisfies this.

Acknowledgments

I would like to thank Manfred Broy and Leslie Lamport for posing an interesting problem and Arend Rensink and Wolfgang Reisig for making me aware at an early stage (one day after I started to work on the problem) that $Spec3$ does not implement $Spec2$. I am very grateful to Maciej Koutny – who found a major problem in a previous definition of being in sequence – and to Burkhard Graves for careful reading at short notice and spotting several mistakes. Johan Lilius – who suggested a basic pattern leading to the solution described in section 6 – and Peter Starke helped me out in the jungle of time(d) Petri nets. Thanks are also due to Hanna Klaudel, Javier Esparza, Hans Fleischhack and two anonymous reviewers for comments on a draft of this paper. Carola Pohl created most of the figures using the 'graphs.sty' package by Frank Drewes.

References

1. B. Berthomieu and M. Diaz: Modeling and Verification of Time Dependent Systems Using Time Petri Nets. IEEE Transactions on Software Engineering Vol. 17/3, 259–273 (1991).
2. E. Best and R. Devillers: Sequential and Concurrent Behaviour in Petri Net Theory. Theoretical Computer Science Vol. 55/1, 87–136 (1988).

3. E. Best, R. Devillers and J.G. Hall: The Petri Box Calculus: a New Causal Algebra with Multilabel Communication. Advances in Petri Nets 1992 (ed. G.Rozenberg), Springer-Verlag, LNCS Vol. 609, 21–69 (1992).

4. E. Best, H. Fleischhack, W. Frączak, R.P. Hopkins, H. Klaudel and E. Pelz: A Class of Composable High Level Petri Nets. Proceedings of Petri Nets'95, Torino, G. De Michelis, M. Diaz (eds), Springer-Verlag, LNCS Vol.935, 103–120 (1995).

5. E. Best and Th. Thielke: Coloured Nets with Curry. Petri Net Newsletters No. 50, 27–44 (1996).

6. M. Broy and L. Lamport: The RPC-Memory Specification Problem. This volume.

7. A. Cerone and A. Maggiolo-Schettini: Time-based Expressivity of Timed Petri Nets. TR 12/95, Goethe-Universität, Frankfurt am Main (1995).

8. H.J. Genrich: Predicate-transition Nets. Advances in Petri Nets 1986, Springer-Verlag, LNCS Vol.254, 207–247 (1987).

9. H.J. Genrich: Equivalence Preserving Transformations of Predicate-transition Nets, Arbeitspapiere der GMD (1987).

10. U. Goltz and W. Reisig: The Non-sequential Behaviour of Petri Nets. Information and Control Vol. 57/2-3, 125–147 (1983).

11. K. Jensen: *Colored Petri Nets. Basic Concepts, Analysis Methods and Practical Use*. Volume 1. EATCS Monographs on Theoretical Computer Science, 1992.

12. H. Klaudel: Modèles algébriques, basés sur les réseaux de Petri, pour la sémantique des langages de programmation concurrents. PhD Thesis, Université Paris-Sud, Orsay, 1995.

13. H. Klaudel, R.-C. Riemann and A. Gronewold: Consistent Equivalence Notion for a Class of High Level Petri Nets. Rapport de Recherche 1054, LRI, Université Paris Sud (June 1996).

14. A. Mazurkiewicz: Concurrent Program Schemes and Their Interpretation. University of Århus, Computer Science Department, DAIMI PB-78 (1977).

15. P.M. Merlin and D.J. Farber: Recoverability of Communication Protocols - Implication of a Theoretical Study. IEEE Transactions on Software Communications 24, 1036–1043 (1976).

16. A.J.R.G. Milner: *Communication and Concurrency*. Prentice Hall (1989).

17. E.R. Olderog: *Nets, Terms and Formulas*. Cambridge Tracts in Theoretical Computer Science Vol. 23 (1991).

18. L. Popova: On Time Petri Nets. Journal of Information Processing and Cybernetics (formerly EIK), Vol. 27/4, 227–244 (1991).

19. V.R. Pratt: The Pomset Model of Parallel Processes: Unifying the Temporal and the Spatial. Springer-Verlag, LNCS Vol. 197: *Seminar on Concurrency*, S.D. Brookes, A.W. Roscoe, G. Winskel (eds), 180–196 (1985).

20. W. Reisig: *Petri Nets. An Introduction*. EATCS Monographs on Theoretical Computer Science Vol. 4 (1985).

21. P.H. Starke: *Analyse von Petri-Netz-Modellen*. Verlag Teubner, Stuttgart (1990).

22. P.H. Starke: A Memo on Time Constraints in Petri Nets. Informatik-Bericht Nr. 46, Humboldt-Universität zu Berlin (August 1995).

A   Proofs

Proof of claim 1

Let T and T' be in sequence in Σ. By definition, either $\forall t \in T : t^\bullet = \{s_{TT'}\}$ or $\forall t' \in T' : {}^\bullet t' = \{s_{TT'}\}$. Assume that ${}^\bullet t' = \{s_{TT'}\}$ for all $t' \in T'$. Let

$$\tau \;=\; \ldots\; M_{i-1}\;\underbrace{(t,\sigma)}_{(1),i}\; M_i\;\underbrace{\ldots\;\ldots}_{(2)}\; M_{j-1}\;\underbrace{(t',\sigma')}_{(3),j}\; M_j\;\ldots$$

be such that $t \in T$, by (1), puts some token m on $s_{TT'}$ which remains there during (2) until it is removed by $t' \in T'$, by (3). We show that by a sequence of $\equiv_0$-permutations, (t',σ') can be moved leftward into a position immediately following (t,σ). Note that in (2) there could be other instances of t or t' (or any other transition of T or T', for that matter). Hence to be precise we consider indices into τ. Let i and j be the initial indices of (t,σ) and (t',σ'), respectively. If $i=j-1$ then there is nothing to prove. So assume $i<j-1$ and consider the index $j-1$. Let (x,ξ) be the transition and binding at index $j-1$.

Assume first that $x \notin T'$. An $\equiv_0$-permutation of the pairs at indices $j-1$ and j could be hindered only by some output place of x, say s, which is also an input place of t', such that x puts a token on this place needed by t' for its occurrence. By the assumption ${}^\bullet t' = \{s_{TT'}\}$, $s = s_{TT'}$, and since t' needs only the token m for its occurrence, the token put there by x must be a different one. Hence the marking M_{j-2} enables (x,ξ) and (t',σ') concurrently, and thus they can be $\equiv_0$-permuted.

Assume next that $x \in T'$ and hence, ${}^\bullet x = \{s_{TT'}\}$ by the above assumption. Because the token m on $s_{TT'}$ removed by t' at index j remains on $s_{TT'}$ all through (2), the token taken from $s_{TT'}$ by x is a different one (even if x is t'). ¿From the fact that x and t' have no other common input places apart from $s_{TT'}$, it follows that the marking M_{j-2} just before (x,ξ) enables (x,ξ) and (t',σ') concurrently, and (x,ξ) and (t',σ') can thus be $\equiv_0$-permuted.

This procedure can be repeated. Moreover, moving t' leftward may temporarily destroy already established neighbourships, say of u and u', but a permutation of t' with u' is always directly followed by another permutation of t' with u, so that neighbourship between u and u' is instantly re-established. Moreover, as a consequence of the fact that t' takes away no more than one token from $s_{TT'}$, once t' has been moved to the right of its corresponding t, there can be no other transition that would lead to any further moving of t'.

Finally, suppose that $\forall t \in T : t^\bullet = \{s_{TT'}\}$, rather than $\forall t' \in T' : {}^\bullet t' = \{s_{TT'}\}$ holds true. Then a symmetric argument shows that (t,σ) can be moved to the right until it is a neighbour of (t',σ'). ∎1

Proof of claim 4

Let τ_1 be a δ-complete sequence of Σ_1. We construct a sequence τ_2 of Σ_2 such that τ_1^δ and τ_2 are $\delta\rho$-related. We do this inductively for finite sequences and appeal to a standard generalisation for infinite sequences. Assume

$$\tau_1^\delta = M^0(t^1, \sigma^1) M^1 \dots M^{n-1}(t^n, \sigma^n) M^n.$$

Note that markings M of Σ_1 such that $M(s)=\emptyset$ and markings K of Σ_2 correspond uniquely to each other.

The construction of τ_2 begins by letting K^0 be the marking corresponding to M^0. Then we distinguish two cases:

Case 1: $t^1 \neq t$. Let $x^1 = t^1$ and $\xi_1 = \sigma_1$ and K^1 the marking corresponding to M^1 and continue the construction with the tail $M^1 \dots$ of τ_1^δ. (Note that by δ-completeness of τ_1^δ, $t^1 \notin T'$.)

Case 2: $t^1 = t$. By δ-respectfulness of τ_1^δ, t^2 exists and satisfies $t^2 \in T'$. Let $x^1 = t^1 t^2$ (i.e. the transition in Σ_2 which has been combined from t^1 and t^2) and let ξ_1 be $\sigma_1 \cup \sigma_2$. Let K^1 be the marking corresponding to M^2 and continue the construction with the tail $M^2 \dots$ of τ_1^δ.

Continuing in this way (either, in case 1, translating transitions of τ_1^δ one-to-one into transitions of τ_2, or, in case 2, combining two successive transitions of τ_1^δ into a single transition of τ_2), one eventually gets $\tau_2 = K^0(x_1, \xi_1) K^1 \dots$ which is $\delta\rho$-related to τ_1^δ. ■4

Proof of claim 5

$Spec0 \sqsupseteq Spec1$ follows with claim 2. The proof of $Spec1 \sqsupseteq Spec2$ is a repeated application of claim 4, first applying it to $\{t_2'\}$ and $\{t_2''\}$ and then to $\{u_1'\}$ and $\{u_1''\}$ (or, what comes to the same, the other way round). $Spec2 \sqsubseteq Spec3$ is a consequence of claim 3. $Speci \sqsubseteq Speciu$ (for all i=0, 1, 2, 3) also follow from claim 3. The proofs of the claims of the middle and lower lines of the claim mirror those of the upper line. ■5

Proof of claim 6

The task is to prove that every occurrence sequence of *Impl* has a corresponding sequence in *Spec*. First, we explain informally how *Impl* and *Spec* correspond to each other. Their interface transitions are related by ρ_{Impl} as defined in table 1. Moreover, the internal transitions of *Spec* are 'somehow' (in a sense to be made precise) simulated by transitions of *Impl*. For example, transition t_2' of *Spec* corresponds to transitions y_1, y_2' and y_2'' of *Impl*. Similarly, u_1'' corresponds to z_1', z_1'' and z_2. In addition, *Impl* contains a feedback loop through transitions t_F and t_R, which can be entered after a *read*, after a *write* or after *BadArg* exceptions q_1 or q_2. This loop can 'somehow' be retrieved in *Spec* by transition $\widetilde{u_1''}$, but in the *read* part of *Spec* there is no such loop. Thus, we need to show its 'harmlessness'. Furthermore, *Impl* contains other intermediate behaviour which needs to be related to behaviour of *Spec*. It is here that the theory of sections 3.2 and 3.3 helps. We will use claims 2–4 in order to construct a series of marked M-nets $\Sigma^0, \dots, \Sigma^m$ such that $Impl = \Sigma^0$ and $\Sigma^m = Spec$, and Σ^{j-1} implements Σ^j for $0 < j \leq m$.

To make the correspondence between the *RemoteCall* transition tu_1 of figure 16 with its two parameters *read* and *write* and the two transitions *ReadCall* (t_1) and *WriteCall* (u_1') of figure 17 transparent, we use unfolding preserving transformations, all of which are incarnations of the principle explained in section 2.2 (cf. figure 3). Such transformations involve splitting of transitions and/or places such that the resulting net has the same unfolding as the original net. In our case, they are driven by suitable partitionings of the type sets of places.

After suitable transformations of this kind, the M-net *Impl'* depicted in figure 24 (with inscriptions as in table 2)[14] is obtained from *Impl* by splitting place s_1 into s_1^{rb}, s_1^r, s_1^w and s_1^{wb} and place s_6 into s_6^r, s_6^{rb}, s_6^{wb} and s_6^w, and correspondingly splitting transition tu_1 into t_1^b, t_1, u_1' and $u_1'^b$ and tu_2 into t_2'', t_2^b, u_2^b and u_2. *Impl'* has the same unfolding as *Impl*, and hence *Impl* implements *Impl'*. The annotations (a)–(l) of figure 24 refer back to the lines of table 1.

$$\iota(t_1^b) = (\{RemoteCall(p, read, arglist_0)\} \mid b=(p, read, arglist_0))$$
$$\iota(t_1) = (\{RemoteCall(p, read, [l])\} \mid b=(p, read, [l]))$$
$$\iota(x^1) = (\{BadCall(p)\} \mid a=(p, read, arglist_0))\ (BADCALL \text{ is true, cf. table 1})$$
$$\iota(s_1^{rb}) = Pcss \times \{read\} \times (Args \setminus \{[l]\})$$
$$\iota(s_1^r) = Pcss \times \{read\} \times \{[l]\}$$
$$\iota(s_0^r) = Pcss \times \{read\} \times Args$$
$$\iota(y_2') = (\emptyset \mid a=(p, l) \wedge c=(l, v) \wedge b=(p, l, v) \wedge d=(l, v))$$
$$\iota(y_2'') = (\emptyset \mid a=(p, l) \wedge c=(p, l, v) \wedge b=(p, read, l, v))$$
$$\iota(\tilde{q}_1) = (\emptyset \mid a=(p, l)=c \wedge b=(p, read, l, badarg) \wedge l \in NonLoc)$$
$$\iota(t_M^r) = (\{RPCMemFail(p, read)\} \mid a=(p, r, arglist))$$
$$\iota(s_6^r) = Pcss \times \{read\} \times Loc \times Val$$
$$\iota(s_6^{rb}) = Pcss \times \{read\} \times NonLoc \times \{badarg\}$$
$$\iota(t_2'') = (\{RemoteReturn(p, read, [l, v])\} \mid a=(p, read, l, v) \wedge v \in Val)$$
$$\iota(t_2^b) = (\{RemoteReturn(p, read, [l, badarg])\} \mid a=(p, read, l, badarg)).$$

Table 2. Some inscriptions of figure 24 (*Impl'*)

Next, consider the M-net obtained from *Impl'* by omitting places s_7 and s_8. By claim 2, this net is implemented by *Impl'* (and hence also by *Impl*). After removal of s_7 and s_8, $\{y_2'\}$ and $\{y_2'', \tilde{q}_1\}$ are in sequence (as they are sequentialised by place $s_{\{y_2'\}\{y_2''\}}=s_4$) and $\{z_1'\}$ and $\{z_1'', \tilde{q}_2\}$ are in sequence (as they are sequentialised by place s_3). Moreover, s_6^{rb} sequentialises $\{\tilde{q}_1\}$ and $\{t_2^b\}$ and s_6^{wb} sequentialises $\{\tilde{q}_2\}$ and $\{u_2^b\}$.

Applying claim 4 four times shows that y_2', s_4 and y_2'' and $\tilde{q}_1$, s_6^{rb} and t_2^b on

---

[14] Actually, table 2 shows only part of the *read* part of the figure. The *write* part is, *mutatis mutandis*, analogous. We use the abbreviation $\{[l]\}=\{[l] \mid l \in (Loc \cup NonLoc)\}$, and similarly $\{[l, v]\}=\{[l, v] \mid l \in (Loc \cup NonLoc) \wedge v \in Val\}$.

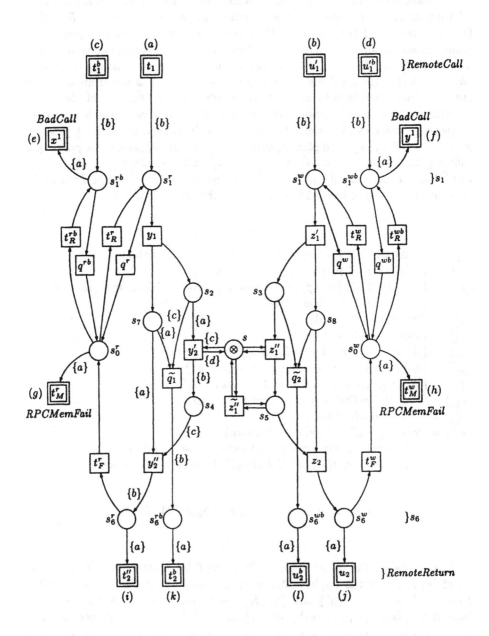

Fig. 24. Implementation *Impl'*

the one hand, and z_1', s_3 and z_1'' and $\widetilde{q}_2$, s_6^{wb} and u_2^b on the other hand, can be replaced by single transitions, say y_2, t_2^b, z_1 and u_2^b, respectively. Also, the singleton factor $\{read\}$ can be omitted at place s_6^r (this is justified by the fact that unfolding is stable with respect to isomorphic type changes, see section 2.2). The result is $Impl''$ as shown in figure 25. Claim 4 shows that $Impl'$ implements $Impl''$ while (as will be seen later) $Impl''$ still implements $Spec$.

Next, consider $Impl''$. Observe that $\{z_2\}$ and $\{u_2, t_F^w\}$ are in sequence by s_6^w. According to claim 4, they can be replaced by two transitions. Moreover, after suitably splitting places s_0^r and s_0^w, the 'null loops' between those places and s_1^{rb}, s_1^r and s_1^w, s_1^{wb} can be collapsed as shown at the end of section 3.3 (cf. figure 7). This yields $Impl'''$ as shown in figure 26.[15] It is still true that $Impl$ implements $Impl'''$.

In the next step, consider $Impl'''$. The sets $\{y_1\}$ and $\{t_2^b, t_2'\}$ are in sequence by s_2; so they can be replaced by two transitions. Moreover, the types of the places $s_1^{rb}, \ldots, s_1^{wb}$ can be modified by identifying all tokens $(p, read, arglist_0)$ on s_1^{rb} with (p, l_0) and identifying all tokens $(p, write, arglist_0')$ on s_1^{rb} with (p, l_0, v_0), as in table 1. This is justified by the fact that the parameters $arglist_0$ and $arglist_0'$ are 'forgotten' in the labels of x^1, y^1 ($BadCall$) and t_M^{r2}, t_M^{w2} ($RPCMemFail$). Moreover, the factors $\{read\}$ and $\{write\}$ can be neglected in the types of places s_1^{rb}, s_1^r, s_1^w and s_1^{wb}, which is justified by the fact, pronounced at the end of section 2.2, that unfolding is stable with respect to isomorphic type changes. Eventually, this yields the M-net $Impl^{(iv)}$ shown in figure 27. By claim 4 (and other claims stated in sections 2 and 3), $Impl$ implements $Impl^{(iv)}$.

$Impl^{(iv)}$ still contains internal loops (t_2', t_F^r and u_1'', t_F^w) that do not directly correspond to a part of $Spec$. We apply partial collapsing, as provided by claim 4, in order to transform $Impl^{(iv)}$ into yet another M-net which is even closer to $Spec$. To this end we exploit the fact that, in $Impl^{(iv)}$, s_1^r sequentialises $\{t_1, t_F^r\}$ and $\{t_2', t_M^{r1}, t_2^b\}$, and s_1^w sequentialises $\{u_1', t_F^w\}$ and $\{u_1'', t_M^{w1}, u_2^b\}$. Of the pairs that can be collapsed in each sequence, we collapse $[t_F^r, t_2']$, $[t_F^r, t_M^{r1}]$ and $[t_F^r, t_2^b]$ in the first sequence and $[t_F^w, u_1'']$, $[t_F^w, t_M^{w1}]$ and $[t_F^w, u_2^b]$ in the second sequence. Note that $[t_F^r, t_2^b]$ and $[t_F^w, u_2^b]$ disappear because their guards are **false**. We also recombine places s_1^{rb} and s_1^r (in $Impl^{(iv)}$) into place s_1^r (in $Impl^{(v)}$) and places s_1^{wb} and s_1^w (in $Impl^{(iv)}$) into place s_1^w (in $Impl^{(v)}$). $Impl^{(v)}$ is shown in figure 28. Transition x corresponds to $[t_F^r, t_2']$ and transition y corresponds to $[t_F^w, u_1'']$, while transition t_M^r corresponds to $[t_F^r, t_M^{r1}]$ and transition t_M^w corresponds to $[t_F^w, t_M^{w1}]$.

The relationship between $Impl^{(v)}$ and $Spec$ is indicated by the $\cong$ in figure 28. We are left with needing to prove that $Impl^{(v)}$ implements $Spec$, i.e. that every occurrence sequence of $Impl^{(v)}$ has a matching (i.e. equivalent on the visible interface) sequence in $Spec$. A difference between $Impl^{(v)}$ and $Spec$ is that $Impl^{(v)}$

---

[15] In going from $Impl''$ to $Impl'''$, we have renamed y_2 into t_2', z_1 into u_1'' and $\widetilde{z_1''}$ into $\widetilde{u_1''}$. This has been done in order to bring $Impl'''$ closer to $Spec$. Moreover, transition t_F^w in $Impl'''$ is really the collapsed counterpart of $[z_2, t_F^w]$ of $Impl''$. Similarly, u_2 in $Impl'''$ is the counterpart of $[z_2, u_2]$ of $Impl''$.

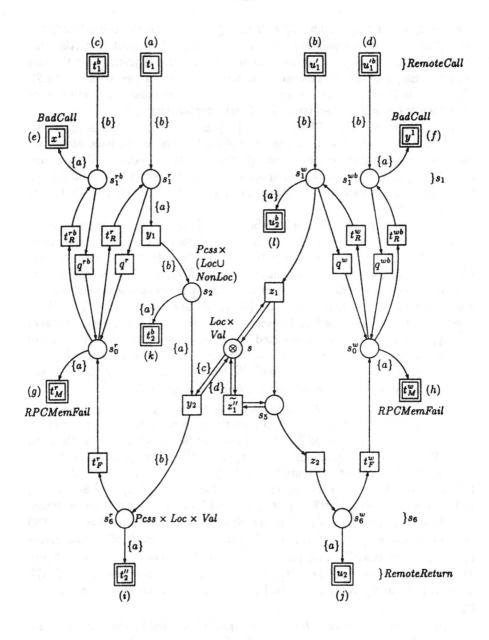

$\iota(s_1^w) = Pcss \times \{write\} \times \{[l, v]\}$

$\iota(u_2^b) = (\{RemoteReturn(p, write, [l, badarg])\} \mid a=(p, write, [l, v]) \wedge l \in NonLoc)$

$\iota(y_2) = (\emptyset \mid a=(p,l) \wedge c=(l,v) \wedge b=(p,l,v) \wedge d=(l,v))$

$\iota(t_2^b) = (\{RemoteReturn(p, read, [l, badarg])\} \mid a=(p,l) \wedge l \in NonLoc)$

$\iota(s_1^r) = Pcss \times \{read\} \times \{[l]\}$

$\iota(y_1) = (\emptyset \mid a=(p, read, [l]) \wedge b=(p,l))$.

Fig. 25. Implementation $Impl''$ and some of its inscriptions

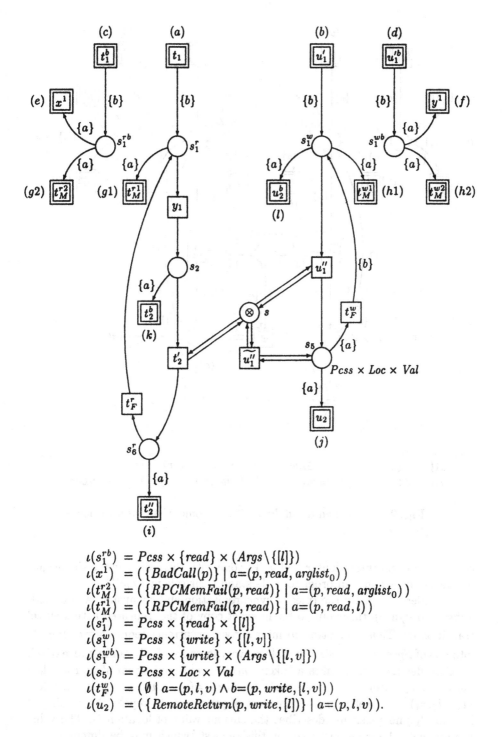

$$\iota(s_1^{rb}) = Pcss \times \{read\} \times (Args \setminus \{[l]\})$$
$$\iota(x^1) = (\{BadCall(p)\} \mid a=(p, read, arglist_0))$$
$$\iota(t_M^{r2}) = (\{RPCMemFail(p, read)\} \mid a=(p, read, arglist_0))$$
$$\iota(t_M^{r1}) = (\{RPCMemFail(p, read)\} \mid a=(p, read, l))$$
$$\iota(s_1^r) = Pcss \times \{read\} \times \{[l]\}$$
$$\iota(s_1^w) = Pcss \times \{write\} \times \{[l,v]\}$$
$$\iota(s_1^{wb}) = Pcss \times \{write\} \times (Args \setminus \{[l,v]\})$$
$$\iota(s_5) = Pcss \times Loc \times Val$$
$$\iota(t_F^w) = (\emptyset \mid a=(p,l,v) \wedge b=(p, write, [l,v]))$$
$$\iota(u_2) = (\{RemoteReturn(p, write, [l])\} \mid a=(p,l,v)).$$

Fig. 26. Implementation $Impl'''$ and some of its inscriptions

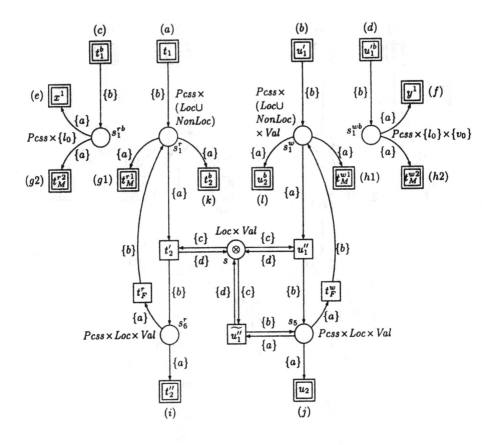

$$\iota(t_2') = (\emptyset \mid a{=}(p,l) \land l{\in}Loc \land c{=}(l,v) \land b{=}(p,l,v) \land d{=}(l,v))$$
$$\iota(t_2^b) = (\{RemoteReturn(p, read, [l, badarg])\} \mid a{=}(p,l) \land l{\in}NonLoc).$$

Fig. 27. Implementation $Impl^{(iv)}$ and some of its inscriptions

contains internal transitions x and y. To cope with this, we examine the origins of transitions x and y in order to understand their role in $Impl^{(v)}$.

Consider first y. By the rules of synchronisation and collapsing, and considering its origins, y turns out to be an exact copy of the 'repeated actual write' transition $\widetilde{u_1''}$. Thus, when transforming a given occurrence sequence τ of $Impl^{(v)}$ into one of $Spec$, we may simply replace every instance of y by an instance of $\widetilde{u_1''}$.

Consider next x. It takes a token $m_1 = (p_1, l_1, w)$ from s_6^r and a token $m_2 = (l_2, v_2)$ from s and returns a token $m_3{=}(p_3, l_3, v_3)$ to s_6^r and a token $m_3{=}(l_4, v_4)$ to s. Token m_1 is a request of process p_1 to repeat the reading of location l_1 and token m_2 describes the current value of location l_2. The value w represents the value last read by this request (which may be different from v_2, the actual value). The inscription of x shows that it identifies $p_1{=}p_3$ and

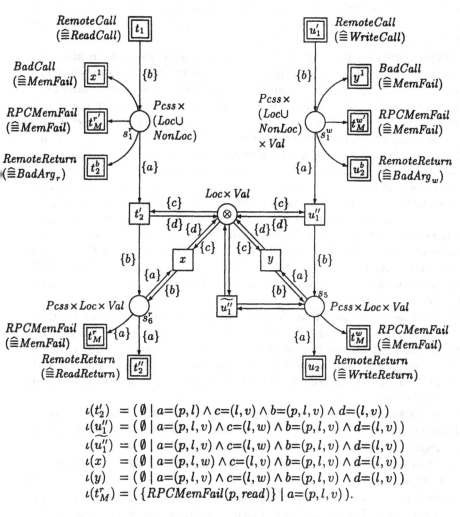

$$\iota(t_2') \; = \; (\,\emptyset \mid a{=}(p,l) \wedge c{=}(l,v) \wedge b{=}(p,l,v) \wedge d{=}(l,v)\,)$$
$$\iota(u_1'') \; = \; (\,\emptyset \mid a{=}(p,l,v) \wedge c{=}(l,w) \wedge b{=}(p,l,v) \wedge d{=}(l,v)\,)$$
$$\iota(\widetilde{u_1''}) \; = \; (\,\emptyset \mid a{=}(p,l,v) \wedge c{=}(l,w) \wedge b{=}(p,l,v) \wedge d{=}(l,v)\,)$$
$$\iota(x) \; = \; (\,\emptyset \mid a{=}(p,l,w) \wedge c{=}(l,v) \wedge b{=}(p,l,v) \wedge d{=}(l,v)\,)$$
$$\iota(y) \; = \; (\,\emptyset \mid a{=}(p,l,v) \wedge c{=}(l,w) \wedge b{=}(p,l,v) \wedge d{=}(l,v)\,)$$
$$\iota(t_M^r) \; = \; (\,\{RPCMemFail(p, read)\} \mid a{=}(p,l,v)\,).$$

Fig. 28. Implementation $Impl^{(v)}$ and some of its inscriptions

$l_1{=}l_2{=}l_3{=}l_4$, as well as values $v_2{=}v_3{=}v_4$. In particular, the token m_1 taken from place s_6^r may be different from token m_3 put back on that place. (Notice the difference to y where the token taken from s, rather than the token taken from s_5, may be different from the one put back there.)

Now let τ be an occurrence sequence of $Impl^{(v)}$. We will gradually transform τ into a matching occurrence sequence of $Spec$. By the previous considerations, we may assume that τ contains no instances of y. Furthermore, instances of t_M^r and t_M^w of $Impl^{(v)}$ may be identified with instances of v_3 and w_3, respectively, of $Spec$, by (g) and (h). A similar remark is true for instances of x^1, $t_M^{r'}$, t_2^b, y^1, $t_M^{w'}$ and u_2^b of $Impl^{(iv)}$. If τ contains no instances of x then there is nothing more to prove. So, assume now that τ contains at least one instance of x, say at index i, and with input tokens $m_1=(p_1,l_1,w)$ and $m_2=(l_1,v_1)$ and output tokens $m_3=(p_1,l_1,v_1)$ and $m_4=(l_1,v_1)$.

Suppose first that after this instance, τ contains some instance, say at index i, of either t_M^r or t_2'' with parameters (p_1,l_1,w') (some arbitrary value w' which may be different from w). Let j be a minimal index of such an occurrence after index i. Because place s_6^r is empty in the initial marking, some token with parameters p_1 and l_1 has been put there by some occurrence of transition t_2'. Let k be a maximal index of such an occurrence before index i. Then the section from k to j in τ can be interpreted in the following way: k is the initial production of a token $(p_1,l_1,.)$ on place s_6^r, all x-instances between k (exclusively) and j (of which there is at least one) are repeated reads of the same location by the same process, and j is the eventual consumption of token $(p_1,l_1,.)$ from place s_6^r. In particular, between k and j, no transition instance (other than the x instances and the instance of t_M^r or t_2'' at j) ever needs a token $(p_1,l_1,.)$ for its occurrence. It follows that when between k (inclusively) and j all instances of t_2' and x are erased, except for the last x instance, which is replaced by an instance of t_2', then the resulting sequence does not lose its property of being an occurrence sequence.

Suppose next (and last) that after the assumed instance of x at index i, there is no further instance of either t_M^r or t_2'' with parameters p_1 and l_1. Then by the same reasoning, it follows that in the entire tail of τ, tokens with parameters $(p_1,l_1,.)$ on s_6^r are used at most for instances of x. It follows that all such instances can be erased from τ without destroying its property of being an occurrence sequence.

This shows, then, that $Impl^{(v)}$ implements $Spec$ (with respect to empty δ and the obvious ρ). In sum, the proof has exhibited a sequence of M-nets, from $Impl$, $Impl'$ to $Impl^{(v)}$, and finally $Spec$, such that every element of the sequence implements its successor (if there is one), proving, in all, that $Impl$ implements $Spec$ as required. ∎6

Note that the last step of the proof cannot be applied to transition $\widetilde{u_1''}$ in the same way as to x. The main reason is that x modifies only place s_6^r, which can be kept under control as shown above, but $\widetilde{u_1''}$ modifies place s upon which other transitions such as t_2' depend, and hence the argument which was valid for x is invalid for $\widetilde{u_1''}$. In particular, it cannot be proved (and is indeed untrue) that $Impl$ implements $Spec2u$, i.e. unreliable memory without repeated writes.

Proof of claim 7

This is a general property of nets which are composed from others by synchronisation and restriction. Suppose that in the composed net some transition t does not progress. If t is a member of one of the constituent nets then this contradicts the progress property of the constituent net. If t is a synchronisation, say of two transitions of two constituent nets, then this contradicts the progress property for both of them. ∎7

Proof of claim 8

Suppose that τ is not *read*-complete. Then there is some last instance of tu_1 with label $\{RemoteCall(p_1, read, [l_1])\}$ in τ, such that τ contains no subsequent occurrence of tu_2 with the same parameters p_1 and $[l_1]$ (and some arbitrary value v_1). By the structure of the net, this implies that in every marking of the tail of τ determined by this last occurrence of tu_1, there is either a token $(p_1, read, [l_1])$ on s_1; or tokens (p_1, l_1) and (p_1, l_1) on s_7 and s_2, respectively; or tokens (p_1, l_1) and (p_1, l_1, v_1) on s_7 and s_4, respectively; or a token $(p_1, read, l_1, v_1)$ on s_6; or a token $(p_1, read, [l_1])$ on s_0. In the first case, this token activates y_1 or q (under the induced binding), and in the other cases, y_2', y_2'', both t_F and tu_2, and t_R are activated, respectively. Progress and the fact that the tail of τ in question does not contain tu_2 for this particular binding imply that the tail of τ contains an infinity of instances of the form $q t_R \ldots$ or $y_1 y_2' y_2'' t_F t_R \ldots$, all with the same bindings. This contradicts fairness towards y_1 or fairness towards tu_2.   ∎8

Proof of claim 10

It has to be shown that the observable part of a behaviour τ of $RPCImpl$ can – under the premise that tokens may not rest on places r_2 and r_3 longer than time ϵ – be retrieved from some behaviour of RPC. This can be seen as follows. Initially, the $RemoteCall$ transition of $RPCImpl$ puts three similar tokens on r_1, r_5 and r_6, say, respectively, m, n and n'. Thereafter, there are three alternatives for m, n and n'.

Firstly, m might get passed through to r_4, either via r_2 or via r_3. When this happens, m appears on r_4 within time $\delta + \epsilon$, since it may stay on r_1 not longer than δ and on r_2 or r_3 not longer than ϵ. In that case, n and n' are still present (at least for time δ) on r_5 and r_6, and thus the $RemoteReturn$ transition is enabled for a time span of δ and may occur during this period.

Secondly, m might get taken away from r_1 by a $BadCall$ transition. In that case, n and n' disappear simultaneously from r_5 and r_6.

Thirdly, m might get taken away from r_1 by t^2 or from r_4 by t^3. If this happens then n and n' are still present on r_5 and r_6, but they have no matching m and henceforth this triple of tokens will not contribute to enabling $RemoteReturn$. Therefore, the timeout transition occurs for n' and takes away n' from place r_6, and the $RPCFailure$ transition may or may not occur for n. (We might strengthen the implementation by requiring it to occur. However as this reduces behaviour, the proof covers the strengthened case as well.)

No other cases are possible. Moreover, the cases mentioned above are mutually exclusive.

In the first case, n and n' leave no observable trace other than together with m, and the trace of m can be simulated by a similar trace through RPC leading from a $RemoteCall$ to a $RemoteReturn$. In the second case, the trace of m (which is also the trace of n and n') can be simulated by a corresponding $BadCall$ execution of RPC. In the third case, both m and (possibly) n leave a trace. However, due to the fact that $RemoteReturn$ does not occur in this trace, it can be simulated by a trace of RPC, using the appropriate one of its $RPCFailure$ transitions, i.e. t'_F if m disappeared through t^2 and t_F if m disappeared through t^3.   ∎10

Observe that the last possibility – simulating the disappearance of token m through t^3 in $RPCImpl$ by executing t_F in RPC – relies crucially on the timing constraint of transition u^2 in $RPCImpl$ (which implies, in particular, that it cannot occur before time δ). Suppose, on the contrary, that u^2 can occur before time δ and consider an execution in $RPCImpl$ by which first u^2 and then y_1 is executed. This particular ordering of the two transitions cannot be simulated in RPC, at least not in the sense defined in section 3.3.

Note that this relies on the property that any transitions that can be synchronised with y_1 and z'_1 are not delayed. In our example, this concerns transitions $ReadCall$ and $WriteCall$ of $Speci$, $Speci'$ and $Speciu$ which satisfy this property because they do not have entry places. Any violation of this property – or, for that matter, any other hidden dependency between transitions u^2 and y_1 or z'_1 of $RPCImpl$ – has an influence on claim 10.

Constraint Oriented Temporal Logic Specification

The Dagstuhl RPC-Memory Specification Problem

Johan Blom, Bengt Jonsson *

Dept. of Computer Systems,Uppsala University,Box 325,S-751 05 Uppsala, SWEDEN

Abstract. We present a partial solution to the Dagstuhl RPC-Memory Specification Problem which is carried out in linear-time temporal logic (LTL). Our language is quite similar to TLA (Temporal Logic of Actions) by Lamport. However, our use of this language provides some (in our opinion) interesting novelties. A major contribution of this paper is in our opinion a demonstration of different structuring mechanisms that exist in LTL. We use flexible predicates to represent synchronizing events, as in e.g., LOTOS, that serve for communication between components. In the specification of a component, the central part is a set of formulas that for each state variable states the constraints under which it may change, and for each event states the constraints (in terms of state changes) under which it may occur. We define a graphical syntax for parts of a temporal logic specification that involve "control".

This contribution contains solutions to the specification problems, except for the timing extension, i.e., we solve Problem 1, 2 and 3 except for the verification parts which is only briefly covered.

1 Introduction

This paper presents a formal specification of a simple memory interface, the Dagstuhl RPC-Memory Specification Problem. This memory interface has been informally described by Broy and Lamport, who have then inspired several researchers to present a formal specification of it in a language of their choice. The overall ambition has been to create a common case study through which different specification formalisms can be compared in a rather precise way. By preparing specifications of (almost) the same system, one can really compare several aspects of different specification formalisms. This is in contrast to some earlier common case studies, such as e.g., the "Lake Arrowhead Workshop" [5], where the contributed specifications were often rather different, making comparison difficult.

---

* e-mail:{johan,bengt}@DoCS.UU.SE

In this paper, we present a specification of the memory interface in linear-time temporal logic (LTL), as in [9] or [6]. The expressiveness of LTL allows a close relationship between specifications and informal requirements in a structured way. Our specification style uses a restricted subset of LTL which is rather similar to TLA. Our structuring of the solution is similar to that of [7] in that we strive to decompose the specification as much as possible into small independent parts. In fact the actual decomposition used is very similar. In the solution based on TLA [1], LTL is used to specify each component as a state machine. The specification represents the effects of each operation on all variables of the component.

Our specification style is constraint based in the following sense. In the specification of a component, the central part is a set of formulas that for each state variable states the constraints under which it may change, and for each event states the constraints (in terms of state changes) under which it may occur. In this way, we hope to arrive at specifications that give the least possible restrictions on the behavior of a component.

Our style is constraint based and we specify only minimal constraints for events and variables. The intention is to give a minimal specification of the behavior of the memory in the sense that we have a close relationship to the informal requirements.

The main contribution of this paper is in our opinion a demonstration of different structuring mechanisms that exist in LTL. We believe that the structure of our specification fairly well reflects the logical structure of the behavior of the memory interface. The mechanisms that we want to emphasize are the following.

- Logical conjunction is used to combine specifications of different components.
- Universal quantification is used to combine parameterized specifications of components with similar behavior.
- Existential quantification is used to hide local variables and events of a component.
- Synchronization between modules is achieved through events. Components are composed into systems by renaming and identification of synchronization events.
- We define a graphical syntax for parts of a temporal logic specification that involve "control".

A specification is based on variables which represent the current state of a system, and events that represent synchronizing interactions between components of a system. As stated, a central part in the specification of a component is a set of constraints. These are of one of the following forms:

1. *Event* $\implies$ *Transition_formula*
2. *Changed(Set_of_variables)* $\implies$ *Set_of_events*

Formula (1) states that the event *Event* can occur only under certain constrains on variable changes (as given by *Transition_formula*), and formula (2) states that only events in the set *Set_of_events* may change any of the variables in the set *Set_of_variables*. We try not to insist on interleaving between actions of different components. This style was used in our earlier work on specifying telephone services [2].

This paper is structured as follows. In the next section, we present rather informally LTL as a specification language. Section 2 contains the formal semantics of LTL. Our specification style is presented in Section 4. Section 5 outlines the overall structure of our specification. Each of the following sections contain specifications of the main components of the specification: Section 6 the Memory Cells, Section 7 the interface to the Memory, Section 8 the RPC Component and Section 9 the Clerk component.

2 Temporal Logic

In this section, we present the version of linear-time temporal logic that will be used in the paper. The logic is essentially that of Lamport's Temporal Logic of Actions (TLA), with the addition of flexible predicate variables. The flexible predicate variables are intended to represent synchronization events, as in e.g., LOTOS [11].

2.1 Syntax and Informal Semantics

We assume a set of *individual variables* and a set of *predicate variables*, where each predicate variable has a nonnegative arity. We also assume a domain $\mathcal{D}$ of individuals into which we interpret the individual variables. A *state s* is a mapping which maps each individual variable to an element of $\mathcal{D}$ and which maps each n-ary predicate variable to an n-ary relation over $\mathcal{D}$ (i.e., a subset of $\mathcal{D}^n$). A *behavior* is an infinite sequence of states. A variable may thus be mapped to different values in different states of a behavior. However, for convenience we may declare some individual variables as *rigid*, meaning that they must be mapped to the same value in all states within a behavior.

Behaviors are intended to represent executions of a system. For example, assuming only a single individual variable x and the predicate variable *inc*, the behavior

$$\sigma \stackrel{\Delta}{=} \{ \begin{matrix} x \stackrel{\Delta}{=} 0, \\ inc \stackrel{\Delta}{=} T \end{matrix} \} \rightarrow \{ \begin{matrix} x \stackrel{\Delta}{=} 1, \\ inc \stackrel{\Delta}{=} F \end{matrix} \} \rightarrow \{ \begin{matrix} x \stackrel{\Delta}{=} 1, \\ inc \stackrel{\Delta}{=} T \end{matrix} \} \rightarrow \{ \begin{matrix} x \stackrel{\Delta}{=} 2, \\ inc \stackrel{\Delta}{=} F \end{matrix} \} \rightarrow \{ \begin{matrix} x \stackrel{\Delta}{=} 2, \\ inc \stackrel{\Delta}{=} F \end{matrix} \} \cdots$$

represents an execution where x is incremented from 0 upwards. We use T and F to denote true and false. The predicate variable *inc* represents an event which is connected to transitions between states in which the variable x is incremented. In the semantics, if *inc* is true in a state, then we informally take this to mean that the event *inc* occurs in the following state transition.

Linear-time temporal logic (LTL), restricted to the future fragment, is a formalism for expressing properties of behaviors. We assume a set of pre-defined constants, functions, and predicate symbols with fixed interpretations over $\mathcal{D}$.

A *term* (in LTL) is constructed from constant symbols and individual variables, using pre-defined function symbols and the unary temporal operator $^+$.

For a term t, the term t^+ means "the next value of t", i.e., the interpretation of t^+ at position i is the interpretation of t at position $i + 1$.

An *atomic formula* is an n-ary predicate symbol or n-ary predicate variable applied to n terms. *Formulas* are built from atomic formulas, using standard first-order logic connectives (including quantification over individual variables) and the unary temporal operators $\Box$ and $\Diamond$. For a formula ϕ, the formula $\Box \phi$ means "always in the future ϕ", and the formula $\Diamond \phi$ means "sometime in the future ϕ".

3   Semantics

In the following paragraphs, we define the semantics of LTL formulas more precisely. The reader who is already familiar with LTL may skip to section 4.

Each term will be given a certain meaning in each state of a behavior. For a term t, let $\sigma[i](t)$ denote the value assigned to the term t in $\sigma[i]$, the ith state of behavior σ. Note that $\sigma[i]$ is a state which gives a value $\sigma[i](v)$ to each variable v. We define $\sigma[i](t)$ as follows.

- $\sigma[i](v)$ is already defined by $\sigma[i]$ for an individual variable or a predicate variable v
- $\sigma[i](f(t_1,\ldots,t_n)) = f(\sigma[i](t_1) , \ldots , \sigma[i](t_n))$ if f is a pre-defined n-ary function symbol. Constant symbols can be treated as 0-ary function symbols. Note that we use the same notation for a function symbol and its intended meaning.
- $\sigma[i](t^+) = \sigma[i+1](t)$, i.e., the value of t^+ in the ith state is the value of t in the $(i+1)^{st}$ state.

Formulas are interpreted with respect to a certain position in a behavior. We use $(\sigma, i) \models \phi$ to denote that the formula ϕ is true in the ith state of the behavior σ. We define $(\sigma, i) \models \phi$ as follows.

- $(\sigma, i) \models P(t_1,\ldots,t_n)$ **iff** $P(\sigma[i](t_1),\ldots,\sigma[i](t_n))$ is true for a pre-defined n-ary predicate symbol P,
- $(\sigma, i) \models e(t_1,\ldots,t_n)$ **iff** $\langle \sigma[i](t_1),\ldots,\sigma[i](t_n) \rangle \in \sigma[i](e)$ for an n-ary predicate variable e,
- $(\sigma, i) \models \neg\phi$ **iff** not $(\sigma, i) \models \phi$
- $(\sigma, i) \models (\phi_1 \land \phi_2)$ **iff** $(\sigma, i) \models \phi_1$ and $(\sigma, i) \models \phi_2$.
  Other boolean connectives ($\lor$, $\implies$, etc.) are treated analogously.
- $(\sigma, i) \models \Box \phi$ **iff** $(\sigma, j) \models \phi$ for all $j \geq i$
- $(\sigma, i) \models \Diamond \phi$ **iff** $(\sigma, j) \models \phi$ for some $j \geq i$

Quantification deserves special attention. Let v be a individual variable. We say that the behavior σ' is a v-*variant* of the behavior σ if for each i the states $\sigma[i]$ and $\sigma'[i]$ differ at most in the interpretation given to v. Similarly we define an e-*variant* for a predicate variable e. (A variant must of course obey the restriction that rigid variables do not change their values in a behavior). Define

$- (\sigma, i) \models \exists e : \phi$ **iff** $(\sigma', i) \models \phi$ for some e-variant σ' of σ.
$- (\sigma, i) \models \exists v : \phi$ **iff** $(\sigma', i) \models \phi$ for some v-variant σ' of σ.
$- (\sigma, i) \models \forall v : \phi$ **iff** $(\sigma', i) \models \phi$ for all v-variants σ' of σ.

4 Using LTL to Specify Concurrent Systems

In this section, we outline how we will use LTL, in this paper, to specify components of concurrent systems.

We model a system by the following primitives A specification of a system is based on the following primitive concepts.

- *individual variables* (also called state variables) represent the state of the system,
- *predicate variables* are used to model events which represent interaction between components, or between components and the environment of the system. Each event can occur at some of the state transitions of a behavior. In a behavior, events may be associated with the transition from one state to the next. More precisely, an *event* is of the form $e(d_1, \ldots, d_n)$, where e is an n-ary predicate variable, and $d_1, \ldots, d_n$ are elements of $\mathcal{D}$. In a behavior σ, we represent the fact that *"event $e(d_1, \ldots, d_n)$ occurs at the ith transition, i.e., the transition between $\sigma[i-1]$ and $\sigma[i]$"* by $\langle d_1, \ldots, d_n \rangle \in \sigma[i-1](e)$. Informally, this means that $e(d_1, \ldots, d_n)$ is true in a state iff the event $e(d_1, \ldots, d_n)$ occurs in the subsequent transition.

A system may consist of a set of components. We regard each components as acting on a set of state variables, each of which can be local to the component or shared with other components. Components may also interact by synchronizing over events, as in e.g., LOTOS [11] or I/O-automata [8]. In the following subsections, we will outline the style that we use for specification a system consisting of components. First, we describe how state transitions of a component are specified, thereafter we describe the structure of component specifications, and finally we outline how component specifications are combined.

4.1 Specification of State Changes

In our specification style, we intend to specify a component by constraints between state changes and events. These constraints will for each event specify conditions, in terms of state changes, under which it may occur, and for each variable specify the conditions under which it may change. To make this idea more precise, define a *change formula* to be either

1. a disjunction of formulas $v^+ \neq v$ for individual variables v, or
2. an atomic formula formed by applying a predicate variable to terms.

Define a *transition formula* to be a formula in which the only temporal operator is the operator $^+$, which may only be applied to individual variables. A *basic constraint* is then of the form

$$\forall v_1, \ldots, v_n : [change \implies trans]$$

where *change* is a change formula, where *trans* is a transition formula, and where $v_1, \ldots, v_n$ are variables. We let $\text{Changed}(v_1, \ldots, v_n)$ stand for $v_1^+ \neq v_1 \vee \cdots \vee v_n^+ \neq v_n$. As an example, suppose we are specifying a memory cell holding one value (represented by the individual variable *val*), to which we can apply a read operation, represented by the unary predicate variable *Read*, and a write operation, represented by the unary predicate variable *Write*. Each state change in a behavior of such a memory would be specified by three basic constraints.

$$\forall v : Read(v) \implies val = v$$
$$\wedge \forall v : Write(v) \implies val^+ = v$$
$$\wedge \text{Changed}(val) \implies \exists v : Write(v)$$

This specification tries to capture the minimal constraints between read operation, write operations, and changes to the individual variable *val*. We refer to the two first conjuncts as *event constraints*, and to the last conjunct as a *frame constraint*. A frame constraint is intended to take care of the conditions under which "nothing else changes", and our solution to this "frame problem" is analogous to the one suggested in [3]. We observe that our specification style does not use the modeling assumption about interleaving between different events of a component, which is common in many specification approaches. The above specification of a memory allows simultaneous read and write operations in a transition between two states, as long as these are not inconsistent with each other. A major reason for not using the interleaving assumption, is that it is not part of the temporal logic framework, and that it must therefore be introduced by an explicit logical formula. To illustrate, an "interleaving" specification of state changes of the above mentioned memory component might look something like

$$\exists v : \quad Read(v) \wedge val = v \wedge val^+ = v$$
$$\wedge \forall v1 \neq v : \neg Read(v1)$$
$$\wedge \forall v : \neg Write(v)$$
$$\vee \exists v : \quad Write(v) \wedge val^+ = v$$
$$\wedge \forall v1 \neq v : \neg Write(v1)$$
$$\wedge \forall v : \neg Read(v)$$

The formula is now considerably larger, due to the fact that exclusion between events must be explicitly specified.

4.2 State transition diagrams

It is often convenient to identify one state variable as *control variable* and use a state transition diagram to define transition formulas. In this paper, we will use this idea in the following way.

A state transition diagram consist of nodes and arcs, see Figure 1. Nodes represents different values of a control variable. The label in a node is the value represented by that node. In Figure 1, there are two possible values ($state_1$ and $state_2$) for the control variable. The control variable is assumed in this paper to always have the name *ctr*. Each arc in the diagram is labeled by

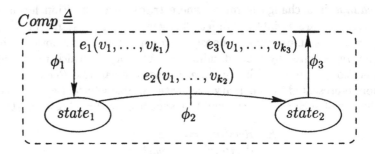

Fig. 1. A state transition diagram representing parts of the formal specification of a component.

1. an atomic formula of the form $e(v_1, \ldots, v_n)$ where e is a predicate variable and $v_1, \ldots, v_n$ individual variables.
2. a transition formula ϕ without predicate variables.

For an arc from $state_1$ to $state_2$ labeled by the transition formula ϕ, let ϕ' denote the transition formula $\phi \wedge ctr = state_1 \wedge ctr^+ = state_2$. Let $e_1, \ldots, e_n$ be the predicate variables that occur in a diagram. For $i = 1, \ldots, n$, let $\phi_{i1} \ldots \phi_{im_i}$ be the m_i transition formulas that label arcs that are also labeled by e_i. The state transition diagram then denotes the conjunction of the formulas

$$e_i \implies \phi'_{i1} \vee \ldots \vee \phi'_{im_i}$$

for $i = 1, \ldots, n$.

In a state transition diagram, arcs may lead from one node to another, or they may lead between nodes and the boundary of the diagram. For an arc from $state_1$ to the boundary labeled by the transition formula ϕ, let ϕ' denote the transition formula $\phi \wedge ctr = state_1 \wedge ctr' = \bot$. For an arc from the boundary to $state_2$ labeled by the transition formula ϕ, let ϕ' denote the transition formula $\phi \wedge ctr' = \bot \wedge ctr = state_2$. We assume that different occurrences of the same predicate variable e are connected with the same tuple $v_1, \ldots, v_n$ of variables. This interpretation of state transition diagrams is similar to that in coloured Petri Nets [10].

We may give a name to such a specification (here *Comp*) as a heading to the state transition diagram, so that the formula represented by the diagram inside the boundary can be used as a component in larger specifications.

4.3 Specifying Components

In general, a specification of a component is a conjunction of the following parts.

- An initial condition over the individual variables
- A formula ϕ_S giving safety requirements for the component, which is the conjunction of event constraints and frame constraints.

– A liveness formula ϕ_L giving progress requirements for the component.

Liveness formulas will often be given as a conjunction of fairness properties. For a transition formula ϕ, define

$$Enabled(\phi) \triangleq \exists c_1, \ldots, c_n : \phi[c_1, \ldots, c_n / v_1', \ldots, v_n']$$

where $v_1', \ldots, v_n'$ are all primed variables in ϕ. Define

$$WF(\phi) \triangleq \Diamond \Box \; Enabled(\phi) \implies \Box \Diamond \phi$$
$$SF(\phi) \triangleq \Box \Diamond \; Enabled(\phi) \implies \Box \Diamond \phi$$

$WF(\phi)$ specifies that if a state transition satisfying ϕ is continuously enabled beyond some point in a behavior, then the behavior must contain infinitely many state transitions that satisfy ϕ. $SF(\phi)$ specifies that if a state transition satisfying ϕ is enabled infinitely many times in a behavior, then the behavior must contain infinitely many state transitions that satisfy ϕ.

Local variables: In addition, state variables and event variables of a component can be made local by existential quantification, which is added on top of the conjunction between initial condition, safety formula and liveness formula. Existential quantification prohibits a variable to be referenced outside the component specification.

Similarly events can be made only internally accessible. Arcs attached to the boundary of the diagram are, by convention, also visible from the outside of the component. Internal events have no connection with the boundary.

4.4 Combining components

Specifications of components with different behavior are combined by conjunctions. Communication between components is specified by a predicate which specifies how event predicates of the participating components are connected. Typically this predicate will specify equivalences between certain change formulas specifying the occurrence of events.

Parameterized components: To specify a collection of components, which exhibit similar behavior and are distinguished only by the value of some parameters, we represent the parameters by rigid variables. The component specification will be a formula $\phi(p)$ which depends on the value of a parameter (p) (the case with several parameters is straight-forward).

A collection of such components is specified by the formula $\forall p \in PId : \phi(p)$ PIdis the set of parameter values of the components in the collection.

5 Overall Structure of the Specification

In the original problem description [4], the unreliable memory is structured into several components. We will structure our specification into the same components. The components are

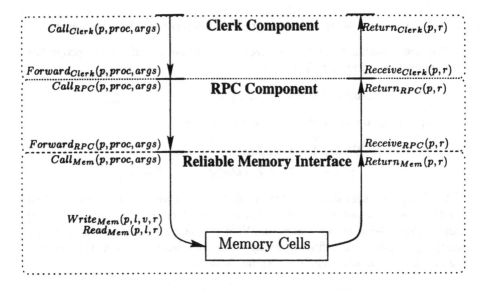

Fig. 2. Overview of the components in the specification

- A Reliable Memory Component containing a memory which can be accessed through an interface. Our specification *MemSpec* of the Memory Component has two parts:
  - A "naked" memory *Memory*, consisting of a set of locations that store values to which synchronizing read and write operations can be performed.
  - An interface, specified by *RelMemInt*, which contains the interface to the "naked" memory, providing a set of callable procedures for performing read and write operations.
- An RPC Component through which remote procedure calls can be made to the Memory Component. The RPC Component is specified by *RPCSpec*.
- A Clerk Component *ClerkSpec* which manages calls to the RPC Component so that all components together can act in the same way as just the Memory Component

Figure 2 gives an overview of the components in the specification.

6 The Memory Cells

In this section, we present a specification of the innermost part of the memory. This part assumes a set MemLocs of locations, each of which can contain a value from a set MemVals. For each location we will specify a corresponding memory cell. The specification of each memory cell assumes

Variables In the specification of each memory cell, we only need one local variable val which takes values from MemVals and is the value of the current location in the memory cell.

Initial Conditions Initially all cells contain the value InitVal.

Events are the following:

$Write_{Mem}(p, l, v, r)$ denotes that a call, identified by p, performs a write operation on the memory, writing value v into location l and getting the return value r.

$Read_{Mem}(p, l, r)$ denotes that a call, identified by p, performs a read operation on the memory, reading from location l and getting the return value r.

There are no liveness properties for this component, since a memory cell is considered to be a passive component in the complete specification of the memory.

$$
\begin{aligned}
MemActs(l) &\triangleq \forall p, v, r : \\[2mm]
&Write_{Mem}(p, l, v, r) \implies \left(\begin{array}{l} \left(\begin{array}{l} (l \notin \mathsf{MemLocs} \vee v \notin \mathsf{MemVals}) \\ \wedge\, r = \text{``BadArg''} \end{array} \right) \\ \vee \left( \begin{array}{l} l \in \mathsf{MemLocs} \wedge v \in \mathsf{MemVals} \\ \wedge\, val^+ = v \\ \wedge\, r = \text{``OK''} \end{array} \right) \end{array} \right) \\[2mm]
\wedge & \\[2mm]
&Read_{Mem}(p, l, r) \implies \left(\begin{array}{l} \left(\begin{array}{l} l \notin \mathsf{MemLocs} \\ \wedge\, r = \text{``BadArg''} \end{array} \right) \\ \vee \left(\begin{array}{l} l \in \mathsf{MemLocs} \\ \wedge\, r = val \end{array} \right) \end{array} \right)
\end{aligned}
$$

$$
Memory \triangleq \left(\begin{array}{l} \forall l : \exists val : \\ \quad val = \mathsf{InitVal} \\ \wedge \Box \left(\begin{array}{l} MemActs(l) \\ \wedge\, \mathrm{Changed}(val) \implies \exists p, v : Write_{Mem}(p, l, v, \text{``OK''}) \end{array} \right) \end{array} \right)
$$

Fig. 3. Specification of the Memory Cell at location l.

The transition formula $MemActs(l)$ specifies the effect of an operation on the single memory location l. The operation represented by $Write_{Mem}(p, l, v, r)$ tries to write value v at memory location l. Assuming that $l \in$ MemLocs, if the arguments to the Write event are well-formed (i.e., $v \in$ MemVals), the value of the location will be v after the event. Return value will be "OK" in this case. Otherwise, an exception occurs, indicated by the return value "BadArg". The operation represented by a $Read_{Mem}(p, l, r)$ returns the value from location l in the memory, still assuming that $l \in$ MemLocs.

Memory completely specifies the behavior of all memory cells. For each value of l the specification prescribes the existence of a local variable *val* such that the action formula, $MemActs(l)$ and the frame formula is satisfied. For all values of MemLocs that are in l, this is in accordance with the behavior of a memory cell. For other values of l, the specification tells to raise exception for all calls to the memory with such an argument. In this case the value of *val* is irrelevant. The frame formula for *Memory* states that the contents of a memory cell l may only be changed by a *Write* operation.

The given specification will allow concurrent Read and Write events at the same location l because the Write event constrains the value of *val* after the operation, whereas Read depends only on the value of *val* before the operation.

7   The Memory Interface

7.1   Unreliable Memory Interface

In this section, we specify the interface to the memory cells that were specified in the previous section

The specification of the Memory Interface (Figure 4) specifies the behavior of calls to the memory. Several calls can be active simultaneously, but at most one call for each process identifier. For each process identifier $p \in PId$ the behavior of a call with process identifier p is specified.

Variables In the specification of a call with process identifier p we use the following individual variables.

    ctr is a control variable. The possible control states are:

        $\perp$ denotes that there is no call with process identifier p currently in the memory interface.

        badarg denotes that the arguments to the call are not syntactically correct and should be neglected.

        incoming denotes that the call has been received and that the corresponding operation must still be carried out (e.g., the "Read" or "Write" operation has not yet been performed on the memory cell by the calling interface).

        done denotes that the call has been received and the corresponding operation has been performed, or that a failure has occurred.

    proc is the procedure name (in this case "Read" or "Write").

    args is a list of the arguments to the procedure.

    ret is the return value in the case that $ctr = done$, otherwise it is insignificant.

Events The synchronizing events between this module and others are

    $Call_{Mem}(p, pr, ar)$ denotes a calling event by process p to the memory interface with procedure pr and arguments ar. The parameter ar is a list which contains all arguments to the procedure.

$Return_{Mem}(p, r)$ denotes the return to process p of a call with return value r.

The $Write_{Mem}(p, l, v, r)$ and $Read_{Mem}(p, l, r)$ events have the same intended meaning as in Section 6.

Initial Conditions Initially there are no calls in the component.

Safety and Liveness properties The safety requirements, $MemIntSafe(p)$, is the conjunction of:

1. $MemIntActs(p)$ which specifies conditions and effects of the events, (to be elaborated below). The formula can more suitably be written as a state-transition diagram in which transitions between control states are labeled with events and procedures on variables, as in Figure 4.

2. Frame axioms telling that ctr and ret can be changed by all events, but $proc$ and $args$ only by $Call_{Mem}(p, pr, ar)$. This is important to keep in mind when reading $MemActs(p)$ where we do not have to say explicitly that $proc$ and $args$ are unchanged.

The liveness requirements for the memory interface states that once a call is in state $incoming$, (1) eventually the corresponding operation is performed and (2) the call must be returned. The first condition is ensured by weak fairness on a step from $incoming$ to $done$. Because of the $Retry_{Mem}$ event, which removes the return value, we can have a situation in which $Return_{Mem}$ events are repeatedly disabled. Therefore the second condition is ensured by strong fairness on a step from $done$ to $\bot$.

A call to the memory is made by the $Call_{Mem}$ event, if the arguments pr and ar are syntactically correct. We assume a predicate $GoodArgs(pr, ar)$ which is true if the arguments pr and ar are syntactically correct. In the next state the individual variables $proc$ and $args$ are initialized.

If a call to $Write_{Mem}$ has been received (i.e., $ctr = incoming$, $proc =$ "Write" , $args = [l, v]$ for some l and v) then the $Write$ event can be performed with value v at memory location l. Note that the effect of the $Write_{Mem}$ event on the memory itself was specified in Section 6, Figure 3. After the Write event there will also be a return value from the memory in ret, either "OK" or "BadArg", indicating whether the Write(l,v) operation was legal or not.

If a call to $Read_{Mem}$ has been received (i.e., $ctr = incoming$, $proc =$ "Read" , $args = [l]$ for some l) then a Read event can be performed. Note that the effect of the $Read_{Mem}$ operation on the memory itself was specified in the previous section. After the Read event there will also be a return value from the memory cell in ret, either the value at memory location l or "BadArg", indicating whether the Read(l) operation was legal or not.

$Return_{Mem}$ can be performed when the procedure call has returned a value or an exception has been raised (i.e., $ctr = done$).

Internal events In addition to the externally visible events defined above there are two internal events. The event $Fail_{Mem}$ specifies that a call has been received (i.e., $ctr = incoming$) but the memory cannot be read. In this case the exception

$MemIntActs(p) \triangleq$

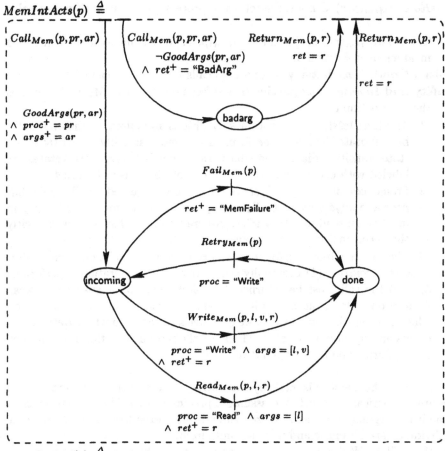

$MemIntInit(p) \triangleq ctr = \bot$

$$MemIntSafe(p) \triangleq \Box \left(\begin{array}{l} MemIntActs(p) \\ \wedge \, \text{Changed}(ctr, ret) \implies \begin{array}{l} \exists pr, ar, l, v, r : \\ \left(\begin{array}{l} Call_{Mem}(p, pr, ar) \\ \vee \, Write_{Mem}(p, l, v, r) \\ \vee \, Read_{Mem}(p, l, r) \\ \vee \, Return_{Mem}(p, r) \\ \vee \, Retry_{Mem}(p) \\ \vee \, Fail_{Mem}(p) \end{array} \right) \end{array} \\ \wedge \, \text{Changed}(proc, args) \implies \exists pr, ar : Call_{Mem}(p, pr, ar) \end{array} \right)$$

$$MemIntLive(p) \triangleq \left(\begin{array}{l} \text{WF}(\, ctr = incoming \wedge ctr^+ = done \,) \\ \wedge \, \text{SF}(\, ctr = done \wedge ctr^+ = \bot \,) \end{array} \right)$$

$MemInt(p) \triangleq \exists Retry_{Mem}, Fail_{Mem} : \exists ctr, ret, proc, args :$
$\qquad MemIntInit(p) \wedge MemIntSafe(p) \wedge MemIntLive(p)$

Fig. 4. The specification of a call with process identifier p in the Memory Interface

"MemFailure" is raised and ctr is changed to $done$ with no communication with the memory.

The $Retry_{Mem}$ event tries to redo an already performed "Write" operation in control state $done$. This is accomplished through remarking the procedure as unperformed i.e., $ctr^+ = incoming$.

7.2   Reliable Memory Interface

The preceding section specified an unreliable Memory Interface through the $Fail_{Mem}$ event. A more reliable memory component, $RelMemInt(p)$ can easily be obtained from $MemInt(p)$ by simply removing the $Fail_{Mem}$ event from the specification. In this case we can define the entire component as

$$RelMemIntSafe(p) \stackrel{\Delta}{=} MemIntSafe(p) \land \Box \neg Fail_{Mem}(p)$$

$$RelMemInt(p) \stackrel{\Delta}{=} \begin{array}{l} \exists Retry_{Mem}, Fail_{Mem} : \exists ctr, ret, proc, args : \\ MemIntInit(p) \land RelMemIntSafe(p) \land MemIntLive(p) \end{array}$$

7.3   Solution to Problem 1

The specification of the entire memory now becomes the following. Define an unreliable memory component to be

$$MemSpec \stackrel{\Delta}{=} \begin{array}{l} \exists Read_{Mem}, Write_{Mem} : \forall p \in PId : \\ MemInt(p) \land Memory \end{array}$$

A more reliable memory component is analogously

$$RMemSpec \stackrel{\Delta}{=} \begin{array}{l} \exists Read_{Mem}, Write_{Mem} : \forall p \in PId : \\ RelMemInt(p) \land Memory \end{array}$$

We can now look more closely at Problem 1:

1 (a) The Memory Component is specified by $MemSpec$, and the Reliable Memory Component is specified by $RMemSpec$.

1 (b) We see that $RMemSpec \implies MemSpec$ because $RelMemIntSafe(p) \implies MemIntSafe(p)$ and the other parts of the specifications stay the same.

1 (c) It is allowed by $MemSpec$ always to raise "MemFailure"-exceptions, since we have no constraints that forbid this. There could be liveness constraints, but no such are mentioned in the problem. The problem description simply says *"The memory must eventually issue a return for every Read and Write call."*

$RPCActs(p) \triangleq$

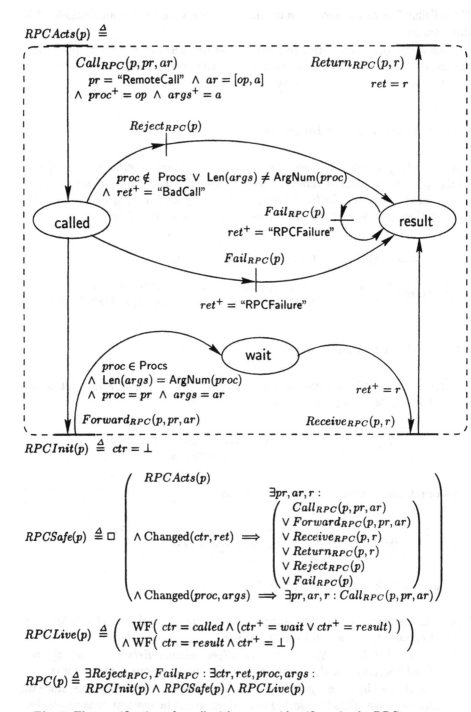

$RPCInit(p) \triangleq ctr = \bot$

$$RPCSafe(p) \triangleq \Box \left(\begin{array}{l} RPCActs(p) \\ \land\, Changed(ctr, ret) \implies \left(\begin{array}{l} \exists pr, ar, r : \\ \quad Call_{RPC}(p, pr, ar) \\ \quad \lor\, Forward_{RPC}(p, pr, ar) \\ \quad \lor\, Receive_{RPC}(p, r) \\ \quad \lor\, Return_{RPC}(p, r) \\ \quad \lor\, Reject_{RPC}(p) \\ \quad \lor\, Fail_{RPC}(p) \end{array} \right) \\ \land\, Changed(proc, args) \implies \exists pr, ar, r : Call_{RPC}(p, pr, ar) \end{array} \right)$$

$$RPCLive(p) \triangleq \left(\begin{array}{l} WF\big(\, ctr = called \land (ctr^+ = wait \lor ctr^+ = result)\, \big) \\ \land\, WF\big(\, ctr = result \land ctr^+ = \bot\, \big) \end{array} \right)$$

$RPC(p) \triangleq \exists Reject_{RPC}, Fail_{RPC} : \exists ctr, ret, proc, args :$
$\qquad\qquad RPCInit(p) \land RPCSafe(p) \land RPCLive(p)$

Fig. 5. The specification of a call with process identifier p in the RPC component

8   Problem 2 – The RPC Component

In this section we give a specification of an RPC component (Figure 5), which relays procedure calls from the sender to the receiver, and relays return values back to the sender. As in the specification of the Memory Interface in Section 7, the component consists of a number of calls parameterized by a process identifier p of the calling process.

Variables In the specification of a call with process identifier p we use the following individual variables.

ctr is a control state. The possible control states are:

$\perp$ denotes that the there is no call with process identifier p currently in the RPC component.

called denotes that the call has been received but not yet forwarded.

wait denotes that the call has been forwarded but not yet received.

result denotes that the call has been forwarded and received but not yet returned.

proc is a procedure name.

args is a list of the arguments to the procedure.

ret is the return value if $ctr = result$.

Events In the specification, certain events are used to synchronize state changes in the *RPC* components and state changes in other components. These synchronizing events are also referred to as events. We describe these as follows.

$Call_{RPC}(p, \text{``RemoteCall''}, ar)$ denotes that process p calls the *RPC* component with procedure "RemoteCall" and parameters ar. The parameter ar is a list that contains the arguments to RemoteCall(op,a) where op is the procedure name and a its arguments.

$Forward_{RPC}(p, pr, ar)$ denotes that the call from process p with procedure pr and arguments ar is forwarded by the *RPC* component to the receiver.

$Receive_{RPC}(p, r)$ denotes that the call from process p is returned from the receiver with return value r.

$Return_{RPC}(p, r)$ denotes that the call from process p is returned to the calling process with return value r.

The formal specification of these events is given in Figure 5.

Initial Conditions Initially there are no calls in the component.

Safety and Liveness properties The safety requirements, $RPCSafe(p)$, is the conjunction of:

1. $RPCActs(p)$ which specifies conditions and effects of the events. In Figure 5 the formula is written as a state-transition diagram.
2. Frame axioms telling that ctr and ret can be changed by all events, but $proc$ and $args$ only by $Call_{RPC}(p, pr, ar)$.

The liveness requirements for the *RPC* components states that once a call is in state *called*, (1) eventually the "RemoteCall" operation is performed and (2) the return value forwarded to the sender, unless a $Fail_{RPC}$ event occur and disables the $Forward_{RPC}$ event. The first condition is ensured by weak fairness on a step from *called* to *wait* or to *result*. The second condition is ensured by weak fairness on a step from *result* to ⊥.

A $Call_{RPC}(p,$ "RemoteCall"$, ar)$ event in the RPC component corresponds to a call to the procedure RemoteCall(op, a) where ar is a list, $[op, a]$, with a procedure op and arguments a. It is only possible to initiate the call if no other call with the process identifier p currently is in the component, i.e., $ctr = \perp$. In the next state, op is stored in $proc$, a in $args$ and the control state is changed to denote that there is a pending call in the component.

The $Forward_{RPC}$ event forwards the call to the receiver if it is a legal procedure call (i.e., $proc \in$ Procs) with the right number of arguments. The predicates Len($args$) and ArgNum($proc$) are assigned for the latter task. To indicate a pending procedure call ctr is changed to $wait$.

A $Receive_{RPC}$ event catches the return value given by the receiver and stores it in ret.

Finally the $Return_{RPC}$ event can be performed when the remote procedure call has returned a value or an exception has been raised (i.e., $ctr = result$ and there exists a return value r).

Internal events In addition to the synchronizing events defined above there are also two internal events. The $Reject_{RPC}$ event may occur when the requested procedure call is not a valid procedure (i.e., $pr \notin$ Procs) or has an illegal number of arguments (i.e., Len(ar) $\neq$ ArgNum(pr)). In this case an exception is raised and stored such that $ret^+ =$ "BadCall".

The $Fail_{RPC}$ event may raise an "RPCFailure" exception at any time when $ctr = called$ or $ctr = result$.

8.1 Solution to Problem 2

The entire component $RPCSpec$ can now finally be defined as

$$RPCSpec \stackrel{\Delta}{=} \forall p \in PId : RPC(p)$$

9 Problem 3 – The Clerk Component

In this section we give a specification of a Clerk component (Figure 6), which translates memory calls into RPC calls. As in the specification of the RPC component in Section 8, the component consists of a number of calls parameterized by a process identifier p.

Variables In the specification of a call with process identifier p we use the following individual variables.

ctr is a control state. The possible control states are:

⊥ denotes that there is no call with process identifier p currently in the Memory Clerk component.

called denotes that the call has been received but not yet forwarded or that it will be tried again.

pend denotes that the call has been forwarded but no result has been received.

result denotes that the call has been forwarded and a result has been received but not yet returned.

proc is a procedure name.

args is a list of the arguments to the procedure.

ret is the return value if $ctr = result$.

Events In the specification, certain events are used to synchronize state changes in the *Clerk* components and state changes in other components. We describe these as follows.

$Call_{Clerk}(p, pr, ar)$ denotes that process p calls the *Clerk* component with procedure pr (i.e., either **Read** or **Write**) and parameters ar. The parameters ar is a tuple which contains the arguments of the procedure.

$Forward_{Clerk}(p, pr, ar)$ denotes that the call from process p with procedure pr and arguments ar is forwarded by the *Clerk* component to the receiver.

$Receive_{Clerk}(p, r)$ denotes that the call from process p is returned from the receiver with return value r.

$Return_{Clerk}(p, r)$ denotes that the call from process p is returned to calling process with return value r.

The formal specification of these events is given in Figure 6.

Initial Conditions Initially there are no calls in the component.

Safety and Liveness properties The safety requirements, *SafeClerk(p)* is the conjunction of:

1. *ClerkActs(p)* which specifies conditions and effects of the events. In Figure 6 the formula is written as a state-transition diagram.
2. Frame axioms telling that *ctr* and *ret* can be changed by all events, but *proc* and *args* only by $Call_{Clerk}(p, pr, ar)$.

The liveness requirements for the *Clerk* components state that once a call is in state *called*, (1) eventually the corresponding operation is performed and (2) the call must be returned. The first condition is ensured by weak fairness on a move from *called* to *pend*. The second condition is ensured by strong fairness on a move from *result* to $\perp$.

A $Call_{Clerk}$ event in the Clerk component corresponds to a call by the *Sender* in the problem description. It is only possible to initiate the call if no other call currently is in the component, i.e., $ctr = \perp$. In the next state pr and ar is stored in *proc*, a in *args* and *ctr* is changed to denote there is a pending call in the component.

The $Forward_{Clerk}$ event forwards the call to the receiver. To indicate a pending procedure call, *ctr* is set to *pend*.

A $Receive_{Clerk}$ event catches the return value given by the receiver and stores it in *ret*. If the return value r is not an "RPCFailure"-exception it is stored in *ret* at the next state. Otherwise either the return value is accepted

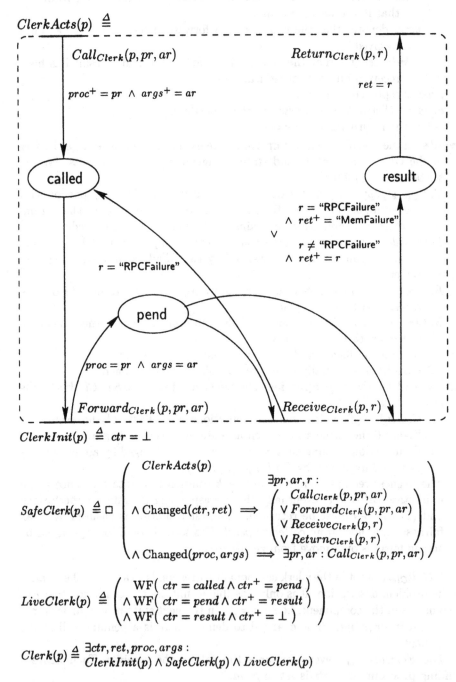

$ClerkActs(p) \triangleq$

$Call_{Clerk}(p, pr, ar)$

$proc^+ = pr \land args^+ = ar$

$Return_{Clerk}(p, r)$

$ret = r$

called

result

$r = \text{“RPCFailure”}$
$\land \ ret^+ = \text{“MemFailure”}$

$\lor$

$r \neq \text{“RPCFailure”}$
$\land \ ret^+ = r$

$r = \text{“RPCFailure”}$

pend

$proc = pr \land args = ar$

$Forward_{Clerk}(p, pr, ar)$

$Receive_{Clerk}(p, r)$

$ClerkInit(p) \triangleq ctr = \bot$

$$SafeClerk(p) \triangleq \Box \left(\begin{array}{l} ClerkActs(p) \\ \land \, \text{Changed}(ctr, ret) \implies \left(\begin{array}{l} \exists pr, ar, r : \\ \quad \left(\begin{array}{l} Call_{Clerk}(p, pr, ar) \\ \lor Forward_{Clerk}(p, pr, ar) \\ \lor Receive_{Clerk}(p, r) \\ \lor Return_{Clerk}(p, r) \end{array} \right) \end{array} \right) \\ \land \, \text{Changed}(proc, args) \implies \exists pr, ar : Call_{Clerk}(p, pr, ar) \end{array} \right)$$

$$LiveClerk(p) \triangleq \left(\begin{array}{l} \text{WF}(\, ctr = called \land ctr^+ = pend \,) \\ \land \, \text{WF}(\, ctr = pend \land ctr^+ = result \,) \\ \land \, \text{WF}(\, ctr = result \land ctr^+ = \bot \,) \end{array} \right)$$

$Clerk(p) \triangleq \exists ctr, ret, proc, args :$
$\qquad ClerkInit(p) \land SafeClerk(p) \land LiveClerk(p)$

Fig. 6. The specification of a call with process identifier p in the Clerk component

and a "MemFailure"-exception is raised setting $ret^+ = $ "MemFailure" or is not accepted and the call reissued by changing the control state (i.e., $ctr^+ = called$).

Finally the $Return_{Clerk}$ event can be performed when the remote procedure call has returned a value or an exception has been raised (i.e., $ctr = result$ and there is a return value r).

9.1 Solution to Problem 3

Problem 3a With the definitions given in the previous section we can now finally define the entire Memory Clerk component $ClerkSpec$ as

$$ClerkSpec \triangleq \forall p \in PId : Clerk(p)$$

Figure 7 gives a graphical overview of all components in the memory. To specify the entire implementation of the memory system, we specify $RPCMemory$ to be

$$
\begin{aligned}
&Links \triangleq \forall p, pr, ar, l, r: \\
&\quad \Box \left(
\begin{array}{l}
Forward_{Clerk}(p, pr, ar) \Leftrightarrow Call_{RPC}(p, \text{"RemoteCall"}, [pr, ar]) \\
\wedge\, Receive_{Clerk}(p, v) \Leftrightarrow Return_{RPC}(p, r) \\
\wedge\, Forward_{RPC}(p, \text{"Write"}, [l, r]) \Leftrightarrow Call_{Mem}(p, \text{"Write"}, [l, r]) \\
\wedge\, Forward_{RPC}(p, \text{"Read"}, [l]) \Leftrightarrow Call_{Mem}(p, \text{"Read"}, [l]) \\
\wedge\, Receive_{RPC}(p, r) \Leftrightarrow Return_{Mem}(p, r)
\end{array}
\right) \\
\\
&RPCMemory \triangleq
\begin{array}{l}
\exists\, Forward_{Clerk}, Call_{RPC}, Forward_{RPC}, Call_{Mem} \\
\quad Return_{Mem}, Receive_{RPC}, Return_{RPC}, Receive_{Clerk}: \\
\quad Links \wedge RMemSpec \wedge RPCSpec \wedge ClerkSpec
\end{array}
\end{aligned}
$$

Problem 3b The problem of verifying the specification can be formalised as

$$
\begin{aligned}
RPCMemory[Call, Return/Call_{Clerk}, Return_{Clerk}] \Longrightarrow \\
MemSpec[Call, Return/Call_{Mem}, Return_{Mem}]
\end{aligned}
$$

where the interface from the $Clerk$ component and $MemSpec$ are renamed to achieve a common interface to both specifications. Expanding the above formula yields

$$
\left(
\begin{array}{l}
\exists\, Forward_{Clerk}, Call_{RPC}, Forward_{RPC}, Call_{Mem} \\
\quad Return_{Mem}, Receive_{RPC}, Return_{RPC}, Receive_{Clerk}: \\
\quad Links \\
\wedge \exists Read_{Mem}, Write_{Mem} : \forall p \in PId : Memory \wedge RelMemInt(p) \\
\wedge\, \forall p \in PId : RPC(p) \\
\wedge\, \forall p \in PId : Clerk(p)[Call, Return/Call_{Clerk}, Return_{Clerk}]
\end{array}
\right)
$$
$$\Longrightarrow$$
$$
\left(
\begin{array}{l}
\exists\, Read_{Mem}, Write_{Mem} : \forall p \in PId : \\
\quad Memory \wedge MemInt(p)[Call, Return/Call_{Mem}, Return_{Mem}]
\end{array}
\right)
$$

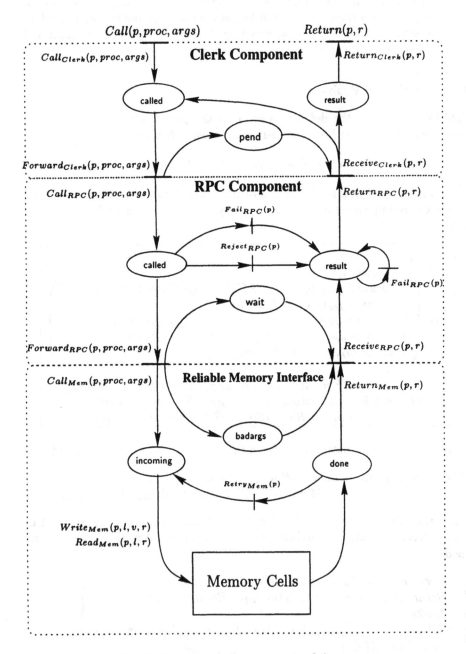

Fig. 7. Overview of all components of the memory

Now it is possible to move all existential quantification before the formula Links to an outermost scope. The existential quantification then becomes universal and can be cancelled. In the same way, we can remove the part

$$\exists Read_{Mem}, Write_{Mem}$$

in the antecedent. We chose to remove it also in the consequent by assuming that the values for $Read_{Mem}$ and $Write_{Mem}$ which satisfy the existential quantification will be the same as those of $Read_{Mem}$ and $Write_{Mem}$ in the antecedent. After renaming of $Call$ and $Return$ in $Clerk(p)$ and $MemInt(p)$ the following formula remains

$$\forall p \in PId : Links \wedge Memory \wedge RelMemInt(p) \wedge RPC(p) \wedge Clerk'(p)$$
$$\implies \forall p \in PId : Memory \wedge MemInt'(p)$$

The predicate $Links$ only specifies the synchronization between components which essentially are renaming of events. After instantiation of the synchronization given by $Links$, moving the universal quantification to an outermost level and cancelling out $Memory$ we are left with the stronger formula

$$\forall p \in PId : RelMemInt'(p) \wedge RPC'(p) \wedge Clerk''(p) \implies MemInt'(p)$$

This formula must now be proven by some means. We have not had the time to investigate how to prove it. We can observe that the formula is "almost finite-state" in that the only unbounded component is the dependency on different memory values and memory locations. These are handled in such a trivial way that it seems likely that some automatic verification algorithm should be able to prove the above formula.

References

1. M. Abadi, L. Lamport, and S. Merz. A TLA Solution to the RPC-Memory Specification Problem. This volume.
2. J. Blom, B. Jonsson, and L. Kempe. Using temporal logic for modular specification of telephone services. In L. G. Bouma and Hugo Velthuijsen, editors, *Feature Interactions in Telecommunications Systems*, pages 197–216, Amsterdam, The Netherlands, May 1994. IOS Press.
3. A. Borgida, J. Mylopoulos, and R. Reiter. On the frame problem in procedure specifications. *IEEE Trans. on Software Engineering*, 21(10):785–798, 1995.
4. M. Broy and L. Lamport. The RPC-Memory Specification Problem. This volume.
5. L. Lamport. Lake arrowhead specification problem, 1987. Manuscript.
6. L. Lamport. The temporal logic of actions. Technical report, DEC/SRC, 1991.
7. K. G. Larsen, B. Steffen, and C. Weise. The Methodology of Modal Constraints. This volume.
8. N. Lynch and M.R. Tuttle. An Introduction to Input/Output Automata. Technical Report MIT/LCS/TM-373, MIT, Nov. 1988. TM-351 Revised.
9. Z. Manna and A. Pnueli. *The Temporal Logic of Reactive and Concurrent Systems*. Springer Verlag, 1992.
10. J.L. Peterson. Petri nets. *Computing Surveys*, 9(3):221–252, 1977.
11. P.H.J. van Eijk, C.A. Vissers, and M. Diaz, editors. *The Formal Description Technique LOTOS*. North-Holland, 1989.

A Functional Solution
to the
RPC-Memory Specification Problem[*]

Manfred Broy

Institut für Informatik
Technische Universität München
80290 München, Germany

Abstract. We give a functional specification of the syntactic interface and the black box behavior of an unreliable and a reliable memory component and a remote procedure (RPC) call component. The *RPC* component controls the access to the memory. In addition, we specify a clerk for driving the *RPC* component. The used method is modular and therefore it allows us to specify each of these components independently and separately. We discuss the specifications shortly and then compose them into a distributed system of interacting components. We prove that the specification of the composed system fulfills again the requirement specification of the unreliable memory component. Finally we give a timed version of the *RPC* component and of a clerk component and compose them.

1 Introduction

For describing the behavior of a reactive component we can either use state transition models or communication/action history based models. Using states, we specify the behavior of a system by a state machine that models its state changes. We specify liveness properties, that we cannot express easily by state transition techniques, separately, for instance by temporal logic.

Besides states we may use history based descriptions of the behavior of components. With them we model the behaviors of systems by their traces or by their input and output histories. In the following, we choose a history based modeling technique and describe the behavior of components by relations on their timed input and output streams. We provide modular specifications that model the behavior of the components independently.

We treat the specification problem of an unreliable memory, a *RPC* component and a clerk as posed in [Broy, Lamport]. In a first chapter, we briefly repeat the basic mathematical concepts of the used approach. Then we give interface

---

[*] This work was partially sponsored by the Sonderforschungsbereich 342 "Werkzeuge und Methoden für die Nutzung paralleler Rechnerarchitekturen" and the industrial research project SysLab.

specifications of the unreliable memory, the reliable memory, the RPC component, and the clerk. We put the latter three components together in parallel. Due to the modularity of our approach the specification of the composed system is obtained in a schematic modular way from the specifications of the components. For the composed system we prove that it is a refinement of the requirement specification for the unreliable memory again. We carry out this proof in the appendix.

We then go through the same exercise for a *RPC* component that reacts within time bounds. In particular, it determines by a time-out that certain *RPC* calls do not return. We specify, compose and verify the components as required in [Broy, Lamport]. So we solve all the tasks of the RPC-Memory Specification Problem. We do not give a proof of the correctness of the timed implementation.

2 The Basic System Model

As a basic model for describing the behavior of system components we use relations on timed streams. Timed streams are streams carrying data messages and time ticks. A timed stream is accordingly a finite or infinite sequence of messages and time ticks. A timed stream is called complete, if it contains an infinite number of time ticks. Apart from the time ticks a complete timed stream may carry a finite or an infinite number of messages. The basic idea is that the time ticks indicate the time bounds (the bounds of the time intervals) in which the messages are sent on a channel. On the basis of this simple model, we introduce a quite flexible notation in this section that we will use throughout the paper when writing specifications. For a detailed introduction into the theory of streams see appendix A.

We model the time flow by a special time signal called a time tick that indicates the end of a time interval. By the symbol

$$\sqrt{}$$

we denote the time tick signal. Let M be a set of messages that does not contain the time signal $\sqrt{}$. By M^ω we denote the set of streams of messages from the set M and by

$$M^{\underline{\omega}}$$

we denote the set of complete timed streams of elements from the set $M \cup \{\sqrt{}\}$ with an infinite number of ticks[2]. Every element in the set $M^{\underline{\omega}}$ denotes a complete timed communication history over an unbounded time period.

In the following, we use the notations and operators as given in Tab. 1 in the formulas specifying the components.

---

[2] Perhaps it is helpful to point out that of course the time ticks are not thought as signals that are actually transmitted. They are introduced rather as an auxiliary concept that allows us to model time.

For a stream $x \in (M \cup \{\surd\})^\omega$ we denote by:

$S©x$ the substream of the elements from the set $S \subseteq M \cup \{\surd\}$ in stream x;
      if $S = \{a\}$ we write $a©x$ instead of $S©x$, $©$ is called the *filter operator*,

$x.i$ the i-th element in the stream x different from the signal $\surd$, more precisely
      the i-th element in the message stream $M©x$,

$x : i$ the least prefix of the stream $M©x$ that contains i elements,

$x \downarrow i$ the largest prefix of the stream x containing i time ticks (the history till time
      point i),

$\#x$ the number of elements in stream x,

$S\ddagger x$ $\#S©x$,

$x^{\mathsf{TM}}i$ the number of time ticks till the i-th message different from $\surd$ in the stream
      x, formally:

$$x^{\mathsf{TM}}i = \min\{\#\surd©z : z \sqsubseteq x \land M\ddagger z \geq i\}$$

Here $\sqsubseteq$ denotes the prefix order which is formally introduced in appendix A.
If $\#M©x < i$ then $x^{\mathsf{TM}}i = \infty$.

Table 1. Table of the Used Notation

Fig. 1 shows a timed stream with its time ticks representing the beginning
and the end of a time interval. In this example we have $x^{\mathsf{TM}}i = k$, since the i-th
message (which is $x.i$) occurs after the k-th time tick.

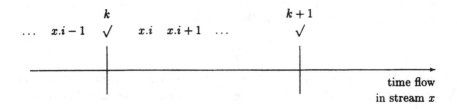

Fig. 1. Stream with Time Ticks

We describe the black box behavior of a component by a behavior relation.
A behavior relation is a relation between the input streams and the output
streams of a component that fulfills certain conditions with respect to their
timing. Let $I_1, \ldots, I_n, O_1, \ldots, O_m$ be message sets where $m, n \in I\!N$. A graphical
representation of a component f with n input channels of the sorts $I_1, \ldots, I_n$
and m output channels of the sorts $O_1, \ldots, O_m$ is shown by Fig. 2.

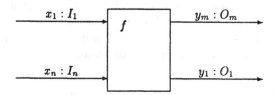

Fig. 2. Graphical representation of component f

A behavior relation for this component is represented by a predicate on the timed streams of input and output messages.

$$f : (I_1^\omega \times \ldots \times I_n^\omega \times O_1^\omega \times \ldots \times O_n^\omega) \to I\!B$$

For a behavior relation we always assume the following timing property (principle of time flow and delay):

$$x \downarrow i = z \downarrow i \Rightarrow \{y \downarrow i + 1 : f(x,y)\} = \{y \downarrow i + 1 : f(z,y)\}$$

The timing property expresses that the set of possible output histories for the first $i + 1$ time intervals only depends on the input histories for the first i time intervals. In other words, the processing of messages in a component takes at least one tick of time. We could work with more liberal conditions by dropping the $+1$ in the formula above. However, this timing condition is very convenient for us, since it leads to guarded recursion which is very useful in proofs.

3 Basic Message Sets Involved

In this section we shortly list the basic message sets and some additional auxiliary functions that we use in our specifications. We introduce the data sets given in Tab. 2.

$MemLocs$		memory locations,
$MemVals$		memory values,
$PrIds$		identifiers for processes,
$Procs$	$= \{Read, Write\}$	procedure names,
$Args$	$= (MemLocs \times MemVals) \cup MemLocs$	arguments,
$RetVals$	$= MemVals \cup \{BadArg, MemFail, Ack\}$	return values,
$RetMem$	$= Calls \times RetVals$	return messages of memory,
$Returns$	$= Calls \times (RetVals$	
	$\cup \{RPCFailure, BadCall\})$	return messages of RPC comp.,
$Calls$	$= (PrIds \times Procs \times Args)$	calls.

Table 2. Table of data sets

By $MemLoc(c)$ we denote for every call $c \in Calls$ the memory location referenced in the arguments of the call c. By $MemVal(c)$ we denote the written value of a write call $c \in Calls$. We use the following subsets of the sets of calls and return values as abbreviations in specifications:

$$W(e) = \{(p, Write, (e, v)) \in Calls : p \in PrIds \wedge v \in MemVals\}$$
$$R(c) = \{(c', b) \in Returns : c = c'\}$$

We assume that for every call $c \in Calls$ the identifier for the process that issued the call is denoted by $PrId(c)$. We define in addition the following sets in specifications:

$$C(p) = \{c \in Calls : PrId(c) = p\}$$
$$RP(p) = \{(c, b) \in Returns : PrId(c) = p\}$$

For simplicity we assume that the set $RetVals$ does not contain the element $RPCFailure$ nor the element $BadCall$ and that the set $MemVals$ does not contain the element $BadArg$.

According to the informal specification some calls are bad. We assume a Boolean function

$$IsBadCall : Calls \rightarrow Bool$$

that allows us to distinguish bad calls from proper calls.

This set of definitions constitutes what software engineers call the *data model* of our little application.

4 The Unreliable and the Reliable Memory Component

The unreliable memory component is a simple device that receives a stream of memory calls and returns a stream of memory return messages. We model the memory component by a relation between its input and output streams, the timed stream of calls and the timed streams of memory return messages.

Note: On the Conceptional Model
In the informal specification as given in [Broy, Lamport] a scenario is used to explain the behavior of the memory component informally in terms of a conceptual model that refers to a particular implementation. It refers to a simple memory and to a clerk component that executes every call several times (or no call at all). Therefore a specification based on this scenario might be most suggestive when starting from the informal specification. We are rather interested in a black box specification that specifies the behavior of the unreliable memory by the relation between its input and output histories represented by streams. Therefore we do not give a specification in terms of an abstract implementation – as suggested by the informal description – but rather isolate its characteristic properties and formalize them.

The particular example of the *RPC* component includes a subtle difficulty for our specification technique. The fact that the memory may assume that for each processor at most one call is active makes it necessary to refer to the time order between output (returns to memory calls) and input (further calls). For (nontimed) stream processing functions it is easy to express that a certain input message is causal for a certain output message. This means that the output does never occur before the input occurred. However, it is difficult to express without time information that an input message occurs only after a particular output message[3]. We can express such a relationship in our model without problems due to the fact that we work with timed input and output streams. Therefore we can formulate the assumption that the next call of a process arrives only after the return to the previous one has been issued. □

The memory component MC with its syntactic interface is graphically shown in Fig. 3. Its behavior is specified formally along the lines of the informal statements (1) - (5) by the relation MC given below.

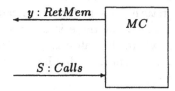

Fig. 3. The Memory Component MC as a Data Flow Node

For all component specifications we use the same format. We specify the syntactic interface that indicates the number of channels, their internal names and which messages are sent along the channels by a data flow node. Then we give an informal description of the properties and finally specify the relation MC by a logical formula describing a relation between input and output streams.

We formulate the specification in the so-called assumption/commitment format. In that format we write a specification by an implicative formula

$$A \Rightarrow C$$

where A is the *assumption* and C is the *commitment*. In the assumption we express the condition about the input streams that have to be fulfilled to be able to guarantee that the component works properly. The commitment C formalizes what it means that the component works properly (for a detailed description of assumption/commitment specifications for stream processing components see [Stølen et al. 93] and [Broy 94b]).

For the unreliable memory the assumption, abbreviated by ProcAssumption, expresses the following property:

---

[3] This can easily be expressed by traces. A trace specification is given in the appendix.

(0) A call of a process to the memory only may occur when no other call of this process is active.

In other words, we require that at every point in time the number of calls of a process in the input stream is at most by one larger than the number of returns.

The commitment (the behavior guaranteed provided the assumption holds) of the unreliable memory component is described by the following basic statements:

There exists a history of calls that we may name the *internal access stream*[4] z with the following properties:

(1) For every call in the input stream exactly one return message is issued.

(2) For every call in the input stream its corresponding return message fits into the set of allowed return messages for that call.

(3) Whenever there occurs a call in the internal access stream z such a call is active at that point of time. A call is called *active* at a time point if it has been issued (received by the memory) but not answered yet.

(4) If a return message is an acknowledgment for a write call then there is an entry in the internal access stream at a moment where this call is active.

(5) If there is a successful return message for a read call c for location e which delivers the value v as the result there is an entry in the internal access stream at a time point where the call c is active such that the last value written for location e (or the special value InitVal, if such a write call does not exist) coincides with v.

The formal specification of the component MC follows exactly these informal statements. It reads as follows:

$MC \equiv (s \in Calls^{\underline{\omega}}, y \in RetMem^{\underline{\omega}})$:

$ProcAssumption(s, y) \Rightarrow$

$\exists z \in Calls^{\underline{\omega}} : \forall v \in MemVals, c \in Calls, i \in [1 : c\ddagger s]$:

(1) $c\ddagger s = R(c)\ddagger y$

(2) $\wedge\ Fit(d.i)$

(3) $\wedge\ \forall k \in [1 : c\ddagger z] : \exists j \in [1 : c\ddagger s] : active(j, (\{c, \sqrt{}\}©z)^{TM}k)$

(4) $\wedge\ (d.i = (c, Ack) \Rightarrow \exists k : active(i, z^{TM}k) \wedge z.k = c)$

(5) $\wedge\ (d.i = (c, v) \Rightarrow\quad \exists k : active(i, z^{TM}k) \wedge v = last(z : k, MemLoc(c)))$

where $b = \{c, \sqrt{}\}©s, d = (R(c) \cup \{\sqrt{}\})©y,$

$active(i, t) \equiv b^{TM}i \leq t \leq d^{TM}i$

---

[4] This internal access stream is introduced as an auxiliary construct. It reflects the informal problem description expressing that every call may perform a sequence of atomic accesses to the memory while active.

In this specification we use the following auxiliary functions and predicates. The term $last(y, e)$ denotes the last value written into the memory location e in the finite stream y; it is $InitVal$ if such a call does not exist. Formally, this is specified by

$$last(y, c) = if \#x = 0 \text{ then } InitVal \text{ else } MemVal(x.\#x)$$

$$\text{where } x = W(MemLoc(c))\textcircled{c}y$$

Here $W(e)$ denotes the set of all return messages to write calls to location e. We define the input assumption as follows:

$$ProcAssumption \equiv (s \in Calls^{\underline{\omega}}, y \in RetMem^{\underline{\omega}}) :$$

$$\forall p \in PrIds : \forall i \in I\!N : C(p)\ddagger(s \downarrow i + 1) \leq 1 + RP(p)\ddagger(y \downarrow i)$$

We specify the predicate Fit that indicates whether a return message fits with a call as follows:

$$Fit \equiv ((j, p, a) \in (PrIds \times Procs \times Args), b \in RetVals) :$$

$$(p = Write \Rightarrow \quad (b = Ack \wedge a \in MemLocs \times MemVals)$$

$$\vee (b = BadArg \wedge a \notin MemLocs \times MemVals)$$

$$\vee (b = MemFail)) \quad \wedge$$

$$(p = Read \quad \Rightarrow \quad (b \in MemVals \wedge a \in MemLocs)$$

$$\vee (b = BadArg \wedge a \notin MemLocs)$$

$$\vee (b = MemFail))$$

This concludes the specification of the unreliable memory.

The assumption/commitment format inhibits a subtle point, which has to be clarified. Obviously the assumption does not only refer to the input stream s, but also to the output stream y. This may seem paradoxical, since then the assumption might be falsified by choosing a respective output stream. As explained in detail in [Broy 94a] the input assumption is – due to the timing property – in fact a restriction of the input stream s. Whenever the assumption $ProcAssumption(s, y)$ yields false, there exists a least time point $i > 0$ such that for all streams s' and y' with

$$s \downarrow i + 1 \sqsubseteq s' \quad and \quad y \downarrow i \sqsubseteq y'$$

we have $\neg ProcAssumption(s', y')$. Furthermore, we have[5]

$$ProcAssumption(s \downarrow i \hat{\ } \sqrt{}^{\infty}, y \downarrow (i - 1) \hat{\ } \sqrt{}^{\infty})$$

---

[5] Here $\sqrt{}^{\infty}$ stands for an infinite stream of time signals $\sqrt{}$.

so $y \downarrow (i-1)\hat{\ }\sqrt{\ }^{\infty}$ fulfills the commitment. This imposes also, by the timing condition, that $y \downarrow i$ fulfills the safety properties of the commitment.

The specification MC is our solution to task 1(a) of [Broy, Lamport].

The reliable memory (task 1(a)) is easily specified similarly to the MC component as follows:

$RMC(s, y) \equiv$ like $MC(s, y)$, but in the definition of predicate Fit the branch
$$\text{"} \ldots \vee b = MemFail \ldots \text{"}$$
is omitted.

With this specification the answer to problem 1(b) is trivially "Yes" Since the reliable memory is specified just like the unreliable memory besides leaving out one disjunctive branch, we have immediately the theorem

$$RMC(s, y) \Rightarrow MC(s, y)$$

This is what we expect, since every behavior the reliable memory shows is also a behavior of the unreliable memory. So the reliable memory component RMC is a property refinement of MC.

Also the answer to problem 1(c) is trivially "Yes". The memory component allows an implementation that always returns $MemFail$. We have not included any liveness assumption that expresses that a memory failure cannot be returned all the time.

5 The Remote Procedure Call Component

In this section, we specify the behavior of the remote procedure call component (Problem 2 in [Broy, Lamport]) that we call RPC. We specify it again by a relation between the input/output streams of the component. The remote procedure call component has two input channels, called x and y and two output channels called s and r. The RPC component is graphically shown as a data flow node in Fig. 4.

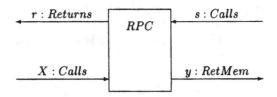

Fig. 4. RPC Component as a Data Flow Node

On its input channel x the component RPC receives calls and forwards them on its output channel s. On its input channel y it receives memory return messages and forwards them on its output channel r as return messages to its environment. We specify this relation again in the assumption/commitment format. The *RPC* assumption expresses that

(1) for each process at most one call is active at a time,
(2) on its return memory line y at most as many return messages are received as resp. calls have been issued on the channel s before and not answered so far,
(3) all calls issued on the channel s eventually receive a memory return message on the channel y.

The specification of the *RPC* component is quite straightforward. It expresses the following four properties. For each call c we require:

(0) If the call c received on its input channel x is a bad call then it is not forwarded on channel s but returned with a *BadCall* return message on the return channel r.
(1) At most those calls are forwarded on channel s that have been received on channel x.
(2) Only memory return messages are forwarded on channel r that have been received on channel y.
(3) For each call on channel x a return message is issued eventually on channel r.

Note that this way we model the calls returned with the *RPC* return message *RPCFailure* quite implicitly as a default by the fact that all calls arriving on channel x eventually return.

The syntactic interface specification of the *RPC* component and its semantic interface defining its black box behavior are given by the following formula:

$$RPC \equiv (x \in Calls^{\underline{\omega}}, y \in RetMem^{\underline{\omega}}, s \in Calls^{\underline{\omega}}, r \in Returns^{\underline{\omega}}) :$$

$$RPCAssumption(x, r, s, y) \Rightarrow \forall c \in Calls, v \in RetVals :$$

$$(0) \quad (IsBadCall(c) \Rightarrow c{\ddagger}x = (c, BadCall){\ddagger}r \wedge c{\ddagger}s = 0)$$

$$(1) \wedge c{\ddagger}s \leq c{\ddagger}x$$

$$(2) \wedge (c, v){\ddagger}r \leq (c, v){\ddagger}y$$

$$(3) \wedge R(c){\ddagger}r = c{\ddagger}x$$

Here we define the assumption *RPCAssumption* as follows:

$$RPCAssumption \equiv (x \in Calls^{\underline{\omega}}, r \in Returns^{\underline{\omega}}, s \in Calls^{\underline{\omega}}, y \in RetMem^{\underline{\omega}}) :$$

$$\forall c \in Calls, i \in \mathbb{N} :$$

$$(1) \quad ProcAssumption(x, r)$$

$$(2) \wedge c{\ddagger}s \downarrow i \geq R(c){\ddagger}y \downarrow i + 1$$

$$(3) \land R(c)\$y \geq c\$s$$

Again we express both safety and liveness properties by the specifying predicate for the *RPC* component.

6   Implementation with the Help of a Clerk

In this section we specify a clerk which can be used to drive an *RPC* component. It has a syntactic interface similar to the *RPC* component, but in contrast to this it forwards calls and receives returns from the *RPC* component and turns them into memory returns. The specification is quite similar. In [Broy, Lamport] the clerk is not mentioned and described explicitly but rather implicitly by describing the way the implementation works.

The clerk component *CLK* (Problem 3) is graphically shown in Fig. 5. It is specified again by an assumption/commitment specification.

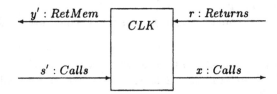

Fig. 5. The Clerk CLK as a Data Flow Node

We use the same assumption for the channels of the clerk as for the respective channels of the *RPC* component.

The commitment of the clerk component formalizes the following properties:

(1) The calls returned with *BadArg* messages on the channel y' are those that are returned with *BadCall* and *BadArg* messages on the channel r.

(2) All memory failures that are received on the channel r are forwarded on the channel y'.

(3) The calls on the channel s', the *RPC* Failure return messages and Memory Failures on r are exactly those calls forwarded on the channel x or returned on the channel y' with a memory failure message.

(4) All returns received on the channel r which are not memory failure return messages are forwarded on the channel y'.

(5) All calls return.

These properties of the clerk are formally specified by a relation between its input and output streams as follows. By this specification we give both the syntactic interface and the history relation:

$CLK \equiv (s' \in Calls^{\underline{\omega}}, r \in Returns^{\underline{\omega}}, x \in Calls^{\underline{\omega}}, y' \in RetMem^{\underline{\omega}}) :$

$RPC\,Assumption(s', y', x, r) \Rightarrow \forall c \in Calls, v \in RetVals\{MemFail\} :$

(1)　$(c, BadArg)\ddagger y' = (c, BadCall)\ddagger r + (c, BadArg)\ddagger r$

(2)　$\wedge\ (c, MemFail)\ddagger y' \geq (c, MemFail)\ddagger r$

(3)　$\wedge\ (c, MemFail)\ddagger y' + c\ddagger x = c\ddagger s' + (c, RPCFailure)\ddagger r + (c, MemFail)\ddagger r$

(4)　$\wedge\ (c, v)\ddagger y' = (c, v)\ddagger r$

(5)　$\wedge\ R(c)\ddagger y' = c\ddagger s'$

Again this is a pure property specification just counting and relating the numbers of calls and return messages for them in the input and output channels.

7　The Composed System

The composition of the RPC component with the reliable memory component RMC and the clark CLK is straightforward along the lines of Fig. 6:

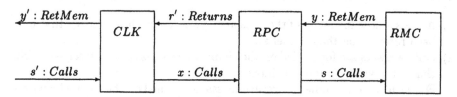

Fig. 6. Data Flow Diagram of the Composed System Called CI

The data flow diagram can be translated in a straightforward way into a logical formula specifying the component CI:

$CI \equiv (s' \in Calls^{\underline{\omega}}, y' \in RetMem^{\underline{\omega}}) :$

$\exists x, s, r, y : CLK(s', r, x, y') \wedge RPC(x, y, s, r) \wedge RMC(s, y)$

We claim that CI is an implementation (or in other words a refinement) for the unreliable memory. Formally this corresponds to the following verification condition:

$$CI(s', y') \Rightarrow MC(s', y')$$

A proof for the verification condition is given in the appendix. This is our solution to problem 3.

8 Specification of the Lossy RPC Component

The lossy *RPC* component can be specified along the lines of the *RPC* component. But now we work with a weaker input assumption. We do no longer assume that all calls that are issued on the output channel s actually return. Furthermore, we now refer to an explicit timing of the messages. Fig. 7 shows a graphical representation of the lossy *RPC* component. Its specification is given below.

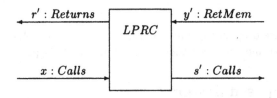

Fig. 7. Lossy *RPC* Component *LRPC* as a Data Flow Node

The specification of the component *LRPC* is quite straightforward. It expresses the following three properties. For each call c we require:

(1) At most those instances of the calls are forwarded on the channel s that have been received on the channel x.
(2) Only answers are forwarded on the channel r that have been received on the channel y within δ units of time.
(3) For each call on channel x a return message is issued on the channel r within δ units of time after the return was received on the channel y or after the call has been received on the channel x (if the call has not been not forwarded on s after δ units of time).

We specify the component *LRPC* by the following formula:

$LRPC \equiv (x \in Calls^{\underline{\omega}}, y \in RetMem^{\underline{\omega}}, s \in Calls^{\underline{\omega}}, r \in Returns^{\underline{\omega}}) :$

$\exists r' : r = NRPCF©r' \wedge$

$((ProcAssumption(x, r') \wedge \forall c \in Calls, i \in I\!N : c{\ddagger}s \downarrow i \geq R(c){\ddagger}y \downarrow i + 1) \Rightarrow$

  $\forall i \in I\!N, c \in Calls, v \in RetVals :$

  (1) $(IsBadCall(c) \Rightarrow R(c){\ddagger}r' = (c, BadCall){\ddagger}r' \wedge c{\ddagger}s = 0)$

  (2) $\wedge\ (c, v){\ddagger}r' \downarrow i + \delta \leq (c, v){\ddagger}y \downarrow i$

  (3) $\wedge\ R(c){\ddagger}r' \downarrow i + \delta = (c{\ddagger}x \downarrow i) - (c{\ddagger}s \downarrow i + \delta) + R(c){\ddagger}y \downarrow i$

    where $NRPCF = (c, b) \in Returns : b \neq RPCFailure) \cup \{\surd\}$

Hint: $(c \ddagger x \downarrow i) - (c \ddagger s \downarrow i + \delta)$ denotes the calls that are not forwarded. The RPCFailure signals are allowed inside the specification and then are filtered out. Note that this way we model the return message RPCFailure like in the case of the nonlossy *RPC* component and filter them out later. This implies that for certain calls no return messages are issued.

The specification *LRPC* is our solution to the problem 3' in [Broy, Lamport].

9 A Clerk for the Lossy RPC Component

In this section we specify a clerk component LCLK for the lossy *RPC* component. It is illustrated in Fig. 8 and specified below.

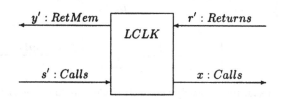

Fig. 8. Clerk of Lossy *RPC* Component as a Data Flow Node

We use the same assumption for the channels of the clerk as for the respective channels of the *RPC* component. The specification formalizes the following properties:

(1) All calls that are received on the channel s' are forwarded on the channel x.
(2) The calls forwarded on the channel x for which return messages are not returned within $2\delta + \epsilon$ time units after issued are returned with a *RPCFailure*, otherwise forwarded on the channel y' as returned.

These properties are formally specified as follows:

$LCLK \equiv (s' \in Calls^{\underline{\omega}}, r \in Returns^{\underline{\omega}}, x \in Calls^{\underline{\omega}}, y' \in RetMem^{\underline{\omega}}):$

$(ProcAssumption(s', y') \wedge$

$\forall c \in Calls, i \in I\!N : c \ddagger x \downarrow i \geq R(c) \ddagger r \downarrow i + 1) \Rightarrow$

$\quad$ (1) $s' : \infty = x : \infty \wedge$

$\quad$ (2) $\forall c \in Calls, i \in [1 : c \ddagger x] :$

$\qquad (R(c) \copyright y').i = \textbf{if } i > R(c) \ddagger r \downarrow ((c, \sqrt{\copyright} x)^{\text{TM}} i + 2\delta + \epsilon)$

$\qquad\qquad\qquad\qquad \textbf{then } (c, RPCFailure)$

$\qquad\qquad\qquad\qquad \textbf{else } r.i \qquad\qquad\qquad \textbf{fi}$

Again this is a pure black box specification just specifying the properties of the external behavior by counting the numbers of calls and corresponding return messages within the required time bounds.

10 Composing the Clerk and the Lossy RPC Component

In this section we compose the clerk with the lossy *RPC* component. We obtain a composed system called CRPC as shown in Fig. 9. Its specification is a straightforward transliteration of the data flow graph into logic.

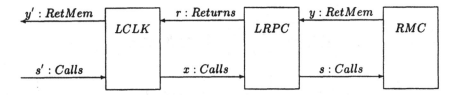

Fig. 9. Data Flow Diagram of the System CRPC Composed of the Lossy *RPC* Component and the Clerk

Again we obtain the component specification in a straightforward way from the data flow diagram:

$$CRPC \equiv (s' \in Calls^{\underline{\omega}}, y \in RetMem^{\underline{\omega}}, s \in Calls^{\underline{\omega}}, y' \in RetMem^{\underline{\omega}}) :$$

$$\exists r, x : LCLK(s', r, x, y') \land LRPC(x, y, s, r)$$

We obtain the following verification condition:

$$CRPC(s', y, s, y') \land (\forall c \in Calls, i \in I\!N : R(c)\ddagger y \downarrow i + \epsilon = c\ddagger s \downarrow i)$$

$$\Rightarrow RPC(s', y, s, y')$$

The verification condition includes the assumption that the calls issued on the channel s are returned within ϵ time ticks.

11 Conclusion

We have given a complete treatment of the problems posed in [Broy, Lamport]. Although these problems were posed mainly in terms of an abstract design we have given requirement specifications and not design specifications. Of course, in cases where the informal problem description is given in terms of an abstract design a design specification using some abstract implementation model may be easier to relate to the informal description.

We demonstrate in appendix B how such a specification of the memory component using an abstract design can be given by functional modeling techniques. Another extreme of a specification is shown in appendix C. There we give a pure black box specification in terms of traces where no auxiliary construct is used such as a simple memory component or an internal access stream.

Acknowledgment

It is a pleasure to thank Stephan Merz and Ketil Stølen for discussions and Birgit Schieder for comments. I am grateful to Peter Scholz and Ursula Hinkel for careful comments on a draft version.

A Mathematical Basis

Throughout this paper interactive systems are supposed to communicate asynchronously through unbounded FIFO channels. Streams are used to denote histories of communications on channels. Given a set M of messages, a *stream* over M is a finite or infinite sequence of elements from M. By M^* we denote the finite sequences over M. M^* includes the empty stream that is denoted by $\langle\rangle$.

By M^∞ we denote the infinite streams over the set M. M^∞ can be represented by the total mappings from the natural numbers $I\!N$ into M. We denote the set of all streams over the set M by M^ω. Formally we have

$$M^\omega = M^* \cup M^\infty.$$

We introduce a number of functions on streams that are useful in system descriptions.

A classical operation on streams is the concatenation that we denote by $\hat{}$. The concatenation is a function that takes two streams (say s and t) and produces a stream $s\hat{}t$ as result, starting with the stream s and continuing with the stream t. Formally the concatenation has the following functionality:

$$\hat{}: M^\omega \times M^\omega \to M^\omega.$$

If the stream s is infinite, then concatenating the stream s with a stream t yields the stream s again:

$$s \in M^\infty \Rightarrow s\hat{}t = s.$$

Concatenation is associative and has the empty stream $\langle\rangle$ as its neutral element:

$$r\hat{}(s\hat{}t) = (r\hat{}s)\hat{}t, \qquad \langle\rangle\hat{}s = s = s\hat{}\langle\rangle.$$

For any message $m \in M$ we denote by $\langle m\rangle$ the one element stream consisting of the element m.

On the set M^ω of streams we define a *prefix ordering* $\sqsubseteq$. We write $s \sqsubseteq t$ for streams s and t if s is a prefix of t. Formally we have

$$s \sqsubseteq t \text{ iff } \exists r \in M^\omega : s\hat{\ }r = t.$$

The prefix ordering defines a partial ordering on the set M^ω of streams. If $s \sqsubseteq t$, then we also say that s is an *approximation* of t. The set of streams ordered by $\sqsubseteq$ is complete in the sense that every directed set $S \subseteq M^\omega$ of streams has a *least upper bound* denoted by $lub\ S$. A nonempty subset S of a partially ordered set is called *directed*, if

$$\forall x, y \in S : \exists z \in S : x \sqsubseteq z \wedge y \sqsubseteq z.$$

By least upper bounds of directed sets of finite streams we may describe infinite streams. Infinite streams are also of interest as (and can also be described by) fixpoints of prefix monotonic functions. The streams associated with feedback loops in interactive systems correspond to such fixpoints.

A *stream processing function* is a function

$$f : M^\omega \to N^\omega$$

that is *prefix monotonic* and *continuous*. The function f is called prefix monotonic, if for all streams s and t we have

$$s \sqsubseteq t \Rightarrow f.s \sqsubseteq f.t.$$

For better readability we often write for the function application $f.x$ instead of $f(x)$. A prefix monotonic function f is called prefix continuous, if for all directed sets $S \subseteq M^\omega$ of streams we have

$$f.lub\ S = lub\ \{f.s : s \in S\}.$$

If a function is prefix continuous, then its results for infinite input can be already determined from its results on all finite approximations of the input.

By $\bot$ we denote the pseudo element that represents the result of diverging computations. We write $M^\bot$ for $M \cup \{\bot\}$. Here we assume that $\bot$ is not an element of M. On $M^\bot$ we define also a simple partial ordering called the flat ordering as follows:

$$x \sqsubseteq y \quad \text{iff} \quad x = y \vee x = \bot$$

We use the following functions on streams

$$ft : M^\omega \to M^\bot,$$

$$rt : M^\omega \to M^\omega.$$

The function ft selects the first element of a nonempty stream. The function rt deletes the first element of a nonempty stream.

For keeping our notation simple we extend the concatenation $\char94$ also to elements of the message set M (treating them like one element sequences) and to tuples of streams (by concatenating the streams elementwise). For the special element $\perp$ we specify $\perp\char94 s = \langle\rangle$. This equation reflects the fact that there cannot be any further message on a channel after trying to send a message that is to be generated by a diverging (and therefore never ending) computation.

The properties of the introduced functions can be expressed by the following equations (let $m \in M, s \in M^\omega$):

$$ft.\langle\rangle = \perp, \quad rt.\langle\rangle = \langle\rangle, \quad ft(m\char94 s) = m, \quad rt(m\char94 s) = s.$$

All the introduced concepts and functions such as the prefix ordering and the concatenation carry over to tuples of streams by pointwise application. Similarly the prefix ordering induces a partial ordering on functions with streams and tuples of streams as range.

We denote the function space of (n, m)-ary prefix continuous stream processing functions by

$$[(M^\omega)^n \sqsubseteq (M^\omega)^m]$$

The operations ft and rt are prefix monotonic and continuous, whereas concatenation $\char94$ as defined above is prefix monotonic and continuous only in its second argument.

B State Transition Specification of the Memory Component

As pointed out in the introduction, an alternative to the functional specification for the description of the unreliable memory is a state transition specification. For the state transition specification we work with a state space. We show how to use state transition techniques to define history relations. A state of the unreliable memory is characterized by a value for each memory location and at most one active call for each process id. For each process at most one call may be active in the unreliable memory. If a call is active we store an optional memory return message from RetMem for that process; otherwise the default value nonactive is stored.

We use the set State to represent the state space of the unreliable memory. It is defined as follows:

$$State = (PrIds \to RetMem \cup \{nonactive\}) \times (MemLocs \to MemVals)$$

For a state $t \in State$ and a process $p \in PrIds$ we denote by $t.p$ the status (the optional return message or nonactive if the process is not active) of the process in the state t and for a memory location $e \in MemLocs$ we denote by $t.e$ the value stored under that location. By $(t.p).2$ we denote the second component of the returned message, that is the returned value.

Each memory location holds a memory value. Initially the memory locations contain the value InitVal and all processes are not active.

We define a function that associates with every state of the memory component a behavior relation:

$$MCS : State \rightarrow [(Calls^{\underline{\omega}} \times RetMem^{\underline{\omega}}) \rightarrow Bool]$$

We specify the behavior relation MCS for each state t with the help of the state transition relations that associates input streams and output streams by the following formula:

$$MCS(t) \equiv (s \in Calls^{\underline{\omega}}, y \in RetMem^{\underline{\omega}}) :$$

$$\exists t' \in State :$$

$$(ft.y \neq \surd \wedge out(ft.y, t, t') \wedge MCS(t').(s, rt.y)) \vee$$

$$(ft.s \neq \surd \wedge ft.y = \surd \wedge ((in(ft.s, t, t') \wedge MCS(t').(rt.s, y)) \vee$$

$$t.PrIds(ft.s) \neq nonactive) \vee$$

$$(ft.s = \surd \wedge ft.y = \surd \wedge MCS(t).(rt.s, rt.y))$$

We require that MCS is the weakest relation that fulfills the equation above. We specify the state transition relations called in and out as follows:

$$in((p, u, a), t, t') \qquad \equiv SR(t[p := (c, MemFail)], t')$$

$$out(((p, u, a), z), t, t') \equiv SR(t[p := nonactive], t')$$

$$\wedge (u = read \Rightarrow z = (t.p).2)$$

$$\wedge (u = write \Rightarrow z = (t.p).2)$$

SR denotes a relation between the states of the memory component. It is specified below. Here we write

$$t[p := v]$$

to express that the state t is updated selectively by changing the entry for process p to v.

$$(t[p := v]).p = v$$

$$(t[p := v]).q = t.q \quad \Leftarrow \quad q \neq p$$

We always give an optional return value for each active process that is $MemFail$ in the beginning. In transitions this value may be changed.

In every state transition all active calls may change the memory locations. This is expressed by the relation SR that specifies the relation between the old and the new state. The relation SR is specified as follows:

$SR(t, t') \equiv$

$\forall p \in PrIds, e \in MemLocs, z \in RetVals,$

$\qquad u \in Procs, a \in Args : \exists z' \in RetVals :$

$\quad (t.p = nonactive \quad \Rightarrow \quad t'.p = nonactive) \quad \wedge$

$\quad (t.p = ((p, u, a), z) \quad \Rightarrow \quad t'.p = ((p, u, a), z') \quad \wedge$

$\quad (u = read \qquad\qquad \Rightarrow \quad z' = t'.a$

$\qquad\qquad\qquad\qquad\qquad \vee\ z' = MemFail$

$\qquad\qquad\qquad\qquad\qquad \vee\ (z' = BadArg \wedge a \notin MemLocs)) \quad \wedge$

$\quad (u = write \qquad\quad \Rightarrow \quad (z' = Ack \wedge CHD(MemLoc(a), t, t'))$

$\qquad\qquad\qquad\qquad\qquad \vee\ z' = z$

$\qquad\qquad\qquad\qquad\qquad \vee\ (z' = BadArg \wedge a \notin MemLocs \times MemVals)) \quad \wedge$

$\quad (t.e = t'.e \vee CHD(e, t, t'))$

The proposition $CHD(e, t, t')$ expresses that the memory location e is accessed by one write action in the transition from state t to state t'.

$$CHD(e, t, t') \equiv \exists p \in PrIds, z \in \{Ack, MemFail\}, v \in MemVals :$$

$$t.p = ((p, write, (e, v)), z) \wedge t'.e = v$$

Note that this specification does not include any liveness specifications. Therefore, by this specification, it is not guaranteed that every call eventually returns. However, it is not difficult to add this as an additional constraint. The same holds for the timing condition.

C   A Trace Solution to the Memory Specification Problem

A pure trace specification may be the most appropriate approach for a history-based specification of the unreliable memory. We give such a specification in the following. We use the following syntactic interface:

$$MC : Action^{\underline{\omega}} \to Bool$$

where the set action includes both the input and output actions of the unreliable memory:

$$Action = Calls \cup RetMem$$

Again we write an assumption/commitment specification. The assumption that for each process identifier at most one call is active can easily be formulated. We specify the commitment predicate of a trace by three conditions:

(1) Every call eventually returns.

(2) Every returned memory message fits to its call.

(3) A return message for a read call c returns a value written by one of the writers active while the call c is active or a value written by a write call that terminates before c is active provided there are no successful read or write calls that starts after the write call terminates and terminates before the read call starts.

Conditions (1) and (2) are obvious. Condition (3) is more sophisticated and requires a more detailed justification. According to the behavior of the memory a write call may be executed many times while it is active (while it is issued but has not returned yet). A read call c may access the memory any time while it was active. Therefore it may return any value written by a write call to the respective location that overlaps in its activity interval with that of the read call c. Besides that, it may read a value that was written before the read call c is issued if this value is stored in the memory at the time the read call c is issued.

A value written by a write call w (or the initial value, if there are no write calls) can only be the value stored in the memory at the time the read call c is issued if there does not exist an output that indicates that the value was definitely overwritten. This is indicated by another read call c' that starts after the write call w for the respective location has been completed and returns a different value and ends before the read call c starts or by a write call w' that starts after the write call w was finished and ends successfully. In both cases the value written by the write call w has been definitely overwritten. If there exists such a write call w and if read calls c' and write calls w' with the specified properties do not exist then there is always a possibility that the written value is still stored and can be read.

This analysis shows that a value returned by a read call either is a value written by a write call with an overlap in the activity interval or it is the last written value.

The trace predicate is specified in the assumption/commitment format again by the following formula:

$MC \equiv (t \in Action^{\omega})$:

$(\forall s : s \sqsubseteq t \Rightarrow (\forall p \in PrIds : \#C(p)\copyright s \leq 1 + \#RP(p)\copyright s)) \Rightarrow$

$\forall c \in Calls$:

(1) $\#c\copyright t = \#R(c)\copyright t \wedge \forall i \in [1 : \#t]$:

(2) $t.i \in RetMem \Rightarrow Fit(t.i)\wedge$

(3) $t.i \in Calls \times MemVals \Rightarrow val(t.i) \in active(t, k, i, e) \cup posval(t, k)$

where

$e = Loc(t.i)$

$j = Call\_to\_Return(t, i)$

$$k = \max\{Call\_to\_Return(t,a) : a < j \ \wedge$$

$$t.a \text{ is a successful write or read for location } e\}$$

$Call_to_Return(t,i) = $ index of the call to the return action $t.i$ in trace t

$Loc(a) = $ Location referenced in action a

$active(t,k,i,e) = \{val(t.w) : Loc(t.w) = e \wedge Proc(t.w) = Write \wedge k \leq w \leq i\}$

$posval(t,k) = \{val(t.w) : Loc(t.w) = e \wedge Proc(t.w) = Write \wedge free(w,j)\}$

$\qquad \cup \{InitVal : free(0,j)\}$

$free(w,j) \ = \forall z : t.z \in RetMem\wedge$

$\qquad w < Call\_to\_Return(t,z)\wedge$

$\qquad z < j\wedge$

$\qquad Loc(t.z) = e \Rightarrow$

$\qquad (t.z \notin Calls \times \{Ack\} \wedge t.z \notin Calls \times MemVals\backslash\{val(t.i)\}$

According to our assumption we can find the unique index j of the call action for which a return message is issued.

The procedure Fit is specified as in section 4.

By this trace specification we obtain a purely extensional specification. Without referring to a simple memory component or to an internal access stream we specify the properties of a trace of the unreliable memory. The same style of specification can be used for the relational component model since all the used concepts can also be expressed, there.

Of course this specification could only be written after a careful analysis of the informal description, understanding all the data dependencies. However, such an analysis is useful and necessary, anyhow in a well-organized development method. The trace specification is very interesting if we only intend to write specifications. It is not so easy to deal with if we want to compose specifications.

D   Proof of the Verification Conditions

In this appendix we give the proof for the first of our two basic correctness theorems. It claims that the composed system CI is a refinement of the memory component MC.

Theorem:
The system CI is a refinement of the unreliable memory component MC:

$$CI(s',y') \Rightarrow MC(s',y')$$

Proof: We may use $CI(s',y')$ as our logical assumptions to prove $MC(s',y')$. Unfolding $CI(s',y')$ yields:

$$\exists x, s, r, y : CLK(s', r, x, y') \wedge RPC(x, y, s, r) \wedge RMC(s, y)$$

Furthermore, we may add the assumption in the specification of $MC(s', y')$

$$ProcAssumption(s', y')$$

to our assumptions. Unfolding yields (we drop all outermost universal quantifiers):

(A') $\quad C(p)\ddagger(s' \downarrow i + 1) \leq 1 + RP(p)\ddagger(y' \downarrow i)$

We have to prove that there exists an internal access stream $z \in Calls^\omega$ such that the following properties hold:

(U1) $\quad c\ddagger s' = R(c)\ddagger y' \wedge$

(U2) $\quad Fit(d.i) \wedge$

(U3) $\quad \forall k \in [1 : c\ddagger z] : \exists j \in [1 : c\ddagger s'] : active(j, (c, \sqrt{}©z)^{TM}k) \wedge$

(U4) $\quad (d.i = (c, Ack) \Rightarrow \exists k : active(i, z^{TM}k) \wedge z.k = c) \wedge$

(U5) $\quad (d.i = (c, v) \Rightarrow \exists k : active(i, z^{TM}k) \wedge v = last(z : k, MemLoc(c)))$

where $\quad b = \{c, \sqrt{}\}©s', d = (R(c) \cup \{\sqrt{}\})©y',$

$\qquad\qquad active(i, t) \equiv b^{TM}i \leq t \leq d^{TM}i$

We unfold the specification CLK, RPC and RMC that are used in the description of CI. For the clerk specification $CLK(s', r, x, y')$ we obtain the following properties:

$RPCAssumption(s', y', x, r) \Rightarrow \forall c \in Calls, v \in MemVals :$

(C1) $\quad (c, BadArg)\ddagger y' = (c, BadCall)\ddagger r + (c, BadArg)\ddagger r \wedge$

(C2) $\quad (c, MemFail)\ddagger y' \geq (c, MemFail)\ddagger r \wedge$

(C3) $\quad (c, MemFail)\ddagger y' + c\ddagger x = c\ddagger s' + (c, RPCFailure)\ddagger r + (c, MemFail)\ddagger r \wedge$

(C4) $\quad (c, v)\ddagger y' = (c, v)\ddagger r \wedge$

(C5) $\quad R(c)\ddagger y' = c\ddagger s'$

For $RPC(x, y, s, r)$ we obtain the following properties:

$RPCAssumption(x, r, s, y) \Rightarrow \forall c \in Calls, v \in RetVals :$

(R0) $\quad (IsBadCall(c) \Rightarrow c\ddagger x = (c, BadCall)\ddagger r \wedge c\ddagger s = 0) \wedge$

(R1) $\quad c\ddagger s \leq c\ddagger x \wedge$

(R2) $\quad (c,v)\ddagger r \leq (c,v)\ddagger y \wedge$

(R3) $\quad R(c)\ddagger r = c\ddagger x$

For $RMC(s,y)$ we get that there exists an internal access stream $z' \in Calls^{\underline{\omega}}$ such that the following properties hold:

$ProcAssumption(s,y) \Rightarrow \forall v \in MemVals, c \in Calls, i \in [1 : c\ddagger s] :$

(M1) $\quad c\ddagger s = R(c)\ddagger y$

(M2) $\quad Fit(d.i)$

(M3) $\quad \forall k \in [1 : c\ddagger z'] : \exists j \in [1 : c\ddagger s] : active(j, (\{c, \sqrt{}\}©z')^{TM}k)$

(M4) $\quad (d.i = (c, Ack) \Rightarrow \exists k : active(i, z'^{TM}k) \wedge z'.k = c)$

(M5) $\quad (d.i = (c, v) \Rightarrow \exists k : active(i, z'^{TM}k) \wedge v = last(z' : k, MemLoc(c)))$

where $\quad b = \{c, \sqrt{}\}©s, d = (R(c) \cup \{\sqrt{}\})©y,$

$\qquad\qquad active(i, t) \equiv b^{TM}i \leq t \leq d^{TM}i$

To be able to make use of the input assumptions of the components above we first show that all the component assumptions hold provided the input assumption for $MC(s', y')$ holds. These assumptions are:

$$ProcAssumption(s,y)$$
$$RPCAssumption(s', y', x, r)$$
$$RPCAssumption(x, r, s, y)$$

Unfolding yields the assumption for the three components (which is abbreviated by $As(y', x, s, y, r, s')$):

(A) $\quad C(p)\ddagger(s \downarrow i + 1) \leq 1 + RP(p)\ddagger(y \downarrow i) \wedge$

(C'1) $\quad C(p)\ddagger(s' \downarrow i + 1) \leq 1 + RP(p)\ddagger(y' \downarrow i) \wedge$

(C'2) $\quad c\ddagger x \downarrow i \geq R(c)\ddagger r \downarrow i + 1 \wedge$

(C'3) $\quad R(c)\ddagger r \geq c\ddagger x \wedge$

(R'1) $\quad C(p)\ddagger(x \downarrow i + 1) \leq 1 + RP(p)\ddagger(r \downarrow i) \wedge$

(R'2) $\quad c\ddagger s \downarrow i \geq R(c)\ddagger y \downarrow i + 1 \wedge$

(R'3) $\quad R(c)\ddagger y \geq c\ddagger s$

We get the following commitment for the three components (which is abbreviated by $Co(y', x, s, y, r, s')$):

$$(C1) - (C5), (R0) - (R3), (M1) - (M5)$$

We structure our proof as follows.

(1) We prove that every tuple of streams (y', x, s, y, r, s') which fulfills the formula

$$As(y', x, s, y, r, s') \Rightarrow Co(y', x, s, y, r, s')$$

fulfills the predicate $As(y', x, s, y, r, s')$ provided it fulfills the input assumption $ProcAssumption(s', y')$.

(2) We prove from $As(y', x, s, y, r, s') \wedge Co(y', x, s, y, r, s')$ the commitment of the unreliable memory.

The step (1) is structured into two steps.

(1a) We prove that if an assumption of a component contains a safety and a liveness part, by the time delay property we can assume that every family of streams that fulfills the safety part of the assumption till time point i fulfills the safety part of the commitment till time point i.

(1b) We prove that every family of streams that fulfills the specification and the safety part of the assumption fulfills the liveness part of the assumption.

Proof of (1): The assumption contains only two liveness properties (C3) and (R3).

Proof of (1a): We prove that from

$$As(y', x, s, y, r, s') \Rightarrow Co(y', x, s, y, r, s')$$

we can deduce the safety assumption $As_S(y', x, s, y, r, s')$ given by the formulas:

(A) $C(p)\ddagger(s \downarrow i + 1) \leq 1 + RP(p)\ddagger(y \downarrow i)$

(C'1) $C(p)\ddagger(s' \downarrow i + 1) \leq 1 + RP(p)\ddagger(y' \downarrow i)$

(C'2) $c\ddagger x \downarrow i \geq R(c)\ddagger r \downarrow i + 1$

(R'1) $C(p)\ddagger(x \downarrow i + 1) \leq 1 + RP(p)\ddagger(r \downarrow i)$

(R'2) $c\ddagger s \downarrow i \geq R(c)\ddagger y \downarrow i + 1$

for $i = n + 1$ from

$$\forall i \in I\!N : i \leq n \Rightarrow As_S(y', x, s, y, r, s') \wedge Co_S(y', x, s, y, r, s')$$

and from the safety part of the commitments.

We may assume the safety assumptions for $n = i$:

(A') $C(p)\ddagger(s' \downarrow n+1) \leq 1 + RP(p)\ddagger(y' \downarrow n)$

(A) $C(p)\ddagger(s \downarrow n+1) \leq 1 + RP(p)\ddagger(y \downarrow n)$

(C'1) $C(p)\ddagger(s' \downarrow n+1) \leq 1 + RP(p)\ddagger(y' \downarrow n)$

(C'2) $c\ddagger x \downarrow n \geq R(c)\ddagger r \downarrow n+1$

(R'1) $C(p)\ddagger(x \downarrow n+1) \leq 1 + RP(p)\ddagger(r \downarrow n)$

(R'2) $c\ddagger s \downarrow n \geq R(c)\ddagger y \downarrow n+1$

and the safety commitments that hold because of the delay property till time
point $i = n+1$:

(C1) $(c, BadArg)\ddagger y' \downarrow n+2 \leq (c, BadCall)\ddagger r \downarrow n+1 + (c, BadArg)\ddagger r \downarrow n+1$

(C3) $(c, MemFail)\ddagger y' \downarrow n+2 + c\ddagger x \downarrow n+2 \leq$

       $c\ddagger s' \downarrow n+1 + (c, RPCFailure)\ddagger r \downarrow n+1 + (c, MemFail)\ddagger r \downarrow n+1$

(C4) $(c, v)\ddagger y' \downarrow n+2 \leq (c, v)\ddagger r \downarrow n+1$

(C5) $R(c)\ddagger y' \downarrow n+2 \leq c\ddagger s' \downarrow n+1$

(R0) $(IsBadCall(c) \Rightarrow c\ddagger x \downarrow n+1 \geq (c, BadCall)\ddagger r \downarrow n+2 \wedge c\ddagger s = 0)$

(R1) $c\ddagger s \downarrow n+2 \leq c\ddagger x \downarrow n+1$

(R2) $(c, v)\ddagger r \downarrow n+2 \leq (c, v)\ddagger y \downarrow n+1$

(R3) $R(c)\ddagger r \downarrow n+2 \leq c\ddagger x \downarrow n+1$

(M1) $c\ddagger s \downarrow n+1 \geq R(c)\ddagger y \downarrow n+2$

(M2) $Fit(d.n+1)$

(M3) $\forall k \in [1:c\ddagger z] : \exists j \in [1:c\ddagger s] : active(j, (c, \sqrt{}©z')^{TM}k)$

(M4) $(d.n+1 = (c, Ack) \Rightarrow \exists k : active(n+1, z'^{TM}k) \wedge z'.k = c)$

(M5) $(d.n+1 = (c, v) \Rightarrow \exists k : active(n+1, z'^{TM}k) \wedge (c, v) = last(z' : k, c))$

where $b' = c, \sqrt{}©s, d' = (R(c) \cup \{\sqrt{}\})©y,$

       $active(n+1, t) \equiv b'^{TM}n+1 \leq t \leq d'^{TM}n+1$

We have to prove:

(A) $C(p)\ddagger(s \downarrow n+2) \leq 1 + RP(p)\ddagger(y \downarrow n+1)$

(C'1) $C(p)\ddagger(s' \downarrow n+2) \leq 1 + RP(p)\ddagger(y' \downarrow n+1)$

(C'2) $c\ddagger x \downarrow n+1 \geq R(c)\ddagger r \downarrow n+2$

(R'1) $C(p)\ddagger(x \downarrow n+2) \leq 1 + RP(p)\ddagger(r \downarrow n+1)$

(R'2) $c\ddagger s \downarrow n + 1 \geq R(c)\ddagger y \downarrow n + 2$

We give only an informal proof outline and do not carry out all the formal steps of the proof. The assumption (C'2) for the clerk follows immediately from (R3). The assumption (C'1) for the clerk follows immediately from the assumption (A'). The assumption (R'1) follows from the commitments by straightforward arithmetic manipulation.

Proof of (1b): We show that from

$$As(y', x, s, y, r, s') \Rightarrow Co(y', x, s, y, r, s')$$

and the safety assumption $As_S(y', x, s, y, r, s')$ we can deduce the liveness part of the assumption

(C'3) $R(c)\ddagger r \geq c\ddagger x$

(R'3) $R(c)\ddagger y \geq c\ddagger s$

Proof of (2): We assume the properties $As(y', x, s, y, r, s') \wedge Co(y', x, s, y, r, s')$ and prove the commitment of the unreliable buffer. We can assume therefore the following properties:

(A) $C(p)\ddagger(s \downarrow i + 1) \leq 1 + RP(p)\ddagger(y \downarrow i)$ $\wedge$

(C'1) $C(p)\ddagger(s' \downarrow i + 1) \leq 1 + RP(p)\ddagger(y' \downarrow i)$ $\wedge$

(C'2) $c\ddagger x \downarrow i \geq R(c)\ddagger r \downarrow i + 1$ $\wedge$

(C'3) $R(c)\ddagger r \geq c\ddagger x$ $\wedge$

(R'1) $C(p)\ddagger(x \downarrow i + 1) \leq 1 + RP(p)\ddagger(r \downarrow i)$ $\wedge$

(R'2) $c\ddagger s \downarrow i \geq R(c)\ddagger y \downarrow i + 1$ $\wedge$

(R'3) $R(c)\ddagger y \geq c\ddagger s$ $\wedge$

(C1) $(c, BadArg)\ddagger y' = (c, BadCall)\ddagger r + (c, BadArg)\ddagger r$ $\wedge$

(C2) $(c, MemFail)\ddagger y' \geq (c, MemFail)\ddagger r$ $\wedge$

(C3) $(c, MemFail)\ddagger y' + c\ddagger x = c\ddagger s' + (c, RPCFailure)\ddagger r + (c, MemFail)\ddagger r$ $\wedge$

(C4) $(c, v)\ddagger y' = (c, v)\ddagger r$ $\wedge$

(C5) $R(c)\ddagger y' = c\ddagger s'$ $\wedge$

(R0) $(IsBadCall(c) \Rightarrow c\ddagger x = (c, BadCall)\ddagger r \wedge c\ddagger s = 0)$ $\wedge$

(R1) $c\ddagger s \leq c\ddagger x$ $\wedge$

(R2) $(c, v)\ddagger r \leq (c, v)\ddagger y$ $\wedge$

(R3) $R(c)\ddagger r = c\ddagger x$ $\wedge$

(M1) $\quad c\ddagger s = R(c)\ddagger y \quad \wedge$

(M2) $\quad Fit(d'.i) \quad \wedge$

(M3) $\quad \forall k \in [1 : c\ddagger z] : \exists j \in [1 : c\ddagger s] : active(j, (c, \sqrt{}\copyright z')^{TM}k) \quad \wedge$

(M4) $\quad (d.i = (c, Ack) \Rightarrow \exists k : active(i, z'^{TM}k) \wedge z'.k = c) \quad \wedge$

(M5) $\quad (d.i = (c, v) \Rightarrow \exists k : active(i, z'^{TM}k) \wedge (c, v) = last(z' : k, c))$

where $\quad b' = c, \sqrt{}\copyright s, d' = (R(c) \cup \{\sqrt{}\})\copyright y,$

$\qquad active(i, t) \equiv b'^{TM}i \leq t \leq d'^{TM}i$

Based on these assumptions we have to prove that there exists $z \in Calls^{\underline{\omega}}$ such that:

(U1) $\quad c\ddagger s' = R(c)\ddagger y' \quad \wedge$

(U2) $\quad Fit(d.i) \quad \wedge$

(U3) $\quad \forall k \in [1 : c\ddagger z] : \exists j \in [1 : c\ddagger s'] : active(j, (c, \sqrt{}\copyright z)^{TM}k) \quad \wedge$

(U4) $\quad (d.i = (c, Ack) \Rightarrow \exists k : active(i, z^{TM}k) \wedge z.k = c) \quad \wedge$

(U5) $\quad (d.i = (c, v) \Rightarrow \exists k : active(i, z^{TM}k) \wedge (c, v) = last(z : k, c))$

where $\quad b = c, \sqrt{}\copyright s', d = (R(c) \cup \{\sqrt{}\})\copyright y',$

$\qquad active(i, t) \equiv b^{TM}i \leq t \leq d^{TM}i$

The statements (U1) and (U2) are logical consequences of our assumptions. (U1) is exactly (C5). (U2) follows from (M2) by (R2) and (R0) and by (C4) and (C2). To prove the properties (U3)-(U5) we have to construct a stream z that has the required properties. We do this based on the stream z'.

Every entry in z corresponds to an entry in z'. We define this correspondence by

$$z.i = \max\{j \in I\!N : \exists k \in I\!N : (z' \downarrow k).j = z.i \wedge R(c) \neq (y' \downarrow k) = i$$

$$\wedge \, c \neq (s' \downarrow k) = i\}$$

By this definition $z.i$ is the last reply to the iterated sending of the call $z'.i$ to the memory component. With the help of this definition we can prove the properties (U3) - (U5) by straightforward arithmetic manipulation.

References

[Broy 94a] M. Broy: Specification and Refinement of a Buffer of Length One. Marktoberdorf Summer School 1994

[Broy 94b] M. Broy: A Functional Rephrasing of the Assumption/Commitment Specification Style. Technische Universität München, Institut für Informatik, TUM-I9417, June 1994

[Broy, Lamport] M. Broy, L. Lamport: The RPC-Memory Specification Problem. This volume.

[Broy, Stølen 94] M. Broy, K. Stølen: Specification and Refinement of Finite Dataflow Networks - a Relational Approach. In: Langmaack, H. and de Roever, W.-P. and Vytopil, J. (eds): Proc. FTRTFT'94, Lecture Notes in Computer Science 863, 1994, 247-267

[Stølen et al. 93] K. Stølen, F. Dederichs, R. Weber: Assumption/Commitment Rules for Networks of Agents. Technische Universität München, Institut für Informatik, TUM-I9302

A Solution Relying on the Model Checking of Boolean Transition Systems

Jorge Cuéllar*, Dieter Barnard and Martin Huber

Siemens R&D, ZT SE 1, D-81730 Munich, Germany

Abstract. In this paper we present the *Temporal Language of Transitions* (TLT) solution to the RPC Memory Specification Problem posed by Lamport for a Dagstuhl seminar. TLT is a framework for the compositional specification and verification of distributed systems. In our solution we show how the TLT specifications can be factorized to extract their finite-state control parts. This leads to straightforward refinement checks. We address all parts of the original problem statement.

0 Introduction

Temporal Language of Transitions (TLT) is a framework for the compositional specification and verification of concurrent programs. In particular, it has been applied to reactive control systems [CWB94, CH95, BC95]. TLT consists of a specification language, in which distributed systems can be specified as modules. The modules have appropriate interfaces (similar to [AG94]), which contain shared variables (similar to Unity [CM88]) and actions (similar to CCS [Mil89]) as a basis for inter-module communication. The interfaces also contain explicit assumptions about the environment of a module and vice versa, commitments by the module to its environment. A subset of the TLT language is a programming language, for which there is a compiler [CBH96].

Methodology
TLT modules can be translated to TLA formulas [Lam94a]. The composition of TLT modules is then defined logically as conjunction and the refinement of TLT modules is defined logically as implication. The semantics of TLT systems can thus be given as the set of traces satisfying a temporal formula. TLT also provides an alternative definition in terms of transition systems (automata) labelled by elements of Boolean algebras of appropriate FOL predicates, similar to [Kur94, CGS91]. Different Boolean algebras allow for different levels of abstraction, as demonstrated in [CW96].

Motivation
TLT provides a notation for specifications (modules or properties in several abstraction levels) which have (infinite) Boolean automata as semantics. The proofs of properties and of refinement relations can be carried out in temporal logic (eg., in TLA) or be done semantically. This provides flexibility, we can use

---

* Correspondence to: Jorge.Cuellar@zfe.siemens.de

model checking when possible, theorem proving when necessary, and mathematical arguments when the generality permits (to reduce complexity). Our theorem prover is based upon a shallow embedding of TLA in the Lambda tool [Bus95].

Solution

In this paper we present the TLT solution to the RPC Memory Specification Problem posed by Broy and Lamport for a Dagstuhl seminar [BL]. The design consists of the separation of the control and data parts of the specification. This allows us to factorize the control parts according to the call parameters, resulting in a *small number* of *finite-state* 'control' modules. The necessary refinement proofs can then be carried out by CAV tools. We address all parts (1-5) of the original problem statement.

Comparison

Our solution differs from others in this volume especially in the way that we separate the 'data' and 'control' parts of the specification and reduce the problem to checking a collection of small automata and data-type refinements.

As indicated above, TLT is closely related to TLA. For the sake of describing all possible traces of a TLT module, and particularly for reasoning about them, we use TLA in combination with automata-theoretic methods in our tools. But a TLT module has additional information (eg., an action is either an input or an output action), that is lost when translating to TLA. For instance, in TLA one can express something like: "if any module performs an action A, then only in such a way that other modules can not distinguish it from an own action", but it is not possible to say "action A can only be performed by one module".

It may be argued, that if there is some loss of information while translating from TLT to TLA, then this information was irrelevant. Of course, if programs are only seen as predicates on traces, then there is no loss of information. But TLT modules may also be regarded as transducers (infinite Mealy automata) representing (nondeterministic) *functions* of inputs and outputs, and not simply as automata accepting traces in inputs and outputs. At least for implementation purposes (eg., for a compiler), this information is indeed very relevant [CBH96].

A TLT specification also has a structure that *may* be lost during the translation. For instance, the datatypes in TLT may be seen as invariants in TLA, and therefore their presence is an *assertion* that certain consistency conditions hold. TLT modules also have assumptions, commitments, annotations, etc. that should be translated as assertions. We do not claim that this not possible to do within TLA (or even better, in TLA+) by introducing appropriate *theories*, *theorems*, etc., but we believe that writing specifications in TLT helps structuring the proofs (that may be carried out in TLA). Also, many small lemmas are already proven while checking the consistency of a TLT specification.

TLT is also closely related to evolving algebras [Gur91] and to Boolean automata [Kur94]. It can also be related to the functional approach of [Bro96], even though this relation is somewhat cumbersome [Mer96].

1 The Procedure Interface

1.1 Data types

Before we start with the TLT specification, we introduce a set of data types that will be used throughout the paper. The data types are based on the original problem formulation in [BL]. Besides MemLocs and MemVals, we assume a set ProcIds of process identifiers. Further, we denote supersets of these data types by MemLocs*, MemVals*, etc. Note that incoming calls and outgoing returns are parameterized amongst others by the memory value range (MemVals), which can be infinite. However, the return values of the (factorized) 'control' modules (Server, RServer, RPC and Clerk) consist of ok for a successful memory operation and appropriate exceptions. Finally, we assume two predicates SConsistent and RConsistent, denoting whether a call is consistent or not, as explained below.

TYPES

MemOps	:=	{ Read, Write }
Buffer_Type	:=	{ nil, forward }
Call_Type	:=	ProcIds* × MemOps* × MemLocs* × MemVals*
Return_Type	:=	MemVals ∪ Svr_Exc
Svr_Return_Type	:=	{ ok, MemFailure, BadArg }
RSvr_Return_Type	:=	{ ok, BadArg }
RPC_Return_Type	:=	{ ok, BadArg, RPCFailure, BadCall }
SConsistent	:=	Call_Type
RConsistent	:=	Call_Type

AXIOMS

SConsistent	⇒	Call_Type
RConsistent	⇒	Call_Type
SConsistent	⇒	RConsistent
SConsistent	⇒	ProcIds × MemOps × MemLocs × MemVals

Call_Type consists of a 4-tuple of process identifiers, memory operations, memory locations and memory values. The predicate RConsistent will be used to indicate whether a call is consistent from the viewpoint of a RPC module. This predicate may be checked 'syntactically', it is true if the operation is an element of MemOps and the other parameters of the call make sense for the selected operation. The predicate SConsistent will be used to indicate whether a call is consistent from the viewpoint of the server. This is a 'semantical' restriction that can not be checked outside of the conjunction of server and memory. Our axioms are slightly more general than in the original problem formulation. Note that in any module factorized by Call_Type, the two predicates naturally reduce to propositional constants.

Note: If the data type is defined as an explicit set, say $D := \{a, b, c\}$, then it is assumed that a, b and c are all different. Given data types D_1 and D_2, the following may be constructed: $D_1 \times D_2$, Array D_1 of D_2 and Table D_1 of D_2. Formally, Array D_1 of D_2 is the set of functions of D_1 to D_2. Table D_1 of D_2 is the set of partial functions from D_1 to D_2 not everywhere undefined, or equivalently, Table D_1 of D_2 is defined as $(D_2 \dot{\cup} \{\bot\})^{D_1} \backslash \{\bot\}^{D_1}$.

The *table* data type will be used to accommodate multiple calls in a single execution step. Other candidates for a result data type are power sets or arrays, however tables firstly represent the fact that for each call there is only one result, and secondly, tables have at least one entry (they are nonempty). This definition thus elegantly excludes the possibility of 'stuttering' when the action occurs.

1.2 Interfaces in TLT

TLT modules may contain a set of interfaces. Each interface describes a protocol of interaction between the module and its environment.

An interface starts with *declarations* of variables and actions. Besides their domain, variables (and actions) are given an environment class: *private* variables belong to the module which declares them as private; they are visible to the environment, but they may not be modified by it; *read* variables are imported from the environment; their values can be read but not modified locally; and finally, *history* variables record the history of visible events between a module and its environment, but are not visible themselves. Further classes are: *specification* variables that are not part of the state space of modules; they are used to define parameterized statements (schemas); *local* variables finally completely belong to a module; they may neither be read nor changed by the environment, and they are not visible.

Actions are used in a CCS-style [Mil89], i.e., matching actions (identified by the same name) allow for synchronous communication among modules. Actions are therefore declared as *input* or *output*, depending on whether they are under the control of the environment or of the given module. A restricted form of broadcasting is assumed, in the sense that only one output action synchronizes with one or more input actions. Furthermore, there are *local* actions that are not visible to the outside and only 'synchronize' within a given module.

For example, consider a protocol where an incoming Call action and an outgoing Return action alternate, starting with a call. We will assume that the protocol is responsible for handling one particular call. Thus, the call can be modelled by a signal (i.e., an action that provides no 'value passing'). Signals are just actions of type unit (denoted by ()). Formally, () is a set which contains exactly one element. For the Return action we assume some arbitrary Return_Type. Often, we are not interested in the exact value that is returned. Thus, $\exists_r Return(r)$ for some specification variable r declared of type *Return_Type* will simply be abbreviated by *Return*. This convention will be used throughout the paper.

To describe this protocol, one Boolean-valued history variable pending is sufficient: pending is true iff a call is pending, that is iff a call already has been issued but the corresponding return action has not yet occurred. In the appendix we will use transition systems labelled with elements of an appropriate Boolean algebra (Boolean Transition Systems, or BTS for short) as formal semantics of specifications. Using this representation, we may visualize the protocol as shown in Figure 1.

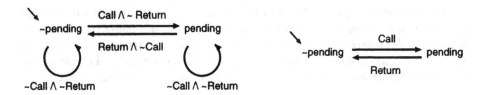

Fig. 1. The BTS shown on the left describes the alternate protocol with 'exact' labels. On the right, the labels on the arcs are incomplete: every transition label should also state that nothing else happens, the stutter loops are omitted.

In TLT, this protocol specified as follows:

```
INTERFACE    2User
  DECLARATIONS
    VARIABLES
      HISTORY  pending  :  Boolean
    ACTIONS
      IN      Call    : ()
      OUT     Return  : Return_Type
  INITIALLY      ¬pending
  ALWAYS

      ‖ Call  =▷  pending′

      ‖ Return  =▷  ¬pending′

  ASSUMPTIONS

      ‖ Call  =▷  ¬pending

  COMMITMENTS

      ‖ Return  =▷  pending

  END
```

The interface is given some name for reference purposes, followed by the declaration section, that declares the actions Call and Return as well as the variable pending as mentioned above.

The declarations are followed by the *initially predicate* specifying the initial values of the variables in the declaration section. In the example this predicate is simply:

$init :\equiv \neg pending$

The *always* section contains a set of always statements. The intuition of these statements is that whenever the *event* on the left side of the 'trigger' symbol ($=\triangleright$) occurs, then the corresponding command on the right is executed. Always statements are used to process input actions and to update the values of history variables.

In the example, there are two always statements:

‖ Call $=\triangleright$ pending$'$

‖ Return $=\triangleright$ $\neg$pending$'$

The first statement describes, that whenever a call occurs, then the history variable pending is set (‖ is used as separator, the primed occurrence of a variable represents its value in the next state). This can be expressed in temporal logic as $\square$ Call $\Rightarrow$ pending$'$, where $\square$ has to be read 'always'.[2]

Further, we require that pending does not occur primed neither in other interfaces nor in the module body (nor in other modules). Thus no other statement changes the value of pending. This is expressed in a local *frame axiom* for pending:

$\square$ (pending$'$ $\neq$ pending $\Rightarrow$ Call $\vee$ Return)

Together the always section is translated as:

$alw\_section :\equiv \square$ [(Call $\Rightarrow$ pending$'$) $\wedge$ (Return $\Rightarrow$ $\neg$ pending$'$) $\wedge$
(pending$'\neq$ pending $\Rightarrow$ Call $\vee$ Return)]

Still, $init \wedge alw\_section$ does not describe the protocol as shown in Figure 1. One reason is that $init \wedge alw\_section$ is *input-enabled*. This means that Call may occur in any state, allowing for a self-loop in state pending that is labelled with $\neg$Return (or equivalently, (Call $\vee\neg$ Call) $\wedge$ $\neg$Return). To disallow such calls, we have to explicitly assume that the environment only executes Call in state $\neg$pending, which will be noted as:

‖ Call $=\triangleright$ $\neg$pending

More general, the *assumptions* section contains assumptions made about the behaviour of the environment . Each assumption consists of a predicate describing an environment event (i.e., a predicate on read variables and input actions), the $=\triangleright$-symbol, and the constraint (a predicate on unprimed variables) posed on this event. In combination with history variables, it is possible to model the (assumed) behaviour of the environment in arbitrary detail, typically as a protocol between the environment and a module.

Similarly, we have to restrict the behaviour of the module itself. The exact moment when the module issues Return may depend on local variables, however

---

[2] The formal semantics of this temporal logic can be found in [CBH95].

at least we require that Return occurs only in state pending. We say, the module commits itself to issue Return only in state pending, and note this by

❙   Return   =▷   pending

More general, the *commitments* section contains commitments about the behaviour of the module itself. That is, the module guarantees to perform an *output* event only if the constraint following the =▷-symbol holds. Translated to logic we get two further constraints:

$assume :\equiv \Box\ Call \Rightarrow \neg pending$
$commit :\equiv \Box\ Return \Rightarrow pending$

The final formula describing the behaviour of the interface in temporal logic is:

$$\exists_{pending}\ (init \wedge alw\_section \wedge assume \wedge commit)$$

where the ∃ quantor hides the (flexible) variable pending (as in TLA [Lam94a]). The reader may validate that this formula and the BTS in Figure 1 have the same observable behaviour. For example, both allow infinite stuttering, i.e., an infinite sequence of ¬Call ∧ ¬Return transitions.

By translating the TLT specifications to either temporal logic or BTS, we loose information about the environment classes, although this information plays a major role in the translation process itself as well as in determining the consistency criteria necessary to guarantee that the different modules (and interfaces) of a system can be composed [CBH95]. For verification purposes based on arguments on the sets of traces of a module, this information is not really necessary. However, for describing the intended distribution of the solution and in order to compile the specifications to a distributed architecture, this information is crucial [CBH96]. This is one of the reasons why we do not simply use TLA from the start.

Instances of the 2User interface will appear several times, e.g. the Clerk module uses one to communicate with some non specified user, the RPC component uses it to describe its view of the communication with the Clerk. In a vertical hierarchy where the User is 'on the top', followed by the Clerk, the RPC-Component, and the Server, the different instances of the 2User interface are directed 'upwards'. Correspondingly, a dual interface is used to describe a view of the same protocol in the other direction:

```
INTERFACE   2Server
  DECLARATIONS
    VARIABLES
      HISTORY   waiting   : Boolean
    ACTIONS
      OUT    Call      : ()
      IN     Return    : Return_Type
    INITIALLY    ¬waiting
  ALWAYS
```

‖ Call ⇒▷ waiting′

‖ Return ⇒▷ ¬waiting′

ASSUMPTIONS

‖ Return ⇒▷ waiting

COMMITMENTS

‖ Call ⇒▷ ¬waiting

END

Sometimes we will use variants of already defined interfaces that differ in the names of some variables or actions, or even in their data types. Instead of repeating the same text with minor changes each time, the new interface will be declared as: USE INTERFACE Name WITH Substitution.

Only one further interface used in this paper needs extra explanation:

INTERFACE   2Memory
  DECLARATIONS
    ACTIONS
      OUT   MemCall   : ()
      IN   MemReturn : ()
  ASSUMPTIONS

  ‖ MemCall ⇒▷ MemReturn

  ‖ MemReturn ⇒▷ MemCall

  COMMITMENTS

  ‖ MemCall ⇒▷ SConsistent

END

This interface is used by a server to connect to a memory automaton. This automaton is expected to react 'immediately' on a MemCall request with Mem-Return (i.e., within the same execution step). This is expressed by the two assumptions: the first one says that MemCall is answered in the same step with MemReturn. The second one states that MemReturn occurs only when triggered by MemCall. The commitment states that the module using this interface executes MemCall only if the module is responsible for a SConsistent call.

2   A Memory Component

In this section we present the TLT solution to Problem 1 of the RPC Memory Specification Problem. The memory component will be specified in TLT as a set of modules and mappings as displayed in Figure 2. The key aspect of this specification is that we specify the (parameterized) server as a set of independent server modules factorized according to each call. Furthermore, the memory value of a successful memory operation is not passed back via the server, but temporarily stored in a result module. This data information is given back to the user using a user connector as a 'glue'. This connector however needs no memory (it only translates). Therefore the memory and the result modules are only 'data' modules, while the control part is only in the server, which is the parameterized conjunction of a fairly simple generic server.

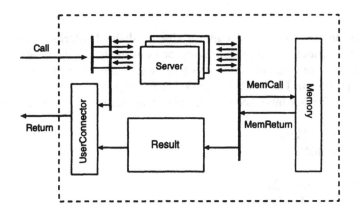

Fig. 2. Memory Component Architecture

Besides those modules (represented in Figure 2), we also use some mappings between the data types of the actions, similar to elementary data refinements. These mappings (represented by the vertical bars in Figure 2) are a consistent set of embeddings of the corresponding Boolean algebras. A (parameterized) call is mapped to a set of call signals for the appropriate servers. Return actions from the servers are mapped to a parameterized return to the user connector, which passes exceptions back unchanged but substitutes successful memory operations by their corresponding values stored in the result module. Finally, call signals to the memory module are mapped to a (parameterized) memory call, and a return from the memory is mapped to return signals for the servers and a (parameterized) return for the result module. These mappings will be made explicit on Subsection 2.4.

The factorization of the server according to calls and the use of the result module lead to *finite-state* server modules, which are responsible purely for control (and not for data). The motivation for this design is that the proofs of properties of and the refinement relations between these modules can now be done efficiently by *automatic* verification tools (or even by hand). The compositional theory presented in the appendix then allows us to lift these results to the parameterized specifications.

2.1 The Memory Specification

The memory module represents a memory automaton. For the RPC Memory Specification Problem and the refinement proofs, the specification of the memory is irrelevant: we can assume an arbitrary Mealy automaton or any other object for that matter (restricted to the data types above). Nevertheless, for the sake of completeness we include our own version of the memory module in TLT below.

MODULE   Memory

  INTERFACE   Memory2Server
   DECLARATIONS
    VARIABLES
     SPEC   id : ProcIds
              op : MemOps
              i : MemLocs
              v : MemVals
    ACTIONS
     IN   MemCall   : Table(Call_Type) Of ()
     OUT   MemReturn : Table(Call_Type) Of MemVals
    ASSUMPTIONS
     $\|_{id,op,i,v}$ MemCall(id, op, i, v) $\Rightarrow\triangleright$ SConsistent(id, op, i, v)

END

  DECLARATIONS
   VARIABLES
    LOCAL   memory : Array(MemLocs) Of MemVals
  INITIALLY $\forall_i$ (memory(i) = InitVal)
  ALWAYS

    $\|_{id,i,v}$ MemCall(id, Read, i, v) $\Rightarrow\triangleright$
        MemReturn(id, Read, i, v, memory(i))

    $\|_{id,i,v}$ MemCall(id, Write, i, v) $\Rightarrow\triangleright$
        MemReturn(id, Write, i, v, v) $\wedge$ memory'(i) = v

END.

The memory is implemented as an array of memory locations, instantiated to some default value. The module contains two parameterized always instructions, responsible for read and write operations. A MemCall input action requesting a read triggers a MemReturn with the value of the given location; a MemCall with a write request triggers a MemReturn with the same value and updates the memory. Note that MemCall and MemReturn happens synchronously, i.e., within a single step.

2.2 The Server Specification

In addition to a set of interfaces, the module body can contain further declaration, initially and always sections, as well as an *instruction* and a *fairness* section. *Instructions* consist of a predicate representing a guard, the → symbol, and a predicate representing a command. Intuitively this means that once in a state where the guard evaluates to true (i.e., the instruction is *enabled*), it is *possible* to execute the command. If several instructions are enabled, any subset of enabled instructions may be executed, as long as they do not contradict each other. This means, that the ‖ -separator for instructions has to be read as disjunction, whereas in all other sections it denotes conjunction. With each instruction comes an implicit consistency criteria that guarantees that the instruction is executable if it's guard is enabled.

The *fairness* section contains weak and strong fairness requirements as pairs of predicates representing a condition (to be fulfilled continuously in case of weak and infinitely often in case of strong fairness) and an event to be executed. Fairness is necessary due to the possible nondeterminism of the guarded-commands. One (minimal) fairness condition, *local progress*, is assumed implicitly: if instructions of the module are enabled continuously, then an instruction is eventually executed.

MODULE Server

   USE   INTERFACE   2User
             WITH   Return ← (SReturn : Svr_Return_Type)

   USE   INTERFACE   2Memory

   DECLARATIONS
      VARIABLES
         LOCAL   buffer   : (RSvr_Return_Type ∪ Buffer_Type)
   INITIALLY   buffer = nil
   ALWAYS

       ‖ Call ∧ SConsistent =▷ buffer′= forward

       ‖ Call ∧ ¬SConsistent =▷ buffer′= BadArg

       ‖ MemReturn =▷ buffer′= ok

       ‖ SReturn =▷ buffer′= nil

   INSTRUCTIONS

       ‖ buffer ≠ nil ∧ buffer ≠ BadArg ⟶ MemCall

       ‖ buffer ∈ RSvr_Return_Type ⟶ SReturn(buffer)

       ‖ buffer ≠ nil ⟶ SReturn(MemFailure)

FAIRNESS

   ‖ WF(buffer = ok, SReturn)

END.

    The control functions of the server are based upon a local variable called buffer. The (internal) states of automata will therefore correspond to the 4 possible values of buffer (the history variable pending that occurs in the 2User interface is just a function of buffer). The incoming call is 'entered' in a buffer, which will store the result for this call. If the call is consistent, then it is marked as forward. If not, then the result is already determined as BadArg. A consistent call is then either forwarded to the memory and acquires the result ok when the memory replies with MemReturn, or it fails and MemFailure is returned as result. When a call is returned, the buffer is 'emptied'.

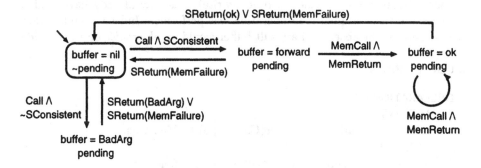

Fig. 3. BTS of Factorized Server

    The factorized server above has the BTS semantics given in Figure 3. Again, for the sake of readability, the labels on the arcs are incomplete. With regards to fairness, the acceptance conditions on the module (implicit local progress and the explicit weak fairness) are equivalent to the single Büchi property that runs 'pass' infinitely often through (buffer = nil). This is denoted by the circled state in Figure 3 and is due to the fact that fairness for the action SReturn is encoded in the internal variable buffer: SReturn $\Leftrightarrow$ (buffer $\neq$ nil) $\wedge$ buffer$'$ = nil).

    We will now use this transition system to justify our TLT specification in view of the requirements stated in [BL]:

– The return of BadArg has no effect on the memory. The consistency check on the operands is performed immediately when the call is received and an inconsistent call never results in a memory operation.

- Each successful read operation on the memory automaton occurs atomically and is performed one or more times. This seems weaker than the original requirement, but the observable behaviour is the same.
- Each successful write operation on the memory automaton occurs atomically and is performed one or more times.
- Each unsuccessful write call involves zero or more write operations on the memory automaton, due to the choice between MemCall and FailCall.
- Each call is eventually returned. This is guaranteed by the fairness requirements in the module body.

2.3   Result and UserConnector Modules

In addition to the factorized server modules, the TLT solution to the first problem is based upon a result module and a user connector. The Result module can be seen as a temporary register to store the value of a successful read operation. This value is irrelevant for control purposes, but essential for the solution. We cannot use the current value of the memory when the final return to the user is made, because the presence of other (write) calls may already have lead to changes since the original read operation was performed. Indeed, counterexamples show that the absence of a result buffer would be *observable* on the outside.

MODULE   Result

DECLARATIONS
 ACTIONS
  IN   MemReturn : Table(Call_Type) Of MemVals
 VARIABLES
  PRIVATE result : Array(Call_Type) Of MemVals
  SPEC c   : Call_Typ
     v   : MemVals
INITIALLY $\forall_c$ (result(c) = InitVal)
ALWAYS

  $\|_{c,v}$ MemReturn(c, v) $\Rightarrow\triangleright$ result'(c) = v

END.

The result module receives a table of calls and memory values from the memory automaton. The individual entries are then stored in a variable called result. Since result is declared as private, it is visible to the environment. Each transition of the BTS of the module Result that we need here is labelled with a predicate on the variables result, result' and on the action MemReturn.

Remember that the separate return signals of the server modules are mapped to a parameterized return, which serves as an input action to the user connector. The task of the connector is simply to return exceptions unchanged but to substitute the ok result (of a successful memory operation) by the real value stored in result.

MODULE   UserConnector

DECLARATIONS
   ACTIONS
     IN   SReturn : Table(Call_Type) Of Svr_Return_Type
     OUT   Return   : Table(Call_Type) Of Return_Type
   VARIABLES
     READ   result   : Array(Call_Type) Of MemVals
     SPEC   c   : Call_Typ
                v   : MemVals
                exc   : Svr_Exc
ALWAYS
   $\|_{c,v}$ SReturn(c, ok) $\wedge$ v = result(c) $=\!\!\triangleright$ Return(c, v)

   $\|_{c,exc}$ SReturn(c, exc) $=\!\!\triangleright$ Return(c, exc)

END.

2.4 Conjunction of Modules

Let us now informally explain the conjunction of identical replicas of a TLT module F (see the appendix for a formal exposé). As an example, let us recall the simple alternating protocol of §1.2. Let F be characterized as follows: F has only two visible actions Call and Return of type unit, the first one an input and the second an output, which may only alternate, starting with Call; further, F always reacts, in the sense that if the input Call happens, eventually F responds with the output Return. To describe F as a an automaton we introduce an internal (local) Boolean variable pending, such that:

(F.1) Initially ¬pending;
(F.2) □(Call ⇔ ¬pending ∧ pending′);
       □(Return ⇔ pending ∧ ¬pending′);
(F.3) □◇ (¬ pending).

Let us call (1) the initially predicate, (2) the next-step equations and (3) the Büchi condition of F. (This last one may also be written as a weak or strong fairness property).

Let C be any data type and let c be a fresh variable of type C. For each $c \in C$ we wish to define F(c) as a replica of F and we want to construct the conjunction $\vec{F} := \bigwedge_{c \in C} F(c)$. F(c) is just a renaming of F: Call will be denoted by Call(c) and Return by Return(c). Think of Call(c) as an action with *name* Call and, if present, passing the *value* c. For the sake of simplicity in the exposition, it is convenient but not necessary to also denote the internal variable pending by pending(c).

The BTS of F is now the conjunction of the BTS of F(c), for $c \in C$. The state space of $\vec{F}$ is the Cartesian product of the state spaces of F(c) for $c \in C$, each of which has two elements. Thus $\vec{F}$ has $2^{|C|}$ internal states. Let $\overrightarrow{\text{pending}}$ be a local variable of type $\{0, 1\}^C$ of $\vec{F}$ denoting the internal state. The variable (function) $\overrightarrow{\text{pending}}$ may be identified with the vector of variables [pending(c) : $c \in C$]. The resulting defining equations for $\vec{F}$ are:

($\vec{F}$.1) Initially $\forall_c$ ¬pending(c)

($\vec{F}$.2) $\Box(\forall_c$ Call(c) $\Leftrightarrow$ ¬pending(c) $\wedge$ pending'(c));
$\qquad \Box(\forall_c$ Return(c) $\Leftrightarrow$ pending(c) $\wedge$ ¬pending'(c));

($\vec{F}$.3) For all $c \in C$, $\Box\Diamond$ (¬pending(c)).

In other words, the initial predicate, the next-step equations and the Büchi (or Fairness) conditions of $\vec{F}$ are respectively, the conjunction of the initial predicate, the next-step equations and the Büchi conditions of F(c). This is sometimes called the free product of the automata F(c) (see [Arn94], pages 26ff).

Thus $\vec{F}$ may be seen as a module having two visible actions, called (as in F) Call and Return. What we still have to explain is the data types of the actions Call and Return in the new module $\vec{F}$. Seen from the outside, $\vec{F}$ is a collection of independent modules F(c), for $c \in C$, all of which may accept a Call or issue a Return in one common step. This may be formalized by saying that Call (and Return) are (in $\vec{F}$) of type Table C of (), that is, on each transition a set C_1 of calls may happen.

More generally, if A is an action of type D in F, then the action A in $\vec{F} :=$ $\bigwedge_{c \in C} F(c)$ has type Table C of D. In a single transition, any number of modules F(c) may perform A with a value $d \in D$, depending on C.

We will use a further convention in TLT: two actions named by the same letter in two modules F and G synchronize in F∧G, even if they have different data types in F and G respectively. In this case, we have to make sure that there is a data refinement relating the data types. In general, it is necessary to explicitly write down those refinements, but in this paper we only use one very simple special case, in which the two data types are Table C of D and Table C of () respectively. (As a particular case, letting $C = ()$, we have a refinement between D and ()).

The refinement is just the projection on the first coordinate of a table (see a table as a subset of $C \times D$, project onto the first component and see this as a table of entries of C). Expressed as logical (FOL) formulas, this amounts to the equivalence $\exists_d A(c, d) \Leftrightarrow A(c)$, which is a TLT convention (in particular, we also have $\exists_d A(d) \Leftrightarrow A$).

In our example, we have: MemReturn is of type () in the server, thus of type Table CallType of () in $\overrightarrow{\text{Server}}$, and of type Table CallType of MemVals in the memory and Result components.

2.5 Solution to Problem 1(a)(i):

1. $\overrightarrow{\text{Server}}(c) := \text{Server}$

2. $\overrightarrow{\text{Server}} := \bigwedge_{c \,\in\, Call\_type} \overrightarrow{\text{Server}}(c)$

3. Abstract_Memory $:= \overrightarrow{\text{Server}} \wedge \text{Memory} \wedge \text{Result} \wedge \text{UserConnector}$

The TLT specification of the memory component is given by Abstract_Memory.

2.6 The Reliable Server Specification

The specification of the reliable server is similar to the one given for the (un-reliable) server, except that the possibility of a memory failure is not included. This constitutes in the following three changes:

1. Rename the module to RServer1.
2. The 2User interface is now used as follows (only the datatype changes):
   USE   INTERFACE   2User
          WITH   Return ← (SReturn : RSvr_Return_Type)
3. Omit the third guarded-command (the one responsible for the return of MemFailure)

We call this server RServer1 to reserve the name RServer for a version of it later.

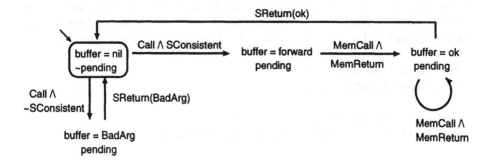

Fig. 4. BTS of Factorized Reliable Server

The semantics of the reliable server is displayed as an automaton in Figure 4. From this transition system is easy to see that the reliable server never returns MemFailure as a result. This is the only additional requirement for the reliable server stated in [BL].

Solution to Problem 1(a)(ii):

1. $\overrightarrow{\text{RServer1}}(c) := \text{RServer1}$

2. $\overrightarrow{\text{RServer1}} := \bigwedge_{c \in Call\_type} \overrightarrow{\text{RServer1}}(c)$

3. $\text{Reliable\_Memory1} := \overrightarrow{\text{RServer1}} \wedge \text{Memory} \wedge \text{Result} \wedge \text{UserConnector}$

The TLT specification of the reliable memory component is given by Reliable_Memory.

2.7 The Refinement of Server

The task is now to prove that the memory component containing the reliable server is a refinement of the memory component containing the (unreliable) server. The proof relies from the fact that the (factorized) reliable server is a refinement of the (factorized) server. Using the compositional theory presented in the appendix, this result can be lifted to the parameterized memory components.

1. $\text{RServer1} \Rightarrow \text{Server}$ (CAV Tool)

2. $\overrightarrow{\text{RServer1}} \Rightarrow \overrightarrow{\text{Server}}$ (from Defs. and 1)

3. $\text{Reliable\_Memory1} \Rightarrow \text{Abstract\_Memory}$ (from Defs. and 2)

The CAV tool used above inputs the TLT specifications of the (factorized) reliable and unreliable servers, constructs their BTS and automatically checks for refinement. This is possible because the factorized modules are finite-state. In fact, since the BTS of the server module and the reliable server module both have 5 reachable states (Figures 3 and 4), the refinement check is trivial.

Solution to Problem 1(b):
Yes, the proof is given above.

Solution to Problem 1(c):
Yes, this is one of the traces of the memory component.

3 A RPC Component

In this section we address the second task of the RPC Memory Specification Problem. We start with the TLT specification of a RPC component. This is followed by the specification of a clerk. The system composed of the clerk, RPC and reliable memory server is then proven to be a refinement of the original (unreliable) memory component. This proof will again exploit the factorization in our specification. First we need to rename the actions of the reliable server to distinguish them from the ones of the user (which now does not communicate with the server directly). Let RServer be identical to RServer1 with the following change:

```
USE   INTERFACE   2User
         WITH   Call ← (SvrCall : () )
         WITH   Return ← (SvrReturn : RSvr_Return_Type)
```

3.1 The RPC Specification

The RPC component is specified in TLT as a module factorized by Call_Type. It has an interface to the clerk (discussed later) and an interface to the reliable memory server. The first interface contains a RPCCall input signal and an RPCReturn output action, the second interface contains a SvrCall output signal and a SvrReturn input action. The history variables pending and waiting will be used in the two interfaces respectively to model the expected behaviour of the environment.

```
MODULE  RPC

  USE   INTERFACE   2User
           WITH   Call ← (RPCCall : () )
           WITH   Return ← (RPCReturn : RPC_Return_Type)


  USE   INTERFACE   2Server

           WITH   Call ← (SvrCall : () )
           WITH   Return ← (SvrReturn : RSvr_Return_Type)

DECLARATIONS
   VARIABLES
     SPEC      r        : RPC_Return_Type
     SPEC      v        : RSvr_Return_Type
     LOCAL     buffer   : ( RPC_Result_Type ∪ Buffer_Type )
   ACTIONS
     LOCAL  FailCall  : ()
INITIALLY      buffer = nil
ALWAYS
```

$\parallel$ RPCCall $\wedge$ RConsistent $\Rightarrow\triangleright$ buffer$'=$ forward

$\parallel$ RPCCall $\wedge$ ¬RConsistent $\Rightarrow\triangleright$ buffer$'=$ BadCall

$\parallel$ SvrCall $\Rightarrow\triangleright$ buffer$'=$ nil

$\parallel_v$ SvrReturn(v) $\Rightarrow\triangleright$ buffer$'=$ v

$\parallel$ RPCReturn $\Rightarrow\triangleright$ buffer$'=$ nil

$\parallel$ FailCall $\Rightarrow\triangleright$ buffer$'=$ RPCFailure

INSTRUCTIONS

| buffer = forward $\longrightarrow$ SvrCall

| buffer $\neq$ nil $\wedge$ buffer $\neq$ RPCFailure $\longrightarrow$ FailCall

|$_r$ buffer = r $\longrightarrow$ RPCReturn(r)

END.

The RPC module uses a local variable called buffer for control purposes. The incoming call is entered in the buffer; if the call is inconsistent the result is fixed as BadCall, otherwise as forward. Consistent calls are relayed via SvrCall to the memory server (and temporarily deleted from buffer). The result via SvrReturn is reentered in the buffer, and eventually returned using RPCReturn. A call that has not yet been forwarded or a call for which a result was obtained but not passed back yet can instead return with a RPCFailure exception.

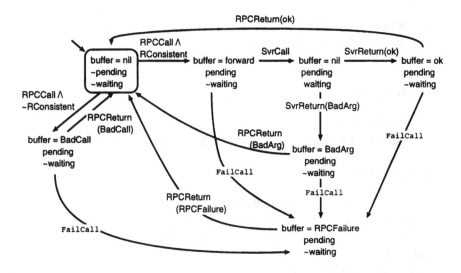

Fig. 5. Factorized Transition System of RPC

The semantics of the factorized RPC module is displayed as a BTS in Figure 5. Using this, we can compare our specification with the requirements for the RPC component stated in [BL]:

– The RPC module returns a BadCall result if the call is not consistent. This check is performed immediately when RPCCall occurs and an inconsistent call is never relayed to the memory server.

- The RPC module can issue a single SvrCall for a consistent call. Once the result has been obtained, (a) this can be passed back, or (b) FailCall can be executed and the result becomes the RPCFailure exception.
- FailCall can also be executed before the call is relayed to the server. In this case, no SvrCall is performed and the result is simply the RPCFailure exception.

Solution to Problem 2:

1. $\overrightarrow{RPC}(c) := RPC$

2. $\overrightarrow{RPC} := \bigwedge_{c \in Call\_type} \overrightarrow{RPC}(c)$

The TLT specification of the RPC component is given by $\overrightarrow{RPC}$.

3.2 The RPC Implementation

The RPC component is to be implemented in such way that it presents the same observable behaviour to its environment as the (unreliable) memory server. However, the RPC module specified above can return a RPCFailure exception, which is not included in the result type of the memory server. The solution is to introduce another component called Clerk. The resulting system is displayed in Figure 6.

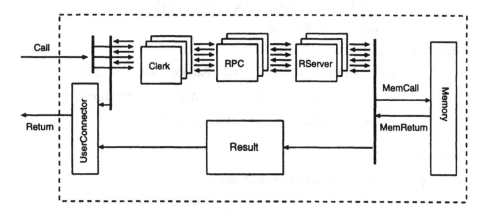

Fig. 6. RPC Component Architecture

The clerk is specified in TLT as a module factorized by Call_Type. It has an interface to the user and an interface to the RPC module. The interface to the user is identical to the interface included in the (factorized) server module (Call input signal and Return output action). The interface to the RPC module contains the RPCCall output signal and RPCReturn input action. The interfaces also make use of pending and waiting history variables respectively.

MODULE Clerk

  USE   **INTERFACE**   2User
        WITH   Return $\leftarrow$ (SReturn : Svr_Return_Type)

  USE   **INTERFACE**   2Server

        WITH   Call $\leftarrow$ (RPCCall : ())
        WITH   Return $\leftarrow$ (RPCReturn : RPC_Return_Type)

DECLARATIONS
  VARIABLES
    SPEC   r   : Svr_Return_Type
    SPEC   v   : RPC_Return_Type
    LOCAL   buffer   : (RPC_Return_Type $\cup$ Buffer_Type)
INITIALLY   buffer = nil
ALWAYS

     ‖   Call $=\!\triangleright$ buffer′ = forward

     ‖   RPCCall $=\!\triangleright$ buffer′ = nil

     ‖   RPCReturn(BadCall) $=\!\triangleright$ buffer′ = BadArg

     ‖$_v$ RPCReturn(v) $\wedge$ v $\neq$ BadCall $=\!\triangleright$ buffer′ = v

     ‖   SReturn $=\!\triangleright$ buffer′ = nil

INSTRUCTIONS

     ‖   buffer = forward $\vee$ buffer = RPCFailure $\longrightarrow$ RPCCall

     ‖$_r$ buffer = r $\wedge$ (r = ok $\vee$ r = BadArg) $\longrightarrow$ SReturn(r)

     ‖   buffer = RPCFailure $\longrightarrow$ SReturn(MemFailure)

FAIRNESS

     ‖ SF(buffer = RPCFailure, SReturn)

END.

The clerk also uses a local buffer for control purposes. Incoming calls are entered in the buffer, and then relayed to the RPC module. The result comes back via the RPCReturn action and is again entered in buffer. If the result was a BadCall exception, this is immediately changed to the BadArg exception. If the result was a RPCFailure, the call can be relayed again. Eventually all calls with their results are returned, RPCFailure exceptions are simply returned as MemFailure exceptions.

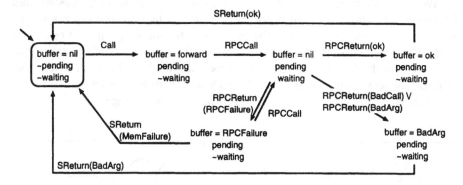

Fig. 7. Factorized Transition System of Clerk

The resulting BTS of the (factorized) clerk is displayed in Figure 7. The acceptance condition is equivalent to the Büchi condition that the initial state is visited infinitely often.

Solution to Problem 3(a):

1. $\overrightarrow{\text{Clerk}}(c) := \text{Clerk}$

2. $\text{DServer} := \text{Clerk} \wedge \text{RPC} \wedge \text{RServer}$

3. $\overrightarrow{\text{DServer}}(c) := \overrightarrow{\text{Clerk}}(c) \wedge \overrightarrow{\text{RPC}}(c) \wedge \overrightarrow{\text{RServer}}(c)$

4. $\overrightarrow{\text{DServer}} := \bigwedge_{c \in Call\_type} \overrightarrow{\text{DServer}}(c)$

5. $\text{Distributed\_Memory} := \overrightarrow{\text{DServer}} \wedge \text{Memory} \wedge \text{Result} \wedge \text{UserConnector}$

The TLT specification of the implementation of the RPC component is given by Distributed_Memory.

3.3 The Refinement of Server

The proof that the Distributed_Memory implements the Abstract_Memory is straightforward (RConsistent and SConsistent are propositional constants for a given call):

0. RConsistent ∧ SConsistent

1. DServer ∧ SConsistent ∧ RConsistent ⇒ Server   (CAV Tool)

2. $\overrightarrow{\text{DServer}} \Rightarrow \overrightarrow{\text{Server}}$ (from Defs. and 1)

3. Distributed_Memory $\Rightarrow$ Abstract_Memory   (from Defs. and 2)

We have to consider the role of the consistency predicates SConsistent and RConsistent in the refinement proof. Since calls can be repeated (by the clerk), we need to rely on the fact that the two predicates (or propositional constants in the factorized version) do not change their values (for a particular call). This is however easily done by modelling the predicates as the BTS RConsistent and SConsistent as shown in Figure 8. The BTS simply state that there is no trace in which the truth value of RConsistent or SConsistent changes.

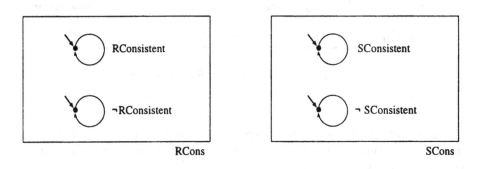

Fig. 8. BTS for the predicates RConsistent and SConsistent.

The composition in (1) above results in a BTS with 4 disjunct parts, corresponding to the 4 possible combinations of SConsistent and RConsistent (for one particular call). We again rely on a tool to check the refinement relation in (7). This is possible because the factorized modules are all finite-state. The refinement is easily checked.

Solution to Problem 3(b):
Given by the proof above.

4   A Lossy RPC Component

In this section we sketch the TLT solution for implementing the RPC component by a lossy RPC and a supervising clerk.

4.1   Timed Instructions

In this section we present a lossy RPC that may loose calls, and a supervising Clerk that keeps track of the time passed after a call is sent forward to the RPC. If the call remains pending for a long time, the supervising Clerk returns a RPC_Failure to the caller. To do this, we introduce in this section a variable t representing the value of a global time and we extend the notion of instructions to timed instructions.

More formally, we assume the existence of a real valued variable t that is increased monotonically and eventually exceeds any value. That is, only traces are considered that fulfill the following two axioms:

1. $\Box t' \geq t$
2. $true \longmapsto t > t_0$ for all $t_0 \in \mathbb{R}$

where $b_1 \longmapsto b_2$ is the usual leads-to: $b_1 \longmapsto b_2 \Leftrightarrow \Box(b_1 \Rightarrow \Diamond b_2)$.

Now, we introduce timed transitions of the form

$$(*) \qquad g \xrightarrow{[\delta_1, \delta_2)} \alpha,$$

$0 \leq \delta_1 < \delta_2 \leq \infty$. For the sake of simplicity, we will assume that initially g is false and that the instruction blocks itself, that is, by executing the instruction α, its guard gets disabled (more precisely, assume $(g \wedge \alpha \Rightarrow \neg g')$ is true in FOL). Further, we assume that actions are instantaneous. That is, they do not consume time. The instruction $(*)$ has two aspects: a safety and a 'liveness' part (in an informal sense). The safety part states that this instruction is enabled only in certain windows of time: let t_0 be any moment where g becomes true; if g remains true for all time in $(t_0, t]$, and $t \in t_0 + [\delta_1, \delta_2)$ then (and only then) the instruction is enabled (at time t).

The liveness part states that if g remains true over the whole window $t \in t_0 + [\delta_1, \delta_2)$, then the instruction has to happen. Let us state this more precisely. Consider first the case where $\delta_2 = \infty$. Then, the fairness of $g \xrightarrow{[\delta_1, \infty)} \alpha$ is a week fairness: if g is from a point on continuously true, then α has to be executed infinitely often. But then, since $g \wedge \alpha \Rightarrow \neg g'$, g will become false. In other words, g may not be continuously true. That means, $\Box \Diamond \neg g$, or $g \mapsto \neg g$ (where $\mapsto$ is leads-to). The weak-fairness of $g \rightarrow \alpha$ is equivalent to saying that g may not be eventually always true, or that g leads-to $\neg g$.

Now, for $\delta_2 < \infty$, $g \xrightarrow{[\delta_1, \delta_2)} \alpha$ contains a stronger liveness condition. It says that if g is true then it will be false before δ_2 time passes.

We formalize timed instructions using history variables as follows: let, for a given state predicate g, the transition predicate $\neg g \wedge g'$ be denoted by '$g \uparrow$'. For a given transition predicate E (which excludes stuttering), let us define t_E as the history variable (of sort real) defined initially as $t_E = -\infty$, and when event E happens, t_E is updated to the current value of t (if E does not occur, then t_E is not updated). That is: $\Box(E \Rightarrow t_E' = t') \wedge \Box(t_E' \neq t_E \Rightarrow E)$. Combining together, given a state predicate g, we have a history variable $t_{g\uparrow}$ which denotes the last time that g became true.

The transition (or next-step) relation of a module F is constructed using the next-step relations defined by the instructions (see Appendix). For an untimed instruction $g \longrightarrow \alpha$, this relation is simply $g \wedge \alpha$, while for the timed version $g \xrightarrow{[\delta_1, \delta_2)} \alpha$ the relation strengthens to $g \wedge \alpha \wedge \delta_1 \leq (t - t_{g\uparrow}) < \delta_2$.

Due to the progress of time, the 'liveness' part of $(*)$ may be formulated (for $\delta_2 < \infty$) as a safety property: $\Box(g \Rightarrow t - t_{g\uparrow} < \delta_2)$. It follows that, $\Box(g \wedge \neg g' \Rightarrow (t' - t_{g\uparrow} < \delta_2))$ and that for all $t_0 \in \mathbb{R}$, $g \wedge t = t_0 \longmapsto g \wedge \neg g' \wedge (t' - t_0 \leq t' - t_{g\uparrow} < \delta_2)$.

4.2 The Lossy RPC Specification

The changes necessary to the original RPC module are straightforward:

1. Exclude RPCFailure as a possible return value, by changing the declaration of RPCReturn;
2. Use timed instructions;
3. Add the assumption

   waiting $\overset{[0,\epsilon)}{\longmapsto}$ SvrReturn

   (or equivalently, waiting $\wedge\ t = t_0 \longmapsto$ SvrReturn $\wedge\ t - t_0 < \epsilon$)

   in the RServer interface;
4. The variable pending on the upper interface of the lossy RPC is more difficult to define. It was used to stipulate the assumption that the clerk will not re-issue a RPCCall if the corresponding RPCReturn has not been sent. Now, since a RPCReturn must not be sent, the lossy RPC can only assume that if a second RPCCall is issued, then either a RPCReturn has been sent or at least $2\delta + \epsilon$ time has passed from the last RPCCall. This assumption is easily discharged in the Clerk.

The last two modifications were not exactly part of the problem statement (in the informal description of the lossy RPC module there is no reference to ϵ). But the user (or the clerk) should somehow be prevented from repeating the same RPCCall before the lossy RPC has returned to the initial state. Another possibility would be to assume the same call is never issued. This could been implemented by distinguishing all calls by an extra id-tag on the value c.

We think that we met the *intended* informal specification (since this lossy RPC is to be used in such an environment). For the purpose of Problems 4 and 5(a), this assumption as well the assumption on the other interface may be removed, but for Problem 5(b), these assumptions will be necessary.

```
MODULE  LossyRPC

  INTERFACE    2SupClerk
    DECLARATIONS
      VARIABLES
        HISTORY   pending  :  Boolean
      ACTIONS
        IN      RPCCall    : ()
        OUT     RPCReturn : RPC_Return_Type \ { RPCFailure }
      INITIALLY    ¬pending
      ALWAYS
```

‖ RPCCall $=\!\!\triangleright$ pending$'$

‖ RPCReturn $\vee$ (t$'$ - t$_{\text{RPCCall}}$) $= 2\delta + \epsilon$
   $=\!\!\triangleright$ ¬pending$'$

ASSUMPTIONS

‖ RPCCall $=\!\!\triangleright$ ¬pending

COMMITMENTS

‖ RPCReturn $=\!\!\triangleright$ pending

END

INTERFACE   2RServer
  DECLARATIONS
    VARIABLES
     HISTORY   waiting : Boolean
    ACTIONS
     OUT   SvrCall   : ()
     IN   SvrReturn : RSvr_Return_Type
  INITIALLY   ¬waiting
  ALWAYS

‖ SvrCall $=\!\!\triangleright$ waiting$'$

‖ SvrReturn $=\!\!\triangleright$ ¬waiting$'$

ASSUMPTIONS

‖ SvrReturn $=\!\!\triangleright$ waiting

‖ SvrCall $\mapsto$ SvrReturn $\wedge$ t $<$ t$_{\text{SvrCall}}$ + ϵ

COMMITMENTS

‖ SvrCall $=\!\!\triangleright$ ¬waiting

END

DECLARATIONS
  VARIABLES
    SPEC   r   : RPC_Return_Type \ { RPCFailure }
    SPEC   v   : RSvr_Return_Type
    LOCAL   buffer : (RPC_Result_Type $\cup$ Buffer_Type)
  ACTIONS
    LOCAL FailCall : ()
INITIALLY   buffer = nil
ALWAYS

‖ RPCCall ∧ RConsistent =▷ buffer′= forward

‖ RPCCall ∧ ¬RConsistent =▷ buffer′= BadCall

‖ SvrCall =▷ buffer′= nil

‖ᵥ SvrReturn(v) =▷ buffer′= v

‖ RPCReturn =▷ buffer′= nil

‖ FailCall =▷ buffer′= nil

INSTRUCTIONS

‖ buffer = forward $\xrightarrow{[0,\delta)}$ SvrCall

‖ buffer ≠ nil $\xrightarrow{[0,\delta)}$ FailCall

‖ᵣ buffer = r $\xrightarrow{[0,\delta)}$ RPCReturn(r)

END.

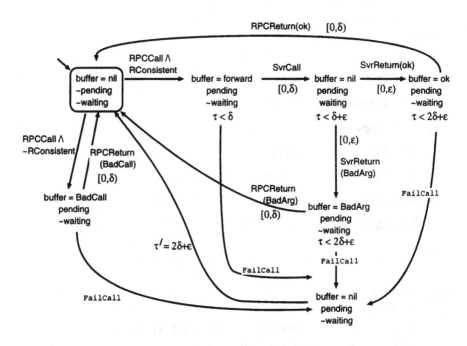

Fig. 9. The BTS of factorized, lossy RPC

Let us define a new variable τ in LossyRPC by $\tau = t - t_{\text{RPCCall}}$ (thus τ is a function of the state). Notice that t and RPCCall are both visible outside of the

LossyRPC (i.e., visible in the 2SupClerk interface). Therefore τ is also visible. The BTS of the lossy RPC module is now presented in Figure 9. This automaton is a simplified version of the automaton obtained directly from the code of the TLT module. There, each state has a transition to the initial state labelled by $\tau' = 2\delta + \epsilon$. But, due to the timing constraints on the transitions of the module, for all states p with buffer $\neq$ nil, we know that $p \wedge \neg p' \Rightarrow \tau' < 2\delta + \epsilon$.

Note that the transition (pending $\wedge \neg$ pending$' \wedge \neg$ RPCReturn) is only enabled when pending has been true for $2\delta + \epsilon$ time. This is only possible when buffer = nil $\wedge \neg$ waiting. The reason is simple: all other states where pending is true are a distance $< 2\delta + \epsilon$ (in time) from the transition RPCCall that made pending become true.

Solution to Problem 4:

1. $\overrightarrow{\text{LossyRPC}}(c) := \text{RPC}$

2. $\overrightarrow{\text{LossyRPC}} := \bigwedge_{c \,\in\, Call\_type} \overrightarrow{\text{LossyRPC}}(c)$

The TLT specification of the lossy RPC component is given by $\overrightarrow{\text{LossyRPC}}$.

4.3 The Supervising Clerk

The supervising clerk is very similar to the clerk. Now it is assumed (on the lower interface) that RPCReturn(RPCFailure) never happens. Also, the buffer never assumes the value RPCFailure. The new instruction section is:

INSTRUCTIONS

$\parallel$ buffer = forward $\longrightarrow$ RPCCall

$\parallel_r$ buffer = r $\longrightarrow$ Return(r)

$\parallel$ waiting $\overset{[2\delta+\epsilon,\infty)}{\longrightarrow}$ Return(MemFailure)

Here the specification variable r ranges only over { ok, BadArg }. The BTS of the supervising clerk is given in Figure 10.

Solution to Problem 5(a):

1. $\overrightarrow{\text{SupClerk}}(c) := \text{SupClerk}$

2. $\text{TServer} := \text{SupClerk} \wedge \text{LossyRPC} \wedge \text{RServer}$

3. $\overrightarrow{\text{TServer}}(c) := \overrightarrow{\text{SupClerk}}(c) \wedge \overrightarrow{\text{LossyRPC}}(c) \wedge \overrightarrow{\text{RServer}}(c)$

4. $\overrightarrow{\text{TServer}} := \bigwedge_{c \,\in\, Call\_type} \overrightarrow{\text{TServer}}(c)$

5. $\text{Timed\_Memory} := \overrightarrow{\text{TServer}} \wedge \text{Memory} \wedge \text{UserConn}$

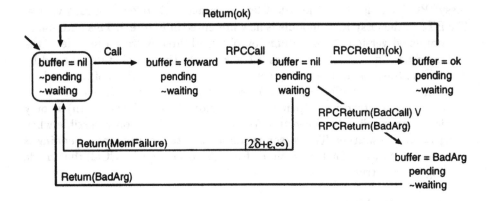

Fig. 10. BTS of the factorized Supervising Clerk

The TLT specification of the lossy RPC implementation is given by Timed_Memory.

4.4 Proof of the Real-time Property in Problem 5(b)

Let us calculate the composition of the supervising clerk and lossy RPC. First, observe that the state (buffer = nil $\wedge$ pending $\wedge \neg$ waiting) may be eliminated, since, the incoming-outgoing instructions are not visible. Instead, we have an invisible transition from (buffer = ok) or (buffer = BadArg) to (buffer = nil).

Let us call the remaining 6 states of Figure 9: 0, BC, f, w, ok, BA for (buffer = nil $\wedge \neg$ waiting), (buffer = BadCall), (buffer = forward), (buffer = nil $\wedge$ waiting), (buffer = ok) and (buffer = BadArg) respectively. Similar abbreviations are used for the states in Figure 10. In their composition, not all $6 \times 5 = 30$ states are reachable. The initial state of the composition is (0,0).

The only enabled transition is the Call from the user, leading to (f,0). From there, the RPCCall can lead to (w,f) or to (w,BC). The second case is somewhat easier: the system moves to (BA,0) (within the time constraint $[0, \delta)$) or FailCall happens (leading to (w,0)). The transition to (0,BC) is constrained to happen in time $[2\delta + \epsilon, \infty)$ and is therefore not enabled. From (BA,0) the system moves back to (0,0).

The state (w,f) is more interesting: three transitions appear enabled: to (w,w) (within time constraint $[0, \delta)$), FailCall to (w,0) or to (0,f) (within time constraint $[2\delta + \epsilon, \infty)$). Due to the time restriction on the first one, the last transition is not enabled. In (w,w), three transitions are candidates: to (w,ok) (time: $[0, \epsilon)$), to (w,BA) (time: $[0, \epsilon)$), or to (0,w). The last transition has time constraints (time: $[\delta + \epsilon, \infty) = [2\delta + \epsilon, \infty) \ominus [0, \delta)$, where $[A, B) \ominus [A_1, B_1) := [A - B_1, B - A_1)$). Therefore, as before, this transition is not enabled, since $\delta + \epsilon > \epsilon$.

Now consider the state (w,ok). (The same tableau will work for (w,BA)). Here there are three possibilities: a transition to (ok,0) (time: $[0, \delta)$), a transition to (0,ok) (time: $[\delta + \epsilon, \infty) \ominus [0, \epsilon) = [\delta, \infty)$), and is therefore not enabled), or

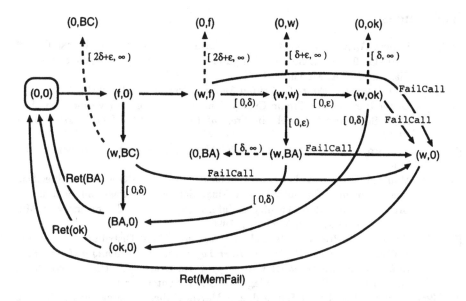

Fig. 11. The Composition of Supervising Clerk and Lossy RPC (the dotted lines are transitions which are not enabled due to the time constraints)

a transition to (w,0) (corresponding to the internal transition FailCall of the RPC). There, at last, the transition Return(MemFailure) is enabled (and *must* happen, due to the time restriction $[\delta, \infty) \ominus [0, \epsilon) = [0, \infty))$, leading back to (0,0).

This discussion is summarized in Figure 11. The rest of the proof is done by simplifying Figure 11 (minimizing states), building the composition with the reliable server and checking the refinement relation.

5 Conclusion

The TLT solutions to the RPC Memory Specification Problem presented in this paper rely on the factorization of parameterized modules and the separation of control and data information. This results in simple but intuitive 'control' modules, making the proofs of properties and of refinement relations straightforward (using CAV tools or even by hand). We have therefore shown that the (semantic) theory of TLT is flexible enough to accommodate mathematical techniques to reduce the complexity of a specification, as well as CAV techniques like theorem proving and model checking to assist the user where possible.

Acknowledgments:
The work presented in this paper is the result of a team effort. In particular, Isolde Wildgruber contributed significantly to the TLT paper presented at the seminar. The current members of the TLT project are Jorge Cuéllar, Isolde Wildgruber, Holger Busch, Dieter Barnard, Martin Huber and Simone Prummer.

References

[AG94] Robert Allen and David Garlan. Formal Connectors. Technical Report CMU-CS-94-115, School of Computer Science, Carnegie Mellon University, Pittsburgh, PA, March 1994.

[Arn94] Andre Arnold. *Finite Transition Systems*. Prentice Hall, 1994.

[BC95] Dieter Barnard and Simon Crosby. The Specification and Verification of an ATM Signalling Protocol. In *Proc. of 15th IFIP PSTV'95*, Warsaw, June 1995.

[BL] M. Broy, L. Lamport. The RPC Memory Specification Problem. This Volume.

[Bro96] Manfred Broy. A Functional Solution to the RPC-Memory Specification Problem. Submitted as a Final Solution to Dagstuhl Seminar of Broy/Lamport, 1994, Faculty of Informatics, Technical University of Munich, D-80290 Munich, Germany, 1996.

[Bus95] H. Busch. A Practical Method for Reasoning About Distributed Systems in a Theorem Prover. In *Higher Order Logic Theorem Proving and its Applications - 8th International Workshop, Aspen Grove, UT, USA, Proceedings*, pages 106–121. Springer-Verlag, LNCS 971, September 1995.

[CBH95] Jorge Cuéllar, Dieter Barnard, and Martin Huber. Dealing with Actions in Assertional Reasoning. Internal report, available by e-mail, ZFE T SE 1, Siemens AG, October 1995.

[CBH96] Jorge Cuéllar, Dieter Barnard, and Martin Huber. Rapid Protyping for an Assertional Specification Language. *TACAS'96, LNCS 1055*, March 1996.

[CGS91] C. Courcoubetis, S. Graf, and J. Sifakis. An Algebra of Boolean Processes. In *Proc. of CAV'91*, pages 454–465, 1991.

[CH95] Jorge Cuéllar and Martin Huber. The FZI Production Cell Case Study: A distributed solution using TLT. In *Formal Development of Reactive Systems: Case Study Production Cell*, volume 891 of *LNCS*. Springer-Verlag, 1995.

[CM88] K. Mani Chandy and J. Misra. *Parallel Program Design - A Foundation*. Addison-Wesley, Reading, Massachusetts, 1988.

[CW96] Jorge Cuéllar and Isolde Wildgruber. The Steam Boiler Problem - A TLT Solution (Presented at a Dagstuhl Seminar). In *Proc. of a Dagstuhl Seminar*, 1996.

[CWB94] J. R. Cuéllar, I. Wildgruber, and D. Barnard. Combining the Design of Industrial Systems with Effective Verification Techniques. In M. Naftalin, T. Denvir, and M. Betran, editors, *Proc. of FME'94*, volume 873 of *LNCS*, pages 639–658, Barcelona, Spain, October 1994. Springer-Verlag.

[Gur91] Y. Gurevich. Evolving Algebras: A Tutorial Introduction. In *Bulletin of the EATCS*, volume 43, pages 264–284. EATCS, 1991.

[Kur90] R.P. Kurshan. Analysis of Discrete Event Systems. *LNCS*, 430:414–453, 1990.

[Kur94] R.P. Kurshan. *Computer Aided Verification of Coordinating Processes*. Princeton University Press, 1994.

[Lam94a] L. Lamport. The Temporal Logic of Actions. *ACM Transactions on Programming Languages and Systems*, 16(3):872–923, May 1994.

[Mer96] Stephan Merz. From TLT modules to stream processing functions. Internal paper, Faculty of Informatics, Technical University of Munich, D-80290 Munich, March 1996.

[Mil89] R. Milner. *Communication and Concurrency*. Prentice-Hall, London, 1989.

A   An Introduction to TLT

A.1   Concrete States and Transitions

Consider a signature consisting of a set V of variables and a set A of actions. Each variable and action is typed such that $D(x)$ denotes the domain of values of the variable x and $D(A)$ denotes the domain of values of the action A.

Given a set of variables V, a concrete state w.r.t. V is an element of

$$V := \prod_{x \in V} D(x)$$

A concrete state ζ may be seen as a valuation of each variable such that:

$$V \ni x \overset{\zeta}{\longmapsto} \zeta(x) \in D(x)$$

If $\zeta(x) = v \in D(x)$, we say that $x = v$ is true in the concrete state ζ. If $p \subseteq D(x)$, and $\zeta(x) \in p$, then we say that $p(x)$ is true in the concrete state ζ (thus we identify sets with predicates). Similarly, a valuation α of the actions is given by:

$$A \ni A \overset{\alpha}{\longmapsto} \alpha(A) \in D_\perp(A)$$

where $D_\perp(A) := D(A) \ \dot\cup \ \{\perp\}$ is called the extended domain of A.

We can now formalize the concept of a concrete transition w.r.t. (V,A). It is a pair of elements of V together with a valuation of each action, i.e., an element of:

$$V \times V \times \prod_{A \in A} D_\perp(A)$$

If $\alpha(A) \in D(A)$, we say that A 'occurs' in the concrete transition, and that it has the value $\alpha(A)$. If $\alpha(A) = \perp$, we say that A 'does not occur' in the concrete transition. The symbol $\perp$ is never used in the TLT syntax for writing modules or properties of programs.

If $v = \alpha(A) \in D(A)$ on a concrete transition α, we do not write $A = v$ (as we would for variables), but simply $A(v)$. We say that $A(v)$ is true in the concrete transition. If $\alpha(A) = \perp$, then we say that $\neg A$ (or equivalently, $\neg \exists_v A(v)$) is true in this concrete transition. If $p \subseteq D(A)$ (note, not $D_\perp(A)$) and $\alpha(A) \in p$, then we say that $A(p)$ is true in the concrete transition α.

A.2   Boolean Algebras

Given a variable x of type (domain) $D(x)$, let the Boolean Algebra $B_x := P(D(x))$ (the power set of $D(x)$). Given an action A of type (domain) $D(A)$, let the Boolean Algebra $B_A := P(D_\perp(A))$. Given a set of variables V and a set of actions A, the definitions extend as follows:

$$B_V = P(\textstyle\prod_{x \in V} D(x)) = \bigotimes_{x \in V} P(D(x))$$
$$B_A = P(\textstyle\prod_{A \in A} (D_\perp(A))) = \bigotimes_{A \in A} P(D_\perp(A))$$

where $\mathcal{B}_1 \otimes \mathcal{B}_2$ denotes the exterior product of algebras $\mathcal{B}_1$ and $\mathcal{B}_2$.

Given a set of variables $\mathcal{V}$ and actions $\mathcal{A}$, let

$$
\begin{aligned}
\mathcal{B}_{(\mathcal{V},\mathcal{A})} &:= \mathcal{B}_\mathcal{V} \otimes \mathcal{B}_\mathcal{V} \otimes \mathcal{B}_\mathcal{A} \\
&= \mathcal{P}(\prod_{x \in \mathcal{V}} \mathcal{D}(x) \times \prod_{x \in \mathcal{V}} \mathcal{D}(x) \times \prod_{A \in \mathcal{A}} \mathcal{D}_\perp(A)) \\
&= \mathcal{P}(V \times V \times \prod_{A \in \mathcal{A}} \mathcal{D}_\perp(A))
\end{aligned}
$$

That is, $\mathcal{B}_{(\mathcal{V},\mathcal{A})}$ is the power set of the set of concrete transitions on $(\mathcal{V},\mathcal{A})$. Since in an exterior product each factor is naturally a subalgebra of the product, we obtain two monomorphisms $i_1, i_2 : \mathcal{B}_\mathcal{V} \hookrightarrow \mathcal{B}_{(\mathcal{V},\mathcal{A})}$ and dually two projections $\Pi_1, \Pi_2 : \mathcal{B}_{(\mathcal{V},\mathcal{A})} \to \mathcal{B}_\mathcal{V}$, corresponding to the first two components of the product $\mathcal{B}_{(\mathcal{V},\mathcal{A})} = \mathcal{B}_\mathcal{V} \otimes \mathcal{B}_\mathcal{V} \otimes \mathcal{B}_\mathcal{A}$. For later reference we also introduce the monomorphism $i_{1,2} : \mathcal{B}_\mathcal{V} \times \mathcal{B}_\mathcal{V} \hookrightarrow \mathcal{B}_{(\mathcal{V},\mathcal{A})}$ and the corresponding projection $\Pi_{1,2} : \mathcal{B}_{(\mathcal{V},\mathcal{A})} \to \mathcal{B}_\mathcal{V} \times \mathcal{B}_\mathcal{V}$.

A.3 Boolean Transition Systems

A Boolean transition system (BTS) is a structure $\Sigma = (V, I, \mathcal{B}, M, \mathcal{F})$ such that (similar to the definitions in [CGS91, Kur90]):

- V is a set of states (vertices);
- $I \subseteq V$ is a set of initial states;
- $\mathcal{B}$ is a complete, atomic Boolean algebra;
- M is a transition matrix, i.e., $M : V \times V \to \mathcal{B}$
- $\mathcal{F}$ is a set of acceptance conditions, each of the form (G, E), where G is a set of states $G \subseteq V$, and E is a set of pairs of states $E \subseteq V \times V$.

A run $(v_1, v_2, \ldots, v_n, \ldots)$, $v_i \in V$ satisfies the acceptance condition (G, E) iff *(if for infinitely many i, $v_i \in G$, then for infinitely many j, $(v_j, v_{j+1} \in E))$.* A run $(v_1, v_2, \ldots, v_n, \ldots)$ is a run of Σ iff $v_1 \in I$, $M(v_i, v_{i+1}) \neq 0$ for all I and $(v_1, v_2, \ldots, v_n, \ldots)$ satisfies all acceptance conditions.

A sequence $(b_1, b_2, \ldots)$ of atoms of $\mathcal{B}$ (where all $b_i \neq 0$) is a trace of Σ iff Σ has a run $(v_1, \ldots)$ such that $M(v_i, v_{i+1}) \geq b_i$.

Remark: We do not deal with general BTS. As in TLA, a predicate Stutter $\in \mathcal{B}$ plays a central role in TLT. The BTS used in this paper are the BTS of TLT modules. They have the (further) property that $\mathcal{B} = \mathcal{B}_{(\mathcal{V},\mathcal{A})}$ and that they allow stuttering on all $v \in \mathcal{V}$.

A.4 Conjunction of Boolean Transition Systems

Given two Boolean transition systems Σ_1 and Σ_2, we wish to define their conjunction (composition) $\Sigma_1 \wedge \Sigma_2$. Semantically, the traces of $\Sigma_1 \wedge \Sigma_2$ will be the intersection of the traces of Σ_1 and the traces of Σ_2, or more precisely, the BTS $\Sigma_1 \wedge \Sigma_2$ is the product of the BTS of Σ_1 and of Σ_2.

We start by restricting our attention to the case where the BTS operate on (use labels of) the same Boolean algebra. Then, if Σ_1 and Σ_2 are two Σ(over the same Boolean algebra $\mathcal{B}$) $\Sigma_i = (V_i, I_i, \mathcal{B}, M_i, \mathcal{F}_i)$, their conjunction (product) is defined as

$$\Sigma_1 \wedge \Sigma_2 = (V_1 \times V_2, I_1 \times I_2, \mathcal{B}, M, \mathcal{F})$$

where

$$M = M_1 \otimes M_2 \text{ with } M((v_1, v_2), (v_1', v_2')) = M_1(v_1, v_1') \wedge M_2(v_2, v_2')$$

and

$$\mathcal{F} = \{\rho_1(F_1) \mid F_1 \in \mathcal{F}_1\} \cup \{\rho_2(F_2) \mid F_2 \in \mathcal{F}_2\}$$

where ρ_1 and ρ_2 are the following natural monomorphisms:

If $F = (G, E) \in \mathcal{F}_i$, then $G \in \mathcal{P}(V_i)$ and $E \in \mathcal{P}(V_i^2)$. The exterior products

$$\mathcal{P}(V_1 \times V_2) \cong \mathcal{P}(V_1) \otimes \mathcal{P}(V_2) \quad \text{and} \quad \mathcal{P}((V_1 \times V_2)^2) \cong \mathcal{P}(V_1^2) \otimes \mathcal{P}(V_2^2)$$

induce injections

$$i_i : \mathcal{P}(V_i) \hookrightarrow \mathcal{P}(V_1 \times V_2) \quad \text{and} \quad j_i : \mathcal{P}(V_i^2) \hookrightarrow \mathcal{P}((V_1 \times V_2)^2).$$

Then $\rho_i = (i_i , j_i)$.

To compute the conjunction of two Σon different Boolean algebras $\mathcal{B}_1$ and $\mathcal{B}_2$, it is necessary to obtain a Boolean algebra $\mathcal{B}$ and two algebra monomorphisms $\phi_i : \mathcal{B}_i \hookrightarrow \mathcal{B}$. That is, the $\Sigma$are imaged to $\mathcal{B}$ before they are conjoined. The resulting product thus depends on the chosen ϕ_i. Formally, the image of a BTS under a Boolean algebra monomorphism is given by the following construction:

If ϕ is an algebra monomorphism $\phi : \mathcal{B}_1 \to \mathcal{B}$ and $\Sigma_1 = (V, I, \mathcal{B}_1, M_1, \mathcal{F})$ is a BTS over $\mathcal{B}_1$, then $\phi\Sigma_1 = (V, I, \mathcal{B}, M, \mathcal{F})$ is a BTS over $\mathcal{B}$ with $M(v, v') := \phi(M_1(v, v'))$.

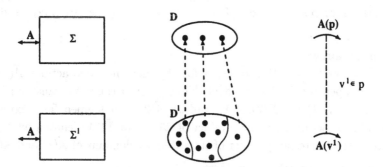

Fig. 12. Conjunction of actions with 'different' domains.

In particular, we wish to compose Σ naming the same action but with apparently 'different' domains (typically, one 'control' domain D can be regarded as a partition of some 'data' domain D^1). This may be seen as a data abstraction on actions.

Let D^1 be a set, $\cong$ be an equivalence relation on D^1 and $D=D^1/_\cong$ the partition generated by $\cong$. Let $[v] \in D$ denote the class of $v \in D^1$. Then $\cong$ induces a Boolean algebra monomorphism:

$$\phi : \mathcal{P}(D \,\dot\cup\, \{\bot\}) \hookrightarrow \mathcal{P}(D^1 \,\dot\cup\, \{\bot\})$$

which extends to a monomorphism $\mathcal{B}_{(V,\mathcal{A})} \hookrightarrow \mathcal{B}_{(V,\mathcal{A}^1)}$ where $\mathcal{A}^1$ is the 'same' set of actions as $\mathcal{A}$, except that the domain of A in $\mathcal{A}^1$ is $\mathcal{D}(A)=D^1$ while $\mathcal{D}(A)=D$ in $\mathcal{A}$. The conjunction of Σ and Σ^1 then is given by $\phi\Sigma \wedge \Sigma^1$. Using this construction, the labels of $\phi\Sigma \wedge \Sigma^1$ fulfil:

$$A(p) \Leftrightarrow \bigvee_{\{v^1 \in D^1 \mid [v^1]=p\}} A(v^1) .$$

Note, that there is no danger of confusion by denoting $A \in \mathcal{A}$ and $A \in \mathcal{A}^1$ with the same letter, since the equation above is equivalent to $A(p) \Leftrightarrow \bigvee_{v \in p} A(v)$, which is the convention introduced in Section A.1.

A.5 Parameterization of Boolean Transition Systems

We will be interested in replicas (or instances) of a 'simple' BTS Σ, and in conjunctions (or products) of such instances. Let I be a set which will be used to index the Boolean transition systems. Consider the parameterized (or indexed) set of Boolean transition systems $\vec{\Sigma}(i) := \Sigma$ for $i \in I$, that is, all $\Sigma\ \vec{\Sigma}(i)$ are identical. Firstly, we assume that the Boolean algebra $\mathcal{B}$ of the BTS Σ is of type $\mathcal{B} = \mathcal{B}_{V,\mathcal{A}}$ for $\mathcal{A} = \{A\}$, that is there is just one action A 'in' Σ, and thus in each $\vec{\Sigma}(i)$.

What we want is to define the product $\vec{\Sigma} := \bigwedge_i \vec{\Sigma}(i)$ (semantically), and in particular to define the action $\vec{A}$ in $\vec{\Sigma}$ with 'components' $\vec{A}(i) = A$ in $\vec{\Sigma}(i)$.

At least four possible cases of interference among the $\vec{A}(i)$ may be distinguished:

(a) **Concurrency:**

In this case (and letting I={1,2} for the moment), two actions $\vec{A}(1)$ and $\vec{A}(2)$ happen totally independent. That is, on a concrete transition in the product of $\vec{\Sigma}(1)$ and $\vec{\Sigma}(2)$, $\vec{A}(1)$ *and/or* $\vec{A}(2)$ *may* happen. The (extended) domain for action $\vec{A}$ in the product of $\vec{\Sigma}(1)$ and $\vec{\Sigma}(2)$, denoted by $\mathcal{D}_\bot(\vec{A})$, is then the Cartesian product of the extended domains of $\vec{A}(1)$ and $\vec{A}(2)$:

$$\mathcal{D}_\bot(\vec{A}) = \mathcal{D}_\bot\vec{A}(1) \times \mathcal{D}_\bot\vec{A}(2)$$
$$= \mathcal{D}_\bot(A) \times \mathcal{D}_\bot(A)$$
$$\cong (\mathcal{D}_\bot(A))^{\{1,2\}}$$

In the general case, where $\vec{\Sigma}$ is a collection of BTS parameterized on $i \in I$, each having an action $\vec{A}(i)$ of type $\mathcal{D}(A)$, this construction leads to an action $\vec{A}$ in the conjunction of the $\vec{\Sigma}(i)$ such that $\mathcal{D}_{\perp}(\vec{A}) = \mathcal{D}_{\perp}(A)^I$. However, $\mathcal{D}_{\perp}(\vec{A})$ should be defined in the form $\mathcal{D}_{\perp}(\vec{A}) = \mathcal{D}(\vec{A}) \,\dot{\cup}\, \{\perp\}$. This is achieved by identifying $\perp$ with the partial function nowhere defined. Then we see that

$$\mathcal{D}(\vec{A}) \cong \mathcal{D}_{\perp}(A)^I \setminus \{\perp\}^I$$

is the set of functions of I to $\mathcal{D}_{\perp}$ which are not identically $\perp$. In the sequel, this domain will be referred to as table with index I and values of type $\mathcal{D}(A)$ and denoted by Table I Of A.

(b) **Synchronization:**
In this case, the two actions $\vec{A}(1)$ and $\vec{A}(2)$ are forced to happen simultaneously. Then each time $\vec{A}(1) \wedge \vec{A}(2)$ happens, both a value for $\vec{A}(1)$ and for $\vec{A}(2)$ are needed, and the domain of $\vec{A}$ is the product of the two domains:

$$\mathcal{D}(\vec{A}) = \mathcal{D}(\vec{A}(1)) \times \mathcal{D}(\vec{A}(2)) \cong (\mathcal{D}(A))^{\{1,2\}}$$

For arbitrary index sets,

$$\mathcal{D}(\vec{A}) = \prod_{i \in I} \mathcal{D}(\vec{A}(i)) = \prod_{i \in I} \mathcal{D}(A) \cong \mathcal{D}(A)^I$$

is the set of (total) functions from I to $\mathcal{D}(A)$. Observe that these are naturally a subset of $\mathcal{D}_{\perp}(A)^I \setminus \{\perp\}$, i.e., just a special case of (a).

(c) **Broadcast:**
In addition to synchronizing the actions $\vec{A}(i)$ as in (b), all $\vec{A}(i)$ are forced to have the same value. Then $\mathcal{D}(\vec{A}) \cong \mathcal{D}(A)$. Obviously $\mathcal{D}(A) \subseteq \mathcal{D}(A)^I$, that is, broadcasting is just a special case of synchronization.

(d) **Interleaving:**
Now assume that $\vec{A}(1)$ and $\vec{A}(2)$ exclude each other. That is, in the conjunction exactly one value is needed plus the indication which of the two actions happened. Thus the domain of $\vec{A}$ is the disjoint union of the domains of $\vec{A}(1)$ and $\vec{A}(2)$:

$$\mathcal{D}(\vec{A}) = \mathcal{D}(\vec{A}(1)) \,\dot{\cup}\, \mathcal{D}(\vec{A}(2)) = \mathcal{D}(A) \,\dot{\cup}\, \mathcal{D}(A) \cong \{1,2\} \times \mathcal{D}(A)$$

In the more general case of arbitrary index sets, $\mathcal{D}(\vec{A}) \cong I \times \mathcal{D}(A)$. Again, $I \times \mathcal{D}(A)$ naturally is a subset of $\mathcal{D}_{\perp}(A)^I \setminus \{\perp\}$ (a special case of (a)), corresponding to the set of partial functions from I to $\mathcal{D}(A)$ defined exactly in one point of I (or, equivalently, the set of (total) functions $\mathcal{F}$ from I to $\mathcal{D}_{\perp}(A)$ with $\mathcal{F}(i) = \perp$ for all but one $i \in I$).

We consider only case (a) for the parameterized BTS in this paper.

Now, let Σ be a BTS over $\mathcal{B}_{V,\mathcal{A}}$ for arbitrary sets of (visible) variables and actions ($V = \{x, y, \ldots\}$, $\mathcal{A} = \{A, B, \ldots\}$) and with state space V. As before, $M : V^2 \to \mathcal{B}_{(V,\mathcal{A})}$ denotes the transition function. We now define a BTS $\vec{\Sigma}$

that is the parameterized composition of (a vector of) identical copies of Σ (see Figure 13).

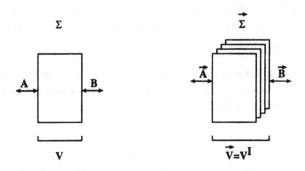

Fig. 13. Parameterized Modules

Let I be an index set and $\vec{V} = \{\vec{x}, \vec{y}, \ldots\}$, $\vec{A} = \{\vec{A}, \vec{B}, \ldots\}$ be fresh variables and actions of type $\mathcal{D}(\vec{x}) = \mathcal{D}(x)^I$ and $\mathcal{D}_\perp(\vec{A}) = \mathcal{D}_\perp(A)^I$.

The state space of the composed Boolean transition systems is defined as the product of state spaces of its components,

$$\vec{V} = \prod_{\vec{x} \in \vec{V}} \mathcal{D}(\vec{x}) = \prod_{x \in V} \prod_{i \in I} \mathcal{D}(x) = \prod_{i \in I} \prod_{x \in V} \mathcal{D}(x) = \prod_{i \in I} V = V^I$$

whereas the algebra the composed Boolean transition systems operate on is described by

$$\mathcal{B}_{(\vec{V}, \vec{A})} = \bigotimes_{i \in I} \mathcal{B}_{(V, A)}.$$

This last equation holds because for all variables

$$\mathcal{B}_{\vec{x}} = \mathcal{P}(\mathcal{D}(\vec{x})) = \mathcal{P}(\mathcal{D}(x)^I) = \bigotimes_{i \in I} \mathcal{P}(\mathcal{D}(x)) = \bigotimes_{i \in I} \mathcal{B}_x$$

and, since we consider concurrent actions as described under (a) from above,

$$\mathcal{B}_{\vec{A}} = \mathcal{P}(\mathcal{D}_\perp(\vec{A})) \stackrel{(a)}{=} \mathcal{P}(\mathcal{D}_\perp(A)^I) = \bigotimes_{i \in I} \mathcal{P}(\mathcal{D}_\perp(A)) = \bigotimes_{i \in I} \mathcal{B}_A.$$

The transition function M is then defined as follows:

$$\vec{M} : \vec{V} \times \vec{V} \to \mathcal{B}_{(\vec{V}, \vec{A})} \quad \text{with} \quad \vec{M}(\vec{v}, \vec{v}') := \bigwedge_{i \in I} i_i(M(\vec{v}(i), \vec{v}'(i))$$

where for all i

$$i_i : \mathcal{B}_{(V, A)} \hookrightarrow \mathcal{B}_{(\vec{V}, \vec{A})} = \bigotimes_{i \in I} \mathcal{B}_{(V, A)}$$

is the injection (Boolean algebra monomorphism) induced by the i-th component of the exterior product.

A.6 Translating the Program Notation

This section informally explains how the transition matrix is extracted from this notation. First we briefly demonstrate how to extract the predicate Δ, which represents the next-state relation of a TLT module.

The *transition relation* is given as conjunction of the translations of all always, assumption and commitment sections of the module and the conjunction of frame predicates for each variable and action controlled by the module (i.e. the local, private and history variables and local and output actions). For each of these controlled actions and each controlled *primed* variable it is required that they occur in at most one section on the right side of the $\rightarrow$ or $\Rightarrow$ symbols.

The always, assumption and commitment sections contribute to the translation in form of a conjunction over all statements in these sections:

$$\bigwedge_{\{lhs \Rightarrow rhs\}} lhs \Rightarrow rhs$$

Further, for each controlled variable and action, a frame axiom is added: For each variable x occurring primed in the instruction section, we get the following translation :

$$x' \neq x \;\Rightarrow\; \bigvee_{\{lhs \rightarrow rhs \mid x' \text{ occurs in } rhs\}} lhs \wedge rhs$$

Similarly, for a variable x occurring primed in an always section, we get

$$x' \neq x \;\Rightarrow\; \bigvee_{\{lhs \Rightarrow rhs \mid x' \text{ occurs in } rhs\}} lhs \,.$$

For each controlled action A, we get accordingly

$$A \;\Rightarrow\; \bigvee_{\{lhs \rightarrow rhs \mid A \text{ occurs in } rhs\}} lhs \wedge rhs$$

and

$$A \;\Rightarrow\; \bigvee_{\{lhs \Rightarrow rhs \mid A \text{ occurs in } rhs\}} lhs \,,$$

depending on whether A belongs to the instruction or one of the always sections.

Assuming the predicates $Init$ and Δ, a TLT module F defines:

- a set of variables Var, of which $\mathcal{V} \subseteq Var$ are visible;
- a set of actions Act, of which $\mathcal{A} \subseteq Act$ are visible;
- an initial predicate $Init \in \mathcal{B}_{Var}$;
- the transition relation $\Delta \in \mathcal{B}_{(Var, Act)}$
- a set $\mathcal{F}$ of fairness relations $F \in \mathcal{B}_{(Var, Act)}$, with $F \Rightarrow \Delta$. Each F is either a *weak-* or a *strong* fairness constraint.

The transition relation includes stuttering, i.e., if

$$Stutter(Var, Act) := \bigwedge_{x \in Var} (x' = x) \wedge \bigwedge_{A \in Act} \neg A$$

then $Stutter(Var, Act) \Rightarrow \Delta$. Given these elements, we show how to construct the standard BTS for F, denoted by $\Sigma(F)$:

- $V := \prod_{x \in Var \setminus \nu} \mathcal{D}(x)$
- $I := \Pi_{Var \setminus \nu} Init$
- $\mathcal{B} := \mathcal{B}_{(\nu, A)}$
- $M : V \times V \to \mathcal{B}$ defined as

$$M(v, v') := \Pi_\mathcal{B}(\Delta \wedge i_1(v) \wedge i_2(v'))$$

where $i_1, i_2 : \mathcal{B}_{Var} \hookrightarrow \mathcal{B}_{(Var, Act)}$ are the two natural monomorphisms described in Section A.2;

- If $F \in \mathcal{B}_{(Var, Act)}$ is a weak-fairness relation, then consider

$$E_1 := \Pi_{1,2}[(\neg i_1(\Pi_1 F) \wedge \Delta) \vee F] \in \mathcal{B}_{Var} \otimes \mathcal{B}_{Var}$$

which translates the weak-fairness relation in an acceptance condition. However, this acceptance condition may still name visible actions and variables. Thus, in a second step, we project it onto the hidden variables

$$E := \Pi_{Var \setminus \nu, Var \setminus \nu} E_1$$

and let the (V, E) be the corresponding acceptance condition (equivalent to the Büchi condition, that the set E has to be crossed infinitely often). Note that this is a faithful translation only if the occurrence of the fair transition can be observed in the changes of the internal state. If necessary, one has to extend the (local) state space first with an extra encoding of the occurrence of the fair transition.

- If $F \in \mathcal{B}_{(Var, Act)}$ is a strong-fairness relation, then $(\Pi_{Var \setminus \nu} F, \Pi_{Var \setminus \nu, Var \setminus \nu} F)$ is the corresponding acceptance condition. Similarly, one has to take care that the translation is faithful.

Applying a Temporal Logic to the RPC-Memory Specification Problem

Reinhard Gotzhein

Department of Computer Science, University of Kaiserslautern
PO 3049, D-67653 Kaiserslautern, Germany

Abstract. The unreliable and the reliable memory component of the RPC-Memory Specification Problem are specified and verified using a formalism that is based on a temporal logic. In that formalism, a system (open and/or distributed) consists of the system architecture and the system behaviour. The architecture is specified by defining the sets of its agents (= active components) and interaction points (= conceptual locations of interactions), and by associating with each agent a set of interaction points. The behaviour is built from external actions and defined by the logical conjunction of all component behaviours. A component behaviour is specified by the conjunction of logical safety and liveness properties. For the memory component, a many-sorted first-order branching time temporal logic with operators to refer to the future, the past, actions, the number of actions, and intervals constructed in the (linear) past are used. It is proven that the reliable memory is a correct implementation of the unreliable memory. The proof obligation takes both the system architecture and the system behaviour into account. Finally, it is discussed whether architectural requirements should be formally expressed.

1 Introduction

The RPC-Memory Specification Problem calls for the specification and verification of a series of components that can be embedded into a larger context that is not known in advance. From the problem description, we infer that it is important to specify how this embedding may be done, and what behaviour the components of the context may perceive when the specified components are stimulated. To formally specify these aspects, we have chosen a formalism based on temporal logic that is able to specify both architectural and behavioural aspects. Furthermore, the formalism suggests a notion of system refinement that involves both architecture and behaviour. This is different from other techniques in this volume which do not give a semantics to structural aspects of a specification and thus to the architecture of the specified system. We argue that specifying the essential system architecture should be among the first development steps, and be as rigorous and formal as the specification of the system behaviour.

In this paper, solutions for Problems 1a, 1b, and 1c are presented in detail. The specifications are formal, the proof is straightforward and involves simple temporal reasoning. Problem 3 is briefly addressed. Problems 4 and 5 are not treated because they include bounded response properties which at the moment are not expressable in our formalism. Although it is technically feasible to solve problems 2 and 3, we have not developed solutions. The reason is that the refinement as suggested in the problem statement introduces a system structure and corresponding behaviour which in our opinion is not a requirement, but one of several possible design decisions. This step is not well supported by our formalism, which should be used for the specification of requirements only. We will explain this in more detail in Sections 3.3 and 4.

The structure of the paper is the following. Section 2 gives a brief introduction to the formalism and its underlying concepts. In Section 3, this formalism is applied to some parts of the RPC-Memory Specification Problem. In Section 4, we discuss whether architectural requirements should be expressed formally. This aspect is not treated in other solutions listed in this volume, and has been a point of controversy during and after the Dagstuhl workshop. Section 5 draws a conclusion.

2 The Formalism

In this section, the formalism applied to the RPC-Memory Specification Problem will be explained. It can be classified as a property-oriented formal description technique, suitable for the specification of requirements for open distributed systems. The view taken throughout this paper and questioned in Section 4 is that these systems consists of system behaviour *and* system architecture. Elementary concepts are used to define these system aspects. For further details and examples, including the modeling, specification and verification of a communication service, see [7].

2.1 Elementary concepts

We start with the informal introduction of a very small number of elementary concepts. Due to their elementary nature, these concepts cannot be formally defined. All that can be stated at this point is that these concepts are disjoint. Elementary concepts form the basis for the definition of several derived concepts.

Definition 1 (elementary concepts).
- An *agent* $ag \in Ag$ is a component performing actions.
- An *interaction point* $ip \in Ip$ is a conceptual location where actions may occur[1].
- An *action*[2] $a \in Act$ is something that happens.
- Agent, interaction point, and action are disjoint concepts, i.e. $Ag \cap Ip = Ag \cap Act = Ip \cap Act = \{\}$.

---

[1] A specialization of the interaction point concept called "procedure interface" is used in [1].

[2] sometimes called *action occurrence*

An action is performed by an agent or a set of agents, it may be internal or external. External actions occur at some interaction point or a set of interaction points. An agent thus is the carrier of actions, it can be characterized by its behaviour. This behaviour (a notion still to be defined) consists of actions local to the agent, i.e. internal and external actions of the agent. For instance, the share an agent has in an interaction is considered external. Actions may also be non-local, such as interactions or transactions as a whole. Non-local actions may be performed by a *set* of agents and may occur at a *set* of interaction points. Interactions and transactions may also be considered as high-level actions, i.e., actions that can be decomposed into smaller units. Depending on what kind of action is taken as atomic on a given level of abstraction, the behaviour of a system can be characterized in different ways.

2.2 System architecture

With the elementary concepts *agent* and *interaction point*, more complex structures termed *system architectures* can be composed:

Definition 2 (system architecture). A *system architecture Arch* is a structure $\langle Ag, Ip, ArchF \rangle$, where
- Ag is a non-empty set of agents,
- Ip is a set of interaction points, and
- $ArchF : Ag \rightarrow 2^{Ip}$ is a total function called *architecture function* associating with each agent a set of interaction points.

A set $Ag^* \subseteq Ag$ of agents has one or more interaction points in common if and only if $\bigcap_{ag \in Ag^*} ArchF(ag) \neq \{\}$. We require as a rule of composition that a common interaction point is introduced explicitly into the architecture whenever a group of agents has the capability to interact directly. Depending on the kind of interaction, two or more agents may in general be involved in interactions. Whether such interactions will actually take place also depends on the behaviour.

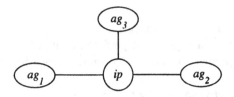

Fig. 1. Graphical representation of an architecture

Figure 1 shows a graphical representation of an architecture $Arch = \langle \{ag_1, ag_2, ag_3\}, \{ip\}, ArchF(ag_1) = ArchF(ag_2) = ArchF(ag_3) = \{ip\} \rangle$ consisting of three agents ag_1, ag_2, and ag_3 that have a common interaction point ip. From this architecture, we can infer that ag_1, ag_2, and ag_3 have the capability to interact, however, we can not yet say whether they will actually do so. This can only be derived from the behaviour of the agents and the interaction point.

With the definition of the system architecture, important structural information about the system to be specified is determined. Since the architecture is part of the requirements, it will have to be respected in subsequent refinement steps. Thus, system architecture will have a semantics, which is taken into account in the correctness notion explained in Section 2.5. Different from other approaches, architecture is therefore not just a means to structure a specification. It will become clear in the following that a system specification can have additional structure without a semantics, which therefore needs not be respected in subsequent refinements.

2.3 System behaviour

With the elementary concept *action*, more complex structures termed *behaviours* can be composed. A behaviour is specified as a conjunction of logical formulas, each expressing a restriction on the behaviour of system components (agents and interaction points). The behaviour refers to external actions, which are associated with system components and therefore contain some reference to the system architecture. In the following definition, we assume that restrictions are syntactically local in the sense that they each refer to aspects of a single system component only: a property referring to local aspects of an agent (interaction point) contains only references to that agent (interaction point) or its attached interaction points (agents)[3]. As a consequence, we can compose system behaviour from component behaviour, which supports modular system development and verification. Additionally, non-local properties can be specified and proven from the composition of component behaviour.

Definition 3 (system behaviour). Let $Arch = \langle Ag, Ip, ArchF \rangle$ be a system architecture, $Behav_{ag}$ be the behavioural specification of agents $ag \in Ag$, and $Behav_{ip}$ be the behaviour of interaction points $ip \in Ip$. The *system behaviour Behav* is given as the conjunction of component behaviour, i.e.:

$$Behav =_{Df} \bigwedge_{ag \in Ag} Behav_{ag} \wedge \bigwedge_{ip \in Ip} Behav_{ip}$$

When system components are specified separately and composed using logical conjunction, the question arises whether this yields a description of the system behaviour. The crucial idea here is the explicit introduction of interaction points as connection links between agents. By this elementary architectural concept,

---

[3] We do not use an explicit assumption – guarantee format. In general, assumptions about the environment will have to be made in order to implement syntactically local restrictions.

sets of local actions forming interactions can be related. How they are related depends on the system architecture and the behaviour of interaction points.

To specify component behaviour, a variety of logics can be used. Since behaviour involves a notion of time, a temporal logic is a possible candidate. Several kinds of temporal logics have been proposed, including linear time and branching time temporal logic, temporal logic based on propositional logic and first-order logic, and for each of these alternatives, a variety of temporal operators to refer to the future, the past, actions, and intervals [6]. These logics differ in expressiveness, availability and completeness of axiomatic bases, and decidability. Consequently, the logic for the specification of component behaviour should be selected carefully with respect to the given problem.

In [7], we have introduced a number of building blocks, each consisting of formation rules, semantics, and an axiomatic basis, which together form a modular temporal logic:

- At_P atomic formulas of propositional logic,
- At_F atomic formulas of first-order logic,
- Pr propositional operators,
- Qu quantifiers,
- F_L linear time temporal operators to refer to the future,
- F_B branching time temporal operators to refer to the future,
- P_L temporal operators to refer to the past,
- A_P action operator,
- A_F operator for the number of actions,
- I operators for interval construction.

For a given problem, a subset of these building blocks can be selected and combined, i.e., the formation rules, semantics, and axiomatic bases are joined together, in order to customize an appropriate temporal logic. A few obvious restrictions apply to the combination of building blocks:

- exactly one of the building blocks At_P and At_F must be selected;
- selection of Pr is mandatory;
- only one of the building blocks F_L and F_B may be selected;
- A_F can not be combined with At_P;
- if I is chosen, A_P must also be selected.
- A_F can not be combined with At_P;
- if I is chosen, A_P must also be selected.

The combination of several groups of temporal operators yields a so-called *mixed* temporal logic. While the formation rules and semantics of a mixed logic obtained by joining together the formation rules and semantics of the selected building blocks are complete, the axiomatic basis needs supplement.

When customizing a temporal logic, the following heuristics are helpful to make an adequate choice:

- select At_F, if architectural aspects have to be expressed in formulas;
- select Qu for quantification over infinite value domains;
- select F_L to express invariance and liveness for reliable systems;
- select F_B to express invariance and liveness for unreliable systems;
- select P_L to avoid history variables;
- select A_P to express actions;
- select A_F to count actions without introducing history variables;
- select I to express contexts in the past and thus to avoid history variables.

For the RPC-Memory Specification Problem, we customize a many-sorted first-order branching time temporal logic with operators to refer to the future, the past, actions, the number of actions, and intervals, i.e. building blocks At_F, Pr, Qu, F_B, P_L, A_P, A_F, and I are selected. Note that we use a branching time logic that will allow us to specify potential behaviour, which is not possible in the linear time version. This way, we can express additional liveness requirements in the case of unreliable systems. We will now summarize the customized logic.

In many-sorted first-order temporal logic, atomic formulas are formed starting from the following sets of symbols:

- a denumerable list S of symbols called *sorts*, including the natural numbers $I\!N_0$.
- a denumerable list V of symbols called *individual variables*; each $x \in V$ is attached to a sort $s \in S$, which is expressed by writing x^s;
- for each integer $n \geq 0$, a denumerable set $\mathcal{F}^{(n)}$ of *n-ary function symbols*; each $f \in \mathcal{F}^{(n)}$ is associated with sorts $s, s_1, ..., s_n \in S$ (written "$f_{s,s_1,...,s_n}$");
- for each integer $n \geq 0$, a denumerable set $\mathcal{R}^{(n)}$ of *n-ary relation symbols*; each $r \in \mathcal{R}^{(n)}$ is associated with sorts $s_1, ..., s_n \in S$ (written "$r_{s_1,...,s_n}$").

With these preparations, the syntax of formulas can be defined as follows:

i) For all $x^s \in V$: x^s is a term of sort s.

ii) For all $n \geq 0$, $f_{s,s_1,...,s_n} \in \mathcal{F}^{(n)}$, and terms $t_1, ..., t_n$ of sorts $s_1, ..., s_n$: $f_{s,s_1,...,s_n}(t_1, ..., t_n)$ is a term of sort s.

iii) For all $n \geq 0$, $r_{s_1,...,s_n} \in \mathcal{R}^{(n)}$, and terms $t_1, ..., t_n$ of sorts $s_1, ..., s_n$: $r_{s_1,...,s_n}(t_1, ..., t_n)$ is a formula.

iv) Let φ be a formula, x^s be an individual variable, then $\exists x^s.\varphi$ and $\forall x^s.\varphi$ are formulas.

v) Let φ be a formula, then $\neg\varphi$ is a formula.

vi) Let φ_1, φ_2 be formulas, then $(\varphi_1 \wedge \varphi_2), (\varphi_1 \vee \varphi_2), (\varphi_1 \supset \varphi_2), (\varphi_1 \equiv \varphi_2)$ are formulas.

vii) Let φ be a formula, then $AG\varphi, AF\varphi$ and $EF\varphi$ are formulas.

viii) Let φ be a formula, then $\blacksquare\,\varphi$ and $\blacklozenge\,\varphi$ are formulas.

ix) Let φ be a formula, then $[\varphi]$ (read "action of type φ") is a formula.

x) Let φ be a formula, then $\#[\varphi]$ (read "number of actions of type φ") is a term of sort $I\!N_0$.

xi) Let φ be a formula, α be an action term, then $[\varphi]$, $\bullet\alpha$ are action terms.

xii) Let α be an action term, β be an interval term, then α, (β) are interval expressions.

xiii) Let δ, δ_1, δ_2 be interval expressions, then $\delta \Rightarrow$, $\delta \Leftarrow$, $\Rightarrow \delta$, $\Leftarrow \delta$, $\delta_1 \Rightarrow \delta_2$, $\delta_1 \Leftarrow \delta_2$, *begin* δ, *end* δ are interval terms.

xiv) Let φ be a formula, β be an interval term, then $\langle\beta\rangle\varphi$ is a formula.

To define the structure of the semantical model and the meaning of formulas, we will use some notational conventions. σ and σ' denote infinite state sequences, σ_i is the $(i+1)$th element of the state sequence σ. $\sigma^{i,j}$ denotes the subsequence $\langle\sigma_i...\sigma_j\rangle$, $\sigma^{0,j} < \sigma'$ expresses that $\sigma^{0,j}$ is a prefix of σ'. π and π' are infinite state trees, $r(\pi)$ is the root state of π. $\sigma \in \pi$ means that σ is a branch of π, so from $\sigma \in \pi$ it follows that $\sigma_0 = r(\pi)$.

The semantics of the temporal operators is defined with respect to a model $\mathcal{M} = \langle E, Q, \Pi, Q_0 \rangle$, where

- $E = (E_1, ..., E_n)$ is a family of non-empty sets of objects (containing agents, interaction points, natural numbers, etc.);
- Q is a set of states, where each state is given by a set $\mathcal{F}$ of functions and a set $\mathcal{R}$ of relations on E (the states are not states in the ordinary sense with state variables, but contain only what will be necessary to characterize architecture and behaviour);
- $Q_0 \subseteq Q$ is a non-empty set of initial states;
- Π is a set of infinite state trees with states from Q, root states from Q_0, i.e. $r(\pi) \in Q_0$ for all $\pi \in \Pi$; furthermore, it is required that for all $\pi, \pi' \in \Pi$, $r(\pi) = r(\pi')$ implies $\pi = \pi'$ (or, $\pi \neq \pi'$ implies $r(\pi) \neq r(\pi')$).

Formulas of many-sorted first-order logic are interpreted in a model $\mathcal{M}$ by associating for each state $q \in Q$ sort symbols with sets of objects, function symbols with functions, relation symbols with relations as follows[4]:

- to every sort symbol $s \in S$, a set $D^s \in \{E_1, ..., E_n\}$ is attached; for notational convenience, we will use the same identifiers as sort symbols and to refer to the attached object sets, i.e.: $E_i \in S$ and $D^{E_i} = E_i$;
- for each integer $n \geq 0$: to each n-ary function symbol $f_{s,s_1,...,s_n} \in \mathcal{F}^{(n)}$, a function $f : D^{s_1} \times ... \times D^{s_n} \to D^s$ is attached;
- for each integer $n \geq 0$: to each n-ary relation symbol $r_{s_1,...,s_n} \in \mathcal{R}^{(n)}$, a relation $r \subseteq D^{s_1} \times ... \times D^{s_n}$ is attached.

The propositional operators $(\neg, \wedge, \vee, \supset, \equiv)$, existential and universal quantification $(\exists, \forall)$ are interpreted as usual. The semantics of the temporal operators and the function $\#[\varphi]$ are defined with respect to a satisfaction relation $\models$, where $\models$ is a relation between $\mathcal{M}$, a tree $\pi \in \Pi$, a sequence $\sigma \in \pi$, positions i, j with $0 \leq i \leq j$, and a formula φ (written "$\mathcal{M}, (\pi, \sigma, i, j) \models \varphi$").

---

[4] Note that this allows for flexible functions. Therefore, constants correspond to flexible state variables. However, we will not exploit the generality of this concept and assume that the interpretation of n-ary function symbols with $n > 0$ is the same across all states.

i) $M, (\pi, \sigma, i, j) \models AG\ \varphi$ iff $\forall \sigma' \in \pi.$
$$(\sigma^{0,j} < \sigma' \text{ implies } \forall k \geq j.M, (\pi, \sigma', i, k) \models \varphi)$$

ii) $M, (\pi, \sigma, i, j) \models AF\ \varphi$ iff $\forall \sigma' \in \pi.$
$$(\sigma^{0,j} < \sigma' \text{ implies } \exists k \geq j.M, (\pi, \sigma', i, k) \models \varphi)$$

iii) $EF\ \varphi =_{Df} \neg AG\ \neg\varphi$

iv) $M, (\pi, \sigma, i, j) \models \blacksquare\ \varphi$ iff $\forall k.(i \leq k \leq j \text{ implies } M, (\pi, \sigma, i, k) \models \varphi)$

v) $\blacklozenge\ \varphi =_{Df} \neg\ \blacksquare\ \neg\varphi$

vi) $M, (\pi, \sigma, i, j) \models [\varphi]$ iff $M, (\pi, \sigma, i, j) \models \varphi$
$$\text{and } (j > 0 \text{ implies } M, (\pi, \sigma, i, j-1) \not\models \varphi)$$

vii) $M, (\pi, \sigma, i, j) \models \#[\varphi] =_{Df}$

$$\begin{cases} 0 & \text{if } j = i \text{ and } M, (\pi, \sigma, i, j) \models \neg[\varphi] \\ 1 & \text{if } j = i \text{ and } M, (\pi, \sigma, i, j) \models [\varphi] \\ M, (\pi, \sigma, i, j-1) \models \#[\varphi] & \text{if } j > i \text{ and } M, (\pi, \sigma, i, j) \models \neg[\varphi] \\ M, (\pi, \sigma, i, j-1) \models \#[\varphi] + 1 & \text{if } j > i \text{ and } M, (\pi, \sigma, i, j) \models [\varphi] \end{cases}$$

The future operators AG, AF, and EF are interpreted as usual:

- $AG\ \varphi$ (read "φ is global") means that φ is true now and will hold in all possible future states.
- $AF\ \varphi$ (read "φ is inevitable") means that φ holds now or will hold for every possible future at some moment in time.
- $EF\ \varphi$ (read "φ is potential") that φ holds now or will hold for some possible future at some moment in time.

The meaning of the past operators $\blacksquare$ and $\blacklozenge$ covers the general case where a context in the past has been established using interval operators:

- $\blacksquare\ \varphi$ (read "always in the past φ") means that φ is true now and has always been true in the current context in the past.
- $\blacklozenge\ \varphi$ (read "sometimes in the past φ") means that φ is true now or has been true sometime in the current context in the past.

Furthermore, there are past operators referring to actions, which are interpreted as follows:

- $[\varphi]$ (read "action of type φ") means that φ has just become true.
- $\#[\varphi]$ (read "number of actions of type φ") denotes the number of actions of type φ in the current context in the past.

The semantics of interval operators is a little involved, therefore, we give an informal idea about their interpretation. For a complete formal semantics, the reader is referred to [7].

To construct intervals, the notion of action is used. With an action, an atomic interval, i.e., a single point in time, is associated. Complex intervals can be constructed with the help of two interval operators $\Rightarrow$ and $\Leftarrow$. Intuitively, the directions of the arrows indicate in which direction and in which order the interval end points are located. The end point of the interval expressed by the interval term at the end of the arrow is located first, followed by a search, in the direction of the arrow, for the end point of the interval denoted by the interval term at the head of the arrow. An explicit operator • to refer to the next/last but one action is introduced.

- $\langle\beta\rangle\varphi$ (read "φ restricted on the context β") means that φ holds in the context established by the interval β. It is vacuously true if the context does not exist.
- •α (read "the last but one action α" and "the next but one action α", respectively) means that if the search direction is backward, •α refers to the last but one action ; if it is forward, •α denotes the next but one action.
- $begin\ \delta$ and $end\ \delta$ denote atomic intervals consisting of the first and the last state of the interval δ, respectively.
- $\delta_1 \Rightarrow \delta_2$ denotes the interval commencing at the end of δ_1 and ending at the end of δ_2, where δ_1 is located first, and δ_2 is searched within the current context in the forward direction, starting with the end of δ_1.
- $\delta_1 \Leftarrow \delta_2$ denotes the interval commencing at the end of δ_1 and ending at the end of δ_2, where δ_2 is located first, and δ_1 is searched within the current context in the backward direction, starting with the end of δ_2.

Example: Let φ_1, φ_2, ψ be formulas, $\sigma^{0,j}$ be a state sequence representing the current context in the past. The interpretation of $\langle[\varphi_1] \Rightarrow [\varphi_2]\rangle\psi$ proceeds as illustrated below: starting from the current state σ_j, the end point of the interval denoted by $[\varphi_1]$ is located first, searching backward. In the diagram, this end point is state σ_i. Next, the end point denoted by $[\varphi_2]$ is located, searching in the direction of the arrow, i.e. forward. In the diagram, this leads to σ_k. Thus, the new current context is evaluated as $\sigma^{i,k}$. Formula ψ is now evaluated in the last state of this context. In case of an open ended arrow, the corresponding end point coincides with the boundary of the search context. For instance, the interpretation of $\langle[\varphi_1] \Rightarrow\rangle\psi$ would yield the new current context $\sigma^{i,j}$.

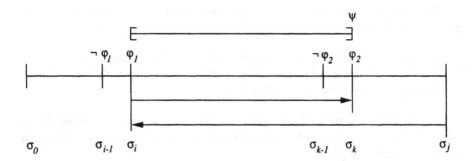

When we use temporal logic to characterize a system, we require that a specification must hold in the *initial* state of execution (properties holding throughout the execution can be defined using the operator AG). To express this formally, we use the notion of initial validity. A formula φ is *initially-satisfied in a model*

$\mathcal{M}$ *for a tree* $\pi \in \Pi$, written $\mathcal{M}, \pi \models_i \varphi$, iff $\mathcal{M}, (\pi, \sigma, 0, 0) \models \varphi$ is true, where $\sigma \in \pi$. φ is *initially-valid in* $\mathcal{M}$ iff φ is initially-satisfied for all $\pi \in \Pi$. Finally, φ is *initially-valid*, written $\models_i \varphi$, iff φ is initially-valid in all models $\mathcal{M}$.

2.4 System

Having introduced system architectures and system behaviours, we can combine them into the derived concept of *system*.

Definition 4 (system). A system S is a structure $\langle Arch, Behav \rangle$, where $Arch$ is a system architecture and $Behav$ is a system behaviour.

2.5 System refinement

A notion of system refinement should take both system architecture and system behaviour into account. In general, it is desirable that the refinement of a single component (architecture and/or behaviour) has no influence on the other components. Only then will it be possible to perform incremental system design and modular verification, which is a prerequisite for the development of large systems. By incremental system design, we mean that we can modify or replace a part of the system without affecting the other parts. Modular verification means that only the modified or replaced parts have to be verified, not the entire system. To allow for incremental system design and modular verification, we have to make suitable restrictions with respect to architecture and behaviour.

A system S' *refines* a system S, if S' is equivalent to or more specific than S. With respect to the system architecture, this is the case if all agents and interaction points of S are represented in S', and if their composition is maintained in S'. This is captured by the notion of architectural refinement below. Concerning the behaviour, S' is equivalent to or more specific than S if the behaviour of S' logically implies the behaviour of S mapped to the abstraction level of S'. This mapping is expressed by a *representation function rep*.

Definition 5 (system refinement). Let $S = \langle Arch, Behav \rangle$ and $S' = \langle Arch', Behav' \rangle$ be systems. S' is a refinement of S under the representation function rep (written "S' *refines*$_{rep}$ S") if and only if the following is satisfied[5]:

  − $Arch'$ *refines* $Arch$
  − $\models_i Behav' \supset rep(Behav)$

When we use temporal logic to characterize system behaviour, we require that a property must hold in the *initial* state of execution (properties holding throughout the execution can be defined using appropriate temporal operators). To express this formally, we use the notion of initial validity. Therefore, it is sufficient to require $Behav' \supset rep(Behav)$ to be initially-valid.

With respect to architectures, we require that agents and interaction points be refined separately. In other words, a single component of the refinement (an

---

[5] *Refinement* as defined here has been termed *conformance* in [7].

agent or interaction point) is uniquely related to a single component of the refined architecture. Also, we require that the number of interaction points an agent is associated with remains the same. These and further architectural constraints can be formalized as follows:

Definition 6 (architectural refinement). Let $Arch = \langle Ag, Ip, ArchF \rangle$ and $Arch' = \langle Ag', Ip', ArchF' \rangle$ be architectures. $Arch'$ is an *architectural refinement* of $Arch$ (written "$Arch'$ refines $Arch$") if and only if there is a refinement function $ref : Ag \cup Ip \to 2^{Ag' \cup Ip'}$ such that the following restrictions hold:

- Each component of $Arch$ is refined, i.e., ref is a total function.
- The refinement of an agent must include at least one agent. Formally: $\forall ag \in Ag.\ ref(ag) \cap Ag' \neq \{\}$.
- The refinement of an interaction point must include at least one interaction point: $\forall ip \in Ip.\ ref(ip) \cap Ip' \neq \{\}$.
- Each agent and each interaction point is refined separately, i.e., the refinement is disjoint: $\forall x, y \in Ag \cup Ip.\ (x \neq y\ implies\ ref(x) \cap ref(y) = \{\})$.
- Ag' is the set of exactly those agents resulting from the refinement, i.e., $Ag' = (\bigcup_{ag \in Ag} ref(ag) \cup \bigcup_{ip \in Ip} ref(ip)) \setminus Ip'$.
- Ip' is the set of exactly those interaction points resulting from the refinement, i.e., $Ip' = (\bigcup_{ip \in Ip} ref(ip) \cup \bigcup_{ag \in Ag} ref(ag)) \setminus Ag'$.
- If an agent $ag \in Ag$ is associated with an interaction point $ip \in Ip$, then exactly one agent of the refinement of ag must be associated with exactly one interaction point of the refinement of ip. Formally:

$\forall ip \in Ip.\ \forall ag \in Ag.\ ip \in ArchF(ag)\ implies$

$$(\mid ref(ip) \setminus Ag' \cap \bigcup_{ag' \in ref(ag) \setminus Ip'} ArchF'(ag') \mid = 1\ and$$

$$\mid \{ag' \in ref(ag) \setminus Ip' \mid ArchF'(ag') \cap ref(ip) \setminus Ag' \neq \{\} \} \mid\ = 1)$$

Figure 2 shows the graphical representation of a possible refinement of the interaction point ip (compare Figure 1), which on a lower level of abstraction comprises an agent ag that can interact with ag_1, ag_2, and ag_3 through ip_1, ip_2, and ip_3, respectively. It is necessary to introduce interaction points in the refinement, because otherwise the rule of composition of architectures about their explicit introduction would be violated. This rule supports the composition of system behaviour from component behaviour. Also, we notice that the duality between agents and interaction points is nicely carried into the refinement.

3 The Memory Component

In this section, we will apply the formalism outlined in Section 2 to the unreliable and the reliable memory component of the RPC-Memory Specification Problem. We will explain why the reliable memory component implements the unreliable memory, and how the memory can be architecturally refined.

The general concepts introduced in Section 2 can be related to the domain-specific concepts of the RPC-Memory Specification Problem as shown in Table 1.

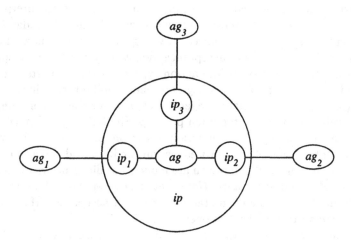

Fig. 2. Graphical representation of architectural refinement

3.1 A temporal logic

To specify the memory component, we use the logic defined in Section 2.3. We introduce sort symbols Ag, Ip, Ao, Pn, $Proc$, Arg, $RetVals$, $MemLocs$, and $MemVals$ interpreted as sets of agents (here: components), interaction points, abstract operations, interaction types (here: procedure names), processes, argument lists, return values, memory locations, and memory values, respectively. Furthermore, we define constants M, Env (of sort Ag), ip (of sort Ip), !, ? (of sort Ao, denoted *offer* and *accept*), R, W (of sort Pn), $InitVal$ (of sort $MemVals$) and $BadArg$, $Fail$, OK (of sort $RetVals$). Individual variables are pn, pn_1, pn_2 (of sort Pn), p, p_1, p_2, p', p'' (of sort $Proc$), a, a_1, a_2, l, v (of sort Arg), r, r', r'', r_1, r_2 (of sort $RetVals$), and n_1, n_2 (of sort $I\!N_0$). There is one function symbol $ArchF$, interpreted as the architecture function and associated with sorts 2^{Ip} and Ag. at_i and $after_i$, for $i \in \{3, 4, 5, 6, 7\}$, are relation symbols of arity i, associated with i sorts Ag, Ip, Ao, Pn, $Proc$, Arg, $RetVals$ (in that order).

general concept	domain-specific concept
agent	component, process
interaction point	(procedure-calling) interface
interaction	call, return

Table 1. Relationship between general and domain-specific concepts

Some restrictions as explained below apply with respect to their interpretation. In the specification of the memory component, we will omit the index i.

An interaction may occur between two agents at a common interaction point and consists of offer and acceptance, denoted by the abstract operations ! and ?, respectively. It has an interaction type pn (e.g., R for *Read* or W for *Write*) and interaction parameters (e.g., arguments and return values). We write $ag.ip.!\ pn(p, a, r)$ to denote that the agent ag offers an interaction of type pn with parameter values p, a, r at interaction point ip. Similarly, $ag.ip.?\ pn(p, a, r)$ denotes that agent ag accepts an interaction, where pn, p, a, and r will have values of a previous interaction offer. A procedure call can be considered as one particular interaction scheme: call and return are modeled as different interactions, each consisting of offer and acceptance. Note that the concepts of call and return are different from the concepts of interaction offer and acceptance, therefore, they do not correspond to the abstract operations ! and ?.

The formula $at_7\ ag.ip.!\ pn(p, a, r)$ (i.e. $(ag, ip, !, pn, p, a, r) \in at_7$) holds when ag is prepared to offer an interaction of type pn with parameter values p, a, r at interaction point ip; $after_7\ ag.ip.!\ pn(p, a, r)$ holds immediately after completion of the offer. We require that any interpretation of at_7 and at_6 satisfies $AG\ \forall pn, p, a, r.\ (at_7\ ag.ip.!\ pn(p, a, r) \supset at_6\ ag.ip.!\ pn(p, a))$, so the formula $at\ ag, ip.!\ pn(p, a)$ holds when the agent ag is prepared to offer an interaction of type pn with parameter values p, a and some additional parameter value r at ip. Similar constraints apply to at_i and $after_i$, for $i \in \{3, 4, 5, 6, 7\}$, and can be stated formally. Since the index i is clear from the context, it will be omitted in the following specification. Also, we omit $after$ and ip.

With these preparations, we can now give a requirement specification of the memory component.

3.2 Specification of the unreliable memory component

The specification of the unreliable memory component is listed in Table 2. As compared to the version presented in Dagstuhl, several improvements have been made to solve problems pointed out by Reino Kurki-Suonio, Leslie Lamport and Stephan Merz. All these versions have avoided the use of process identities for procedure calls. Finally, further problems discovered by Reino Kurki-Suonio have led to the present version which makes use of process identities (which is in line with the problem statement) in order to establish a relationship between calls and returns.

The architecture consists of the memory component M, the environment Env and an interaction point ip. The behaviour of M is given as the conjunction of properties P_1 through P_6, the interaction point behaviour is captured by properties P_7 through P_9. No properties are specified for the environment, which means that its behaviour is not restricted. All specified properties will be explained informally below. Additionally, some restrictions are placed on the sets of memory locations, memory values, arguments, and return values.

The first part of property P_1 specifies that for each process p and argument a, the number of *Read/Write* returns must not exceed the number of *Read/Write* calls. More technically, the number of actions where M has offered an interaction of type $Read/Write$ with parameter values p and a at interaction point ip (i.e. returns) is less or equal to the number of actions where M has accepted a corresponding interaction at ip (i.e. calls). This captures part of the semantics of the procedure calling mechanism from M's point of view. The second part of property P_1 states that for each process p, only one procedure call can be pending at any time.

Next, P_2 states that if $BadArg$ is returned as the result of a $Read/Write$ call, then the argument is not in the proper domain, therefore an exception is raised.

P_3 reads as follows: if value r is returned as the result of a $Read$ call of process p on location l, one of the following must hold:

- $r \in \{BadArg, Fail\}$, or
- $r = InitVal$, and no $Write$ into location l has ever ended successfully, or
- a successful $Write$ into location l has occurred in the past before the $Read$ call corresponding to the $Read$ return in the antecedents, and some $Write$ of value r into location l has been pending at some point in time since the call of the successful $Write$, or
- no successful $Write$ into location l has occurred in the past before the $Read$ call corresponding to the $Read$ return in the antecedents, and some $Write$ of value r into location l has been pending at some point in time.

The interval constructed in P_3 needs some explanation: starting from the current state, the starting point denoted by the expression $(([\varphi_1] \Leftarrow [\varphi_2]) \Leftarrow [\varphi_3])$ is located by searching backward first for $[\varphi_3]$, then for $[\varphi_2]$, and finally for $[\varphi_1]$.

If some $Write$ of value r into location l is pending, an atomic write into that location may occur. Whether it actually *does* occur may only become externally visible through the completion of a pending or subsequent $Read$. It is, however, possible that atomic writes may no longer become externally visible, namely if there is a successful $Write$ afterwards. The precise characterization of this scenario is given in the third alternative of P_3.

Property P_4 specifies an additional constraint to exclude illegal behaviour not ruled out by P_3. Consider the following scenario: two subsequent successful $Read$ operations on location l are performed such that no atomic writes may have changed the value of the memory cell between the corresponding atomic reads. Then both $Read$ operations must return the same value, unless there is some memory failure which may result in the return value $Fail$. This condition is stated in two parts, distinguishing between possible orderings of the $Read$ calls (for all processes p' and return values r'):

- If a $Read$ call and a return of process $p' \neq p$ have occurred since the last $Read$ call of process p, then the returned values are the same, $Fail$ is returned, or some atomic write may have happened in that interval.
- If no $Read$ call and return of process p' have occurred since the last $Read$ call of process p, but before the current $Read$ return of process p, then again

$S = \langle Arch, Behav \rangle$

$Arch = \langle \{M, Env\}, \{ip\}, ArchF \rangle$ with $ArchF(M) = ArchF(Env) = \{ip\}$

$Behav = \bigwedge_{1 \le i \le 10} P_i$

> $MemLocs \cup (MemLocs \times MemVals) \subseteq Arg$
>
> $BadArg \notin MemVals \wedge Fail \notin MemVals$
>
> $MemVals \subseteq RetVals$

$P_1.$ $AG\ \forall p, a.\ (\#[M.?\ R(p,a)] \ge \#[M.!\ R(p,a)]\ \wedge\ \#[M.?\ W(p,a)] \ge \#[M.!\ W(p,a)])\ \wedge$
$\quad AG\ \forall p.\ (0 \le \#[M.?\ W(p)] + \#[M.?\ R(p)] - \#[M.!\ W(p)] - \#[M.!\ R(p)] \le 1)$

$P_2.$ $AG\ \forall p, a.\ ([M.!\ R(p,a,BadArg)] \supset a \notin MemLocs)\ \wedge$
$\quad AG\ \forall p, a.\ ([M.!\ W(p,a,BadArg)] \supset a \notin MemLocs \times MemVals)$

$P_3.$ $AG\ \forall p, l, r.\ ([M.!\ R(p,l,r)]$
$\quad \supset (r \in \{BadArg, Fail\}\ \vee$
$\qquad r = InitVal\ \wedge\ \neg\ \exists p', r'.\ \blacklozenge\ [M.!\ W(p,(l,r'),OK)]\ \vee$
$\qquad \blacklozenge\ ([M.?\ R(p,l)]\ \wedge\ \exists p', r'.\ \blacklozenge\ [M.!\ W(p',(l,r'),OK)])\ \wedge$
$\qquad \exists p', r'.\ \langle begin\ (([M.?\ W(p',(l,r'))] \Leftarrow [M.!\ W(p',(l,r'),OK)]) \Leftarrow [M.?\ R(p,l)]) \Rightarrow)$
$\qquad\qquad\qquad \exists p'.\ \blacklozenge\ (\#[M.?\ W(p',(l,r))] > \#[M.!\ W(p',(l,r))]))\ \vee$
$\qquad \neg\ \blacklozenge\ ([M.?\ R(p,l)]\ \wedge\ \exists p', r'.\ \blacklozenge\ [M.!\ W(p',(l,r'),OK)])\ \wedge$
$\qquad\qquad\qquad \exists p'.\ \blacklozenge\ (\#[M.?\ W(p',(l,r))] > \#[M.!\ W(p',(l,r))]))))$

$P_4.$ $AG\ \forall p, p', l, r, r'.\ ([M.!\ R(p,l,r)] \wedge r \notin \{BadArg, Fail\}$
$\quad \supset \langle [M.?\ R(p,l)] \Rightarrow) (p' \ne p\ \wedge\ \blacklozenge\ ([M.!\ R(p',l,r')]\ \wedge\ \blacklozenge\ [M.?\ R(p',l)])$
$\qquad \supset (r' \in \{r, Fail\}\ \vee\ \blacklozenge\ \exists p''.\ (\#[M.?\ W(p'',(l,r))] > \#[M.!\ W(p'',(l,r))])))\ \wedge$
$\quad \langle [M.?\ R(p,l)] \Rightarrow) \neg\ (p' \ne p\ \wedge\ \blacklozenge\ ([M.!\ R(p',l,r')]\ \wedge\ \blacklozenge\ [M.?\ R(p',l)]))$
$\qquad \supset (begin([M.?\ R(p',l)] \Leftarrow [M.!\ R(p',l,r')]) \Rightarrow)$
$\qquad\qquad (r' \in \{r, Fail\}\ \vee\ \blacklozenge\ \exists p''.\ (\#[M.?\ W(p'',(l,r))] > \#[M.!\ W(p'',(l,r))])))$

$P_5.$ $AG\ \forall pn, p.\ (\#[M.?\ pn(p)] > \#[M.!\ pn(p)] \supset AF\ at\ M.!\ pn(p))$

$P_6.$ $AG\ \forall pn, p, a.\ \exists r.\ ([M.?\ pn(p,a)] \supset EF\ (at\ M.!\ pn(p,a,r) \wedge r \ne Fail))$

$P_7.$ $AG\ \forall pn_1, pn_2, p_1, p_2, a_1, a_2, r_1, r_2, n_1, n_2.$
$\quad ((\#[M.?\ pn_1(p_1,a_1)] = n_1\ \wedge\ \#[M.?\ pn_2(p_2,a_2)] = n_2$
$\qquad \supset\ \blacklozenge\ (\#[Env.!\ pn_1(p_1,a_1)] = n_1\ \wedge\ \#[Env.!\ pn_2(p_2,a_2)] = n_2))\ \wedge$
$\quad ((\#[Env.?\ pn_1(p_1,a_1,r_1)] = n_1\ \wedge\ \#[Env.?\ pn_2(p_2,a_2,r_2)] = n_2$
$\qquad \supset\ \blacklozenge\ (\#[M.!\ pn_1(p_1,a_1,r_1)] = n_1\ \wedge\ \#[M.!\ pn_2(p_2,a_2,r_2)] = n_2)))$

$P_8.$ $AG\ (at\ M.! \wedge at\ Env.? \supset AF\ [M.!] \wedge AF\ [Env.?])\ \wedge$
$\quad AG\ (at\ Env.! \wedge at\ M.? \supset AF\ [Env.!] \wedge AF\ [M.?])$

$P_9.$ $AG\ (at\ M.? \wedge \#[Env.!] > \#[M.?] \supset AF\ [M.?])\ \wedge$
$\quad AG\ (at\ Env.? \wedge \#[M.!] > \#[Env.?] \supset AF\ [Env.?])$

Table 2. Specification of the unreliable memory component

the returned values are the same, *Fail* is returned, or some atomic write may have happened in the interval starting with the earlier *Read* call.

As P_1 through P_3, P_4 is a safety property. Properties P_5 and P_6 are liveness properties stating that

- for each *Read/Write* call of process p, a corresponding *Read/Write* return is eventually offered (P_5), and
- a *Read/Write* call potentially leads to a return with a return value other than *Fail* (P_6).

P_6 is the reason why we have used a branching time temporal logic. With linear time, we could, for instance, specify strong fairness with respect to a return value other than *Fail*, which in our opinion would solve the issue raised in Problem 1c. P_6 is a different solution to this issue, since it is orthogonal to strong fairness: systems satisfying P_6 may not implement strong fairness, and vice versa.

The specification of the system behaviour is not complete without the behaviour of the interaction point *ip* [5]. So far, we have addressed the ability and readiness of the memory component M to interact with its environment *Env* through *ip*. It is still left open under what circumstances interactions can occur. E.g., interactions can be synchronous, in which case offer and acceptance must occur simultaneously, or asynchronous, meaning that the offer occurs before the acceptance. Synchronous interaction is a frequent assumption for process algebras, while asynchronous interaction is typical for communicating state machines. In an early development stage, it may also be left open whether interactions occur synchronously or asynchronously. Another difference is whether an interaction offered at some point in time may "cancel" an interaction offered earlier, but not yet accepted, or whether interactions offered are always kept until they are accepted. The first case can be related to the concept of a shared variable with a single value, while in the second case, we may think of a set or - more specifically - a queue.

We require that only interactions that have been offered by *Env* (M) can be accepted by M (*Env*). In addition, we require that the order of interactions is maintained (FIFO-property). However, no restriction is made whether interactions between M and *Env* have to occur synchronously or asynchronously. Thus, a decision for one particular form of interaction can be made in a later design stage. The above requirements are captured by property P_7. Note that P_7 is a safety property, expressing that for all combinations of interaction types pn_1, pn_2, and parameter vectors p_1, a_1, p_2, a_2, if at some point in time the interactions $pn_1(p_1, a_1)$ and $pn_2(p_2, a_2)$ have been accepted n_1 times and n_2 times at *ip*, respectively, then there must be some previous point in time where $pn_1(p_1, a_1)$ and $pn_2(p_2, a_2)$ have been offered n_1 times and n_2 times, respectively (similar for $pn_1(p_1, a_1, r_1)$ and $pn_2(p_2, a_2, r_2)$) This is provably equivalent to the FIFO-property (for a proof, see [5]).

Since P_7 is already satisfied in case of inaction, it should be complemented by liveness requirements. Property P_8 expresses that if M is prepared to offer and

Env is prepared to accept an interaction, then both agents will eventually proceed. Progress does not have to occur simultaneously, and may concern different interactions. Again, it is left open whether interactions occur synchronously or asynchronously. Therefore, P_8 should be augmented by P_9, which expresses that if more interactions have been offered than accepted, and M (*Env*) is prepared to accept, then it will eventually proceed. Interestingly, P_7, P_8, and P_9 together prevent loss of interactions: if an interaction would be lost, this would violate P_7, because to satisfy P_7 and P_8, an interaction would have to be created.

3.3 Refinements of the unreliable memory component

In this section, the unreliable memory component will be refined in two respects. Firstly, we will give a specification of a reliable memory component and argue that this is a system refinement (see Section 2.5). Secondly, we will make one step in the direction of a distributed implementation of the unreliable memory component by refining the architecture.

The specification of the reliable memory S' is identical with the specification of the unreliable memory component S (see Table 2) with the exception of properties P_3 and P_6. In P_3, *Fail* has to be removed, since in the reliable memory, this is no longer a possible return value. In P_6, the temporal operator EF has to be replaced by AF, because the reliable memory inevitably has to return a value other than *Fail*. For better readability, the second part of the conjunction, i.e. $r \neq Fail$, could be removed, since that is already covered by $P3$.

Proposition 7. *Let rep be the identical mapping between formulas, i.e. $\forall\, \varphi$. $rep(\varphi) = \varphi$. Then the reliable memory $S' = \langle Arch', Behav'\rangle$ is a refinement of the unreliable memory $S = \langle Arch, Behav\rangle$ under rep, i.e. S' refines$_{rep}$ S.*

Proof. With the definition of system refinement in Section 2.5, there are two proof obligations:

a) to show: $Arch'$ *refines* $Arch$

   Define *ref* to be the identical mapping between architectures, i.e.
   $\forall\, x \in Ag \cup Ip.\ ref(x) = \{x\}$.

b) to show: $\models_i Behav' \supset rep(Behav)$

   With *rep* as defined, and $\models \varphi$ implies $\models_i \varphi$, it suffices to show: $\models Behav' \supset$ *Behav*. With *Behav* and *Behav'* as given, this follows from $\models P_3' \supset P_3$ and $\models P_6' \supset P_6$:

   i) $\models P_3' \supset P_3$

       $AG\ \forall p,l,r.\ ([M.!\ R(p,l,r)] \supset (r \in \{BadArg\}\ \vee\ ...))$

       implies[6]

       $AG\ \forall p,l,r.\ ([M.!\ R(p,l,r)] \supset (r \in \{BadArg\}\ \vee\ r \in \{Fail\}\ \vee\ ...))$

---

[6] due to $\models (\varphi \supset \varphi') \supset (\varphi \supset (\varphi' \vee \varphi''))$

iff[7]

$$AG\ \forall p,l,r.\ ([M.!\ R(p,l,r)] \supset (r \in \{BadArg, Fail\} \lor \ldots))$$

ii) $\models P_6' \supset P_6$

$$AG\ \forall pn,p,a.\ \exists r.\ ([M.?\ pn(p,a)] \supset AF\ (at\ M.!\ pn(p,a,r)\ \land\ r \neq Fail))$$

implies[8]

$$AG\ \forall pn,p,a.\ \exists r.\ ([M.?\ pn(p,a)] \supset EF\ (at\ M.!\ pn(p,a,r)\ \land\ r \neq Fail))$$

q.e.d.

Next, we refine the memory component M into a reliable memory component RM, an RPC component, a clerk C and two interaction points ip_1 and ip_2. Formally, we get the architecture $Arch'' = \langle\{RM, RPC, C, Env\}, \{ip, ip_1, ip_2\}, ArchF''\rangle$ with $ArchF''(RM) = \{ip_2\}$, $ArchF''(RPC) = \{ip_1, ip_2\}$, $ArchF''(C) = \{ip_1, ip\}$, and $ArchF''(Env) = \{ip\}$ (see Figure 3). With the refinement function $ref(M) = \{RM, RPC, C, ip_1, ip_2\}$, $ref(Env) = \{Env\}$, $ref(ip) = \{ip\}$, this qualifies as a legal architectural refinement, i.e. $Arch''$ *refines* $Arch$.

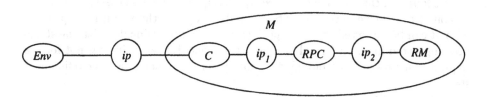

Fig. 3. Graphical representation of the refined memory architecture $Arch''$

Some comments are in place here. Although it is technically feasible to refine M as described, and to specify the behaviour of the components in a property-oriented way, we would prefer a different approach in this particular case. The reason for this is that the refinement as suggested in the problem statement introduces a system structure which in our opinion is not a requirement, but one of several possible design decisions, and which therefore should not be prescribed. It would be sufficient here to respect the original architecture consisting of M, Env and ip, and to introduce the refined structure in a more informal way, e.g., in order to improve the readability of the specification. This, however, is not supported by our formalism. Also, the refinement of M is given in operational terms in the problem statement. Thus, it would be more appropriate to use an

---

[7] due to $\models \forall x.\ ((x \in A \lor x \in B) \equiv (x \in A \cup B))$

[8] due to $\models AF\ \varphi \supset EF\ \varphi$

operational specification style together with a specification structure that does not express an architectural requirement in this particular case.

4 Are Architectural Requirements Important?

It has been argued that architectural requirements are not essential and should therefore be omitted. This argument manifests itself in equivalence or correctness notions abstracting away from specification structure. A typical example here are LOTOS specifications which may be composed from a number of LOTOS processes [3]. Transformations may be such that the specification structure is changed, while the visible behaviour remains the same, thus resulting in equivalent specifications. E.g., a monolithic specification consisting of a single LOTOS process may be equivalent to a resource oriented specification composed of several processes [9]. This way, structure is exploited to improve readability and modularity of a specification. However, if specifications with different structure can be equivalent, the structure does not have a formal semantics and therefore does not form an architectural requirement. Consequently, architectural requirements cannot be expressed in languages like LOTOS. If they are considered essential, they can only be dealt with informally.

Other examples where the structure of a specification has no formal semantics can be found in this volume (e.g., see [1], [2], [4], [8]). In these cases, structure is exploited to achieve better readability, and to support the verification process. Also, it can be observed that the specification structure coincides with the structure suggested in the informal problem statement. However, it does not form a requirement and may be modified by the system designer in a later refinement step.

In Section 2.5, we have introduced a correctness notion respecting architectural requirements. Recall that one condition for a system S' refining a system S is that all agents and interaction points of S are represented in S', and that their composition is maintained in S'. Consequently, systems with different architectures cannot be equivalent, or, stated otherwise, system architecture forms a requirement.

While we agree with the view that the structure of a specification may serve better readability and modularity, we argue that in certain cases, structure carries essential information about the specified system and therefore should have a formal semantics. E.g., consider a communication service with two service users ag_1 and ag_2 exchanging messages via interaction points ip_1 and ip_2. When ag_1 sends a message at ip_1, this message should be delivered to ag_2 through ip_2. However, any system delivering this message back to ag_1 through ip_1 would obviously not be correct. Abstracting away from the system architecture would prevent us from distinguishing the two cases, therefore, architectural reference points are necessary if such a distinction is considered important. Distinctions of this kind are typically drawn in the area of distributed systems when distribution is a requirement as in the case of a communication system.

In the example of the communication service, it may be argued that one can make a distinction by introducing additional message parameters, e.g. a destination address. However, this can be seen as just another way of introducing architectural aspects, with the clear disadvantage that no formal architectural meaning is associated with these parameters. Instead, this approach heavily relies on background knowledge not expressed in the specification and therefore is an informal way of treating architectural aspects.

In summary, architectural requirements are important in some cases and therefore should be expressable. This creates reference points that can be used when specifications on different abstraction levels have to be related, e.g., for verification purposes. On the other hand, a specification structure may just serve better readability and modularity, and does not form a requirement for the implementor. A specification technique for distributed systems should be able to distinguish between structure forming a requirement and structure that does not. If structure is important, it should be possible to express this explicitly and formally. If it is not important, it should not be a requirement.

5 Conclusion

The RPC-Memory Specification Problem partially treated in this report can be classified as an informal design specification. It is largely operational and relies on an intuitive understanding of well-known mechanisms, such as procedure calls and the reading and writing of memory cells. This makes it well suited for techniques directed towards design specifications, i.e. constructive FDTs that are able to model these mechanisms by closely following structure and style of the informal specification and then putting the parts together. However, the formalism applied above is more suited for requirement specifications which usually are more abstract. The goal here has been to capture the externally visible behaviour of each component by a conjunction of logical formulas. Therefore, our first step has been to fathom the external behaviour implicitly stated by the informal specification, and, as the second step, to capture it by logical properties. We have limited confidence that the resulting specification does not exclude legal memory behaviour. Also, we are not completely convinced that all illegal behaviour according to the problem statement is ruled out. The reason is that we had to insert a reengineering step in order to get from the operational style to the property style, a step which certainly must be considered as extremely errorprone. However, if we understand our result as a requirement specification, i.e. a specification that does not rule out legal behaviour – in contrast to a design specification capturing legal behaviour only –, then that result appears in a different light.

Acknowledgements. Special thanks go to Reino Kurki-Suonio and Stephan Merz, who have provided very detailed, constructive comments and extremely valuable feedback.

References

1. M. Abadi, L. Lamport and S. Merz. *A TLA Solution to the RPC-Memory Specification Problem*, this volume
2. J. Blom and B. Jonsson. *Constraint Oriented Temporal Logic Specification*, this volume
3. T. Bolognesi and E. Brinksma. *Introduction to the ISO Specification Language LOTOS*, Computer Networks, 14(1), Jan. 1989
4. M. Broy. *A Functional Solution to the RPC-Memory Specification Problem*, this volume
5. R. Gotzhein. *Formal Definition and Representation of Interaction Points*, Computer Networks and ISDN Systems 25 (1992) 3-22
6. R. Gotzhein. *Temporal Logic and Applications – A Tutorial*, Computer Networks and ISDN Systems 24 (1992) 203-218
7. R. Gotzhein. *Open Distributed Systems - On Concepts, Methods and Design from a Logical Point of View*, Vieweg Wiesbaden, 1993
8. K. G. Larsen, B. Steffen and C. Weise. *The Methodology of Modal Constraints*, this volume
9. C. A. Vissers, G. Scollo and M. van Sinderen. *Architecture and Specification Style in Formal Descriptions of Distributed Systems*, in: S. Aggarwal, K. Sabnani (eds.), Protocol Specification, Verification, and Testing VIII, Proceedings, Atlantic City, USA, June 7-10, 1988, 16p.

Using PVS for an Assertional Verification of the RPC-Memory Specification Problem

Jozef Hooman

Dept. of Computing Science
Eindhoven University of Technology
P.O. Box 513, 5600 MB Eindhoven, The Netherlands
e-mail: wsinjh@win.tue.nl

Abstract. The RPC-Memory Specification Problem has been specified and verified in an assertional method, supported by the verification system PVS. Properties of the components are expressed in the higher-order logic of PVS and all implementations have been verified by means of the interactive proof checker of PVS. A simplification of the memory specification - allowing multiple atomic reads - has been proved correct. Additionally, to increase the confidence in the specification, an implementation-oriented specification of the inner memory is shown to be equivalent to our original property-oriented formulation.

0 Introduction

A solution of the RPC-Memory Specification Problem is presented using an assertional method supported by the verification system PVS[1] (Prototype Verification System) [ORS92]. The PVS specification language is a higher-order typed logic, with many built-in types including booleans, integers, rationals, sequences, lists, and sets. Specifications can be structured into a hierarchy of parameterized theories. The tool contains an interactive proof checker with powerful commands for, e.g., inductive proofs, automatic rewriting, and the use of decision procedures for propositional and arithmetical simplification.

All components mentioned in the RPC-Memory Specification Problem are specified in the PVS specification language. Events are used to model the occurrence of actions such as a procedure call, a return of a procedure, and an atomic read or write. Causality relations between events are represented by a partial order. Further we use the notation of event attributes from [JPZ94] to express, for instance, the arguments and the timing of an action.

Moreover, all implementations given in the formulation of the specification problem are verified by means of the PVS proof checker, using a compositional rule for parallel composition. This rule is taken from previous work, where a framework based on assumption/commitment pairs has been devised for the top-down design of distributed real-time systems. In [Hoo94a], a mixed formalism in which programs and assumption/commitment based specifications are combined, has been defined in the PVS specification language.

---

[1] PVS is free available, see WWW page http://www.csl.sri.com/sri-csl-pvs.html

To our experience, the use of the tool PVS significantly increases both the speed with which a complete solution can be obtained and the size of the problems that can solved by an assertional approach. Having a mechanical check of the correctness proofs, tedious proof reading is avoided and more attention can be paid to the essential issues, such as a discussion about the axioms and the correctness of the definitions. Since proofs are stored and can be rerun, it is relatively easy to make modifications and check which assumptions are essential. However, when constructing a proof with an interactive tool such as PVS, it is important to have a clear outline of the proof. Starting without a good intuition about the proof could undo a possible gain of time.

In our assertional approach we specify a component by listing its properties. An advantage is that this does not give any implementation bias and one obtains insight in the essential properties that are needed for correctness. There is, however, a danger that the specification does not correspond to the informal specification and it is relatively easy to introduce inconsistencies (see also the remarks about axiomatic specifications in [Lam94]). In the specification given here we have tried to stay as close as possible to the informal formulation of the specification problem. When needed, the resulting formal specification can be transformed into an equivalent, more convenient, specification. E.g., in section 2.4 the original specification of the memory component, in which exactly one atomic read is performed for each successful read operation, is shown to be equivalent to a specification where multiple atomic reads are allowed.

Another technique in PVS is the use of "putative" theorems, that is, one tries to prove properties that should follow from the specification (see [ORSvH95]). Especially the failure of such a proof is helpful because it might reveal errors in the specification or the understanding of the system. As an illustration of this method, in section 2.2 an implementation-oriented specification of the inner memory is proved to be equivalent to our original, property-oriented, formulation.

A brief background of our formal method is presented in section 0.1. In section 0.2, the basic formalism is formulated in the PVS specification language and the use of the PVS proof checker is illustrated by a small example. In section 1 we start with the specification and verification of the RPC-Memory Specification Problem, following the arrangement of the original description. Concluding remarks can be found in section 5.

0.1 Formal Background

Starting point of our approach is a formal method for the specification and verification of distributed real-time systems [Hoo91]. The method has been inspired by Hoare triples (precondition, program, postcondition), which have been extended to deal with the timing of events [Hoo94b]. To distinguish the resulting framework from classical Hoare logic, we use "assumption" and "commitment" instead of "precondition" and "postcondition".

The assumption-commitment structure of specifications is especially convenient for the formulation of compositional proof rules for sequential constructs.

Compositionality means that the specification of a compound programming construct can be derived from the specifications of its components, without knowing the implementation of these components. This makes it possible to verify design steps during the process of program design.

For parallel composition we have formulated a proof rule which essentially expresses that the specification of a parallel system can be derived from the conjunction of the specifications of its components. To obtain such a rule, the assumption-commitment style specification of a component is extended with a static part describing the interface of the component (its alphabet), i.e. the events that could occur during execution. Note that the assertions (assumption and commitment) describe the dynamic part of a system, that is, the events that actually occur during execution, their order, and maybe other attributes of events such as their timing. Then a compositional rule for parallel composition has been formulated by requiring that the assertions of a component only refer to events of its own static interface.

In previous work, our framework for the top-down design of distributed real-time programs has been formulated in PVS [Hoo94a]. There the semantics of programs is essentially a relation on states with some additional components to record the timing behavior of systems. Based on this semantics, the soundness of a number of proof rules for programming constructs (e.g., sequential composition, iteration, parallel composition) have been proved. Since program design is not part of the RPC-Memory Specification, the semantic framework with states is not needed. To avoid unnecessary notation, the states are left out in this paper and the only programming construct considered here is parallel composition.

For simplicity, also the syntactic constraints of the parallel composition rule, which require that the assertions of a component only refer to its static interface, are omitted. We refer to [Hoo91] for more details and a soundness proof of the parallel composition rule. Here the proof rules are simply postulated as axioms. Further, it should be mentioned that the assumption-commitment framework has been used here mainly because it was available in PVS from earlier examples [Hoo94a]. In the RPC-Memory Specification the assumption is not relevant and will be true in all specifications.

0.2 Basic PVS Framework

In general, a PVS specification consists of a number of theories. First the basic specification primitives are defined in a theory specs which can be imported by other theories. In this theory we first declare uninterpreted types Value and Program. The symbol "+" indicates that these types are nonempty.

```
specs : THEORY
BEGIN
Value, Program : TYPE+
```

Next we define variables of type Program and of the predefined type bool. Specifications consist of a pair of boolean formulas (predicates on states in the full framework of [Hoo94a]), called assumption and commitment. To achieve a flexible framework in which programs and specifications can be mixed freely, a specification is also considered as a program. Hence we define `spec(A, C) : Program` in PVS, saying that `spec(A, C)` has type `Program`, given boolean variables `A` and `C`. Note that this equivalent to `spec : [bool, bool -> Program]`.

As usual one should be able to express that a program satisfies a specification and, in general, that one program refines another. For refinement we overload the infix operator `=>` and make it a pre-order on programs by defining `=>` as a constant of the type `(preorder?[Program])` which is constructed using the predefined predicate `preorder?`.

```
prog, prog1, prog2, prog3, prog4 : VAR Program
A, A1, A2, C, C1, C2              : VAR bool

spec(A, C) : Program

=> : (preorder?[Program])
```

Reflexivity and transitivity of `=>` can be made explicit by proving two lemmas, with labels `refrefl` and `reftrans`.

```
refrefl : LEMMA prog => prog

reftrans : LEMMA (prog1 => prog2) IFF
                 (EXISTS prog : (prog1 => prog) AND
                                (prog => prog2))
```

The next two axioms correspond to the usual consequence and conjunction rules of Hoare logic.

```
rulecons : AXIOM (A IMPLIES  A1) AND (C1 IMPLIES C)
                 IMPLIES
                 (spec(A1, C1) => spec(A, C))

ruleconj : AXIOM (prog => spec(A1, C1)) AND (prog => spec(A2, C2))
                 IMPLIES
                 (prog => spec(A1 AND A2, C1 AND C2) ;
```

Finally we define the parallel composition operation on programs, using the infix operator `//`, axiomatize two properties, and derive a convenient proof rule which combines some of the axioms.

```
// : [Program, Program -> Program]

rulepar : AXIOM  spec(A1, C1) // spec(A2, C2)
                 =>
                 spec(A1 AND A2, C1 AND C2)
```

```
% monotonicity property
monopar : AXIOM  (prog3 => prog1) AND (prog4 => prog2)
                       IMPLIES
                 (prog3 // prog4 => prog1 // prog2)


% combined proof rule for parallel composition
% including monotonicity and consequence
specpar : THEOREM (EXISTS A1, A2, C1, C2 :
                      (prog1 => spec(A1, C1)) AND
                      (prog2 => spec(A2, C2)) AND
                      (A IMPLIES A1 AND A2) AND
                      (C1 AND C2 IMPLIES C) )
                  IMPLIES
                  prog1 // prog2 => spec(A, C)
END specs
```

The PVS parser and type-checker can be applied to such a theory to check consistency. Lemmas and theorems can be proved by means of the interactive proof checker of PVS. As an illustration of its user interface, we briefly show a simple proof of lemma reftrans. By invoking a certain command on this lemma, the PVS system creates a new EMACS buffer (PVS uses EMACS as its interface), displays the formula, and asks the user for a command by the Rule? prompt. (In the text below, only the part after this prompt is typed in by the user, the rest is generated by the system.)

```
reftrans :
  |-------
{1}    (FORALL (prog1: Program, prog2: Program):
          (prog1 => prog2)
               IFF (EXISTS (prog: Program):
                      (prog1 => prog) AND (prog => prog2)))
Rule?
```

Now a proof command of PVS can be invoked. By typing the (skolem!) command, Skolem constants prog1!1 and prog2!1 are introduced for prog1 and prog2. Observing the IFF in the goal, we decide to split the proof of formula 1 into two subgoals, and the system presents the first one.

```
Rule? (skolem!)
Skolemizing, this simplifies to:
reftrans :
  |-------
{1}    (prog1!1 => prog2!1)
          IFF (EXISTS (prog: Program):
                  (prog1!1 => prog) AND (prog => prog2!1))
Rule? (split 1)
Splitting conjunctions, this yields  2 subgoals:
```

```
reftrans.1 :
  |-------
{1}    (prog1!1 => prog2!1)
          IMPLIES (EXISTS (prog: Program):
                    (prog1!1 => prog) AND (prog => prog2!1))
```

This goal is flattened and we ask the system to find a suitable instantiation of the quantified variable by means of the command (inst?).

```
Rule? (flatten)
Applying disjunctive simplification to flatten sequent,
this simplifies to:
reftrans.1 :
{-1}   (prog1!1 => prog2!1)
  |-------
{1}    (EXISTS (prog: Program):
          (prog1!1 => prog) AND (prog => prog2!1))
Rule? (inst?)
Found substitution:
prog gets prog2!1,
Instantiating quantified variables, this simplifies to:
reftrans.1 :
[-1]   (prog1!1 => prog2!1)
  |-------
{1}    (prog1!1 => prog2!1) AND (prog2!1 => prog2!1)
```

Simplifying the formula and using the reflexivity lemma completes this case.

```
Rule? (assert)
Simplifying, rewriting, and recording with decision procedures,
this simplifies to:
reftrans.1 :
[-1]   (prog1!1 => prog2!1)
  |-------
{1}    (prog2!1 => prog2!1)
Rule? (use "refrefl")
Using lemma refrefl,
This completes the proof of reftrans.1.

reftrans.2 :
  |-------
{1}    (EXISTS (prog: Program):
          (prog1!1 => prog) AND (prog => prog2!1))
        IMPLIES (prog1!1 => prog2!1)
```

For this second subgoal, we first use command (skosimp*) to simplify it and then introduce the type of the => operator.

Rule? (skosimp*)
Repeatedly Skolemizing and flattening, this simplifies to:
reftrans.2 :
{-1}   (prog1!1 => prog!1)
{-2}   (prog!1 => prog2!1)
 |-------
{1}   (prog1!1 => prog2!1)

Rule? (typepred "specs.=>")
Adding type constraints for specs.=>, this simplifies to:
reftrans.2 :
{-1}   preorder?[Program](specs.=>)
[-2]   (prog1!1 => prog!1)
[-3]   (prog!1 => prog2!1)
 |-------
[1]   (prog1!1 => prog2!1)

By expanding the definition of **preorder?** into
reflexive?(specs.=>) & transitive?(specs.=>),
hiding reflexivity, and next expanding transitivity, we obtain:

reftrans.2 :
{-1}   FORALL (x: Program), (y: Program), (z: Program):
            specs.=>(x, y) & specs.=>(y, z) => specs.=>(x, z)
[-2]   (prog1!1 => prog!1)
[-3]   (prog!1 => prog2!1)
 |-------
[1]   (prog1!1 => prog2!1)

By an instantiation of -1 and the command (**assert**), the proof is completed.

Rule? (inst -1 "prog1!1" "prog!1" "prog2!1")
Instantiating the top quantifier in -1 with the terms:
prog1!1, prog!1, prog2!1, this simplifies to:
reftrans.2 :
{-1}   (specs.=>(prog1!1, prog!1)) & (specs.=>(prog!1, prog2!1))
            => (specs.=>(prog1!1, prog2!1))
[-2]   (prog1!1 => prog!1)
[-3]   (prog!1 => prog2!1)
 |-------
[1]   (prog1!1 => prog2!1)

Rule? (assert)
Simplifying, rewriting, and recording with decision procedures,
This completes the proof of reftrans.2.
Q.E.D.
Run time = 5.83 secs.
Real time = 216.45 secs.

Note that reasoning in PVS is based on the sequent calculus; the last sequent above consists of antecedents numbered -1, -2, and -3, and a succedent numbered 1. Please note that the proof above is just to show the user interface and not the power of the theorem prover. There are several more powerful commands, combining skolemization, simplification, instantiation, decision procedures, etc., which allow a reduction of the number of proof steps. For instance, the proof above, with 14 commands, can be easily reduced to 7 commands.

Since the amount of run time, indicated above, depends heavily on the equipment used, we will henceforth mention the number of commands as a measure for the complexity of a proof. Note that we have not tried to minimize proofs, so it gives an indication about the number of interactions that are required by an average user to perform the proofs.

Henceforth, declarations of variables are not repeated. So in subsequent theories A is a variable of type bool, prog a variable of type Program, etc.

1 The Procedure Interface

The procedure interface is defined in a theory procinterface which imports the theory specs. The occurrence of actions is represented by an uninterpreted nonempty type Event. We define a strict order < on events to represent a "happens before" relation, indicating potential causality. Transitivity of this relation is made explicit in lemma caustrans.

```
procinterface : THEORY
BEGIN
IMPORTING specs
Event     : TYPE+
E, E1, E2, E3, E4, E5 : VAR Event

< : (strict_order?[Event]) ;

caustrans : LEMMA (EXISTS E2 : E1 < E2 AND E2 < E3)
                  IMPLIES E1 < E3
```

Similar to [JPZ94] we introduce event attributes. For the current specification problem we start with five attributes, event type etype, component number comp, process identity ident, argument argu, and name name. The event type Etype is defined as an enumeration type consisting of three elements, which implies in PVS that these three elements are different. This fact is used by the PVS decision procedures. The component number is used later to distinguish between different components with the same interface. The argument of an event is a list of values (list is a built-in type in PVS). For the name of a procedure we use an uninterpreted type Name and declare the names read and write as constants. We have not used the enumeration type here, since also other names should be allowed (e.g. for the RPC component). Hence we have an explicit axiom to express that read and write are different. Further we define a constant

ProcName? which has type [Name -> bool], with the additional constraint that read and write are procedure names. Similarly, the constant function ArgNum : [(ProcName?) -> nat] specifies the number of arguments of these procedures.

```
Etype        : TYPE = {call, return, atomic}
Identity     : TYPE+
Arg          : TYPE = list[Value]
Name         : TYPE+
etype : [Event -> Etype]
comp  : [Event -> nat]
ident : [Event -> Identity]
argu  : [Event -> Arg]
name  : [Event -> Name]

read, write : Name
RWDiff  : AXIOM read /= write

ProcName? : {PN : [Name -> bool] | PN(read) AND PN(write)}
ArgNum    : {AN : [(ProcName?) -> nat] | AN(read) = 1 AND
                                         AN(write) = 2}
```

Next we define, by proced, when a pair of events forms a procedure.

```
NoEventBetween(E1,E2) : bool =
  NOT (EXISTS E : name(E) = name(E1) AND ident(E) = ident(E1) AND
                  comp(E) = comp(E1) AND
                  (etype(E) = call OR etype(E) = return) AND
                  E1 < E AND E < E2)

proced (E1,E2) : bool =
    E1 < E2 AND etype(E1) = call AND etype(E2) = return AND
    name(E1) = name(E2) AND ident(E1) = ident(E2) AND
    comp(E1) = comp(E2) AND NoEventBetween(E1,E2)
```

Assuming that events with the same identity are totally ordered (as expressed by axiom IdentTotal), two overlapping procedures (i.e. there is an event between both call/return pairs) with the same name, identity, and component number are proved to be identical.

```
IdentTotal : AXIOM NOT (E1 < E2) AND NOT (E2 < E1) AND
                   ident(E1) = ident(E2)
                   IMPLIES E1 = E2

UniqueProced : LEMMA
    proced (E1,E2) AND proced (E3,E4) AND name(E1) = name(E3) AND
    ident(E1) = ident(E3) AND comp(E1) = comp(E3) AND
    E1 < E5 AND E5 < E2 AND E3 < E5 AND E5 < E4
    IMPLIES
    E1 = E3 AND E2 = E4
```

Finally, we axiomatize that each return has a corresponding call, i.e. is part of a procedure.

```
ReturnCallAx: AXIOM etype(E2) = return
                    IMPLIES (EXISTS E1 : proced (E1,E2))
END procinterface
```

2   A Memory Component

First, in section 2.1, a few basic primitives of memory are defined. Then, in section 2.2, we axiomatize an inner memory component which is used, in section 2.3, to specify the memory component. In section 2.4 we show that this specification can be simplified by not restricting the number of atomic read actions. A reliable memory component is specified in section 2.5. Section 2.6 contains a description of a failing memory component.

2.1   Basic Properties of Memory

Theory membasic contains predicates MemLoc? and MemVal? to describe which values are considered as locations and memory values, respectively. They are extended to arguments, i.e. lists of values, using the short-hand notation (: v1, v2, v3 , .. :) of PVS for a list of values. Further we declare four special values and axiomatize a few properties of these values.

```
membasic : THEORY
BEGIN
IMPORTING   procinterface

l, v         : VAR Value
MemLoc?(l)   : bool
MemVal?(v)   : bool


arg            : VAR Arg
MemLoc(arg)    : bool = (EXISTS l : MemLoc?(l) AND arg = (:l:))
MemVal(arg)    : bool = (EXISTS v : MemVal?(v) AND arg = (:v:))
MemLocVal(arg) : bool = (EXISTS l, v : MemLoc?(l) AND
                                    MemVal?(v) AND arg = (:l, v:))


InitVal, WriteOK, BadArg, MemFailure : Value

ValDiff : AXIOM InitVal /= WriteOK AND InitVal /= BadArg AND
                InitVal /= MemFailure AND WriteOK /= BadArg AND
                WriteOK /= MemFailure AND BadArg /= MemFailure


SpecVal: AXIOM MemVal(InitVal) AND NOT MemVal(WriteOK) AND
               NOT MemVal(BadArg) AND NOT MemVal(MemFailure) AND
```

```
        NOT MemLoc(InitVal) AND NOT MemLoc(WriteOK) AND
        NOT MemLoc(BadArg) AND NOT MemLoc(MemFailure)
END membasic
```

2.2 Inner Memory

The RPC-Memory Specification mentions in section 2:

> The memory behaves as if it maintains an array of atomically read and
> written locations ...

Hence we model the access to the inner memory by a sequence of atomic read
and write events, using the PVS predefined type **sequence** which gives infinite
sequences (i.e., a function from **nat** to a certain type). To include finite sequences
in the model, a special atomic "undefined" event UE with name undef is declared.

The type **Atoms** consist of events that are either undefined or represent read
or write actions. In the subtype **AtomsRW** the undefined ones are excluded. Note
that the argument of read and write events is a list of a location and a value.
Functions loc and val are defined to select these elements.

```
innermem : THEORY
BEGIN
IMPORTING membasic

undef        : Name
UndefDiff    : AXIOM undef /= read AND undef /= write
UndefExists  : AXIOM (EXISTS E : etype(E) = atomic AND
                                 name(E) = undef)

UE  : { E | etype(E) = atomic AND name(E) = undef }

Atoms : TYPE = { E | etype(E) = atomic AND
                     (name(E) = undef OR
                       ((name(E) = read OR name(E) = write) AND
                        MemLocVal(argu(E)) ) ) }

AtomsRW : TYPE = { At : Atoms | name(At) /= undef }
A       : VAR AtomsRW
loc(A)  : (MemLoc?) = car(argu(A))        % first of argument
val(A)  : (MemVal?) = car(cdr(argu(A)))   % second of argument
```

By axiom **TotalOrderSeq**, it is assumed that a sequence of atomic events corresponds to the causal ordering of these events. Finally, predicate **ReadCorrect**
expresses that an atomic read event either reads the initial value if there is no
preceding write event or it reads the value of the last preceding write event.

```
AtomSeq               : VAR sequence[Atoms]
i, j, j0, j1, j2, k, n : VAR nat
```

```
loca                        : VAR (MemLoc?)

TotalOrderSeq : AXIOM j1 < j2 IFF AtomSeq(j1) < AtomSeq(j2)

% define value read, using two auxiliary predicates

NoWriteBefore(j,loca,AtomSeq) : bool =
   NOT (EXISTS j0 : j0 < j AND name(AtomSeq(j0)) = write AND
                    loc(AtomSeq(j0)) = loca)

NoWriteBetween(j0,j,loca,AtomSeq) : bool =
   NOT (EXISTS j1 : j0 < j1 AND j1 < j AND
                    name(AtomSeq(j1)) = write AND
                    loc(AtomSeq(j1)) = loca)

ReadCorrect ( AtomSeq ) : bool = (FORALL j :
  name(AtomSeq(j)) = read IMPLIES
  ((val(AtomSeq(j)) = InitVal AND
                  NoWriteBefore(j,loc(AtomSeq(j)),AtomSeq)) OR
    (EXISTS (j0 | j0 < j) : name(AtomSeq(j0)) = write AND
                  argu(AtomSeq(j)) = argu(AtomSeq(j0)) AND
                  NoWriteBetween(j0,j,loc(AtomSeq(j)),AtomSeq) )))
END innermem
```

Equivalent Formulation of the Inner Memory Clearly it is easy to make
mistakes in specifications, in the sense that the specification does not express the
intended behavior. For instance, in the specification above one could forget the
initial case. Therefore it is important to have a way to increase the confidence
in the specification, e.g. using simulations. In PVS one can try to prove putative
theorems, expressing properties that should hold for a correct specification.

Here we give an alternative formulation of the inner memory, in terms of a
state-based implementation, and show that it is equivalent to the formulation
above. In theory inmemimpl we define the state of the inner memory as a function
from memory locations to memory values. The behavior of the inner memory is
then modeled by a sequence of states. An atomic read does not change the state
and returns the value of the location involved in the current state, whereas an
atomic write changes the value of the location (represented by the WITH construct
in PVS by which a new value can be assigned to an element of a sequence or a
function).

```
inmemimpl : THEORY
BEGIN
IMPORTING innermem
State     : TYPE = [ (MemLoc?) -> (MemVal?) ]
InitState : State = (LAMBDA loca : InitVal)
mval      : VAR (MemVal?)
```

```
ss          : VAR sequence[State]

MemSeqImpl(AtomSeq,ss) : bool =
 ss(0) = InitState AND
 (FORALL i :
  IF  name(AtomSeq(i)) = read
  THEN val(AtomSeq(i)) = ss(i)(loc(AtomSeq(i))) AND
       ss(i+1) = ss(i)
  ELSIF name(AtomSeq(i)) = write
  THEN ss(i+1) = ss(i) WITH [(loc(AtomSeq(i))) := val(AtomSeq(i))]
  ELSE ss(i+1) = ss(i)
  ENDIF )


MemImpl(AtomSeq) : bool = (EXISTS ss : MemSeqImpl(AtomSeq,ss))
```

The aim is to show that the alternative formulation MemImpl is equivalent to the specification ReadCorrect of innermem. In order to prove that ReadCorrect implies MemImpl, a sequence of states is constructed by the recursive function ConstrStatSeq. Such a recursive definition in PVS requires a MEASURE function which should be shown to decrease for recursive calls (which is trivial here).

```
ConstrStatSeq(AtomSeq) (i) : RECURSIVE State =
    IF i = 0
    THEN InitState
    ELSIF name(AtomSeq(i-1)) = write
    THEN ConstrStatSeq(AtomSeq)(i-1)
            WITH [(loc(AtomSeq(i-1))) := val(AtomSeq(i-1))]
    ELSE ConstrStatSeq(AtomSeq)(i-1)
    ENDIF
    MEASURE (LAMBDA n : n)


impllem1 : LEMMA ReadCorrect(AtomSeq) IMPLIES MemImpl(AtomSeq)
```

For the proof in the other direction we have to show, for each read action that does not read the initial value, the existence of a preceding write with the same value. This is done by the following recursive function.

```
FirstWriteBefore(AtomSeq,loca) (j) : RECURSIVE nat =
    IF j=0 THEN j+1        % some value
    ELSIF name(AtomSeq(j-1)) = write AND loc(AtomSeq(j-1)) = loca
    THEN j-1
    ELSE FirstWriteBefore(AtomSeq,loca)(j-1)
    ENDIF
    MEASURE (LAMBDA n : n)


impllem2 : LEMMA MemImpl(AtomSeq) IMPLIES ReadCorrect(AtomSeq)
```

```
memimplcor : THEOREM ReadCorrect(AtomSeq) IFF MemImpl(AtomSeq)

END inmemimpl
```

Of course one could very well imagine that one starts with the operational description of inmemimpl and then proves the formulation as given in innermem. We have presented the theories here in the order in which they were written originally. In subsequent theories the predicate ReadCorrect is used.

2.3 Memory

Next we specify the memory component in the theory memory. This theory is parameterized by a natural number N to represent the component number. First a few simple properties are defined, expressing the values returned after a call of a read or write event.

```
memory [ N : nat ] : THEORY
BEGIN
IMPORTING innermem

MRead : bool = (FORALL E1 :
 etype(E1) = call AND name(E1) = read AND comp(E1) = N
  IMPLIES (EXISTS E2 : proced(E1,E2) AND
          IF MemLoc(argu(E1))
          THEN argu(E2) = (:MemFailure:) OR MemVal(argu(E2))
          ELSE argu(E2) = (:MemFailure:) OR argu(E2) = (:BadArg:)
          ENDIF ) )

MWrite : bool = (FORALL E1 :
 etype(E1) = call AND name(E1) = write AND comp(E1) = N
  IMPLIES (EXISTS E2 : proced(E1,E2) AND
          IF MemLocVal(argu(E1))
          THEN argu(E2) = (:MemFailure:) OR argu(E2) = (:WriteOK:)
          ELSE argu(E2) = (:MemFailure:) OR argu(E2) = (:BadArg:)
          ENDIF ) )
```

Note that we allow a MemFailure if the argument is not correct, although this is not completely clear from the informal formulation. The implementation given later, however, allows this possibility.

Property MReadInternal specifies, using predicate NoReadBetween, that a successful read procedure performs a single atomic read on the inner memory. A similar specification is given for write procedures, with the difference that a successful write procedure may perform one or more atomic write events.

```
NoReadBetween(E1,E2,j,AtomSeq) : bool =
NOT (EXISTS (j0 | j0 /= j) :
        E1 < AtomSeq(j0) AND AtomSeq(j0) < E2 AND
```

```
            name(AtomSeq(j0)) = read AND name(AtomSeq(j)) = read AND
            ident(AtomSeq(j0)) = ident(AtomSeq(j)) AND
            loc(AtomSeq(j0)) = loc(AtomSeq(j)) )

MReadInternal (AtomSeq ) : bool = (FORALL E1, E2:
 comp(E1) = N AND name(E1) = read AND proced(E1,E2) AND
 MemVal(argu(E2))
   IMPLIES (EXISTS j :
   name(AtomSeq(j)) = read AND ident(AtomSeq(j)) = ident(E1) AND
   argu(E1) = (:loc(AtomSeq(j)):) AND
   argu(E2) = (:val(AtomSeq(j)):) AND
   E1 < AtomSeq(j) AND AtomSeq(j) < E2 AND
   NoReadBetween(E1,E2,j,AtomSeq)))

MWriteInternal ( AtomSeq ) : bool = (FORALL E1, E2 :
     comp(E1) = N AND name(E1) = write AND
     proced(E1,E2) AND argu(E2) = (:WriteOK:)
     IMPLIES (EXISTS j : name(AtomSeq(j)) = name(E1) AND
                         ident(AtomSeq(j)) = ident(E1) AND
                         argu(AtomSeq(j)) = argu(E1) AND
                         E1 < AtomSeq(j) AND AtomSeq(j) < E2))
```

According to the informal specification, an operation that raises a BadArg exception has no effect on the memory. We strengthen this property by expressing that for any internal atomic action there is a causally related procedure which does not raise this exception. Although this is not mentioned in the informal specification, it seems unreasonable to allow spurious internal actions, which might even change the state in case of a write action.

```
MInternalRead ( AtomSeq ) : bool = (FORALL j :
   name(AtomSeq(j)) = read
     IMPLIES (EXISTS E1, E2 : proced(E1,E2) AND comp(E1) = N AND
                              name(E1) = read AND
                              ident(E1) = ident(AtomSeq(j)) AND
                              argu(E1) = (:loc(AtomSeq(j)):) AND
                              argu(E2) /= (:BadArg:) AND
                              E1 < AtomSeq(j) AND AtomSeq(j) < E2))

MInternalWrite ( AtomSeq ) : bool = (FORALL j :
   name(AtomSeq(j)) = write
     IMPLIES (EXISTS E1, E2 : proced(E1,E2) AND comp(E1) = N AND
                              name(E1) = name(AtomSeq(j)) AND
                              ident(E1) = ident(AtomSeq(j)) AND
                              argu(E1) = argu(AtomSeq(j)) AND
                              argu(E2) /= (:BadArg:) AND
                              E1 < AtomSeq(j) AND AtomSeq(j) < E2))
```

Finally, the commitment of the memory component requires the existence of a sequence of atomic read and write events satisfying the predicates defined above.

```
CMem : bool = MRead AND MWrite AND
              (EXISTS AtomSeq : ReadCorrect(AtomSeq) AND
                                MReadInternal(AtomSeq) AND
                                MWriteInternal(AtomSeq) AND
                                MInternalRead(AtomSeq) AND
                                MInternalWrite(AtomSeq) )
END memory
```

2.4 Simplifying the Memory Specification

The informal specification of the memory component requires that a successful read operation performs exactly one atomic read on the inner memory. This is formalized above by NoReadBetween in property MReadInternal. In this section we show that this specification is equivalent to a specification that allows multiple atomic reads. First we formulate this simplified specification CMemSimp in theory memsimp, replacing MReadInternal by MReadInternalSimp.

```
memsimp [ N : nat ] : THEORY
BEGIN
IMPORTING memory[N]

MReadInternalSimp ( AtomSeq ) : bool = (FORALL E1, E2:
    comp(E1) = N AND name(E1) = read AND proced(E1,E2) AND
    MemVal(argu(E2))
    IMPLIES (EXISTS j : name(AtomSeq(j)) = read AND
                        ident(AtomSeq(j)) = ident(E1) AND
                        argu(E1) = (:loc(AtomSeq(j)):) AND
                        argu(E2) = (:val(AtomSeq(j)):) AND
                        E1 < AtomSeq(j) AND AtomSeq(j) < E2))

CMemSimp : bool = MRead AND MWrite AND
              (EXISTS AtomSeq : ReadCorrect(AtomSeq) AND
                                MReadInternalSimp(AtomSeq) AND
                                MWriteInternal(AtomSeq) AND
                                MInternalRead(AtomSeq) AND
                                MInternalWrite(AtomSeq) )
```

The aim is to prove CMem IFF CMemSimp. Observe that CMem IMPLIES CMemSimp is trivial, and it remains to show the implication CMemSimp IMPLIES CMem. Assuming a sequence AtomSeq!1 satisfying
ReadCorrect(AtomSeq!1) AND MReadInternalSimp(AtomSeq!1) AND
MWriteInternal(AtomSeq!1) AND MInternalRead(AtomSeq!1) AND
MInternalWrite(AtomSeq!1),
we have to show the existence of a sequence AtomSeq such that

ReadCorrect(AtomSeq) AND MReadInternal(AtomSeq) AND
MWriteInternal(AtomSeq) AND MInternalRead(AtomSeq) AND
MInternalWrite(AtomSeq).

In our proof, the required sequence is constructed by means of a refinement function R. This function does not affect write operations but, to achieve property MReadInternal(AtomSeq), the atomic read operations between a call/return pair of a read procedure are reduced to one. To select such an atomic read, we first define for a certain event AtomSeq(i) the set of indices of atomic reads between the same call/return pair with identical attributes.

```
ReadIndexSet(AtomSeq,i) : setof[nat] =
{ j | name(AtomSeq(i)) = read AND name(AtomSeq(j)) = read AND
      ident(AtomSeq(j)) = ident(AtomSeq(i)) AND
      argu(AtomSeq(j)) = argu(AtomSeq(i)) AND
      (EXISTS E1, E2 : proced(E1,E2) AND comp(E1) = N AND
                       name(E1) = read AND
                       ident(E1) = ident(AtomSeq(i)) AND
                       E1 < AtomSeq(i) AND AtomSeq(i) < E2 AND
                       E1 < AtomSeq(j) AND AtomSeq(j) < E2 AND
                       argu(E1) = (:loc(AtomSeq(i)):) AND
                       argu(E2) = (:val(AtomSeq(i)):)}
```

Note that by lemma UniqueProced the surrounding procedure proced(E1,E2) is unique. Further observe that this set is empty if AtomSeq(i) is not a read event or the surrounding procedure does not return its value. Now R is defined using the predefined PVS function choose, a choice function for nonempty sets, which yields an arbitrary element of the set. A read operation is copied by R if its index is selected by this choice function. All other atomic read events are transformed into the undefined event UE.

```
R (AtomSeq) : sequence[Atoms] =
    (LAMBDA i : IF (name(AtomSeq(i)) /= read OR
                   (nonempty?(ReadIndexSet(AtomSeq,i)) AND
                        choose(ReadIndexSet(AtomSeq,i)) = i))
              THEN AtomSeq(i)
              ELSE UE
              ENDIF )
```

```
ReadInternalImpl : LEMMA MReadInternalSimp(AtomSeq)
                         IMPLIES MReadInternal(R(AtomSeq))
```

```
MemSimpTh : THEOREM CMem IFF CMemSimp
END memsimp
```

Theorem MemSimpTh has been proved using 14 auxiliary lemmas, and around 300 commands have been used to complete all proofs. (Note that no attempt has been made to minimize the number of commands.)

2.5   Reliable Memory

A simple specification of a reliable memory component, which never raises the
MemFailure exception, can be obtained by adding a predicate Reliable to the
memory specification.

```
relmem [ N : nat ] : THEORY
BEGIN
IMPORTING memory[N]

Reliable : bool = (FORALL E: comp(E) = N AND
    etype(E) = return AND (name(E) = read OR name(E) = write)
      IMPLIES argu(E) /= (:MemFailure:) )

CRelMem : bool = CMem AND Reliable
```

When using the specification of the reliable memory it is often convenient to have
a more explicit specification. Such a specification can be derived easily from the
one above.

```
RelRead : bool = (FORALL E1 :
   etype(E1) = call AND name(E1) = read AND comp(E1) = N
     IMPLIES (EXISTS E2 : proced(E1,E2) AND
                          IF MemLoc(argu(E1))
                          THEN MemVal(argu(E2))
                          ELSE argu(E2) = (:BadArg:)
                          ENDIF ) )

RelWrite : bool = (FORALL E1:
   etype(E1) = call AND name(E1) = write AND comp(E1) = N
     IMPLIES (EXISTS E2 : proced(E1,E2) AND
                          IF MemLocVal(argu(E1))
                          THEN argu(E2) = (:WriteOK:)
                          ELSE argu(E2) = (:BadArg:)
                          ENDIF ) )

CRelExpl : bool = RelRead AND RelWrite AND
                  (EXISTS AtomSeq : ReadCorrect(AtomSeq) AND
                                    MReadInternal(AtomSeq) AND
                                    MWriteInternal(AtomSeq) AND
                                    MInternalRead(AtomSeq) AND
                                    MInternalWrite(AtomSeq) )

RelExplLem : LEMMA CRelMem IFF CRelExpl
END relmem
```

Correctness of Reliable Memory In the theory `relmemcor` we show that a reliable memory component is a correct implementation of a memory component. The main point of the proof is expressed in lemma `RelMemSimp` where we show that the commitment of the reliable memory component implies commitment `CMem` of the memory component. The proof is trivial (and indeed requires one command by the PVS prover), since `CRelMem` equals `CMem AND Reliable`. By `RelMemSimp` and rule `rulecons` of theory `specs` it is easy to prove (two commands in PVS) theorem `RelMemImpl` which expresses that the specification of the reliable memory component implements the specification of the memory component.

```
relmemcor   : THEORY
BEGIN
M : nat
IMPORTING  relmem[M]

RelMemSimp : LEMMA CRelMem IMPLIES CMem

RelMemImpl : LEMMA spec(true,CRelMem) => spec(true,CMem)
END relmemcor
```

2.6   Failing Memory

A failing memory component always returns the `MemFailure` exception, as specified in theory `memfail`.

```
memfail [ N : nat ] : THEORY
BEGIN
IMPORTING memory[N]

FailRead : bool = (FORALL E1 :
   etype(E1) = call AND name(E1) = read AND comp(E1) = N
      IMPLIES (EXISTS E2: proced(E1,E2) AND
                            argu(E2) = (:MemFailure:) ) )

FailWrite : bool = (FORALL E1 :
   etype(E1) = call AND name(E1) = write AND comp(E1) = N
      IMPLIES (EXISTS E2: proced(E1,E2) AND
                            argu(E2) = (:MemFailure:) ) )

CMemFail : bool = FailRead AND FailWrite
END memfail
```

Correctness of Failing Memory Since the specification of the memory component does not restrict the number of times that the `MemFailure` exception can be raised, we can easily prove that a failing component correctly implements a memory component. The main idea is that a failing memory never accesses the inner memory, so we prove CMem using an empty sequence of atomic events. Since sequences are infinite in PVS, this is modeled by the sequence which only contains the undefined event UE.

```
memfailcor  : THEORY
BEGIN
M : nat
IMPORTING memfail[M]

EmptyAtomSeq : sequence[Atoms] = (LAMBDA (j:nat) : UE )

MemFailSimp : THEOREM CMemFail IMPLIES CMem

MemFailImpl : THEOREM spec(true,CMemFail) => spec(true,CMem)
END memfailcor
```

Here the proof of MemFailImpl is again trivially done by two commands. The proof of MemFailSimp requires a lot of case distinctions and has been proved by approximately 50 commands. The main point is to show that CMem allows the possibility of never accessing the inner memory.

3 Implementing the Memory

3.1 The RPC Component

To specify an RPC component we first formulate a theory with a few basic primitives. Two special values are added to model exceptions. Moreover RemoteCall is added as a new procedure name. The argument of this procedure is of type RPCArg, a tuple consisting of a name and an argument. The elements of such a tuple are selected by the functions namearg and argarg.

```
rpcbasic : THEORY
BEGIN
IMPORTING membasic

RPCFailure, BadCall  : Value      % exceptions

RPCValDiff : AXIOM RPCFailure /= BadCall AND
                   WriteOK /= BadCall AND RPCFailure /= WriteOK

RPCSpecVal : AXIOM NOT MemVal?(BadCall) AND
                   NOT MemVal?(RPCFailure)

RemoteCall : Name

RPCArg : TYPE = [ Name, Arg ]
```

```
rpcarg(E)   : RPCArg
namearg(E) : Name = proj_1(rpcarg(E))
argarg(E)   : Arg  = proj_2(rpcarg(E))

END rpcbasic
```

Consider an RPC component with component number RPC, which relays calls to a component with component number N and relays returns from N to the caller. First we specify by RPCReturn that it contains a single procedure RemoteCall and that a call to the RPC always leads to a return. Commitment RPCRelay expresses that a procedure of the RPC either returns RPCFailure without any call to N, or returns BadCall without any call to N if the argument is not correct, or leads to one procedure call to N where either the value returned is forwarded or RPCFailure is raised.

```
rpc [ RPC, N : nat ] : THEORY
BEGIN
IMPORTING rpcbasic

RPCReturn : bool = (FORALL E1 :
  etype(E1) = call AND comp(E1) = RPC
    IMPLIES name(E1) = RemoteCall AND (EXISTS E2 : proced(E1,E2)))

% first three auxiliary definitions used in RPCRelay

CorrectArg(E1) : bool = ProcName?(namearg(E1)) AND
                        ArgNum(namearg(E1)) = length(argarg(E1))

NoCallsBetween(E1,E2) : bool =
 NOT (EXISTS E3 : etype(E3) = call AND comp(E3) = N AND
            ident(E1) = ident(E3) AND name(E3) = namearg(E1) AND
            argu(E3) = argarg(E1) AND E1 < E3 AND E3 < E2)

NoOtherCall(E1,E2,E3) : bool =
 NOT (EXISTS E4 : E4 /= E3 AND etype(E4) = call AND
         comp(E4) = N AND ident(E1) = ident(E4) AND
         name(E4) = namearg(E1) AND argu(E4) = argarg(E1) AND
         E1 < E4 AND E4 < E2)

RPCRelay : bool = (FORALL E1, E2 :
  proced(E1,E2) AND comp(E1) = RPC IMPLIES
    (argu(E2) = (:RPCFailure:) AND NoCallsBetween(E1,E2))
    OR
    IF NOT CorrectArg(E1)
    THEN (argu(E2) = (:BadCall:) AND NoCallsBetween(E1,E2))
    ELSE (EXISTS E3 , E4 : E1 < E3 AND E4 < E2 AND
```

```
                    proced(E3,E4) AND comp(E3) = N AND
                    ident(E1) = ident(E3) AND
                    name(E3) = namearg(E1) AND argu(E3) = argarg(E1) AND
                    NoOtherCall(E1,E2,E3) AND
                    (argu(E2) = argu(E4) OR argu(E2) = (:RPCFailure:)))
                    ENDIF)
```

Note that the informal specification does not explicitly mention that no call is issued in case of a BadCall, but it seems reasonable to require this to avoid spurious calls to component N. This is also the reason for adding RPCBackw which expresses that any procedure of N is causally related to a corresponding procedure of RPC. Finally we formulate commitment CRPC of the RPC component.

```
RPCBackw : bool = (FORALL E3, E4 :
  proced(E3,E4) AND comp(E3) = N
    IMPLIES (EXISTS E1, E2 : E1 < E3 AND E4 < E2 AND
            proced(E1,E2) AND comp(E1) = RPC AND
            ident(E1) = ident(E3) AND
            name(E3) = namearg(E1) AND
            argu(E3) = argarg(E1) AND
            (argu(E2) = argu(E4) OR argu(E2) = (:RPCFailure:)) AND
            CorrectArg(E1) ) )

CRPC : bool = RPCReturn AND RPCRelay AND RPCBackw
END rpc
```

3.2 The Implementation

A memory component with identification M is implemented using a clerk component which forwards read and write calls to the RPC component, say with number RPC. In the normal situation, this RPC component then relays these calls to a reliable memory component RM (see figure 1).

In the theory clerk we first give two axioms relating exceptions from an RPC component to special values of a memory component. Further, by ClerkReturn the clerk guarantees that a call to M always leads to a return.

```
clerk [M, RPC, RM : nat ] : THEORY
BEGIN
IMPORTING memsimp[M], rpc[RPC,RM]

ClerkValDiff: AXIOM BadArg /= RPCFailure AND BadArg /= BadCall AND
                    WriteOK /= RPCFailure AND WriteOK /= BadCall

ClerkSpecialVal : AXIOM NOT MemVal?(RPCFailure) AND
                    NOT MemVal?(BadCall) AND
                    NOT MemLoc?(RPCFailure) AND
                    NOT MemLoc?(BadCall)
```

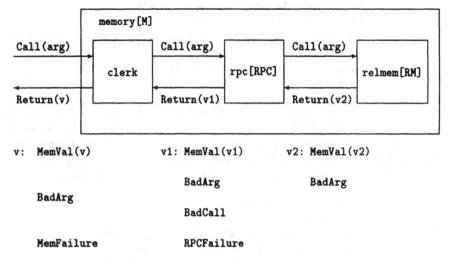

v: MemVal(v)   v1: MemVal(v1)   v2: MemVal(v2)

                         BadArg   BadArg

        BadArg

                         BadCall

    MemFailure   RPCFailure

Fig. 1. Implementation of a memory component

```
ClerkReturn : bool =
    (FORALL E1 : etype(E1) = call AND comp(E1) = M
                  IMPLIES (EXISTS E2 : proced(E1,E2)))
```

Next we define abbreviation `ClerkReturnValue` to describe how values received
from the RPC component are relayed to the caller. Note that, in addition to the
informal description, the clerk transforms the `BadCall` exception into the `BadArg`
exception. Property `ClerkRelay` expresses that a procedure call to M eventually
leads to a procedure call to the RPC component, where the corresponding return
value is described by `ClerkReturnValue`. Finally `ClerkBackw` expresses that a
call/return pair of RPC is surrounded by a corresponding call/return pair of M.

```
ClerkReturnValue(E2,E4) : bool =
   (argu(E4) = (:RPCFailure:) AND argu(E2) = (:MemFailure:)) OR
   (argu(E4) = (:BadCall:) AND argu(E2) = (:BadArg:)) OR
   (argu(E4) /= (:RPCFailure:) AND argu(E4) /= (:BadCall:) AND
       argu(E2) = argu(E4))

ClerkRelay : bool = (FORALL E1, E2 :
   proced(E1,E2) AND comp(E1) = M IMPLIES
     (EXISTS E3, E4 : E1 < E3 AND E4 < E2 AND
              proced(E3,E4) AND comp(E3) = RPC AND
              name(E3) = RemoteCall AND ident(E3) = ident(E1) AND
              name(E1) = namearg(E3) AND argu(E1) = argarg(E3) AND
              ClerkReturnValue(E2,E4) ) )
```

```
ClerkBackw : bool = (FORALL E3, E4 :
   proced(E3,E4) AND comp(E3) = RPC IMPLIES
      (EXISTS E1, E2 : E1 < E3 AND E4 < E2 AND proced(E1,E2) AND
            comp(E1) = M AND ident(E3) = ident(E1) AND
            name(E1) = namearg(E3) AND argu(E1) = argarg(E3) AND
            ClerkReturnValue(E2,E4) ) )

CClerk : bool = ClerkReturn AND ClerkRelay AND ClerkBackw
END clerk
```

Correctness of the Implementation The correctness of the implementation
is proved in theory clerkcor. The aim is to prove theorem MemImpl, expressing that the parallel composition of a clerk, an RPC component, and a reliable
memory component implements the memory module. This can be shown easily,
by rule specpar, if CClerk AND CRPC AND CRelMem IMPLIES memory[M].CMem.
(Different instances of a predicate are distinguished by preceding them with a
theory name and an actual parameter.) Observe that the implementation of the
memory can retry an atomic read to the inner memory of the reliable memory arbitrarily many times because of RPCFailure exceptions. Therefore we use
CMemSimp instead of CMem, which is justified by theorem MemSimpTh (see section 2.4). Further, using lemma RelExplLem of section 2.5, CRelMem is replaced
by CRelExpl. Then for each property of CMemSimp we formulate a lemma, showing on which properties of the implementation it depends. The proof of these
lemmas is rather straightforward (in fact, the main work has been done in section 2.4).

```
clerkcor : THEORY
BEGIN
M, RPC, RM  : nat
IMPORTING clerk[M,RPC,RM], relmem[RM]

RLem : LEMMA ClerkReturn AND ClerkRelay AND RPCRelay AND RelRead
            IMPLIES memory[M].MRead

WLem : LEMMA ClerkReturn AND ClerkRelay AND RPCRelay AND RelWrite
            IMPLIES memory[M].MWrite

ReadInternalLem : LEMMA ClerkRelay AND RPCRelayRead AND
                  memory[RM].MReadInternal(AtomSeq)
                  IMPLIES MReadInternalSimp(AtomSeq)

WriteInternalLem : LEMMA ClerkRelay AND RPCRelayWrite AND
                  memory[RM].MWriteInternal(AtomSeq)
                  IMPLIES memory[M].MWriteInternal(AtomSeq)
```

```
InternalReadLem : LEMMA memory[RM].MInternalRead(AtomSeq) AND
                        RPCBackw AND ClerkBackw AND RelRead
                        IMPLIES memory[M].MInternalRead(AtomSeq)

InternalWriteLem : LEMMA memory[RM].MInternalWrite(AtomSeq) AND
                        RPCBackw AND ClerkBackw AND RelWrite
                        IMPLIES memory[M].MInternalWrite(AtomSeq)

ClerkImpl : LEMMA CClerk AND CRPC AND CRelMem
                        IMPLIES memory[M].CMem

MemImpl : THEOREM (( spec(true,CClerk) //
                     spec(true,CRPC) ) //
                     spec(true,CRelMem) ) =>
                                          spec(true,memory[M].CMem)
END clerkcor
```

Besides the lemmas shown above, 8 auxiliary lemmas have been introduced to split up the proof in small parts. The proofs of all lemmas and the final theorem required approximately 500 commands in the PVS prover.

4 Implementing the RPC Component

Next we consider a lossy RPC component, which is specified informally using timing information. To express these real-time properties, theory procinterface is extended with the type Time which is equal to the built-in type real. Further the timing of events is defined as an attribute.

```
Time : TYPE = real
time : [Event -> Time]
```

4.1 A Lossy RPC

We specify a lossy RPC component, with component number LRPC, which relays procedures to component N. First we specify the values returned in LRPCRetVal and the treatment of an incorrect call. The main differences with theory rpc are that lrpc does not raise the RPCFailure exception, a call need not lead to a return, and there is some timing information. We start with a specification which is close to the informal description.

```
lrpc [ LRPC, N : nat ] : THEORY
BEGIN
IMPORTING rpc[LRPC,N]

delta       : Time
```

```
NoRPCFailure : bool = (FORALL E :
   comp(E) = LRPC AND etype(E) = return
        IMPLIES argu(E) /= (:RPCFailure:))

BadCallreturn : bool = (FORALL E1, E2 :
   proced(E1,E2) AND comp(E1) = LRPC AND argu(E2) = (:BadCall:)
        IMPLIES time(E2) < time(E1) + delta)

CallReturnTiming : bool = (FORALL E1, E2, E3, E4 :
   proced(E1,E2) AND comp(E1) = LRPC AND
   proced(E3,E4) AND comp(E3) = N AND ident(E1) = ident(E3) AND
   name(E3) = namearg(E1) AND argu(E3) = argarg(E1) AND
   E1 < E3 AND E4 < E2
     IMPLIES time(E3) < time(E1) + delta AND
     (argu(E2) /= (:BadCall:) IMPLIES time(E2) < time(E4) + delta))

CLRPC : bool = RPCRelay AND RPCBackw AND NoRPCFailure AND
                BadCallreturn AND CallReturnTiming
```

Next we show that CLRPC implies a simplified relay property LRPCRelay.

```
LRPCRelay : bool = (FORALL E1, E2 :
  proced(E1,E2) AND comp(E1) = LRPC IMPLIES
     IF NOT CorrectArg(E1)
     THEN (argu(E2) = (:BadCall:) AND NoCallsBetween(E1,E2))
     ELSE (EXISTS E3, E4 : E1 < E3 AND E4 < E2 AND
             proced(E3,E4) AND comp(E3) = N AND
             ident(E1) = ident(E3) AND
             name(E3) = namearg(E1) AND argu(E3) = argarg(E1) AND
             NoOtherCall(E1,E2,E3) AND argu(E2) = argu(E4) )
     ENDIF )

LRPCExplLem : LEMMA CLRPC IMPLIES LRPCRelay
END lrpc
```

4.2 The RPC Implementation

An RPC component is implemented by means of a lossy RPC component using an rpcclerk component (see figure 2).

In the specification of rpcclerk, property RPCClerkReturn asserts it contains a single procedure RemoteCall and that a call to RPC always leads to a return. By property RPCClerkRelay we express that this rpcclerk component relays remote procedure calls to the lossy RPC component LRPC and, as expressed by RPCClerkReturn, it relays return values back to the caller, raising an RPCFailure if there is no return before a certain deadline. Since the value of this deadline is not yet determined, it is represented by a timing constant IDel.

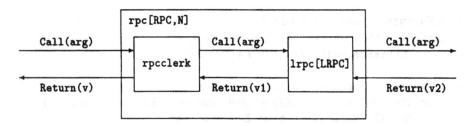

Fig. 2. Implementation of the RPC component

```
rpcclerk [ RPC, LRPC : nat ] : THEORY
BEGIN
IMPORTING rpcbasic

RPCClerkReturn : bool = (FORALL E1 :
   etype(E1) = call AND comp(E1) = RPC
     IMPLIES name(E1) = RemoteCall AND (EXISTS E2 : proced(E1,E2)))

IDel : Time

RPCClerkReturn(E2,E3) : bool =
   (EXISTS E4 : proced(E3,E4) AND time(E4) < time(E3) + IDel AND
                argu(E2) = argu(E4) AND E4 < E2)
   OR
   (NOT (EXISTS E4 : proced(E3,E4) AND
                     time(E4) < time(E3) + IDel) AND
                     argu(E2) = (:RPCFailure:))

NoOtherLRPCCall(E1,E2,E3) : bool =
  NOT (EXISTS E4 : E4 /= E3 AND etype(E4) = call AND
                comp(E4) = LRPC AND E1 < E4 AND E4 < E2 AND
                ident(E3) = ident(E4) AND rpcarg(E3) = rpcarg(E4))

RPCClerkRelay : bool = (FORALL E1, E2 :
  proced(E1,E2) AND comp(E1) = RPC
    IMPLIES (EXISTS E3 : E1 < E3 AND etype(E3) = call AND
                  comp(E3) = LRPC AND ident(E1) = ident(E3) AND
                  rpcarg(E1) = rpcarg(E3) AND
                  RPCClerkReturn(E2,E3) AND
                  NoOtherLRPCCall(E1,E2,E3)))

RPCClerkBackw : bool = (FORALL E3, E4 :
  proced(E3,E4) AND comp(E3) = LRPC
    IMPLIES (EXISTS E1 , E2 : E1 < E3 AND E4 < E2 AND
```

```
               proced(E1,E2) AND comp(E1) = RPC AND
               ident(E1) = ident(E3) AND
               rpcarg(E1) = rpcarg(E3) AND argu(E2) = argu(E4)))

CRPCClerk : bool = RPCClerkReturn AND RPCClerkRelay AND
                   RPCClerkBackw
END rpcclerk
```

Correctness of the RPC Implementation In theory rpcclerkcor we verify that the parallel composition of the rpcclerk component and the lossy RPC component implements the RPC component under certain conditions. One of these conditions is that every call of a procedure of component N returns within epsilon time units, as expressed in CallReturnProp. This is needed for the proof of RPCRelay, where also a condition on IDel is needed. The complete proof of all lemmas and the resulting theorem required approximately 250 user interactions.

```
rpcclerkcor  : THEORY
BEGIN
RPC, LRPC, N  : nat
IMPORTING rpcclerk[RPC,LRPC], lrpc[LRPC,N], rpc[RPC,N]

epsilon : Time

CallReturnProp : bool = (FORALL E1 :
  etype(E1) = call AND comp(E1) = N
    IMPLIES
     (EXISTS E2 : proced(E1,E2) AND time(E2) < time(E1) + epsilon))

ImplRPCReturn : LEMMA RPCClerkReturn IMPLIES rpc[RPC,N].RPCReturn

ImplRPCBackw : LEMMA RPCClerkBackw AND rpc[LRPC,N].RPCBackw
                     IMPLIES rpc[RPC,N].RPCBackw

ImplRPCRelay : LEMMA RPCClerkRelay AND LRPCRelay AND
                     rpc[LRPC,N].RPCBackw AND
                     RPCClerkBackw AND CallReturnTiming AND
                     CallReturnProp AND RPCClerkReturn AND
                     IDel >= 2 * delta + epsilon
                     IMPLIES rpc[RPC,N].RPCRelay

ImplRPCImpl : LEMMA IDel >= 2 * delta + epsilon AND CallReturnProp
                    AND CRPCClerk AND CLRPC
                    IMPLIES rpc[RPC,N].CRPC
```

```
RPCImpl : THEOREM IDel >= 2 * delta + epsilon AND CallReturnProp
              IMPLIES
              ( spec(true,CRPCClerk) // spec(true,CLRPC) )
              =>
              spec(true,rpc[RPC,N].CRPC)
END rpcclerkcor
```

5 Concluding Remarks

Using the tool PVS, all components of the RPC-Memory Specification Problem have been specified and the implementations of the memory component and the RPC component have been verified mechanically. An important aspect of such a formalization is that it reveals ambiguities in the informal specification. For instance, in the current example the treatment of exceptions is not always clear:

- For the memory component it is not clear whether a MemFailure can be returned if the argument is not correct. We decided to allow this, motivated by the implementation of section 3.2.
- In the clerk component we extended the informal description by transforming any BadCall exception from the RPC component into a BadArg return to the caller.

Further, as usual when writing an assertional specification, one also has to state explicitly that spurious events are not allowed. For instance:

- We have assumed that for any internal atomic action there is a causally related procedure which does not raise the BadArg exception.
- In the rpc component we have added the property that no call is issued in case of a BadCall. Similarly, we require that any procedure of N is causally related to a corresponding procedure of RPC.

Also implicit in the informal specification are the properties if the inner memory (e.g., the meaning of atomicity).

In the RPC-Memory example only a small part of our real-time framework has been used. In [Hoo94a] we show how PVS can be used during the design of real-time systems by an example of the top-down derivation of a distributed real-time control system (a chemical batch processing system). Another example of the formalization of an informal specification can be found in [Hoo95] where part of an ACCESS.bus protocol, connecting a host computer with a dynamically changing number of devices, has been specified and verified.

Acknowledgments

We are grateful to Job Zwiers for the suggestion to use event attributes, thus simplifying our initial solution. The reviewers are thanked for valuable comments which have led to several improvements. Finally, many thanks goes to the participants of the Dagstuhl seminar on the RPC-Memory Specification Problem for many interesting discussions which have significantly contributed to the current version of our solution.

References

[Hoo91]   J. Hooman. *Specification and Compositional Verification of Real-Time Systems.* LNCS 558, Springer-Verlag, 1991.

[Hoo94a]   J. Hooman. Correctness of real time systems by construction. In *Formal Techniques in Real-Time and Fault-Tolerant Systems*, pages 19–40. LNCS 863, 1994.

[Hoo94b]   J. Hooman. Extending Hoare logic to real-time. *Formal Aspects of Computing*, 6(6A):801–825, 1994.

[Hoo95]   J. Hooman. Verifying part of the ACCESS.bus protocol using PVS. In *Proceedings 15th Conference on the Foundations of Software Technology and Theoretical Computer Science*, pages 96–110. LNCS 1026, Springer-Verlag, 1995.

[JPZ94]   W. Janssen, M. Poel, and J. Zwiers. The compositional approach to sequential consistency and lazy caching. Memoranda informatica 94-37, University of Twente, 1994.

[Lam94]   L. Lamport. Verification and specification of concurrent programs. In *A Decade of Concurrency*, pages 347–374. LNCS 803, 1994.

[ORS92]   S. Owre, J. Rushby, and N. Shankar. PVS: A prototype verification system. In *11th Conference on Automated Deduction*, volume 607 of *Lecture Notes in Artificial Intelligence*, pages 748–752. Springer-Verlag, 1992.

[ORSvH95] S. Owre, J. Rushby, N. Shankar, and F. von Henke. Formal verification for fault-tolerant architectures: Prolegomena to the design of PVS. *IEEE Transactions on Software Engineering*, 21(2):107–125, 1995.

Specification and Verification Using a Visual Formalism on Top of Temporal Logic

Hardi Hungar

Kuratorium OFFIS
Oldenburg, Germany
hungar@informatik.uni-oldenburg.de

Abstract. The problem is treated with a method whose main concern is the formal verification of key properties of a design. Availability of largely automatic verification procedures is, for this purpose, considered the most important point, less emphasis is put on completeness of the specification. Another distinguishing characteristic of this solution is the rôle of the remote procedure call protocol. Any implementation of the protocol must include some mechanism to ensure responsiveness. To obtain specifications of components which can be implemented independently, something must be known about the protocol mechanism. So, appropriate assumptions are made explicitly, here. These of course enter the specification and verification process.

Technically, the specification is done in an assumption/commitment variant of CTL. The verification methodology for this logic combines model checking, compositional reasoning and abstraction techniques. It indeed relies to a large extent on automatic procedures and is supported in a prototype tool, which has been used to verify partially an implementation.

1 Specifics of this Solution

1.1 Methodology

This article sketches how to treat the problem with a methodology developed at the University of Oldenburg in different variants [Hun93, Jos93, DDH+96]. The main motivation of this methodology is to provide a way to verify a design, resp. to find bugs as early as possible, with as much support by automatic tools as possible. If a rigid verification is in some case not feasible, one restricts the attention to the verification or validation of key properties only, i.e. properties which are considered to be critical or particularly important. So it is a merely pragmatic view of verification which is adopted here. The process of specification itself is not the main concern.

Model checking, that is deciding the validity of a propositional temporal-logic specification for the computations of a finite automaton, is at the core of the verification method. There are two main problems encountered when trying to apply model-checking techniques to problems occurring in practice: the complexity of the system to be verified and difficulties in formalizing requirements in (propositional) temporal logic. The methodology includes ways to cope with both problems.

Two techniques are used to reduce the sizes of automata models: *decomposition* and *abstraction*. Decomposition is a step which distributes a specification over the parallel components of a system, which can thereafter be verified separately. I.e. a global specification of the system behavior is replaced by a set of specifications of the components which together imply the system specification. Abstraction replaces a system description by a simpler description where this can safely be done. I.e. it is guaranteed that if the simpler system satisfies the specification, then also the original system does so.

On the specification side, temporal-logic formulas can be given in a graphical format, called *symbolic timing diagrams*, by which a concise representation of otherwise lengthy formulas is achieved.

This methodology has been instantiated for several scenarios. The one used here was developed within the KORSO project[1], described in [BH95]. The implementation language borrows its main features from OCCAM [INM88]. Programs are parallel compositions of sequential components which communicate synchronously via directed channels. Abstractions for this language work by reducing the data domain, or by neglecting some variables, or by simplifying the channel protocol where this can safely be done. The logic is an assumption-commitment extension of computation tree logic [CE81]. Assumptions are added to CTL to provide additional expressiveness needed for decomposition steps. The logic is closely related to Josko's logic MCTL, only that assumptions are interpreted as branching-time formulas, similar as in cf. [GL94]. The prototype tool TRAVERDI includes a model checker and an interactive prover component and supports decomposition and abstraction reasoning. Also, an LTL tautology checker (by Gert Janssen, Eindhoven) is available in the system. TRAVERDI does not support symbolic timing diagrams. They had to be imported manually from the conceptually similar, but much further developed toolbox coming from the ESPRIT-project FORMAT.

1.2 Problem Coverage

A specification of the memory component is given and the distribution step, which implements the memory component, is verified. As the logic does not include real-time constructs (time enters qualitatively, not quantitatively), the lossy RPC component which works with timeouts is not treated here. But additionally, program implementations of the distributed components are given and verified w.r.t. their specifications.

A few changes have been made to the original problem formulation. As observed by most other contributors, the mechanism of RPC calls and replies was described too vaguely. To allow the specifier to match calls and replies properly, the obvious thing to do was to add an identification tag to the messages. But in opinion of the author, the problem with the RPC mechanism goes beyond that.

---

[1] Funded by the BMFT.

How can, in real life, a call/reply mechanism be implemented? As any device has only finite memory, it must be ensured that not too many incoming calls are sent to it.

There are several ways to solve this problem in an implementation. How that is done cannot be ignored completely, as it will affect the component interaction in any distributed implementation. The solution assumed here is essentially the following: Sender and receiver synchronize on calls and replies, with the additional requirement that calls will eventually be accepted if the sender does not block replies. I.e. the receiver has the choice to reject calls if it cannot process them, e.g. if it runs out of memory. On the technical side, this is mapped to an OCCAM-like language with one channel for each different RPC call and one each for replies. Other protocol implementations would lead to different component requirements and accordingly to different proof obligations and component programs.

To simplify the specifications technically, all aspects concerning the exception BadArg have been neglected. They pose no conceptual difficulty. Since raising of this exception is determined by the arguments to remote procedure calls, and calls leading to BadArg do not change future behavior of the receiving side, it would be easy but boring to add cases to the specifications accordingly. This contribution does not intend to simulate a real-life situation, nor does it try to convey the impression that the prototype tools are close to be applicable in practice (which they are not). And the methodology is better presented with the scenario simplified.

There is one aspect of the approach pursued here which influenced drastically the form of the specification. It is the decision to specify the behavior of the RPC memory in terms of its interface, not in terms of the internal memory variables. To compare with the problem description: "The memory behaves *as if* it maintains an array of automatically read and written location [...]". I.e. the behavior is specified (operationally) as that of a virtual machine which has an appropriate set of memory cells. Such "virtual cells" are not available in CTL. They would — in the terminology of [MP91] — be representable in temporal logic as existentially quantified "flexible variables". Satisfaction of an appropriately extended CTL remains decidable in finite structures, see [KV95]. But there was no model checker available for such constructs. So, proceeding accordingly was out of question. Besides, there is a drawback coming with a "virtual-cell" specification: All properties must refer to the same choice of virtual cells, resulting in one big formula of the form

$$\exists \, cell_1, \ldots, cell_n. \, \phi_1 \wedge \ldots \wedge \phi_m \, .$$

Of course, it would not be sound to verify the formulas $\exists \, cell_1, \ldots, cell_n. \, \phi_i$ separately. This contrast with our approach where each single conjunct in a specification may be verified on its own. Two alternatives remained. Either

- making the internal structure of the memory visible and specifying in terms of values of memory cells, i.e. dropping the "as if" in the problem description, or

– specifying just the behavior at the RPC interface, i.e. sequences of calls and replies, without referring to memory cells at all.

The first alternative would have been the easy way. All requirements could have been translated directly into the language of temporal logic. But the resulting specification would have had the undesirable property of being implementation dependent.[2]

The second alternative is conceptually cleaner, and it is the one which was chosen. The remote procedure call protocol was easy to specify. It was not necessary to explicate any details. Just general requirements such as "Every call is answered at most once," and "The calling side will accept replies to unanswered calls" were sufficient to describe a distributed solution. These requirements are still very abstract, leaving room for many different implementations. Nevertheless, the term 'distributed' may be interpreted in a strict sense. It is said which component has to guarantee what part of the property. Each component specification is implementable, and they can indeed be implemented independently, and nevertheless the combined system will show the correct behavior.

What proved to be more difficult was to specify the *functional behavior*. In fact, the given formalization does not completely capture the informal problem description. It is, however, in the spirit of the methodology to trade completeness for efficient verification support. In case of the memory component, the incompleteness does not seem to leave room for implementation errors anyhow.

The practical experiments have been conducted mostly with the tool TRAVERDI. They covered essential parts of the verification of an implementation, including the distribution step which implements a memory component by three parallel units, and the separate implementations of the three units.

2 The Implementation Language

2.1 Processes and Programs

Programs are parallel compositions of a finite number of sequential *processes*. Processes interact via synchronous channels which establish directed connections between two processes. We use an interleaving semantics with built-in fairness constraints.

The syntax of processes and programs is given in Figure 1. We assume a set of channels and a set of variables, each having an associated type, $type(ch)$ resp. $type(x)$. Typed function and relation symbols are used to form *terms* and *boolean expressions*.

---

[2] As an intermediate way, one could have chosen to classify the occurring memory cells as "probes". Probes [DDH+96] are observables introduced only for the purpose of verification. To prove an implementation correct, the proof engineer would have to annotate the implementation with statements setting those probes. In effect, the engineer would have to provide manually a simulation relation.

```
<prc> ::= x:= t | ch ? x | ch ! t | stop | skip |
          <prc> ; <prc> |
          alt b & ch ? x→ <prc>, ... , b → <prc>, ... tla |
          while b do <prc> od

<prg>::=   <prc> | hide_ch(<prg>) | <prg> || ... || <prg>
```

Fig. 1. Syntax of Programs

A set of well-formedness conditions, which we do not list here, is used to guarantee that each channel is a directed connection either between two processes or between one process and the environment. I.e. we forbid broadcast and multiple synchronization. Our channels are unidirectional. In the semantics, every variable is considered to be local, such that there is no interaction via shared variables.

2.2 The Semantics of Programs

The intuitive meaning of all the constructs should be clear. Perhaps the only thing which needs some explanation are the clauses in an **alt**-statement. A branch b & $ch?x→$ <prc> may be chosen if b is true for the current (internal) state of the process and the environment offers an output on ch. The first step of its execution is the communication, then the control passes to the process behind the arrow. A branch $b →$ <prc> (where the input statement is missing) may be chosen simply if b is true for the current (internal) state of the process. The first execution step of that branch is that of the process behind the arrow. If no branch of an **alt** is open, the program waits for one to become open.

Important for the computational power of the programming language is its built-in fairness. If the control reaches some **alt**-statement infinitely often and one branch could always be taken at that point, then this branch will indeed infinitely often be executed. This kind of fairness requirement is operationally motivated. It is stronger than what is usually called "weak fairness" and it is in fact more useful, but it is still easily implemented. It is sufficient to cyclically switch the alternative which is tested first. I.e. try the first alternative the first time the **alt**-statement is reached, the second alternative the next time, and so on.

The formal definition of the semantics translates each process to a Kripke structure with fairness.

Definition 1 Kripke Structure. A *generalized Kripke structure* is a sextuple $(S, R, A, L, I, \mathcal{F})$ where S is a set of *states*, $R \subseteq S \times S$ is the *transition relation*, A is a set of *atoms*, $L : S \to \mathcal{P}(A)$ is the *labeling function*, $I \subseteq S$ is the set of *initial states*, and $\mathcal{F} \subseteq \mathcal{P}(S) \times \mathcal{P}(S)$ is a set of *fairness requirements*.

The *paths* of a generalized Kripke structure are those words w over S satisfying

- $\forall i.\,(w_i, w_{i+1}) \in R$,
- $\forall (G, H) \in \mathcal{F}.\,|\{\,i \mid w_i \in G\,\}| = \infty \to |\{\,i \mid w_i \in H\,\}| = \infty$.

A formal definition of the semantical mapping would be rather lengthy. To provide a concise description, the translation process is sketched and exemplified.

The state set of the resulting Kripke structure is essentially the set of control points of the process times the set of variable and channel valuations. The valuation of a channel ch is an element of $\mathcal{P}(\{\mathbf{rts}, \mathbf{rtr}\}) \cup \{\,\mathbf{rtx}(v) \mid v \in D_{type(ch)}\,\}$, where $D_{type(ch)}$ is the set of values of type $type(ch)$. $\mathbf{rtx}(v)$ means that v is communicated over the channel. $\mathbf{rts}$ says that the sender wants to transmit a value (*ready to send*), and $\mathbf{rtr}$ expresses that the receiver would accept a value (*ready to receive*). Both $\mathbf{rts}$ and $\mathbf{rtr}$ have to be true before a communication can happen. The atom set of the Kripke structure contains elements to describe the channel valuation appropriately, i.e. $\mathbf{rts}_{ch}, \mathbf{rtr}_{ch}, \mathbf{rtx}_{ch}$ and atoms for the value v.

In a first step, the process is mapped to a flowgraph with first-order annotations. Each variable of the process is also a variable in the flowgraph, and for a channel ch, a variable of the same name and type is introduced, plus a boolean variable $\mathbf{rts}_{ch}$ for an input channel, resp., $\mathbf{rtr}_{ch}$ for an output channel. These represent the environment component in a channel valuation. The atom values for the process side of the channel valuation can be extracted from the flowgraph node and the variable valuations.

An example is given in in Fig. 2. The example program is a simplified version of a memory cell which is only able to process write calls.

The annotations of the edges may consist of a boolean condition and a set of assignment statements. A question mark on the right hand side of an assignment means a random assignment. The flowgraph drawn in Fig. 2 is not complete. Each node except those labeled by some $\mathbf{rtx}$ should have a cycling edge. And each edge annotation (including the cycling edges) is to be extended with random assignments to the boolean channel variables ($\mathbf{rtr}_{\mathbf{reply}}$ and $\mathbf{rts}_{\mathbf{call}}$). With those additions, the flowgraph correctly represents the program.

The Kripke structure defining the semantics of the program is generated from its flowgraph representation. States of the Kripke structure are pairs of nodes of the flowgraph and variable valuations (remember that channels now count as variables). A transition connects two states if the nodes are connected by an edge and the first-order annotation of the edge is in accordance with their variable valuations. E.g. the copy of the node in the right lower corner with valuation ($x=0$, $y=1$, $\mathbf{rtr}_{\mathbf{reply}}$=false, $\mathbf{rts}_{\mathbf{call}}$=true) is related to four copies of the node above it. One of them has the valuation ($x=1$, $y=1$, $\mathbf{rtr}_{\mathbf{reply}}$=false, $\mathbf{rts}_{\mathbf{call}}$=false). The labels of the states are derived canonically, only that $\mathbf{rtx}_{ch}$ excludes $\mathbf{rts}_{ch}$ and $\mathbf{rtr}_{ch}$ from the label set (the same effect could be achieved by eliminating such states during the construction).

The fairness sets are defined to ensure progress (if continually possible) along the edges in the figure, and fairness of choice between them. Formally, for an

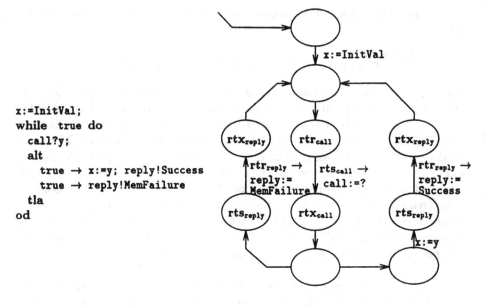

```
x:=InitVal;
while true do
  call?y;
  alt
    true → x:=y; reply!Success
    true → reply!MemFailure
  tla
od
```

Fig. 2. Example program and its flowgraph

edge $n \to n'$ with $n \neq n'$ which is annotated by $b \to \alpha$, the pair $(\{\,(n,\nu) \mid \nu \models b\,\}, \{\,(n'',\nu') \mid n'' = n' \vee (n'' = n \wedge \nu' \not\models b)\,\})$ is a fairness pair. In the example, the fairness properties e.g. ensure that all state sets $\{\,(n,\nu) \mid \nu \models \text{true}\,\}$, except those where n is predecessor of an **rtx**-node, must be left, and that both edges leaving the lowest node in the middle column will be taken infinitely often if this node is entered infinitely often. It is *not* guaranteed that infinitely many communications do occur, nor that input values are fairly chosen (indeed, input is not restricted), nor that the boolean channel variables do change their value.

To define the semantics of programs consisting of more than one process, a simple parallel composition operator for generalized Kripke structures is used. Roughly speaking, this operator is a synchronous product where compatible labeling of parallel states is required.

Definition 2. Let $K_1, \ldots, K_n$ be generalized Kripke structures. Then their parallel composition, $synpar(K_1, \ldots, K_n)$ is the following structure.

$$S =_{df} \{\,(s_1, \ldots, s_n) \mid \forall i,j.\, L_i(s_i) \cap A_j = L_j(s_j) \cap A_i\,\}$$

$$(s_1, \ldots, s_n)R(s'_1, \ldots, s'_n) \Leftrightarrow_{df} \forall i.\, s_i R_i s'_i$$

$$A =_{df} \bigcup_{i=1}^{n} A_i$$

$$L(s_1, \ldots, s_n) =_{df} \bigcup_{i=1}^{n} L_i(s_i)$$

$$I =_{df} \left(\prod_{i=1}^{n} I_i \right) \cap S$$

$$F =_{df} \{ (S_1 \times \ldots \times G_i \times \ldots \times S_n \cap S,$$
$$S_1 \times \ldots \times H_i \times \ldots \times S_n \cap S)$$
$$\mid (G_i, H_i) \in F_i, \ i = 1, \ldots, n \}$$

To get an interleaving of communications (as it is assumed in the verification tools), states where more than one channel is active (rtx) are eliminated. The interleaving assumption is used implicitly when formulating the specifications. In some cases, it allows us to use shorter diagrams or formulas.

This parallel composition operator is accompanied by means for renaming and hiding of atoms. These are simple, standard operators and need not be described in more detail here.

3 The Specification Language

3.1 The Logic

The basic formalism is ACTL, the universal fragment of computation tree logic [CES83], that is, CTL without negation and existential path quantifiers. Negated versions of atomic observations are assumed to be available, which allows us to use negations of non-temporal formulas as abbreviations. ACTL is extended to an assumption-commitment logic as it is done in [GL94]. The resulting logic is called AC-ACTL. Its formulas have the form $A \rightsquigarrow C$, where A is called the *assumption* and C is the *commitment*. Intuitively, the formula means that the module in question guarantees C, whenever it is run in a context (with other parallel components), so that A is true of the combined system. A branching-time logic like ACTL needs an additional operator to express this concept, whereas in a linear-time logic, implication could be used for that purpose.

Note that there are assumption-commitment logics with a different flavor, where e.g. the assumption is viewed as a property of the environment only, or where the module is forced to guarantee the commitment as long as the environment does not violate the assumption. With AC-ACTL, the interpretation is a purely logical one, resembling intuitionistic implication. One may use assumptions which cannot be ensured by the environment on its own, or which are already guaranteed by the module in question. In the extreme, if the module falsifies an assumption A regardless of the environment, for any C, the specification $A \rightsquigarrow C$ will be valid.

There are complexity arguments which favor AC-ACTL over a linear-time logic [KV95]. Compared to CTL, we profit from the additional assumption operator when specifying components of a distributed system. Also, reasoning about parallel compositions is simplified, because the existential path quantifier has been dropped. The reader may note that *synpar* essentially intersects the computation trees of the components. Therefore, any formula valid for some component is valid for the complete system. Thus, the transition from component properties, which may have been established by model checking, to system properties is trivial. And to draw conclusions from some set of assumption-commitment formulas on system level, one can use the axioms for implication from intuitionistic propositional logic. E.g. $A \rightsquigarrow B$ and $B \rightsquigarrow C$ imply $A \rightsquigarrow C$.

Here, the logic AC-ACTL must be instantiated for the specification of synchronously communicating processes. The necessary atoms correspond to the observables (atoms) of the Kripke structures: $\mathbf{rtx}_{ch}(v)$ (communication), $\mathbf{rts}_{ch}$ (ready to send), and $\mathbf{rtr}_{ch}$ (ready to receive). To refer to data values like v in $\mathbf{rtx}_{ch}(v)$, a first-order term language is used, and first-order quantifiers stand for (possibly infinite) disjunctions and conjunctions.

3.2 Symbolic Timing Diagrams

To arrive at more concise specifications than possible in first-order temporal logic, a shorthand visual representation of ACTL formulas may be used. The formalism STD of *symbolic timing diagrams* offers graphical constructs to express qualitative temporal relations. Each diagram can be translated to an ACTL formula. Two diagrams may be used to represent an assumption-commitment formula: One for the assumption and one for the commitment. Or we can take a set of diagrams for a conjunction of formulas in the assumption. The main advantage of diagrams over formulas shows when some behavior involving a number of basic steps has to be described where some partial order on the steps is to be obeyed. A formula would have to enumerate all possible linearizations of the events, while this is done implicitly in a diagram. The diagram in Fig. 6 is an example. The point in time when the final reply to a write call with parameter *val* (the last one in the line named **reply** write) occurs is not fixed with respect to the events on the read channels. So, there are a number of linearizations hidden in the diagram. The savings effect was even more prominent in previous versions of that diagram. These were more complicated, and have been simplified step-by-step until we arrived at this comparatively simple diagram.

A full formal definition of the semantics of STD is beyond the scope of this paper. The reader may refer to [DJS95], where a linear-time interpretation of timing diagrams is given. Replacing the linear-time operators by their branching-time correspondents (yielding a stronger formula) gives the semantics assumed in this paper. Below, a very short informal introduction to STD is given, followed by a more detailed example.

A diagram has a *mode* (*dynamic* or *initial*) and it may have *parameters* which latter are implicitly universally quantified variables. The mode *initial* means that the diagram holds in the initial state, otherwise it expresses a property which should hold whenever its activation condition (to be explained below) is met. I.e. an initial diagram will denote a formula $\forall x. (activation \wedge \phi)$, whereas a dynamic diagram will denote a formula of the form $\forall x. (\mathbf{AG}(activation \rightarrow \phi))$.

A diagram consists of a set of finite sequences of first-order formulas. Conjoining the first elements of those sequences yields the activation condition. Each sequence now restricts the future behavior in that the system must not violate the order prescribed by the formulas. E.g. a sequence $\phi\ \psi\ \rho$ translates to the temporal restriction

$$A[\phi \text{ unless } (\psi \wedge A[\psi \text{ unless } \rho])].$$

Further ordering restrictions between elements from different sequences may be introduced by precedence arcs ($\longrightarrow$) or simultaneity arcs ($=$). To require progress (resulting in **until** instead of **unless**), arcs of the form ($\cdots\!\!\succ$) may be used. Finally, if instead of the formulas in the sequences, additionally given exit conditions ($[\psi]$) are met, the timing diagrams counts as satisfied. In these cases, the denoting formula contains appropriate ∨-parts.

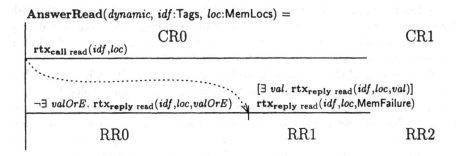

AnswerRead(*dynamic, idf*:Tags, *loc*:MemLocs) =

Fig. 3. Example diagram

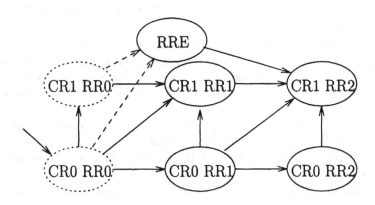

Fig. 4. The restrictions expressed by the example diagram in automata notation.

As an example, consider the diagram from Figure 3. It has two sequences, one (of length one) referring to the channel on which the memory component receives read calls, and one (of length two) for its replies to read calls. The entry point of the timing diagram is connected by a progress arc to the second element of the second sequence, and that element is accompanied by an exit condition. The first-order variable *val* is assumed to be of type MemVals, whereas *valOrE* has type MemVals+MemFailure.

We will use this diagram to exemplify the translation from timing diagrams to temporal logic. The formal definition of this process would be too long to be included here. The intuitive meaning of the diagram is that each read call must be answered either by MemFailure or by some value. If additionally it is assumed that the calling side will eventually accept replies to each issued read call, this is a behavior the memory component should show. This diagram is, however, not part of the specification in Section 4. It is included just to illustrate the semantics of STD. It is in fact a bit artificial. There is no necessity to distinguish between ordinary and exceptional return of the read call, here. That would only be necessary if some additional restrictions were imposed on the behavior in the non-exit case, which is not done in this small diagram.

The elements of the sequences have been given names CR0, CR1 resp., RR0, RR1, RR2 where CR1 and RR2 denote additional endpoints labeled by 'true'. The first step in the translation replaces the diagram by the graph (automaton) in Fig. 4. Its node set is the cross product of the sequences, arrows are a subset of the next-step relation (one may pass a diagram only step by step from left to right). Each node in the graph is labeled by the conjunction of the first-order formulas corresponding to the sequence element names in the figure (where RRE should denote the exit). Intuitively, the graph restricts computations in the following way[3]:

- Each node drawn with a dotted line must be left.
- One may pass from node to node along any solid line.
- One may follow a dashed arrow, but only if one can neither stay in the current node nor follow a solid line.

It is the eventuality arc which causes that the nodes whose labels include RR0 are drawn with a dotted line. Arrows leading to some exit are dashed. Precedence arcs (not present in the example) would result in the removal of solid arrows, simultaneity arcs remove those nodes where only one of two simultaneous sequent elements occurs.

In the mode *dynamic*, every computation must comply to these restrictions at each point which matches the initial node of the graph. In the mode *initial*, from the start of every computation onwards the graph would have to be matched (i.e. only once).

This informal description is captured by a straightforward translation to ACTL. Each node n is associated with a formula ϕ_n, e.g.

$$\phi_{\text{CR0 RR0}} = \text{CR0 RR0} \land \text{A}[\text{CR0 RR0 } \textbf{until } (\phi_{\text{CR0 RR1}} \lor \phi_{\text{CR1 RR1}} \lor \phi_{\text{CR1 RR0}} \lor$$
$$(\lnot\text{RR0} \land \lnot\text{RR1} \land \phi_{\text{RRE}}))] \tag{1}$$

---

[3] This intuitive description could be formalized in terms of automata homomorphisms. Here, of course, the satisfaction relation of temporal logic is employed.

Note that the recursive definition of the ϕ_n is well-founded because the graph is cycle-free (not only in this example). Taking into account the mode *dynamic* and the parameters of the diagram, we get the overall formula (2).

$$\mathbf{AG}[\mathrm{CR0\ RR0} \to \phi_{\mathrm{CR0\ RR0}}] \tag{2}$$

In fact, (2) is equivalent to the comparatively simple (3).

$$\forall idf, loc.\ \mathbf{AG}[\mathbf{rtx_{call\ read}}(idf, loc) \wedge \neg \exists valOrE.\ \mathbf{rtx_{reply\ read}}(idf, loc, valOrE) \to$$
$$\mathbf{AF}\ \exists valOrE.\ \mathbf{rtx_{reply\ read}}(idf, loc, valOrE)] \tag{3}$$

4 Specification of the Memory Component

Most of the specification is given in the form of symbolic timing diagrams, whereas in most places formulas could have been used as well. When interpreting the diagrams (or the formulas), the reader should bear in mind the underlying interleaving semantics. Some of the property formalizations make implicitly use of it. For a non-interleaving semantics, in some places case distinctions would have had to be added.

4.1 The Protocol of Calls and Replies

As already mentioned, the remote procedure call mechanism is realized here with synchronous channels. For each remote procedure p, two channels are introduced: **call_p** and **reply_p**. Over those channels, tuples consisting of a tag value and the parameters of the call resp., reply, may be sent. E.g. the type of **call_write** is Tag×MemLocs×MemVals. The reply repeats the parameters of the call together with its result[4]. The result of a reply to Write may be Success or MemFailure. The result of a read is either *val* ∈ MemVals or MemFailure.

Fig. 5 contains the diagrams necessary to specify how the RPC protocol works on those channels. Below each diagram, it is written which side is responsible for the diagram's validity, under which assumptions. The assumption-commitment pairs of the protocol requirements for the memory component are collected in Table 2. Only the diagrams for the remote procedure Write are listed in Fig. 5. This is indicated by the string 'write' which has been added as a form of parameter to the names of the diagrams and by enclosing references to 'write' in the diagrams in curly braces. The diagrams for Read, which are not given here, are similar. Besides replacing {write} by {read}, parameter lists in annotations have to be adapted in some cases.

The diagrams are written in an abbreviated notation. Each sequence refers to one channel only. Tuples refer to values transmitted on the channel, where arbitrary values are replaced by dots. E.g. in the diagram

---

[4] It would have been sufficient to require repetition of the tag. The temporal logic specification gets simpler if also the other parameters are repeated.

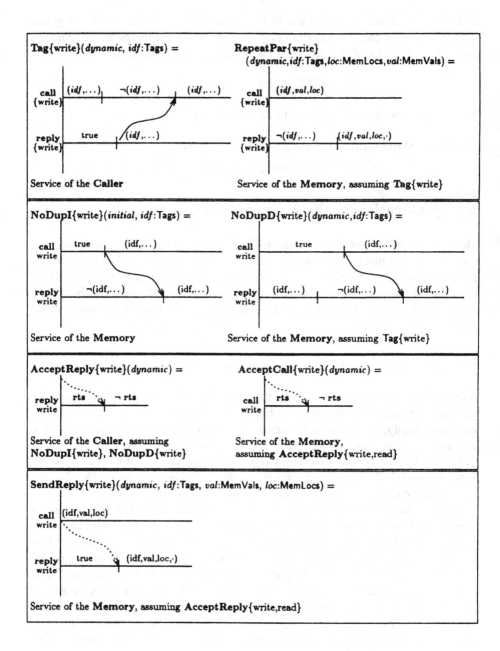

Fig. 5. Symbolic Timing Diagrams for specification of the protocol

Tag{write}, the annotation $(idf, \ldots)$ in the line for channel **call**$_{\{write\}}$ abbreviates the condition $\exists loc, val.\, \mathbf{rtx_{call\,\{write\}}}(idf, loc, val)$. And $\neg(idf, \ldots)$ stands for $\neg\exists loc, val.\, \mathbf{rtx_{call\,\{write\}}}(idf, loc, val)$.

All those diagrams have short formula equivalents given in Table 1. Informally, **Tag**{write} says that the reply to a write must precede the next write using the same tag, or in other words: overlapping write calls must use different tags. **RepeatPar**{write} assures that each reply repeats the parameters of the call. The **NoDup**-diagrams state that the Memory sends at most one reply to each call. The **Accept**-diagrams express that each message the partner wants to send is finally accepted. To understand this, it is important to remember that the signal **rts** goes down during the transmission of a message. So if the diagrams are satisfied and the message-sending component keeps **rts** up continuously until the message is transmitted (by trying to execute a command $ch!x$), this transmission is guaranteed to happen.

Tag{write}	$\forall idf : \text{Tags. } \mathbf{AG}[\mathbf{rtx_{call\,\{write\}}}(idf, \ldots) \rightarrow$ $\mathbf{A}[\mathbf{rtx_{call\,\{write\}}}(idf, \ldots) \text{ unless } (\neg\mathbf{rtx_{call\,\{write\}}}(idf, \ldots)\wedge$ $\mathbf{A}[\neg\mathbf{rtx_{call\,\{write\}}}(idf, \ldots) \text{ unless } \mathbf{rtx_{reply\,\{write\}}}(idf, \ldots)])]]$
RepeatPar{write}	$\forall idf : \text{Tags}, val : \text{MemVals}, loc : \text{MemLocs}.$ $\mathbf{AG}[\mathbf{rtx_{call\,\{write\}}}(idf, val, loc) \rightarrow$ $\mathbf{A}[\neg\mathbf{rtx_{reply\,\{write\}}}(idf, \ldots) \text{ unless }$ $\mathbf{rtx_{reply\,\{write\}}}(idf, val, loc, \cdot)]$
NoDupI{write}	$\forall idf : \text{Tags. } \neg\mathbf{rtx_{reply\,\{write\}}}(idf, \ldots) \wedge$ $\mathbf{A}[\neg\mathbf{rtx_{reply\,\{write\}}}(idf, \ldots) \text{ unless } \mathbf{rtx_{call\,\{write\}}}(idf, \ldots)]$
NoDupD{write}	$\forall idf : \text{Tags. } \mathbf{AG}[\mathbf{rtx_{reply\,\{write\}}}(idf, \ldots) \rightarrow$ $\mathbf{A}[\mathbf{rtx_{reply\,\{write\}}}(idf, \ldots) \text{ unless } (\neg\mathbf{rtx_{reply\,\{write\}}}(idf, \ldots)\wedge$ $\mathbf{A}[\neg\mathbf{rtx_{reply\,\{write\}}}(idf, \ldots) \text{ unless } \mathbf{rtx_{call\,\{write\}}}(idf, \ldots)])]]$
AcceptReply{write}	$\mathbf{AF}\ \neg\mathbf{rts_{reply\ write}}$
AcceptCall{write}	$\mathbf{AF}\ \neg\mathbf{rts_{call\ write}}$
SendReply{write}	$\forall idf : \text{Tags.}$ $\mathbf{AG}[\mathbf{rtx_{call\,\{write\}}}(idf, \ldots) \rightarrow \mathbf{AF}\ \mathbf{rtx_{reply\,\{write\}}}(idf, \ldots)]$

Table 1. Formulas for specification of the protocol.

4.2 Specification of the Functional Behavior

The diagrams in Figures 6 and 7 serve to specify the main behavior of the memory. To denote the diagrams, further abbreviations are used in the annotations.

AC_{MEM}**RepeatPar**{write}   **Tag**{write} $\rightsquigarrow$ **RepeatPar**{write}
AC_{MEM}**NoDupI**{write}   **NoDupI**{write}
AC_{MEM}**NoDupD**{write}   **Tag**{write} $\rightsquigarrow$ **NoDupD**{write}
AC_{MEM}**AcceptCall**{write}   **AcceptReply**{write} $\rightsquigarrow$ **AcceptCall**{write}
AC_{MEM}**SendReply**{write}   **AcceptReply**{write} $\rightsquigarrow$ **SendReply**{write}

Table 2. Assumption-commitment specification of the protocol for the memory component

WriteD($dynamic,val$:MemVals, loc:MemLocs, idf,idf':Tags) =

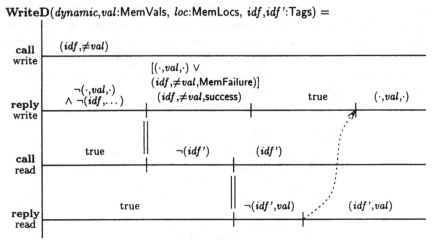

Assumptions: **Tag**{write,read} and **AcceptReply**{write,read}.

Fig. 6. Functional behavior of the memory component

First, the diagram parameter loc should be added as location parameter to all tuples in the diagrams. And the notation $\neq val$ means transmission of an arbitrary value different from val. For instance, "$(idf,\neq val,$Success)" in the **reply**$_{write}$-line of **WriteD** abbreviates the formula $\exists v \neq val.$ **rtx**$_{reply\ write}(idf, v, loc,$ Success).

The diagram **WriteD** expresses that each successful write changes the contents of a location, and that a write with result MemFailure may change it. **ReadI** and **ReadD** together assert that a write call is needed to change a location. A more detailed explanation of **WriteD** and **ReadD** will follow below. In contrast to the protocol diagrams, the formula representations of these diagrams, in particular that of **WriteD**, are rather long.

The specification of the functional behavior requires **WriteD** and **ReadD** under the assumptions **Tag**{write,read} and **AcceptReply**{write,read}, and **ReadI** without assumptions. This covers essential parts of the respective requirements in the RPC-memory specification problem.

The restriction of specifying the behavior only in terms of the (observable) interface is responsible for some of the complications in the specification. For **WriteD**, this implies e.g. that only those successful writes which are followed by a read action can enter the specification (This resembles a bit the problem

ReadD(*dynamic*, *val*:MemVals, *loc*:MemLocs, *idf*:Tags) =

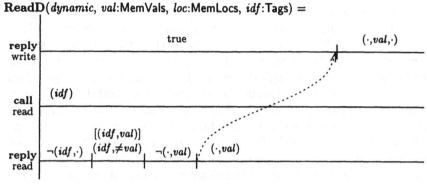

Assumptions: **Tag**{write,read} and **AcceptReply**{write,read}.

ReadI(*initial*,*loc*:MemLocs) =

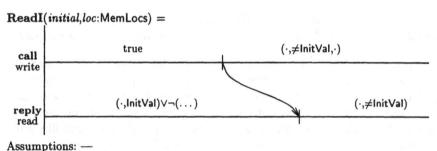

Assumptions: —

Fig. 7. Functional behavior of the memory component [ctd.]

with Schrödinger's cat). As well as this restriction, also the inability to refer to the past in a timing diagram makes things more difficult. One can think of a timing diagram of mode *dynamic* as being a sliding window, which starts observing the system at a state meeting its activating condition. So one has to build up all of the required past in the diagram, i.e. one has to start the observation early enough.

In **WriteD**, one such "window" containing a critical observation sequence is constructed. If there is some successful write (which destroys *val*), and a subsequent read does return *val*, then there must have been some call requesting *val* to be written. This restoring call Write(...,*val*) itself need not be visible in the diagram, it could have been initiated before activation of the diagram (i.e. before the call Write(*idf*,(loc),≠*val*)). But its reply must occur, either before the answer to Write(*idf*,(loc),≠*val*) (covered by the exit condition), or later (required by the progress arc at the end). This is expressed in the diagram by requiring the system to reach a state (after the read reply with value *val*) where it will issue the write reply. Since the system is not allowed to invent replies (as formulated in the protocol specification), there must be an open write call with value *val*.

Note the different rôles of the outcomes of a write call in this diagram: A successful write will have an impact on future reads unless the result is overwritten due to some other write. The overwriting call need not be successful, though.

The diagram **ReadD** is easier to explain. If two reads yield different values, the second value must have been written by a write which has not been answered before initiation of the first read. So that answer must be visible in the window covered by the diagram (although the call might be outside of its scope). This diagram captures part of the following defect noted at the workshop in some of the solutions. If a write call is unsuccessful, it either sets the internal variable or it does not affect it. It will not be possible for the environment to once read the new value and afterwards the old. That is not excluded by **WriteD**. It is still not completely excluded, even after adding **ReadD**, but now contradicting interface behavior gets harder to construct. The following – unwanted – sequence is not ruled out:

v_0 in memory — call Read — call Write(v_1) — reply Write(MemFailure) — call Write(v_2) — reply Write(MemFailure) — reply Read(v_2) — v_1 in memory

It is the presence of read calls overlapping unsuccessful writes which is now necessary to produce erratic observations. To capture the requirements completely withs diagrams specifying the interface behavior seems to be at least very difficult, if not impossible. However, it could be argued that it would not even be worth the effort. The errors which are not covered now do not seem likely to be introduced into any implementation, or they could be considered to be not harmful. Anyway, a high degree of confidence in an implementation's correctness would already be achieved by verifying the given specification.

4.3 Reliability

A reliable memory component is an implementation of the specification above. It could be specified by adding the requirement that no reply raises MemFailure – a simple formula.

Also a module which always raises MemFailure is a valid implementation of the memory specification. There is no direct way of ruling out this behavior in AC-ACTL, because AC-ACTL only specifies what is guaranteed, and does not mention positively what is possible. There is not much what can be done bearing in mind that the problem formulation does not exclude MemFailure implementations, either.

To add just the requirement that MemFailure is not the guaranteed answer, one could adopt the following, indirect way. First, one specifies a memory component which always raises MemFailure (if the arguments are in range). Here is the formula in informal notation.

$$\mathbf{AG}[\mathbf{rtx}_{\text{reply write}}(\ldots) \rightarrow \mathbf{rtx}_{\text{reply write}}(\ldots, \text{MemFailure})]$$

A module which does *not* satisfy that formula is one which may sometimes answer with Success. Note that this is an indirect way of formulating the requirement, because no temporal operator may be in the scope of a negation in

AC-ACTL. And only parts of the methodology may be applied in establishing such negative results. Most importantly, a decomposition step cannot be performed.

A sensible, positive requirement could be that every infinite sequence of operations will include successful ones.

$$\mathbf{AG\ AF}[\mathbf{rtx_{reply\ write}}(\dots)] \leadsto \mathbf{AG\ AF}[\mathbf{rtx_{reply\ write}}(\dots, \mathsf{Success})]$$

While certainly manageable, such qualitative statements are obviously of limited use. Quantitative performance requirements like "At least for fifty percent of the calls, the memory component will not raise an exception," however, are outside of the scope of the methodology. They cannot be specified adequately in temporal logic, and indeed it seems very difficult to include things like that in a formal method.

5 Implementing the Memory

The structure of the implementation is given in Fig. 8. As described in the RPC-

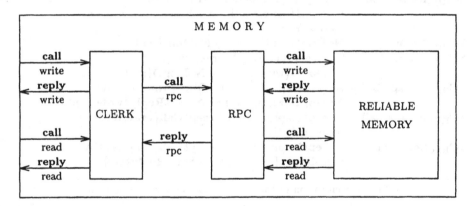

Fig. 8. The structure of the implementation

memory specification problem, CLERK translates incoming write calls to calls of RemoteCall with procedure Write (similar for Read), and reverses the translation for the replies. RPC does essentially the oppposite. The main difference between the components is that RPC issues a call at most once, and may raise the exception RPCFailure unconditionally, while CLERK may reissue a call if the answer was RPCFailure. Correspondingly, their specifications will be very similar. In this paper, only the specification of RPC will be presented.

5.1 Specification and Verification of the Protocol

The remote procedure call protocol differs a bit from that to be satisfied by the memory component. The reason is that RPC must act like a channel. According to [BL], if it issues a translated call of RemoteCall, it must wait for the reply to the issued translation before it is allowed to reply to the RemoteCall. So it cannot guarantee replies: If the component breaks to which the call is issued, RPC too will not reply. Thus, replies are only guaranteed under the assumption that issued calls are replied. This is different from the specification of the remote procedure call protocol of the memory component, which does not issue calls itself and is thus not dependent on replies.

The properties expressed in the diagrams in Fig. 5, however, are sufficient for the specification, here, and can be reused. We only have to rearrange the assumption-commitment pairs. The result is shown in Table 3. A point which is not represented adequately in the notation is the fact that the name of the remote procedure is viewed as part of the tag in RPC. I.e. **Tag**$\{rpc\}$ is meant to denote a formula restricting only tags of overlapping calls to each single procedure.

AC_{RPC}**Tag**	**Tag**$\{$rpc$\} \leadsto$ **Tag**$\{$write, read$\}$
AC_{RPC}**RepeatPar**	**Tag**$\{$rpc$\} \wedge$ **RepeatPar**$\{$write, read$\}\wedge$ **NoDupI**$\{$write, read$\} \wedge$ **NoDupD**$\{$write, read$\} \leadsto$ **RepeatPar**$\{rpc\}$
AC_{RPC}**NoDupI**	**NoDupI**$\{$write, read$\} \leadsto$ **NoDupI**$\{$rpc$\}$
AC_{RPC}**NoDupD**	**Tag**$\{$rpc$\} \wedge$ **NoDupI**$\{$write, read$\}\wedge$ **NoDupD**$\{$write, read$\} \leadsto$ **NoDupD**$\{$rpc$\}$
AC_{RPC}**AcceptReply**	**AcceptReply**$\{$rpc$\} \wedge$ **NoDupI**$\{$write, read$\}\wedge$ **NoDupD**$\{$write, read$\} \leadsto$ **AcceptReply**$\{$write, read$\}$
AC_{RPC}**AcceptCall**	**AcceptReply**$\{$rpc$\} \wedge$ **AcceptCall**$\{$write, read$\} \leadsto$ **AcceptCall**$\{$rpc$\}$
AC_{RPC}**SendReply**	**AcceptReply**$\{$rpc$\} \wedge$ **AcceptCall**$\{$write, read$\}\wedge$ **SendReply**$\{$write, read$\} \leadsto$ **SendReply**$\{rpc\}$

Table 3. Specification of the protocol for the RPC component

Using the protocol properties of the (reliable) memory component, we can derive for the parallel composition of RPC and RELIABLE MEMORY the formulas from Table 4. These formulas constitute the same protocol as the one for the memory component, only reformulated for the different interface.

$AC_{RPC\|RMEM}$**RepeatPar**	**Tag**$\{rpc\} \leadsto$ **RepeatPar**$\{rpc\}$
$AC_{RPC\|RMEM}$**NoDupI**	**NoDupI**$\{$rpc$\}$
$AC_{RPC\|RMEM}$**NoDupD**	**Tag**$\{rpc\} \leadsto$ **NoDupD**$\{rpc\}$
$AC_{RPC\|RMEM}$**AcceptCall**	**AcceptReply**$\{rpc\} \leadsto$ **AcceptCall**$\{rpc\}$
$AC_{RPC\|RMEM}$**SendReply**	**AcceptReply**$\{rpc\} \leadsto$ **SendReply**$\{rpc\}$

Table 4. Protocol of RPC ∥ RELIABLE MEMORY

Only the embedding principle (everything valid for a component is valid for the parallel composition) and simple assumption-commitment reasoning is needed in the derivation. I.e. $\rightsquigarrow$ is treated like propositional implication. For instance, we use $\text{AC}_{\text{MEM}}\text{NoDupI}\{\text{write,read}\}$, $\text{AC}_{\text{MEM}}\text{NoDupD}\{\text{write,read}\}$ and $\text{AC}_{\text{RPC}}\text{Tag}$ to eliminate assumptions in $\text{AC}_{\text{RPC}}\text{NoDupD}$ and derive $\text{AC}_{\text{RPC}\|\text{RMEM}}\text{NoDupD}$.

5.2 Specification and Verification of the Functional Behavior

RPC and CLERK are essentially channels, and since messages carry identification tags here, a specification of their functionality can easily be formulated in temporal logic (resp., symbolic timing diagrams). Fig. 9 and Fig. 10 contain the diagrams for RPC, and Table 5 lists the assumption-commitment pairs. Assumptions are just some protocol properties of the environment of RPC, i.e. commitments of the protocol specification of CLERK and MEMORY. It would be correct to require the complete set of these properties in each case. But since assumptions increase the complexity of the model-checking procedure considerably, it helps to suppress unnecessary assumptions.

$\text{AC}_{\text{RPC}}\text{ActOnRPC}\{\text{read}\}$	$\text{AcceptCall}\{\text{read}\} \wedge \text{AcceptReply}\{\text{rpc}\} \rightsquigarrow$ $\text{ActOnRPC}\{\text{read}\}$
$\text{AC}_{\text{RPC}}\text{AwaitReply}\{\text{read}\}$	$\text{NoDupI}\{\text{read}\} \wedge \text{NoDupD}\{\text{read}\}$ $\text{Tag}\{\text{rpc}\} \rightsquigarrow \text{AwaitReply}\{\text{read}\}$
$\text{AC}_{\text{RPC}}\text{NotForward}\{\text{read}\}$	$\text{NoDupI}\{\text{read}\} \wedge \text{NoDupD}\{\text{read}\} \wedge$ $\text{Tag}\{\text{rpc}\} \rightsquigarrow \text{NotForward}\{\text{read}\}$
$\text{AC}_{\text{RPC}}\text{ForwardReply}\{\text{read}\}$	$\text{NoDupI}\{\text{read}\} \wedge \text{NoDupD}\{\text{read}\}$ $\text{Tag}\{\text{rpc}\} \rightsquigarrow \text{ForwardReply}\{\text{read}\}$
$\text{AC}_{\text{RPC}}\text{NoDupForwardI}\{\text{read}\}$	$\text{NoDupForwardI}\{\text{read}\}$
$\text{AC}_{\text{RPC}}\text{NoDupForwardD}\{\text{read}\}$	$\text{Tag}\{\text{rpc}\} \rightsquigarrow \text{NoDupForwardD}\{\text{read}\}$

Table 5. Specification of the functional behavior of RPC

For an explanation of the requirements, let us recall the fundamental properties of a channel.

1. It does not *invent* messages.
2. It does not *duplicate* messages.
3. It does not *lose* messages.
4. It does not *change* messages.
5. It does not *block* message transmission.

These properties are already covered partly by the protocol specification (namely 5, but also the others), and part of them have to be relaxed (1,3,4) because RPC is not really a channel. The additions to the protocol specification concern mainly 4 (by tying the contents of the messages to the identification tags), and the permitted deviations from channel behavior.

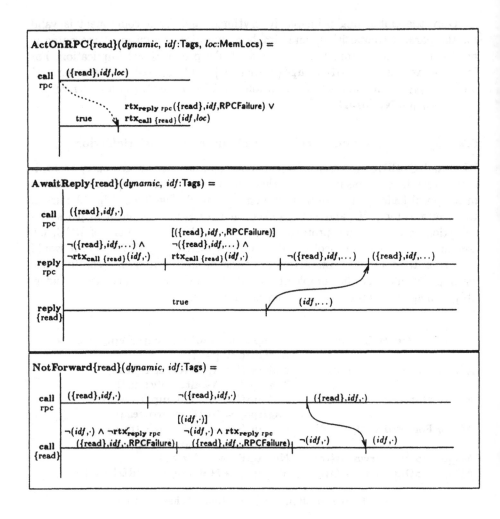

Fig. 9. Diagrams for the functional specification of the RPC component

ActOnRPC expresses that RPC cannot ignore RPC calls. It must either call the procedure (*forward* the call) or answer with RPCFailure. If it forwards the call, it must wait for the reply before the remote call is answered. This is stated in **AwaitReply**.[5] On the other hand, if it answers with RPCFailure, it must not forward the call afterwards (**NotForward**). Any reply is forwarded as received, with the exception that RPCFailure may be raised unconditionally. That is expressed by **ForwardReply**. The remaining two requirements forbid

---

[5] This behavior is required in the problem description. Actually, for the other two components it would make no difference if the RPC component was allowed to reply with RPCFailure before the reply arrived, and ignore the subsequent reply.

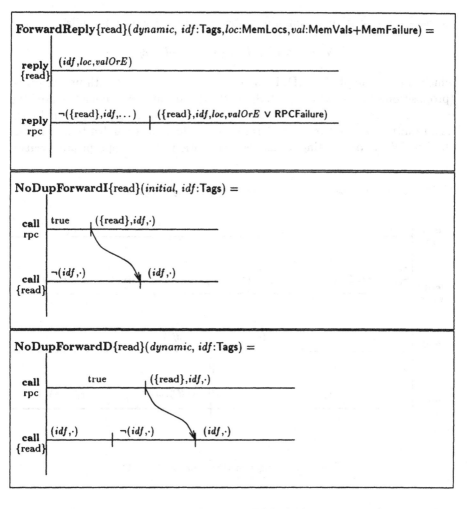

Fig. 10. Diagrams for the functional specification of the RPC component [ctd.]

that RPC issues calls which it has not been asked to forward. (A component might do so without violating any of the other requirements, if it ignores replies to those invented calls). Their formulation is simplified by assuming that RPC reuses the identification tags from the RPC calls it gets.

To verify the functional behavior, we have to combine the specifications of the three components (RELIABLE MEMORY, RPC and CLERK) and derive **WriteD, ReadD** and **ReadI** for their composition. This step is more difficult than the protocol verification.

We first apply the embedding principle and eliminate assumptions, and then first-order temporal implication on the commitment side must allow us to conclude the memory function. First-order (quantifier) reasoning reduces the task to check a propositional temporal implication. I.e. to show a formula

$$\forall val, loc, idf, idf'.\phi(val, loc, idf, idf')$$

which is the form of **WriteD**, it suffices to show $\phi(v, l, i, i')$ with uninterpreted (propositional) constants v, l, i, i'. Similarly, the formulas which may be used (i.e. established commitments) are instantiated (weakened) to a propositional form. The resulting propositional temporal-logic implication is handed to a tautology checker. With the existing tools, the verification of the appropriate **WriteD**

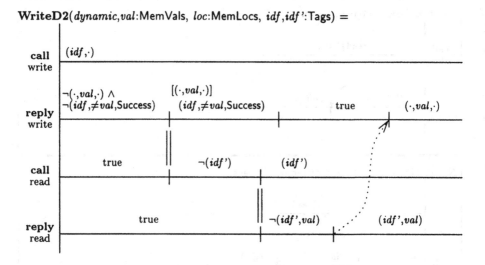

WriteD2(*dynamic,val*:MemVals, *loc*:MemLocs, *idf,idf'*:Tags) =

Fig. 11. Strengthened version of **WriteD**

variant first for RPC ∥ RELIABLE MEMORY, and then for the full memory implementation with CLERK, has been done. The complexity of deciding the full implication (even after propositional reduction) proved to be prohibitive. The implication was then reduced, some lemmas were introduced, propositions were reencoded manually. Finally, the implication for RPC ∥ RELIABLE MEMORY had the form

$$\text{write cycle} \land \text{read cycle} \land \textbf{WriteD}\{\text{MEM}\} \rightarrow \textbf{WriteD}\{\text{RPC}\}.$$

The formulas "write cycle" and "read cycle" were derived from the combined protocol properties of both modules. The implication was recognized as a tautology after three minutes CPU time on a SPARC 10. A previous, weaker version of **WriteD** required a more detailed description of the write and read cycles, and the tautology checker had needed more than one hour. The step to include CLERK is similar, only that a more complex write cycle must be described. To proceed slightly differently proved to be advantageous. Fig. 11 shows a stronger version of **WriteD**, which is better suited for the verification. **WriteD2** differs from **WriteD** in that it already includes part of the write protocol, it is a consequence of **WriteD** and the **NoDup**, **Tag** and **RepeatPar** properties. Using **WriteD2**, the write-cycle description can be made very short, resulting in less than one minute checking time for the implication justifying the composition with CLERK.

Since no tautology checker for ACTL was available, all those experiments have been performed with an LTL checker. The complexity of deciding ACTL implications could be expected to be of the same degree of complexity, cf. [KV95]. The reductions did not make use of specific linear-time features.

Deriving **WriteD** was certainly the most challenging task in the correctness proof. The steps concerning **ReadI** and **ReadD** can be expected to be much simpler. W.r.t. the practical applicability of the method it must be said that a manually reduced formula equivalent of **WriteD**, resp. **WriteD2** has been used throughout the process. The experiment has not been repeated with the mechanically produced formula translations. Certainly, the verification times would have been higher. With the former version of **WriteD** (which had needed more than one hour), this would perhaps have caused a prohibitive blow-up. With **WriteD** in its present form, or with **WriteD2**, we would expect the verification to go through. Nevertheless, it is not clear whether user intervention (encoding, lemmas) would not be necessary.

So it seems that with present-day tools, the verification of the implementation step in this methodology cannot be expected to be completely automatic. But already the existing tools provide very valuable proof support. In many cases, a verification engineer will be able to construct a proof, which is completely checked by a computer, spending a reasonable amount of time.

6 Verifying an Implementation

After the implementation step in the previous section, each of the three components can be implemented and verified separately. If a component is chosen to be implemented again by a parallel system, further distribution steps like the previous one may be performed. For sequential systems, model checking has to be applied, and using that technique is also an option for distributed systems.

In most cases, complexity will forbid to use model checking right away. The state space of the systems will be too large, even for the so-called *symbolic* techniques relying on BDDs [BCM+90]. With the help of *abstraction techniques* one avoids to build an unnecessarily detailed system representation. There are two main abstraction techniques which can be applied within our methodology. One is *data-independence* reasoning in the spirit of [Wol86], the other relies on *homomorphic* abstractions as in [CGL94].

Indeed, we will need to apply abstraction to verify the implementations of the three components which are provided in Tables 6, 7 and 8. These program texts are high-level representations of the OCCAM-like programs which are input to TRAVERDI. We have used a **let** construct to handle the case distinction necessary to cope with union types. The type set of the progamming language supported by TRAVERDI is much simpler, and complex types have to be coded.

The given programs do not just constitute an arbitrary implementation. The general philosophy underlying the programming was to provide an implementation with considerable nondeterminism. It was our intention to try the verification for an unrestricted and therefore hard case. As in the specifications in the previous sections, the exception BadArgs does not occur. This is assumed here to be handled by typing.

The RELIABLE MEMORY program can handle two write calls and two read calls simultaneously. It has two "slots" for each remote procedure. RPC does not store calls or replies, it directly forwards them, resp. raises the exception RPCFailure. Raising RPCFailure is controlled by the boolean variable working, which is flipped nondeterministically. CLERK, too, does not store calls or replies. But it uses a bookkeeping mechanism to decide what to do when RPCFailure has been raised. Then it is allowed to repeat the remote call, but not infinitely often. To ensure an eventual reply, the internal fairness mechanism of the alt-statement has been used. This is the reason for the case distinction on the tag value when RPCFailure is raised. We could also have used a mechanism relying on slots for open calls, where each slot stores a tag value.

The main abstraction technique we will use is a variant of data independence. Data independence was introduced in [Wol86] to cope with communication systems. Very often, the behavior of a communication system does not depend on the content of the messages: They are neither inspected nor changed, just forwarded. Here, this would apply to the RPC component, which need not inspect the arguments of write and read calls (except for checking their type, in the presence of BadArgs). CLERK is not interested in locations and values, and even the memory component does not care for the values it stores. They are *independent* of the value of certain "fields" of the transmitted values: If the inputs on those fields were renamed, the outputs would change accordingly. One such field is the component type MemVals+MemFailure in a read reply of RPC, and there is a corresponding component in replies to remote procedure calls with procedure Read. Renaming the inputs in the first field leads to consistently renamed outputs in the second (while raising RPCFailure is not affected by the renaming operation). This semantical invariance under renaming allows us to drastically reduce the data domain before starting the model checker.

For the formal definition of a message "field", we view the type of each input and output channel as constructed by + (disjoint union) and × (cross product) from basic types β. So, a type corresponds to a labeled tree with basic types at the leaves and + or × at inner nodes. A *field* of a type can be fixed by an assignment of one of $\{\bot, \iota, \top\}$ to each leaf. The intuition is that the assignment specifies a conditional projection from the type to a component type. $\bot$ says that the smallest surrounding alternative is not in the domain of the projection, $\top$ says that the value of this component does not matter for the result. ι specifies values which should be preserved by the projection, unless this is overruled by some $\bot$. This interpretation is formalized in the following rewrite rules. The first

```
Mem[...]:=InitVal; writeSlot[1,2]:=free; readSlot[1,2]:=free;
while true do
  alt
    writeSlot[1]=free & callWrite?(tagW[1],locW[1],valW[1]) →
      writeSlot[1]:=unprocessed,
    ¬(writeSlot[1]=free)→ Mem[locW[1]]:=valW[1]; writeSlot[1]:=processed,
    writeSlot[1]=processed→
      replyWrite!(tagW[1],locW[1],valW[1],Success); writeSlot[1]:=free,
    writeSlot[2]=free & callWrite?(tagW[2],locW[2],valW[2]) →
      writeSlot[2]:=unprocessed,
    ¬(writeSlot[2]=free)→ Mem[locW[2]]:=valW[2]; writeSlot[2]:=processed,
    writeSlot[2]=processed→
      replyWrite!(tagW[2],locW[2],valW[2],Success); writeSlot[2]:=free,
    readSlot[1]=free & callRead?(tagR[1],locR[1])) →
      readSlot[1]:=unprocessed,
    ¬(readSlot[1]=free)→ valR[1]:=Mem[locR[1]]; readSlot[1]:=processed,
    readSlot1=processed→
      replyRead!(tagR[1],locR[1],valR[1]); readSlot[1]:=free,
    readSlot[2]=free & callRead?(tagR[2],locR[2]) →
      readSlot[2]:=unprocessed,
    ¬(readSlot[2]=free)→ valR[2]:=Mem[locR[2]]; readSlot[2]:=processed,
    readSlot[2]=processed→
      replyRead!(tagR[2],locR[2],valR[2]); readSlot[2]:=free,
  tla
od
```

Table 6. RELIABLE MEMORY

row tells what to do with annotated basic types, the others say how $\top$ and $\bot$ affect compound types. τ denotes an arbitrary type or annotation.

$$(\beta, \iota) \to \beta \qquad\qquad (\beta, \bot) \to \bot \qquad\qquad (\beta, \top) \to \top$$
$$\top \times \tau \to \tau \qquad\qquad \tau \times \top \to \tau \qquad\qquad \top + \top \to \top$$
$$\bot + \tau \to \tau \qquad\qquad \tau + \bot \to \tau \qquad\qquad \bot \times \tau \to \bot \qquad\qquad \tau \times \bot \to \bot$$

Not every assignment is meaningful. For instance, there is no computation rule for $\top + \beta$. Annotations leading to that situation during evaluation are not permitted.

As an example, consider the following assignments to channels of RPC. The types of the channels of RPC are given in Table 9.

$$\alpha(\mathbf{reply}_{\mathrm{rpc}}) = (\top \times (\top \times \top \times (\iota + (\iota + \bot)))) +$$
$$(\bot \times (\bot \times \bot \times \bot \times (\bot + \bot + \bot)))$$
$$\alpha(\mathbf{reply}_{\mathrm{read}}) = \top \times \top \times (\iota + \iota)$$

```
working:= true;
while  true do
  alt
    callRPC?(proc,args) →
      let
        (proc,args) = (Read,(tag,loc)) →
          alt
            working → callRead!(tag,loc),
            ¬ working → replyRPC!(Read,(tag,loc,RPCFailure))
          tla
        (proc,args) = (Write,(tag,loc,val)) →
          alt
            working → callWrite!(tag,loc,val),
            ¬ working → replyRPC!(Write,(tag,loc,val,RPCFailure))
          tla
      tel
    replyRead?(tag,loc,valOrE) →
        alt
          working → replyRPC!(Read,(tag,loc,valOrE)),
          ¬ working → replyRPC!(Read,(tag,loc,RPCFailure))
        tla
    replyWrite?(tag,loc,val,res) →
        alt
          working → replyRPC!(Write,(tag,loc,val,res)),
          ¬ working → replyRPC!(Write,(tag,loc,val,RPCFailure))
        tla
    true → working:=¬working
  tla
od
```

Table 7. RPC

They specify the functions which extract the information provided by the memory in a read reply, which is then forwarded (or changed to RPCFailure) by RPC. The resulting type is MemVals+MemFailure in both cases.

A *set of fields* is specified by fixing a subset of the channels and providing one assignment for each channel of the subset, s.t. there is one type τ to which all the assignments evaluate. The set of fields in the example above has the interesting property that no other message fields are influenced by the values in that set, nor will by changing those values the behavior of RPC be affected in any other form (e.g. RPC's willingness to communicate): RPC is *syntactically data independent* on this set of fields.

More precisely, syntactic data independence means that a (syntactic) data-

```
while  true do
  alt
    callWrite?(tag,loc,val) →
      callRPC!(Write,(tag,loc,val)),
    callRead?(tag,loc) →
      callRPC!(Read,(tag,loc)),
    replyRPC?(proc,args) →
      let
        (proc,args)=(Read,(0,loc,RPCFailure)) →
          alt
            true → replyRead(0,loc,MemFailure),
            true → callRPC(Read,(0,loc)),
          tla
          . . .
        (proc,args)=(Read,(2,loc,RPCFailure)) →
          alt
            true → replyRead(2,loc,MemFailure),
            true → callRPC(Read,(2,loc)),
          tla
        (proc,args)=(Read,(tag,loc,valOrE)) →
          replyRead(tag,loc,valOrE)
        (proc,args)=(Write,(0,loc,val,RPCFailure)) →
          alt
            true → replyWrite(0,loc,val,MemFailure),
            true → callRPC(Write,(0,loc,val)),
          tla
          . . .
        (proc,args)=(Write,(tag,loc,val,Success)) →
          replyWrite(tag,loc,val,Success)
      tel
  tla
od
```

Table 8. CLERK (with three Tags)

$Exceptions = \text{MemFailure} + \text{RPCFailure}$
$type(\textbf{call}_{rpc}) = (\text{Read} \times (\text{Tags} \times \text{MemLocs})) +$
$\qquad\qquad (\text{Write} \times (\text{Tags} \times \text{MemLocs} \times \text{MemVals}))$
$type(\textbf{reply}_{rpc}) = (\text{Read} \times (\text{Tags} \times \text{MemLocs} \times (\text{MemVals} + \text{Exceptions}))) +$
$\qquad\qquad (\text{Write} \times (\text{Tags} \times \text{MemLocs} \times \text{MemVals} \times (\text{Success} + \text{Exceptions})))$
$type(\textbf{call}_{write}) = \text{Tags} \times \text{MemLocs} \times \text{MemVals}$
$type(\textbf{reply}_{write}) = \text{Tags} \times \text{MemLocs} \times \text{MemVals} \times (\text{Success} + \text{MemFailure})$
$type(\textbf{call}_{read}) = \text{Tags} \times \text{MemLocs}$
$type(\textbf{reply}_{read}) = \text{Tags} \times \text{MemLocs} \times (\text{MemVals} + \text{MemFailure})$

Table 9. Channel types of RPC

flow analysis establishes the following, for a given set of fields.[6]

- Input values of fields do not affect conditions,
- output values of fields are values of previous inputs of fields, and
- the values of non-field outputs are not affected by input values of fields.

Syntactic data independence has semantical consequences.

- The program never outputs a field value which it has not previously received, and
- the program semantics is invariant under renaming and identification of field values.

The second property above can be formalized as follows. Let D be the data domain of of the field, and let $f : D \to D$ be a total function. f can then also be viewed as a function on the observables of the program, by applying it to elements of the field set in communication predicates $rtx_{ch}(\ldots, d, \ldots)$. And finally, $\hat{f}$ is this function lifted to the program semantics domain (consisting of sets of fair computation trees). I.e. $\hat{f}$ is the pointwise application of f. Then, we require

$$[\pi] \cap ran(\hat{f}) \subseteq \hat{f}([\pi]), \text{ and}$$
$$[\pi] \cap dom(\hat{f}) \subseteq \hat{f}^{-1}([\pi]) .$$

In the above, $[\pi]$ denotes the semantics of the program π. The set comparison "$\subseteq$", which could be taken literally for a linear-time (trace) semantics as in [Wol86], must be interpreted adequately for the branching-time semantics we use (homomorphical mapping to a subtree). The technical details are a bit cumbersome and not relevant for this case study.

The semantical invariance properties of data-independent programs can be used profitably for the verification of temporal specifications of a specific form. Let $\phi(x_1, \ldots, x_n)$ be a formula with free variables $x_1, \ldots, x_n$ s.t.

- a term referring to a field-set value in ϕ is either some x_i or an existentially quantified variable as in $\exists y_1, \ldots, y_i, \ldots, y_m . rtx_{ch}(\ldots, y_i, \ldots)$,
- the only other occurrences of the x_i are tests for equality among them.

Then Wolper's result states that an LTL formula $\forall x_1, \ldots, x_n . \phi(x_1, \ldots, x_n)$ holds if and only if it holds if the domain of the type of the field set is restricted to $n+1$ elements. This result carries over to AC-ACTL because AC-ACTL is restricted to use only universal path quantifiers.

---

[6] This definition ignores the possibility of outputs being initial values of variables. Initializations can be integrated into the picture by regarding them as field inputs and treating them accordingly, in the data-flow analysis as well as in the consequences.

Consider the property **ForwardReply**{read} as an example. Its formula representation has the form

$\forall valOrE$: MemVals + MemFailure, idf : Tags, loc : MemLocs.

$\textbf{AG}[\textbf{rtx}_{\textbf{reply} \{\text{read}\}}(idf, loc, valOrE) \land \neg \exists y, z. \textbf{rtx}_{\textbf{reply rpc}}(\{\text{read}\}, idf, z, y) \rightarrow$

$\quad \textbf{A}[\neg \exists y, z. \textbf{rtx}_{\textbf{reply} \{\text{rpc}\}}(\{\text{read}\}, idf, z, y) \textbf{ unless}$

$\qquad \textbf{rtx}_{\textbf{reply} \{\text{rpc}\}}(\{\text{read}\}, idf, loc, valOrE) \lor$

$\qquad \textbf{rtx}_{\textbf{reply} \{\text{rpc}\}}(\{\text{read}\}, idf, loc, \text{RPCFailure})]\,.$

This formula meets the criteria for the field set specified above, with only one universally quantified variable. So we can replace the domain for Mem-Vals+MemFailure both in the program RPC and the formula by a two-elemented one and still decide the correctness of the original program.

Similarly, the programs are data-independent on other field sets. The only types which cannot be reduced because of data independence are: MemLocs for the memory component and Tags for CLERK. The latter is due to the fact that CLERK has to do bookkeeping on the tags to organize repetitions and final answers.

A look at the programs will convince the reader that their behavior is comparably uniform in these parameters as in the others, which meet the formal criterion of data independence. To cope with that case, we would have to generalize the notion of data independence further. Effectively, that is what has been done to perform the experiments and is described later on. This was inspired by another kind of abstraction, coming from the framework of *homomorphic abstractions* [CGL94]. So let us have a brief look at homomorphic abstractions to explain the idea.

Given a Kripke structure $K = (S, R, \mathcal{A}, L, I, \mathcal{F})$, a mapping $h : S \rightarrow S'$ gives rise to a homomorphic image K_h of K.

$$S_h =_{\text{df}} h(S)$$

$$R_h =_{\text{df}} \{ (s_h, s'_h) \mid \exists (s, s') \in R. h(s) = s_h \land h(s') = s'_h \}$$

$$L_h(s_h) =_{\text{df}} \bigcap_{h(s) = s_h} L(s)$$

$$I_h =_{\text{df}} h(I)$$

$$\mathcal{F} =_{\text{df}} \{ (S_h \setminus h(S \setminus \bigcup_{i \in I} G_i), h(\bigcup_{i \in I} H_i)) \mid \{ (G_i, H_i) \mid i \in I \} \subseteq \mathcal{F} \}$$

The intention is that K_h shows at least the behaviors as K, and that henceforth each formula valid for K_h holds in K. For this to work it is (technically) important that $\mathcal{A}$ contains for each atom A a negation $\neg A$. If, both, states labeled with A and labeled with $\neg A$ are mapped to one abstract state, it cannot safely be told whether A holds in the abstract state. Accordingly, with the definition above, neither A nor $\neg A$ will be true in that state. A further assumption concerns the transition relation R, which must be total on S (or we could require of h that it maps all deadlocks of K to deadlocks of K_h). Finally, we can extend the notion of homomorphic abstraction by allowing the abstraction to have less atoms, i.e. $L_{abs} \subseteq L_h$.

With homomorphic abstractions one can reduce the system representations e.g. by neglecting channels which are not addressed in one specification, or by eliminating irrelevant fields completely, or by leaving out some program segments.

There is a specific type of homomorphic abstraction which has much in common with data-independence. A *symbolic* homomorphic abstraction [CGL94] is parameterized by some value, resulting in a Kripke structure where each state is parameterized by a value, and transitions also may depend on the value. In our case of the memory component we choose one parameter of type MemLocs. The abstraction neglects all memory cells except the one addressed by the parameter. I.e. the assignment Mem[loc]:=val will effectively be replaced by alt loc=par → Mem:=val, loc≠par → skip tla , and instead of val:=Mem[loc] we will have alt loc=par → val:=Mem, loc≠par → val:=? tla . Let us denote the parameterized structure by $K(par)$. *Symbolic* model checking can be performed on such parameterized structures, see [CGL94], resulting in a condition on *par* for the truth of a formula $\phi(par)$. If the condition is simply true, the formula $\forall par. \phi(par)$ is true for the original system. This applies to the specification at hand. No formula has more than one universally quantified location. But no symbolic model checker was available.

An alternative which does not need symbolic model checking uses (again) a data-flow analysis. It suffices to show that the parameter does enter only such conditions where it is tested for equality with values from the location fields of read and write calls. I.e. exchanging values l_1 and l_2 in the location fields of observations produces the behavior of $K(l_2)$ from that of $K(l_1)$. That means that it will suffice to verify the program for one parameter value. In this way, the memory component can be reduced to a manageable size, and a similar argument works for the tags in CLERK.

The reader may have noted the informality of the argumentation above. A formalization would proceed by defining a (syntactic) flowgraph representation of the structure $K(par)$ and a suitable criterion for the data-flow analysis.

6.1 Practical Experiments

The practical experiments were performed using the model-checking features of TRAVERDI. The implementation of data independence in the verification tool proved to be not flexible enough to handle the problems at hand. Those abstractions were performed manually. Other (mainly homomorphic) abstractions were done automatically by the Kripke-structure generator. As a result, the model checker was able to handle the problem complexities, despite the fact that it does not rely on BDDs. The Kripke structures had between 5,000 and 30,000 states, depending on the specification, in the case of the RELIABLE MEMORY implementation, which was the largest of the three systems. The model-checking times on a SPARC 10 ranged from seconds to a few minutes.

7 Observations

7.1 Timing Diagrams Versus Temporal Logic

At early stages of the work, some of the diagrams were very complicated. In particular, one would certainly not have wanted to look at the formula representation of the first version of **WriteD**, while the diagram was still comprehensible. During the specification and verification process, the specifications have been simplified considerably. As already said, the property expressed by **WriteD2** was not only stronger and resulted in less complex verification subtasks, but it was also easier to translate to temporal logic. However, that does not imply that one should not use timing diagrams at all. They proved to be valuable in early stages of the specification process, as they helped to formalize first versions of the properties. Also, there might of course be cases where no similar complexity reduction is possible.

7.2 Adequateness of Temporal Logic

Even in its final version, the specification of the functional behavior of the memory component is incomplete. As already explained, this is due to the difficulty of giving an interface specification without resorting to the use of existentially quantified flexible variables ("virtual cells"). Perhaps, already past operators may have helped. Anyway, this incompleteness shows a weakness of the method, the limited expressivity of the logic. This weakness must be weighed against the method's strengths, i.e. the automatizability of the verification process.

To do so, we compare our solution with others [CBH, KNS, LSW] which also used automatic tools. These approaches did not try the verification of a program implementation (the problem did not call for that) which was done here (Section 6). We have to restrict the comparison to the distribution step (Section 5 in this paper), although our method is supposed to show its advantages mainly when it comes to verify a particular implementation. Also, the other approaches did not introduce a protocol for the remote procedure call mechanism. Abstracting from that protocol makes the specifications simpler, and it will also be more difficult to relate them to program implementations. So, the results of the comparison are of limited significance.

The three other contributions handle the problem differently. Even the accuracy of modeling the requirements is not the same. It is the "as if"-clause for the read calls in the requirements which makes this apparent. For a successful read, the memory is to behave "as if" it performs exactly one atomic read. Now, the RPC component might turn a successful read reply of the reliable memory into RPCFailure, after which CLERK might initiate a second read operation. Therefore, the distributed implementation behaves "as if" a successful read is the result of one or more atomic read operations. Of course, since only the last atomic operation counts for the reply, and none changes the internal state, this is equivalent to "'as if' exactly one atomic read". But this equivalence would have to be established in the verification of the distributed implementation.

In [KNS], this is done. Existentially quantified flexible variables are available in the employed second-order formalism. Their use lead to a rather direct logical representation of the requirements. The implication characterizing correctness of the distributed implementation has the form

$$\exists x.\,\phi(x) \;\rightarrow\; \exists y.\,\psi(y)\,. \qquad (4)$$

It required a nontrivial proof, because the simple sufficient $\forall x.(\phi(x) \rightarrow \psi[x/y])$ does not hold, according to the fact that "one or more atomic reads" (expressed in ϕ) and "exactly one atomic read" (in ψ) are not the same. The tool MONA was not able to verify the general implication (4). A strengthened formula, where the relation between x and y was partially specified, passed the tool. I.e. this step in the proof required some human intervention.

The solution given in [CBH] avoided such problems. The formalization of the requirements already allowed a successful read to do more than one atomic read, although existentially quantified variables were available. In [LSW], the specification was done in terms of internal actions, i.e. the "as if" was ignored. Consequently, the proof attempt was successful only after the specification was relaxed (as in [CBH]). Both approaches applied techniques of structuring the specifications to facilitate verification, and in both cases no further human intervention was necessary.

In our approach, as an interface specification was used, the problem arises in a slightly different form. Since the two versions of successful read calls result in the same interface behavior, our specification would be the same in both cases. But still, we have to verify the equivalence in some form, because we cannot match external read calls and read calls issued to the reliable memory component, and there are no atomic calls which could be matched. So we experience similar difficulties as described in [KNS].

Summarizing, it can be said that the RPC-memory specification problem was already difficult for automatic tools. There is some evidence that an accurate specification in terms of "virtual cells", although easy to produce, might not be easy to verify. The amount of intervention is difficult to compare, and we also cannot say whether the methods of [CBH, LSW] would not have been able to cope with the original requirements. Taking the results in their present form, as no other method verified a program implementation, our method does certainly not look inferior.

8 Conclusion

The main objective of this contribution was to demonstrate how well the specification problem could be handled with the particular temporal-logic based methodology. The main observations are:

- The operational specification in the problem description was in parts difficult to capture with the restricted temporal-logic dialect. On the other hand, the formalized requirements could be verified rigidly and completely, down to the level of a program implementation.

– It seems feasible to provide helpful machine assistance for all verification steps. But to permit a machine-checked and largely automatic verification in this methodology, the tools must support a considerable set of complementary techniques. For applications like this one, the basic principles (e.g. data independence) have to be generalized to yield more flexible and powerful techniques.

So we may conclude that the strong point of this methodology is indeed the fact that adequate machine support could be provided for it, though this requires (still) quite some effort. The result could be a tool useful for, among other purposes, partial verification and validation. In conjunction with an operational informal specification, the value of verified properties formalized independently of the implementation process seems particularly high.

Acknowledgment The presentation of this work profited very much from the comments of many people. In particular, it was Stephan Merz who discovered several shortcomings and inconsistencies, and who suggested numerous improvements.

References

[BCM+90] J.R. Burch, E.M. Clarke, K.L. McMillan, D.L. Dill, and J. Hwang. Symbolic model checking: 10^{20} states and beyond. In *5th IEEE Symp. on Logic in Comp. Sc.*, pages 428–439, 1990.

[BH95] J. Bohn and H. Hungar. Traverdi — transformation and verification of distributed systems. In M. Broy and S. Jähnichen, editors, *KORSO: Methods, Languages, and Tools for the Construction of Correct Software*, LNCS 1009, pages 317–338. Springer, 1995.

[BL] M. Broy and L. Lamport. The RPC-Memory Specification problem. This volume.

[CBH] Jorge Cuellar, Dieter Barnard, and Martin Huber. A Solution Relying on the Model Checking of Boolean Transition Systems. This volume.

[CE81] E.M. Clarke and E.A. Emerson. Design and synthesis of synchronization skeletons using branching time temporal logic. In D. Kozen, editor, *Workshop on Logics of Programs*, LNCS 131, pages 52–71. Springer, 1981.

[CES83] E.M. Clarke, E.A. Emerson, and A.P. Sistla. Automatic verification of finite state concurrent systems using temporal logic specifications. In *POPL10*, pages 117–126, 1983. also appeared in ACM Transact. on Prog. Lang. and Systems 8, 244–263, 1986.

[CGL94] E.M. Clarke, O. Grumberg, and D.E. Long. Model checking and abstraction. *ACM Trans. on Prog. Lang. and Systems*, 16:1512–1542, 1994.

[DDH+96] W. Damm, G. Döhmen, R. Herrmann, P. Kelb, H. Pargmann, and R. Schlör. Verification flow. In C.D. Kloos, J. Goicolea, and W. Damm, editors, *Formal Methods for Hardware Verification*. Springer, 1996. to appear.

[DJS95] W. Damm, B. Josko, and R. Schlör. Specification and verification of VHDL-based system-level hardware designs. In E. Börger, editor, *Specification and Validation Methods*, pages 331–410. Oxford Univ. Press, 1995.

[GL94]   O. Grumberg and D.E. Long. Model checking and modular verification. *ACM Trans. on Prog. Lang. and Systems*, 16:843–871, 1994. Extended version of GrLo91.

[Hun93] H. Hungar. Combining model checking and theorem proving to verify parallel processes. In C. Courcoubetis, editor, *5th Int. Conf. on Computer Aided Verification*, LNCS 697, pages 154–165. Springer, 1993.

[INM88] INMOS Ltd. *OCCAM 2 Reference Manual*. Prentice Hall, 1988.

[Jos93] B. Josko. Modular specification and verification of reactive systems. Technical report, CvO Univ. Oldenburg, 1993. Habilitation Thesis.

[KNS]   Nils Klarlund, Mogens Nielsen, and Kim Sunesen. A Case Study in Verification Based on Trace Abstractions. This volume.

[KV95]   O. Kupfermann and M.Y. Vardi. On the complexity of branching modular model checking. In I. Lee and S.A. Smolka, editors, *6th Int. Conf. on Concurrency Theory*, LNCS 962, pages 408–422. Springer, 1995.

[LSW]   Kim G. Larsen, Bernhard Steffen, and Carsten Weise. The Methodology of Modal Constraints. This volume.

[MP91]   Z. Manna and A. Pnueli. *The temporal logic of reactive and concurrent systems: Specification*. Springer, 1991.

[Wol86] P. Wolper. Expressing interesting properties of programs in propositional temporal logic. In *13th ACM Symp. on Principles of Programming Languages*, pages 184–193, 1986.

A Case Study in Verification Based on Trace Abstractions

Nils Klarlund* Mogens Nielsen Kim Sunesen
BRICS**
Department of Computer Science
University of Aarhus
Ny Munkegade
DK-8000 Aarhus C.
{klarlund,mnielsen,ksunesen}@daimi.aau.dk

Abstract. In [14], we proposed a framework for the automatic verification of reactive systems. Our main tool is a decision procedure, MONA, for Monadic Second-order Logic (M2L) on finite strings. MONA translates a formula in M2L into a finite-state automaton. We show in [14] how *traces*, i.e. finite executions, and their abstractions can be described behaviorally. These state-less descriptions can be formulated in terms of customized temporal logic operators or idioms.

In the present paper, we give a self-contained, introductory account of our method applied to the RPC-memory specification problem of the 1994 Dagstuhl Seminar on Specification and Refinement of Reactive Systems. The purely behavioral descriptions that we formulate from the informal specifications are formulas that may span 10 pages or more.

Such descriptions are a couple of magnitudes larger than usual temporal logic formulas found in the literature on verification. To securely write these formulas, we use FIDO [16] as a reactive system description language. FIDO is designed as a high-level symbolic language for expressing regular properties about recursive data structures.

All of our descriptions have been verified automatically by MONA from M2L formulas generated by FIDO.

Our work shows that complex behaviors of reactive systems can be formulated and reasoned about without explicit state-based programming. With FIDO, we can state temporal properties succinctly while enjoying automated analysis and verification.

1 Introduction

In *reactive systems*, computations are regarded as sequences of events or states. Thus programming and specification of such systems focus on capturing the

---

* Author's current address: AT&T Research, Room 2C-410, 600 Mountain Ave., Murray Hill, NJ 07974; E-mail: klarlund@research.att.com
** Basic Research in Computer Science,
Centre of the Danish National Research Foundation.

sequences that are allowed to occur. There are essentially two different ways of defining such sets of sequences.

In the *state approach*, the state space is defined by declarations of program variables, and the state changes are defined by the program code.

In the *behavioral approach*, the allowed sequences are those that satisfy a set of temporal constraints. Each constraint imposes restrictions on the order or on the values of events.

The state approach is used almost exclusively in practice. State based descriptions can be effectively compiled into machine code. The state concept is intuitive, and it is the universally accepted programming paradigm in industry.

The behavioral approach offers formal means of expressing temporal or behavioral patterns that are part of our understanding of a reactive system. As such, descriptions in this approach are orthogonal to the state approach—although the two essentially can express the same class of phenomena.

In this paper, we pursue the purely behavioral approach to solve the RPC-memory specification problem [4] posed by Manfred Broy and Leslie Lamport in connection with the Dagstuhl Seminar on Specification and Refinement of Reactive Systems. The main part of the problem is to verify that a distributed system P *implements* a distributed system S, that is, that every behavior of P is a behavior of S. Both systems comprise a number of processes whose behaviors are described by numerous informally stated temporal requirements like "Each successful Read(l) operation performs a single atomic read to location l at some time between the call and return."

The behavioral approach that we follow is the one we formulated in [14]. This approach is based on expressing behaviors and their abstractions in a decidable logic. In the present paper, we give an introductory and self-contained account of the method as applied to the RPC-memory specification problem.

We hope to achieve two goals with this paper:

- to show that the behavioral approach can be used for verifying complicated systems—whose descriptions span many pages of dense, but readable, logic— using decision procedures that require little human intervention; and
- to show that the FIDO language is an attractive means of expressing finite-state behavior of reactive systems. (FIDO is a programming language designed to express regular properties about recursive data structures [16].)

An overview of our approach

Our approach is based on the framework for automatic verification of distributed systems that we described in [14]. There, we show how *traces*, ie. finite computations, can be characterized behaviorally. We use *Monadic Second-order Logic* (M2L) on finite strings as the formal means of expressing constraints. This decidable logic expresses regular sets of finite strings, that is, sets accepted by finite-state machines. Thus, when the number of processes and other parameters of the verification problem is fixed, the set L_P, of traces of P can be expressed by finite-state machines synthesized from M2L descriptions of temporal constraints. Similarly, a description of the set L_S of traces of the specification can be synthesized.

The *verifier*, who is trying to establish that P implements S, cannot just directly compare L_P and L_S. In fact, these sets are usually incomparable, since they involve events of different systems. As is the custom, we call the events of interest the *observable events*. These events are common to both systems. The *observable behaviors* $Obs(L_P)$ of L_P are the traces of L_P with all non-observable events projected away. That P implements S means that $Obs(L_P) \subseteq Obs(L_S)$.

One goal of the automata-theoretic approach to verification is to establish $Obs(L_P) \subseteq Obs(L_S)$ by computing the product of the automata describing $Obs(L_P)$ and $Obs(L_S)$. Specifically, we let A_P be an automaton accepting $Obs(L_P)$ and we let A_S be a automaton representing the complement of $Obs(L_S)$. Then $Obs(L_P) \subseteq Obs(L_S)$ holds if and only if the product of A_P and A_S is empty. Unfortunately, the projection of traces may entail a significant blow-up in the size of A_S as a function of the size of the automaton representing L_S. The reason is that the automaton A_S usually can be calculated only through a subset construction.

The use of state abstraction mappings or homomorphisms may reduce such state space blow-ups. But the disadvantage to state mappings is that they tend to be specified at a very detailed level: each global state of P is mapped to a global state of S.

In [14], we formulate well-known verification concepts, like *abstractions* and *decomposition principles* for processes in the M2L framework. The resulting trace based approach offers some advantages to conventional state based methods.

For example, we show how trace abstractions, which relate a trace of P to a corresponding trace of S, can be formulated loosely in a way that reflects only the intuition that the verifier has about the relation between P and S—and that does not require a detailed, technical understanding of how every state of P relates to a state of S. A main point of [14] is that even such loose trace abstractions may (in theory at least) reduce the non-determinism arising in the calculation of A_S.

The framework of [14] is tied closely to M2L: traces, trace abstractions, the property of implementation, and decomposition principles for processes are all expressible in this logic—and thus all amenable, in theory at least, to automatic analysis, since M2L is decidable.

In the present paper, we have chosen the FIDO language both to express our concrete model of the RPC-memory specification problem and to formulate our exposition of the framework of [14]. FIDO is a notational extension of M2L that incorporates traditional concepts from programming languages, like recursive data types, functions, and strongly typed expressions. FIDO is compiled into M2L.

An overview of the RPC-memory specification problem

The Specification Problem of the Dagstuhl Seminar on Specification and Refinement of Reactive Systems is a four page document describing interacting components in distributed memory systems. Communication between components takes place by means of procedures, which are modeled by call and return events. At the highest level, the specification describes a system consisting of a memory component that provides read and write services to a number of processes. These services are implemented by the memory component in terms of basic i/o procedures. The relationships among service events, basic events, and failures are described in behavioral terms.

Problem 1 in the problem description document calls for the comparison of this memory system with a version in which a certain type of memory failure cannot occur.

Problem 2 calls for a formal specification of another layer added to the memory system in form of an RPC (Remote Procedure Call) component that services read and write requests.

Problem 3 asks for a formal specification of the system as implemented using the RPC layer and a proof that it implements the memory system of Problem 1.

In addressing the problems, we deal with safety properties of finite systems.

Problems 4 and 5 address certain kinds of failures that are described in a real-time framework. Our model is discrete, and we have not attempted to solve this part.

Previous work

The TLA formalism by Lamport [19] and the temporal logic of Manna and Pnueli [23, 13] provide uniform frameworks for specifying systems and state mappings. Both logics subsume predicate logic and hence defy automatic verification in general. However, work has been done on providing mechanical support in terms of proof checkers and theorem provers, see [8, 9, 22].

The use of state mappings have been widely advocated, see e.g. [20, 18, 19, 13]. The theory of state mappings tend to be rather involved, see [2, 15, 21, 25].

The Concurrency Workbench [6] offers automatic verification of the existence of certain kinds of state-mappings between finite-state systems.

Decomposition is a key aspect of any verification methodology. In particular, almost all the solutions of the RPC-memory specification problem [4] in [1] use some sort of decomposition. In [3], Lamport and Abadi gave a proof rule for compositional reasoning in an assumption/guarantee framework. A non-trivial decomposition of a closed system is achieved by splitting it into a number of open systems with assumptions reflecting their dependencies. In our rule, dependencies are reflected in the choice of trace abstractions between components and a requirement on the relationship between the trace abstractions.

For finite-state systems, the COSPAN tool [10], based on the automata-theoretic framework of Kurshan [17], implements a procedure for deciding language containment for ω-automata.

In [5], Clarke, Browne, and Kurshan show how to reduce the language containment problem for ω-automata to a model checking problem in the restricted case where the specification is deterministic. The SMV tool [24] implements a model checker for the temporal logic CTL [7]. In COSPAN and SMV, systems are specified using typed C-like programming languages.

In the rest of the paper

In Section 2, we first explain M2L and then introduce the FIDO notation by an example. Section 3 and 4 discuss our verification framework and show how all concepts can be expressed in FIDO. We present our solutions to the RPC-memory specification problem [4] in the remaining sections. In Section 5, we describe the distributed system that constitutes the specification. In Section 6, we describe the implementation, which is an elaboration on the specification. In Section 7, we prove that the implementation satisfies the specification.

Acknowledgements

We would like to thank the referees for their comments and remarks.

2   Monadic Second-Order Logic on Strings

The logical notations we use are based on the monadic second-order logic on strings (M2L). A closed M2L formula is interpreted relative to a natural number n (the *length*). Let $[n]$ denote the set $\{0, \ldots, n-1\}$. First-order variables range over the set $[n]$ (the set of *positions*), and second-order variables range over subsets of $[n]$. We fix countably infinite sets of first and second-order variables $Var_1 = \{p, q, p_1, p_2, \ldots\}$ and $Var_2 = \{P, P_1, P_2, \ldots\}$, respectively. The *syntax* of M2L formulas is defined by the abstract syntax:

$$t ::= p < q \mid p \in P$$
$$\phi ::= t \mid \neg\phi \mid \phi \vee \phi \mid \exists p.\phi \mid \exists P.\phi$$

where p,q and P range over Var_1 and Var_2, respectively.

The standard *semantics* is defined as follows. An M2L formula ϕ with free variables is interpreted relative to a natural number n and an interpretation (partial function) $\mathcal{I}$ mapping first and second-order variables into elements and subsets of $[n]$, respectively, such that $\mathcal{I}$ is defined on the free variables of ϕ. As usual, $\mathcal{I}[a \leftarrow b]$ denotes the partial function that on c yields b if $a = c$, and otherwise $\mathcal{I}(c)$. We define inductively the *satisfaction relation* $\models_\mathcal{I}$ as follows.

$$n \models_\mathcal{I} p < q \overset{\text{def}}{\Longleftrightarrow} \quad \mathcal{I}(p) < \mathcal{I}(q)$$
$$n \models_\mathcal{I} p \in P \overset{\text{def}}{\Longleftrightarrow} \quad \mathcal{I}(p) \in \mathcal{I}(P)$$

$$n \models_\mathcal{I} \neg\phi \overset{\text{def}}{\Longleftrightarrow} \quad n \not\models_\mathcal{I} \phi$$
$$n \models_\mathcal{I} \phi \vee \psi \overset{\text{def}}{\Longleftrightarrow} \quad n \models_\mathcal{I} \phi \vee n \models_\mathcal{I} \psi$$

$$n \models_\mathcal{I} \exists p.\phi \overset{\text{def}}{\Longleftrightarrow} \quad \exists k \in [n].n \models_{\mathcal{I}[p \leftarrow k]} \phi$$
$$n \models_\mathcal{I} \exists P.\phi \overset{\text{def}}{\Longleftrightarrow} \quad \exists K \subseteq [n].n \models_{\mathcal{I}[P \leftarrow K]} \phi$$

As defined above M2L is rich enough to express the familiar atomic formulas such as successor $p = q + 1$ (albeit only for numbers less than n), as well as formulas constructed using the Boolean connectives such as $\wedge, \Rightarrow$ and $\Leftrightarrow$, and the universal first and second-order quantifier $\forall$, following standard logical interpretations. Throughout this paper we freely use such M2L derived operators.

There is a standard way of associating a language over a finite alphabet with an M2L formula. Let $\alpha = \alpha_0 \ldots \alpha_{n-1}$ be a string over the alphabet $\{0,1\}^l$. Then the length $|\alpha|$ of α is n and $(\alpha_j)_i$ denotes the ith component of the l-tuple denoted by α_j. An M2L formula ϕ with free variables among the second-order variables $P_1, \ldots, P_l$ defines the language:

$$L(\phi) = \{\alpha \in (\{0,1\}^l)^* \mid |\alpha| \models_{\mathcal{I}_\alpha} \phi\}$$

of strings over the alphabet $\{0,1\}^l$, where $\mathcal{I}_\alpha$ maps P_i to the set $\{j \in [n] \mid (\alpha_j)_i = 1\}$.

Any language defined in this way by an M2L formula is regular; conversely, any regular language over $\{0,1\}^l$ can be defined by an M2L formula. Moreover, given an M2L formula ϕ a minimal finite automaton accepting $L(\phi)$ can effectively be constructed using the standard operations of product, subset construction, projection, and minimization. This leads to a decision procedure for M2L, since ϕ is a tautology if and only if $L(\phi)$ is the set of all strings over $\{0,1\}^l$. The approach extends to any finite alphabet. For example, letters of the alphabet $\Sigma = \{a, b, c, d\}$ are encoded by letters of the alphabet $\{0,1\}^2$ by enumeration: a, b, c and d are encoded by $(0,0), (1,0), (0,1)$ and $(1,1)$, respectively. Thus, any language over Σ can be represented as a language over $\{0,1\}^2$ and hence any regular language over Σ is the language defined by some M2L formula with two free second-order variables P_1 and P_2. For example, the formula ϕ:

$$\forall p.p \notin P_1 \wedge p \notin P_2$$

defines the language $\{a\}^*$, that is, $L(\phi) = \{(0,0)\}^*$. In particular, since $L(\phi)$ is not the set of all strings over $\{0,1\}^2$, ϕ is not valid, and any string not in $L(\phi)$ corresponds to a length n and an interpretation relative to n that falsifies ϕ.

2.1 FIDO

As suggested above, any regular language over any finite alphabet can be defined as the language of an open M2L formula by a proper encoding of letters as bit patterns, that is, by enumerating the alphabet. In our initial solution to the RPC-memory specification problem, we did the encoding "by hand" using only the Unix M4 macro processor to translate our specifications into M2L. This is an approach we cannot recommend, since even minor syntactic errors are difficult to find. The FIDO notation helps us overcome these problems. Below, we explain the FIDO notation by examples introducing all needed concepts one by one.

Consider traces, i.e. finite strings, over an alphabet Event consisting of events Read and Return with parameters that take on values in finite domains and the event τ. A Read may carry one parameter over the domain $\{l_0, l_1, l_2\}$, and a Return may carry two parameters, one from the domain $\{v_0, v_1\}$, and one from the domain $\{normal, exception\}$. In FIDO, the code:

```
type Loc     = l0,l1,l2;
type Value   = v0,v1;
type Flag    = normal,exception;
```

declares the enumeration types Value, Flag, and Loc. They define the domains of constants $\{l_0, l_1, l_2\}$, $\{v_0, v_1\}$, and $\{normal, exception\}$, respectively. The type definitions:

```
type Read   = Loc;
type Return = Value & Flag;
```

declare a new name Read for the type Loc and the record type Return, which defines the domain of tuples $\{[v, f] \mid v \in Value \wedge f \in Flag\}$. The alphabet Event is the union of Read, Return and $\{\tau\}$:

```
type Event = Read | Return | τ;
```

The union is a disjoint union by default, since the FIDO type system requires the arguments to define disjoint domains. The types presented so far all define finite domains. FIDO also allows the definition of recursive data types. For our purposes, recursively defined types are of the form:

```
type Trace = Event(next: Trace) | empty;
```

Thus, Trace declares the infinite set of values $\{e_1 e_2 \ldots e_n empty \mid e_i \in Event\}$. In other words, the type Trace is the set of all finite strings of parameterized events in Event with an empty value added to the end. The details of coding the alphabet of events in second-order M2L variables are left to the FIDO compiler.

FIDO provides (among others) four kinds of variables ranging over *strings*, *positions*, *subsets of positions* and *finite domains*, respectively. The FIDO code:

```
string γ: Trace;
```

declares a free variable γ holding an element (a string) of Trace. We often refer to γ just as a string.

A first-order variable p may be declared to range over all positions in the string γ by the FIDO declaration:

pos p: γ;

Similarly, a second-order variable P ranging over subsets of positions of the string can be declared as:

set P: γ;

A variable event holding an element of the finite domain Event is declared by:

dom event: Event;

The FIDO notation includes, besides M2L syntax for formulas, existential and universal quantification over all the kinds of variables. For example, we can specify as a formula that the event Read:[l_0] from the domain Event occurs in γ:

$\exists$**pos** p :γ.(γ(p) = Read:[l_0])

which is true if and only if there exists a position p in γ such that the pth element in γ is the event Read:[l_0].

If we want to refer to a Read event without regard to the value of its parameter, then we write:

$\exists$**pos** p :γ; **dom** l: Loc.(γ(p) = Read:[l?])

which is true if and only if there exists a position p in γ and an element l in Loc such that the pth element in γ is the event Read:[l] (the question mark in l? is just a synthetic FIDO convention necessary for variables used in pattern matching expressions). To make the above formula more succinct, we can use the pattern matching syntax of FIDO, where a "dont't care" value is specified by a question mark:

$\exists$**pos** p :γ.(γ(p) = Read:[?])

The FIDO compiler translates such question marks into explicit existential quantifications over the proper finite domain.

A FIDO *macro* is a named formula with type-annotated free variables. Below, we formulate some useful temporal concepts in FIDO that formalize high-level properties of intervals. In the rest of the paper, we use strings to describe behaviors over time. Therefore, we refer to positions in strings as time instants in traces.

In order to say that a particular event event of type Event occurred before a given time instant t in trace α of type Trace, we write:

func Before(**string** α: Trace; **pos** t: α; **dom** event: Event): **formula**;
  $\exists$**pos** time: α.(time$<$t $\wedge$ α(time)=event)
end;

To express that event occur sometime in the interval from t_1 to t_2 (both excluded), we write:

func Between(**string** α: Trace; **pos** t_1,t_2: α; **dom** event: Event): **formula**;
  $\exists$**pos** time: α.(t_1 $<$time $\wedge$ time$<t_2$ $\wedge$ α(time)=event)
end;

The property that in a trace γ a Return is always preceded by a Read is expressed as:

$\forall$**pos** t: $\gamma.(\gamma(t)$=Return:[?,?] $\Rightarrow$ Before(γ,t,Read:[?]));

We can also express that a Return event occurs exactly once in an interval:

func ExactlyOneReturnBetween(**string** α: Trace; **pos** t_1,t_2: α): **formula**;
$\exists$**pos** time: $\alpha.(t_1<$time $\wedge$ time$<t_2 \wedge \alpha$(time)=Return:[?,?] $\wedge$
$\neg$Between(α,t_1,time,Return:[?,?]) $\wedge$
$\neg$Between(α,time,t_2,Return:[?,?])
end;

That a Read event occurred at both end points of the interval, but not in the interval, is expressed as:

func ConseqReads(**string** α: Trace; **pos** t_1,t_2: α): **formula**;
$t_1<t_2 \wedge \alpha(t_1)$ =Read:[?] $\wedge \alpha(t_2)$=Read:[?] $\wedge$
$\neg$Between(α,t_1,t_2,Read:[?])
end;

Using the macros above it is easy to specify more complicated properties. For example, to specify that a Read event is blocking, in the sense that any Return is issued in response to a unique Read event and no two Read events occurs consecutively without a return in between, we write:

func ReadProcs(**string** α: Trace): **formula**;
$\forall$**pos** t_1: α.
$\alpha(t_1)$=Return:[?,?]
$\Rightarrow$
$\exists$**pos** t_0: $\alpha.(t_0 <t_1 \wedge \alpha(t_0)$=Read:[?] $\wedge$
$\neg$Between(α,t_0,t_1, Return:[?,?])) $\wedge$
$\forall$**pos** time$_1$,time$_2$: α.
ConseqReads(α,time$_1$,time$_2$)
$\Rightarrow$
ExactlyOneReturnBetween(α,time$_1$,time$_2$)
end;

Finally in this FIDO overview, we mention that strings may be quantified over as well. For example, the formula:

$\exists$**string** α: γ; **pos** t: γ. ($\gamma(t)$=$\alpha(t)$);

expresses that there is a string α of the same type and length as γ and some time instant t in γ (and therefore also in α) such that the tth element of γ and α, respectively, are the same.

2.2 Automated translation and validity checking

Any well-typed FIDO formula is translated by the FIDO compiler [16] into an M2L formula. Hence, the FIDO compiler together with the MONA tool [11] provides a decision procedure for FIDO. For any formula in FIDO, the procedure either gives the answer "yes" (when the formula is valid) or a counter-example, which specifies a set of values of all free variables for which the formula does not hold:

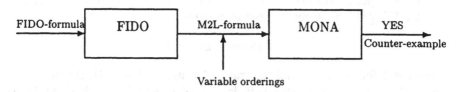

Variable orderings

In the negative case, the counter-example is translated back to the FIDO level from a MONA counter-example calculated on the basis of a path of minimal length to a non-accepting state in the canonical automaton recognizing $L(\phi)$.

We will not describe the efficient translation of the high-level syntax of FIDO into M2L formulas here. Instead, we emphasize that the translation is in principle straightforward: a string over a finite domain D is encoded using as many second-order variables (bits) as necessary to enumerate D; quantification over strings amounts to quantification over the second-order variables encoding the alphabet; and existential (universal) quantification over finite domains amounts to quantification over propositional variables (which are easily encoded in M2L).

The MONA tool provides an efficient implementation of the underlying M2L decision procedure [11].

3 Systems

We reason about computing systems through specifications of their behaviors in FIDO, i.e. viewed as traces over parameterized events specified in terms of FIDO formulas.

A system A determines an alphabet Σ_A of *events*, which is partitioned into *observable events* Σ_A^{Obs} and *internal events* Σ_A^{Int}. It is the observable events that matters when systems are compared. A *behavior* of A is a finite sequence over Σ_A. The system A also determines a prefix–closed language L_A of behaviors called *traces* of A. We write $A = (L_A, \Sigma_A^{Obs}, \Sigma_A^{Int})$. The *projection* π from a set Σ^* to a set Σ'^* ($\Sigma' \subseteq \Sigma$) is the unique string homomorphism from Σ^* to Σ'^* given by $\pi(a) = a$, if a is in Σ' and $\pi(a) = \epsilon$, otherwise, where ϵ is the empty string. The *observable behaviors* of a system A, $Obs(A)$, are the projections onto Σ_A^{Obs} of the traces of A, that is $Obs(A) = \{\pi(\alpha) \mid \alpha \in L_A\}$, where π is the projection from Σ_A^* onto $(\Sigma_A^{Obs})^*$.

A system A is thought of as existing in a *universe* of the systems with which it may be composed and compared. Formally, the universe is a global alphabet $\mathcal{U}$, which contains Σ_A and all other alphabets of interest. Moreover, $\mathcal{U}$ is assumed to contain the distinguished event τ which is not in the alphabet of any system. The set $N_\Sigma(A)$ of *normalized traces* over an alphabet $\Sigma \supseteq \Sigma_A$ is the set $h^{-1}(L_A) = \{\alpha \mid h(\alpha) \in L_A\}$, where h is the projection from Σ^* onto Σ_A^*. Normalization plays an essential rôle when composing systems and when proving correctness of implementation of systems with internal events.

A system can conveniently be expressed in FIDO. Following the discussion in Section 2 a finite domain U representing the universal alphabet $\mathcal{U}$, and a data type, Trace$_U$, representing the traces over U are defined. A system $A = (L_A, \Sigma_A^{Obs}, \Sigma_A^{Int})$ is then represented by a triple:

$$A = (\mathsf{Norm_A, Obs_A, Int_A})$$

of macros defining the normalized traces, Norm$_A$, of A over U, the observable events, Obs$_A$, and the internal events, Int$_A$. That is, let γ be a string over Trace$_U$ then Norm$_A(\gamma)$ is true if and only if γ denotes a trace of $N_\mathcal{U}(A)$ and let u be an element of U then Obs$_A$(u) and Int$_A$(u) are true if and only if u denotes an element of Σ_A^{Obs} and Σ_A^{Int}, respectively. When writing specifications in FIDO, we often confuse the name of a system with the name of the macro defining its set of normalized traces.

Our first example of a system in FIDO is the system ReadProcs, which resides in the universe given by Event from Section 2. The normalized traces of ReadProcs are defined by the macro ReadProcs, the alphabet of observable events by:

```
func ObsReadProcs(dom v: Event; dom id: Ident): formula;
  v=Read:[?] ∨ v=Return:[?,?]
end;
```

and the alphabet of internal events by:

```
func IntReadProcs(dom v: Event; dom id: Ident): formula;
  false
end;
```

That is, ReadProcs has observable events Read:[?] and Return:[?,?], and no internal events:

$$\mathsf{ReadProcs = (ReadProcs, ObsReadProcs, IntReadProcs)}$$

3.1 Composition

Our notion of composition of systems is essentially that of CSP [12], adjusted to cope with observable and internal events. We say that systems A and B are *composable* if they agree on the partition of events, that is, if no internal event of A is an observable event of B and vice versa, or symbolically, if $\Sigma_A^{Int} \cap \Sigma_B^{Obs} = \emptyset$ and $\Sigma_B^{Int} \cap \Sigma_A^{Obs} = \emptyset$. Given composable systems A and B, we define their *composition* $A \parallel B = (L_{A\parallel B}, \Sigma_{A\parallel B}^{Obs}, \Sigma_{A\parallel B}^{Int})$, where

- the set of observable events is the union of the sets of observable events of the components, that is, $\Sigma_{A\parallel B}^{Obs} = \Sigma_A^{Obs} \cup \Sigma_B^{Obs}$,
- the set of internal events is the union of the sets of internal events of the components, that is, $\Sigma_{A\parallel B}^{Int} = \Sigma_A^{Int} \cup \Sigma_B^{Int}$, and
- the set of traces is the intersection of the sets of normalized traces with respect to the alphabet $\Sigma_{A\parallel B}$, that is, $L_{A\parallel B} = N_{\Sigma_{A\parallel B}}(A) \cap N_{\Sigma_{A\parallel B}}(B)$.

As in CSP, a trace of $A \parallel B$ is the interleaving of a trace of A with a trace of B in which common events are synchronized. Composition is commutative, idempotent and associative, and we adopt the standard notation, $A_1 \parallel \ldots \parallel A_n$ or just $\parallel A_i$, for the composition of n composable systems A_i.

In FIDO, composability of A and B is expressed by:

$$\forall \textbf{pos } t:\gamma. \ (\mathsf{Int}_A(\gamma(t)) \ \Rightarrow \ \neg \ \mathsf{Obs}_B(\gamma(t))) \ \wedge \ (\mathsf{Int}_B(\gamma(t)) \ \Rightarrow \ \neg \ \mathsf{Obs}_A(\gamma(t)))$$

and given composable systems A and B, composition is defined by:

$$A \parallel B = (\mathsf{Norm}_{A \parallel B}, \ \mathsf{Obs}_{A \parallel B}, \ \mathsf{Int}_{A \parallel B})$$

where the set of normalized traces are defined by conjunction:

func $\mathsf{Norm}_{A \parallel B}(\textbf{string } \alpha: \mathsf{Trace}_U)$: **formula**;
  $\mathsf{Norm}_A(\alpha) \ \wedge \ \mathsf{Norm}_B(\alpha)$
end;

and the alphabets by disjunction:

func $\mathsf{Obs}_{A \parallel B}(\textbf{dom } v: U)$: **formula**;
  $\mathsf{Obs}_A(v) \ \vee \ \mathsf{Obs}_B(v)$
end;

func $\mathsf{Int}_{A \parallel B}(\textbf{dom } v: U)$: **formula**;
  $\mathsf{Int}_A(v) \ \vee \ \mathsf{Int}_B(v)$
end;

To exemplify composition, we extend the universe Event with *atomic memory events*:

type Mem = Loc & Value & Flag;

A Mem event Mem:[l,v,f] denotes an atomic read operation from location l with return value v and status f, which may be normal or exceptional. The type Event is now:

type Event = Mem | Read | Return | τ;

The macro:

func MemBetween(**string** α: Trace): **formula**;
  $\forall$ **dom** l: Loc; **dom** v: Value;**pos** t_1,t_2: α.
    $t_1 < t_2 \wedge \alpha(t_1) = \mathsf{Read}:[l?] \wedge \alpha(t_2) = \mathsf{Return}:[v?,?]$
    $\Rightarrow$
    $\exists$**pos** t_0: α. $t_1 < t_0 \wedge t_0 < t_2 \wedge \alpha(t_0) = \mathsf{Mem}:[l?,v?,?]$
end;

is true on a trace if and only if there exists an atomic read event Mem:[l,v,?] between any read event Read:[l] to location l and return event Return:[v,?] with value v. We define the system MemBetween with observable events Read:[?] and Return:[?,?], and internal events Mem:[?,?,?]:

    MemBetween = (MemBetween,ObsMemBetween,IntMemBetween)

where

```
func ObsMemBetween(dom v: Event; dom id: Ident): formula;
   v=Read:[?] ∨ v=Return:[?,?]
end;
```

and

```
func IntMemBetween(dom v: Event; dom id: Ident): formula;
   Mem:[?,?,?]
end;
```

The systems ReadProcs and MemBetween are composable, since they do not disagree on the partition of their alphabets. We define their composition:

$$MReadProcs = ReadProcs \parallel MemBetween$$

Hence, MReadProcs has observable events Read:[?] and Return:[?,?], and internal events Mem:[?,?,?], and the normalized traces of MReadProcs specify the behaviors of read procedure calls with atomic reads.

3.2 Implementation

We formalize the notion of implementation in terms of language inclusion, again adjusted to cope with observable and internal events. We say that systems A and B are *comparable* if they have the same set of observable events Σ^{Obs}, that is, $\Sigma^{Obs} = \Sigma_A^{Obs} = \Sigma_B^{Obs}$. In the following A and B denote comparable systems with $\Sigma_A^{Obs} = \Sigma_B^{Obs} = \Sigma^{Obs}$.

Definition 1. Let A and B denote comparable systems. A *implements* B if and only if $Obs(A) \subseteq Obs(B)$

In FIDO, comparability between systems is easily expressible:

$$\forall pos\ t:\gamma.Obs_A(\gamma(t)) \Leftrightarrow Obs_B(\gamma(t)) \tag{1}$$

Implementation is less obvious. One sound approach is to attempt a proof of $N_U(A) \subseteq N_U(B)$, which is expressible in FIDO as the formula $Norm_A(\gamma) \Rightarrow Norm_B(\gamma)$. However, when the systems A and B have different internal behaviors the approach does not work in general.

We may specify a variation RMReadProcs of our system above that contains no exceptional atomic reads:

$$RMReadProcs = (RMReadProcs, ObsRMReadProcs, IntRMReadProcs)$$

where ObsRMReadProcs and IntRMReadProcs are defined to be the same as ObsMReadProcs and IntMReadProcs, respectively, and where RMReadProcs

```
func RMReadProcs(string α: Trace): formula;
   MReadProcs(α) ∧ ¬∃pos t: α.α(t)=Mem:[?,?,exception]
end;
```

The systems RMReadProcs and ReadProcs are comparable since they have the same set of observable events. The former system implements the latter since the implication:

$$\text{RMReadProcs}(\gamma) \Rightarrow \text{ReadProcs}(\gamma)$$

holds for all traces γ over Trace. The opposite implication does not hold; a simple counterexample is the trace

Read:[l_0] Mem:[l_0,v_0,exception] Return:[v_0,normal] empty.

However, the observable behaviors of the systems RMReadProcs and ReadProcs are clearly identical. In the next section, we show how to prove the implementation property using FIDO.

4 Relational Trace Abstractions

A *trace abstraction* is a relation on traces preserving observable behaviors. In the following A and B denote comparable systems with $\Sigma_A^{Obs} = \Sigma_B^{Obs} = \Sigma^{Obs}$ and π denotes the projection of $\mathcal{U}^*$ onto $(\Sigma^{Obs})^*$.

Definition 2. [14] A trace abstraction $\mathcal{R}$ from A to B is a relation on $\mathcal{U}^* \times \mathcal{U}^*$ such that:

1. If $\alpha \mathcal{R} \beta$ then $\pi(\alpha) = \pi(\beta)$
2. $N_{\mathcal{U}}(A) \subseteq dom\ \mathcal{R}$
3. $rng\ \mathcal{R} \subseteq N_{\mathcal{U}}(B)$

The first condition states that any pair of related traces must agree on observable events. The second and third condition require that any normalized trace of A should be related to some normalized trace of B, and only to normalized traces of B.

Theorem 3. [14] There exists a trace abstraction from A to B if and only if A implements B.

Hence, looking for a trace abstraction is a sound and complete technique for establishing the implementation property. In the following, we incorporate the method in the FIDO framework, where the main technical obstacle is that trace relations in general cannot be represented.

Given strings $\alpha = \alpha_0 \ldots \alpha_n \in \Sigma_1^*$ and $\beta = \beta_0 \ldots \beta_n \in \Sigma_2^*$, we write $\alpha^\wedge \beta$ for the string $(\alpha_0, \beta_0) \ldots (\alpha_n, \beta_n) \in (\Sigma_1 \times \Sigma_2)^*$. Every language $L_{\mathcal{R}}$ over a product alphabet $\Sigma_1 \times \Sigma_2$ has a canonical embedding as a relation $\mathcal{R}_L \subseteq \Sigma_1^* \times \Sigma_2^*$ on strings of equal length given by $\alpha^\wedge \beta \in L_{\mathcal{R}} \stackrel{\text{def}}{\Leftrightarrow} \alpha \mathcal{R}_L \beta$. We say that a trace abstraction is *regular* if it is the embedding of a regular language over $\mathcal{U} \times \mathcal{U}$.

Not all trace abstractions between finite-state systems are regular. However, to use FIDO we have to restrict ourselves to regular abstractions.

Definition 4. Given a subset Σ' of Σ, we say that strings $\alpha, \beta \in \Sigma^*$ are Σ'-*synchronized* if they are of equal length and if whenever the ith position in α contains a letter in Σ' then the ith position in β contains the same letter, and vice versa.

The property of being Σ^{Obs}-synchronized is FIDO expressible:

```
func Observe(string α: Traceᵤ; string β: α): formula;
    ∀pos t: α.(Obsₐ(α(t)) ∨ Obs_B(β(t)) ⇒ α(t)= β(t))
end;
```

Definition 5. Let $\hat{\mathcal{R}}$ be the language over $\mathcal{U} \times \mathcal{U}$ given by $\alpha^\wedge \beta \in \hat{\mathcal{R}}$ if and only if

$$\beta \in N_{\mathcal{U}}(B) \text{ and } \alpha, \beta \text{ are } \Sigma^{Obs}\text{-synchronized}$$

Since $N_{\mathcal{U}}(B)$ is a regular language, so is $\hat{\mathcal{R}}$, and furthermore it may be expressed in FIDO by:

```
func R(string α: Traceᵤ; string β: α): formula;
    Observe(α, β) ∧ Norm_B(β)
end;
```

The next proposition gives a sufficient condition for $\hat{\mathcal{R}}$ and any regular subset of $\hat{\mathcal{R}}$ to be a trace abstraction. We return to the significance of the last part when dealing with automated proofs.

Proposition 6. [14] (a) If $N_{\mathcal{U}}(A) \subseteq dom\ \hat{\mathcal{R}}$, then $\hat{\mathcal{R}}$ is a regular trace abstraction from A to B. (b) Moreover in general, for any regular language $\mathcal{C} \subseteq (\mathcal{U} \times \mathcal{U})^*$, if $N_{\mathcal{U}}(A) \subseteq dom\ \hat{\mathcal{R}} \cap \mathcal{C}$, then $\hat{\mathcal{R}} \cap \mathcal{C}$ is a regular trace abstraction from A to B.

Importantly, the condition in (a) can in fact be expressed in FIDO:

```
Normₐ(α) ⇒ ∃string β: α.R(α,β)
```

Thus, letting FIDO decide this formula is in principle a sound and complete and fully automated verification method.

To prove that the system MReadProcs implements ReadProcs, we instantiate macro Observe and R properly and then we check that

```
MReadProcs(α) ⇒ ∃string β:α.R(α,β)
```

holds.

4.1 Decomposition

Trace abstractions allow compositional reasoning [14], which enables us to drastically reduce the state spaces arising from our specifications.

Theorem 7. [14] Let A_i and B_i be pairwise comparable systems forming the compound systems $\| A_i$ and $\| B_i$. If

$$\mathcal{R}_i \text{ is a trace abstraction from } A_i \text{ to } B_i. \tag{2}$$

$$\bigcap_i \text{ dom } \mathcal{R}_i \subseteq \text{ dom } \bigcap_i \mathcal{R}_i \tag{3}$$

then

$$\| A_i \text{ implements } \| B_i$$

We call the extra condition (3) the *compatibility requirement*. By allowing components of a compound systems to also interact on internal events, we allow systems to be non-trivially decomposed. This is why the compatibility requirement (3) is needed; intuitively, it ensures that the choices defined by the trace abstractions can be made to agree on shared internal events. Formally, the intuition is expressed by the corollary:

Corollary 8. [14] If additionally the components of the specification are non-interfering on internal events, that is, $\Sigma_{B_i}^{Int} \cap \Sigma_{B_j}^{Int} = \emptyset$, for every $i \neq j$, then A_i implements B_i implies $\| A_i$ implements $\| B_i$.

Again, the compatibility requirement is expressible in FIDO:

$$\bigwedge_{i=1,\ldots,n} (\exists \textbf{string } \beta_i \colon \gamma.(\mathsf{R}_i(\gamma,\beta_i))) \Rightarrow \exists \textbf{string } \beta \colon \gamma.(\bigwedge_{i=1,\ldots,n} \mathsf{R}_i(\gamma,\beta)) \tag{4}$$

where R_i is a FIDO macro taking as parameters two strings of type Trace and n is some fixed natural number.

The use of Theorem 7 for compositional reasoning about non-trivial decompositions of systems is illustrated in Section 7.

5 The RPC-Memory Specification Problem

We can now describe our solution to the RPC-memory specification problem proposed by Broy and Lamport [4]. We consider only the safety properties of the untimed part. We intersperse the original informal description (in *italic*) with our exposition.

5.1 The procedure interface

The problem [4] calls for the specification and verification of a series of components interacting with each other using a procedure-calling interface. In our specification, components are systems defined by FIDO formulas. Systems interact by synchronizing on common events, internal as well as observable. There is no notion of sender and receiver on this level. A procedure call consists of a *call* and the corresponding *return*. Both are indivisible (atomic) events. There are two kinds of returns, *normal* and *exceptional*. A component may contain a number of concurrent processes each carrying a unique identity. Any call or return triggered by a process communicates its identity. This leads us to declare the parameter domains:

```
type Flag  = normal,exception;
type Ident = id₀,...,idₖ;
```

of return flags and process identities for some fixed k, respectively.

5.2 A memory component

The first part of the problem [4] calls for a specification of a memory component. The component should specify a memory that maintains the contents of a set MemLocs of locations such that the contents of a location is an element of a set MemVals. We therefore introduce the domains:

```
type MemLocs = l₀,...,lₙ;
type MemVals = initVal,v₁,...,vₘ;
```

of locations and of values for some fixed n and m, respectively. The reason for defining the distinguished value initVal follows from: *The memory behaves as if it maintains an array of atomically read and written locations that initially all contain the value InitVal.* Furthermore, we define the atomic memory events, Mem, as carrying five parameters:

```
type Mem = Operation & MemLocs & MemVals & Flag & Ident;
```

The first parameter defined by the domain

```
type Operation = rd,wrt;
```

indicates whether the event denotes an atomic read or write operation. The second and third carry the location and the value read or written, respectively. The fourth indicates whether the operation succeeded. Finally, the fifth parameter carries a process identity (meant to indicate the identity of the process engaged in in the event).

The component has two procedure calls: *reads* and *writes*. The informal description [4] notes that *being an element of* MemLocs *or* MemVals *is a "semantic" restriction, and cannot be imposed solely by syntactic restrictions on the types of arguments.*

Procedure calls and returns have arguments of type Loc and Value, which are both associated with a Tag:

```
type Tag   = ok,error;
type Loc   = MemLocs & Tag;
type Value = MemVals & Tag;
```

The location or value is semantically correct if and only if the value of the corresponding Tag component is ok.

In the informal description [4], a read procedure is described as:

Name	Read
Arguments	loc : *an element of* MemLocs
Return Value	*an element of* MemVals
Exception	BadArg : *argument* loc *is not an element of* MemLocs.
	MemFailure: *the memory cannot be read.*
Description	*Returns the value stored in address* loc.

In our specification, a read procedure is called when a Read event of type

type Read = Loc & Ident & Visible;

happens. A Read event takes as first parameter an element of Loc that might not be a "semantically" correct element of MemLocs and as second parameter a process identity. The last parameter is an element of the domain:

type Visible = internal, observable;

When verifying the implementation, we need the parameter Visible to be able to regard reads, writes and returns as both observable and internal events.

The return of a read procedure call is modelled as a Return event:

type Return = Value & Flag & RetErr & Ident & Visible;

The first parameter is the value returned. The second indicates whether the return is normal or exceptional. If it is exceptional, then the third parameter is an element of the domain:

type RetErr = BadArg,MemFailure;

of possible errors returned by an exceptional return as described above.

Again, the fourth and fifth parameter are elements of the domains Ident and Visible with the intended meaning as for Read events. Similarly, a write procedure is specified in terms of Write events defined by:

type Write = Loc & Value & Ident & Visible;

and Return events. Hence, the universe for our systems is given by:

type Event = Mem | Read | Write | Return | τ;

and traces (strings) over the universe by:

type Trace = Event(next: Trace) | empty;

We specify the memory component Spec by the compound system:

$$\text{Spec} = \text{MemSpec}(id_0) \parallel \ldots \parallel \text{MemSpec}(id_k) \parallel \text{InnerMem}$$

constructed from systems MemSpec(id) that specify read and write procedures for fixed process identities id and a system InnerMem that specifies the array maintained by the memory component. Each of the systems MemSpec(id) is itself a compound system:

$$\text{MemSpec}(id) = \text{ReadSpec}(id) \parallel \text{WriteSpec}(id)$$

defined by composing the systems ReadSpec(id) and WriteSpec(id) specifying respectively read and write procedures for fixed process identities id.

For a fixed process identity id in Ident, the system ReadSpec(id) with observable events Read:[?,id,observable] and Return:[?,?,?,id,observable] and internal events Mem:[rd,?,?,?,id] specifies the allowed behaviors of read procedure calls involving the process with identity id. In FIDO notation, a *logical and* ($\wedge$) can alternatively be written as a semicolon (;). The normalized traces of ReadSpec(id) are defined by the macro:

```
func ReadSpec(string α: Trace; dom id: Ident; dom vis: Visible): formula;
    BlockingCalls(α,id,vis);
    CheckSuccessfulRead(α,id,vis);
    WellTypedRead(α,id,vis);
    ReadBadArg(α,id,vis);
    OnlyAtomReadsInReadCalls(α,id,vis)
end;
```

That is, γ is a normalized trace of ReadSpec(id) if and only if ReadSpec(γ,id, observable) is true.

Before we explain ReadSpec, let us make a couple of conventions. We often implicitly specialize macros, e.g. we write ReadSpec(id,observable) for the macro obtained from ReadSpec by instantiating the parameters id and vis. The system ReadSpec(id) is then given by the triple:

$$(\text{ReadSpec(id,observable)},\text{ObsReadSpec(id,observable)},\text{IntReadSpec(id)})$$

where

```
func ObsReadSpec(dom v: Event; dom id: Ident; dom vis: Visible): formula;
    v=Read:[?,id?,vis?] ∨ v=Return:[?,?,?,id?,vis?]
end;
```

and

```
func IntReadSpec(dom v: Event; dom id: Ident): formula;
    v=Mem:[rd,?,?,?,id?]
end;
```

The macro **ReadSpec** is the conjunction of five clauses. The first clause BlockingCalls specifies as required in [4] that procedure calls are blocking in the sense that a process stops after issuing a call in order to wait for the corresponding return to occur. The last clause OnlyAtomReadsInReadCalls specifies that an atomic read event occurs only during the handling of read calls. This requirement is not described in [4]. Reading in between the lines however, it seems clear that the specifier did not mean for atomic reads to happen without being part of some read procedure call. Both clauses are straightforwardly defined in FIDO using interval temporal idioms similar to those explained in Section 2.1.

In order to explain the other clauses, we follow [4] and defined an *operation* to consist of a procedure call and the corresponding return: We define the macro:

```
func Opr(string α: Trace; pos t₁,t₂: α;
            dom call,return: Event; dom id: Ident; dom vis: Visible): formula;
    t₁<t₂ ∧ α(t₁)=call ∧ α(t₂)=return;
    ¬Between(α,t₁,t₂,Read:[?,id?,vis?]);
    ¬Between(α,t₁,t₂,Write:[?,?,id?,vis?]);
    ¬Between(α,t₁,t₂,Return:[?,?,?,id?,vis?])
end;
```

This macro holds for a trace γ, time instants t_1 and t_2 in γ and events call and return if and only if the events call and return occurred at t_1 and t_2, respectively, and none of the events Read, Write and Return occurred between t_1 and t_2 (both excluded). An operation is *successful* if and only if its return is normal (non-exceptional).

The informal description from [4] quoted above (excluding the last line that describes the return value) then essentially states:

```
func WellTypedRead(string α: Trace; dom id: Ident; dom vis: Visible): formula;
  ∀dom vt,lt: Tag; dom retErr: RetErr; dom flg: Flag; pos t₁,t₂: α.
    Opr(α,t₁,t₂, Read:[[?,lt?],id?,vis?],Return:[[?,vt?],flg?,retErr?,id?,vis?],id,vis)
    ⇒
    (flg=normal;lt=MemLocs;vt=MemVals) ∨
    (flg=exception;retErr=MemFailure) ∨
    (flg=exception;¬lt=MemLocs;retErr=BadArg)
  end;
```

This macro encodes that whenever a read call and the corresponding return have occurred, either the return is normal and the value as well as the location passed are of the right types (respectively MemVals and MemLocs), or the return is exceptional and the error returned is MemFailure or the return is exceptional and the location passed is not of the right type (MemLocs) and the returned error is BadArg.

Furthermore, it is stated in [4] that:

An operation that raises a BadArg exception has no effect on the memory.

We transcribe this into the macro:

```
func ReadBadArg(string α: Trace; dom id: Ident; dom vis: Visible): formula;
  ∀ pos t₁,t₂: α.
    Opr(α,t₁,t₂,Read:[?,id?,vis?],Return:[?,exception,BadArg,id?,vis?],id,vis)
    ⇒
    ¬Between(α,t₁,t₂,Mem:[?,?,?,?,id?])
  end;
```

It says that between the call and the return of a read operation resulting in an exceptional return with return error BadArg no atomic read or write is performed. Note that we interpret *no effect on the memory* as the absence of atomic reads and writes.

Finally, a read procedure must satisfy that:

Each successful Read(l) operation performs a single atomic read to location l at some time between the call and return.

Thus the value returned should be the value read in the atomic read. This relation between a successful read and the corresponding return is captured by the macro:

```
func CheckSuccessfulRead(string α: Trace; dom id: Ident; dom vis: Visible): formula;
  ∀ dom v: MemVals; dom l: MemLocs; dom flg: RetErr; pos t₁: α; pos t₂: α.
    (Opr(α,t₁,t₂, Read:[[l?,?],id?,vis?],Return:[[v?,ok],normal,?,id?,vis?],id,vis)
    ⇒
```

∃ **pos** time: α.
    $(t_1 <$time$\wedge$ time$<t_2 \wedge \alpha($time$)=$Mem:[rd,l?,v?,normal,id?];
    $\neg$Between$(\alpha,t_1,$time,Mem:[rd,?,?,?,id?]);
    $\neg$Between$(\alpha,$time,$t_2,$Mem:[rd,?,?,?,id?])))
end;

requiring that if the return is normal (and thus the read successful) then exactly one atomic read is performed between the call and the return on the requested location. Furthermore, the value returned is the value read.

The systems WriteSpec(id) are defined similarly to the systems ReadSpec(id) though slightly more complicated, since write calls carry more parameters. The observable events of WriteSpec(id) are Write:[?,id,observable] and Return:[?,?,?,id,observable], and the internal events are Mem:[wrt,?,?,?,id].

The system InnerMem defines the behaviors allowed by the array maintained by the memory component. The informal description [4] refers to define an array without defining it. We apply the informal description: whenever a successful atomic read to a location occurs the value thus returned is the value last written by a successful atomic write on the location or if no such atomic write has occurred its the initial value initVal. The normalized traces of InnerMem are defined by the macro:

func InnerMem(**string** α: Trace): **formula**;
  $\forall$ **dom** v: MemVals; **dom** l: MemLocs; **pos** t: α.
    $\alpha($t$)=$Mem:[rd,l?,v?,normal,?]
    $\Rightarrow$
    $\exists$ **pos** t_0: α.($t_0 <$t$\wedge \alpha($$t_0$$)=$Mem:[wrt,l?,v?,normal,?] $\wedge$
      $\neg$Between$(\alpha,t_0,$t,Mem:[wrt,l?,?,normal,?])) $\vee$
    v$=$initVal $\wedge \neg$Before$(\alpha,$t,Mem:[wrt,l?,?,normal,?])
end;

The system InnerMem has internal events Mem:[?,?,?,?,?] and no observable events and is hence given by the triple:

$$\text{InnerMem} = (\text{InnerMem,ObsInnerMem,IntInnerMem})$$

where ObsInnerMem is a macro yielding false on every v of Event and

func IntInnerMem(**dom** v: Event): **formula**;
  v$=$Mem:[?,?,?,?,?]
end;

The informal description [4] also calls for the specification of a *reliable memory component* which is a variant of the memory component in which no Mem-Failure exceptions can be raised. We specify the reliable memory component by the compound system:

$$\text{RSpec} = \text{RMemSpec(id}_0) \parallel \ldots \parallel \text{RMemSpec(id}_k) \parallel \text{InnerMem}$$

where

$$\text{RMemSpec(id)} = \text{MemSpec(id)} \parallel \text{Reliable(id)}$$

and Reliable(id) is the system with the same alphabets as MemSpec(id) and with normalized traces given by the following macro specifying that no exceptional return with process identity id raising MemFailure occurs.

func Reliable(**string** α: Trace; **dom** id: Ident; **dom** vis: Visible): **formula**;
$\quad \neg$ **∃pos** t: $\alpha.(\alpha(t)=$Return:[?,exception,MemFailure,id?,vis?])
end;

That is, γ is a normalized trace of Reliable(id) if and only if Reliable(γ,id,observable) is true.

Below, when we say that have proven a formula $F(\gamma)$ by means of our tool, we mean that the tool has processed with answer "yes" a file consisting of all appropriate type declarations for fixed k, m, and n, together with the macro definitions given above and the code

string γ: Trace;
$F(\gamma)$

In what follows, we fix $k = m = n = 1$, that is, we have two process identities, two locations and two values.

Problem 1 *(a) Write a formal specification of the Memory component and of the Reliable Memory component.*

These are defined by Spec and RSpec, respectively.

(b) Either prove that a Reliable Memory component is a correct implementation of a Memory component, or explain why it should not be.

We prove that:
$$\text{RSpec}(\gamma) \Rightarrow \text{Spec}(\gamma) \tag{5}$$

is a tautology by feeding the formula to our tool.

(c) If your specification of the Memory component allows an implementation that does nothing but raise MemFailure exceptions, explain why this is reasonable.

We first define the following macro stating that any return occurring is exceptional and raises a MemFailure exception.

func NothingButMemFailure(**string** α: Trace): **formula**;
$\quad \forall$ **dom** retErr: RetErr; **dom** flg: Flag; **pos** t: α.
$\quad\quad (\alpha(t)=$Return:[?,flg?,retErr?,id?,vis?] $\Rightarrow$ flg=exception $\wedge$ retErr=MemFailure)
end;

Then we prove that:
$$\text{Spec}(\gamma) \wedge \text{NothingButMemFailure}(\gamma) \Rightarrow \text{Spec}(\gamma) \tag{6}$$

is a tautology by running our tool. This seems reasonable for two reasons. First, there is nothing in the informal description specifying otherwise. Second, from a practical point of view disallowing such an implementation would mean disallowing an implementation involving an inner memory that could be physically destroyed or removed.

6 Implementing the Memory

We now turn to the implementation of the memory component using an RPC component.

6.1 The RPC component

The problem [4] calls for a specification of an RPC component that interfaces with two components, a *sender* at a local site and a *receiver* at a remote site. Its purpose is to forward procedure calls from the local to the remote site, and to forward the returns in the other direction.

Parameters of the component are a set Procs *of procedure names and a mapping* ArgNum, *where* ArgNum(p) *is the number of arguments of each procedure* p.

We thus declare the domains:

type Procs   = ReadProc,WriteProc;
type NumArgs = n_1,n_2;

of procedure names Procs and of possible numbers of arguments NumArgs. As for elements of MemLocs and MemVals, we adopt the convention that being an element of Proc is a "semantic" restriction, and cannot be imposed solely by syntactic restrictions on the types of arguments. Therefore we declare:

type TProc = Procs & Tag;

The idea is that a remote procedure call passes arguments of type TProc whose first component denotes a semantically correct element of Procs if and only if the value of the Tag component is ok. The mapping ArgNum is specified by the macro:

func ArgNum(**dom** n: NumArgs; **dom** proc: TProc): **formula**;
   proc↓Procs=ReadProc ⇒ n=n_1;
   proc↓Procs=WriteProc ⇒ n=n_2
end;

where we use the FIDO notation ↓ to access a field in a record. That is, proc↓Procs denotes the Procs field in the record denoted by proc.

In the informal description [4], a remote call procedure is described as:

Name	RemoteCall
Arguments	proc : *name of a procedure*
	args : *list of arguments*
Return Value	*any value that can be returned by a call to* proc
Exception	RPCFailure : *the call failed*
	BadCall: proc *is not a valid name or* args *is not a*
	syntactically correct list of arguments for proc.
	Raises any exception raised by a call to proc.
Description	*Calls procedure* proc *with arguments* args.

We declare the domains:

type Args   = Loc & Value;
type RpcErr = RPCFailure,BadCall | RetErr;

of argument lists and of possible exceptions raised by exceptional return errors, respectively. (Note that we restrict ourselves to lists of length at most two.) In our specification, a remote procedure is called by issuing a RemoteCall event of the type:

type RemoteCall = TProc & NumArgs & Args & Ident;

A RemoteCall event takes as first parameter an element of TProc that might not be a "semantically" correct element of Procs and as second parameter an element of NumArgs denoting the length of the list from Args carried by the third parameter. The last parameter is a process identity from Ident. The return of a remote procedure is an RpcReturn event given by the declaration:

type RpcReturn = Value & Flag & RpcErr & Ident;

The first parameter is the value returned. The second indicates whether the return is normal or exceptional. In case, it is exceptional the third parameter is an element of the domain RetErr. The last parameter carries a process identity from Ident. Hence, the universe for our systems is given by:

type Event = Mem | Read | Write | Return | RemoteCall | RpcReturn | τ;

and traces (strings) over the universe by:

type Trace = Event(next: Trace) | empty;

We specify the RPC component RPC by the compound system:

$$RPC = RPC(id_0) \parallel \ldots \parallel RPC(id_k)$$

defined by composing the systems RPC(id).

For a fixed process identity id in Ident, the system RPC(id) with no observable events and internal events Mem:[?,?,?,?,id], Read:[?,id,internal], Write:[?,id,internal], Return:[?,?,?,id,internal], RemoteCall:[?,?,?,id] and RpcReturn:[?,?,?,id] specifies the allowed behaviors of RPC procedure calls involving the process with identity id. The normalized traces of RPC(id) are defined by the macro:

func RPC(**string** α: Trace; **dom** id: Ident): **formula**;
    RemoteCallAndReturnAlternates(α,id);
    RPCBehavior(α,id);
    WellTypedRemoteCall(α,id);
    OnlyInternsInRemoteCalls(α,id)
end;

That is, γ is a normalized trace of RPC(id) if and only if RPC(γ,id) is true. The system RPC(id) is then given by the triple:

$$RPC(id) = (RPC(id),ObsRPC(id),IntRPC(id))$$

where ObsRPC(id) is a macro that yields false on every v of Event and

func IntRPC(**dom** v: Event; **dom** id: Ident): **formula**;
    v=Mem:[rd,?,?,?,id?] $\vee$
    v=Read:[?,id,internal] $\vee$ v=Write:[?,id,internal] $\vee$ v=Return:[?,?,?,id,internal] $\vee$
    v=RemoteCall:[?,?,?,id] $\vee$ v=RpcReturn:[?,?,?,id] $\vee$
end;

The macro RPC is defined as the conjunction of four clauses each of which except for the last one describes properties explicitly specified in [4]. The last clause OnlyInternsInRemoteCalls specifies that any of the events Read:[?,id,internal], Write:[?,id,internal] and Return:[?,?,?,id,internal] only occurs during the handling of RPC calls. It seems clear that it was not the intention of [4] to allow read and write procedure calls on the remote site to happen without being triggered by some remote procedure call. The first clause, RemoteCallAndReturnAlternates specifies as required in [4] that remote procedure calls are blocking in the sense that a process stops after issuing a call while waiting for the corresponding return to occur. Hence, there may be multiple outstanding remote calls but not more than one triggered by the same process. Both clauses are straightforwardly defined in FIDO.

For convenience, we define the following macro specifying an RPC operation by associating a RemoteCall with the corresponding RpcReturn.

func RpcOpr(**string** α: Trace; **pos** t_1, t_2: α;
   dom call,return: Event; **dom** id: Ident): **formula**;
 $t_1 < t_2 \wedge \alpha(t_1) = $call$\wedge \alpha(t_2) = $return;
 $\neg$Between(α, t_1, t_2,RemoteCall:[?,?,?,id?]);
 $\neg$Between(α, t_1, t_2,RpcReturn:[?,?,?,id?])
end;

The second clause is a fairly direct transcription of the quoted lines above (excluding the last line):

func WellTypedRemoteCall(**string** α: Trace; **dom** id: Ident): **formula**;
 $\forall$ **dom** proc: TProc; **dom** num: NumArgs;
   dom flg: Flag; **dom** rpcErr: RpcErr; **pos** t_1, t_2: α.
  RpcOpr(α, t_1, t_2,RemoteCall:[proc?,num?,?,id?],RpcReturn:[?,flg?,rpcErr?,id?],id)
  $\Rightarrow$
   flg=normal $\Rightarrow$ proc$\downarrow$Tag=ok;ArgNum(num,proc);
   flg=exception;rpcErr=BadCall $\Leftrightarrow$ $\neg$(proc$\downarrow$Tag=ok;ArgNum(num,proc))
end;

stating the relationship between the parameters of a remote call and the corresponding return. The third clause specifies the properties described by:

A call of RemoteCall(proc,args) *causes the RPC component to do one of the following:*

- *Raise a* BadCall *exception if* args *is not a list of* ArgNum(proc) *arguments.*
- *Issue one call to procedure* proc *with arguments* args, *wait for the corresponding return (which the RPC component assumes will occur) and either (a) return the value (normal or exceptional) returned by that call, or (b) raise the* RPCFailure *exception.*
- *Issue no procedure call, and raise the* RPCFailure *exception.*

This description is translated into the macro:

```
func RPCBehavior(string α: Trace; dom id: Ident): formula;
  ∀ dom proc: TProc; dom num: NumArgs; dom lst: Args; dom val: Value;
    dom flg: Flag; dom rpcErr: RpcErr; pos t₁,t₂: α.
    RpcOpr(α,t₁,t₂,RemoteCall:[proc?,num?,lst?,id?],RpcReturn:[val?,flg?,rpcErr?,id?],id)
    ⇒
    ABadCall(α,t₁,t₂proc,num,flg,rpcErr) ∨
    OneSuccessfulRpcCall(α,t₁,t₂,proc,lst,val,flg,rpcErr,id) ∨
    OneUnSuccessfulRpcCall(α,t₁,t₂,proc,lst,val,flg,rpcErr,id) ∨
    NoCallOfAnyProcedure(α,t₁,t₂,flg,rpcErr,id)
end;
```

where

```
func ABadCall(string α: Trace; pos t₁,t₂: α;dom proc: TProc;
        dom num: NumArgs; dom flg: Flag; dom rpcErr: RpcErr): formula;
  (¬proc↓ProcTag=Procs ∨ ¬ArgNum(num,proc)) ∧
  rpcErr=BadCall ∧ flg=exception ∧
  ¬Between(α,t₁,t₂,Read:[?,id?,internal]) ∧
  ¬Between(α,t₁,t₂,Write:[?,?,id?,internal]) ∧
  ¬Between(α,t₁,t₂,Return:[?,?,?,id?,internal])
end;
```

```
func OneSuccessfulRpcCall(string α: Trace; pos t₁: α; pos t₂: α;
        dom proc: TProc; dom lst: Args; dom val: Value;
        dom flg: Flag; dom rpcErr: RpcErr; dom id: Ident): formula;
  ∃ dom retErr: RetErr.
    ExactlyOneProcCallBetween(α,t₁,t₂,proc,lst↓Loc,lst↓Value,val,flg,retErr,id);
    flg=exception ⇒ (retErr=BadArg ⇔ rpcErr=BadArg;
                     retErr=MemFailure ⇔ rpcErr=MemFailure)
end;
```

```
func OneUnSuccessfulRpcCall(string α: Trace; pos t₁: α; pos t₂: α;
        dom proc: TProc; dom lst: Args; dom val: Value;
        dom flg: Flag; dom rpcErr: RpcErr; dom id: Ident): formula;
  flg=exception;rpcErr=RPCFailure;
  ∃ dom val₁: Value; dom flg₁: Flag; dom err: RetErr.
    ExactlyOneProcCallBetween(α,t₁,t₂,proc,lst↓Loc,lst↓Value,val₁,flg₁,err,id);
end;
```

```
func NoCallOfAnyProcedure(string α: Trace; pos t₁: α; pos t₂: α;
        dom flg: Flag; dom rpcErr: RpcErr; dom id: Ident): formula;
  flg=exception ∧ rpcErr=RPCFailure ∧
  ¬Between(α,t₁,t₂,Read:[?,id?,internal]) ∧
  ¬Between(α,t₁,t₂,Write:[?,?,id?,internal]) ∧
  ¬Between(α,t₁,t₂,Return:[?,?,?,id?,internal])
end;
```

The macro ExactlyOneProcCallBetween specifies that exactly one call of procedure proc with parameters l,v,flg and retErr occurred between t_1 and t_2, and no other internal procedure call occurred. Note that macro ABadCall additionally to the description specifies that no internal procedure call occurs.

Problem 2 *Write a formal specification of the RPC component.*
The RPC component is specified by the system RPC.

6.2 The implementation

A Memory component is implemented by combining an RPC component with
a reliable memory component. A read or write call is forwarded to the reliable
memory by an appropriate call to the RPC component, and the return event
from the RPC component is transmitted back to the caller.

We specify the implementation of the memory component Impl by the compound system:

$$\text{Impl} = \text{MemImpl}(id_0) \parallel \ldots \parallel \text{MemImpl}(id_k) \parallel \text{InnerMem}$$

defined by composing the systems MemImpl(id) specifying the allowed read and
write procedures for fixed process identities id. Each of the systems MemImpl(id)
are themselves compound systems:

$$\text{MemImpl}(id) = \text{Clerk}(id) \parallel \text{RPC}(id) \parallel \text{IRMemSpec}(id)$$

For a fixed process identity id in Ident, the system Clerk(id) with observable events
Read:[?,id,observable], Write:[?,id,observable] and Return:[?,?,?,id,observable], and
internal events Mem:[?,?,?,?,id], Read:[?,id,internal], Write:[?,id,internal],
Return:[?,?,?,id,internal], RemoteCall:[?,?,?,id] and RpcReturn:[?,?,?,id] specifies the
allowed behaviors of read and write procedure calls involving the process with
identity id. That is, it specifies how a local procedure call is forwarded to a remote procedure call and how the return of a remote procedure call is forwarded
back as the return of the procedure call. The normalized traces of Clerk(id) are
defined by the macro:

```
func Clerk(string α: Trace; dom id: Ident): formula;
    BlockingCalls(α,id,observable);
    RPCReadStub(α,id);
    RPCWriteStub(α,id);
    RPCReturnStub(α,id);
    RetryOnlyOnRPCFailure(α,id);
    RpcOnlyInObsCall(α,id)
end;
```

That is, γ is a normalized trace of Clerk(id) if and only if Clerk(γ,id) is true. The
system Clerk(id) is then given by the triple:

$$\text{Clerk}(id) = (\text{Clerk}(id), \text{ObsClerk}(id), \text{IntClerk}(id))$$

where ObsClerk(id) and IntClerk(id) are the obvious macros.

The second, third, fourth and fifth clauses of Clerk(id) are fairly direct translations of the informal description [4].

*A Read or Write call is forwarded to the Reliable Memory by issuing
the appropriate call to the RPC component.*

```
func RPCReadStub(string α: Trace; dom id: Ident): formula;
  ∀ dom l: Loc; pos t₁,t₂: α.
    (Opr(α,t₁,t₂, Read:[l?,id?,observable],Return:[?,?,?,id?,observable],id,observable)
    ⇒
    ∃ pos tc,tr: α.
    (t₁<tc; tr<t₂;
    RpcOpr(α,tc,tr,RemoteCall:[[ReadProc,ok],n1,[l?,?],id?],RpcReturn:[?,?,?,id?],id)))
end;
```

The macro **RPCWriteStub** is similar.

If this call returns without raising an RPCFailure exception, the value returned is
returned to the caller. (An exceptional return causes an exception to be raised.)

```
func RPCReturnStub(string α: Trace; dom id: Ident): formula;
  ∀ dom val₁: Value; dom flg: Flag; dom retErr: RetErr; pos t₁: α.
    α(t₁)=Return:[val₁?,flg?,retErr?,id?,observable]
    ⇒
    ∃ dom val₂: Value; dom rpcErr: RpcErr; pos t₀: α.
    t₀<t₁; α(t₀)=RpcReturn:[val₂?,flg?,rpcErr?,id?];
    ¬Between(α,t₀,t₁,RpcReturn:[?,?,?,id?]);
    flg=normal ⇒ val₁=val₂;
    (flg=exception;rpcErr=RPCFailure) ⇒ (retErr=MemFailure;
    (flg=exception;¬rpcErr=RPCFailure) ⇒ (retErr=BadArg ⇔ rpcErr=BadArg;
                                          retErr=MemFailure ⇔ rpcErr=MemFailure)
end;
```

If the call raises an RPCFailure exception, then the implementation may either
reissue the call to the RPC component or raise a MemFailure exception.

```
func RetryOnlyOnRPCFailure(string α: Trace; dom id: Ident): formula;
  ∀ pos t₁,t₂: α.
    t₁<t₂;
    α(t₁)=RemoteCall:[?,?,?,id?];
    α(t₂)=RemoteCall:[?,?,?,id?];
    ¬Between(α,t₁,t₂,Read:[?,id?,observable]) ∧
    ¬Between(α,t₁,t₂,Write:[?,?,id?,observable]) ∧
    ¬Between(α,t₁,t₂,Return:[?,?,?,id?,observable])
    ⇒
    ∃ pos t: α. t₁<t;t<t₂; α(t)=RpcReturn:[?,exception,RPCFailure,id?]
end;
```

The last clause, RpcOnlyInObsCall(α,id) specifies that a remote procedure call
only occurs as the forwarding of an observable procedure call.

The systems IRMemSpec(id) specify a reliable memory with no observable
events and internal events Mem:[?,?,?,?,id], Read:[?,id,internal], Write:[?,id,internal]
and Return:[?,?,?,id,internal]:

$$\text{IRMemSpec(id)} = \text{IMemSpec(id)} \parallel \text{IReliable(id)}$$

where IReliable(id) are the systems with the same alphabets as IMemSpec(id) and with normalized traces given by Reliable(id,internal), and where IMemSpec(id) are defined by composition:

$$\text{IMemSpec(id)} = \text{IReadSpec(id)} \parallel \text{IWriteSpec(id)}$$

of the systems:

$$\text{IReadSpec(id)} = (\text{ReadSpec(id,internal)},\text{ObsReadSpec(id,internal)},\text{IntReadSpec(id)})$$

and the similarly defined systems IWriteSpec(id).

Problem 3 *Write a formal specification of the implementation, and prove that it correctly implements the specification of the Memory component of Problem 1.*

The implementation is specified by the system Impl. We devote the next section to proving the correctness of the implementation.

7 Verifying the Implementation

We want to verify that the system Impl is an implementation of the system Spec. The trivial part is to check that the systems are comparable by instantiation of formula (1).

Now the obvious way to attempt verifying that the implementation is correct is to check if the formula:

$$\text{MemImpl}(\gamma,id_0) \Rightarrow \text{MemSpec}(\gamma,id_0) \tag{7}$$

holds. This is however not the case. Feeding it to the MONA tool results in the following counterexample of length 13:

```
Read:[[l1,ok],id0,observable]
RemoteCall:[[ReadProc,ok],n1,[[l1,ok],?],id0]
Read:[[l1,ok],id0,internal]
Mem:[rd,l1,v1,normal,id0]
Return:[[v1,ok],normal,?,id0,internal]
RpcReturn:[[initVal,?],exception,RPCFailure,id0]
RemoteCall:[[ReadProc,ok],n1,[[l1,ok],?],id0]
Read:[[l1,ok],id0,internal]
Mem:[rd,l1,v1,normal,id0]
Return:[[v1,ok],normal,?,id0,internal]
RpcReturn:[[v1,ok],normal,?,id0]
Return:[[v1,ok],normal,?,id0,observable]
empty
```

where we have left out most of the typing information. The counterexample tells us that a successful read operation of the implementation may contain two RPC procedure calls each triggering an atomic read whereas such a read operation is not allowed by the specification. Hence, the counterexample reflects that whereas the specification requires a successful read to contain exactly one atomic read the implementation of the memory allows more than one.

An atomic read is however an internal event and fortunately, we can follow our method explained in Section 4.

To avoid explicitly building the compound system $\text{Impl}(\gamma)$ of the implementation, we apply the proof rule of Theorem 7.

First, we check and see that the systems $\text{MemImpl}(\gamma,\text{id}) \parallel \text{InnerMem}(\gamma)$ and $\text{MemSpec}(\gamma,\text{id}) \parallel \text{InnerMem}(\gamma)$ for $\text{id} = \text{id}_0,\text{id}_1$ are comparable by running the proper instantiations of formula (1). Let Obs denote a macro defining their common alphabet of observable events and note that the internal events are defined by $\text{IntMemImpl}(\text{id})$ and $\text{IntMemSpec}(\text{id})$, respectively. Let

> **func** Observe(**string** α: Trace; **string** β: α; **dom** id: Ident): **formula**;
> $\forall$**pos** t: α.(Obs(α(t),id) $\vee$ Obs(β(t),id)) $\Rightarrow$ α(t)= β(t)
> **end**;

and let

> **func** R(**string** α: Trace; **string** β: α; **dom** id: Ident): **formula**;
>   Observe(α,β,id); MemSpec(β,id);InnerMem(β)
> **end**;

We then prove that:

$$(\text{MemImpl}(\gamma,\text{id});\text{InnerMem}(\gamma)) \Rightarrow \exists\textbf{string } \beta: \gamma.R(\gamma,\beta,\text{id}) \tag{8}$$

is a tautology (for $\text{id} = \text{id}_0,\text{id}_1$; the formulas are symmetric) using our tool. Thus by Proposition 6 and Theorem 3, the system $\text{MemImpl}(\gamma,\text{id}) \parallel \text{InnerMem}(\gamma)$ implements $\text{MemSpec}(\gamma,\text{id}) \parallel \text{InnerMem}(\gamma)$ for $\text{id} = \text{id}_0,\text{id}_1$.

As discussed in Section 4, the compatibility requirement of Theorem 7 amounts to checking the formula (4). However, the MONA tool can not handle the state explosion caused by the existential quantification on the right hand side of the implication. Intuitively, the existential quantification guesses the internal behavior of the trace β needed to match the observable behavior of the trace γ. We can however help guessing by constraining further for each trace γ of the implementation the possible choices of matching traces β of the specification. To do this we formulate more precise (smaller) trace abstractions based on adding information of the relation between the internal behavior on the implementation and specification level.

In particular, we formalize the intuition we gained from the counterexample above that between a successful read call and the corresponding return on the implementation level exactly the last atomic read should be matched by an atomic read on the specification level. This is formalized by the macro:

> **func** Map$_1$(**string** α: Trace; **string** β: α; **dom** id: Ident): **formula**;
> $\forall$**pos** t_1,t_2: α.
>   Opr(α,t_1,t_2,Read:[?,id?,observable],Return:[?,normal,?,id?,observable],id,observable)
> $\Rightarrow$
> $\exists$**pos** t: α.
> $t_1<t;t<t_2$;

$\alpha(t)=Mem:[rd,?,?,?,id?];$
$\alpha(t)=\beta(t);$
$\neg Between(\beta,t_1,t,Mem:[rd,?,?,?,id?]);$
$\neg Between(\beta,t,t_2,Mem:[rd,?,?,?,id?]);$
$\neg Between(\alpha,t,t_2,Mem:[rd,?,?,?,id?])$
end;

Also, we define the macro Map$_2$ specifying that an atomic read on the implementation level is matched either by the same atomic read or by a τ on the specification level:

func Map$_2$(**string** α: Trace; **string** β: α; **dom** id: Ident): **formula**;
  $\forall$**pos** t: $\alpha.\alpha(t)=Mem:[rd,?,?,?,id?] \Rightarrow (\alpha(t)=\beta(t) \lor \beta(t)=\tau)$
end;

and the macro Map$_3$ specifying that any internal event but an atomic read on the implementation level is matched by the same atomic read on the specification level and conversely, that any internal event on the specification level is matched by the same event on the implementation level:

func Map$_3$(**string** α: Trace; **string** β: α; **dom** id: Ident): **formula**;
  $\forall$**pos** t: $\alpha.$
    $(IntMemImpl(\alpha(t),id) \land \neg\alpha(t)=Mem:[rd,?,?,?,id?]) \lor IntMemSpec(\beta(t),id)$
  $\Rightarrow$
    $\alpha(t)=\beta(t)$
end

We sum up the requirements in the macro:

func C(**string** α: Trace; **string** β: α): **formula**;
  Map$_1$(α,β,id$_0$); Map$_2$(α,β,id$_0$); Map$_3$(α,β,id$_0$);
  Map$_1$(α,β,id$_1$); Map$_2$(α,β,id$_1$); Map$_3$(α,β,id$_1$)
end;

We prove using our tool that:

$$MemImpl(\gamma,id_0);InnerMem(\gamma) \Rightarrow \exists\textbf{string }\beta: \gamma.(C(\gamma,\beta)) \land R(\gamma,\beta,id_0)) \qquad (9)$$

is a tautology (for id = id$_0$,id$_1$; the formulas are symmetric) and conclude by Proposition 6 that C $\cap$ R(id) is a trace abstraction from the system MemImpl(γ,id) $\|$ InnerMem(γ) to the system MemSpec(γ,id) $\|$ InnerMem(γ) for id = id$_0$,id$_1$. Finally, by running our tool we prove that the formula:

$$\exists\textbf{string }\beta_0: \gamma.(C(\gamma,\beta_0) \land R(\gamma,\beta_0,id_0)) \land \exists\textbf{string }\beta_1: \gamma.(C(\gamma,\beta_1) \land R(\gamma,\beta_1,id_1))$$
$$\Rightarrow \qquad\qquad\qquad\qquad\qquad\qquad\qquad\qquad\qquad\qquad\qquad\qquad\qquad (10)$$
$$\exists\textbf{string }\beta: \gamma. (C(\gamma,\beta) \land R(\gamma,\beta,id_0) \land R(\gamma,\beta,id_1))$$

is a tautology and hence verify the compatibility requirement of Theorem 7 and conclude that Impl(γ) implements Spec(γ).

An alternative reaction to the failure of proving (7) is to claim to have found an error in the informal description and change the description such that it allows the behavior described by the counterexample. In our formal specification, this would amount to simply changing the macro CheckSuccessfulRead to require that at least one atomic read occurs instead of exactly one. Hence modified, we prove using our tool that the formula (7) is a tautology. Likewise, we prove the symmetric formula with id_0 replaced for id_1 and conclude by propositional logic that:

$$\begin{array}{c} \mathsf{MemImpl}(\gamma,id_0);\mathsf{MemImpl}(\gamma,id_1);\mathsf{InnerMem}(\gamma) \\ \Rightarrow \\ \mathsf{MemSpec}(\gamma,id_0);\mathsf{MemSpec}(\gamma,id_1);\mathsf{InnerMem}(\gamma) \end{array} \qquad (11)$$

and therefore by definition that:

$$\mathsf{Impl}(\gamma) \Rightarrow \mathsf{Spec}(\gamma)$$

Note that when dealing with automatic verification, the difference between the two solutions may be significant since the first, in contrast to the second, involves the projecting out of internal behavior and hence a potential exponential blow-up in the size of the underlying automata.

The full solution is written in 11 pages of FIDO code. All the formulas (5), (6), (7), (8), (9) and (10) are decided within minutes. The largest FIDO formulas specify M2L formulas of size half a million characters. During processing the MONA tool handles formulas with more than 32 free variables corresponding to deterministic automata with alphabets of size 2^{32}. The proofs of (8), (9) and (10) required user intervention in terms of explicit orderings of the BDD variables

References

1. *This volume.*
2. M. Abadi and L. Lamport. The existence of refinement mappings. *Theoretical Computer Science*, 82(2):253–284, 1991.
3. M. Abadi and L. Lamport. Conjoining specifications. Technical Report Report 118, Digital Equipment Corporation, Systems Research Center, 1993.
4. M. Broy and L. Lamport. The RPC-Memory Specification Problem. A case study for the Dagstuhl Seminar 9439. This volume.
5. E.M. Clark, I.A. Browne, and R.P. Kurshan. A unified approach for showing language containment and equivalence between various types of ω-automata. In A. Arnold, editor, *CAAP, LNCS 431*, pages 103–116, 1990.
6. R. Cleaveland, J. Parrow, and B. Steffen. The Concurrency Workbench: A semantics-based tool for the verification of concurrent systems. *ACM Transactions on Programming Languages and Systems*, 15(1):36–72, jan 1993.
7. E.A. Emerson. Temporal and modal logic. In J. van Leeuwen, editor, *Handbook of Theoretical Computer Science*, volume B, chapter 16, pages 995–1072. MIT Press/Elsevier, 1990.
8. U. Engberg, P. Grønning, and L. Lamport. Mechanical verification of concurrent systems with tla. In *Computer Aided Verification, CAV '92*. Springer-Verlag, 1993. Lecture Notes in Computer Science, Vol. 663.
9. U. Engberg. Reasoning in temporal logic of actions. Ph.D. Thesis, 1996.
10. Z. Har'El and R.P. Kurshan. Software for analytical development of communications protocols. Technical report, AT&T Technical Journal, 1990.

11. J.G. Henriksen, O.J.L. Jensen, M.E. Jørgensen, N. Klarlund, R. Paige, T. Rauhe, and A.B. Sandholm. Mona: Monadic second-order logic in practice. In U.H. Engberg, K.G. Larsen, and A. Skou, editors, *Procedings of the Workshop on Tools and Algorithms for the Construction and Analysis of Systems*, pages 58–73, 1995. BRICS Notes Series NS-95-2.

12. C.A.R. Hoare. *Communicating Sequential Processes*. Prentice-Hall, 1985.

13. Y. Kesten, Z. Manna, and A. Pnueli. Temporal verification and simulation and refinement. In *A Decade of Concurrency*, pages 273–346. ACM, Springer-Verlag, 1993. Lecture Notes in Computer Science, Vol. 803, Proceedings of the REX School/Symposium, Noordwijkerhout, The Netherlands, June 1993.

14. N. Klarlund, M. Nielsen, and K. Sunesen. Automated logical verification based on trace abstractions. In *Proc. Fifteenth ACM Symp. on Princ. of Distributed Computing (PODC)*. ACM, 1996.

15. N. Klarlund and F.B. Schneider. Proving nondeterministically specified safety properties using progress measures. *Information and Computation*, 107(1):151–170, 1993.

16. N. Klarlund and M.I. Schwartzbach. Logical programming for regular trees. In preparation, 1996.

17. R. Kurshan. *Computer-Aided Verification of Coordinating Processes*. Princeton Univ. Press, 1994.

18. L. Lamport. Specifying concurrent program modules. *ACM Transactions on Programming Languages and Systems*, 5(2):190–222, 1983.

19. L. Lamport. The temporal logic of actions. *ACM Transactions on Programming Languages and Systems*, 16(3):872–923, 1994.

20. N. Lynch and M. Tuttle. Hierarchical correctness proofs for distributed algorithms. In *Proc. Sixth Symp. on the Principles of Distributed Computing*, pages 137–151. ACM, 1987.

21. N. Lynch and F. W. Vaandrager. Forward and backward simulations – part i: untimed systems. Technical Report CS-R9313, Centrum voor Wiskunde en Informatica, CWI, Computer Science/Department of Software Technology, 1993.

22. Z. Manna and et al. STeP: The stanford temporal prover. In *Theory and Practice of Software Development (TAPSOFT)*. Springer-Verlag, 1995. Lecture Notes in Computer Science, Vol. 915.

23. Z. Manna and A. Pnueli. *The Temporal Logic of Reactive and Concurrent Systems*. Springer-Verlag, 1991.

24. K. L. McMillan. *Symbolic Model Checking*. PhD thesis, Carnegie Mellon University, 1993.

25. A.P. Sistla. On verifying that a concurrent program satisfies a nondeterministic specification. *Information Processing Letters*, 32(1):17–24, July 1989.

Incremental Specification with Joint Actions: The RPC-Memory Specification Problem

Reino Kurki-Suonio

Tampere University of Technology
Software Systems Laboratory
P.O. Box 553, FIN-33101 Tampere, Finland

Abstract. Solutions to the RPC-Memory Specification Problem are developed incrementally, using an object-oriented modeling formalism with multi-object actions. Incrementality is achieved by superposition-based derivation steps that make effective use of multiple inheritance and specialization of inherited actions. Each stage models collective behaviors of objects at some level of abstraction, and the preservation of all safety properties is guaranteed in each step. The aim of the approach is to support a design methodology that combines operational intuition with formal reasoning in TLA and is suited for the use of animation tools.

1 Introduction

The execution model of joint actions was introduced in 1983 [5, 6]. Since then it has been used both in connection with refinement calculus [4] and as a basis for an object-oriented specification language (DisCo) for reactive systems [11, 10]. Conceptually this execution model is related to production system languages, although the aims are different. Basically, a joint action system behaves like a single guarded loop in Dijkstra's guarded command language, where repeated nondeterministic selections are made for the "action" to be executed next. A similar execution model has also been adopted in Unity [9], but with a different approach to guards and fairness.

Based on this execution model, DisCo has been developed as an object-oriented specification language with multi-object actions instead of single-object methods. An important concern in its design has been to support incremental development of specifications with superposition-based transformations. A tool is also available for graphical animation and testing of DisCo specifications [17]. Temporal Logic of Actions (TLA) [15] is used as the formal basis, and PVS [16] is used for the development of proof support [13].

Specifications derived using this approach are formal models that allow rigorous reasoning in TLA. They also have an operational interpretation that conforms to software engineer's intuition about software, although they need not be executable without human assistance. The aim of the approach is to combine the advantages of operational intuition and formal reasoning, using a formal basis in logics and a formally based design methodology.

This paper demonstrates how the approach can be used to derive solutions to the RPC-Memory Specification Problem [8]. The notations are different from

DisCo, although the facilities used are available in it. (Syntactically DisCo looks more like a programming language, it has only typed variables, relations between objects are currently given in terms of explicit pointer variables, and action refinement and inheritance are included in a somewhat different form.) Incrementality is utilized in the manner supported by the language. A specification style with many simple objects is used, instead of the alternative of having fewer objects with heavier data structures.

Model-oriented solutions are derived for all parts of the specification problem. For simplicity, some of the initial conditions are given only verbally instead of formal expressions. The models are formal, but it is beyond the language to distinguish which of their variables must be represented in an implementation, and which are auxiliary specification variables that need not be implemented. In general, implementation correctness therefore depends on information that has to be supplied in addition to the model. In this example such information is needed for the correctness proofs, which use known proof techniques (see e.g. [1, 12]), and are only outlined in this paper.

In the rest of the paper, Section 2 describes the theoretical foundations of the approach in TLA. After that, solutions to the problem are derived in seven steps, and the paper ends with some concluding remarks.

2 Foundations in TLA

The theoretical foundations of the approach are in Temporal Logic of Actions (TLA). A detailed description of TLA can be found in [15]; the reader is also referred to another article in this volume [3], which gives a TLA solution to the RPC-memory specification problem. Some of the fundamental aspects of the approach are related to TLA in this section.

2.1 Correspondence to Canonical TLA Expressions

There is a close correspondence between DisCo and *canonical* TLA expressions. A model given in DisCo always corresponds to a TLA expression of the form

$$P \wedge \Box[\mathcal{A}_1 \vee \cdots \vee \mathcal{A}_m]_U \wedge \mathrm{SF}(\mathcal{F}_1) \wedge \mathrm{SF}(\mathcal{F}_2) \wedge \cdots, \qquad (1)$$

where

- U is the collection of program variables that are of interest,
- P is an initial condition, which is assumed to be satisfiable,
- $\mathcal{A}_i$ are TLA actions that correspond to the actions given as syntactic units in DisCo, and
- $\mathrm{SF}(\mathcal{F}_j)$ are strong fairness formulas with respect to actions $\mathcal{F}_j$, each $\mathcal{F}_j$ being a special case of some $\mathcal{A}_i$, i.e., $\mathcal{F}_j \Rightarrow \mathcal{A}_i$.

Expression (1) has a natural operational interpretation: execution may start in any state that satisfies P, each execution step must satisfy one of actions $\mathcal{A}_i$, and a "scheduler" is assumed to see to it that none of actions $\mathcal{F}_j$ is infinitely often enabled without being executed infinitely often. In particular, execution may not terminate in a state where any $\mathcal{F}_j$ is enabled.

Since each $\mathcal{F}_j$ implies some $\mathcal{A}_i$, the execution can never lead to a situation which could not be completed into a legal behavior. This is true also with a countably infinite number of fairness formulas.

Usually actions $\mathcal{A}_i$ are non-stuttering (i.e., they necessarily modify some variable in U) and disjoint (i.e., conjunctions $\mathcal{A}_i \wedge \mathcal{A}_j$ are identically false for $i \neq j$). When this is the case, there is a unique correspondence between the non-stuttering steps in a behavior and the given DisCo actions.

Compared to the general possibilities of canonical TLA formulas, there are syntactic restrictions on the (strong) fairness requirements that can be expressed. For simplicity, the possibility of modeling weak fairness requirements is left out of the language. It should be noticed, however, that arbitrary additional TLA properties can be taken as additional assumptions in formal proofs.

2.2 Objects and Actions

The notion of *objects* is used to impose structure on the collection of program variables U in (1). A program variable may be local to an object, and objects of the same *class* have the same structure of local variables. *Relations* between objects can also be introduced. In terms of TLA, relations represent additional program variables that are not local to objects.

The number of objects in each class is either finite or countably infinite. A specification can often be given independently of these sizes. The possibility for infinite classes is needed for the modeling of unbounded situations without burdening the language with facilities for dynamic creation of objects. (Some simple restrictions are used to guarantee finite representability of an infinite state.) While proofs can be carried out independently of class sizes, animation tools, for instance, require specific instantiations, where class sizes (and all other aspects of the intial state) are fixed.

For the operational interpretation, *actions* are atomic units of execution. That is, once an action is started, it will eventually be completed, and no other action can interfere with it during its execution. Therefore, the simplistic idea of a sequential action scheduler is not in conflict with concurrency in implementation.

DisCo actions are multi-object actions that may involve several objects as "participants." Indicating only the classes of the participants means that actions are patterns for similar actions between all possible combinations of participants. Therefore, a TLA action $\mathcal{A}_i$, corresponding to a single DisCo action, contains existential quantification over all objects in the participant classes. Classes and the associated actions can be displayed graphically, as illustrated in Figure 1.

Syntactically, actions are given in the form $g \rightarrow S$, where g is an enabling condition or *guard*, and S is the *body* that indicates how the action modifies the local states of the participants and the relations in which they are involved. To keep S deterministic and still allow nondeterministic effects, an action may have *parameters*, which are existentially quantified values that can be constrained

Fig. 1. Graphical illustration of actions.

by the guard. In terms of TLA, the parameter notation is also understood as a shorthand for further (list-valued) program variables (different variables for each action and different subsets of participants) to which the parameter values are implicitely appended in action bodies.

Unlike in conventional programming languages, actions are not executed as a result of explicit calls. Instead, an implicit scheduler invokes enabled actions non-deterministically. Another difference to programming languages is that objects are unnamed, and they can be referenced only as participants within actions, and by expressions that are quantified over classes.

The notion of objects makes the possibility for distributed implementation explicit. An implementation is always allowed to execute concurrently actions that involve disjoint sets of objects.

Fairness requirements are given by marking some participants as "fair." An action cannot be infinitely often enabled for the same object as a fair participant without being infinitely often executed for it. Similarly, an action parameter can be fair, indicating that the action cannot be infinitely often enabled for the same parameter value without being infinitely often executed for it. With infinite classes or infinite domains for parameters, one fairness marking in DisCo may therefore give rise to an infinite number of fairness formulas in (1).

With more than one fairness marking it is required that an action cannot be infinitely often enabled for any set of objects (and/or values) as fair participants (and/or parameters), without being infinitely often executed for this set. This interpretation avoids the danger that addition of fairness markings might invalidate some liveness properties in the presence of infinite classes.

2.3 Refinement by Superposition

DisCo supports extension and refinement of a model by *superposition*. Omitting fairness formulas for a moment, this means in terms of TLA that a formula

$$P \wedge \Box[\mathcal{A}_1 \vee \cdots \vee \mathcal{A}_m]_U \tag{2}$$

is transformed into

$$Q \wedge \Box[\mathcal{B}_1 \vee \cdots \vee \mathcal{B}_n]_V, \tag{3}$$

where

- the set of program variables is extended to V, $U \subseteq V$,
- the initial condition P is strengthened into Q, $Q \Rightarrow P$, and
- each action $\mathcal{B}_j$ is either a *refinement* of some old action $\mathcal{A}_i$, $\mathcal{B}_j \Rightarrow \mathcal{A}_i$, or a *new* action that has no affect on variables in U.

Obviously, (3) then implies (2), i.e., superposition preserves all safety properties.

For liveness properties, consider safety formula (2) together with a fairness requirement $\mathrm{SF}(\mathcal{F})$, where $\mathcal{F}$ is a special case of some action $\mathcal{A}_i$, and let $\mathcal{A}_i$ be refined in (3) into $\mathcal{B}_j$. To preserve the operational interpretation, $\mathrm{SF}(\mathcal{F})$ needs then to be weakened in connection with (3) into $\mathrm{SF}(\mathcal{F} \wedge \mathcal{B}_j)$, which means that liveness properties cannot always be preserved.

A simple special case where the weakened fairness condition is equivalent to the original one is the situation where the enabling conditions of $\mathcal{F}$ and $\mathcal{F} \wedge \mathcal{B}_j$ are the same. More generally, it is sufficient that enabling of $\mathcal{F}$ always leads to enabling of $\mathcal{F} \wedge \mathcal{B}_j$,

$$Enabled(\mathcal{F}) \rightsquigarrow Enabled(\mathcal{F} \wedge \mathcal{B}_j).$$

This provides a practical proof obligation for showing that also liveness properties are preserved in a superposition step.

In terms of object-oriented concepts, extending the set of program variables means extension of classes with further local variables, and introduction of new classes. *Subclasses* can be introduced when one does not want to extend all objects of a given (super)class. As default, capability to participate in actions is *inherited* to subclasses. Refining an action for a given subclass gives a possibility to specialize inherited actions, as illustrated in Figure 2.

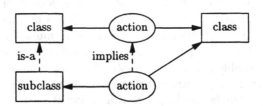

Fig. 2. Specialization of an inherited action.

No special complications are caused by multiple inheritance, i.e., by allowing a subclass to have several superclasses. In this case objects of the subclass have all the attributes and capabilities of all its superclasses, with all (combined) action specializations introduced for them.

2.4 Combination of Specifications

DisCo supports the combination of specifications in a way that provides superposition on each of them. The general situation, where the specifications to be combined are independent refinements of the same original system, is illustrated in Figure 3. Actions $\mathcal{A}$ and $\mathcal{B}$ are there refined independently in two different systems, which also introduce new actions $\mathcal{C}_1$ and $\mathcal{C}_2$. For purposes of explanation, consider the two refinements also to contain stuttering actions $Stut_1$ and $Stut_2$ that do not modify any variables.

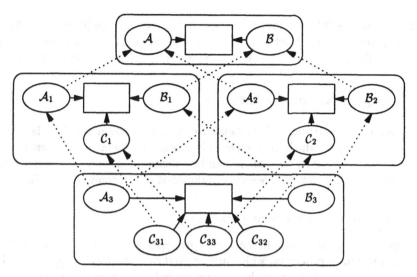

Fig. 3. Combining independent refinements.

When the two specifications are combined (and possibly refined further), actions A_1 and A_2 are "synchronized" into action A_3 that implies both of them, and similarly for B. No synchronization of A_1 and B_2, or A_2 and B_1, is produced, since these would give identically false actions, if A and B are non-stuttering and disjoint. The same would hold for synchronizing A_1 or B_1 with $Stut_2$, or one of A_2 and B_2 with $Stut_1$. As for C_1 and C_2, their possible synchronizations are with each other (action C_{33}) and with $Stut_2$ and $Stut_1$, respectively (actions C_{31} and C_{32}).

The simple format of actions has the consequence that synchronized combinations of actions can always be formed by conjuncting their guards and concatenating their bodies.

Obviously, all class extensions, subclasses, and new classes of the independent refinements are also included in the combined system, although such aspects have been omitted from Figure 3.

2.5   Modeling vs. Specification

This approach gives *closed models* that always model also the environment where the specified system is supposed to operate. The language makes, however, no distinction between the two. Therefore, to implement a system in reality, one also has to know which of the actions are on the responsibility of the system to be implemented, and which describe assumptions about the environment.

For a model-oriented specification it is also important to know, which program variables are needed in an implementation, and which need not be represented. The latter are often called *specification variables*. In the TLA formalism specification variables are quantified by a (boldface) existential quantifier.

In DisCo this information is also left outside of the language. This means that, in proving that a model is a correct implementation of another, one may need to utilize information that is not expressed in the modeling language.

3   Components and Processes

An incremental derivation of solutions to the specification problem is started with a simple layer, which introduces only the basic notions of *components* and *processes*. In principle, a component can be thought of as a static structure that determines how the processes executing the code of the component behave.

3.1   Component and Process Classes

A component may have both independent processes, which are executed without calls, and interface processes, which are invoked by calls to the component. The given specification problem needs also components that may lose calls issued to them, or give up calls issued by them. Component class C_{00} is introduced for this level of generality by a trivial definition without any local variables:

$$\textbf{class } C_{00} : \{\}.$$

A process $p \in P_0$ is modeled as an object whose current state (the value computed by the process so far) is given by a single untyped local variable:

$$\textbf{class } P_0 : \{value\}.$$

Each process $p \in P_0$ is associated with a fixed component $c \in C_{00}$. This relation is denoted as "*of*," and we write $p \cdot of \cdot c$ when the relation holds. Definition

$$\textbf{const relation } (+) \cdot of \cdot (1) : P_0 \times C_{00}$$

indicates that the relation cannot be modified by any action, that for each $p \in P_0$ there is exactly one $c \in C_{00}$ for which $p \cdot of \cdot c$ holds, and for each $c \in C_{00}$ there is at least one $p \in P_0$ for which it holds ("+" standing for "at least one").
    Notice that no restrictions have been given for the number of components, or for the number of processes associated with each of them. These numbers can therefore be arbitrary, either finite or (countably) infinite.

3.2   Computational Steps by Processes

This first layer models a system of processes with only one kind of actions, which represents a computational step for modifying the value computed by a process:

$$step(p : P_0; \ c : C_{00}; \ val) \ : \ p \cdot of \cdot c$$
$$\rightarrow p.value' = val.$$

Both a process p and the associated component c are given as participants, and the new value for $p.value$ is given as parameter val. The actual parameter value is not constrained by the guard at this level, but it will be contrained by refinements to be introduced in subsequent layers.

Action bodies are written as sequences of "assignments," with primed variables denoting the updated values. Variables that are left unchanged are not explicitly indicated. No fairness requirements have been associated with the actions at this stage. Therefore, there are no requirements for executing *step*.

For each variable introduced in a layer, all actions that modify its value have to be given in the same layer. When sufficient information is not yet available to give such actions in a deterministic form, nondeterminism needs to be utilized as demonstrated here. Notice that later introduction of new ways to modify variables would violate safety properties.

This aspect of the design methodology is contrary to the common practice in object-oriented design that the local states of objects are designed in great detail before any actions or methods are given for their modification. It should be noticed, however, that a meaning can be given to variables only by actions that modify their values.

4 Procedure Calls

The basic mechanism for procedure calls is specified in this layer. *Interface processes* are defined as a subclass of processes, with the capability to be invoked by procedure calls and to respond to them.

4.1 Interface Processes

Compared to their superclass P_0, interface processes (class P) have three additional local variables:

$$\textbf{class } P : P_0 + \{i\_state : (Free,\ Called,\ Computing);\ proc;\ args\}.$$

The enumeration variable i_state can be understood as a state machine with three exclusive states, *Free*, *Called*, and *Computing*, indicating whether an interface process is free to be used, freshly associated with a procedure call, or computing a response. Variables $proc$ and $args$ indicate the called procedure and the arguments associated with the call. Initially, $p.i\_state = Free$ for all $p \in P$.

To allow processes to invoke procedure calls properly, their local states are extended in this connection with another attribute p_state modeling a two-state transition system,

$$\textbf{class } P_0 : P_0 + \{p\_state : (Normal,\ Waiting)\},$$

where *Waiting* indicates that the process is waiting for a response to a call. The applied occurrence of P_0 in this definition refers to the non-extended class. Since all objects of class P_0 are extended, this applies also to objects of class P. Initially, $p.p\_state = Normal$ for all $p \in P_0$, including all $p \in P$.

In the following we will be mostly interested in components that have no independent processes, i.e., for which all processes are interface processes. Such components are defined as a subclass of C_{00}:

$$\textbf{class } C_0 : C_{00};$$
$$\forall c \in C_0 : p \cdot of \cdot c \Rightarrow p \in P.$$

Procedure calls establish a relation between objects of classes P and P_0. When an interface process $q \in P$ has been called by process $p \in P_0$, we write $q \cdot called\_by \cdot p$. This is a dynamic relation, which is assumed to be initially empty, but can be modified by the actions of this layer,

$$\textbf{relation } (0..1) \cdot called\_by \cdot (0..1) : P \times P_0.$$

The ranges $0..1$ indicate that a process can call at most one process at a time, and it can itself be called by at most one process at a time. Although these properties are stated here, they are to be considered as *intended invariants*, whose preservation by actions still needs to be verified.

4.2 Calls and Returns

The actions of this layer model the dynamics of processes at a level where the main concern is in procedure calls. Before giving these actions, their intended effects are illustrated by the statechart of Figure 4. This consists of the two parallel state systems of an interface process, corresponding to enumeration variables *p_state* and *i_state*, respectively. A process that is not an interface process possesses the upper part only.

Arrows labeled by $call_p$ and $call_q$ correspond to a procedure call, indicating state transitions in the caller and the callee, respectively. Correspondingly, $return_p$ and $return_q$ describe the effects of a return. Arrows *give_up* and *lose* correspond to events where a process gives up waiting for a return, or loses a call that has been issued to it.

A process p can issue a procedure call when it is in state *Normal*:

$$
\begin{aligned}
call(p : P_0;\ c : C_{00};\ q : P;\ d : C_{00};\ n;\ a)\ :\ & p \cdot of \cdot c \\
& \wedge\ q \cdot of \cdot d \\
& \wedge\ p.p\_state = Normal \\
& \wedge\ q.i\_state = Free \\
& \rightarrow\ q \cdot called\_by' \cdot p \\
& \wedge\ p.p\_state' = Waiting \\
& \wedge\ q.i\_state' = Called \\
& \wedge\ q.proc' = n \\
& \wedge\ q.args' = a.
\end{aligned}
$$

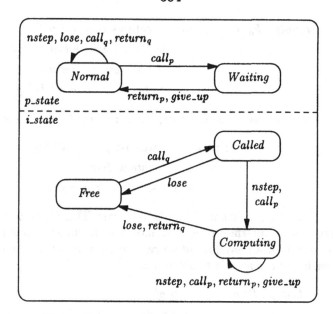

Fig. 4. State transitions of an interface process.

Parameters n and a stand for the name of the procedure to be called and the list of arguments. The guard contains no conjunct $q.p\_state = Normal$, but this will be invariantly true when $q.i\_state = Free$.

For an interface process to issue a procedure call, its i_state must not be $Free$, and after execution it must be $Computing$. Therefore, action $call$ is specialized for interface processes to impose these additional constraints:

$$call(p : P;\ c : C_{00};\ q : P;\ d : C_{00};\ n;\ a)\ :\ \textbf{refines}\ call(p, c, q, d, n, a)\ \textbf{for}\ p \in P$$
$$\&\ p.i\_state \neq Free$$
$$\rightarrow p.i\_state' = Computing.$$

The **for** clause gives the condition for which the previous version of $call$ is no longer available. Separator "&" is used between the applied occurence of $call$ and the additions to the specialized action. The complete form of the action is obtained by combining the old action (for the participants and parameters given in the applied occurrence) with these additions.

Considering action $step$, we need to decide on its effect on the new attributes of participant p. Two cases are to be distinguished. If the state is $Normal$, no new effects are needed. For state $Waiting$ the action is refined to enter state $Normal$ and to modify relation $called\_by$ accordingly, modeling a situation where the caller gives up a call that it has issued. This leads to the following refinements, which replace the previous definition of $step$:

$$nstep(p : P_0;\ c : C_{00};\ val)\ :\ \textbf{refines}\ step(p, c, val)$$
$$\&\ p.p\_state = Normal;$$

$$give\_up(p : P_0; \ c : C_{00}; \ val) \ : \ \textbf{refines } step(p, c, val)$$
$$\& \ p.p\_state = Waiting$$
$$\rightarrow p.p\_state' = Normal$$
$$\wedge \ \forall q \in P : \neg q \cdot called\_by' \cdot p.$$

For interface processes we specialize *nstep* further to modify *i_state* as follows:

$$nstep(^*p : P; \ c : C_{00}; \ val) \ : \ \textbf{refines } nstep(p, c, val) \ \textbf{for } p \in P$$
$$\& \ p.i\_state \neq Free$$
$$\rightarrow p.i\_state' = Computing.$$

The asterisk prefixing participant *p* marks it as fair. This fairness requirement has the effect that an interface process cannot stay indefinitely in state *Called*.

Since we also need a lossy procedure call mechanism, where the callee may lose a call, we introduce an additional action

$$lose(p : P; \ c : C_{00}) \ : \ p \cdot of \cdot c$$
$$\wedge \ p.p\_state = Normal$$
$$\wedge \ p.i\_state \neq Free$$
$$\rightarrow p.i\_state' = Free$$
$$\wedge \ \forall q \in P_0 : \neg p \cdot called\_by' \cdot q,$$

which is restricted to situations where the interface process is not itself waiting for a return from another procedure call.

The return from a procedure call is modeled as a third refinement of action *step* (for the caller process), in which the callee also participates:

$$return(p : P_0; \ c : C_{00}; \ ^*q : P; \ d : C_{00}; \ val) \ : \ \textbf{refines } step(p, c, val)$$
$$\& \ q \cdot of \cdot d$$
$$\wedge \ q \cdot called\_by \cdot p$$
$$\wedge \ q.i\_state = Computing$$
$$\wedge \ q.p\_state = Normal$$
$$\wedge \ p.p\_state = Waiting$$
$$\wedge \ val = q.value$$
$$\rightarrow q.i\_state' = Free$$
$$\wedge \ p.p\_state' = Normal$$
$$\wedge \ \neg q \cdot called\_by' \cdot p.$$

Giving *q* as a fair participant forces an eventual return to the caller, if *return* is enabled continually or repeatedly. In other words, once a possible return value has been computed (i.e., the callee has entered state *Computing*), if the caller stays *Waiting* (i.e., does not execute *give_up*), and the callee stays *Normal* (or repeatedly enters this state), then *return* must eventually be executed. Giving

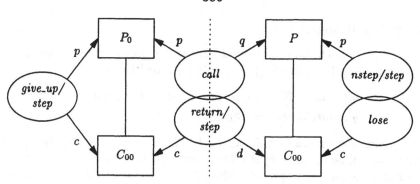

Fig. 5. Actions modeling the procedure interface.

val as a parameter for *return* would not be necessary, but this has been done to make the transmitted value visible in the action heading.

Figure 5 now illustrates the actions and their participants. The caller component and the calling process are on the left, and the callee component and the associated interface process are on the right. Solid lines indicate fixed relations between objects. In cases where actions have the same participants, the ovals standing for them are drawn overlapped, and only one set of arrows is given to indicate the participants. Action labels, like *return/step*, indicate the refinement history. The dotted vertical line separates the caller from the callee. Although not indicated in the figure, the callee may also use the procedure mechanism for further calls.

4.3 Notes on the Formalism

State machines, given as enumeration variables, can in DisCo be both nested and parallel, similarly to Statecharts. Statecharts are here used only as graphical illustrations that can be derived from the textual representation of class and action definitions. Diagrams like Figure 5 can be used as a basis for animation, showing which actions are enabled or executed, and for which participants.

Extending a class with new attributes can be understood as a shorthand for defining a subclass and requiring that all objects of the superclass belong to this subclass. From the language point of view, a dedicated extension mechanism is useful for deriving classes incrementally.

In each layer, new actions and refinements of old actions are allowed to affect only the newly introduced variables and relations, and this can be checked mechanically. Also, once a layer has been completed, no further action specializations can be given for its subclasses. (The given specializations can be refined later, like any other actions.) In the absence of explicit refinements, an old action is always implicitly refined not to modify any of the new variables.

The program variables that are relevant for the procedure interface specification are the (implicit) variables that correspond to the parameters in actions *call* and *return*. All other variables are specification variables only.

4.4 Safety Properties

If a state predicate holds in the initial state and is preserved by all actions, it is a state invariant. Denoting $S(q) = \{p \in P_0 \mid q \cdot called\_by \cdot p\}$, predicates

$$q.i\_state = Free \Rightarrow q.p\_state = Normal \wedge |S(q)| = 0,$$
$$q.i\_state \neq Free \Rightarrow |S(q)| \leq 1$$

are examples of such invariants for all $q \in P$. This shows that an interface process cannot, indeed, be in *called_by* relation to more than one process at a time.

Another simple safety property that can be proved at this level is that for each return
$$return(p, c, q, d, val)$$
there has been a corresponding call
$$call(p, c, q, d, \ldots),$$
and that no call gives rise to more than one return. This can be proved by showing that there is a state predicate Q that is turned on only by a call,

$$\Box[\neg Q \wedge Q' \Rightarrow call(p, c, q, d, \ldots)]_U,$$

and is turned off by a corresponding return,

$$\Box[return(p, c, q, d, \ldots) \Rightarrow Q \wedge \neg Q']_U.$$

Obviously, the predicate $q \cdot called\_by \cdot p$ satisfies these conditions.

4.5 Reliable Procedure Calls

Components that never lose procedure calls issued to them can be introduced as a subclass C_1 for which action *lose* is specialized into an identically false action. Similarly, components that do not give up calls issued by them can be introduced as another subclass C_2, for which action *give_up* is not possible. Considering only components in C_0 we can express this as

$$\textbf{class } C_1 : C_0;$$
$$\textbf{class } C_2 : C_0;$$
$$\textbf{remove } lose(p, c) \textbf{ for } c \in C_1;$$
$$\textbf{remove } give\_up(p, c) \textbf{ for } c \in C_2.$$

A subclass C that inherits the properties of both C_1 and C_2,

$$\textbf{class } C : C_1 + C_2;$$

gives components that belong to both of them and therefore have both of the above constraints. In the presence of components in C only, the procedure mechanism is reliable. Notice, however, that even then a procedure call need not lead to a corresponding return, since it may give rise to an infinite number of nested procedure calls.

4.6 Call Structures

In the following there is a need for structures where components are not free to call arbitrary other components. Therefore, another relation is introduced for components, and actions *call* is refined to observe it as follows:

$$\textbf{const relation } (*)\cdot may\_call\cdot(*) \; : \; C_{00} \times C_{00};$$
$$call(p : P_0; \; c : C_{00}; \; q : P; \; d : C_{00}; \; n; \; a) \; : \; \textbf{refines } call(p, c, q, d, n, a)$$
$$\& \; c\cdot may\_call\cdot d.$$

Obviously, action *return* must then also obey the same constraint.

5 Memory Components

After these preparations the specification of memory components can be given.

5.1 Memory Class

Memory components are introduced as a subclass M_0 of C,

$$\textbf{class } M_0 : C + \{\textbf{const } mem\_vals\},$$

where the constant value of variable *mem_vals* gives the set of legal values in the memory. Having this as an attribute instead of using a fixed set MemVals allows different memories to have different sets of values. The value InitVal is always assumed to belong to this set, and all exceptional values are assumed to be outside of it.

The set of memory locations MemLocs could be introduced either as another attribute of memory components, or as separate objects with a suitable relation to memory components. To avoid introduction of complex attributes, the latter alternative is chosen. A memory location is then an object of class L,

$$\textbf{class } L : \{\textbf{const } addr; \; value\},$$

where *addr* is the (fixed) address of a location, and *value* is the value stored in it. Each memory location $l \in L$ is assumed to be associated with a unique memory component indicated by relation

$$\textbf{const relation } (*)\cdot in\cdot(1) : L \times M_0,$$

and to be initialized with $l.value =$ InitVal. The locations associated with the same memory component are assumed to have distinct addresses $l.addr$.

The number of interface processes associated with a memory component determines the maximum number of concurrent read and write operations for it. Not specifying this number means that there may or may not be such a bound for a given memory.

5.2 Memory Actions

Actions for issuing calls to memory components are specialized to issue only read and write operations:

$$call\_r(p : P_0; \ c : C_{00}; \ q : P; \ d : M_0; \ loc) :$$
$$\textbf{refines } call(p, c, q, d, \mathsf{Read}, \langle loc \rangle) \textbf{ for } d \in M_0;$$
$$call\_w(p : P_0; \ c : C_{00}; \ q : P; \ d : M_0; \ loc; \ val) :$$
$$\textbf{refines } call(p, c, q, d, \mathsf{Write}, \langle loc, val \rangle) \textbf{ for } d \in M_0.$$

A memory interface process does not itself issue further procedure calls:

$$\forall c \in M_0 : |\{d \mid c \cdot may\_call \cdot d\}| = \emptyset.$$

Attempts for atomic reads and writes are given as specializations of *nstep*, where the boolean parameter b indicates whether the memory fails:

$$read(^*p : P; \ m : M_0; \ l : L; \ b : \mathsf{bool}) \ : \ \textbf{refines } nstep(p, m, val) \textbf{ for } m \in M_0$$
$$\&\ l \cdot in \cdot m$$
$$\wedge\ p.i\_state = Called$$
$$\wedge\ p.proc = \mathsf{Read}$$
$$\wedge\ l.addr = \mathsf{first}(p.args)$$
$$\wedge\ val = \text{if } b \text{ then } l.value \text{ else } \mathsf{MemFailure};$$
$$write(^*p : P; \ m : M_0; \ l : L; \ b : \mathsf{bool}) \ : \ \textbf{refines } nstep(p, m, val) \textbf{ for } m \in M_0$$
$$\&\ l \cdot in \cdot m$$
$$\wedge\ p.proc = \mathsf{Write}$$
$$\wedge\ l.addr = \mathsf{first}(p.args)$$
$$\wedge\ \mathsf{scnd}(p.args) \in m.range$$
$$\wedge\ val = \text{if } b \text{ then } \mathsf{FixedVal} \text{ else } \mathsf{MemFailure}$$
$$\rightarrow\ l.value' =$$
$$\text{if } b \text{ then } \mathsf{scnd}(p.args) \text{ else } l.value.$$

Notice that the guard of *read* allows only one atomic read for a read operation (in state *Called*), while more than one atomic writes are possible (in states *Called* and *Computing*). The indicated fairness requirements will be discussed below.

To allow bad calls, a third specialization of *nstep* is needed:

$$bad\_arg(^*p : P; \ m : M_0) \ : \ \textbf{refines } nstep(p, m, \mathsf{BadArg}) \textbf{ for } m \in M_0$$
$$\&\ (\forall l \in L : l \cdot in \cdot m \Rightarrow l.addr \neq \mathsf{first}(p.args)) \ \vee$$
$$p.proc = \mathsf{Write} \wedge \mathsf{scnd}(p.args) \notin m.range.$$

Figure 6 now illustrates the actions for memory, and their refinement histories.

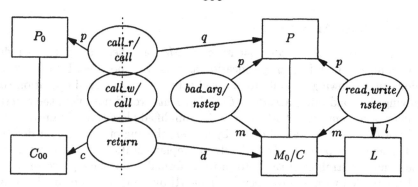

Fig. 6. Actions for memory.

5.3 Liveness Properties

Action *nstep*, which had a fairness requirement associated with it, has been specialized for memories as three different actions. Whenever the guard of *nstep* is true, one of their guards is also true. Therefore, the fairness markings imply that the fairness requirement with respect to *nstep* has not been violated.

By construction, all safety properties of the previous layers are preserved. In particular, each return from a memory component corresponds to a unique call, and no read or write operation gives rise to more than one return. The absence of further calls by a memory component allows us to strengthen this into the liveness property that each read and write call by a process in C_2 also leads to a return. Each *call_r*, for instance, enables either *read* or *bad_arg*, which in its turn enables *return*, and fairness forces their eventual execution. Notice that this property holds also when there is no bound for concurrent read and write operations.

The specification has been constructed so that an implementation which always returns MemFailure is also correct. This is a deliberate choice that slightly simplifies the construction of an RPC implementation of memory. For avoiding this possibility, consider splitting action *read* into different cases for $b = true$ and $b = false$, and marking also m as a fair participant in the former. Then no memory component could respond to all read requests by MemFailure. Doing the same with *write* actions would still allow MemFailure for all write operations, but some of the writes would then necessarily affect the memory.

Notice that marking both m and b as fair in *read* would also avoid the trivial implementation, but it would be an overspecification that would not allow a memory to be reliable.

5.4 Reliable Memory

Reliable memory components are specified as a subclass M of M_0, for which actions *read* and *write* are refined by an additional constraint $b = true$. Since this has no effect on the enabling of these actions, no liveness properties are violated, and M therefore satisfies all properties of M_0.

5.5 Simplified Memory

The actions for memory components $m \in M_0$ have been designed to reflect the wording of the informal specification as closely as possible. Intuitively it is obvious that allowing several atomic read attempts in one read operation (i.e., removing the condition $p.i\_state = Called$ in $read$) would not affect the external behavior of a memory. Let M_1 denote the simplified class thus obtained.

Since M_0 can be obtained of M_1 by a strengthening of actions that does not affect liveness properties, M_0 is clearly an implementation of M_1, but the converse is not as straightforward. To prove it formally, interface processes of M_1 can be extended with a "prophecy" variable [1] by which it can be distinguished whether a $read$ action is the last one for a given read operation or not. In a refinement relation, all but the last one of successive $read$ actions in M_1 are then determined to simulate a stuttering action in M_0. It does not matter that the values of $m.i\_state$, $m.value$ and $m.status$ do not always agree in this simulation, since these are quantified program variables. It is, however, important that memory locations always have identical contents, and that the returned values are the same.

The construction of a refinement relation will be discussed below in some more detail for a somewhat less obvious situation. We also omit here the proof that the added prophecy variable is, indeed, a prophecy variable that affects no behavioral properties.

6 The RPC Component

The specification of RPC components is independent of memories. Therefore, it can be given as another refinement of the layer where procedure calls were modeled.

6.1 RPC Component Class

An RPC component interfaces with two components, a $sender$ and a $receiver$, relaying procedure calls from the former to the latter. The relation may_call is used to express these connections. To facilitate the construction of lossy RPC components, a weaker class C^0_{rpc} is first given that may also lose calls:

$$\textbf{class } C^0_{\text{rpc}} : C_2 + \{\textbf{const } pairs\};$$
$$\forall c \in C^0_{\text{rpc}} : |\{d \mid d \cdot may\_call \cdot c\}| = |\{d \mid c \cdot may\_call \cdot d\}| = 1$$
$$\wedge\ d \cdot may\_call \cdot c \Rightarrow d \in C_1 \wedge c \cdot may\_call \cdot d \Rightarrow d \in C.$$

The value of $pairs$ is assumed to be a set of pairs $\langle proc, n \rangle$, giving the available remote procedure names and the associated numbers of parameters. This provides the required mapping $\mathsf{ArgNum}(proc)$.

Ordinary RPC components (class C_{rpc}) are easily constructed as a subclass,

$$\textbf{class } C_{\text{rpc}} : C^0_{\text{rpc}} + C;$$
$$\forall c \in C_{\text{rpc}} : d \cdot may\_call \cdot c \Rightarrow d \in C.$$

The only effect of having C as another superclass of C_{rpc} is to inherit the refinement that removes action *lose*.

6.2 RPC Actions

An RPC component accepts calls only from the associated sender, and only calls of one procedure, RemoteCall, with an argument list of length two, where the first argument is the name of a remote procedure, and the second is an argument list to be supplied with the remote call:

$$call(p : P; \ s : C_1; \ q : P; \ d : C^0_{rpc}; \ n; \ a) \ : \ \textbf{refines } call(p, s, q, d, n, a) \textbf{ for } d \in C^0_{rpc}$$
$$\& \ n = \mathsf{RemoteCall}$$
$$\wedge \ \mathsf{length}(a) = 2.$$

Proper calls should be transmitted to the receiver at most once. These are the only calls that an RPC component can issue:

$$call(^*p : P; \ c : C^0_{rpc}; \ q : P; \ r : C; \ n; \ a) \ : \ \textbf{refines } call(p, c, q, r, n, a) \textbf{ for } c \in C^0_{rpc}$$
$$\& \ p.Called$$
$$\wedge \ n = \mathsf{first}(p.args)$$
$$\wedge \ a = \mathsf{scnd}(p.args)$$
$$\wedge \ \langle n, \mathsf{length}(a) \rangle \in c.pairs.$$

For bad calls and RPC failures action *nstep* is specialized as

$$bad\_call(^*p : P; \ c : C^0_{rpc}) \ : \ \textbf{refines } nstep(p, c, \mathsf{BadCall}) \textbf{ for } c \in C^0_{rpc}$$
$$\& \ \langle \mathsf{first}(p.args), \mathsf{length}(\mathsf{scnd}(p.args)) \rangle \notin c.pairs;$$
$$rpc\_fail(p : P; \ c : C^0_{rpc}) \ : \ \textbf{refines } nstep(p, c, \mathsf{RPCFailure}) \textbf{ for } c \in C^0_{rpc}.$$

Figure 7 illustrates the situation for a non-lossy RPC component. The two dotted vertical lines correspond to interfaces towards the sender and the receiver.

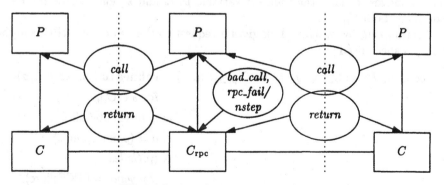

Fig. 7. Actions for remote procedures.

7 Implementing the Memory

Memory is implemented by using a special non-lossy RPC component (class $C_{\text{rpc\_m}}$) together with a clerk component (class C_{clerk}) that acts as a sender to the RPC component, and with a receiver (class M_{rpc}) that is a reliable memory component. A memory that is part of such an implementation is not allowed to communicate with any other components except the associated RPC component.

7.1 RPC-Memory Classes

The classes needed and their constraints are the following:

> **class** $C_{\text{rpc\_m}} : C_{\text{rpc}}$;
>
> **class** $C_{\text{clerk}} : C$;
>
> **class** $M_{\text{rpc}} : M$;
>
> $\forall c \in C_{\text{rpc\_m}} : (d \cdot may\_call \cdot c \Rightarrow d \in C_{\text{clerk}}) \wedge (c \cdot may\_call \cdot d \Rightarrow d \in M_{\text{rpc}})$;
>
> $\forall c \in C_{\text{clerk}} : |\{d \mid c \cdot may\_call \cdot d\}| = 1 \wedge c \cdot may\_call \cdot d \Rightarrow d \in C_{\text{rpc\_m}}$;
>
> $\forall c \in M_{\text{rpc}} : |\{d \mid d \cdot may\_call \cdot c\}| = 1 \wedge d \cdot may\_call \cdot c \Rightarrow d \in C_{\text{rpc\_m}}$;
>
> $\forall c \in C_{\text{rpc\_m}} : c.pairs = \{\langle \text{Read}, 1 \rangle, \langle \text{Write}, 2 \rangle\}$.

7.2 RPC-Memory Actions

To reflect the behavior of memory components, the clerk accepts only read and write calls:

$$call\_r(p : P_0; \; c : C_{00}; \; q : P; \; s : C_{\text{clerk}}; \; loc) :$$
$$\textbf{refines } call(p, c, q, s, \text{Read}, \langle loc \rangle) \textbf{ for } s \in C_{\text{clerk}};$$
$$call\_w(p : P_0; \; c : C_{00}; \; q : P; \; s : C_{\text{clerk}}; \; loc; \; val) :$$
$$\textbf{refines } call(p, c, q, s, \text{Write}, \langle loc, val \rangle) \textbf{ for } s \in C_{\text{clerk}}.$$

This removes, in fact, the need for variable *pairs* and action *bad_call* for RPC components in $C_{\text{rpc\_m}}$.

Action *call*, by which a clerk gives a request to the associated RPC component, is specialized as

$$call(^{*}p : P; \; s : C_{\text{clerk}}; \; q : P; \; c : C_{\text{rpc\_m}}; \; n; \; a) \; : \; \textbf{refines } call(p, s, q, c, n, a)$$
$$\textbf{for } s \in C_{\text{clerk}}$$
$$\& \; n = \text{RemoteCall}$$
$$\wedge \; a = \langle p.proc, p.args \rangle$$
$$\wedge \; (p.Called$$
$$\vee \; p.value = \text{RPCFailure}),$$

which allows repeated calls in the case of RPCFailure. The added fairness requirement guarantees that at least one call is eventually made.

In the case of RPC failure, the clerk returns exception MemFailure instead of RPCFailure. Therefore, action *nstep* for a clerk must be specialized to change the error condition:

$$change(^*p : P; \; s : C_{\text{clerk}}) \; : \; \textbf{refines } nstep(p, s, \textsf{MemFailure}) \textbf{ for } s \in C_{\text{clerk}}$$
$$\& \; p.value = \textsf{RPCFailure}.$$

In this situation, return from the clerk may not take place before this change has taken place:

$$return(q : P_0; \; c : C_{00}; \; ^*p : P; \; s : C_{\text{clerk}}; \; val) \; : \; \textbf{refines } return(q, c, p, s, val)$$
$$\textbf{for } s \in C_{\text{clerk}}$$
$$\& \; p.value \neq \textsf{RPCFailure}.$$

Infinite repetition of calls is avoided by the fairness requirement in *change*.

The classes and actions of this implementation are illustrated in Figure 8.

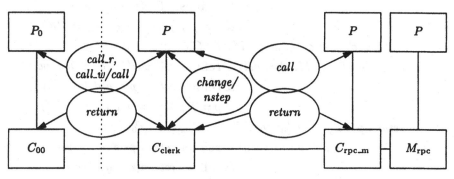

Fig. 8. RPC implementation of memory.

7.3 Correctness of the Implementation

Since this implementation has not been directly derived by superposition from the specification of a memory, its correctness is not obvious. An outline for a proof is given here. The proof is based on combining the specification and implementation together and proving certain properties of this combined system.

The layer with memory specifications is taken as the specification system (*Spec*), and the refined layer with RPC-memory implementation is taken as the implementation system (*Impl*), but all class names in the latter are changed (by using primed names) in order to keep objects of the two systems separate. Without losing generality we can restrict the objects in *Spec* and *Impl* to correspond to each other as follows. There is exactly one (unprimed) memory in *Spec*, which is a simplified memory, and there is exactly one (primed) memory in *Impl*, which is part of an RPC-memory implementation. The two memories have the same addresses and memory values, and there is a one-to-one correspondence f between the interface processes of the (primed) clerk component and those of the unprimed memory. As for other objects, there is a one-to-one correspondence (also denoted by f) between objects in *Impl* and *Spec*, the corresponding objects being identical, except for the priming of class names. *Impl* is now claimed to simulate *Spec* so that the RPC-memory implementation simulates the memory in *Spec*, and f indicates how the objects otherwise correspond to each other.

For a formal proof the two systems are combined into a system *Comb* in the manner explained in Section 2.4, and their actions are synchronized as follows, to run the two memories in tandem:

- Actions *call_r*, *call_w* and *return*, which determine the read/write requests and responses in both systems, are synchronized so that the callers correspond to each other and the transmitted parameters are the same,

$$call\_r(p' : P_0'; \; c' : C_{00}'; \; q' : P'; \; d' : C_{\text{clerk}}'; \; p : P_0; \; c : C_{00};$$
$$q : P; \; d : M_1; \; loc) \; : \; \textbf{refines } call\_r(p', c', q', d', loc)$$
$$\& \; \textbf{refines } call\_r(p, c, q, d, loc)$$
$$\& \; p = f(p') \wedge c = f(c') \wedge q = f(q');$$

$$call\_w(p' : P_0'; \; c' : C_{00}'; \; q' : P'; \; d' : C_{\text{clerk}}' : \; p : P_0; \; c : C_{00};$$
$$q : P; \; d : M_1; \; loc; \; val) \; : \; \textbf{refines } call\_w(p', c', q', d', loc; \; val)$$
$$\& \; \textbf{refines } call\_w(p, c, q, d, loc; \; val)$$
$$\& \; p = f(p') \wedge c = f(c') \wedge q = f(q');$$

$$return(p' : P_0'; \; c' : C_{00}'; \; {}^*q' : P'; \; d' : C_{\text{clerk}}'; \; p : P_0; \; c : C_{00};$$
$$q : P; \; d : M_1; \; val) \; : \; \textbf{refines } return(p', c', q', d', val)$$
$$\& \; \textbf{refines } return(p, c, q, d, val)$$
$$\& \; p = f(p') \wedge c = f(c') \wedge q = f(q').$$

- Successful actions *read*, *write*, and actions *bad_arg* are synchronized as

$$read({}^*p' : P'; \; m' : M_{\text{rpc}}'; \; l' : L'; \; p : P; \; m : M_1; \; l : L) \; :$$
$$\textbf{refines } read(p', m', l', true)$$
$$\& \; \textbf{refines } read(p, m, l, true)$$
$$\& \; p' \cdot called\_by \cdot f^{-1}(p);$$

$$write({}^*p' : P'; \; m' : M_{\text{rpc}}'; \; l' : L'; \; p : P; \; m : M_1; \; l : L) \; :$$
$$\textbf{refines } write(p', m', l', true)$$
$$\& \; \textbf{refines } write(p, m, l, true)$$
$$\& \; p' \cdot called\_by \cdot f^{-1}(p);$$

$$bad\_arg({}^*p' : P; \; m' : M_{\text{rpc}}'; \; p : P; \; m : M_1) \; :$$
$$\textbf{refines } bad\_arg(p', m')$$
$$\& \; \textbf{refines } bad\_arg(p, m)$$
$$\& \; p' \cdot called\_by \cdot f^{-1}(p).$$

- Action *change*, which changes exception RPCFailure into MemFailure in *Impl*, is synchronized with failing *read* and *write* of *Spec*,

$$fail\_r({}^*p' : P'; \, s' : C'_{clerk}; \, p : P; \, m : M_1) \; : \; \textbf{refines } change(p', s')$$
$$\& \textbf{ refines } read(p, m, false)$$
$$\& \, p = f(p')$$
$$\& \, p'.proc = \textsf{Read};$$
$$fail\_w({}^*p' : P'; \, s' : C'_{clerk}; \, p : P; \, m : M_1) \; : \; \textbf{refines } change(p', s')$$
$$\& \textbf{ refines } write(p, m, false)$$
$$\& \, p = f(p')$$
$$\& \, p'.proc = \textsf{Write}.$$

- Other memory-related actions of *Impl* (calls to the RPC and memory components, returns from them, as well as *bad_call* and *rpc_fail* for the RPC component) are synchronized with the stuttering action in *Spec*.
- All other actions, i.e., actions not concerning memories, are synchronized pairwise so that the participants correspond to each other under f.

Fairness requirements for all combined actions are taken from the implementation; fairness requirements of *Spec* are omitted in the construction.

As far as other objects than the memory and its implementation are concerned, it stays invariantly true that objects corresponding to each other under f have identical local states. Another important safety property is that the two memories always have identical contents.

The idea of the correctness proof now is to prove that

(1) *Impl* is a correct implementation of *Comb*, and
(2) *Comb* is a correct implementation of *Spec*,

which implies that *Impl* is a correct implementation of *Spec*. By using a simplified memory in *Spec* we have avoided the need to augment *Impl* for this proof with auxiliary "history" and "prophecy" variables [1].

To prove (1), it is sufficient to show that *Comb* does not restrict the execution of implementation actions, i.e., whenever the guard of an implementation action is true, the corresponding combined action is also enabled. This is a safety property that can easily be proved with the aid of suitable invariants.

To prove (2), we first notice that, by construction, *Comb* satisfies all safety properties of *Spec*. Therefore, it is sufficient to show that *Comb* exhibits its liveness properties. In this case, liveness properties of *Spec* are determined by its fairness requirements for *return* and for the three mutually exclusive specializations of *nstep*. For the former it suffices to show that each call to the combined memory always leads to a return. The latter property is then a consequence of the fact that no return is possible without executing some refinement of *nstep*.

8 Lossy RPC Component

8.1 Superposing Real-Time Properties

Real-time properties can be superposed on action systems as presented in [14]. Comparing to other related approaches, like [2], for instance, the main difference is that no separate actions are used for incrementing time. Instead, the passing of time is registered in connection with ordinary actions.

In mapping action executions to real time, it will be assumed for simplicity that actions are executed instantaneously. In order to model temporal properties, two special variables are taken, Ω and Δ. Variable Ω is initialized as 0, and it will always show the most recent value of time (measured in seconds) when some action was executed. Variable Δ is initialized as $\emptyset$, and its value is always a set of unique time values that are used as deadlines. All deadlines in Δ are assumed to have different identities, even if their time values are the same.

An implicit parameter τ is also added to each action, denoting the time when the execution takes place, together with an implicit guarding condition

$$\Omega \leq \tau \leq \min(\Delta)$$

and implicit updating of Ω,

$$\Omega' = \tau.$$

This forces actions to be executed in a non-decreasing order of time, and without ever exceeding any of the deadlines in Δ.

Time can now be used to affect behavioral properties by using the parameter τ and variable Δ in actions. Instead of using variable Δ directly, two special operations are provided. By

$$\Delta\text{on}(x, \delta),$$

where x is a program variable and $\delta > 0$, a deadline $\tau + \delta$ is inserted in Δ and also assigned to x. Storing of the deadline is needed in order to be able to remove it from Δ by operation

$$\Delta\text{off}(x).$$

In these operations variable x must be one that is introduced in the same layer where the operations are given.

Unlike for ordinary variables, superposition steps may invalidate safety properties that involve variables Ω and Δ. All safety properties that do not explicitly refer to them are, however, preserved.

8.2 Zeno Behaviors

Fairness is still the only "force" that can force actions into execution. Time, as shown by Ω, is advanced only by actions. Therefore, without fairness requirements, Ω could stay unchanged by no further actions being executed. Also, if there is a deadline that can be removed only by actions that stay disabled, time will never pass that deadline. If fairness still forces the execution of an infinite number of actions, this necessarily results in a Zeno behavior [2], where an infinite number of actions is executed within a finite interval of real time.

Obviously, Zeno behaviors cannot be implemented in reality. Since all behaviors of a specification need not be implemented, Zeno behaviors are harmful only if a situation may arise where Zeno behaviors can no longer be avoided. The following are sufficient conditions under which such situations cannot arise: deadlines in Δ are the only upper bounds given for τ, there is a lower bound $\epsilon > 0$ for δ in Δon, and each deadline in Δ is eventually removed from it. These conditions will hold in the real-time specifications to be given below.

8.3 Classes for Lossy RPC

Class C_{rpc}^0 models RPC components that may lose calls issud to them. However, lossy RPC components do not raise RPCFailure. Therefore, another subclass is introduced to model them:

$$\textbf{class } C_{lrpc} : C_{rpc}^0;$$
$$\textbf{remove } rpc\_fail(p, c) \textbf{ for } c \in C_{lrpc}.$$

To allow all interface processes to store deadlines for some actions, we extend them with another local variable d,

$$\textbf{class } P : P + \{d\}.$$

8.4 Actions for Lossy RPC

The required temporal properties can now be imposed as follows. A call to a lossy RPC sets a deadline with delay δ:

$$call(p : P; \ c : C_1; \ q : P; \ d : C_{lrpc}; \ n; \ a) \ : \ \textbf{refines } call(p, c, q, d, n, a)$$
$$\textbf{for } d \in C_{lrpc} \ \&$$
$$\rightarrow \Delta\text{on}(p.d, \delta).$$

If the call is lost or transmitted (within this deadline), the deadline is removed:

$$lose(p : P; \ c : C_{lrpc}) \ : \ \textbf{refines } lose(p, c) \textbf{ for } c \in C_{lrpc} \ \&$$
$$\rightarrow \Delta\text{off}(p.d);$$
$$call(^*p : P; \ c : C_{lrpc}; \ q : P; \ r : C) \ : \ \textbf{refines } call(p, c, q, r)$$
$$\textbf{for } c \in C_{lrpc} \ \&$$
$$\rightarrow \Delta\text{off}(p.d).$$

Another deadline is set in connection with a return from the receiver:

$$return(p : P; \ c : C_{lrpc}; \ ^*q : P; \ d : C; \ val) \ : \ \textbf{refines } return(p, c, q, d, val)$$
$$\textbf{for } c \in C_{lrpc} \ \&$$
$$\rightarrow \Delta\text{on}(p.d, \delta),$$

and this is removed from Δ either by action *lose* or in the final return:

$$return(p : P;\ c : C_1;\ {}^*q : P;\ d : C_{lrpc};\ val)\ :\ \textbf{refines}\ return(p, c, q, d, val)$$
$$\textbf{for}\ d \in C_{lrpc}\ \&$$
$$\rightarrow \Delta\text{off}(p.d).$$

No changes are needed in *bad_call*. When it is enabled, fairness forces its execution before δ seconds have passed, and the deadline is kept in Δ until removed by *return* or *lose*.

Notice that once a call has been transmitted, a lossy RPC component is committed to wait for a response from the receiver, independently of how long this takes.

9 RPC Implementation

9.1 Classes for RPC Implementation

Similarly to the implementation of memory, implementing an RPC component in terms of a lossy RPC component needs a special sender or clerk (class S):

$$\textbf{class}\ S\ :\ C_1;$$
$$\forall c \in S\ :\ |\{d\ |\ c \cdot may\_call \cdot d\}| = 1$$
$$\land\ c \cdot may\_call \cdot d \Rightarrow d \in C_{lrpc}$$
$$\land\ d \cdot may\_call \cdot c \Rightarrow d \in C.$$

Here its role will be to implement the proper timeout behavior.

Class P is also extended with another variable e for the timeouts and deadlines needed in this layer:

$$\textbf{class}\ P\ :\ P + \{e\}.$$

An RPC component has an interface both to the sender and to the receiver, as shown in Figure 7. In order that a lossy RPC component would provide a correct implementation, its total interface, consisting of interactions both with the sender and with the receiver, must be correct. In particular, an implementation would work incorrectly, if it would respond with RPCFailure after relaying the request to the receiver but before getting a reply from it. This can be avoided only if the receiver is guaranteed to return each call within some deadline. To constrain receivers in this respect, a special receiver subclass is introduced,

$$\textbf{class}\ R\ :\ C.$$

However, in accordance with the problem statement in [8], the construction does not require receivers to belong to this subclass.

9.2 Actions for RPC Implementation

The actions for sender objects in S are specialized to transmit any call to the lossy RPC exactly once, and to give up and indicate RPCFailure if the return does not take place in the specified time.

No *nstep* actions are needed in this case:

remove $nstep(p, c)$ **for** $c \in S$.

When a sender gives a call to the lossy RPC, it stores the deadline by which the reply is expected:

$$call(^*p : P;\ c : S;\ q : P;\ d : C_{\text{lrpc}};\ n;\ a)\ :\ \textbf{refines}\ call(p, c, q, d, n, a)$$
$$\textbf{for}\ c \in S$$
$$\&\ p.i\_state = Called$$
$$\wedge\ n = p.proc$$
$$\wedge\ a = p.args$$
$$\rightarrow p.e' = \tau + 2\delta + \epsilon.$$

If a reply is not obtained within this time, the sender gives up waiting for it. The deadline that has been stored is used as a timeout to enable action *give_up*:

$$give\_up(^*p : P;\ c : S)\ :\ \textbf{refines}\ give\_up(p, c, \text{RPCFailure})$$
$$\textbf{for}\ c \in S$$
$$\&\ \tau > p.e.$$

The fairness requirement means that this action will eventually be executed, if a response is not obtained.

The implementation is illustrated in Figure 9.

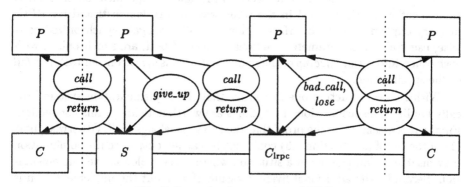

Fig. 9. Lossy implementation of RPC.

9.3 Receivers with Bounded Response Times

Receivers belonging to subclass R are guaranteed to return calls within deadline ϵ. The associated safety property is enforced by specializing calls to components in R and returns from them as

$$call(^*p : P;\ c : C_{\text{lrpc}};\ q : P;\ d : R;\ n;\ a)\ :\ \textbf{refines } call(p, c, q, d, n, a)$$
$$\textbf{for } d \in R\ \&$$
$$\rightarrow \Delta\text{on}(p.e, \epsilon);$$

$$return(p : P;\ c : C_{\text{lrpc}};\ ^*q : P;\ d : R;\ val)\ :\ \textbf{refines } return(p, c, q, d, val)$$
$$\textbf{for } d \in R\ \&$$
$$\rightarrow \Delta\text{off}(p.e).$$

This guarantees only that a return never comes after the deadline. In addition, the liveness property is needed that each call will eventually lead to a return. However, because of the possibility for an infinite number of nested calls, this property cannot be directly built into the model. This is an example of a situation that requires an additional TLA assumption which is not included in the model.

In fact, with receivers in R, the model allows situations that lead only to Zeno behaviors where an infinite number of actions is executed, but the deadline for a return is never reached. The additional liveness assumption that a component in R will eventually return each call guarantees, however, that each deadline is eventually removed from Δ, which excludes such situations. Without this liveness assumption the system would not be acceptable as a specification.

9.4 Correctness of the Implementation

The lossy implementation with a receiver in R, and the specification of an RPC component can be combined in the same way as was demonstrated for RPC-memory implementation. Interface actions of both are again synchronized pairwise, using identical parameters, actions *bad_call* of both are synchronized with each other, and action *give_up* of the implementation is synchronized with *rpc_fail* of the specification.

With this construction one can prove that the implementation system logically implies the specification. Two things are worth noticing in this connection. Firstly, it is essential for the proof that the receiver belongs to R. Otherwise, part (1) of the proof (see Section 7.3) could not be carried out, since the combination may disable action *give_up* in a situation where it is enabled in the implementation. Secondly, the additional liveness assumption about the implementation is not needed in part (2) of the proof, since also the specification allows situations where a receiver never returns a call. Logical implication is not affected by the fact that some behaviors are Zeno behaviors.

10 Concluding Remarks

In the absence of any built-in control structure, the execution model of joint actions is very primitive. Therefore, the aim of the original DisCo project was to investigate, whether some structuring would make this execution model manageable for large numbers of actions. This led to object-orientation with multi-object actions, using statecharts to model control structures within objects, and to facilities for superposition-based modularity. These ideas of structuring are the most important characteristics of this approach.

The language was designed as a programming language-like modeling language for distributed and reactive systems. Except for the fact that superposition was included in a form that preserves safety properties, not much attention was initially paid to formal proofs. Instead, animation tools were built to aid in the inspection of proposed specifications. Since rigorous discussion of behavioral properties was made possible already at high levels of abstraction, one aim was to use high-level animations to replace the scenarios that are conventionally used in the design and documentation of behaviorally complex systems.

When the relationship to canonical TLA expressions was noticed, a suitable basis was obtained for formal reasoning. Proof support is currently under development. As a whole, the approach represents the position that an operational specification language with programming language-like features, and a closely related logic provide two complementary views that should be used to support each other in the engineering of complex systems.

The models derived using this approach are *closed models* that always model also the environments where the specified systems are supposed to operate. Therefore, assumptions about the environment are also made explicit in a model. Operational modeling of liveness properties as fairness requirements with respect to syntactic actions leads, however, easily to overspecification, even if also weak fairness requirements are allowed. Such overspecification can be avoided by leaving some fairness assumptions out of the model, and giving them as additional assumptions in TLA.

As closed models our specifications always model collective behaviors of objects, where the number of objects can be allowed to be arbitrary. In this example this was useful, for instance, in the modeling of procedure calls, where arbitrary collections of components were allowed to coexist and issue calls to each other. An arbitrary number of objects means that the properties to be proved involve quantification over classes. This does not seem to cause essential complications for proofs using inference rules, but it renders ordinary model checking techniques inapplicable.

As for design methodology, the approach provides strong support for incrementality. In general it seems recommendable to start with a very primitive model, which only gives some basic notions to build on. In practice we have found it important that the model can be animated already at this stage. This also supports the experiences of Brooks about incremental development – or growing – of software [7].

In terms of TLA, incremental development is based on superposition. Proofs of safety properties are therefore not affected by later introduction of additional detail. This is different from Unity [9], with which our approach has otherwise much in common, since combination of Unity specifications (called "union" in Unity) may invalidate safety properties. On the other hand, superposition in Unity preserves also liveness properties, but it is therefore too restricted for the design methodology described here.

It can be claimed that incrementality also adds to the understandability of specifications by providing several levels at which they can be inspected. This may have its cost in the length of specifications, and possibly also in the effort required to design the layers suitably, but this is difficult to valuate objectively. Looking into the specifications discussed in this paper, one can notice that 35% of the formally given lines were used for describing such basic notions as procedure calls. This should not be unexpected, as the execution model of joint actions has no built-in notions for such purposes. Each of the five subsequent models could, however, then be built with a relatively small effort, with about 20 lines each.

References

1. M. Abadi, L. Lamport, The existence of refinement mappings. *Theoretical Computer Science 82*, 2, 1991, 253-284.
2. M. Abadi, L. Lamport, An old-fashioned recipe for real time. *ACM Trans. Programming Languages Syst. 16*, 5, September 1994, 1543-1571.
3. M. Abadi, L. Lamport, S. Merz, A TLA solution to the RPC-memory specification problem. In this volume.
4. R. J. R. Back, Refinement calculus II: parallel and reactive programs. *Stepwise Refinement of Distributed Systems: Models, Formalisms, Correctness*, LNCS 430, Springer-Verlag, 1990, 67-93.
5. R. J. R. Back, R. Kurki-Suonio, Decentralization of process nets with a centralized control. *Distributed Computing 3*, 1989, 73-87. An earlier version in *Proc. 2nd ACM SIGACT-SIGOPS Symp. on Principles of Distributed Computing*, 1983, 131-142.
6. R. J. R. Back, R. Kurki-Suonio, Distributed cooperation with action systems. *ACM Trans. Programming Languages Syst. 10*, 4, October 1988, 513-554.
7. F. P. Brooks, Jr., No silver bullet – Essence and accidents of software engineering. *Computer 20*, 4, April 1987, 10-19.
8. M. Broy, L. Lamport, The RPC-memory specification problem. In this volume.
9. K. M. Chandy, J. Misra, *Parallel Program Design - A Foundation*. Addison-Wesley, 1988.
10. H.-M. Järvinen, *The design of a specification language for reactive systems*. Tampere University of Technology, Publication 95, 1992.
11. H.-M. Järvinen, R. Kurki-Suonio, M. Sakkinen, K. Systä, Object-oriented specification of reactive systems. *Proc. 12th Int. Conf. on Software Eng.*, 1990, 63-71.
12. B. Jonsson, Simulations between specifications of distributed systems. *CONCUR '91*, LNCS 527, Springer-Verlag, 1991, 346-360.
13. P. Kellomäki, Mechanizing invariant proofs of joint action systems. *Proc. Fourth Symposium on Programming Languages and Software Tools*, Department of General Computer Science, Eötvös Loránd University, Budapest, June 1995, 141-152.

404

14. R. Kurki-Suonio, Hybrid models with fairness and distributed clocks. *Hybrid Systems*, (eds. R. L. Grossman, A. Nerode, A. P. Ravn, H. Rischel), LNCS 736, Springer-Verlag, 1993, 103-120.
15. L. Lamport, The temporal logic of actions. *ACM Trans. Programming Languages Syst. 16*, 3, May 1994, 872-923.
16. S. Owre, J. M. Rushby, N. Shankar, PVS: A prototype verification system. *11th International Conference on Automated Deduction*, (ed. D. Kanpur), Lecture Notes in Artificial Intelligence 607, Springer-Verlag, 1992, 748-752.
17. K. Systä, A graphical tool for specification of reactive systems. *Proc. Euromicro '91 Workshop on Real-Time Systems*, 1991, 12-19.

The Methodology of Modal Constraints

Kim G. Larsen*[1], Bernhard Steffen[2], Carsten Weise[3]

[1] BRICS[†], Aalborg Univ., Denmark, kgl@iesd.auc.dk
[2] FB Math. u. Informatik, Univ. of Passau, Germany, steffen@fmi.uni-passau.de
[3] Lehrstuhl fuer Informatik I, Univ. of Tech. Aachen, Germany,
carsten@informatik.rwth-aachen.de

Abstract. We present a complete solution of the RPC-Memory Specification Problem, by applying a constraint-oriented state-based proof methodology for concurrent software systems. Our methodolgy exploits compositionality and abstraction for the reduction of the verification problem under investigation. Formal basis for this methodology are Modal Transition Systems allowing loose state-based specifications, which can be refined by successively adding constraints. Key concepts of our method are *projective views, separation of proof obligations, Skolemization* and *abstraction*. Central to the method is the use of *Parametrized* Modal Transition Systems. The method extends elegantly to real-time systems.

1 Introduction

We present a constraint-oriented state-based proof methodology for concurrent software systems which exploits compositionality and abstraction for the reduction of the investigated verification problem. Formal basis for this methodology are Modal Transition Systems (MTS) [LT88] allowing loose state-based specifications, which can be refined by successively adding constraints. In particular, this allows extremely fine-granular specifications, which are characteristic of our approach: each aspect of a system component is specified by a number of independent constraints, one for each parameter configuration. This leads to a usually infinite number of extremely simple constraints which must all be satisfied by a corresponding component implementation. Besides the compositionality in the standard (vertical) fashion, which exploits the syntactic structure of the system and of the property representations, this extreme component decomposition also supports *horizontal* decompostion, which separates the proof obligations for the various parameter instantiations. This is the key for the success of the following three step reduction, which may reduce even a verification problem for infinite state systems to a small number of automatically verifiable problems about finite state systems:

---

* This author has been partially supported by the European Communities under CONCUR2, BRA 7166.
† Basic Research in Computer Science, Centre of the Danish National Research Foundation.

- *Separating the Proof Obligations.* Sect. 3.4 presents a proof principle justifying the separation and specialization of the various proof obligations, which prepare the ground for the subsequent reduction steps.
- *Skolemization.* The separation of the first step leaves us with problems smaller in size but larger in number. Due to the nature of their origin, these problems often fall into a small number of equivalence classes requiring only one prototypical proof each.
- *Abstraction.* After the first two reduction steps the representation of the reduced problem may still be of infinite size. However, the extreme specialization of the problem supports the power of abstract interpretation, which may finally reduce all the proof obligations to a small finite size.

After the reduction process, the resulting simplified problems can hopefully be solved automatically. In the example we used the verification tool EPSILON ([CGL93]) to establish the required refinements. Further application examples of our method can be found in [LSW95a, LSW95b].

Our proof methodology is not complete, i.e., there is neither a guarantee for the existence of a finite state reduction nor a straightforward method for finding the right amount of separation for the success of the subsequent steps or the adequate abstraction for the final verification. Still, as should be clear from the example in the paper, there is a large class of problems and systems, where the method can be applied quite straightforwardly. Of course, the more complex the system structure the more involved will be the required search of appropriate granularity and abstraction.

Whereas complex data dependencies may exclude any possibility of 'horizontal' decomposition into small constraints, our approach elegantly extends to real time systems, even over a dense time domain. In fact, this extension does not affect the possibility of a finite state reduction. For the real-time case, the basis are Timed Modal Transition Systems (TMS), where (weak) refinement is decidable. This is exploited in the TMS tool EPSILON for establishing refinement relations on demand [CGL93].

The treatment of the timed version requires to deal with *parametrized* timed modal transition systems, where parameters may appear either in actions (so-called *parametrized actions*) or in timing constraints. As the underlying parameter domain is potentially infinite, specifications may in general have an infinite number of actions and transitions. Unfortunately, in the presence of timing parameters, the corresponding reduction technique proposed in our method does not apply in general. However the full treatment of the timed version of the case study can be achieved by eliminating all timing parameters, which puts the problem back into the range of our method and of existing verification tools.

Profile of our Solution: We will present a complete solution of the RPC-Memory Specification Problem. Only the qualitative liveness property "every call eventually returns" will be delayed until we provide a quantitative treatment by means of Timed Modal Specifications.

On the technical side, we added the following requirement to the specification of the memory, which is essential for the correctness of the specification: *The memory engages in actions only when it is called.*

Additionally, the specification requires that a read request will result in exactly one read if successful. As the clerk is allowed to repeat read requests after a failed call – which could already have caused a read operation – it is quite clear that this property will not hold for the composition of clerk, RPC and memory. Nevertheless, we formalized this property (as M_{2c}) for completeness. We became aware of this problem in the specification by the error diagnostics of our verification tool.

We interpret the rather vague formulation "The memory behaves as if it maintains an array of atomically read and written locations ..." such that an internal read of the memory will result in the value written by the last internal write to the same location.

We have modelled the exceptions of the memory and the RPC (BadArg, BadCall) in the most simple way that the informal specification allows: the raise of an exception is a non-determinstic alternative in the corresponding states. This abstracts from the actual determination of the fact, whether the raise of an exception is required or not. We consider this abstraction as adequate due to the remark "Note that being an element of memLocs or memVals is a "semantic" restriction, and cannot be imposed solely by syntactic restrictions on the types of arguments".

Overview of the Paper: The paper is divided into three parts: 1) establishing the formal background, 2) treating the untimed problem and 3) extending the method to real time: In the first part, after introducing Modal Transition Systems – our basic (untimed) specification formalism – and explaining abstract/parametrized actions and projective views, we will present our proof method, which is tailored to verification of specific design patterns. The second part gives an untimed specification of the memory, the RPC and the clerk, and applies our proof methodology to the verification problem 3. Similarly, the third part introduces Timed Modal Specifications, an extension of MTS to real-time, specifies the systems components and applies our methodology to solve the timed verification problems.

2 Modal Transition Systems

In this section we give a brief introduction to the existing theory of modal transition systems. We assume familiarity with CCS. For more elaborate introductions and proofs we refer the reader to [LT88, HL89, Lar90].

When specifying reactive systems by traditional Process Algebras like e.g. CCS [Mil89], one defines the set of action transitions that can be performed (or observed) in a given system state. In this approach, any valid implementation *must* be able to perform the specified actions, which often constrains the set of possible implementations unnecessarily. One way of improving this situation within the framework of operational specification is to allow specifications where one can explicitly distinguish between transitions that are *admissible* (or allowed) and those that are *required*. This distinction allows a much more flexible specification and a much more generous notion of implementation, and therefore improves the practicality of the operational approach. Technically, this is made precise through the following notion of *modal transition systems*:

Definition 1. *A modal transition system is a structure* $S = (\Sigma, A, \rightarrow_\Box, \rightarrow_\diamond)$, *where Σ is a set of states, A is a set of actions and* $\rightarrow_\Box$, $\rightarrow_\diamond \subseteq \Sigma \times A \times \Sigma$ *are transition relations, satisfying the well-definedness condition* $\rightarrow_\Box \subseteq \rightarrow_\diamond$. $\quad\Box$

Intuitively, the requirement $\rightarrow_\Box \subseteq \rightarrow_\diamond$ expresses that anything which is required should also be allowed hence ensuring the well-definedness of modal specifications. When the relations $\rightarrow_\Box$ and $\rightarrow_\diamond$ coincide, the above definition reduces to the traditional notion of labelled transition systems.

Syntactically, we represent modal transition systems by means of a slightly extended version of CCS. The only change in the syntax is the introduction of two prefix constructs $a_\Box.P$ and $a_\diamond.P$ with the following semantics: $a_\diamond.P \xrightarrow{a}_\diamond P$, $a_\Box.P \xrightarrow{a}_\Box P$ and $a_\Box.P \xrightarrow{a}_\diamond P$. The semantics for the other constructs follow the lines of CCS in the sense that each rule has a version for $\rightarrow_\Box$ and $\rightarrow_\diamond$ respectively. We will call this version of CCS *modal* CCS.

As usual, we consider a design process as a sequence of *refinement steps* reducing the number of possible implementations. Intuitively, our notion of when a specification S refines another (weaker) specification T is based on the following simple observation. Any behavioural aspect *allowed* by S should also be allowed by T; and dually, any behavioural aspect which is already guaranteed by the weaker specification T must also be guaranteed by S. Using the derivation relations $\rightarrow_\Box$ and $\rightarrow_\diamond$ this may be formalized by the following notion of refinement:

Definition 2. *A refinement $\mathcal{R}$ is a binary relation on Σ such that whenever $S\mathcal{R}T$ and $a \in A$ then the following holds:*

1. *Whenever $S \xrightarrow{a}_\diamond S'$, there is some T' such that $T \xrightarrow{a}_\diamond T'$ and $S'\mathcal{R}T'$,*
2. *Whenever $T \xrightarrow{a}_\Box T'$, there is some S' such that $S \xrightarrow{a}_\Box S'$ and $S'\mathcal{R}T'$,*

S is said to be a refinement of T in case (S, T) is contained in some refinement $\mathcal{R}$. We write $S \vartriangleleft T$ in this case. $\quad\Box$

Note that when applied to traditional labelled transition systems (where $\rightarrow = \rightarrow_\Box = \rightarrow_\diamond$) this defines the well-known bisimulation equivalence [Par81, Mil89]. Using standard techniques, one straightforwardly establishes that $\vartriangleleft$ is a preorder preserving all modal CCS operators.

$\vartriangleleft$ allows *loose* specifications. This important property can be best explained by looking at the 'weakest' specification $\mathcal{U}$ constantly allowing any action, but never requiring anything to happen. Operationally, $\mathcal{U}$ is completely defined by $\mathcal{U} \xrightarrow{a}_\diamond \mathcal{U}$ for all actions a. It is easily verified that $S \vartriangleleft \mathcal{U}$ for any modal specification S.

Intuitively, S and T are *consistent* if they are not contradictory, i.e. any action required by one is not constraint by the other. The following formal definition is due to the fact that for S and T to be consistent all 'simultaneously' reachable specifications S' and T' must be consistent too:

Definition 3. *A consistency relation $\mathcal{R}$ is a binary relation on Σ such that whenever $S \mathcal{R} T$ and $a \in A$ then the following holds:*

1. *Whenever $S \overset{a}{\to}_\square S'$, there is a unique T' such that $T \overset{a}{\to}_\circ T'$,*
2. *Whenever $T \overset{a}{\to}_\square T'$, there is a unique S' such that $S \overset{a}{\to}_\circ S'$,*
3. *Whenever $S \overset{a}{\to}_\circ S'$ and $T \overset{a}{\to}_\circ T'$ then $S' \mathcal{R} T'$.*

S and T are said to be consistent in case (S, T) is contained in some consistency relation $\mathcal{R}$. □

Note in particular that two specifications are consistent if none of them requires any actions. Consistency is important, as it allows to define conjunction on modal transition systems by:

$$\frac{S \overset{a}{\to}_\square S' \quad T \overset{a}{\to}_\circ T'}{S \land T \overset{a}{\to}_\square S' \land T'} \qquad \frac{S \overset{a}{\to}_\circ S' \quad T \overset{a}{\to}_\square T'}{S \land T \overset{a}{\to}_\square S' \land T'}$$

$$\frac{S \overset{a}{\to}_\circ S' \quad T \overset{a}{\to}_\circ T'}{S \land T \overset{a}{\to}_\circ S' \land T'}$$

Of course, $S \land T$ is always a well-defined modal specifications (i.e. any required transition is also allowed), and in fact, for consistent arguments S and T it defines their *logical* conjunction:

Theorem 4. Let S and T be consistent modal specifications. Then $S \land T \triangleleft S$ and $S \land T \triangleleft T$. Moreover, if $R \triangleleft S$ and $R \triangleleft T$ then $R \triangleleft S \land T$.

In order to compare specifications at different levels of abstraction, it is important to abstract from transitions resulting from internal communication. This can be done as usual: For a given modal transition system $\mathcal{M} = (\Sigma, A \cup \{\tau\}, \to_\square, \to_\circ)$ we derive the modal transition system $\mathcal{M}_\varepsilon = (\Sigma, A \cup \{\varepsilon\}, \Rightarrow_\square, \Rightarrow_\circ)$, where $\overset{\varepsilon}{\Rightarrow}_\square$ is the reflexive and transitive closure of $\overset{\tau}{\to}_\square$, and where $T \overset{a}{\Rightarrow}_\square T', a \neq \varepsilon$, means that there exist T'', T''' such that

$$T \overset{\varepsilon}{\Rightarrow}_\square T'' \overset{a}{\to}_\square T''' \overset{\varepsilon}{\Rightarrow}_\square T'$$

The relation $\Rightarrow_\circ$ is defined in a similar fashion.

The notion of *weak refinement* can now be introduced as follows: S weakly refines T in $\mathcal{M}$, $S \trianglelefteq T$, iff there exists a refinement relation on $\mathcal{M}_\varepsilon$ containing S and T.

Weak refinement $\trianglelefteq$ essentially enjoys the same pleasant properties as $\triangleleft$: it is a preorder preserved by all modal CCS operators except + [HL89] (including restriction, relabelling and hiding), and Theorem 4 is also valid for weak refinement. Moreover, for ordinary labelled transition systems weak refinement reduces to the usual notion of weak bisimulation ($\approx$). In our examples, we will deal with weak refinement and (in general) infinite action sets.

Given a modal transition system S, we call S^+ the *saturated* version of S iff it arises from S by adding a τ-may-loop to each state. Saturated MTS's are important because they allow to adopt the same definitions of conjunction and consistency in the context of weak refinement as introduced in the context of strong refinement above. Moreover, we can restrict our attention to saturated MTS's without loosing generality, as weak refinement is not sensitive to τ-loops:

$$S \trianglelefteq S^+ \quad \text{and} \quad S^+ \trianglelefteq S$$

In the following we will assume that all MTS's are saturated without mentioning this explicitly.

3 Actions, Design Patterns and Projective Views

3.1 Abstract Actions

Most of the time we will define specifications graphically, i.e. by pictures of transition systems. Dotted lines indicate allowed, solid lines required transitions. Start states are indicated by an ingoing, unlabelled arc. We assume the sets memLocs of memory locations, memVals of memory values and procId of process identifiers with typical elements val, loc and id.

The actions used in our specifications have parameters: a read issued by process id requesting the data stored in location loc is written as Read(id, loc), where id, loc are the *parameters* of the action. Such an action will sometimes be called a *parametrized action*. The tag Read indicates the type of the action, and is referred to as an *abstract action*.

For simplicity, we label transitions by sets of actions. Note that a transition $s \xrightarrow{\alpha}_\square s'$ (α a set of actions) is a shorthand for the set $\{s \xrightarrow{a}_\square s' \mid a \in \alpha\}$. Often, these sets are abstract actions where some parameters range over the whole parameter domain. In such cases, we use *bar notation*, where a bar in a parameter suggests all possible values for this parameter position, e.g. ReqRd(id, _) is the set $\{\text{ReqRd}(id, loc) \mid loc \in \text{memLocs}\}$. A singleton set is denoted by its element, i.e. we write ReqRd(id,loc) instead of $\{\text{ReqRd}(id, loc)\}$, and we use the usual set operators $\cup$ (set union), $\cap$ (intersection), $\neg$ (complement), $\setminus$ (set minus).

We decompose the specification into parts constraining one calling process id only. The behaviour of all other processes is not affected by these specifications. It is the conjunction of all the properties for all processes which captures the behaviour of the whole system. To make 'not affected' precise in our framework, we introduce for Act(id) (the set of the actions associated with process id) the complement $\neg$Act(id), i.e. the set of actions associated with all processes apart from id. Moreover, we use the following abbreviation: a square box indicates a state where all the actions from $\neg$Act(id) are allowed, i.e.

$$\square \quad = \quad \text{(} \neg \text{Act(id))}$$

3.2 Projective Views

Our specifications consist of *projective views*:

Definition 5. Let A, V be MTS's. Then V is called *a projective view of A* if $V \trianglelefteq A$. A set $\{A(i) \mid i \in I\}$ of projective views of A, all pairwise consistent, is called *a complete set of projective views of A* if

$$A \trianglelefteq \bigwedge_{i \in I} A(i) \trianglelefteq A$$

This general definition does not say anything about the granularity of the decomposition into projective views – especially the set $\{A\}$ is a complete set of projective views of A. To establish that a set of constraints is a complete set of projective views two pre-conditions have to be examined: completeness and consistency. Completeness is mainly the responsibility of the specification designer, who must ensure that the conjunction of constraints captures the given problem. In our formalization consistency of the constraint sets is guaranteed by employing special design patterns, which reduces consistency checking to a simple syntactic test.

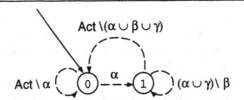

Fig. 1. The Design Pattern for the Memory Component

Design Pattern 1: The first of our design patterns is re-used in the specification of the memory component: Assuming an action set Act and subsets α, β, γ, the property modelled by the pattern can be stated informally as: *after an action in α was observed, no action from β is allowed until an action not in γ is executed*. This pattern can be specified by the modal transition system given in Fig. 1. The property can be expressed as the following formula of CTL with modalities (see [CES83, Ste93] for details):

$$\mathbf{AG}_{\mathbf{Act}} ([\alpha] \mathbf{AG}_\gamma \neg \beta)$$

This specification pattern belongs to the large class of *may-only specifications*:

Definition 6. A state of a specification is called *initially may-only* iff no must-transition leaves this states. If all states reachable from a start state of a specification S are initially may-only, then the specification S is called *may-only*.

As may-only specifications have no required transitions, they are consistent by definition. For the RPC (and the Clerk), may-only specifications are not sufficient. For these specifications we use a special pattern which directly implies consistency of the constraints. The idea is that any two constraints either behave the same, or one focuses on a certain behaviour of the system, while the other constraint must allow this behaviour. Further both constraints must return to their start states by the same set of actions.

Design Pattern 2: For a given set C of constraints the pattern can be explained as follows. Let R be the set of return-actions of all the constraints, i.e. the set of all actions by which one of the constraints returns to its start state. Then every constraint has an auxiliary state s' such that

- for all actions not in R there is a may-loop in s', and
- for all actions in R there is a may-transition from s' back to the start state of the constraint.

Note that s' is a "universal state" as it allows every action in the sort of the constraints.

Now every pair of constraints in the set C must start in the same way, i.e. they must have identical initial segments. There is a further requirement for the endpoints of these identical initial segments: Let s_1, s_2 be states reachable from the start by identical paths in both constraints, which differ in their outgoing transitions. Then

- for every must-transition leaving s_1, there is a may-transition from s_2 to the auxiliary state, and
- for every must-transition leaving s_2, there is a may-transition from s_1 to the auxiliary state.

Fig. 2 gives a small example: the constraint set $\{X1, X2, Y\}$ complies to the pattern. The return-set R is $\{\overline{\mathrm{rok}}, \overline{\mathrm{rerr}}\}$, and the auxiliary states s' are the states no. 4 in all constraints. In the case of $X1$ and $X2$, s_1 and s_2 are their respective states no. 2. For the pair $X1, Y$ resp. $X2, Y$ the states s_1 and s_2 are the start states. The figure also gives their conjunction $X1 \wedge X2 \wedge Y$.

As our specifications use only constraints which are either may-only or conform to design pattern 2 we have the following important property:

Proposition 7. *All constraint sets $\{S_i \mid i \in I\}$ used in the RPC-Memory specification are pairwise consistent, thus $\bigwedge_{i \in I} S_i$ defines logical conjunction.*

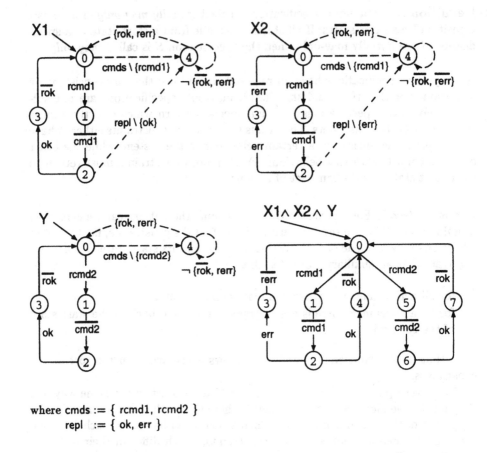

where cmds := { rcmd1, rcmd2 }
     repl := { ok, err }

Fig. 2. Example of Pattern 2

3.3 Generalizations

In the verification, the following generalization of a specification is important:

- first changing all must transitions into may transitions,
- then eliminating a universal quantification of an MTS by replacing the parameterized action by the set of actions arising from instantiating the parameter.

Given a parametrized specification $P(m)$, where m is from a domain D, and a set $M \subseteq D$, we write $P(M)$ for the generalization of $P(m)$ w.r.t. M. Then the following important property holds:

$$\bigwedge_{m \in M} P(m) \trianglelefteq P(M)$$

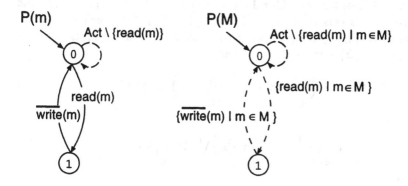

Fig. 3. Example of a Generalization

Thus generalizations are useful to reduce the number of states in the proof. Fig. 3 gives an example, where $P(m)$ is a simple buffer forwarding values. Note that the main difference between the conjunction over the $P(m)$ and the generalization $P(M)$ is that in the conjunction, it is required that the value written is the same as the value read, while $P(M)$ just requires that when a value in M is read, some value from M is written, making the elements of M indistinguishable. Therefore generalizations can be used for abstracting from the domain of a parameter. Note that our specifications have in general several parameters, and that different parameters can be generalized simultaneously.

3.4 Sufficient Proof Condition

Our method will apply a general proof principle to reduce the verification problem. The proof principle is motivated by the idea that typically a verification problem has the form

$$(A^1 \mid \ldots \mid A^k) \trianglelefteq C$$

where the A^ℓ and the specification C consist of large number of conjunctions. If the conjuncts of C are specifications C_j (for some index set J), then it is sufficient to establish

$$\forall j \in J. \, (A^1 \mid \ldots \mid A^k) \trianglelefteq C_j$$

Typically, establishing these refinements will not depend on all the conjuncts in the definitions of the A^ℓ, but only of some. This is reflected by the following theorem:

Theorem 8 Sufficient Proof Condition. *Assume index sets* $I_1, \ldots I_k, I$, *and modal transition systems* $A_i^\ell, C_j (\ell \in \{1, \ldots, k\}, i \in I_\ell, j \in I)$ *such that all* C_j *and (for all* ℓ*) all the* A_i^ℓ *are pairwise consistent. If there are subsets* $I_{\ell,j} \subseteq I_\ell$ *for each* $\ell \in \{1, \ldots, k\}$ *and* $j \in I$, *such that*

$$\forall j \in I. \ \Big(\bigwedge_{i \in I_{1,j}} A_i^1 \mid \ldots \mid \bigwedge_{i \in I_{k,j}} A_i^k \Big) \backslash L \ \trianglelefteq \ C_j \tag{1}$$

then

$$\Big(\bigwedge_{i \in I_1} A_i^1 \mid \ldots \mid \bigwedge_{i \in I_k} A_i^k \Big) \backslash L \ \trianglelefteq \ \bigwedge_{j \in I} C_j \tag{2}$$

holds as well.

Of course, in general the power of this proof principle strongly depends on a good choice of the $I_{\ell,j}$.

4 Specification of the Untimed Problem

In this section, the memory component and the RPC mechanism are specified as modal transition systems. They will be defined as large conjunctions over projective views, each focusing on a certain aspect of the specification. The idea of having a large number of simple specifications is crucial for the application of our method.

4.1 Specification of the Memory Component

Problem 1(a): Write a formal specification of the Memory component and of the Reliable Memory component.

The specification of the memory can be split into the following six properties, where property M_5 is used for the reliable memory:

M_0 The memory component engages in actions only when it is called.

M_1 An operation that raises a BadArg exception has no effect on the memory.

M_2 Each successful read operation performs a single atomic read to the correct location at some time between the call and return.

M_3 Each write operation (successful or not) performs a sequence of one or more atomic writes of the correct value to the correct location at some time between the call and return.

M_4 The memory behaves as if it maintains an array of atomically read and written locations.

M_5 A memory failure never occurs.

The memory is capable of the following actions: accepting a read- or write-request, performing read's and write's, and issuing returns, which are either values or exceptions. A list of all actions of the memory is given in Fig. 4. The set of all actions of the memory component is denoted by Act_M (including the

ReqRd(id, loc) : accept a read-request for location loc from process id
ReqWr(id, loc, val) : accept a write-request of value val to location loc
from process id
Read(id, loc) : perform a read of location loc initiated by process id
Write(id, loc, val) : perform a write of value val to location loc initiated
by process id
$\overline{\text{RetRd}}$(id, val) : send return value val of a read-request to process id
$\overline{\text{RetWr}}$(id) : send return of a write-request to process id
$\overline{\text{BadArg}}$(id) : signal BadArg-exception to process id
$\overline{\text{MemFailure}}$(id) : signal MemFailure-exception to process id

Fig. 4. Actions of the Memory Component

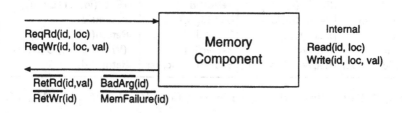

Fig. 5. Sorting Information of the Memory Component

invisible action τ). The sorting information of the memory component is given in Fig. 5. Note that output actions are always written with a bar on top.

Further we use the following shorthands for sets used in the specifications:

$$\text{Ex(id)} := \{\overline{\text{BadArg}}(\text{id}), \overline{\text{MemFailure}}(\text{id})\}$$
$$\text{Return(id)} := \overline{\text{RetRd}}(\text{id}, \_) \cup \overline{\text{RetWr}}(\text{id}) \cup \text{Ex(id)}$$
$$\text{ActRd(id)} := \text{ReqRd}(\text{id}, \_) \cup \text{Read}(\text{id}, \_) \cup \overline{\text{RetRd}}(\text{id}, \_) \cup \text{Ex(id)}$$
$$\text{ActWr(id)} := \text{ReqWr}(\text{id}, \_, \_) \cup \text{Write}(\text{id}, \_, \_) \cup \overline{\text{RetWr}}(\text{id}) \cup \text{Ex(id)}$$
$$\text{BadRd(id,loc)} := \text{Read}(\text{id}, \_) \setminus \{\text{Read}(\text{id}, \text{loc})\}$$
$$\text{BadWr(id,loc, val)} := \text{Write}(\text{id}, \_, \_) \setminus \{\text{Write}(\text{id}, \text{loc}, \text{val})\}$$

Now we can give modal constraints for M_0 through M_5. All constraints take parameters id, loc or val. In all constraints – apart from M_4 – the complement operator ($\neg$) has to be interpreted w.r.t. $\text{Act}_M(\text{id})$.

In the case of M_0, we give a specification for each value of id. The idea is that the memory may only perform internal actions (w.r.t. to id) between a call and a return from id. The specification is split into constraints $M_0^{rd}(\text{id})$ for the case of read actions and $M_0^{wr}(\text{id})$ for write requests as given in Fig. 6. The starte state of $M_0^{rd}(\text{id})$ does not constrain any actions relating to write requests, so it continuously permits actions from ActWr(id). The actions of a read call are restricted to read requests ReqRd(id, _). On seeing a read request, state 1 is entered, which continuously allows internal read actions. Return of id from

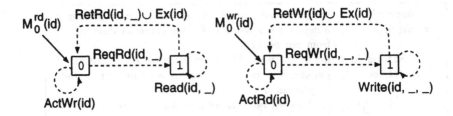

Fig. 6. Specification of M_0(id)

specification	α	β	γ
M_1(id)	Write(id, _, _)	BadArg(id)	¬RetWr(id)
M_{2a}(id)	ReqRd(id, _)	$\overline{\text{RetRd}}$(id, _)	¬ (Read(id, _) ∪ Ex(id))
M_{2b}(id, loc)	ReqRd(id, loc)	BadRd(id, loc)	¬Return(id)
M_{2c}(id)	Read(id, _)	Read(id, _)	¬Return(id)
M_{3a}(id)	ReqWr(id, _, _)	$\overline{\text{RetWr}}$(id)	¬ (Write(id, _, _) ∪ Ex(id))
M_{3b}(id, loc, val)	ReqWr(id, loc, val)	BadWr(id, loc, val)	¬Return(id)

Fig. 7. Pattern Instantiations for Specifications $M_1, M_{2a}, M_{2b}, M_{2c}, M_{3a}, M_{3b}$

a read is permitted as well, but these actions force M_0^{rd}(id) back into its start state, once again waiting for calls from id. M_0^{wr}(id) is defined analogously. The specification of M_0(id) is then the conjunction of both constraints.

The rest of the properties can be formulated using the pattern from Fig. 1. To do this, properties M_2 and M_3 have to be split into properties M_{2a}, M_{2b}, M_{2c} and M_{3a}, M_{3b}.

M_1(id)   after a Write(id, _, _) is observed, no BadArg(id) is allowed until a successful return for id (i.e. RetWr(id)) occurs,

M_{2a}(id)   after a ReqRd(id, _) is observed, no un-exceptional return (i.e. $\overline{\text{RetRd}}$(id, _)) is allowed until a Read(id, _) or an exceptional return (i.e. Ex(id)) occurs,

M_{2b}(id, loc)   after a ReqRd(id,loc) is observed, no read from a different location (i.e. BadRd(id, loc)) is allowed until a Return(id) occurs,

M_{2c}(id)   after a Read(id, _) was observed, no Read(id, _) is allowed until a Return(id) occurs,

M_{3a}(id)   after a ReqWr(id,_,_) is observed, no un-exceptional return (i.e. RetWr(id)) is allowed until a Write(id,_,_) or an exceptional return (i.e. Ex(id)) occurs,

M_{3b}(id, loc, val) after a ReqWr(id,loc,val) is observed, no write to a different location or of a different value (i.e. BadWr(id, loc, val)) is allowed until a Return(id) occurs.

From these intuitions, MTS's for M_{2a}(id), M_{2b}(id, loc), M_{2c}(id), M_{3a}(id) and M_{3b}(id, loc, val) can be derived. The sets α, β, γ used for the individual properties are given in Fig. 7.

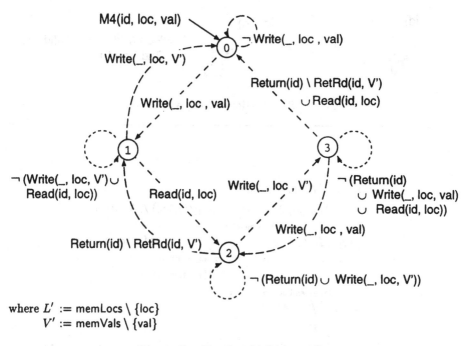

where $L' := \text{memLocs} \setminus \{\text{loc}\}$
$V' := \text{memVals} \setminus \{\text{val}\}$

Fig. 8. Specification $M_4(\text{id}, \text{loc}, \text{val})$

The specification of property M_4 is composed from constraints $M_4(\text{id}, \text{loc}, \text{val})$. Each constraint specifies when a read of location loc issued by process id will result in returning the value val. This constrains the legal reads to those consistent with previous writes. The constraint can be found in Fig. 8.

Specification M_4 differs from M_0 to M_3 as it is sensitive to actions (precisely: write actions) from other processes. Therefore states are not represented as squares, but by plain circles. The complement operator ($\neg$) has to be interpreted w.r.t. the whole action set Act_M. The states of $M_4(\text{id}, \text{loc}, \text{val})$ code the following properties:

- p_1 = the value in location loc is val
- p_2 = a Read(id, loc) has occured when p_1 was true, but yet no return action has been seen

Then states $0, 1, 2$, and 3 represent $\neg p_1 \wedge \neg p_2$, $p_1 \wedge \neg p_2$, $p_1 \wedge p_2$ and $\neg p_1 \wedge p_2$. The transitions in the specification can easily be inferred from this. Note that in state 3, observing Read(id, loc) will lead back to state 0. By this the value returned by a read will always be the value read by the last read action before the return (in the presence of multiple reads within one request). The complete specification of the memory M is defined by

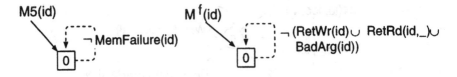

Fig. 9. Specifications $M_5(\text{id})$ and $M^f(\text{id})$

$$M(\text{id}) := M_0(\text{id}) \wedge M_1(\text{id})$$
$$\wedge\ M_{2a}(\text{id}) \wedge \bigwedge_{loc \in memLocs} M_{2b}(\text{id, loc}) \wedge M_{2c}(\text{id})$$
$$\wedge\ M_{3a}(\text{id}) \wedge \bigwedge_{loc \in memLocs, val \in memVals} M_{3b}(\text{id, loc, val})$$
$$\wedge \bigwedge_{loc \in memLocs, val \in memVals} M_4(\text{id, loc, val})$$
$$M := \bigwedge_{id \in procId} M(\text{id})$$

The specification of $M_5(\text{id})$ is trivial: a simple loop allowing anything but MemFailure(id), as given in Fig. 9. The reliable memory RM is derived from the memory by simply adding the constraint $M_5(\text{id})$.

$$RM(\text{id}) := M(\text{id}) \wedge M_5(\text{id})$$
$$RM := \bigwedge_{id \in procId} RM(\text{id})$$

This completes the specification of the memory and the reliable memory. Note that the exceptional returns MemFailure, BadArg are modelled non-deterministically, assuming that the decision is internal to the memory component. If more detailed information on the conditions under which a BadArg is raised were available, corresponding constraints could easily be added to the specification.

Problem 1(b): Either prove that a Reliable Memory component is a correct implementation of a Memory component, or explain why it should not be.

Within our framework, this means to establish the weak refinement

$$RM \trianglelefteq M$$

This refinement holds trivially, as adding constraints refines a specification.

Problem 1(c): If your specification of the Memory component allows an implementation that does nothing but raise MemFailure exceptions, explain why this is reasonable.

We specify the memory that always fails by adding the constraint $M^f(\text{id})$ given in Fig 9. This constraint specifies that no return other than a MemFailure is allowed. The ever-failing memory is then specified by

$$M^f := \bigwedge_{id \in procId} M^f(id)$$
$$FM := M \wedge M^f$$

As before, the refinement $FM \unlhd M$ holds trivially.

Although this is surely a behaviour not wanted by a user of the memory, we think that within this framework it is reasonable to allow this pathological case. In practice, there will be no difference between a memory that never works and one that almost never works. Therefore to rule out the extreme case of "not working" seems not to be reasonable. A specification as e.g. a memory wich works 80% the time is however out of scope of this paper.

4.2 Specification of the RPC Mechanism

Problem 2: Write a formal specification of the RPC component.

Now we give the specification of the RPC mechanism. Following [BL], the RPC knows exactly one procedure remoteCall which takes as arguments a procedure name and the arguments of the procedure.

For simplicity, instead of using actions remoteCall(id, ReqRd, loc)[5] we will directly write this as rReqRd(id, loc)[6], and similarly for all legal read- and write-calls. The rest of the calls are written proc(id, args), where proc $\in$ Procs, and args $\in$ ArgsList is a list of arguments. For the modelling of execptions we partition the set of all calls into:

$$
\begin{aligned}
\text{invalid(id)} \quad &:= \{\text{proc(id, args)} \mid \text{proc} \notin \text{Procs}\} \\
\text{wrongArgs(id)} &:= \{\text{proc(id, args)} \mid \text{proc} \in \text{Procs}, \text{args} \in \text{ArgsList}, \\
&\quad |\text{args}| \neq \text{ArgNum(proc)}\} \\
\text{CallOk(id)} \quad &:= \text{ReqRd(id, \_)} \cup \text{ReqWr(id, \_, \_)}
\end{aligned}
$$

The RPC then has essentially the same actions as the memory, given in Fig. 10. It lacks however the internal write's and read's, but instead is equipped with an additional RPCFail.

The sorting information of the RPC is given in Fig. 11. We can directly translate the informal operational specification of the RPC into a set of projective views. All projective views have the same structure (see Fig. 12): accept a command, pass the command, wait for a return, and pass the return. This is the loop through states 0 to 3. We allow the occurrence of an RPCFail along this loop, but not in-between passing of a call and waiting for a return. State 4 is the auxiliary state s' of pattern 2 as explained in Sect. 3.2. The action sets used here are:

---

[5] Note that due to our notational conventions the id parameter must come first!

[6] note that the prefix r is added to the action!

$$\overline{\text{ReqRd}}(\text{id}, \text{loc}) : \text{proc. id issues read-request for location loc}$$

$\overline{\text{ReqRd}}(\text{id}, \text{loc})$	: proc. id issues read-request for location loc
$\overline{\text{ReqWr}}(\text{id}, \text{loc}, \text{val})$	: proc. id issues write-request of value val to location loc
$\text{RetRd}(\text{id},\text{val})$	: return-value val of a read initiated by proc. id
$\text{RetWr}(\text{id})$	: return from a write initiated by proc. id
$\text{BadArg}(\text{id})$	: memory component raised a BadArg
$\text{MemFailure}(\text{id})$	: memory component raised a MemFailure
$\text{rReqRd}(\text{id}, \text{loc})$	: RPC receives a remote read of location loc from proc. id
$\text{rReqWr}(\text{id}, \text{loc}, \text{val})$	: RPC receives a remote write of value val to location loc from proc. id
$\text{proc}(\text{id}, \text{args})$	: a call which is not a legal read- or write-request
$\overline{\text{rRetRd}}(\text{id}, \text{val})$	: RPC returns from read issued by proc. id with value val
$\overline{\text{rRetWr}}(\text{id})$	: RPC returns from write issued by proc. id
$\overline{\text{rBadArg}}(\text{id})$	: RPC returns an exception from a call issued by proc. id
$\overline{\text{rMemFailure}}(\text{id})$	: RPC returns an exception from a call issued by proc. id
$\overline{\text{BadCall}}(\text{id})$	: RPC issues a BadCall-exception to proc. id
$\overline{\text{RPCFail}}(\text{id})$	: RPC failed for a call from proc. id

Fig. 10. Actions of the RPC

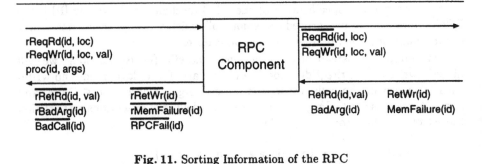

Fig. 11. Sorting Information of the RPC

$$\text{rCall}(\text{id}) := \text{rReqRd}(\text{id}, \_) \cup \text{rReqWr}(\text{id}, \_, \_) \cup \text{invalid}(\text{id}) \cup \text{wrongArgs}(\text{id})$$
$$\text{rRet}(\text{id}) := \overline{\text{rRetRd}}(\text{id}, \_) \cup \overline{\text{rRetWr}}(\text{id}, \_, \_) \cup$$
$$\overline{\text{rBadArg}}(\text{id}) \cup \overline{\text{rMemFailure}}(\text{id}) \cup \overline{\text{RPCFail}}(\text{id}) \cup \overline{\text{BadCall}}(\text{id})$$
$$\text{rRdRet}(\text{id}) := \text{RetRd}(\text{id}, \_) \cup \text{BadArg}(\text{id}) \cup \text{MemFailure}(\text{id})$$
$$\text{rWrRet}(\text{id}) := \text{RetWr}(\text{id}) \cup \text{BadArg}(\text{id}) \cup \text{MemFailure}(\text{id})$$

We specify constraints for the case of a read- and a write-request each. Each constraint models a possible read- resp. write-call with either a successful return, a BadArg or a MemFailure. Fig. 12 shows the general pattern for the case of a read- and a write-request. This pattern has two action-placeholders a and b. The values for a and b for the different cases are given in Fig. 13. The constraints R_{1a}, R_{1b}, R_{1c} use the pattern Rrd, constraints R_{2a}, R_{2b}, R_{2c} use pattern Rwr. From these simple constraints we define the basic read- and write-constraint:

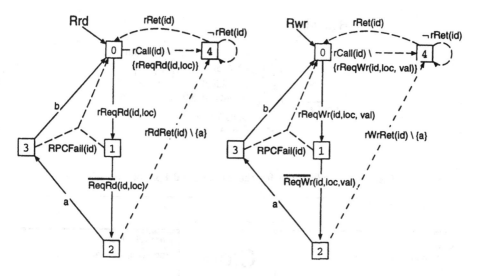

Fig. 12. Pattern for Rea- and Write-Part of the RPC

	a	b
R_{1a}(id, loc, val)	RetRd(id, val)	$\overline{\text{rRetRd}}$(id, val)
R_{1b}(id, loc, val)	BadArg(id)	$\overline{\text{rBadArg}}$(id)
R_{1c}(id, loc, val)	MemFailure(id)	$\overline{\text{rMemFailure}}$(id)
R_{2a}(id, loc, val)	RetWr(id, loc, val)	$\overline{\text{rRetWr}}$(id, loc, val,)
R_{2b}(id, loc, val)	BadArg(id)	$\overline{\text{rBadArg}}$(id)
R_{2c}(id, loc, val)	MemFailure(id)	$\overline{\text{rMemFailure}}$(id)

Fig. 13. Instantiations for RPC

$$R_1(\text{id}, \text{loc}, \text{val}) := R_{1a}(\text{id}, \text{loc}, \text{val}) \wedge R_{1b}(\text{id}, \text{loc}, \text{val}) \wedge R_{1c}(\text{id}, \text{loc}, \text{val})$$
$$R_2(\text{id}, \text{loc}, \text{val}) := R_{2a}(\text{id}, \text{loc}, \text{val}) \wedge R_{2b}(\text{id}, \text{loc}, \text{val}) \wedge R_{2c}(\text{id}, \text{loc}, \text{val})$$

Fig. 14 gives the constraint for calls different from read- and write-request. There are principal two behaviours: either a call has an incorrect number of arguments, or it has an invalid name. Both cases lead to a BadArg(id). The complete RPC can now be specified as follows, solving Problem 2:

$$R(\text{id}) := \bigwedge_{\text{loc}\in\text{memLocs},\text{val}\in\text{memVals}} \left(R_1(\text{id}, \text{loc}, \text{val}) \wedge R_2(\text{id}, \text{loc}, \text{val}) \right)$$
$$R := \bigwedge_{\text{id}\in\text{procId}} \left(R(\text{id}) \wedge R_{err}(\text{id}) \right)$$

Note that all constraints of the RPC follow the design pattern 2 from Sect. 3.2. The return-set R here is rRet(id), the auxiliary state is state no. 4 in the patterns

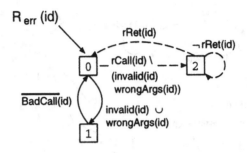

Fig. 14. Specifications for the Exceptional Part of the RPC

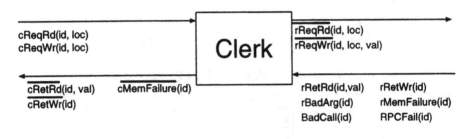

Fig. 15. Sorting Information of the Clerk

for read and write, and state no. 2 in the exception constraint. For a pair of two read or two write constraints, the states $s1, s2$ are their states no. 2. For all other pairs, the states $s1, s2$ are the start states.

4.3 The Clerk

In order to give a complete specification of the implementation, we need an additional component, the clerk. The clerk is specified in the same way as the RPC, with the only difference that if it receives an RPCFail from the RPC, it may choose between a re-issue of the request or signaling a MemFailure.

The actions of the clerk are the same as that of the RPC, with the prefix r replaced by c. Their names are in Fig. 15, which shows the clerk's sorting information.

The clerk has components C_i, $i \in \{1a, \ldots, 1d, 2a, \ldots, 2d\}$. As in the case of the RPC, these constraints model a read (write) with all possible returns. The general pattern for the read-part is given in Fig. 16, the instantiations for a and b are in Fig. 17. The action sets used are:

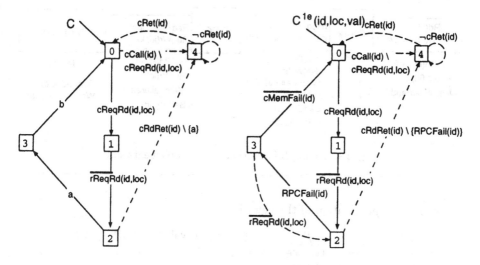

Fig. 16. Specification Patterns of the Clerk

	a	b
C_{1a}(id, loc, val)	cReqRd(id, val)	$\overline{\text{rReqRd}}$(id, val)
C_{1b}(id, loc, val)	BadArg(id)	$\overline{\text{cMemFailure}}$(id)
C_{1c}(id, loc, val)	MemFailure(id)	$\overline{\text{cMemFailure}}$(id)
C_{1d}(id, loc, val)	BadCall(id)	$\overline{\text{cMemFailure}}$(id)

Fig. 17. Instantiations for Clerk Read-Part

$$\text{cCall(id)} := \overline{\text{cReqRd(id, \_)} \cup \text{cReqWr(id, \_, \_)}}$$
$$\text{cRet(id)} := \overline{\text{cRetRd}}\text{(id, \_)} \cup \overline{\text{cRetWr}}\text{(id)} \cup \overline{\text{cMemFailure}}\text{(id)}$$
$$\text{cRdRet(id)} := \text{rRetRd(id, \_)} \cup$$
$$\text{rBadArg(id)} \cup \text{rMemFailure(id)} \cup \text{BadCall(id)} \cup \text{RPCFail(id)}$$
$$\text{cWrRet(id)} := \text{rRetWr(id)} \cup$$
$$\text{rBadArg(id)} \cup \text{rMemFailure(id)} \cup \text{BadCall(id)} \cup \text{RPCFail(id)}$$

In the same figure, an additional specification C_{1e}(id, loc, val) is given, which models the possible repetition of the call after an RPCFail. There is a corresponding specification C_{2e}. The read- and write-constraint of the clerk are defined using these small constraints:

$$C_1(\text{id, loc, val}) := \bigwedge_{i \in \{1a,\dots,1e\}} C_i(\text{id, loc, val})$$
$$C_2(\text{id, loc, val}) := \bigwedge_{i \in \{2a,\dots,2e\}} C_i(\text{id, loc, val})$$

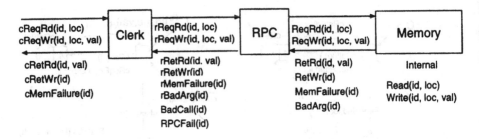

Fig. 18. Sorting Information of the Implementation

The complete specification of the clerk is

$$C(\text{id}) := \bigwedge_{\text{loc}\in\text{memLocs},\text{val}\in\text{memVals}} \big(C_1(\text{id},\text{loc},\text{val}) \wedge C_2(\text{id},\text{loc},\text{val})\big)$$

$$C := \bigwedge_{\text{id}\in\text{procId}} C(\text{id})$$

Note that again all these constraints follow the pattern 2 explained in Sect. 3.2. The return-set here is cRet(id), and the states s', s_1, s_2 are as in the case of the RPC.

5 Applying the Method

Problem 3: Write a formal specification of the implementation, and prove that it correctly implements the specification of the Memory component of Problem 1.

As we already mentioned in the discussion, there is a problem with using M_{2c} in the verification (see p. 407). From now on assume the (reliable) memory is specified without using M_{2c}.

5.1 Formal Specification of the Implementation

The implementation is based on the composition of the reliable memory, the RPC and the clerk shown in Fig. 18. However, in order to compare the implementation to the memory component, we need to restrict its visible actions to the set consisting of the actions of the clerk and the internal actions of the memory:

$$A := \{\ \text{cReqRd}(\text{id},\text{loc}), \text{cReqWr}(\text{id},\text{loc},\text{val}), \overline{\text{cRetRd}}(\text{id},\text{val}), \overline{\text{cRetWr}}(\text{id}),$$
$$\overline{\text{cMemFailure}}(\text{id}), \text{Read}(\text{id},\text{loc}), \text{Write}(\text{id},\text{loc},\text{val})\ |$$
$$\text{id}\in\text{procId}, \text{loc}\in\text{memLocs}, \text{val}\in\text{memVals}\}$$

Further we have to rename the actions of the clerk to the external actions of the memory. The renaming function f simply skips the leading 'c' of all actions that possess a corresponding external action of the memory. Summarizing this leads to the following process term:

$$I := ((C \,|\, R \,|\, RM) \setminus A)[f]$$

5.2 Proof of Correctness

In our framework, this requires the verification of the following refinement:

$$I \trianglelefteq M \qquad (3)$$

As shown in the following subsections, the three reduction steps of our method suffice to complete the correctness proof by automatic verification.

Step 1: Application of the Sufficient Proof Condition Concentrating on a specific process id, our claim follows from

$$\forall \, \text{id} \in \text{procId}. \ I(\text{id}) \trianglelefteq M(\text{id}) \qquad (4)$$

where $I(\text{id}) := \left((C(\text{id}) \mid R(\text{id}) \mid RM(\text{id})) \setminus A \right)[f]$. Of course, such an extreme decomposition is not always successful, but as we will see, it suffices here. In fact, the problem can be broken down into even smaller parts, by concentrating on specific triples (id, loc, val). In the case of the memory this yields:

$$
\begin{aligned}
M(\text{id}, \text{loc}, \text{val}) := \ & M_0(\text{id}) \wedge M_1(\text{id}) \\
& \wedge \ M_{2a}(\text{id}) \wedge M_{2b}(\text{id}, \text{loc}) \\
& \wedge \ M_{3a}(\text{id}) \wedge M3b(\text{id}, \text{loc}, \text{val}) \\
& \wedge \ M_4(\text{id}, \text{loc}, \text{val})
\end{aligned}
$$

This decomposition can be used on the right-hand side of (4), but not on the left-hand side, as this would result in too much freedom when read's and write's with parameters different from loc, val are concerned. Property M_4 is the only property on the left-hand side which can be decomposed in this way. To make use of this we define:

$$
\begin{aligned}
M_2(\text{id}) \quad &:= M_{2a}(\text{id}) \wedge \bigwedge_{\text{loc} \in \text{memLocs}} M_{2b}(\text{id}, \text{loc}) \\
M_3(\text{id}) \quad &:= M_{3a}(\text{id}) \wedge \bigwedge_{\text{loc} \in \text{memLocs}, \text{val} \in \text{memVals}} M_{3b}(\text{id}, \text{loc}, \text{val}) \\
RM(\text{id}, \text{loc}, \text{val}) &:= M_0(\text{id}) \wedge M_1(\text{id}) \wedge M_2(\text{id}) \wedge M_3(\text{id}) \\
& \quad \wedge \ M_4(\text{id}, \text{loc}, \text{val}) \\
& \quad \wedge \ M_5(\text{id}) \\
I(\text{id}, \text{loc}, \text{val}) \quad &:= \left((C(\text{id}) \mid R(\text{id}) \mid RM(\text{id}, \text{loc}, \text{val})) \setminus A \right)[f]
\end{aligned}
$$

This leads to the following sufficient proof condition for (4):

$$\forall \, \text{id}, \text{loc}, \text{val}. \ I(\text{loc}, \text{val}, \text{id}) \trianglelefteq M(\text{id}, \text{loc}, \text{val}) \qquad (5)$$

Step 2: Skolemization It is easy to see that the proof of

$$I(\text{loc}, \text{val}, \text{id}) \trianglelefteq M(\text{id}, \text{loc}, \text{val}) \tag{6}$$

does not depend on the particular choice of the triple $(\text{id}, \text{loc}, \text{val})$. Therefore it suffices to prove the above for prototypical values id, loc and val. However, the transition system for $I(\text{loc}, \text{val}, \text{id})$ is still infinite state, and the transition system for $M(\text{id}, \text{loc}, \text{val})$ has infinitely many transitions, although it is small in the number of states. This problem can be overcome in the subsequent abstraction step.

Step 3(a): Abstraction by Refinement We use generalizations (cf. Sect. 3.3) to reduce the number of states in $I(\text{id}, \text{loc}, \text{val})$. Assume id, loc, val to be fixed from now on. We use auxiliary sets $L' := \text{memLocs} \setminus \{\text{loc}\}$ and $V' := \text{memVals} \setminus \{\text{val}\}$ in order to define:

$$
\begin{aligned}
M_2'(\text{id}) \quad &:= M_{2a}(\text{id}) \wedge M_{2b}(\text{id}, \text{loc}) \wedge M_{2b}(\text{id}, L') \\
M_3'(\text{id}) \quad &:= M_{3a}(\text{id}) \wedge M_{3b}(\text{id}, \text{loc}, \text{val}) \wedge M_{3b}(\text{id}, \text{loc}, V') \\
&\quad \wedge M_{3b}(\text{id}, L', \text{val}) \wedge M_{3b}(\text{id}, L', V') \\
RM'(\text{id}, \text{loc}, \text{val}) &:= M_0(\text{id}) \wedge M_1(\text{id}) \wedge M_2'(\text{id}) \wedge M_3'(\text{id}) \\
&\quad \wedge M_4(\text{id}, \text{loc}, \text{val}) \\
&\quad \wedge M_5(\text{id}) \\
R_1'(\text{id}) \quad &:= R_1(\text{id}, \text{loc}, \text{val}) \wedge R_1(\text{id}, \text{loc}, V') \wedge R_1(\text{id}, L', \text{val}) \wedge R_1(\text{id}, L', V') \\
R_2'(\text{id}) \quad &:= R_2(\text{id}, \text{loc}, \text{val}) \wedge R_2(\text{id}, \text{loc}, V') \wedge R_2(\text{id}, L', \text{val}) \wedge R_2(\text{id}, L', V') \\
R'(\text{id}) \quad &:= R_1'(\text{id}) \wedge R_2'(\text{id}) \wedge R_{err}(\text{id}) \\
C_1'(\text{id}) \quad &:= C_1(\text{id}, \text{loc}, \text{val}) \wedge C_1(\text{id}, \text{loc}, V') \wedge C_1(\text{id}, L', \text{val}) \wedge C_1(\text{id}, L', V') \\
C_2'(\text{id}) \quad &:= C_2(\text{id}, \text{loc}, \text{val}) \wedge C_2(\text{id}, \text{loc}, V') \wedge C_2(\text{id}, L', \text{val}) \wedge C_2(\text{id}, L', V') \\
C'(\text{id}) \quad &:= C_1'(\text{id}) \wedge C_2'(\text{id}) \\
I'(\text{id}, \text{loc}, \text{val}) &:= \big((C'(\text{id}) \mid R'(\text{id}) \mid RM'(\text{id}, \text{loc}, \text{val})) \setminus A \big) [f]
\end{aligned}
$$

Due to the properties of generalizations we have

$$I(\text{id}, \text{loc}, \text{val}) \trianglelefteq I'(\text{id}, \text{loc}, \text{val})$$

Thus it suffices to prove

$$I'(\text{id}, \text{loc}, \text{val}) \trianglelefteq M(\text{id}, \text{loc}, \text{val}) \tag{7}$$

Using abstraction, we have successfully reduced the problem to one of finite states.

Step 3(b): Abstraction by Factorization While the specifications in (7) are finite-state now, they still have an infinite number of transitions. This section applies abstraction to reduce the number of actions, using collapsed transition systems:

Definition 9. Let P be an MTS over Act with transition relations $\to_\square, \to_\diamond$. Each equivalence relation $\equiv$ on Act induces a *collapsed MTS* $P^\equiv$ over the alphabet $\text{Act}_\equiv := \{[a] \mid a \in \text{Act}\}$ and transition relations $\to'_\square, \to'_\diamond$ defined by

$$\frac{p \xrightarrow{a}_\square p'}{p \xrightarrow{[a]'}_\square p'} \qquad \frac{p \xrightarrow{a}_\diamond p'}{p \xrightarrow{[a]'}_\diamond p'}$$

An equivalence relation $\equiv$ on Act is *compatible* with P iff for all $a' \in [a]$ and all reachable states p, p' of P:

$$p \xrightarrow{a}_\square p' \text{ iff } p \xrightarrow{a'}_\square p' \quad \text{and} \quad p \xrightarrow{a}_\diamond p' \text{ iff } p \xrightarrow{a'}_\diamond p'$$

For compatible equivalence relations, we have the following reduction lemma:

Lemma 10. *Let P and Q be two MTS's and $\equiv$ be an equivalence relation on their common alphabet compatible with P and Q. Then the following holds:*

- *$P^\equiv \trianglelefteq Q^\equiv$ implies $P \trianglelefteq Q$,*
- *if $[\tau] = \{\tau\}$ then $\equiv$ is compatible with $P \mid Q$, and $(P \mid Q)^\equiv = P^\equiv \mid Q^\equiv$*
- *if $[\tau] = \{\tau\}$ and for $L \subseteq \text{Act}$ and every $a \in \text{Act}$ either $[a] \cap L = [a]$ or $[a] \cap L = \emptyset$, then $\equiv$ is compatible with $P \setminus L$, and $(P \setminus L)^\equiv = P^\equiv \setminus L^\equiv$ (where $L^\equiv$ is L factorized w.r.t. $\equiv$).*

This Reduction Lemma allows us to collapse the transition system in our proof.

A suitable abstraction here is the one which distinguishes between actions with parameters id, loc or val and ones with at least one parameter different from id, loc or val. Intuitively, this is best seen with the specification M_{3b}, which clearly distinguishes between a correct write (where parameters must be loc and val), and a incorrect write operation (either a write to a location different from loc or of a value different from val).

To ensure compatibility of the equivalence relation, every equivalence class must be a subset of an action set which is a label in the specification. From this reasoning the following compatible equivalence relation can be found:

For fixed loc $\in$ memLocs, val $\in$ memVals, id $\in$ procId, let $L' :=$ memLocs $\setminus$ {loc}, $V' :=$ memVals $\setminus$ {val}, and $P' :=$ procId $\setminus$ {id}.

The actions of processes id' $\in P'$ fall into the following equivalence classes:

- $\bigcup_{\text{id'} \in P'} \text{Act}(\text{id'}) \setminus \{\text{Write}(\text{id'}, \text{loc'}, \text{val'}) \mid \text{id'} \in P', \text{loc'} \in \text{memLocs}, \text{val'} \in \text{memVals}\}$,
- $\{\text{Write}(\text{id'}, \text{loc}, \text{val}) \mid \text{id'} \in P'\}$,
- $\{\text{Write}(\text{id'}, \text{loc}, \text{val'}) \mid \text{id'} \in P', \text{val'} \in V'\}$
- $\{\text{Write}(\text{id'}, \text{loc'}, \text{val}) \mid \text{id'} \in P', \text{loc'} \in L'\}$
- $\{\text{Write}(\text{id'}, \text{loc'}, \text{val'}) \mid \text{id'} \in P', (\text{loc'}, \text{val'}) \in L' \times V'\}$

Splitting the actions of processes id' into these equivalence classes is necessary due to constraint M_4. It is obvious that the classes are compatible with M_4.

We list the equivalence classes for an abstract action α of process id. If α has

$$a_\diamond.P \overset{\varepsilon(d)}{\to}_\square a_\diamond.P \qquad\qquad a_\diamond.P \overset{\varepsilon(d)}{\to}_\diamond a_\diamond.P$$

$$a_\square.P \overset{\varepsilon(d)}{\to}_\square a_\square.P \qquad\qquad a_\square.P \overset{\varepsilon(d)}{\to}_\diamond a_\square.P$$

$$\varepsilon(d).P \overset{\varepsilon(d)}{\to}_\square P \qquad\qquad \varepsilon(d).P \overset{\varepsilon(d)}{\to}_\diamond P$$

$$\varepsilon(c+d).P \overset{\varepsilon(c)}{\to}_\square \varepsilon(d).P \qquad\qquad \varepsilon(c+d).P \overset{\varepsilon(c)}{\to}_\diamond \varepsilon(d).P$$

Fig. 19. Rules for TMS

- only a process parameter: $\{\alpha(\mathsf{id})\}$
- a process and a location parameter: $\{\alpha(\mathsf{id},\mathsf{loc})\}$, $\{\alpha(\mathsf{id},\mathsf{loc}') \mid \mathsf{loc}' \in L'\}$
- a process and a value parameter: $\{\alpha(\mathsf{id},\mathsf{val})\}$, $\{\alpha(\mathsf{id},\mathsf{val}') \mid \mathsf{val}' \in V'\}$
- has all three parameters: $\{\alpha(\mathsf{id},\mathsf{loc},\mathsf{val})\}$, $\{\alpha(\mathsf{id},\mathsf{loc},\mathsf{val}') \mid \mathsf{loc}' \in L'\}$, $\{\alpha(\mathsf{id},\mathsf{loc}',\mathsf{val}) \mid \mathsf{val}' \in V'\}$, $\{\alpha(\mathsf{id},\mathsf{loc}',\mathsf{val}') \mid (\mathsf{loc}',\mathsf{val}') \in L' \times V'\}$

By replacing the transition systems in (7) by their collapsed counterparts, we arrive at a problem which is small in the number of states and actions. The resulting problem has been successfully verified using the EPSILON tool, yielding a complete formal proof for Problem 3. The EPSILON tool has neither a conjunction nor a renaming operator, and it does not support action sets as transition labels. Two simple preprocessors (300 and 100 lines of awk-source) were written to allow the use conjunction and action sets. Moreover, instead of applying the renaming f to the left-hand side of (7), we applied the renaming f^{-1} to the right-hand side. This was done by hand using the find-and-replace operation of the editor. The implementation has 116 states, and the memory has 19 states. On a double-processor SPARCstation 20 it takes little less than 40 CPU-seconds to establish the refinement, which has 162 pairs of states.

6 Timed Modal Specification

In the following, we will show how to verify the timed part of the RPC-Memory problem. This section gives an introduction to Timed Modal Specifications (TMS), an extension of MTS to real time. Using TMS, we give a specification of the lossy RPC and a timed version of the clerk. Both are very similar in structure to their untimed counterparts.

To model real time behaviour, modal transition systems can be extended to *Timed Modal Specifications* (TMS) by means of delay-transitions. Delay-transitions are labelled by actions $\varepsilon(d)$, where d is a positive real number. Syntactically, delays are written as prefixes $\varepsilon(d)$: the specification $\varepsilon(d).P$ will delay for time d, and then behave as P. The interpretation of $a_\square.P$ (resp. of $a_\diamond.P$) changes: action a is ready immediately, but may be taken after any delay. These changes and extensions are reflected by the rules given in Fig. 19.

Timed Modal Specifications come equipped with operators such as restriction, non-deterministic choice and parallel composition, which are defined as conservative extension of Wang's TCCS[Yi91]. TCCS relies on *maximal progress*:

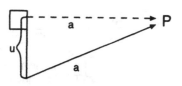

Fig. 20. Representation of $a[0, u].P$

---

internal communication takes place as soon as it becomes available. Therefore, in TMS parallel composition satisfies:

1. a TMS will not allow time-steps if it requires an internal action
2. a TMS will not require time-steps if it allows an internal action

Intuitively by (1) a state requiring a τ may not delay for any amount of time, thus forcing either the communication or another discrete change to happen, while by (2) if a delay is required, no internal communication may be enabled.

Lower time bounds are easily specified in TMS, but for upper time bounds maximal progress is required. We will use a macro operator to specify intervals. The specification $a[\ell, u].P$ ($\ell, u \in \mathbb{R}^{\geq 0}, \ell \leq u$) allows a to happen within ℓ and requires a to be enabled after u time units. The macro is defined as $(\varepsilon(l).a_\diamond + \varepsilon(u).a_\square).P$. The upper bound u will only be fulfilled due to maximal progress. Fig. 20 gives the transition system representation of $a[0, u].P$.

The notion of refinement, weak refinement, consistency and conjunction carry over from Modal Specifications to TMS without problem, so there is no difference in applying our method to MTS or TMS. More elaborated introductions to Timed Modal Specifications can be found in [CGL93, God94].

7 Specification of the Timed Problem

Problem 4: Write a formal specification of the Lossy RPC component.

The specification of the *lossy RPC* demands an RPC R^δ which passes calls and returns within time δ. Further a timed clerk $C^{2\delta+\epsilon}$ is required which raises an exception if a return is outstanding for a delay greater than $2\delta + \epsilon$.

The specifications for R^δ and $C^{2\delta+\epsilon}$ have very much the same structure as their untimed counterparts, and the few differences uniformly apply to all the involved constraints. We will therefore discuss these differences only for some constraints, and leave the straightforward adaptation for the others to the reader.

Instead of signaling an RPCFail, the timed RPC never returns. This is modelled by an non-deterministic choice between passing calls resp. returns and an internal transition back to the start state, where the latter models the choice of not returning from the call.

Calls and returns (exceptional or not) must be passed within time δ. This is modelled by adding an interval $[0, \delta]$ to the transitions which pass the calls resp. returns. The resulting specification pattern for the lossy RPC is given in Fig. 21.

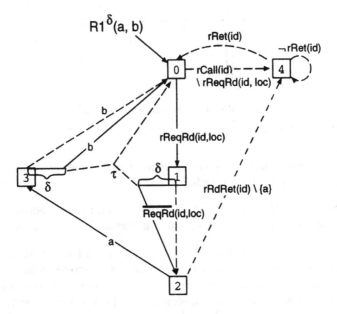

Fig. 21. Pattern for Lossy RPC

The lossy RPC R^δ is then composed from constraints $R_1^\delta(\text{id, loc, val})$, $R_2^\delta(\text{id, loc, val})$ as before. This solves Problem 4.

The timed clerk $C^{2\delta+\epsilon}$ passes calls and returns as before, but if a return is not seen within time $2\delta + \epsilon$, a cMemFailure is raised. This is modelled by a timeout construct as was done with R^δ. The pattern for the timed clerk is given in Fig. 22.

Problem 5(a): Write a formal specification of this implementation. The implementation of the lossy RPC is then defined by

$$R^\delta \mid C^{2\delta+\epsilon}$$

8 Applying the Method

The proof given in this section follows the same pattern as the correctness proof of the untimed case. Therefore we will not discuss the problem at the same level of detail as before.

Problem 5(b): Prove that, if every call to a procedure in Procs *returns within* ϵ *seconds, then the implementation satisfies the specification of the RPC component in Problem 2.*

We model the assumption that any call issued by the RPC returns within time ϵ by a TMS Δ^ϵ. The specification Δ^ϵ is a conjunction of constraints $\Delta_1^\epsilon(\text{id, loc, val})$ and $\Delta_2^\epsilon(\text{id, loc, val})$, built up from constraints Δ_{1a}^ϵ, etc. following the pattern of the RPC. We only give $\Delta_{1a}^\epsilon(\text{id, loc, val})$ in Fig. 23. Each constraint

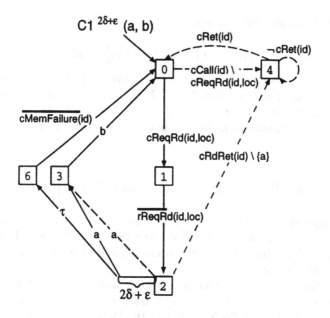

Fig. 22. Specification Pattern of the Timed Clerk

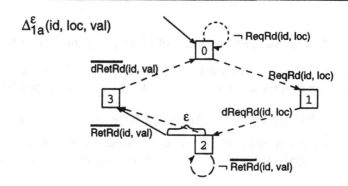

Fig. 23. Example of the Delay Component

models the assumption that a call issued by process id will send some return (exceptional or not) within ϵ. Further every action is echoed (e.g. in the case of a **ReqRd** as **dReqRd**). This is necessary as otherwise the interface from the RPC to the memory would be absorbed by Δ^ϵ. The specification of Δ^ϵ is the conjunction over all these constraints:

$$\Delta^\epsilon(\text{id}) := \bigwedge_{\text{loc}\in\text{memLocs},\text{val}\in\text{memVals}} \left(\Delta_1^\epsilon(\text{id}, \text{loc}, \text{val}) \wedge \Delta_2^\epsilon(\text{id}, \text{loc}, \text{val})\right)$$

$$\Delta^\epsilon := \bigwedge_{\text{id}\in\text{procId}} \Delta^\epsilon(\text{id})$$

Problem 5(b) can now be formalized:

$$((C^{2\delta+\epsilon} \mid R^\delta \mid \Delta^\epsilon) \setminus B)\,[g] \trianglelefteq R \qquad (8)$$

where B restricts the visible actions to the inputs of the clerk and the echo-actions of the delay specification (e.g. dReqRd), while g renames these actions to the in- and output-actions of the RPC.

By the same arguments as for the untimed problem, we can reduce this to problems of the form

$$((C^{2\delta+\epsilon}(\text{id}, \text{loc}, \text{val}) \mid R^\delta(\text{id}, \text{loc}, \text{val}) \mid \Delta^\epsilon(\text{id}, \text{loc}, \text{val})) \setminus B)\,[g] \trianglelefteq R(\text{id}, \text{loc}, \text{val})$$
$$(9)$$

All the components here have a small number of states and transitions, so the refinement could in general be verified using the EPSILON tool. However, there is a certain problem here: EPSILON cannot handle the timing parameters δ and ϵ occurring within the specifications.

Luckily there is a simple transformation reducing this problem of two parameters δ and ϵ into a problem with only one parameter. The parallel composition of the timed RPC $R^\delta(\text{id}, \text{loc}, \text{val})$ and the Delay Component $\Delta^\epsilon(\text{id}, \text{loc}, \text{val})$ is equivalent to a specification $P^{2\delta+\epsilon}(\text{id}, \text{loc}, \text{val})$ with timing parameter $2\delta + \epsilon$ only:

$$((C^{2\delta+\epsilon}(\text{id}, \text{loc}, \text{val}) \mid P^{2\delta+\epsilon}(\text{id}, \text{loc}, \text{val})) \setminus B)\,[g] \trianglelefteq R(\text{id}, \text{loc}, \text{val}) \qquad (10)$$

The parameter $2\delta + \epsilon$ can be safely eliminated by multiplying all timing constraints with its reciprocal. This leaves us with the verification problem

$$((C^1(\text{id}, \text{loc}, \text{val}) \mid P^1(\text{id}, \text{loc}, \text{val})) \setminus B)\,[g] \trianglelefteq R(\text{id}, \text{loc}, \text{val}) \qquad (11)$$

which has no parameters left in the timing constraint, but only constants. This refinement was again successfully verified using EPSILON, which solves Problem 5(b).

9 Conclusion and Future Work

We have successfully applied our constraint-oriented method for the (automated) verification of concurrent systems to the RPC-Memory Specification Problem. We showed that the complete specification can be expressed as Modal Transition Systems or Timed Modal Specifications (in the real-time case). All subproblems could be solved using our method.

Key concepts of our 'divide and conquer' method are *projective views, separation of proof obligations, Skolemization* and *abstraction*, which together support a drastic reduction of the complexity of the relevant subproblems. Of course, our proof methodology does neither guarantee the possibility of a finite state reduction nor a straightforward method for finding the right amount of separation or the adequate abstraction. Still, there is a large class of problems and systems, where the method can be applied quite straightforwardly. Typical examples are systems with limited data dependence. Whereas involved data dependencies may exclude any possibility of 'horizontal' decomposition, our approach elegantly extends to real time systems, even over a dense time domain. In fact, the resulting finite state problems can be automatically verified using the EPSILON verification system.

Note that a major advantage of our method over other approaches is that the original specification matches the informal specification quite naturally, and that the abstractions used in the proof can be proved correct on the basis of very simple syntactic conditions. We are currently investigating how to use the theorem prover Isabelle ([Pau94]) to verify these conditions. Note that the problem with these conditions is that although they are simple, in general they involve infinite sets.

Beside the specification and verification of the RPC-Memory Problem, additional case studies of our method can be found in [LSW95a] and [LSW95b].

Despite further case studies and the search for good heuristics for proof obligation separation and abstraction, we are investigating the limits of tool support during the construction of constraint based specifications and the application of the three reduction steps. Whereas support by graphical interfaces and interactive editors is obvious and partly implemented in META-Frame, a management system for synthesis, analysis and verification currently developed at the university of Passau, the limits of consistency checking and tool supported search for adequate separation and abstraction are still an interesting open research topic.

As pointed out, one major problem are parameters in the timing constraints. We are currently investigating methods – similar to the approach presented for parametrized timed automata in [AHV93] – for checking bisimulation and (weak) refinement for *parametrized modal transition systems*.

For those interested in more detailed information, we have set up a page on the WWW: http://www-il.informatik.rwth-aachen.de/~carsten/com.html

References

[AHV93] R. Alur, T.A. Henzinger, M.Y. Vardi. *Parametric real-time reasoning.* Proc. 25th STOC, ACM Press 1993, pp. 592–601.

[BL] M. Broy, L. Lamport. *The RPC-Memory Specification Problem.* This volume.

[CES83] E. Clarke, E.A. Emerson, A.P. Sistla. *Automatic Verification of Finite State Concurrent Systems using Temporal Logic Specifications: A Practical Approach.* In Proceedings 10th POPL'83, 1983

[CGL93] K. Čerāns, J.C. Godsken, K.G. Larsen. *Timed Modal Specification - Theory and Tools.* in: C. Courcoubetis (Ed.), Proc. 5th Int. Conf. on Computer Aided Verification (CAV '93), Elounda, Greece, June/July 1993. LNCS 697, Springer Berlin 1993, pp. 253–267.

[God94] J. C. Godskesen. Timed Modal Specifications – A Theory for Verification of Real–Time Concurrent Systems. Ph.D.Thesis, Aalborg Univ., R–94–2039, Oct. '94.

[HL89]   H. Hüttel and K. Larsen. *The use of static constructs in a modal process logic.* Proceedings of Logic at Botik'89. LNCS 363, 1989.

[Lar90]   K.G. Larsen. *Modal specifications.* In: Proceedings of Workshop on Automatic Verification Methods for Finite State Systems LNCS 407, 1990.

[LT88]   K. Larsen and B. Thomsen. *A modal process logic.* In: Proceedings LICS'88, 1988.

[LSW95a]   K.G. Larsen, B. Steffen, C. Weise. *A constraint oriented proof methodology based on modal transition systems.* in: Proceedings 1st Workshop Tools and Algorithms for the Construction and Analysis of Systems, Lecture Notes in Computer Science Vol. 1019, Springer Verlag 1995, S. 17–40.

[LSW95b]   K.G. Larsen, B. Steffen, C. Weise. *Fischer's Protocol Revisited: A Simple Proof Using Modal Constraints.* in: Proc. Workshop on Verification and Control of Hybrid Systems, New Brunswick, 1995, to appear in LNCS.

[LSW96]   K.G. Larsen, B. Steffen, C. Weise. *A Case Study in Modal Constraint Methodology: The RPC-Memory Problem.* Aachener Informatik Berichte, Technical Report, Aachen University of Technology, to appear.

[Mil89]   R. Milner. *Communication and Concurrency.* Prentice-Hall, 1989.

[Par81]   D. Park. *Concurrency and automata on infinite sequences.* In P. Deussen (ed.), 5th GI Conference, LNCS 104, pp. 167–183, 1981.

[Pau94]   L. C. Paulson. *Isabelle.* LNCS 828, Springer New York 1994.

[Ste93]   B. Steffen. *Generating data flow analysis from modal specifications.* in: Science of Computer Programming 21, (1993), pp. 115-139.

[Yi91]   W. Yi. *CCS + Time = an Interleaving Model for Real-Time Systems,* Proc.18th Int. Coll. on Automata, Languages and Programming (ICALP), Madrid, July 1991. LNCS 510, Springer New York 1991, pp. 217-228.

Tackling
the
RPC-Memory Specification Problem
with
I/O Automata*

Judi Romijn

CWI

P.O. Box 94079, 1090 GB Amsterdam, The Netherlands
judi@cwi.nl

Abstract. An I/O automata solution to the problem posed in 1994 by Broy & Lamport at the Dagstuhl Workshop on Reactive Systems is presented. The problem calls for specification and verification of memory and remote procedure call components. The problem specification consists of an untimed and a timed part. In this paper, both parts are solved completely.

Keywords. Concurrency, protocol verification, I/O automata, fairness, liveness, real time.

1 Introduction

An example of an distributed system specification problem was stated at the Workshop on Reactive Systems, held in Dagstuhl, Germany in September 1994. The problem concerned the specification of a memory component and a remote procedure call (RPC) component, and the implementation of both. The specification problem is stated in full elsewhere in this volume. In the remainder of this paper, we assume that the reader is familiar with it.

The workshop's main intention was to compare different formalisms by applying them to this example, in order to understand the similarities and differences of the various approaches, as well as their strengths and weaknesses. The problem has been solved completely in [1, 5, 6, 9, 12, 13, 22]. Other papers on this topic are [2, 3, 4, 8, 10, 11, 23] which only solve the untimed part, and [20] which simplifies the problem to a situation with only one sender and one receiver.

This paper is the result of a successful attempt to model and verify the RPC-Memory problem with the I/O automata model [7, 16, 17, 18, 21, 14]. The next

---

* The results reported in this paper have been obtained as part of the research project "Specification, Testing and Verification of Software for Technical Applications", which is being carried out by the Stichting Mathematisch Centrum for Philips Research Laboratories under Contract RWC-061-PS-950006-ps.

two sections dwell on the obstacles that were encountered during the birth of this paper, and on the merits of I/O automata.

1.1 Notes on the problem specification

Ambiguities The informal descriptions of the memory component in Problem 1 and the RPC component in Problem 2 are slightly ambiguous. It is not clear whether these components may issue a failure when a bad call is received. In both cases we have chosen to allow this, because it yields a more general specification. For the memory component this decision conforms with the implementation proposed in Problem 3.

Observable versus internal behaviour Problem 3 requires a proof that a composition of components implements the memory component. The memory component can perform at most one internal read action between call and return. The proposed implementation, however, can do this an arbitrary (but finite!) number of times. The proof for the implementation relation is simplified substantially if one assumes that the memory component can perform an arbitrary number of internal read actions instead of at most one. The solution of Abadi, Lamport & Merz [1] uses such a more convenient memory component, and thus implicitly assumes that the two memory components are observationally equivalent. We prove formally that this assumption is correct, which requires a backward simulation proof of about four pages.

In the solution of Hooman [9] the correctness of this assumption is also proved, with seemingly much less effort. This is due to a difference in view on executions. Hooman introduces safety restrictions on the set of all possible executions. In this manner, unwanted behaviour is avoided. His approach also allows executions with an infinite number of internal actions between two external actions. Our executions are built in an operational manner by concatenating states and transitions. Hence safety restrictions are posed only on single actions, and not on executions. Besides, since each execution contains at most a countable number of actions, there is at most a finite number of actions between any two actions. We feel that the operational view is more natural and closer to any real-world implementation of this problem specification.

Fairness and real time In Problem 5, a timed implementation is compared with an untimed specification. The untimed behaviour is restricted by fairness, whereas the timed behaviour is completely determined by timing constraints. To be able to compare these behaviours, we defined the *fair timed I/O automaton*. This ad hoc notion is explained in Appendix B.

1.2 Notes on the I/O automata model

Benefits I/O automata provide a natural way to describe processes with an input/output behaviour. Most distributed systems can be specified in this way.

The specifications are highly readable, and can be explained without too much trouble to most non-experts.

In the untimed part of our solution, simulation relations provide the major part of proofs for implementation relations, the rest is taken care of by inclusion of fairness properties. All these are standard ingredients of verifications with I/O automata.

Real time aspects of specifications are also captured in I/O automata quite easily. When comparing timed specifications, simulation relations prove implementation relations in a straightforward way.

Imperfections When reasoning about an I/O automaton with more than five state variables and more than five locally controlled actions, proofs for safety properties involve an enormous amount of tedious detail, and are prone to typos and more serious errors. The amount of paper needed to get these proofs done in a semi-readable way is terrifying, whereas in general the properties being proved seem so trivial and intuitively correct. However, we are not aware of the existence of a similar formalism without this problem.

I/O automata theory lacks a proof system for fairness proofs. Many fairness proofs are constructed in an intuitive, ad-hoc manner and thus error prone. The construction of a formal framework for this certainly qualifies as future research.

Another gap in current I/O automata theory is that it is not possible to impose restrictions on the behaviour of the environment. Especially when using timed I/O automata, one sometimes needs to assume that events controlled by the environment will occur within certain time bounds. This is another potential benefit deserving further investigation.

What we added to the classic model A desired property of any specification with fairness requirements is liveness (receptivity, machine closure). In the I/O automata model proposed by Lynch & Tuttle [15], liveness is guaranteed for any weak fairness restriction that holds a countable number of actions. However, the RPC-Memory problem requires strong fairness restrictions on the behaviour of the proposed implementation of the memory component in Problem 3. Secondly, this problem holds a parameter whose cardinality is unknown, namely the number of calling processes for a memory or RPC component. Well-known results for liveness with respect to fairness conditions deal with at most a countable number of fairness sets or actions, and cannot be applied to this problem.

The desire to establish liveness for any specification with uncountably many fairness sets has led to the invention of the *fair I/O automaton* [21]. This is a slight variant of the I/O automaton in [15], and a special case of the live I/O automaton in [7] provided that two conditions hold. These conditions require that each reachable state enables at most a countable number of fairness sets, and that input actions do not disturb the enabledness of these sets. In this paper, each specification is proved to be a live I/O automaton by checking these two conditions. To our knowledge, no other solution to the RPC-Memory problem includes proofs of this kind.

1.3 Further remarks

The outline of this paper is as follows. Section 2 lists some preliminaries which are necessary for a good understanding of the specifications, as well as the proofs. Sections 3 to 7 solve parts 1 to 5 of the problem consecutively. Appendices A and B list the basics of the I/O automata model.

Since endless listings of highly detailed proofs guarantee a boring paper instead of a higher degree of understanding, we have omitted unnecessary detailed proofs and replaced some by sketches. The full formal proofs can be obtained by e-mail request to the author.

Acknowledgements Frits Vaandrager put me on the RPC-Memory problem to 'get to know the field of protocol verification'. We both thought that it would take much less time and energy than it did. Yet I have learned so much about protocol verification in general and more specifically about I/O automata, that I have almost developed a taste for obstacles. While I was working on this paper, enlightening e-mail correspondence has taken place with Jozef Hooman, Leslie Lamport and Stephan Merz. Frits Vaandrager and Stephan Merz are thanked for carefully reading previous versions of this paper and suggesting lots of improvements.

2 Preliminaries

2.1 Fair I/O automata

The set-up of specification and verifications is as follows. All untimed specifications use the *fair I/O automata* model from [21]. The basics of this model are listed in Appendix A. The model is a generalisation from the classic model by Lynch & Tuttle [15], and, under two restrictions, a special case of the live I/O automaton model by Gawlick et al. [7].

The timed specifications use the *fair timed I/O automata* model, which extends the timed I/O automata model of [17] with an ad hoc notion of fairness in the timed setting. The basics of this model are listed in Appendix B. Section 7 explains why we need to use fairness in the timed setting.

2.2 Details on fair I/O automata

Specification Each action is indexed with the process, for which this action is performed. Some of the state variables are also indexed with a process. The state space is roughly partitioned by the value of the *program counters*, the state variables pc_P. These variables keep track of what the automaton should be doing for process P. All automata initially wait for some action by the environment, and each pc_P has a value that expresses this waiting condition. As soon as input is received for process P, pc_P changes accordingly, and each next input for P is discarded (the state is not changed), if pc_P does not satisfy the waiting condition.

For each internal action, the precondition requires pc_P to have a specific value in order to ensure that the right actions are taken at the right moment. After the input for some process P has been handled, pc_P is set to the waiting condition again.

To give the values of each program counter the right meaning, we assume that the interpretation of the domain of each program counter is free, in the sense that different constants symbols are mapped to different elements in its domain ("no confusion"), and each element in the domain is denoted by some constant symbol ("no junk").

Presentation The following conventions are used.

- We omit the precondition of an input action (since this equals true by definition).
- In the effect part of transition types we omit assignments of the form $x := x$.
- We write if c then $[z_1 := f_1, \ldots, z_k := f_k]$ as an abbreviation for

$$z_1 := \text{if } c \text{ then } f_1 \text{ else } z_1$$

$$\vdots$$

$$z_k := \text{if } c \text{ then } f_k \text{ else } z_k$$

- We write $x \in \{A, B, C\}$ for $x=A \lor x=B \lor x=C$, etc.
- To improve readability we often use Lamport's list notation for conjunction or disjunction. Thus we write

$$\wedge\ b_1$$
$$\wedge\ b_2$$
$$\vdots$$
$$\wedge\ b_n$$

for $b_1 \wedge b_2 \wedge \cdots \wedge b_n$.

Proofs We prove an implementation relation between two fair I/O automata A and B by proving that $fairtraces(A) \subseteq fairtraces(B)$. To ease this proof, we mostly start out by proving inclusion on the ordinary and quiescent traces of A and B using refinements and simulations.

Since the only difference between the fair and classic I/O automata model lies in the fairness properties, all results in the latter that do not concern fairness carry over to the fair I/O automata model. This is used when proving ordinary and quiescent trace inclusion.

3 Specifications and Verifications for Problem 1

3.1 Problem 1(a): Specification of two Memory Components

In this section, we present the formal specification of the Memory component and the Reliable Memory component.

Data types We start the specification with a description of the various data types that play a role. We assume a typed signature Σ_1 and a Σ_1-algebra $\mathcal{A}_1$ which consist of the following components:

- a type **Bool** of booleans with constant symbols true and false, and a standard repertoire of function symbols $(\wedge, \vee, \neg, \rightarrow)$, all with the standard interpretation over the booleans. Also, we require, for all types **S** in Σ, an equality, inequality, and if-then-else function symbol, with the usual interpretation:

$$.=. : S \times S \rightarrow Bool$$
$$.\neq. : S \times S \rightarrow Bool$$
$$if . then . else . : Bool \times S \times S \rightarrow S$$

Note the (harmless) overloading of the constants and function symbols of type **Bool** with the propositional connectives used in formulas. We will frequently view boolean valued expressions as formulas, i.e., we use b as an abbreviation of b=true.

- a type **Process** of process identifiers. We frequently use the variable P ranging over **Process** as a subscript.
- a type **MemLocs** of legal memory locations.
- a type **MemVals** of legal memory values, with constant symbol InitVal. None of the memory values is equal to BadArg.
- a type **Locs** of memory locations, such that **MemLocs** $\subseteq$ **Locs**, and a function memloc : **Locs** $\rightarrow$ **Bool**, telling us whether an element of **Locs** is also an element of **MemLocs**.
- a type **Vals** of memory values, such that **MemVals** $\subseteq$ **Vals**, and a function memval : **Vals** $\rightarrow$ **Bool**, telling us whether an element of **Vals** is also an element of **MemVals**.
- a type **Ack** of acknowledgement values, such that **Ack** = **MemVals** $\cup$ WriteOk.
- a type **Memory** of functions from **MemLocs** to **MemVals** We need two functions to actually access the memory: find : **MemLocs**$\times$**Memory** $\rightarrow$ **MemVals** and change : **MemLocs**$\times$**MemVals**$\times$**Memory** $\rightarrow$ **Memory**. These operations are fully characterised by the axioms:

$find(l, m) = m(l)$
$change(l, v, m) = m'$ where $m'(l)=v \wedge \forall l' : (l' \neq l \rightarrow m'(l')=m(l))$
$(l, l'$ are variables of type **MemLocs**, v is a variable of type **MemVals**, and m, m' are variables of type **Memory**)

- a type **Mpc** of program counter values of the Memory component, with constant symbols WC, R and W. The intended meaning of these constants will be explained further on in this section.

The Memory component

We present the fair I/O automaton *Memory*, which models a Memory component. The state variable pc_P of *Memory* gives the current value of the program counter of the Memory component for calling process P. Note that there are as many program counters as calling processes. Each of them may have one of the following values:

- WC: Waiting for a $READ_P$ or $WRITE_P$ call,
- R: Reading from memory,
- W: Writing to memory.

Initially, the program counter value is WC for every process P.

Every possible action of *Memory* is indexed with the process that issued the call leading to this action. Since the state variables are also indexed in this manner (except for *memory!*), we can determine in any situation what is going on for each process P.

$READ_P$ and $WRITE_P$ model an incoming read or write call from a process P. They do not change the state when *Memory* is still handling a previous call from the same process. In this case, we call the input action *discarded*. If *Memory* is ready for handling an incoming call, its state is updated according to the parameter(s) of the call.

GET_P actions model an atomic read operation, PUT_P actions model an atomic write operation. Reading is allowed only once between call and return, writing is allowed for an arbitrary number of times.

A $MEM\_FAILURE_P$ action can occur in any 'busy' state.

BAD_ARG_P is the only action enabled if the parameters of the call from process P were not legal. $RETURN_P$ delivers the requested memory value or a general WriteOk acknowledgement, after *performed$_P$* has been set to true by a GET_P or PUT_P action. The fact that PUT_P actions are in another weak fairness set than $RETURN_P$ and $MEM\_FAILURE_P$, ensures that writing will stop at some point.

The code for *Memory* is listed in Figure 1.

Liveness We show that fair I/O automaton *Memory* is a live I/O automaton in the sense of [7]. To do this, we have to check that *Memory* satisfies two conditions. After this, Theorem 1 from [21] applies immediately.

The next lemma checks a restriction of one of the two conditions.

Lemma 1. *Each reachable state in Memory enables at most finitely many locally controlled actions.*

Proof. For each process P, locally controlled actions can only be enabled if $pc_P \neq WC$. Suppose there is an execution with n actions leading to state s. Then there are at most n processes P such that $s \models pc_P \neq WC$, hence s enables at most $5n$ locally controlled actions.

Proposition 2. *live(Memory) is a live I/O automaton.*

```
Input:     READ_P, WRITE_P
Output:  RETURN_P, BAD_ARG_P, MEM_FAILURE_P
Internal: GET_P, PUT_P
WFair:   ⋃_P{{GET_P, PUT_P}, {BAD_ARG_P, MEM_FAILURE_P, RETURN_P}}
SFair:   ∅
```

State Variables: pc_P: **Mpc**   **Initial:** $\bigwedge_P pc_P = $ WC
　　　　　　　　loc_P: **Locs**　　　　　　　　　$\bigwedge_l$ find(l, $memory$) = InitVal
　　　　　　　　val_P: **Vals**
　　　　　　　　$memory$: **Memory**
　　　　　　　　$performed_P$: **Bool**
　　　　　　　　$legal_P$: **Bool**

$READ_P(l : \textbf{Locs})$
　Effect:
　　if (pc_P=WC) then $[loc_P := l$
　　　　　　　　　　　$performed_P := $ false
　　　　　　　　　　　$legal_P := $ memloc(l)
　　　　　　　　　　　$pc_P := $ R]

$WRITE_P(l : \textbf{Locs}, v : \textbf{Vals})$
　Effect:
　　if (pc_P=WC) then $[loc_P := l$
　　　　　　　　　　　$val_P := v$
　　　　　　　　　　　$performed_P := $ false
　　　　　　　　　　　$legal_P := $ memloc(l) ∧ memval(v)
　　　　　　　　　　　$pc_P := $ W]

BAD_ARG_P
　Precondition:
　　∧ $pc_P \in$ {R, W}
　　∧ ¬$legal_P$
　Effect:
　　$pc_P := $ WC

$MEM\_FAILURE_P$
　Precondition:
　　$pc_P \in$ {R, W}
　Effect:
　　$pc_P := $ WC

GET_P
　Precondition:
　　∧ pc_P=R
　　∧ $legal_P$
　　∧ ¬$performed_P$
　Effect:
　　$val_P := $ find(loc_P, $memory$)
　　$performed_P := $ true

PUT_P
　Precondition:
　　∧ pc_P=W
　　∧ $legal_P$
　Effect:
　　$memory := $ change(loc_P, val_P, $memory$)
　　$performed_P := $ true

$RETURN_P(a : \textbf{Ack})$
　Precondition:
　　∧ $pc_P \in$ {R, W}
　　∧ $performed_P$
　　∧ a=if (pc_P=R) then val_P else WriteOk
　Effect:
　　$pc_P := $ WC

Fig. 1. Fair I/O automaton *Memory*

Proof. We can apply Theorem 1 in [21] if we can show that (1) each reachable state of *Memory* enables at most countably many weak and strong fairness sets, and (2) each set in *sfair*(*Memory*) is input resistant.

Condition (1) is satisfied by Lemma 1, since each locally controlled action is in exactly one weak fairness set. Condition (2) is trivially satisfied, since there are no strong fairness sets.

The Reliable Memory component

We present the fair I/O automaton *RelMemory*, which models a Reliable Memory component. This component behaves exactly like the Memory component, except that it can never issue a *MEM_FAILURE*.

Since the code for *RelMemory* can be obtained from the code for *Memory* by omitting the *MEM_FAILURE* action, *wfair*(*RelMemory*) becomes

$$\bigcup_P \{\{GET_P, PUT_P\}, \{BAD\_ARG_P, RETURN_P\}\}$$

Liveness Knowing that *Memory* is a live I/O automaton, it is easy to prove that *RelMemory* is also a live I/O automaton.

Proposition 3. *live*(*RelMemory*) *is a live I/O automaton.*

Proof. The proof is almost identical to the proof of Proposition 2, since the only difference between *Memory* and *RelMemory* is the absence of *MEM_FAILURE_P* actions.

3.2 Problem 1(b): *RelMemory* implements *Memory*

We show that *fairtraces*(*RelMemory*) ⊆ *fairtraces*(*Memory*), using the properties safety and deadlock freeness.

Safety Since *RelMemory* and *Memory* are so very much alike, a weak refinement appears the most natural construction for proving safety.

Theorem 4. *The function* REF, *which is the identity function on state variables with the same name, is a weak refinement from RelMemory to Memory, with respect to the reachable states in both RelMemory and Memory.*

Proof. The requirements in [18] are trivially fulfilled, since REF is the identity function, and the actions in *RelMemory* form a subset of those in *Memory*.

Corollary 5. *RelMemory is safe with respect to Memory.*

Proof. Directly from Theorem 4 and [18]'s Theorem 6.2.

Deadlock freeness

Theorem 6. *For each reachable and quiescent state s of RelMemory, REF(s) is a quiescent state of Memory.*

Proof. Suppose s is a quiescent state of *RelMemory*. Observing the preconditions of *RelMemory*, we see that $s \models \bigwedge_P RelMemory.pc_P = \text{WC}$.
Clearly, REF(s) $\models \bigwedge_P Memory.pc_P = \text{WC}$, hence REF($s$) is quiescent.

Corollary 7. *RelMemory is deadlock free with respect to Memory.*

Proof. By Theorems 4 and 6 we can, for each quiescent execution of *RelMemory*, construct a corresponding quiescent execution of *Memory* with the same trace.

Implementation

Theorem 8. *RelMemory implements Memory.*

Proof. We prove *fairtraces(RelMemory)* $\subseteq$ *fairtraces(Memory)*.
Assume that $\beta \in$ *fairtraces(RelMemory)*. Let α be a fair execution of *RelMemory* with trace β.

If α is finite then α is quiescent and it follows by Corollary 7 that *Memory* has a quiescent execution with trace β. Since each quiescent execution is also fair, this implies $\beta \in$ *fairtraces(Memory)*. So we may assume without loss of generality that α is infinite.

Using the fact that REF is a weak refinement (Theorem 4) we can easily construct an execution α' of *Memory* with trace β. It remains to prove that α' is fair.

The only case in which α is fair but α' is not, is obtained as follows. From a certain state in α', for some P, $MEM\_FAILURE_P$ is enabled continuously, but no action from $\{RETURN_P, BAD\_ARG_P, MEM\_FAILURE_P\}$ is performed. In this case, α must contain an infinite suffix in which PUT_P occurs infinitely many times and is enabled continuously continuously. Since α is weakly fair, this is impossible.

The interpretation of all the other actions are equal in both automata, even with respect to to the weak fairness sets, so the weak fairness requirements for α' are satisfied by the weak fairness requirements for α.

Since *Memory* has no strong fairness sets, the above shows that α' is fair.

3.3 Problem 1(c): Nothing but $MEM\_FAILURE_P$ actions?

We can construct a very trivial automaton that implements *Memory*, and does nothing but raise $MEM\_FAILURE_P$ actions. It can have the same state variables as *Memory*, but only actions $READ_P$, $WRITE_P$ and $MEM\_FAILURE_P$. A weak refinement like REF will provide us safety and deadlock freeness results. Such a refinement is even enough to show that this automaton implements

Memory, since each fair execution in this automaton can be imitated by a fair execution in *Memory*, using the refinement.

Is it reasonable that such an implementation is possible? Since the specification of the Memory component is presented as a black box that does not remember success nor failure, it is reasonable to think of it as a dice, harbouring the same chances at success with every throw. So while one can expect such a Memory component to yield the right return at some time in an infinite sequence of trials, the possibility of infinitely many failures exists and must therefore be included in the specification we have presented here.

4 Specifications and Verifications for Problem 2

4.1 Problem 2: Specification of the RPC component

Data types We assume a typed signature Σ_2 and a Σ_2-algebra $\mathcal{A}_2$ which consist of the following components:

- the type **Bool** as defined in Section 3.1
- a type **Nat** of natural numbers
- a type **Procs** of procedure names
- a type **Names**, such that **Procs** $\subseteq$ **Names**, and a function legal_proc : **Names** $\rightarrow$ **Bool**, telling us whether a given name is a legal procedure name (that is, an element of **Procs**), and a function arg_num : **Names** $\rightarrow$ **Nat**, giving the expected number of arguments for each name.
- a type **Args** of function arguments, and a function num : **Args** $\rightarrow$ **Nat**, giving the number of actual arguments.
- a function legal_call : **Names**×**Args** $\rightarrow$ **Bool**, such that legal_call$(p, a) =$ legal_proc$(p) \wedge$ (arg_num(p)=num(a)) for each p in **Names** and a in **Args**.
- a type **ReturnVal** of possible return values. All exceptions raised by remote procedure calls are expected to be included in this type.
- a type **Rpc** of program counter values of the RPC component, with constant symbols WC, IC, WR and IR.

Specification We present the fair I/O automaton *RPC*, which models an RPC component. RPC stands for Remote Procedure Call. *RPC*'s program counters may have one of the following values:

- WC: Wait for remote calls from the sender
- IC: Issue a call to the receiver or an exceptional return to the sender
- WR: Wait for a return from the receiver
- IR: Issue a return (possibly exceptional) to the sender

Initially, the program counter value is WC for every process P.

The code for *RPC* is listed in Figure 2.

```
Input:    REM_CALLₚ, I_RETURNₚ
Output:   I_CALLₚ, REM_RETURNₚ, BAD_CALLₚ, RPC_FAILUREₚ
WFair:    ⋃ₚ{{I_CALLₚ, REM_RETURNₚ, BAD_CALLₚ, RPC_FAILUREₚ}}
SFair:    ∅
```

State Variables: pc_P: **Rpc**   **Initial:** $\bigwedge_P pc_P = \text{WC}$
$proc_P$: **Names**
$args_P$: **Args**
$legal_P$: **Bool**
$return_P$: **ReturnVal**

REM_CALLₚ(p : Names, a : Args)
  Effect:
  if $(pc_P = \text{WC})$ then $[proc_P := p$
      $args_P := a$
      $legal_P := \text{legal\_call}(p, a)$
      $pc_P := \text{IC}]$

RPC_FAILUREₚ
  Precondition:
  $pc_P \in \{\text{IC}, \text{IR}\}$
  Effect:
  $pc_P := \text{WC}$

BAD_CALLₚ
  Precondition:
  $\wedge\ pc_P = \text{IC}$
  $\wedge\ \neg legal_P$
  Effect:
  $pc_P := \text{WC}$

I_CALLₚ(p : Names, a : Args)
  Precondition:
  $\wedge\ pc_P = \text{IC}$
  $\wedge\ legal_P$
  $\wedge\ p = proc_P$
  $\wedge\ a = args_P$
  Effect:
  $pc_P := \text{WR}$

I_RETURNₚ(r : ReturnVal)
  Effect:
  if $(pc_P = \text{WR})$ then $[pc_P := \text{IR}$
      $return_P := r]$

REM_RETURNₚ(r : ReturnVal)
  Precondition:
  $\wedge\ pc_P = \text{IR}$
  $\wedge\ r = return_P$
  Effect:
  $pc_P := \text{WC}$

Fig. 2. Fair I/O automaton *RPC*

Liveness *RPC* is a live I/O automaton.

Lemma 9. *Each reachable state in RPC enables at most finitely many locally controlled actions.*

Proposition 10. *live(RPC) is a live I/O automaton.*

5 Specifications and Verifications for Problem 3

5.1 Problem 3: Specification of the composition

Data types We reuse Σ_1 (section 3.1) and Σ_2 (section 4.1) to obtain a typed signature Σ_3 and a Σ_3-algebra, such that:

- Read and Write are different constants of type **Procs** (and therefore also of type **Names**)
- arg_num(Read) = 1, and arg_num(Write) = 2
- the domain of **ReturnVal** is equal to the domain of **Ack**, plus an extra constant BadArg
- for each l, l' of type **Locs** and v, v' of type **Vals**, (l) and (l, v) are elements of type **Args**, $(l) = (l') \rightarrow l = l'$, $(l, v) = (l', v') \rightarrow l = l' \wedge v = v'$, num$((l)) = 1$ and num$((l, v)) = 2$.

A front end for the RPC component We need another component to make the RPC component retry a call to the reliable memory component. This component is a clerk, which can translate incoming calls to RPC's format, and reissue such a call if RPC should fail. Therefore we present the fair I/O automaton $ClerkR$, which models a front end to the RPC component RPC. The program counters of $ClerkR$ are of type **Rpc**, and therefore have the same possibilities as the program counters of RPC. Initially, the program counter value is WC for every process P.
The code for $ClerkR$ is listed in Figure 3.

Liveness Fair I/O automaton $ClerkR$ is a live I/O automaton.

Lemma 11. *Each reachable state in ClerkR enables at most finitely many locally controlled actions.*

Proposition 12. *live(ClerkR) is a live I/O automaton.*

Proof. As before, we apply Theorem 1 in [21] after showing that (1) each reachable state of RPC enables at most countably many weak and strong fairness sets, and (2) each set in $sfair(ClerkR)$ is input resistant.

Condition (1) is satisfied by Lemma 11, since each locally controlled action is in exactly one weak fairness set.

Condition (2) relies upon the input resistance of action $MEM\_FAILURE$. Suppose that $MEM\_FAILURE_P$ is enabled in the reachable state s. Clearly, $s \models ClerkR.pc_P = \text{IC}$. If an input action a for P occurs in s, by definition of $ClerkR$ the transition $s \xrightarrow{a} s$ is taken, and $MEM\_FAILURE_P$ is still enabled. If an input action a for another P' occurs in s, the transition taken does not affect $ClerkR.pc_P$. Hence $MEM\_FAILURE_P$ is input resistant and the second condition is satisfied.

Renaming component *RelMemory* The front end $ClerkR$ is not enough to establish the intended implementation. We also need to rename $RelMemory$ to avoid name clashing, and to get the proper synchronisation. So we define a new

Input: $READ_P, WRITE_P, REM\_RETURN_P, BAD\_CALL_P, RPC\_FAILURE_P$
Output: $REM\_CALL_P, RETURN_P, BAD\_ARG_P, MEM\_FAILURE_P$
WFair: $\bigcup_P\{\{REM\_CALL_P, RETURN_P, BAD\_ARG_P, MEM\_FAILURE_P\}\}$
SFair: $\bigcup_P\{\{MEM\_FAILURE_P\}\}$

State Variables:	pc_P:	**Rpc**	**Initial:** $\bigwedge_P pc_P$=WC
	$proc_P$:	**Names**	
	loc_P:	**Locs**	
	val_P:	**Vals**	
	$failed_P$:	**Bool**	
	$return_P$:	**ReturnVal**	

$READ_P(l : \textbf{Locs})$
  Effect:
    if (pc_P=WC) then [$proc_P$:= Read
               loc_P := l
               $failed_P$:= false
               pc_P := IC]

$WRITE_P(l : \textbf{Locs}, v : \textbf{Vals})$
  Effect:
    if (pc_P=WC) then [$proc_P$:= Write
               loc_P := l
               val_P := v
               $failed_P$:= false
               pc_P := IC]

$REM\_CALL_P(p : \textbf{Names}, a : \textbf{Args})$
  Precondition:
    $\wedge\ pc_P$=IC
    $\wedge\ p$=$proc_P$
    $\wedge\ a$=if ($proc_P$=Read) then (loc_P) else (loc_P, val_P)
  Effect:
    pc_P := WR

BAD_CALL_P
  Effect:
    if (pc_P=WR) then [$return_P$:= BadArg
               pc_P := IR]

BAD_ARG_P
  Precondition:
    $\wedge\ pc_P$=IR
    $\wedge\ return_P$=BadArg
  Effect:
    pc_P := WC

$RPC\_FAILURE_P$
  Effect:
    if (pc_P=WR) then [$failed_P$:= true
               pc_P := IC]

$MEM\_FAILURE_P$
  Precondition:
    $\wedge\ pc_P$=IC
    $\wedge\ failed_P$
  Effect:
    pc_P := WC

$REM\_RETURN_P(r : \textbf{ReturnVal})$
  Effect:
    if (pc_P=WR) then [$return_P$:= r
               pc_P := IR]

$RETURN_P(r : \textbf{ReturnVal})$
  Precondition:
    $\wedge\ pc_P$=IR
    $\wedge\ return_P\neq$BadArg
    $\wedge\ r$=$return_P$
  Effect:
    pc_P := WC

Fig. 3. Fair I/O automaton *ClerkR*

fair I/O automaton $RMemory' \triangleq rename(RelMemory)$, where for every P:

$$
\begin{aligned}
\text{rename}(READ_P(l)) &= I\_CALL_P(\text{Read}, (l)) \\
\text{rename}(WRITE_P(l,v)) &= I\_CALL_P(\text{Write}, (l,v)) \\
\text{rename}(RETURN_P(a)) &= I\_RETURN_P(a) \\
\text{rename}(BAD\_ARG_P) &= I\_RETURN_P(\text{BadArg}) \\
\text{rename}(x) &= x \qquad\qquad\qquad \text{otherwise}
\end{aligned}
$$

(l is a variable of type **Locs**, v is a variable of type **Vals**, a is a variable of type **Ack**, and x is a action variable)

The code for $RMemory'$ is listed in Figure 4.

Liveness It is easily shown that $RMemory'$ is a live I/O automaton.

Proposition 13. *live($RMemory'$) is a live I/O automaton.*

Proof. Trivially, $live(RMemory') = rename(live(RelMemory))$. Combining this with Theorem 3 and [7]'s Proposition 3.23, we obtain that $live(RMemory')$ is a live I/O automaton.

The implementation $MemoryImp$ is defined as the parallel composition of I/O automata $ClerkR$, RPC and $RMemory'$, with all communication between those components hidden:

$$MemoryImp \triangleq \text{HIDE } I \text{ IN } (ClerkR \| RPC \| RMemory')$$

where $I \triangleq \bigcup_P \{REM\_CALL_P(p,a), REM\_RETURN_P(r), BAD\_CALL_P,$
$RPC\_FAILURE_P, I\_CALL_P(p,a), I\_RETURN_P(r)$
$\mid p$ in **Names**, a in **Args**, r in **ReturnVal**$\}$.

$RPCImp$'s behaviour is illustrated in the following figure.

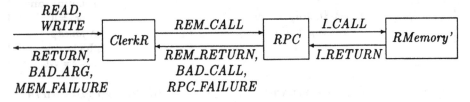

Liveness

Proposition 14. *live($MemoryImp$) is a live I/O automaton.*

Proof. We use Propositions 10, 12, 13, [7]'s Propositions 3.22 and 3.28, and [21]'s Theorem 2.

```
Input:    I_CALL_P
Output:   I_RETURN_P
Internal: GET_P, PUT_P
WFair:    ⋃_P{{GET_P, PUT_P}, {I_RETURN_P}}
SFair:    ∅
State Variables: pc_P:       Mpc        Initial: ⋀_P pc_P=WC
                 loc_P:      Locs                ⋀_l find(l, memory)=InitVal
                 val_P:      Vals
                 memory:     Memory
                 performed_P: Bool
                 legal_P:    Bool


I_CALL_P(Read, (l : Locs))                          I_RETURN_P(BadArg)
  Effect:                                             Precondition:
    if (pc_P=WC) then [loc_P := l                       ∧ pc_P ∈ {R, W}
                       performed_P := false             ∧ ¬legal_P
                       legal_P := memloc(l)           Effect:
                       pc_P := R]                       pc_P := WC


I_CALL_P(Write, (l : Locs, v : Vals))
  Effect:
    if (pc_P=WC) then [loc_P := l
                       val_P := v
                       performed_P := false
                       legal_P := memloc(l) ∧ memval(v)
                       pc_P := W]


GET_P                                PUT_P
  Precondition:                        Precondition:
    ∧ pc_P=R                             ∧ pc_P=W
    ∧ legal_P                            ∧ legal_P
    ∧ ¬performed_P                     Effect:
  Effect:                                memory := change(loc_P, val_P, memory)
    val_P := find(loc_P, memory)         performed_P := true
    performed_P := true


I_RETURN_P(a : Ack)
  Precondition:
    ∧ pc_P ∈ {R, W}
    ∧ performed_P
    ∧ a=if (pc_P=R) then val_P else WriteOk
  Effect:
    pc_P := WC
```

Fig. 4. Fair I/O automaton *RMemory'*

5.2 Set-up for the verification

A direct proof of trace inclusion between *MemoryImp* and *Memory* is not very straightforward. This stems from the fact that *Memory* can only read its memory once for every read call. However, by *MemoryImp*'s fail retry-mechanism, it is able to read multiple times for one read call.

An intermediate automaton To show trace inclusion, we are seem to need a forward backward simulation. However, since this is rather complicated, and [18]'s Theorem 4.1 states that we can just as well look for an intermediate automaton, we will keep things clear by constructing an intermediate automaton, which we allow to read its memory multiple times for one read call. This intermediate automaton will be called *Memory**, the * indicating the possibility of multiple reads instead of one. The code for *Memory** is obtained from *Memory* as follows. The precondition for GET_P is weakened, and a new state variable $hist_P$ is added, in which the value of val_P is stored each time a return is issued. Figure 5 lists the code for fair I/O automaton *Memory**. Boxes highlight the places where the code for *Memory** differs from *Memory*.

A forward simulation establishes trace inclusion between *MemoryImp* and *Memory**; a backward simulation does the same for *Memory** and *Memory*. The new state variable *Memory**.$hist_P$ substantially simplifies the backward simulation and also makes it image-finite.

Liveness Fair I/O automaton *Memory** is a live I/O automaton.

Lemma 15. *Each reachable state in Memory* enables at most finitely many locally controlled actions.*

Proposition 16. *live(Memory*) is a live I/O automaton.*

5.3 Problem 3: *MemoryImp* implements *Memory*

Section 5.3 shows that *Memory** implements *Memory*, Section 5.3 shows that *MemoryImp* implements *Memory**. Both results are reached via safety and deadlock freeness. Transitivity of the implementation relation yields the desired result in Section 5.3.

Memory** implements *Memory We need an invariant to show that between the previous output action and the next internal action, *Memory**'s history variable $hist_P$ is up to date with respect to val_P for each P.

Lemma 17. *The following property* Inv1 *is an invariant of Memory*.*

$$\bigwedge_P (pc_P \in \{\mathsf{WC}, \mathsf{R}\} \wedge \neg performed_P) \rightarrow val_P = hist_P$$

The next invariant expresses that *Memory** will not read or write if it has received illegal arguments.

Input: $READ_P, WRITE_P$
Output: $RETURN_P, BAD\_ARG_P, MEM\_FAILURE_P$
Internal: GET_P, PUT_P
WFair: $\bigcup_P\{\{GET_P, PUT_P\}, \{BAD\_ARG_P, MEM\_FAILURE_P, RETURN_P\}\}$
SFair: $\emptyset$
State Variables: pc_P: Mpc   **Initial:** $\bigwedge_P pc_P$=WC
            loc_P: Locs $\bigwedge_l$ find($l, memory$)=InitVal
            val_P: Vals $\boxed{\bigwedge_P hist_P = val_P}$
            $memory$:   Memory
            $performed_P$: Bool
            $legal_P$:   Bool
            $\boxed{hist_P: \text{ Vals}}$

$READ_P(l : \text{Locs})$
  Effect:
    if (pc_P=WC) then $[loc_P := l$
                      $performed_P := \text{false}$
                      $legal_P := \text{memloc}(l)$
                      $pc_P := \text{R}]$

BAD_ARG_P
  Precondition:
    $\wedge\ pc_P \in \{\text{R}, \text{W}\}$
    $\wedge\ \neg legal_P$
  Effect:
    $pc_P := \text{WC}$
    $\boxed{hist_P := val_P}$

$WRITE_P(l : \text{Locs}, v : \text{Vals})$
  Effect:
    if (pc_P=WC) then $[loc_P := l$
                      $val_P := v$
                      $performed_P := \text{false}$
                      $legal_P := \text{memloc}(l) \wedge \text{memval}(v)$
                      $pc_P := \text{W}]$

$MEM\_FAILURE_P$
  Precondition:
    $pc_P \in \{\text{R}, \text{W}\}$
  Effect:
    $pc_P := \text{WC}$
    $\boxed{hist_P := val_P}$

GET_P
  Precondition:
    $\boxed{\begin{array}{l}\wedge\ pc_P=\text{R} \\ \wedge\ legal_P\end{array}}$
  Effect:
    $val_P := \text{find}(loc_P, memory)$
    $performed_P := \text{true}$

PUT_P
  Precondition:
    $\wedge\ pc_P=\text{W}$
    $\wedge\ legal_P$
  Effect:
    $memory := \text{change}(loc_P, val_P, memory)$
    $performed_P := \text{true}$

$RETURN_P(a : \text{Ack})$
  Precondition:
    $\wedge\ pc_P \in \{\text{R}, \text{W}\}$
    $\wedge\ performed_P$
    $\wedge\ a=\text{if } (pc_P=\text{R}) \text{ then } val_P \text{ else WriteOk}$
  Effect:
    $pc_P := \text{WC}$
    $\boxed{hist_P := val_P}$

Fig. 5. Fair I/O automaton *Memory**

Lemma 18. *The following property* Inv2 *is an invariant of Memory**.

$$\bigwedge_P pc_P \neq \mathsf{WC} \to (\neg legal_P \to \neg performed_P)$$

A weak backward simulation enables us to construct the behaviour of *Memory*, given the behaviour of *Memory**. We can start in the last state of such a sequence, and work our way back to the beginning. The relation that induces this simulation needs to be image-finite.

Lemma 19. *The relation* BACK *defined by the following formula is an image-finite relation over* rstates(*Memory**) *and* states(*Memory*).

$$
\begin{aligned}
&\bigwedge_P Memory.pc_P && = Memory^*.pc_P \\
&\bigwedge_P Memory.loc_P && = Memory^*.loc_P \\
&\bigwedge_P Memory.val_P && = \text{if} \quad Memory.pc_P = \mathsf{R} \wedge \neg Memory.performed_P \\
&&& \quad \text{then } Memory^*.hist_P \\
&&& \quad \text{else } Memory^*.val_P \\
&\bigwedge_P Memory.legal_P && = Memory^*.legal_P \\
&\wedge \quad Memory.memory && = Memory^*.memory \\
&\bigwedge_P \neg Memory^*.performed_P && \to \neg Memory.performed_P \\
&\bigwedge_P Memory^*.pc_P \neq \mathsf{R} && \to (Memory^*.performed_P \to Memory.performed_P)
\end{aligned}
$$

Theorem 20. *Relation* BACK *is a weak backward simulation from Memory** *to Memory, with respect to the reachable states in Memory**.

Proof. We satisfy the three requirements in [18], which is a bit complicated and takes a lot of paper. The most difficult part is caused by the *GET* action, since *Memory* does not always perform this action along with *Memory**. Here, the history variable of *Memory** proves its value.

Corollary 21. *Memory** *is safe with respect to Memory.*

Proof. Combining Lemma 19 and Theorem 20 with [18]'s Theorem 6.2, we obtain the desired result.

Theorem 22. *For each reachable, quiescent state s of Memory**, *each state r* $\in$ BACK(s) *is a quiescent state of Memory.*

Proof. Considering the preconditions of *Memory**, in each quiescent state s, *Memory*$^*.pc_P$ must be equal to WC for every P. For each $r \in$ BACK(s) $: r \models \bigwedge_P Memory.pc_P = \mathsf{WC}$, hence r is quiescent.

Corollary 23. *Memory** *is deadlock free with respect to Memory.*

Proof. By Theorems 20 and 22 we can construct, for each quiescent execution of *Memory**, a corresponding quiescent execution of *Memory* with the same trace.

Theorem 24. *Memory** *implements Memory.*

Proof. Assume that $\beta \in$ *fairtraces(Memory*)*. Let α be a fair execution of *Memory** with the same trace β. If α is finite then α is quiescent and it follows by Corollary 23 that *Memory* has a quiescent execution with trace β. Since each quiescent execution is also fair, this implies $\beta \in$ *fairtraces(Memory)*. So we may assume without loss of generality that α is infinite.

Using the fact that BACK is a weak image-finite backward simulation (see Lemma 19, Theorem 20), we can easily construct an execution α' of *Memory* with trace β. It remains to prove that α' is fair.

We need to show that α' must be infinite. Again, the GET_P action causes trouble, since *Memory* does not always perform it when *Memory** does. However, fairness helps us establish the fact that *Memory** cannot perform infinitely many GET_P actions for P, without performing other actions for P in between. Since *Memory* imitates each of these other actions, the infinity of α' is inevitable.

Using the above, the fairness of α' is satisfied quite trivially because of three facts. Firstly, *wfair(Memory)* = *wfair(Memory*)* and *sfair(Memory)* = *sfair(Memory*)* = $\emptyset$. Secondly, if a weak fairness set is not enabled in *Memory**, it is certainly not enabled in *Memory*. Thirdly, infinitely many occurrences of action a in α cause infinitely many occurrences of a in α'.

MemoryImp implements *Memory**

Invariants The following list of invariants is rather dull. They are necessary for ensuring that the arguments of an incoming call are transmitted properly among the components of *MemoryImp*, and no component will act before it receives permission to do so.

Component *RPC* will remain quiescent until a request is issued by component *ClerkR*:

Lemma 25. *The following property* Inv3 *is an invariant of MemoryImp.*

$$\bigwedge_P \ ClerkR.pc_P \neq \mathsf{WR} \rightarrow RPC.pc_P = \mathsf{WC}$$

Component *RMemory'* will remain quiescent until a request is issued by component *RPC*:

Lemma 26. *The following property* Inv4 *is an invariant of MemoryImp.*

$$\bigwedge_P \ RPC.pc_P \neq \mathsf{WR} \rightarrow RMemory'.pc_P = \mathsf{WC}$$

Component *ClerkR* only handles read or write calls:

Lemma 27. *The following property* Inv5 *is an invariant of MemoryImp.*

$$\bigwedge_P \ ClerkR.pc_P \neq \mathsf{WC} \rightarrow \vee \wedge ClerkR.proc_P = \mathsf{Read}$$
$$\wedge \exists l : ClerkR.loc_P = l$$
$$\vee \wedge ClerkR.proc_P = \mathsf{Write}$$
$$\wedge \exists l : ClerkR.loc_P = l$$
$$\wedge \exists v : ClerkR.val_P = v$$

Component RPC receives the same calls and arguments from $ClerkR$, as $ClerkR$ received from the environment:

Lemma 28. *The following property* Inv6 *is an invariant of MemoryImp.*

$$\bigwedge_P RPC.pc_P{\neq}\mathsf{WC} \;\rightarrow\; \wedge\, RPC.proc_P{=}ClerkR.proc_P$$
$$\wedge\, RPC.args_P{=}\;\text{if}\quad ClerkR.proc_P{=}\mathsf{Read}$$
$$\text{then}\;(ClerkR.loc_P)$$
$$\text{else}\;(ClerkR.loc_P,\, ClerkR.val_P)$$

Component RPC only receives read or write calls:

Corollary 29. *The following property* Inv7 *is an invariant of MemoryImp.*

$$\bigwedge_P RPC.pc_P{\neq}\mathsf{WC} \;\rightarrow\; \vee\, RPC.proc_P{=}\mathsf{Read} \wedge \exists l : RPC.args_P{=}(l)$$
$$\vee\, RPC.proc_P{=}\mathsf{Write} \wedge \exists l, v : RPC.args_P{=}(l, v)$$

Proof. Directly from invariants Inv3, Inv5 and Inv6.

Since Read and Write are proper procedure names, and RPC receives no other procedure calls, the action BAD_CALL_P is never enabled:

Corollary 30. *The following property* Inv8 *is an invariant of MemoryImp.*

$$\bigwedge_P \neg enabled(BAD\_CALL_P)$$

If $RMemory'$ is busy, it is by request of RPC, and the arguments have been transmitted properly:

Lemma 31. *The following property* Inv9 *is an invariant of MemoryImp.*

$$\bigwedge_P RMemory'.pc_P{=}\mathsf{R} \;\rightarrow\; \wedge\, RPC.pc_P{=}\mathsf{WR}$$
$$\wedge\, RPC.proc_P{=}\mathsf{Read}$$
$$\wedge\, RPC.args_P{=}(l) \rightarrow RMemory'.loc_P{=}l$$
$$\bigwedge_P RMemory'.pc_P{=}\mathsf{W} \;\rightarrow\; \wedge\, RPC.pc_P{=}\mathsf{WR}$$
$$\wedge\, RPC.proc_P{=}\mathsf{Write}$$
$$\wedge\, RPC.args_P{=}(l, v) \rightarrow \wedge\, RMemory'.loc_P{=}l$$
$$\wedge\, RMemory'.val_P{=}v$$

RPC can only issue a return to $ClerkR$, following a (possibly exceptional) return by $RMemory'$, and the return value is transmitted properly:

Lemma 32. *The following property* Inv10 *is an invariant of MemoryImp.*

$$\bigwedge_P RPC.pc_P{=}\mathsf{IR} \;\rightarrow\; \vee\, \wedge\, RMemory'.performed_P$$
$$\wedge\, RPC.return_P{=}\;\text{if}\quad RPC.proc_P{=}\mathsf{Read}$$
$$\text{then}\; RMemory'.val_P$$
$$\text{else}\;\mathsf{WriteOk}$$
$$\vee\, \wedge\, \neg RMemory'.legal_P$$
$$\wedge\, RPC.return_P{=}\mathsf{BadArg}$$

Inv11 states the same result as Inv10, for component *ClerkR*:

Lemma 33. *The following property* Inv11 *is an invariant of MemoryImp.*

$$
\begin{aligned}
\textstyle\bigwedge_P \ ClerkR.pc_P{=}\mathsf{IR} \to\ &\vee \wedge RMemory'.performed_P \\
&\quad\ \wedge ClerkR.return_P = \text{if} \quad ClerkR.proc_P{=}\mathsf{Read} \\
&\qquad\qquad\qquad\qquad\qquad \text{then } RMemory'.val_P \\
&\qquad\qquad\qquad\qquad\qquad \text{else } \mathsf{WriteOk} \\
&\vee \wedge \neg RMemory'.legal_P \\
&\quad\ \wedge ClerkR.return_P{=}\mathsf{BadArg}
\end{aligned}
$$

$RMemory'.legal_P$ behaves just like we expect it to, as long as $RMemory'$ is busy:

Lemma 34. *The following property* Inv12 *is an invariant of MemoryImp.*

$$
\begin{aligned}
\textstyle\bigwedge_P RMemory'.pc_P{=}\mathsf{R} &\to RMemory'.legal_P = \mathrm{memloc}(RMemory'.loc_P) \\
\textstyle\bigwedge_P RMemory'.pc_P{=}\mathsf{W} &\to RMemory'.legal_P = \wedge\ \mathrm{memloc}(RMemory'.loc_P) \\
&\qquad\qquad\qquad\qquad\quad\ \wedge\ \mathrm{memval}(RMemory'.val_P)
\end{aligned}
$$

$RMemory'.legal_P$ is not changed after $RMemory'$ returns to RPC:

Lemma 35. *The following property* Inv13 *is an invariant of MemoryImp.*

$$
\begin{aligned}
\textstyle\bigwedge_P RPC.pc_P &\in \{\mathsf{WR}, \mathsf{IR}\} \vee ClerkR.pc_P{=}\mathsf{IR} \\
&\to \vee \wedge ClerkR.proc_P{=}\mathsf{Write} \\
&\qquad \wedge RMemory'.legal_P = \wedge\ \mathrm{memloc}(ClerkR.loc_P) \\
&\qquad\qquad\qquad\qquad\qquad\ \wedge\ \mathrm{memval}(ClerkR.val_P) \\
&\quad\ \vee \wedge ClerkR.proc_P{=}\mathsf{Read} \\
&\qquad \wedge RMemory'.legal_P = \mathrm{memloc}(ClerkR.loc_P)
\end{aligned}
$$

$Memory^*.legal_P$ behaves just like we expect it to, as long as $Memory^*$ is busy:

Lemma 36. *The following property* Inv14 *is an invariant of Memory*.*

$$
\begin{aligned}
\textstyle\bigwedge_P pc_P{=}\mathsf{R} &\to legal_P{=}\mathrm{memloc}(loc_P) \\
\textstyle\bigwedge_P pc_P{=}\mathsf{W} &\to legal_P{=}\mathrm{memloc}(loc_P) \wedge \mathrm{memval}(val_P)
\end{aligned}
$$

Safety We use a weak forward simulation, instead of a weak refinement. In fact, a weak refinement does not exist from *MemoryImp* to *Memory**. Suppose *RPC* receives a call from P for the first time, and *MemoryImp* transits to state s. We can only ensure that *Memory** returns the same value as $RMemory'$ if they read and write simultaneously. So in the image state of s, $Memory^*.performed_P$ must be false. If *RPC* returns a fail to *ClerkR*, *ClerkR* is allowed to retry the call. This may lead to the same state s again. However, *Memory** has imitated the read or write actions performed by $RMemory'$, and $Memory^*.performed_P$ may be true. So a refinement should map s onto a state in which $Memory^*.performed_P$ is both true and false, which is a contradiction.

Theorem 37. *The relation SIM defined by the following formula is a weak forward simulation from MemoryImp to Memory*, with respect to the reachable states in both MemoryImp and Memory*.*

$$
\begin{aligned}
\bigwedge_P Memory^*.pc_P \quad &= \text{ if } \quad ClerkR.pc_P{=}\mathsf{WC} \\
&\quad \text{ then } \mathsf{WC} \\
&\quad \text{ else if } ClerkR.proc_P{=}\mathsf{Read} \text{ then } \mathsf{R} \text{ else } \mathsf{W} \\
\bigwedge_P Memory^*.loc_P \quad &= ClerkR.loc_P \\
\wedge \quad Memory^*.memory &= RMemory'.memory \\
\bigwedge_P ClerkR.proc_P{=}&\mathsf{Write} \to Memory^*.val_P{=}ClerkR.val_P \\
\bigwedge_P RMemory'.performed_P &\wedge \vee\, RPC.pc_P{\in}\{\mathsf{WR},\mathsf{IR}\} \\
&\qquad\qquad\quad \vee\, ClerkR.pc_P{=}\mathsf{IR} \\
\to \wedge\, &Memory^*.performed_P \\
\wedge\, &Memory^*.val_P{=}RMemory'.val_P
\end{aligned}
$$

Proof. We use the following property.
For each two reachable states s in *MemoryImp*, r in *Memory**:

$$
\begin{aligned}
r, s \models \bigwedge_P &Memory^*.pc_P{=}\mathsf{R} \to Memory^*.legal_P{=}\mathrm{memloc}(ClerkR.loc_P) \\
\bigwedge_P &Memory^*.pc_P{=}\mathsf{W} \to Memory^*.legal_P{=} \wedge\,\mathrm{memloc}(ClerkR.loc_P) \\
&\qquad\qquad\qquad\qquad\qquad\qquad\qquad \wedge\,\mathrm{memval}(ClerkR.val_P)
\end{aligned}
$$

This follows directly from Inv5, Inv14 and the definition of SIM. Using this property, and the invariants Inv3, Inv5, Inv6, Inv8, Inv9, Inv11 and Inv13, the proof is obtained by fulfilling the two requirements in [18] in a straightforward manner.

Corollary 38. *MemoryImp is safe with respect to Memory*.*

Proof. Directly from theorem 37 and [18]'s Theorem 6.2.

Deadlock freeness In order to establish that *MemoryImp* is deadlock free with respect to *Memory**, we need an additional invariant. It expresses that as long as *ClerkR* is waiting for a return, *RPC* is busy. Likewise, if *RPC* is waiting for a return, *RMemory'* is busy.

Lemma 39. *The following property Inv15 is an invariant of MemoryImp.*

$$
\begin{aligned}
\bigwedge_P ClerkR.pc_P{=}\mathsf{WR} &\to RPC.pc_P{\neq}\mathsf{WC} \\
\bigwedge_P RPC.pc_P{=}\mathsf{WR} &\to RMemory'.pc_P{\in}\{\mathsf{R},\mathsf{W}\}
\end{aligned}
$$

Theorem 40. *For each reachable and quiescent state s of MemoryImp, each reachable state $r \in Memory^*$ such that $r, s \models$ SIM is a quiescent state of Memory*.*

Proof. From the action types of *MemoryImp* and Inv15, we can conclude that *MemoryImp* is quiescent in state s iff $s \models ClerkR.pc_P=$WC. Since $r, s \models$ SIM, obviously $r \models Memory^*.pc_P=$WC, hence r is quiescent.

Corollary 41. *MemoryImp is deadlock free with respect to Memory*.*

Proof. By Theorems 37 and 40 we can construct for each quiescent execution of *MemoryImp*, a corresponding quiescent execution of *Memory** with the same trace.

Theorem 42. *MemoryImp implements Memory*.*

Proof. We prove $fairtraces(MemoryImp) \subseteq fairtraces(Memory^*)$.
Assume that $\beta \in fairtraces(MemoryImp)$. Let α be a fair execution of *Memory-Imp* with trace β. If α is finite then α is quiescent and it follows by Corollary 41 that *Memory** has a quiescent execution with trace β. Since each quiescent execution is also fair, this implies $\beta \in fairtraces(Memory^*)$. So we may assume without loss of generality that α is infinite.

Using the fact that SIM is a weak forward simulation (Theorem 37) we can easily construct an execution α' of *Memory** with the same trace β. It remains to prove that α' is fair.

First we show that α' is infinite. Then we observe that each non-discarded call to *MemoryImp* will lead to a return within a finite number of steps. Using these two facts, we can easily show for each class in $wfair(Memory^*)$, that α' satisfies the requirements for weak fairness. Since $sfair(Memory^*)$ is empty, this is enough to show that α' is fair.

The main result

Theorem 43. *MemoryImp implements Memory.*

Proof. Theorems 24, 42 yield $fairtraces(MemoryImp) \subseteq fairtraces(Memory)$.

6 Specifications for Problem 4

6.1 Problem 4: Specification of a lossy RPC

The lossy RPC is a timed component whose behaviour is similar to the behaviour of the RPC component from section 4.1.

The difference between timed and untimed I/O automata is that time-passage is made explicit by the action *TIME*, and that the fairness constraints are translated into timing restrictions. However, we will see in Section 7 that fairness restrictions are still needed for a timed I/O automaton. To avoid comparing different types of timed I/O automata, all specifications are in the format of the *fair timed I/O automaton*. A brief introduction to ordinary and fair timed I/O automata is given in Appendix B.

Data types We reuse the ingredients of Σ_2 and $\mathcal{A}_2$, given in section 4.1, and add the data type **Time** to obtain a typed signature Σ_4 and a Σ_4-algebra $\mathcal{A}_4$. **Time** is the set R^+ of positive real numbers, with the usual interpretation and functions for addition (+) and multiplication (.).

We will now present the fair timed I/O automaton *Lossy*, which models a lossy RPC component. It has a new state variable $clock_P$ for each calling process, to keep track of the time elapsed since the last call was received from the sender, or issued to the receiver.

Its behaviour is almost equal to that of the fair I/O automaton *RPC* component, except that the output action *RPC_FAILURE* is replaced by an internal action *LOSE*. After each $LOSE_P$ action, *Lossy* is ready for a new call from the sender for process P.

Also a time-passing action *TIME* is added. We let time increase without bounds, except in states where a certain output action should be issued within δ seconds. Here we forbid time passing if it violates this bound. Clocks are only updated in states where their value is actually used.

Since all fairness restrictions have been replaced by timing constraints, both *wfair(Lossy)* and *sfair(Lossy)* are empty.

The code for *Lossy* is given in Figure 6. Boxes highlight the places where the code differs from the code for *RPC*.

7 Specifications and Verifications for Problem 5

To model an implementation as specified, we need more than the specification of *Lossy*. There has to be some sort of clerk component, that signals the need for a failure output action and issues this failure.

Suppose *Lossy* performs a $LOSE_P$ action. Now, $Lossy.pc_P = \mathsf{WC}$, and new calls from the sender for process P can be handled. However, the clerk will wait until the $2\delta + \epsilon$ bound is reached to issue the necessary $RPC\_FAILURE_P$. Before this $RPC\_FAILURE_P$, all calls for process P should be discarded. So the clerk must also monitor the calls from the sender to *Lossy*.

7.1 Problem 5(a): The RPC implementation *RPCImp*

Data types We reuse the ingredients of Σ_4 and $\mathcal{A}_4$, given in Section 6.1, and add the data type **Cpc** to obtain a typed signature Σ_5 and Σ_5-algebra $\mathcal{A}_5$. **Cpc** contains the constants WC, IC and WR. Note that the domain of **Cpc** is included in the domain of **Rpc**.

Specification We will now present the fair timed I/O automaton *ClerkL*, which models a clerk for the lossy RPC component *Lossy*.

ClerkL catches each *REM_CALL* from the sender. If it is ready for an incoming call, then this call is forwarded with *PASS* to *Lossy*. If it is busy, incoming

Input: REM_CALL_P, I_RETURN_P
Output: $I\_CALL_P, REM\_RETURN_P, BAD\_CALL_P$
Internal: $LOSE_P$
WFair: $\emptyset$
SFair: $\emptyset$

State Variables:	pc_P:	**Rpc**
	$proc_P$:	**Names**
	$args_P$:	**Args**
	$legal_P$:	**Bool**
	$return_P$:	**ReturnVal**
	$clock_P$:	**Time**

Initial: $\bigwedge_P pc_P = \text{WC}$

$REM\_CALL_P(p : \textbf{Names}, a : \textbf{Args})$
Effect:
  if $(pc_P = \text{WC})$ then $[proc_P := p$
    $args_P := a$
    $legal_P := \text{legal\_call}(p, a)$
    $pc_P := \text{IC}$
    $clock_P := 0 \,]$

$LOSE_P$
Precondition:
  $pc_P \in \{\text{IC}, \text{IR}\}$
Effect:
  $pc_P := \text{WC}$

BAD_CALL_P
Precondition:
  $\wedge\ pc_P = \text{IC}$
  $\wedge\ \neg legal_P$
Effect:
  $pc_P := \text{WC}$

$I\_CALL_P(p : \textbf{Procs}, a : \textbf{Args})$
Precondition:
  $\wedge\ pc_P = \text{IC}$
  $\wedge\ legal_P$
  $\wedge\ p = proc_P$
  $\wedge\ a = args_P$
Effect:
  $pc_P := \text{WR}$

$I\_RETURN_P(r : \textbf{ReturnVal})$
Effect:
  if $(pc_P = \text{WR})$ then $[pc_P := \text{IR}$
    $return_P := r$
    $clock_P := 0 \,]$

$REM\_RETURN_P(r : \textbf{ReturnVal})$
Precondition:
  $\wedge\ pc_P = \text{IR}$
  $\wedge\ r = return_P$
Effect:
  $pc_P := \text{WC}$

$TIME(t : \textbf{Time})$
Precondition:
  $\bigwedge_P pc_P \in \{\text{IC}, \text{IR}\} \rightarrow clock_P + t < \delta$
Effect:
  for P in $\{Q \mid pc_Q \in \{\text{IC}, \text{IR}\}\}$
  do $clock_P := clock_P + t$

Fig. 6. I/O automaton *Lossy*

calls are discarded. *ClerkL* signals all output actions from *Lossy*, to ensure that whenever the $2\delta + \epsilon$ bound is reached, the corresponding $RPC\_FAILURE_P$ is really needed. To signal the $2\delta + \epsilon$ bound, *ClerkL* has a clock for each process P.

The code for *ClerkL* is listed in Figure 7.

The composition Since REM_CALL is an input action for both *Lossy* and *ClerkL*, but should only be received by the latter, we need to rename *Lossy*:

$$Lossy' \triangleq \text{rename}(Lossy)$$

where $\quad \text{rename}(REM\_CALL_P(p,a)) = PASS_P(p,a)$
$\qquad \text{rename}(x) \qquad\qquad = x \qquad\qquad$ otherwise

Note that the output actions BAD_CALL, I_CALL and REM_RETURN should be received by both *ClerkL* and the environment. The only output action which must be hidden is $PASS$.

The implementation *RPCImp* is defined as follows:

$$RPCImp \triangleq \text{HIDE } (\bigcup_P \{PASS_P\}) \text{ IN } (ClerkL \| Lossy')$$

RPCImp's behaviour is illustrated in the following figure.

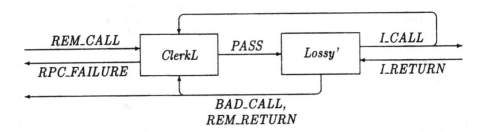

Note that the behaviour of *RPCImp* includes the scenario where *ClerkL* issues a $RPC\_FAILURE_P$ and *Lossy'* issues a REM_RETURN_P for a call from process P, that is, one call leads to two returns. This situation arises whenever the receiver takes too long before returning a procedure call to *Lossy'*. However, since the specification is only required to implement specification *RPC* under the assumption that each I_CALL from *Lossy'* is followed by a I_RETURN within ϵ seconds, this situation is excluded from the desired behaviour.

7.2 Problem 5(b): *RPCImp* implements *RPC*

At this point we have an implementation *RPCImp* with real-time aspects, and an untimed specification *RPC*. To be able to compare these, we can add time to *RPC* and prove admissible trace-inclusion. Since we already specified all components as fair timed I/O automata, we are able to keep the weak and strong fairness sets in *RPC*.

Input: $REM\_CALL_P, BAD\_CALL_P, I\_CALL_P, REM\_RETURN_P$
Output: $PASS_P, RPC\_FAILURE_P$
WFair: ∅
SFair: ∅

State Variables: | pc_P: | **Cpc** | Initial: $\bigwedge_P pc_P = $WC
$proc_P$:	**Names**
$args_P$:	**Args**
$call_P$:	**Bool**
$clock_P$:	**Time**

$REM\_CALL_P(p : \textbf{Names}, a : \textbf{Args})$
  Effect:
    if $(pc_P=$WC$)$ then $[pc_P := $IC
                $proc_P := p$
                $args_P := a$
                $clock_P := 0]$

$PASS_P(p : \textbf{Names}, a : \textbf{Args})$
  Precondition:
    $\wedge\ pc_P=$IC
    $\wedge\ p=proc_P$
    $\wedge\ a=args_P$
  Effect:
    $pc_P := $WR
    $call_P := $false
    $clock_P := 0$

BAD_CALL_P
  Effect:
    $pc_P := $WC

$I\_CALL_P(p : \textbf{Procs}, a : \textbf{Args})$
  Effect:
    $call_P := $true

$REM\_RETURN_P(r : \textbf{ReturnVal})$
  Effect:
    if $(pc_P=$WR $\wedge\ (clock_P < 2\delta+\epsilon))$
    then $[pc_P := WC]$

$RPC\_FAILURE_P$
  Precondition:
    $\wedge\ pc_P=$WR
    $\wedge\ clock_P=2\delta+\epsilon$
  Effect:
    $pc_P := $WC

$TIME(t : \textbf{Time})$
  Precondition:
    $\bigwedge_P pc_P=$IC $\rightarrow clock_P+t < \zeta$
    $\bigwedge_P pc_P=$WR $\rightarrow clock_P+t \leq 2\delta+\epsilon$
  Effect:
    for P in $\{Q \mid pc_Q \in \{$IC, IR$\}\}$
    do $clock_P := clock_P+t$

Fig. 7. Timed I/O automaton *ClerkL*

```
Input:   I_CALL_P
Output:  I_RETURN_P
WFair:   ∅
SFair:   ∅
State Variables: busy_P:     Bool          Initial: ⋀_P ¬busy_P
                 clock_P:    Time

I_CALL_P(p : Procs, a : Args)               I_RETURN_P(r : ReturnVal)
  Effect:                                     Precondition:
    if ¬busy_P then [clock_P := 0               busy_P
                     busy_P := true]          Effect:
                                                busy_P := false


TIME(t : Time)
  Precondition:
    ⋀_P busy_P → clock_P + t < ε
  Effect:
    for P in {Q | busy_Q}
    do clock_P := clock_P + t
```

Fig. 8. Timed I/O automaton *Rec*

The timed I/O automaton *TimeRPC* combines the code for *RPC* with the action *TIME*(t : **Time**). The precondition of *TIME* is true, the effect is empty (no state variables change).

If we could prove that each fair admissible trace of *RPCImp* is in the intersection of the admissible traces and fair timed traces of *TimeRPC*, we would be done. However, we still need to formalise the restriction on the environment, namely that the receiver will return each forwarded procedure-call within ε seconds.

Since there is no straightforward way to express this type of restrictions in I/O automata theory, we choose to specify a very general receiver by means of the fair timed I/O automaton *Rec*. *Rec* returns some answer for each call from *Lossy'* within ε seconds.

Now, *RPCImp* implements *TimeRPC* if the behaviour of *RPCImp* is included in the fair behaviour of *TimeRPC*, provided that both are communicating with the receiver *Rec*.

The code for *Rec* is listed in Figure 8.

A new implementation and specification For the new implementation and specification, we take two copies of *Rec*, and call them *RecLossy* and *RecRPC*. The composition for the implementation is

$$Imp \triangleq \text{HIDE } I \text{ IN } (RPCImp \| RecLossy)$$

where $I \triangleq \bigcup_P \{\mathsf{IC}(p,a), \mathsf{IR}(r) \mid p$ in **Names**, a in **Args**, r in **ReturnVal**$\}$.

The composition for the specification is

$$Spec \triangleq \mathsf{HIDE}\ I\ \mathsf{IN}\ (TimeRPC \| RecRPC)$$

where $I \triangleq \bigcup_P \{\mathsf{IC}(p,a), \mathsf{IR}(r) \mid p$ in **Names**, a in **Args**, r in **ReturnVal**$\}$.

Note that each discrete action in $Spec$ is persistent, and that each admissible execution of Imp is fair. Using these two facts, the implementation relation is proved by the inclusion

$$t\text{-}traces(Imp) \subseteq (t\text{-}traces(Spec) \cap fair\text{-}t\text{-}traces(Spec))$$

First we prove $t\text{-}traces(Imp) \subseteq t\text{-}traces(Spec)$, by means of a weak refinement, and then $t\text{-}traces(Imp) \subseteq fair\text{-}t\text{-}traces(Spec)$.

In the remainder, we will mostly reason about 'sampling' executions instead of timed executions. Since Lemmas 2.11 - 2.13 in [17] state that both induce the same set of timed traces, and we only consider inclusion on sets of traces, this does not make a difference.

Admissible trace inclusion Some invariants are needed to enable the use of a weak timed refinement. The first one states that in the particular states, no clocks violate their bounds.

Lemma 44. *The following property* InvT1 *is an invariant of Imp:*

$\bigwedge_P ClerkL.pc_P{=}\mathsf{IC} \quad \rightarrow (ClerkL.clock_P{<}\gamma)$
$\bigwedge_P ClerkL.pc_P{=}\mathsf{WR} \quad \rightarrow (ClerkL.clock_P{\leq}2\delta{+}\epsilon)$
$\bigwedge_P Lossy'.pc_P{\in}\{\mathsf{IC},\mathsf{IR}\} \rightarrow (Lossy'.clock_P{<}\delta)$
$\bigwedge_P Lossy'.pc_P{=}\mathsf{WR} \quad \rightarrow (RecLossy.clock_P{<}\epsilon)$

The next invariant states that all components synchronise in some way, which is reflected in their program counters and clocks. The formula looks rather complicated, but readability cannot be improved by splitting it into smaller pieces. This is due to the precondition of action $RPC\_FAILURE$.

Lemma 45. *The following property* InvT2 *is an invariant of Imp:*

$\bigwedge_P Lossy'.pc_P{\neq}\mathsf{WC} \rightarrow ClerkL.pc_P{=}\mathsf{WR}$
$\bigwedge_P Lossy'.pc_P{=}\mathsf{WR} \leftrightarrow RecLossy.busy_P$
$\bigwedge_P Lossy'.pc_P{=}\mathsf{IC} \rightarrow (ClerkL.clock_P{=}Lossy'.clock_P)$
$\bigwedge_P Lossy'.pc_P{=}\mathsf{WR} \rightarrow (ClerkL.clock_P{<}RecLossy.clock_P{+}\delta)$
$\bigwedge_P Lossy'.pc_P{=}\mathsf{IR} \rightarrow (ClerkL.clock_P{<}Lossy'.clock_P{+}\delta{+}\epsilon)$

Whenever $Lossy'$ or $ClerkL$ is ready to issue a return to the sender, the other of the two is not doing something unexpected.

Corollary 46. *The following property* InvT3 *is an invariant of Imp:*

$\bigwedge_P$ $enabled(BAD\_CALL_P)$ $\rightarrow$ $ClerkL.pc_P{=}\mathsf{WR}$
$\bigwedge_P$ $enabled(RPC\_FAILURE_P)$ $\rightarrow$ $Lossy'.pc_P{=}\mathsf{WC}$
$\bigwedge_P$ $enabled(REM\_RETURN_P)$ $\rightarrow$ $\wedge$ $ClerkL.pc_P{=}\mathsf{WR}$
$\wedge$ $(C.clock_P{<}2\delta{+}\epsilon)$

ClerkL records every call from Lossy' to RecLossy correctly.

Lemma 47. *The following property* InvT4 *is an invariant of Imp:*

$\bigwedge_P$ $Lossy'.pc_P{=}\mathsf{IC}$ $\rightarrow$ $\neg ClerkL.call_P$
$\bigwedge_P$ $Lossy'.pc_P{\in}\{\mathsf{IR},\mathsf{WR}\}$ $\rightarrow$ $ClerkL.call_P$

Lossy' does not unexpectedly change its state variables.

Lemma 48. *The following property* InvT5 *is an invariant of Lossy':*

$\bigwedge_P$ $pc_P{\neq}\mathsf{WC}$ $\rightarrow$ $legal_P{=}legal\_call(proc_P, args_P)$

Lossy' and ClerkL agree on the arguments of the last call.

Lemma 49. *The following property* InvT6 *is an invariant of Imp:*

$\bigwedge_P$ $Lossy'.pc_P{\neq}\mathsf{WC}$ $\rightarrow$ $\wedge$ $Lossy'.proc_P{=}ClerkL.proc_P$
$\wedge$ $Lossy'.args_P{=}ClerkL.args_P$

Corollary 50. *The following property* InvT7 *is an invariant of Imp:*

$\bigwedge_P$ $Lossy'.pc_P{\neq}\mathsf{WC}$
$\rightarrow$ $Lossy'.legal_P{=}legal\_call(ClerkL.proc_P, ClerkL.args_P)$

Weak refinement The weak timed refinement does not look very straight-forward. This is due to *Lossy'*'s possibility to *LOSE* every now and then. If this happens, the program counter value in *TimeRPC* suddenly relies on the information in *ClerkL*.

Theorem 51. *The function* TREF, *which is defined by the identity function on variables with the same name from RecLossy to RecRPC and by the following formula, is a weak timed refinement from Imp to Spec, with respect to the reachable states in Imp and Spec.*

$\bigwedge_P$ $TimeRPC.pc_P$ $=$ if $Lossy'.pc_P{\neq}\mathsf{WC}$
then $Lossy'.pc_P$
else if $ClerkL.pc_P{\in}\{\mathsf{WC},\mathsf{IC}\}$
then $ClerkL.pc_P$
else if $ClerkL.call_P$
then IR
else IC
$\bigwedge_P$ $TimeRPC.proc_P$ $=$ $ClerkL.proc_P$
$\bigwedge_P$ $TimeRPC.args_P$ $=$ $ClerkL.args_P$
$\bigwedge_P$ $TimeRPC.legal_P$ $=$ $legal\_call(ClerkL.proc_P, ClerkL.args_P)$
$\bigwedge_P$ $TimeRPC.return_P$ $=$ $Lossy'.return_P$

Proof. Using the invariants, this is not too hard. We simply check the requirements in [17].

Corollary 52. *t-traces(Imp)* $\subseteq$ *t-traces(Spec)*

Proof. Directly from Theorem 51 and [17]'s Theorem 8.2.

Fairness is preserved We prove that each *REM_CALL* to *Imp* leads to a return (*BAD_CALL, REM_RETURN* or *RPC_FAILURE*) within bounded time.

Lemma 53. *Let* $\alpha = s_0 a_1 s_1 a_2 s_2 \dots$ *be an admissible execution of Imp.*
Then $a_i = REM\_CALL_P$ *and* $s_{i-1} \models pc_P$=WC *implies that there is some j such that* $j > i$, $a_j \in \{BAD\_CALL_P, REM\_RETURN_P, RPC\_FAILURE_P\}$, *and the sum of time elapsing between* s_{i-1} *and* s_j *is bounded.*

Proof. First we observe that all discrete actions in *Imp* are persistent. This is easily checked by examining the effect of *TIME*, the preconditions of the discrete actions and invariant InvT1.

Suppose $\alpha = s_0 a_1 s_1 a_2 s_2 \dots$ is an admissible execution of *Lossy'*,
$a_i = REM\_CALL_P$ and $s_{i-1} \models pc_P$=WC.

Clearly, $s_i \models pc_P$=IC $\wedge$ *clock*$_P$=0. So either s_i enables *TIME, BAD_CALL*$_P$ and *LOSE*$_P$ or s_i enables *TIME, I_CALL*$_P$ and *LOSE*$_P$. By persistency, InvT1, InvT2 and the action types we know that idling after state s_i can only disable *TIME*, but not enable other discrete actions. Since α is admissible, time must pass without bound. So within bounded time, one of the discrete actions mentioned must be performed:

$$\exists k : \wedge \ k > i$$
$$\wedge \ a_k \in \{BAD\_CALL_P, I\_CALL_P, LOSE_P\}$$
$$\wedge \ \text{the sum of time elapsing between } s_{i-1} \text{ and } s_k \text{ is bounded}$$

Take such a k.

1. Suppose $a_k = BAD\_CALL_P$. The lemma is fulfilled.
2. Suppose $a_k = I\_CALL_P$.
   Then $s_k \models RecLossy.busy_P \wedge RecLossy.clock_P$=0, and s_k apparently enables *I_RETURN*$_P$ and *TIME*. As before, idling after state s_k can only disable *TIME*, but not enable other discrete actions. So within bounded time, *I_RETURN*$_P$ must be performed:

$$\exists l : \wedge \ l > k$$
$$\wedge \ a_l = I\_RETURN_P$$
$$\wedge \ \text{the sum of time elapsing between } s_k \text{ and } s_l \text{ is bounded}$$

   Take such an l.
   We know that $s_l \models Lossy'.pc_P$=IR $\wedge$ *Lossy'.clock*$_P$=0, and s_l must enable

REM_RETURN$_P$, *LOSE$_P$* and *TIME*. Again we see that within bounded time, *REM_RETURN$_P$* or *LOSE$_P$* must be performed:

$$\exists m : \wedge\ m > l$$
$$\wedge\ a_m \in \{REM\_RETURN_P, LOSE_P\}$$
$$\wedge\ \text{the sum of time elapsing between } s_l \text{ and } s_m \text{ is bounded}$$

Take such an m.

(a) Suppose $a_m = REM\_RETURN_P$. The lemma is fulfilled.

(b) Suppose $a_m = LOSE_P$. We know that $m > l > k > i$, so Case 3 applies.

3. Suppose $a_k = LOSE_P$.

Then $s_k \models ClerkL.pc_P$=WR $\wedge$ $Lossy'.pc_P$=WC. Now s_k enables only *TIME*, but idling is only allowed up to (and not beyond!) the state that enables *RPC_FAILURE$_P$*. So within bounded time, *RPC_FAILURE$_P$* must be performed:

$$\exists l : \wedge\ l > k$$
$$\wedge\ a_l = RPC\_FAILURE_P$$
$$\wedge\ \text{the sum of time elapsing between } s_k \text{ and } s_l \text{ is bounded}$$

The lemma is fulfilled.

Theorem 54. *t-traces(Imp) $\subseteq$ fair-t-traces(Spec)*

Proof. Suppose β is a timed trace of *Imp*, and $\alpha = s_0 a_1 s_1 a_2 s_2 \ldots$ is an admissible execution of *Imp* such that $t\text{-}trace(\alpha) = \beta$. Using the fact that TREF is a weak timed refinement (Theorem 51), we can easily construct an admissible execution α' of *Spec* such that $t\text{-}trace(\alpha') = \beta$. It remains to prove that α' is fair.

Initially, $Lossy'.pc_P$=WC for each P. Whenever $Lossy'.pc_P$=WC, the first action that changes $Lossy'.pc_P$ must be I_CALL_P. By Lemma 53, we know that each occurrence of I_CALL_P is followed within bounded time by a state in which $Lossy'.pc_P$ = WC. Combining this with InvT2 and the fact that α is admissible, we see that for each P, α must contain infinitely many occurrences of states such that both $Lossy'.pc_P$=WC and $RecLossy.busy_P$=false.

Using the above and the fact that α' is admissible, we see that for each P, α' must contain infinitely many occurrences of states such that $TimeRPC.pc_P$=WC and $RecRPC.busy_P$=false. Since in such a state no locally controlled actions are enabled for P, α' must be weakly fair. Combining this with the fact that there are no strong fairness sets in *Spec*, we obtain that α' is fair.

References

1. M. Abadi, L. Lamport, and S. Merz. A TLA solution to the RPC-Memory specification problem, 1996. This volume.
2. E. Astesiano and G. Reggio. A dynamic specification of the RPC-Memory problem, 1996. This volume.
3. E. Best. A memory module specification using composable high level nets, 1996. This volume.

4. J. Blom and B. Jonsson. Constraint oriented temporal logic specification, 1996. This volume.

5. M. Broy. A functional solution to the RPC-Memory specification problem, 1996. This volume.

6. J.R. Cuéllar, D. Barnard, and M. Huber. A solution relying on the model checking of boolean transition systems, 1996. This volume.

7. R. Gawlick, R. Segala, J.F. Søgaard-Andersen, and N. Lynch. Liveness in timed and untimed systems. In S. Abiteboul and E. Shamir, editors, *Proceedings* 21th *ICALP*, Jerusalem, volume 820 of *Lecture Notes in Computer Science*. Springer-Verlag, 1994. A full version appears as MIT Technical Report number MIT/LCS/TR-587.

8. R. Gotzhein. Applying a temporal logic to the RPC-Memory specification problem, 1996. This volume.

9. J. Hooman. Using PVS for an assertional verification of the RPC-Memory specification problem, 1996. This volume.

10. H. Hungar. Specification and verification using symbolic timing diagrams, 1996. This volume.

11. N. Klarlund, M. Nielsen, and K. Sunesen. A case study in verification based on trace abstractions, 1996. This volume.

12. R. Kurki-Suonio. Incremental specification with joint actions: The RPC-Memory specification problem, 1996. This volume.

13. K.G. Larsen, B. Steffen, and C. Weise. The methodology of modal constraints, 1996. This volume.

14. N.A. Lynch. *Distributed Algorithms*. Morgan Kaufmann Publishers, Inc., San Fransisco, California, 1996.

15. N.A. Lynch and M.R. Tuttle. Hierarchical correctness proofs for distributed algorithms. In *Proceedings of the 6th Annual ACM Symposium on Principles of Distributed Computing*, pages 137–151, August 1987. A full version is available as MIT Technical Report MIT/LCS/TR-387.

16. N.A. Lynch and M.R. Tuttle. An introduction to input/output automata. *CWI Quarterly*, 2(3):219–246, September 1989.

17. N.A. Lynch and F.W. Vaandrager. Forward and backward simulations – part II: Timing-based systems. Technical Report MIT/LCS/TM-487.c, Laboratory for Computer Science, Massachusetts Institute of Technology, Cambridge, MA, USA, April 1995. To appear in *Information and Computation*.

18. N.A. Lynch and F.W. Vaandrager. Forward and backward simulations. part I: Untimed systems. *Information and Computation*, 121(2):214–233, September 1995.

19. Z. Manna and A. Pnueli. Verifying hybrid systems. In R.L. Grossman, A. Nerode, A.P. Ravn, and H. Rischel, editors, *Hybrid Systems*, volume 736 of *Lecture Notes in Computer Science*, pages 4–35. Springer-Verlag, 1993.

20. M. Rinderspacher. The solution of the RPC-Memory specification problem using reachability analysis, 1996. This volume.

21. J.M.T. Romijn and F.W. Vaandrager. A note on fairness in I/O automata. Report CS-R9579, CWI, Amsterdam, December 1995. To appear in *Information Processing Letters*.

22. K. Stølen. Using relations on Streams to solve the RPC-Memory specification problem, 1996. This volume.

23. R.T. Udink and J.N. Kok. The RPC-Memory specification problem: UNITY plus refinement calculus, 1996. This volume.

24. Wang Yi. Real-time behaviour of asynchronous agents. In J.C.M. Baeten and J.W. Klop, editors, *Proceedings CONCUR 90*, Amsterdam, volume 458 of *Lecture Notes in Computer Science*, pages 502–520. Springer-Verlag, 1990.

A Safe and Fair I/O Automata

In this appendix we review some basic definitions from [7, 21].

A.1 Safe I/O automata

A *safe I/O automaton* B consists of the following components:

- A set $states(B)$ of *states* (possibly infinite).
- A nonempty set $start(B) \subseteq states(B)$ of *start states*.
- A set $acts(B)$ of *actions*, partitioned into three sets $in(B)$, $int(B)$ and $out(B)$ of *input*, *internal* and *output* actions, respectively.
  Actions in $local(B) \triangleq out(B) \cup int(B)$ are called *locally controlled*.
- A set $steps(B) \subseteq states(B) \times acts(B) \times states(B)$ of *transitions*, with the property that for every state s and input action $a \in in(B)$ there is a transition $(s, a, s') \in steps(B)$.

We let $s, s',..$ range over states, and $a,..$ over actions. We write $s \xrightarrow{a}_B s'$, or just $s \xrightarrow{a} s'$ if B is clear from the context, as a shorthand for $(s, a, s') \in steps(B)$.

Enabling of actions An action a of a safe I/O automaton B is *enabled* in a state s iff $s \xrightarrow{a} s'$ for some s'. Since every input action is enabled in every state, safe I/O automata are said to be *input enabled*. The intuition behind the input-enabling condition is that input actions are under control of the environment and that the system that is modeled by an safe I/O automaton cannot prevent the environment from doing these actions.

Executions An *execution fragment* of a safe I/O automaton B is a finite or infinite alternating sequence $s_0 a_1 s_1 a_2 s_2 \cdots$ of states and actions of B, beginning with a state, and if it is finite also ending with a state, such that for all i, $s_i \xrightarrow{a_{i+1}} s_{i+1}$. An *execution* is an execution fragment that begins with a start state. We write $execs^*(B)$ for the set of finite executions of B, and $execs(B)$ for the set of all executions of B. A state s of B is *reachable* if it is the last state of some finite execution of B. We write $rstates(B)$ for the set of reachable states of B.

Traces Suppose $\alpha = s_0 a_1 s_1 a_2 s_2 \cdots$ is an execution fragment of A. Then the *trace* of α is the subsequence of $a_1 a_2 \cdots$ consisting of the input and output actions of A. With $traces^*(A)$ we denote the set of traces of finite executions of A. For s, s' states of A and β a finite sequence of input and output actions of A, we define $s \xRightarrow{\beta}_A s'$ iff A has a finite execution fragment with first state s, last state s' and trace β.

A.2   Fair I/O automata

A *fair I/O automaton* A is a triple consisting of

- a safe I/O automaton *safe*(A), and
- sets *wfair*(A) and *sfair*(A) of subsets of *local*(*safe*(A)), called the *weak fairness sets* and *strong fairness sets*, respectively.

Enabling of sets   Let U be a set of locally controlled actions of a fair I/O automaton A. Then U is *enabled* in a state s iff an action from U is enabled in s. Set U is *input resistant* if and only if, for each pair of reachable states s, s' and for each input action a, s enables U and $s \xrightarrow{a} s'$ implies s' enables U. So once U is enabled, it can only be disabled by the occurrence of a locally controlled action.

Fair executions   An execution α of a fair I/O automaton A is *weakly fair* if the following conditions hold for each $W \in wfair(A)$:

1. If α is finite then W is not enabled in the last state of α.
2. If α is infinite then either α contains infinitely many occurrences of actions from W, or α contains infinitely many occurrences of states in which W is not enabled.

Execution α is *strongly fair* if the following conditions hold for each $S \in sfair(A)$:

1. If α is finite then S is not enabled in the last state of α.
2. If α is infinite then either α contains infinitely many occurrences of actions from S, or α contains only finitely many occurrences of states in which S is enabled.

Execution α is *fair* if it is both weakly and strongly fair. In a fair execution each weak fairness set gets turns if enabled continuously, and each strong fairness set gets turns if enabled infinitely many times. We write *fairexecs*(A) for the set of fair executions of A.

Fair traces   We write *fairtraces*(A) for the set of traces of fair executions of a fair I/O automaton A.

Implementation relation   Let A and B be fair I/O automata. *A implements B* if *fairtraces*(A) $\subseteq$ *fairtraces*(B).

A number of constructions exist that help establish an implementation relation. This paper uses a weak refinement, a weak backward simulation and a weak forward simulation. For definition and use of these, we refer to [18].

Fairness as a liveness condition   We write *live*(A) for the underlying safe I/O automaton of A paired with *fairexecs*(A): *live*(A) $\triangleq$ (*safe*(A), *fairexecs*(A)).

B Timed and Fair Timed I/O Automata

In this appendix we review some basic definitions from [17], and introduce the *fair timed I/O automaton*, which extends the timed I/O automaton in [17] with the property fairness.

B.1 Timed I/O automata

A *timed I/O automaton* A is a safe I/O automaton whose set of actions includes R^+, the set of positive reals. Actions from R^+ are referred to as *time-passage actions*. Other actions are referred to as *discrete actions*. Performing one or more consecutive time-passage actions is called *idling*.

We let $d, d', \ldots$ range over R^+ and, more generally, $t, t', \ldots$ over the set R of real numbers. The set of *visible* actions is defined by $vis(A) \triangleq (in(A) \cup out(A)) - R^+$.

We assume that a timed I/O automaton satisfies the following axioms.

S1 If $s' \xrightarrow{d} s''$ and $s'' \xrightarrow{d'} s$, then $s' \xrightarrow{d+d'} s$.

For the second axiom, an auxiliary definition is needed. A *trajectory* for a step $s' \xrightarrow{d} s$ is a function $w : [0, d] \to states(A)$ such that $w(0) = s'$, $w(d) = s$, and

$$w(t) \xrightarrow{t'-t} w(t') \text{ for all } t, t' \in [0, d] \text{ with } t < t'.$$

Now we can state the second axiom.

S2 Each step $s \xrightarrow{d} s'$ has a trajectory.

Axiom **S1** gives a natural property of time, namely that if time can pass in two steps, then it also pass in a single step. The *trajectory axiom* **S2** is a kind of converse to **S1**; it says that any time-passage step can be "filled in" with states for each intervening time, in a "consistent" way.

Executions of timed I/O automata correspond to what are called *sampling computations* in [19].

Timed Traces The full externally visible behaviour of a timed I/O automaton can be inferred from its executions as follows: suppose $\alpha = s_0 a_1 s_1 a_2 s_2 \cdots$ is an execution fragment of a timed I/O automaton A. For each index j, let t_j be given by

$$t_0 = 0,$$
$$t_{j+1} = \text{if } a_{j+1} \in R^+ \text{ then } t_j + a_{j+1} \text{ else } t_j.$$

The *limit time* of α, notation $\alpha.ltime$, is the smallest element of $R^{\geq 0} \cup \{\infty\}$ larger than or equal to all the t_j. We say α is *admissible* if $\alpha.ltime = \infty$, and *Zeno* if it is an infinite sequence but with a finite limit time. The *timed trace* $t\text{-}trace(\alpha)$ associated with α is defined by

$$t\text{-}trace(\alpha) \triangleq (((a_1, t_1)(a_2, t_2) \cdots) \lceil (vis(A) \times R^{\geq 0}), \alpha.ltime).$$

Thus, $t\text{-}trace(\alpha)$ records the visible actions of α paired with their times of occurrence, as well as the limit time of the execution.

A pair β is a *timed trace* of A if it is the timed trace of some finite or admissible execution of A. Thus, we explicitly exclude the timed traces that originate from Zeno executions. We write $t\text{-}traces(A)$ for the set of all timed traces of A, $t\text{-}traces^*(A)$ for the set of *finite* timed traces (the timed traces derived from the finite executions), and $t\text{-}traces^\infty(A)$ for the set of *admissible* traces (the timed traces derived from the admissible executions).

B.2 Fair timed I/O automata

In Problem 5 in the RPC-Memory specification problem a timed implementation is required for an untimed specification. In our model, this means that we have to compare the admissible behaviour of a timed specification with the fair behaviour of an untimed specification. This may be solved by adding time to the untimed specification. However, the fairness restrictions are lost in this manner, and we may prove the wrong implementation relation. Our final solution is to consider the traces that are both admissible, and fair in the sense that we know from the untimed model. For this purpose, we define the *fair timed I/O automaton*, which is a timed I/O automaton with additional fairness requirements.

Although carrying fairness semantics over from the untimed model to a timed model is very tricky in general, we can get away with the same definition as for the untimed case as long as the discrete actions used in the fairness sets cannot be overruled by the passage of time. This property is known as *persistency* [24] and can be summarised as follows:

> If a discrete action a is enabled in state s, then a is enabled in each state s' that can be reached from s by idling.

All fair timed I/O automata in this paper meet the persistency requirement.

We now list the basic definitions that enable us to use fairness for timed I/O automata.

A *fair timed I/O automaton* A is a triple consisting of

- a timed I/O automaton $timed(A)$, and
- sets $wfair(A)$ and $sfair(A)$ of subsets of $local(timed(A))$, called the *weak fairness sets* and *strong fairness sets*, respectively.

Enabling of sets Let U be a set of locally controlled actions of a fair timed I/O automaton A. Then U is *enabled* in a state s iff an action from U is enabled in s. Set U is *input resistant* if and only if, for each pair of reachable states s, s' and for each input action a, s enables U and $s \xrightarrow{a} s'$ implies s' enables U. So once U is enabled, it can only be disabled by the occurrence of a locally controlled action.

Fair executions An execution α of a fair timed I/O automaton A is *weakly fair* if the following conditions hold for each $W \in wfair(A)$:

1. If α is finite then W is not enabled in the last state of α.
2. If α is infinite then either α contains infinitely many occurrences of actions from W, or α contains infinitely many occurrences of states in which W is not enabled.

Execution α is *strongly fair* if the following conditions hold for each $S \in sfair(A)$:

1. If α is finite then S is not enabled in the last state of α.
2. If α is infinite then either α contains infinitely many occurrences of actions from S, or α contains only finitely many occurrences of states in which S is enabled.

Execution α is *fair* if it is both weakly and strongly fair. In a fair execution each weak fairness set gets turns if enabled continuously, and each strong fairness set gets turns if enabled infinitely many times. We write *fairexecs*(A) for the set of fair executions of A.

Fair timed traces We write *fair-t-traces*(A) for the set of timed traces derived from the fair executions of fair timed I/O automaton A.

Implementation relation Let A and B be fair timed I/O automata. A *implements* B if $(t\text{-}traces^{\infty}(A) \cap fair\text{-}t\text{-}traces(A)) \subseteq (t\text{-}traces^{\infty}(B) \cap fair\text{-}t\text{-}traces(B))$.

A number of constructions exist that help establish an implementation relation. This paper only uses a weak timed refinement. For definition and use of this construction, we refer to [17].

Using Relations on Streams to Solve the RPC-Memory Specification Problem

Ketil Stølen*

Institut für Informatik, TU München, D-80290 München

Abstract. We employ a specification and refinement technique based on streams to solve the RPC-memory specification problem. Streams are used to represent the communication histories of channels. We distinguish between input and output streams. Each input stream represents the communication history of an input channel; each output stream represents the communication history of an output channel. Specifications are *relations* between input and output streams. These relations are expressed as logical formulas. Composition corresponds to logical *conjunction*. We distinguish between time-independent and time-dependent specifications. A time-independent specification is based on untimed streams; a time-dependent specification employs timed streams. Timed streams are needed to capture *timing* constraints and *causalities*. A specification *refines* (or alternatively, *implements*) another specification if any input/output behavior of the former is also an input/output behavior of the latter. This means that refinement corresponds to logical *implication*.

1 Introduction

We use streams and relations on streams to solve the the RPC-memory specification problem, as described in [BL]. We address all parts of the problem statement with one exception: we do not impose the hand-shake protocol on which [BL] is based. This means for example, a user may send a new call before the memory component issues a reply to the previous call sent by the same user. The hand-shake protocol is not considered because our approach is tailored towards asynchronous communication with *unbounded* buffering. More correctly, our approach is based on the hypotheses that asynchronous communication with unbounded buffering simplifies specifications and the verification of refinement steps — simplifies in the sense that it allows us to abstract from synchronization requirements needed in system descriptions based on bounded communication buffers. In our approach this kind of synchronization is first introduced when it is really needed, namely when a specification is mapped into its final implementation. How system specifications based on asynchronous communication with unbounded buffering can be refined into system specifications based on

---

* Address from September 1, 1996: Institute for Energy Technology, P.O.Box 173, 1751 Halden, Norway. Email:Ketil.Stoelen@hrp.no

hand-shake communication is explained in the appendix. More explicitly, in the appendix we show how the implementation of the memory component can be refined into an implementation which differs from the first in only one respect: the communication is conducted via hand-shakes. Thus, we do not ignore the hand-shake protocol because we cannot handle it. On the contrary, we can easily specify hand-shake communication. We ignore the hand-shake protocol because we see asynchronous communication with unbounded buffering as a helpful feature of our method.

Any sensible specification language allows specifications to be expressed in many different ways and styles, and this is of course also true for our approach. In this paper we have tried to find the right balance between readability and brevity. In particular, we characterize nondeterministic behavior in terms of *oracles*.

The rest of the paper is structured as follows. In Sect. 2 we introduce streams and the most basic operators for their manipulation. In Sect. 3 we specify the memory components. The RPC component is the subject of Sect. 4, and in Sect. 5 we show how it can be used to implement the memory component. Similarly, the lossy RPC component is specified in Sect. 6 and used to implement the RPC component in Sect. 7. In Sect. 8 we give a brief summary and draw some conclusions. Finally, as mentioned above, there is an appendix dealing with the introduction of hand-shake communication.

2　Streams and Operators on Streams

We use *streams* to model the communication histories of channels. A stream is a finite or infinite sequence of *messages*. The messages occur in the order they are transmitted. For any set of messages M, by M^∞, M^* and M^ω we denote respectively the set of all infinite streams over M, the set of all finite streams over M, and the set of all finite and infinite streams over M.

We now introduce the most basic operators for the manipulation of streams. $\mathbb{N}$ denotes the set of natural numbers; $\mathbb{N}_+$ denotes $\mathbb{N}\setminus\{0\}$; $\mathbb{N}_\infty$ denotes $\mathbb{N}\cup\{\infty\}$; $[1..n]$ denotes $\{1,..,n\}$; $\mathbb{B}$ denotes the Booleans. Let $r, s \in M^\omega$ and $j \in \mathbb{N}_\infty$:

- $\#r$ denotes the *length* of r. This means ∞, if r is infinite, and the number of messages in r otherwise.
- a^j denotes the stream consisting of exactly j *copies* of the message a.
- $\text{dom}(r)$ denotes $\mathbb{N}_+$ if $\#r = \infty$, and $\{1, 2, \ldots, \#r\}$, otherwise.
- $r[j]$ denotes the jth message of r if $j \in \text{dom}(r)$.
- $\langle a_1, a_2, .., a_n \rangle$ denotes the stream of length n whose first message is a_1, whose second message is a_2, and so on. As a consequence, $\langle\rangle$ denotes the *empty* stream.
- $r|_j$ denotes the *prefix* of r of length j if $0 \leq j < \#r$, and r otherwise. This means that $r|_\infty = r$.
- $r \frown s$ denotes the result of *concatenating* r and s. Thus, $\langle a, b \rangle \frown \langle c, d \rangle = \langle a, b, c, d \rangle$. If r is infinite we have that $r \frown s = r$.
- $r \sqsubseteq s$ holds if r is a *prefix* of or equal to s. In other words, if $\exists v \in M^\omega$: $r \frown v = s$.

For any n-tuple t, we use $\Pi_j.t$ to denote the jth component of t (counting from the left to the right). For example, $\Pi_3.(a, b, c) = c$. When convenient we use t_k as a short-hand for $\Pi_k.t$.

We also need a *filtration* operator $\circledS$ for tuples of streams. For any n-tuple of streams t and natural number $j \in \mathbb{N}_+$ less than or equal to the shortest stream in t, by t/j we denote the n-tuple of messages whose kth component is equal to $(\Pi_k.t)[j]$. For example, if $t = (\langle a, b \rangle, \langle c, d \rangle)$ then $t/1 = (a, c)$ and $t/2 = (b, d)$. For any set of n-tuples of messages A and n-tuple of streams t, by $A \circledS t$ we denote the n-tuple of streams obtained from t by

- truncating each stream in t at the length of the shortest stream in t,
- selecting or deleting t/j depending on whether t/j is in A or not.

For example, if $n = 1$ we have that

$$\{a, b\} \circledS \langle a, b, d, c, d, a, d \rangle = \langle a, b, a \rangle$$

and if $n = 2$ we have that

$$\{(a, a), (b, b)\} \circledS (\langle a, b, a, b, a, b, a \rangle, \langle a, a, a, b \rangle) = (\langle a, a, b \rangle, \langle a, a, b \rangle)$$

Moreover, if $n = 3$ we have that

$$\{(a, b, c)\} \circledS (\langle a, a, a \rangle, \langle b, b, b \rangle, \langle a, b, c \rangle) = (\langle a \rangle, \langle b \rangle, \langle c \rangle)$$

3 Problem I: The Memory Component

In this section we specify the *reliable* and the *unreliable* memory components,[2] as described in Sect. 2 of the problem statement [BL]. To give a smooth introduction to our specification technique, we construct these specifications in a stepwise fashion. We first specify a simple memory component with a *sequential* interface. This component has exactly one input and one output channel. We refer to this memory component as the sequential memory component. Then we consider memory components with a *concurrent* interface. More explicitly, as indicated by Fig. 1, memory components which communicate with n user components in a *point-to-point* fashion. These components we call concurrent. We first explain how the specification of the sequential memory component can be generalized to handle a concurrent interface. This specification is then step-by-step generalized to capture the requirements to the reliable and unreliable memory components, as described in [BL].

---

[2] What we call the "unreliable memory component" corresponds to the "memory component" in [BL].

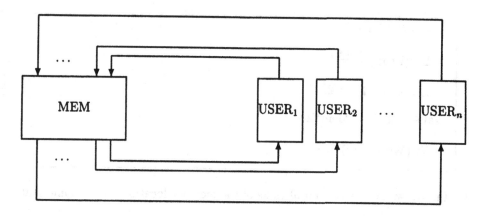

Fig. 1. Network with Concurrent Memory Component.

3.1 Basic Definitions

We first give some basic definitions.

$$
\begin{aligned}
\text{Call} &\overset{\text{def}}{=} \{\text{Read}(l) \mid l \in L\} \cup \{\text{Write}(l, v) \mid l \in L \wedge v \in V\} \\[4pt]
\text{Rpl} &\overset{\text{def}}{=} \{\text{OkRd}(v) \mid v \in V\} \cup \{\text{OkWr}, \text{BadArg}, \text{MemFail}\} \\[4pt]
\text{VldRd} &\overset{\text{def}}{=} \{\text{Read}(l) \mid l \in \text{MemLocs}\} \\[4pt]
\text{Wr} &\overset{\text{def}}{=} \{\text{Write}(l, v) \mid l \in L \wedge v \in V\} \\[4pt]
\text{VldWr}(l) &\overset{\text{def}}{=} \{\text{Write}(l, v) \mid v \in \text{MemVals}\} \\[4pt]
\text{VldWr} &\overset{\text{def}}{=} \{\text{VldWr}(l) \mid l \in \text{MemLocs}\} \\[4pt]
\text{VldCall} &\overset{\text{def}}{=} \text{VldRd} \cup \text{VldWr}
\end{aligned}
$$

L is a set of locations; V is a set of values. Call and Rpl are the sets of all possible calls and replies, respectively. VldRd and VldWr are the sets of all valid read and write calls, respectively. Wr is the set of all possible write calls, and VldWr(l) is the set of all write calls whose value is valid. VldCall is the set of all valid calls. We also introduce two auxiliary functions which are used to access the contents of calls.

$$\begin{array}{l}
\text{Loc} \in \text{Call} \to L \\[4pt]
\quad \text{Loc}(\text{Read}(l)) \stackrel{\text{def}}{=} l \\[4pt]
\quad \text{Loc}(\text{Write}(l, v)) \stackrel{\text{def}}{=} l \\[4pt]
\text{Val} \in \text{VldWr} \to \text{MemVals} \\[4pt]
\quad \text{Val}(\text{Write}(l, v)) \stackrel{\text{def}}{=} v
\end{array}$$

By InitVal we denote the initial value of the memory locations. We assume that

$$\text{InitVal} \in \text{MemVals} \tag{1}$$

3.2 The Sequential Memory Component

As already mentioned, we start by specifying a simple sequential memory component. This component communicates with exactly one user component via exactly one input and one output channel. The component is reliable in the sense that each call results in exactly one memory access and that a call never fails. It can be specified as follows.

$$\begin{array}{l}
\underline{}\text{SeqMc}\underline{}\text{time\_independent}\underline{} \\[4pt]
\textbf{in} \quad i \in \text{Call}^\omega \\[4pt]
\textbf{out} \quad o \in \text{Rpl}^\omega \\[4pt]
\hline \\[2pt]
\#o = \#i \\[4pt]
\forall j \in \text{dom}(o): \\[4pt]
\quad \text{let } w = [\,\text{VldWr}(\text{Loc}(i[j]))\textcircled{S}(i|_j)\,] \\[4pt]
\quad \text{in SeqMcBehavior}(i[j], o[j], w)
\end{array}$$

SeqMc is the *name* of the specification. The keyword time_independent is used to state that the specification is expressed in a *time-independent* setting. Thus, SeqMc does not impose any timing requirements. The keywords in and out separate the declarations of the *input streams* from the declarations of the *output streams*. In the specification above there is one input stream i of type Call^ω and one output stream o of type Rpl^ω. The input stream i models the communication history of the input channel. Similarly, the output stream o models the communication history of the output channel. We refer to these declarations as the specification's *syntactic interface*. The formula constituting the rest of the specification characterizes the required input/output behavior. We refer to this formula as the I/O-relation. For any specification with name S, we use R_S to denote its I/O-relation.

Throughout this paper we often use line breaks to fix *scoping* and represent *conjunction*. We indicate scoping dependency by *indenting* the new line with respect to the previous one. For example, in the I/O-relation above, this technique is used to indicate that the let construct is in the scope of the universal quantifier. We indicate that a line break represents *conjunction* by not indenting the new line with respect to the previous one. For example, in the I/O-relation above the first line break represents a conjunction. The same does not hold for the third line break. The reason is of course that the third and fourth line do not represent formulas.

The I/O-relation of SeqMc has two main conjuncts. The first main conjunct requires that the number of output messages is equal to the number of input messages. This implies that exactly one reply is issued for each call. The second main conjunct determines the output messages as a function of the input messages. For any j, the let construct defines w to be the sub-stream of $i|_j$ of valid write calls to location $Loc(i[j])$. The body of the let construct refers to an auxiliary function which is defined below.

```
─SeqMcBehavior(i, o, w)────────────────────────────

  Call × Rpl × Wr* → 𝔹
  ─────────────────────────

  i ∈ VldWr ⇒ o = OkWr

  i ∈ VldRd ⇒

     w = ⟨⟩ ⇒ o = OkRd(InitVal)

     w ≠ ⟨⟩ ⇒ o = OkRd(Val(w[#w]))

  i ∉ VldCall ⇒ o = BadArg
```

Note that the types of i, o differ from their types in SeqMc. The auxiliary function SeqMcBehavior has three main conjuncts. The first conjunct states that if the call is a valid write call, then the reply is an OkWr. The second conjunct states that if the call is a valid read call then the reply is OkRd(InitVal) if the actual memory location has not yet been updated (w is the empty stream); otherwise the reply is OkRd(v), where v is the value of the last update of this memory location (last message of w). The third conjunct states that if the call is not a valid call then BadArg is returned.

3.3 The Concurrent Memory Component

We now generalize SeqMc to handle a concurrent interface consisting of n input and n output channels. This new component, whose behavior is captured by the specification ConMc below, communicates with n user components, as indicated by Fig. 1.

ConMc ════════════════════════════ time_independent ══

in $ip \in (\mathrm{Call}^\omega)^n$

out $op \in (\mathrm{Rpl}^\omega)^n$

$\exists\, p \in [1..n]^\infty, i \in \mathrm{Call}^\omega, o \in \mathrm{Rpl}^\omega :$

  $\mathrm{Merged}(ip, i, p)$

  $\mathrm{Merged}(op, o, p)$

  $R_{\mathrm{SeqMc}(i,o)}$

---

ip and op are n-tuples of streams. The variable p is an *oracle* (or, alternatively, a *prophecy*) characterizing the order in which the input messages access the memory. Obviously, there are infinitely many interpretations of p. For each interpretation of p such that the first conjunct holds, the output history op is a function of the input history ip. Thus, the nondeterminism allowed by this specification is completely captured by p. Strictly speaking, also i and o are oracles. However, for any interpretation of p and input history ip their interpretations are fixed. The oracle i can be thought of as an internal buffer in which the input messages are placed in the same order as they access the memory — in other words, in accordance with p. Similarly, o can be seen as a buffer which stores the replies in the same order. This is expressed by the first two conjuncts. The third conjunct makes sure that i and o are related as in the sequential case. The auxiliary function Merged is defined below.

Merged(ap, a, p) ──────────────────────

$(\alpha^\omega)^n \times \alpha^\omega \times [1..n]^\infty \to \mathbb{B}$

$\forall\, k \in [1..n] : ap_k = \Pi_1.[(\alpha \times \{k\}) \circledS (a, p)]$

α is a type variable. The filtration operator is used to make sure that the n streams in ap are merged into a in accordance with p.

3.4 The Repetitive Memory Component

The reliable memory component described in [BL] differs from ConMc in several respects. In particular, ConMc does not allow the same call to access the memory more than once. We now generalize ConMc to allow each call to result in an unbounded, finite, nonzero number of memory accesses. Note that we allow a read call to result in more than one memory access. Strictly speaking, this is in conflict with the problem statement. However, we are only interested in specifying the externally observable behavior. In that case this deviation from the problem statement does not matter. Let

$$\text{RpEx} \overset{\text{def}}{=} \{\text{Rep}, \text{Exit}\}$$

The repetitive memory component can then be specified as below.

```
╔═ RepMc ═══════════════════════════════════ time_independent ═══
║  in    ip ∈ (Call^ω)^n
║  out   op ∈ (Rpl^ω)^n
║─────────────────────────────────────────────────────────────────
║  ∃ p ∈ [1..n]^∞, r ∈ RpEx^∞, i ∈ Call^ω, o ∈ Rpl^ω :
║
║     RepMerged(ip, i, p, r)
║
║     RepMerged(op, o, p, r)
║
║     Compatible(i, p, r)
║
║     R_{SeqMc(i,o)}
╚═════════════════════════════════════════════════════════════════
```

Another oracle r has been introduced. It determines the number of memory accesses for each call. The final memory access for a call has Exit as its corresponding element in r; any other memory access corresponds to a Rep in r. As before the amount of nondeterminism is completely captured by the oracles. The output history op is a function of the input history ip for each choice of p and r such that the first and third conjuncts hold. The merge of the input and output histories is captured by the auxiliary function RepMerged which is defined as follows.

```
╔═ RepMerged(ap, a, p, r) ═════════════════════════════════════
║  (α^ω)^n × α^ω × [1..n]^∞ × RpEx^∞ → 𝔹
║─────────────────────────────────────────────────────────────
║  ∀ k ∈ [1..n] : ap_k = Π_1.[(α × {k} × {Exit})Ⓢ(a, p, r)]
╚═════════════════════════════════════════════════════════════
```

It differs from the earlier merge function in that it considers only the entries whose element in r is Exit. In other words, we filter away those elements of i and o that correspond to Rep in r. The third conjunct in the I/O-relation of RepMc makes sure that also those entries that correspond to Rep in r are related to i in the correct way. In other words, that the memory accesses which correspond to Rep are compatible with the input streams, and that for each call the entry representing the last memory access has Exit as its element in r. This is captured by the auxiliary function defined below.

$\underline{\text{Compatible}(i, p, r)}$ —————————————————————

$\text{Call}^\omega \times [1..n]^\infty \times \text{RpEx}^\infty \to \mathbb{B}$

———————————————————————————

$\forall j \in \text{dom}(i) : r[j] = \text{Rep} \Rightarrow$

$\quad \exists l \in \text{dom}(i) :$

$\quad\quad l > j \wedge i[l] = i[j] \wedge p[l] = p[j] \wedge r[l] = \text{Exit}$

$\quad\quad \forall t \in \mathbb{N} : j < t < l \Rightarrow r[t] \neq \text{Exit} \vee p[t] \neq p[j]$

Although RepMc is closer to the reliable memory component of [BL] than ConMc, some requirements are still missing. Firstly, as already mentioned in the introduction, we do not impose the hand-shake protocol on which [BL] is based. Our approach is based on asynchronous communication with unbounded buffering. Thus, we do not need the the environment assumption that a user never sends a new call before the memory component has issued a reply to its previous call.

However, this is not the only respect in which RepMc differs from the reliable memory component of [BL]; it also differs in the sense that it does not require the memory accesses to take place in the time interval between the arrival of the corresponding call and the issue of its reply. Moreover, RepMc does not say anything about the timing of the output with respect to the timing of the input. We now show how the missing causality and timing requirements can be imposed. To do so, we first have to explain what we mean by a timed stream.

3.5 Timed Streams and Operators on Timed Streams

To express *timing* constraints and also *causality* requirements between the input and output streams we use *timed streams*. A timed stream is a finite or infinite sequence of messages and *time ticks*. A time tick is represented by $\sqrt{}$. The interval between two consecutive ticks represents the least unit of time. A tick occurs in a timed stream at the end of each time unit.

An infinite timed stream represents a *complete* communication history; a finite timed stream represents a *partial* communication history. Since time never halts, any infinite timed stream is required to have *infinitely* many ticks. We do not want timed streams to end in the middle of a time unit. Thus, we insist that a timed stream is either empty, infinite or *ends* with a tick. For any set of messages M, by M^∞, $M^\pm$ and M^ω we denote respectively the set of all infinite timed streams over M, the set of all finite timed streams over M, and the set of all finite and infinite timed streams over M.

All the operators for untimed streams are also defined for timed streams. Their definitions are the the same as before given that $\sqrt{}$ is interpreted as an ordinary message. We also introduce some operators specially designed for timed streams. Let $r \in M^\omega$ and $j \in \mathbb{N}_\infty$:

- $\overline{r}$ denotes the result of *removing* all ticks in r. Thus, $\overline{\langle a, \sqrt{}, b, \sqrt{} \rangle} = \langle a, b \rangle$. This operator is overloaded to tuples of timed streams in the obvious way.
- $\mathrm{tm}(r, j)$ denotes the time unit in which the jth message ($\sqrt{}$ is not a message) of r occurs if $j \in \mathrm{dom}(\overline{r})$. For example, if $r = \langle a, b, \sqrt{}, \sqrt{}, b, \sqrt{} \rangle$ then $\mathrm{tm}(r, 1) = \mathrm{tm}(r, 2) = 1$ and $\mathrm{tm}(r, 3) = 3$.
- $r{\downarrow}_j$ denotes the prefix of r characterizing the behavior until the end of time unit j. This means that $r{\downarrow}_j$ denotes r if j is greater than the number of ticks in r, and the shortest prefix of r containing j ticks, otherwise. Note that $r{\downarrow}_\infty = r$ and also that $r{\downarrow}_0 = \langle \rangle$. Note also the way $\downarrow$ differs from $|$. For example, if $r = \langle a, b, \sqrt{}, c, \sqrt{} \rangle$ then $r{\downarrow}_1 = \langle a, b, \sqrt{} \rangle$ and $r|_1 = \langle a \rangle$.

We also introduce a specially designed *filtration* operator. For any set of pairs of messages A ($\sqrt{}$ is not a message), timed infinite stream $t \in M^\infty$, untimed infinite stream $s \in M^\infty$, let $A\circledR(t, s)$ denote the timed infinite stream such that

$$\overline{A\circledR(t, s)} = \Pi_1.[\, A\circledS(\overline{t}, s)\,]$$

$$\forall j \in \mathbb{N} : \#\overline{(A\circledR(t, s)){\downarrow}_j} = \#\{m \in \mathrm{dom}(\overline{t{\downarrow}_j}) \mid (\overline{t}[m], s[m]) \in A\}$$

Roughly speaking, $A\circledR(t, s)$ denotes the timed infinite stream obtained from t by removing the messages for which there are no corresponding pairs in A with respect to the untimed stream s. For example, if

$$A = \{(a, a), (b, b)\}$$

$$t = \langle a, b, \sqrt{}, a, b, \sqrt{} \rangle \frown \sqrt{}^\infty$$

$$s = \langle a, a \rangle \frown b^\infty$$

then

$$A\circledR(t, s) = \langle a, \sqrt{}, b, \sqrt{} \rangle \frown \sqrt{}^\infty$$

3.6 The Reliable Memory Component

As explained above, the component specified by RepMc is quite close to the reliable memory component described in [BL]. However, we still have to impose the requirement that any memory access takes place in the time interval between the transmission of the corresponding call and the issue of its reply, and that the reply is issued first after the call is transmitted. To do so, we introduce another oracle t. Informally speaking, it assigns a time stamp to each memory access. The specification of the reliable memory component is given below.

$$\boxed{\begin{array}{l}
\text{RelMc} \hspace{6cm} \text{time\_dependent} \\[4pt]
\textbf{in} \quad ip \in (\text{Call}^{\underline{\infty}})^n \\[2pt]
\textbf{out} \quad op \in (\text{Rpl}^{\underline{\infty}})^n \\[6pt]
\hline \\[-6pt]
\exists\, p \in [1..n]^{\infty},\, r \in \text{RpEx}^{\infty},\, t \in \mathbb{N}^{\infty},\, i \in \text{Call}^{\omega},\, o \in \text{Rpl}^{\omega}: \\[6pt]
\quad \text{RepMerged}(\overline{ip},\, i,\, p,\, r) \\[4pt]
\quad \text{RepMerged}(\overline{op},\, o,\, p,\, r) \\[4pt]
\quad \text{Compatible}(i,\, p,\, r) \\[4pt]
\quad \text{Timed}(ip,\, op,\, p,\, r,\, t,\, i) \\[4pt]
\quad R_{\text{SeqMc}(i,o)}
\end{array}}$$

In contrast to earlier the input and output streams are timed infinite streams. When this is the case we say that a specification is *time-dependent*. In a time-independent specification we represent the input and output histories by untimed streams; in a time-dependent specification we use timed infinite streams. Thus, strictly speaking, the keyword occurring in the frame is redundant; it is used to emphasize something that is already clear from the declarations of the input and output streams.

The reason why we allow the the input and output streams to be finite in the time-independent case is that a timed infinite stream with only finitely many ordinary messages degenerates to a finite stream when the time information is removed. For example $\sqrt{}^{\infty} = \langle\rangle$. In fact, any time-independent specification S can be understood as syntactic sugar for a time-dependent specification S'; namely the time-dependent specification obtained from S by replacing the keyword by time-dependent; replacing any occurrence of $^{\omega}$ by $\underline{\infty}$ in the declarations of the input and output streams; replacing any free occurrence of any input or output stream v in the I/O-relation by $\overline{v}$.

In the specification of the reliable memory component there is one "new" conjunct with respect to the RelMc. It requires the externally observable behavior to be *compatible* with an interpretation where any memory access takes place in the time interval between the transmission of the corresponding call and the issue of its reply. Moreover, it requires the reply to be delayed by at least one time unit with respect to the transmission of the call. The auxiliary function Timed is defined below.

$\overline{\quad}$ Timed(ip, op, p, r, t, i) $\underline{\hspace{5cm}}$

$(\text{Call}^{\infty})^n \times (\text{Rpl}^{\infty})^n \times [1..n]^{\infty} \times \text{RpEx}^{\infty} \times \mathbb{N}^{\infty} \times \text{Call}^{\omega} \to \mathbb{B}$

$\forall j \in \mathbb{N}_+ : t[j] \leq t[j+1]$

$\forall j \in \text{dom}(i) :$

$\quad$ let $k = p[j]$

$\qquad w = \Pi_1.[(\text{RpEx} \times \{k\}) \textcircled{S} (r|_j, p)]$

$\qquad m = \text{CallNumb}(w, \{\text{Exit}\})$

$\quad$ in $\text{tm}(ip_k, m) < t[j] \leq \text{tm}(op_k, m)$

The first conjunct states that the infinite stream of time stamps is nondecreasing. The let construct introduces three variables: the channel number k of the considered memory access; the sub-stream w of r containing the entries for the channel k until this memory access; the number m of the call transmitted on the channel ip_k for which this memory access is performed. Thus, the second conjunct requires each memory access to take place between the transmission of the corresponding call and the issue of its reply. Note that this requirement also makes sure that there is a delay of at least one time unit between the transmission of a call and the issue of its reply. This is a sensible requirement under the assumption that the least unit of time is chosen sufficiently small.

The auxiliary function CallNumb is defined below.

$\overline{\quad}$ CallNumb(w, A) $\underline{\hspace{5cm}}$

$\alpha^{\omega} \times \mathbb{P}(\alpha) \to \mathbb{N}$

---

let $n = \#(A \textcircled{S} w)$ in if $w[\#w] \in A$ then n else $n+1$

α is a type variable. $\mathbb{P}(\alpha)$ denotes the power set of α.

3.7 The Unreliable Memory Component

The unreliable memory component (called the "memory component" in [BL]) differs from the reliable memory component in that calls may fail. Let

$\quad$ OkFail $\stackrel{\text{def}}{=}$ $\{\text{Ok}, \text{Pfail}, \text{Tfail}\}$

Once more an oracle is introduced. This time of type OkFail$^{\infty}$. This new oracle q determines whether a memory access is successful or not. Any memory access whose corresponding element in q is Tfail has no effect on the memory. Thus, the difference between Pfail (partial failure) and Ok, on the one hand, and Tfail (total failure), on the other hand, is that the latter has no effect on the memory locations. In addition, any call whose final memory access corresponds to a Pfail or a Tfail in q results in a MemFail. Note that a write call that fails may result in several memory updates, but it may also leave the memory unchanged.

UnrelMc ════════════════════════════ time_dependent ═══

in $\quad ip \in (\text{Call}^\infty)^n$

out $\quad op \in (\text{Rpl}^\infty)^n$

$\exists\, p \in [1..n]^\infty, r \in \text{RpEx}^\infty, t \in \mathbb{N}^\infty, q \in \text{OkFail}^\infty, i \in \text{Call}^\omega, o \in \text{Rpl}^\omega :$

$\quad \text{RepMerged}(\overline{ip}, i, p, r)$

$\quad \text{RepMerged}(\overline{op}, o, p, r)$

$\quad \text{Compatible}(i, p, r)$

$\quad \text{Timed}(ip, op, p, r, t, i)$

$\quad \text{UnrelSeqMc}(i, o, q)$

As before, for each interpretation of the oracles such that the first, third and fourth conjuncts hold, the output history is completely determined by the input history (if the timing of the output is ignored). The specification SeqMc is no longer sufficient to characterize the relationship between i and o. Instead we introduce an auxiliary function.

UnrelSeqMc(i, o, q) ──────────────────────────────

$\text{Call}^\omega \times \text{Rpl}^\omega \times \text{OkFail}^\infty \to \mathbb{B}$

$\#o = \#i$

$\forall j \in \text{dom}(o) :$

$\quad q[j] = \text{Ok} \Rightarrow$

$\quad\quad \text{let } w = \Pi_1.[\,(\text{VldWr}(\text{Loc}(i[j])) \times \{\text{Ok}, \text{Pfail}\})\,\textcircled{S}(i|_j, q)\,]$

$\quad\quad \text{in SeqMcBehavior}(i[j], o[j], w)$

$\quad q[j] \in \{\text{Pfail}, \text{Tfail}\} \Rightarrow o[j] = \text{MemFail}$

Note that w is defined to ignore memory accesses which correspond to Tfail. The rest is a straightforward adaptation of the SeqMc specification.

3.8 Implementation

In order to discuss whether RelMc is a *refinement* (or alternatively, an *implementation*) of UnrelMc or not, we have to define what we mean by refinement. Since any time-independent specification can be understood as syntactic sugar for an equivalent time-dependent specification, we consider only specifications written in the time-dependent format.

Let S and S' be specifications of the same syntactic interface. We define S' to be a *refinement* of S if the I/O-relation of S' implies the I/O-relation of S. More explicitly, if

$$R_{S'} \Rightarrow R_S$$

under the assumption that any free variable is typed in accordance with its declaration in the syntactic interface.

Since UnrelMc is equal to RelMc if q is fixed as Ok^∞, it follows that RelMc is a refinement of UnrelMc. It is also clear that UnrelMc allows an implementation which returns MemFail to any call — it is enough to fix q as $Tfail^\infty$. It is straightforward to strengthen UnrelMc to avoid this. In fact the required behavior can be characterized by imposing additional constraints on the distribution of Ok's in q. This is the normal way of imposing fairness constraints in our method.

4 Problem II: The RPC Component

The second problem described in [BL] is to specify a *remote procedure call* component — from now on called the RPC component. As indicated by Fig. 2, the RPC component interfaces with two environment components, a sender and a receiver. It relays procedure calls from the sender to the receiver, and relays the return values back to the sender.

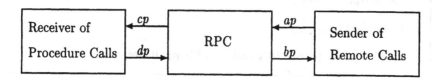

Fig. 2. The RPC Component and its Environment.

4.1 Basic Definitions

We first give some basic definitions.

PrCall	$\stackrel{\text{def}}{=} \{p(a) \mid p \in \text{Procs} \wedge \#a = \text{ArgNum}(p)\}$
ReCall	$\stackrel{\text{def}}{=} \{\text{RemoteCall}(p, a) \mid p \in \text{P} \wedge a \in \text{A}^*\}$
VldReCall	$\stackrel{\text{def}}{=} \{\text{RemoteCall}(p, a) \mid p \in \text{Procs} \wedge \#a = \text{ArgNum}(p)\}$
NotVldReCall	$\stackrel{\text{def}}{=}$ ReCall $\setminus$ VldReCall
ReRpl	$\stackrel{\text{def}}{=}$ PrRpl $\cup$ {RPCFail, BadCall}

P is a set of identifiers; A is a set of arguments. PrCall and ReCall are the sets of all possible procedure and remote calls, respectively. VldReCall is the set of all valid remote calls. PrRpl and ReRpl are the sets of all possible replies to procedure and remote calls, respectively. We assume that

$$\text{PrRpl} \cap \{\text{RPCFail}, \text{BadCall}\} = \{\} \tag{2}$$

We also introduce three auxiliary functions.

$\text{Map} \in \alpha^\omega \times (\alpha \to \beta) \to \beta^\omega$

$\quad \text{Map}(a, m) \stackrel{\text{def}}{=} b$

$\quad$ **where** $\#b = \#a \wedge \forall j \in \text{dom}(b) : b[j] = m(a[j])$

$\text{Cl} \in \text{VldReCall}^\omega \to \text{PrCall}^\omega$

$\quad \text{Cl}(e) \stackrel{\text{def}}{=} \text{Map}(e, m)$

$\quad$ **where** $m(\text{RemoteCall}(p, a)) = p(a)$

$\text{Rp} \in \text{ReRpl}^\omega \to \text{ReRpl}^\omega$

$\quad \text{Rp}(e) \stackrel{\text{def}}{=} \text{Map}(e, m)$

$\quad$ **where** $m(r) = (\text{if } r = \text{RPCFail then MemFail else } r)$

α, β are type variables.

4.2 The Sequential RPC Component

We first specify a *sequential* RPC component — in other words, an RPC component with respect to one user. As indicated by Fig. 3, the general (concurrent) RPC component can be thought of as a network of n sequential RPC components.

```
╔═SeqRPC══════════════════════════════ time_dependent ═
║ in    a ∈ ReCall^∞, d ∈ PrRpl^∞
║ out   b ∈ ReRpl^∞, c ∈ PrCall^∞
╠─────────────────────────────────────────────────────
║ #d̄ = #c̄
║
║ Delayed(c, d)
║
║   ⇒
║
║ ∃ q ∈ OkFail^∞ :
║
║   RPCBehavior(ā, d̄, b̄, c̄, q)
║
║   RPCDelayed(a, d, b, c, q)
╚═════════════════════════════════════════════════════
```

Throughout the paper we use the convention that an indented implication operator on a separate line is the main operator of an I/O-relation. Thus, SeqRPC can be understood as an assumption/commitment specification. The antecedent characterizes the environment *assumption*, and the *commitment* is characterized by the consequent. If the environment behaves in accordance with the assumption then the specified component is required to behave in accordance with the commitment. The first conjunct of the assumption requires that the environment issues exactly one reply on d for each call received on c. The second imposes the constraint that the environment never sends a reply on d before at least one time unit after the call is transmitted on c. This is a sensible assumption given that the least unit of time is chosen sufficiently small. The auxiliary function Delayed is defined below.

```
╔═Delayed(a, b)───────────────────────────────────────
║ α^∞ × α^∞ → 𝔹
╠─────────────────────────────────────────────────────
║ ∀ j ∈ ℕ : #(b↓_{j+1}) ≤ #(a↓_j)
╚═════════════════════════════════════════════════════
```

$α$ is a type variable. The function requires that for any j, the number of messages transmitted along b until time $j+1$ is less than or equal to the number of messages transmitted along a until time j.

The commitment employs an oracle q to determine whether a call terminates normally or with a BadCall exception (Ok); terminates with an RPCFail after having made the procedure call (Pfail); or terminates with an RPCFail without doing anything (Tfail). There are two main conjuncts; both represented by auxiliary functions. The first one is defined below.

$\text{RPCBehavior}(a, d, b, c, q)$ ────────────────────

$\text{ReCall}^\omega \times \text{PrRpl}^\omega \times \text{ReRpl}^\omega \times \text{PrCall}^\omega \times \text{OkFail}^\infty \to \mathbb{B}$

$\forall k \in \text{dom}(a) : q[k] = \text{Pfail} \Rightarrow a[k] \in \text{VldReCall}$

$\#b = \#a$

$\text{let } (w, x) = (\text{VldReCall} \times \{\text{Ok}, \text{Pfail}\})\text{\textcircled{S}}(a, q) \text{ in}$

$\quad c = \text{Cl}(w)$

$\quad \text{PrRpl\textcircled{S}}b = \Pi_1.[\,(\text{PrRpl} \times \{\text{Ok}\})\text{\textcircled{S}}(d, x)\,]$

$\forall j \in \text{dom}(b) :$

$\quad q[j] \neq \text{Ok} \Rightarrow b[j] = \text{RPCFail}$

$\quad q[j] = \text{Ok} \wedge a[j] \notin \text{VldReCall} \Rightarrow b[j] = \text{BadCall}$

Note that the types of a, d, b, c differ from their types in SeqRPC. There are four main conjuncts. The first conjunct makes sure that q is chosen in such a way that there is no invalid remote call in a whose corresponding element in q is Pfail. The second conjunct requires that a reply is issued for any remote call received.

The let construct of which the third conjunct consists defines two local variables w and x. w can be thought of as a buffer in which any remote call which leads to a procedure call is inserted. x contains the corresponding elements of q. Thus, $x \in \{\text{Ok}, \text{Pfail}\}^\omega$ since a valid call, whose corresponding element in p is Tfail, does not lead to a procedure call. The body of the let construct consists of two sub-conjuncts. The first sub-conjunct requires that the output along c is equal to the stream obtained by executing the call of every valid RemoteCall in w. The second sub-conjunct requires that the stream of PrRpl sent along b is equal to the stream of PrRpl received on d minus those replies which correspond to Pfail in x.

Also the fourth conjunct consists of two sub-conjuncts. The first sub-conjunct requires that any remote call, that fails, results in an RPCFail. The second sub-conjunct requires that any invalid RemoteCall, that does not fail, results in a BadCall.

The second main conjunct in the commitment of SeqRPC refers to the auxiliary function RPCDelayed. It makes sure that any response to a message is issued first one time unit after the message has been received. This function is defined below.

RPCDelayed(a, d, b, c, q) ───────────────────

$$\text{ReCall}^{\infty} \times \text{PrRpl}^{\infty} \times \text{ReRpl}^{\infty} \times \text{PrCall}^{\infty} \times \text{OkFail}^{\infty} \rightarrow \mathbb{B}$$

$\text{Delayed}((\text{VldReCall} \times \{\text{Ok}, \text{Pfail}\}) \circledR (a, q), c)$

$\text{Delayed}(a, b)$

$\text{Delayed}(d, ((\text{ReRpl} \setminus \{\text{BadCall}\}) \times \{\text{Ok}, \text{Pfail}\}) \circledR (b, q))$

4.3 The RPC Component

The RPC component can be thought of as a network of n sequential RPC components (see Fig. 3). This network is specified as follows.

RPC ═══════════════════════════ time_dependent ═══

in	$ap \in (\text{ReCall}^{\infty})^n, dp \in (\text{PrRpl}^{\infty})^n$
out	$bp \in (\text{ReRpl}^{\infty})^n, cp \in (\text{PrCall}^{\infty})^n$

$\otimes_{j=1}^{n} \text{SeqRPC}(ap_j, dp_j, bp_j, cp_j)$

The I/O-relation of RPC is equivalent to

$$\bigwedge_{j=1}^{n} R_{\text{SeqRPC}(ap_j, dp_j, bp_j, cp_j)}$$

We use $\otimes$ instead of $\wedge$ to *emphasize* that we compose component specifications. The $\otimes$ operator is employed only when the specifications have mutually disjoint output alphabets — in other words, when for any pair of specifications the sets of identifiers representing output streams are disjoint. Since $\{bp_k, cp_k\}$ is disjoint from $\{bp_l, cp_l\}$ if $k \neq l$ this clearly holds in the case of RPC. We say that the specifications *interfere* if the sets of output identifiers are not mutually disjoint in this sense.

To implement such a *composite* specification it is enough to implement the n component specifications. These implementations can be designed independently of each other in a compositional manner. This is always the case when a network is specified by the $\otimes$ operator. Note the difference with respect to an ordinary *basic* specification based on auxiliary functions. For example, the five conjuncts of UnrelMc cannot be understood as independent component specifications. First of all, the oracles cannot easily be interpreted as local input and output channels. Secondly, the conjuncts interfere.

The RPC component as specified by us deviates from the informal specification in [BL]. Firstly, since we do not impose the hand-shake protocol, our specification does not disallow a sequential RPC component to transmit a new call before the environment has issued a reply to its previous call. Secondly, it can be argued that the environment assumptions of the sequential RPC specifications are too strong. If the environment never replies to a call then we allow arbitrary behavior. However, since a component never knows in advance whether a reply eventually comes or not, it is not possible for a component to exploit this. After all, computer programs cannot predict the future. Thus, we do not see this as a problem.

5 Problem III: Implementing the Unreliable Memory Component

The unreliable memory component is implemented by combining the RPC component with the reliable memory component and a driver. We refer to the latter as the *clerk*. As in the case of the RPC component the clerk is divided into n sequential clerk components. The overall network is pictured in Fig. 3.

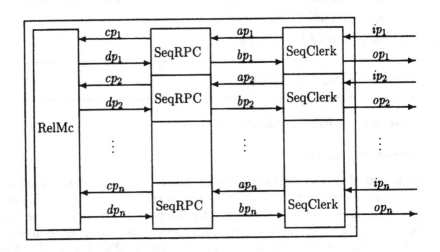

Fig. 3. Network Implementing the Unreliable Memory Component.

5.1 Basic Assumptions

In the following we assume that

$$\text{Call} \subseteq \text{PrCall} \tag{3}$$

$$\text{Rpl} \subseteq \text{PrRpl} \tag{4}$$

$$\{\text{Read}, \text{Write}\} \subseteq \text{Procs} \tag{5}$$

$$\text{ArgNum}(\text{Read}) = 1 \tag{6}$$

$$\text{ArgNum(Write)} = 2 \qquad\qquad (7)$$

5.2 The Sequential Clerk Component

We first specify the sequential clerk component. It has the same main structure as the specification of the sequential RPC component.

═SeqClerk═══════════════════ time_dependent ═

in $i \in \text{Call}^{\infty}, b \in \text{ReRpl}^{\infty}$

out $o \in \text{ReRpl}^{\infty}, a \in \text{ReCall}^{\infty}$

$\#\overline{b} = \#\overline{a}$

$\text{Delayed}(a, b)$

$\Rightarrow$

$\exists\, r \in \text{RpEx}^{\infty} :$

   $\text{ClerkBehavior}(\overline{i}, \overline{b}, \overline{o}, \overline{a}, r)$

   $\text{ClerkDelayed}(i, b, o, a, r)$

The environment assumption corresponds to that for SeqRPC. For each remote call sent along a the environment is assumed to send exactly one reply along b delayed by at least one time unit. In the commitment the oracle r is used to determine whether a call which results in an RPCFail should be retried or not. There are two sub-conjuncts. Both refer to auxiliary functions. The first one is defined below.

┌ClerkBehavior(i, b, o, a, r) ─────────────

$\text{Call}^{\omega} \times \text{ReRpl}^{\omega} \times \text{ReRpl}^{\omega} \times \text{ReCall}^{\omega} \times \text{RpEx}^{\infty} \to \mathbb{B}$

$\forall j \in \text{dom}(b) : r[j] = \text{Rep} \Rightarrow$

   $b[j] = \text{RPCFail}$

   $\exists\, l \in \text{dom}(b) : l > j \wedge r[l] = \text{Exit} \wedge \forall t \in \mathbb{N} : j < t \leq l \Rightarrow a[t] = a[j]$

$\text{let } (w, z) = \Pi_{1,2}.[\,(\text{ReCall} \times \text{ReRpl} \times \{\text{Exit}\})\text{\textcircled{S}}(a, b, r)\,] \text{ in}$

   $\text{Cl}(w) = i$

   $o = \text{Rp}(z)$

Note that the types of i, b, o, a differ from their types in SeqClerk. There are two main conjuncts. The first conjunct requires that r is chosen in such a way that each occurrence of a Rep in $r|_{\#b}$ corresponds to an RPCFail in b. It also makes sure that any remote call is repeated only a finite number of times.

The second conjunct consists of a let construct that defines w to be the stream of remote calls which correspond to Exit in r, and z to contain the corresponding replies. The body consists of two sub-conjuncts. The first requires i to be equal to w if each remote call in w is replaced by the corresponding call. The second requires that the stream of replies sent along o is equal to z given that each RPCFail is replaced by MemFail.

The second conjunct in the commitment of SeqClerk refers to an auxiliary function ClerkDelayed. In the same way as RPCDelayed, it captures that there is a delay of at least one time unit between input and output.

ClerkDelayed(i, b, o, a, r)

$\text{Call}^{\infty} \times \text{ReRpl}^{\infty} \times \text{ReRpl}^{\infty} \times \text{ReCall}^{\infty} \times \text{RpEx}^{\infty} \to \mathbb{B}$

$\text{Delayed}((\text{ReRpl} \times \{\text{Exit}\})\circledR(b, r), o)$

$\forall j \in \text{dom}(\overline{a}) : \text{let } m = \text{CallNumb}(r|_j, \{\text{Exit}\}) \text{ in } \text{tm}(a, j) > \text{tm}(i, m)$

5.3 The Clerk Component

As already explained, the clerk can be understood as a network of n sequential clerk components. It is specified as follows.

Clerk ═══════════════════════════ **time_dependent** ═

in $ip \in (\text{Call}^{\infty})^n, bp \in (\text{ReRpl}^{\infty})^n$

out $op \in (\text{ReRpl}^{\infty})^n, ap \in (\text{ReCall}^{\infty})^n$

$\otimes_{j=1}^{n} \text{SeqClerk}(ip_j, bp_j, op_j, ap_j)$

5.4 The Implementation

The network pictured in Fig. 3 can now be specified as follows.

McImpl ═══════════════════════ **time_dependent** ═

in $ip \in (\text{Call}^{\infty})^n$

out $op \in (\text{Rpl}^{\infty})^n$

loc $cp \in (\text{Call}^{\infty})^n, dp \in (\text{Rpl}^{\infty})^n, ap \in (\text{ReCall}^{\infty})^n, bp \in (\text{ReRpl}^{\infty})^n$

$\text{RelMc}(cp, dp) \otimes \text{RPC}(ap, dp, bp, cp) \otimes \text{Clerk}(ip, bp, op, ap)$

---

cp, dp, ap, bp represent tuples of local channels. This motivates the keyword loc. We have already explained that $\otimes$ corresponds to conjunction. The logical interpretation of the loc declarations is existential quantification. Thus, the composite specification McImpl is equivalent to a basic specification with the same external interface and the following I/O-relation

$$\exists\, cp \in (\text{Call}^\infty)^n,\, dp \in (\text{Rpl}^\infty)^n,\, ap \in (\text{ReCall}^\infty)^n,\, bp \in (\text{ReRpl}^\infty)^n :$$

$$R_{\text{RelMc}(cp,dp)} \wedge R_{\text{RPC}(ap,dp,bp,cp)} \wedge R_{\text{Clerk}(ip,bp,op,ap)}$$

5.5 Verification

We now prove that McImpl is a refinement of UnrelMc. Remember that for any specification S, we use R_S to denote its I/O-relation. If the I/O-relation has $\Rightarrow$ as its main operator, we use A_S to denote its antecedent (assumption) and C_S to denote its consequent (commitment). Although in most cases this is not pointed out explicitly, the validity of the many deductions depends on the type definitions listed in Sect. 3.1, 4.1, and also the assumptions 1-7 listed in Sect. 3.1, 4.1, 5.1. In the following we assume that

$$ip \in (\text{Call}^\infty)^n \tag{8}$$

$$cp \in (\text{Call}^\infty)^n \tag{9}$$

$$op \in (\text{Rpl}^\infty)^n \tag{10}$$

$$dp \in (\text{Rpl}^\infty)^n \tag{11}$$

$$ap \in (\text{ReCall}^\infty)^n \tag{12}$$

$$bp \in (\text{ReRpl}^\infty)^n \tag{13}$$

$$j \in [1..n] \tag{14}$$

It must be shown that

$$R_{\text{RelMc}(cp,dp)} \wedge R_{\text{RPC}(ap,dp,bp,cp)} \wedge R_{\text{Clerk}(ip,bp,op,ap)} \Rightarrow R_{\text{UnrelMc}(ip,op)} \tag{15}$$

From the definitions of RepMerged and Timed it follows straightforwardly that

$$R_{\text{RelMc}(cp,dp)} \Rightarrow A_{\text{SeqRPC}(ap_j,dp_j,bp_j,cp_j)} \tag{16}$$

From the second conjunct of RPCBehavior and the second conjunct of RPCDelayed it follows that

$$A_{\text{SeqRPC}(ap_j,dp_j,bp_j,cp_j)} \wedge C_{\text{SeqRPC}(ap_j,dp_j,bp_j,cp_j)} \tag{17}$$

$$\Rightarrow A_{\text{SeqClerk}(ip_j,bp_j,op_j,ap_j)}$$

16, 17 imply it is enough to show that

$$R_{\text{RelMc}(cp,dp)} \wedge (\wedge_{k=1}^n C_{\text{SeqRPC}(ap_k,dp_k,bp_k,cp_k)} \wedge C_{\text{SeqClerk}(ip_k,bp_k,op_k,ap_k)}) \tag{18}$$

$$\Rightarrow R_{\text{UnrelMc}(ip,op)}$$

Let ip, cp, op, dp, ap, bp be such that

$$R_{\text{RelMc}(cp,dp)} \tag{19}$$

$$C_{\text{SeqRPC}(ap_j,dp_j,bp_j,cp_j)} \tag{20}$$

$$C_{\text{SeqClerk}(ip_j,bp_j,op_j,ap_j)} \tag{21}$$

It must be shown that

$$R_{\text{UnrelMc}(ip,op)} \tag{22}$$

19 implies there are $p' \in [1..n]^\infty$, $r' \in \text{RpEx}^\infty$, $t' \in \mathbb{N}^\infty$, $i' \in \text{Call}^\omega$, $o' \in \text{Rpl}^\omega$ such that

$$\text{RepMerged}(\overline{cp}, i', p', r') \tag{23}$$

$$\text{RepMerged}(\overline{dp}, o', p', r') \tag{24}$$

$$\text{Compatible}(i', p', r') \tag{25}$$

$$\text{Timed}(cp, dp, p', r', t', i') \tag{26}$$

$$\text{SeqMc}(i', o') \tag{27}$$

20 implies there are $q_1, .., q_n \in \text{OkFail}^\infty$ such that

$$\text{RPCBehavior}(\overline{ap_j}, \overline{dp_j}, \overline{bp_j}, \overline{cp_j}, q_j) \tag{28}$$

$$\text{RPCDelayed}(ap_j, dp_j, bp_j, cp_j, q_j) \tag{29}$$

21 implies there are $r_1, .., r_n \in \text{RpEx}^\infty$ such that

$$\text{ClerkBehavior}(\overline{ip_j}, \overline{bp_j}, \overline{op_j}, \overline{ap_j}, r_j) \tag{30}$$

$$\text{ClerkDelayed}(ip_j, bp_j, op_j, ap_j, r_j) \tag{31}$$

22 follows if we can find $p \in [1..n]^\infty$, $r \in \text{RpEx}^\infty$, $t \in \mathbb{N}^\infty$, $q \in \text{OkFail}^\infty$, $i \in \text{Call}^\omega$, $o \in \text{Rpl}^\omega$ such that

$$\text{RepMerged}(\overline{ip}, i, p, r) \tag{32}$$

$$\text{RepMerged}(\overline{op}, o, p, r) \tag{33}$$

$$\text{Compatible}(i, p, r) \tag{34}$$

$$\text{Timed}(ip, op, p, r, t, i) \tag{35}$$

$$\text{UnrelSeqMc}(i, o, q) \tag{36}$$

The remaining of the proof is structured as follows. We first argue the existence of oracles p, r, t, q, i, o satisfying a number of useful properties. Then we show the validity of 32-36.

Definition of oracles: We start by defining the new oracles p, t, i. Informally speaking, they are constructed from the oracles $p', r', t', i', q_1, .., q_n$ and the communication history ap by inserting one new entry for each call that reaches the RPC component but is not forwarded to the reliable memory component — in other words, for each call received on ap that is not forwarded along cp. It follows from 28 that the only calls that reach the jth sequential RPC component without being forwarded to the reliable memory component are those calls

- whose corresponding element in q_j is Tfail,
- that are contained in NotVldReCall and whose corresponding element in q_j is Ok.

3, 5, 6, 7, 8, 30 imply that each remote call is a valid remote call. Thus, it is enough to insert new entries for those elements of ap_j whose corresponding elements in q_j are Tfail. Let $p \in [1..n]^\infty$, $t \in \mathbb{N}^\infty$, $i \in \mathrm{Call}^\omega$, $y \in \mathrm{RpExIns}^\infty$, where $\mathrm{RpExIns} \stackrel{\mathrm{def}}{=} \{\mathrm{Ins}, \mathrm{Rep}, \mathrm{Exit}\}$, be such that

$$i' = \Pi_1.[\,(\mathrm{Call} \times \mathrm{RpEx})\textcircled{S}(i, y)\,] \tag{37}$$

$$(p', r', t') = ([1..n] \times \mathrm{RpEx} \times \mathbb{N})\textcircled{S}(p, y, t) \tag{38}$$

The idea is that any inserted call has Ins as its corresponding element in y. Any other call corresponds to Exit or Rep in y depending on whether the call's corresponding element in r' is Exit or Rep. Since 37, 38 hold if $p = p', t = t', i = i', y = r'$ it follows that such oracles exist. The fact that 37, 38 do not constrain entries whose element in y is Ins imply that this is still the case if we also impose the requirement that

$$\mathrm{Cl}(\Pi_1.[\,(\mathrm{ReCall} \times \{\mathrm{Tfail}\})\textcircled{S}(\overline{ap_j}, q_j)\,]) = \tag{39}$$

$$\Pi_1.[\,(\mathrm{Call} \times \{j\} \times \{\mathrm{Ins}\})\textcircled{S}(i, p, y)\,]$$

39 allows us to insert the new entries at arbitrary positions in the old oracles as long as the order of the new entries is maintained. This is obviously too liberal. Give that $\mathrm{ExIns} \stackrel{\mathrm{def}}{=} \{\mathrm{Exit}, \mathrm{Ins}\}$, we therefore also require that

$$\forall l \in \mathbb{N}_+ : \tag{40}$$

$$\mathrm{let}\ k\ = p[l]$$

$$w = \Pi_1.[\,(\mathrm{RpExIns} \times \{k\})\textcircled{S}(y|_l, p)\,]$$

$$m = \mathrm{CallNumb}(w, \mathrm{ExIns})$$

$$\mathrm{in}\ y[l] = \mathrm{Ins} \Rightarrow q_k[m] = \mathrm{Tfail}$$

40 guarantees that each Ins entry is correctly ordered with respect to the Exit entries in r'. To make sure that the Ins entries are correctly ordered with respect to the old Rep entries we also assume that

$$\forall l \in \mathbb{N}_+ : \tag{41}$$

$$\text{let } k = p[l]$$

$$w = \Pi_1.[\,(\text{RpExIns} \times \{k\})\textcircled{S}(y|_{l-1}, p)\,]$$

$$\text{in } y[l] = \text{Ins} \Rightarrow w = \langle\rangle \vee w[\#w] \neq \text{Rep}$$

Thus, an Ins entry does not interfere with the memory accesses belonging to the next call by the same user. 26 implies

$$\forall l \in \text{dom}(i') : \tag{42}$$

$$\text{let } k = p'[l]$$

$$w = \Pi_1.[\,(\text{RpEx} \times \{k\})\textcircled{S}(r'|_l, p')\,]$$

$$m = \text{CallNumb}(w, \{\text{Exit}\})$$

$$\text{in } \text{tm}(cp_k, m) < t'[l] \leq \text{tm}(dp_k, m)$$

37, 38, 42 imply

$$\forall l \in \text{dom}(i) : y[l] \neq \text{Ins} \Rightarrow \tag{43}$$

$$\text{let } k = p[l]$$

$$w = \Pi_1.[\,(\text{RpExIns} \times \{k\})\textcircled{S}(y|_l, p)\,]$$

$$m = \text{CallNumb}(w, \{\text{Exit}\})$$

$$\text{in } \text{tm}(cp_k, m) < t[l] \leq \text{tm}(dp_k, m)$$

29 implies

$$\text{Delayed}((\text{VldReCall} \times \{\text{Ok}, \text{Pfail}\})\textcircled{R}(ap_j, q_j), cp_j) \tag{44}$$

$$\text{Delayed}(dp_j, ((\text{ReRpl} \setminus \{\text{BadCall}\}) \times \{\text{Ok}, \text{Pfail}\})\textcircled{R}(bp_j, q_j)) \tag{45}$$

3, 5, 6, 7, 8, 30 imply that any remote call is a valid remote. Thus, 44, 45 imply

$$\text{Delayed}((\text{ReCall} \times \{\text{Ok}, \text{Pfail}\})\textcircled{R}(ap_j, q_j), cp_j) \tag{46}$$

$$\text{Delayed}(dp_j, (\text{ReRpl} \times \{\text{Ok}, \text{Pfail}\})\textcircled{R}(bp_j, q_j)) \tag{47}$$

39, 40, 43, 46, 47 imply

$$\forall l \in \text{dom}(i) : y[l] \neq \text{Ins} \Rightarrow \tag{48}$$

$$\text{let } k = p[l]$$

$$w = \Pi_1.[\,(\text{RpExIns} \times \{k\})\textcircled{S}(y|_l, p)\,]$$

$$m = \text{CallNumb}(w, \text{ExIns})$$

$$\text{in } \text{tm}(ap_k, m) < t[l] \leq \text{tm}(bp_k, m)$$

26, 37, 38 imply

$$\forall k, l \in \mathbb{N}_+ : k < l \wedge \{y[k], y[l]\} \subseteq \mathrm{RpEx} \Rightarrow t[k] \leq t[l] \tag{49}$$

28 and 29 guarantee that the replies to the calls received on ap_j are output along bp_j in the FIFO manner and with a delay of at least one time unit. Moreover, 41 implies that the inserted Ins entries do not interfere with the memory accesses of the other calls by the same user. Thus, since neither of the requirements imposed on the new oracles so far say anything about the entries in t that correspond to Ins in y, it follows from 48, 49 that we may also assume that

$$\forall l \in \mathbb{N}_+ : t[l] \leq t[l+1] \tag{50}$$

$$\forall l \in \mathrm{dom}(i) : \tag{51}$$

$\quad$ let $k = p[l]$

$\qquad w = \Pi_1.[\,(\mathrm{RpExIns} \times \{k\})\textcircled{S}(y|_l, p)\,]$

$\qquad m = \mathrm{CallNumb}(w, \mathrm{ExIns})$

$\quad$ in $\mathrm{tm}(ap_k, m) < t[l] \leq \mathrm{tm}(bp_k, m)$

We now chose $q \in \mathrm{OkFail}^\infty$ and $r \in \mathrm{RpEx}^\infty$ such that

$$\Pi_1.[\,(\mathrm{OkFail} \times \mathrm{ExIns} \times \{j\})\textcircled{S}(q, y, p)\,] \sqsubseteq q_j \tag{52}$$

$$\Pi_1.[\,(\mathrm{OkFail} \times \{\mathrm{Rep}\})\textcircled{S}(q, y)\,] \sqsubseteq \mathrm{Ok}^\infty \tag{53}$$

$$\Pi_1.[\,(\mathrm{RpEx} \times \mathrm{ExIns} \times \{j\})\textcircled{S}(r, y, p)\,] \sqsubseteq r_j \tag{54}$$

$$\Pi_1.[\,(\mathrm{RpEx} \times \{\mathrm{Rep}\})\textcircled{S}(r, y)\,] \sqsubseteq \mathrm{Rep}^\infty \tag{55}$$

Since 37-51 do not constrain q, r, they are clearly not in conflict with 52-55. Moreover, since 52, 53 do not constrain r, and 54, 55 do not constrain q, it follows that 52, 53 are not in conflict with 54, 55. Finally, since 52, 54 only constrain those entries that are marked by Exit or Ins in y, and since 53, 55 only constrain those entries that are marked by Rep in y, it follows that 52, 54 are not in conflict with 53, 55. Finally, we define $o \in \mathrm{Rpl}^\omega$ to be such that

$$\mathrm{Rp}(\overline{bp_j}) = \Pi_1.[\,(\mathrm{Rpl} \times \{j\} \times \mathrm{ExIns})\textcircled{S}(o, p, y)\,] \tag{56}$$

$$(\mathrm{Rpl} \times \{\mathrm{Rep}\})\textcircled{S}(o', r') = (\mathrm{Rpl} \times \{\mathrm{Rep}\})\textcircled{S}(o, y) \tag{57}$$

Since the earlier constraints do not refer to o, and since 56 and 57 clearly are not in conflict with each other, we have shown that there are type correct oracles p, r, t, q, i, o, y such that 37-57 hold.
It remains to prove that 32-36 hold.

Proof of 32: 23, 37, 38 imply

$$\overline{cp_j} = \Pi_1.[\,(\text{Call} \times \{j\} \times \{\text{Exit}\})\text{\textcircled{S}}(i,p,y)\,] \tag{58}$$

28 implies

$$\overline{cp_j} = \text{Cl}(\Pi_1.[\,(\text{VldReCall} \times \{\text{Ok},\text{Pfail}\})\text{\textcircled{S}}(\overline{ap_j},q_j)\,]) \tag{59}$$

3, 5, 6, 7, 8, 30 imply that each remote call is a valid remote call. Thus, 59 implies

$$\overline{cp_j} = \text{Cl}(\Pi_1.[\,(\text{ReCall} \times \{\text{Ok},\text{Pfail}\})\text{\textcircled{S}}(\overline{ap_j},q_j)\,]) \tag{60}$$

39, 40, 58, 60 imply

$$\text{Cl}(\overline{ap_j}) = \Pi_1.[\,(\text{Call} \times \{j\} \times \text{ExIns})\text{\textcircled{S}}(i,p,y)\,] \tag{61}$$

61 implies

$$\Pi_1.[\,(\text{Call} \times \{\text{Exit}\})\text{\textcircled{S}}(\text{Cl}(\overline{ap_j}),r_j)\,] = \tag{62}$$

$$\Pi_1.[\,(\text{Call} \times \{\text{Exit}\})\text{\textcircled{S}}(\Pi_1.[\,(\text{Call} \times \{j\} \times \text{ExIns})\text{\textcircled{S}}(i,p,y)\,],r_j)\,]$$

Clearly

$$\Pi_1.[\,(\text{Call} \times \{\text{Exit}\})\text{\textcircled{S}}(\text{Cl}(\overline{ap_j}),r_j)\,] = \tag{63}$$

$$\text{Cl}(\Pi_1.[\,(\text{ReCall} \times \{\text{Exit}\})\text{\textcircled{S}}(\overline{ap_j},r_j)\,])$$

30 implies

$$\overline{ip_j} = \text{Cl}(\Pi_1.[\,(\text{ReCall} \times \{\text{Exit}\})\text{\textcircled{S}}(\overline{ap_j},r_j)\,]) \tag{64}$$

62, 63, 64 imply

$$\overline{ip_j} = \tag{65}$$

$$\Pi_1.[\,(\text{Call} \times \{\text{Exit}\})\text{\textcircled{S}}(\Pi_1.[\,(\text{Call} \times \{j\} \times \text{ExIns})\text{\textcircled{S}}(i,p,y)\,],r_j)\,]$$

54, 55, 65 imply

$$\overline{ip_j} = \Pi_1.[\,(\text{Call} \times \{j\} \times \{\text{Exit}\})\text{\textcircled{S}}(i,p,r)\,] \tag{66}$$

65 implies 32.

Proof of 33: 30 implies

$$\overline{op_j} = \text{Rp}(\Pi_1.[\,(\text{ReRpl} \times \{\text{Exit}\})\text{\textcircled{S}}(\overline{bp_j},r_j)\,]) \tag{67}$$

56, 67 imply

$$\overline{op_j} = \Pi_1.[\,(\text{Rpl} \times \{\text{Exit}\})\text{\textcircled{S}} \tag{68}$$

$$(\Pi_1.[\,(\text{Rpl} \times \{j\} \times \text{ExIns})\text{\textcircled{S}}(o,p,y)\,],r_j)\,]$$

54, 55, 68 imply

$$\overline{op_j} = \Pi_1.[\,(\text{Rpl} \times \{j\} \times \{\text{Exit}\})\text{\textcircled{S}}(o,p,r)\,] \tag{69}$$

69 implies 33.

Proof of 34: 25, 37, 38, 41 imply

$$\forall k \in \text{dom}(i) : y[k] = \text{Rep} \Rightarrow \tag{70}$$

$$\exists l \in \text{dom}(i) :$$

$$l > k \land i[l] = i[k] \land p[l] = p[k] \land y[l] = \text{Exit}$$

$$\forall t \in \mathbb{N} : k < t < l \Rightarrow y[t] \neq \text{Exit} \lor p[t] \neq p[k]$$

28, 30 imply

$$\forall k \in \text{dom}(\overline{ap_j}) : r_j[j] = \text{Rep} \Rightarrow \tag{71}$$

$$\exists l \in \text{dom}(\overline{ap_j}) : l > k \land r_j[l] = \text{Exit}$$

$$\forall t \in \mathbb{N} : k < t \leq l \Rightarrow \overline{ap_j}[t] = \overline{ap_j}[k]$$

54, 55, 61, 70, 71 imply

$$\forall k \in \text{dom}(i) : r[k] = \text{Rep} \Rightarrow \tag{72}$$

$$\exists l \in \text{dom}(i) :$$

$$l > k \land i[l] = i[k] \land p[l] = p[k] \land r[l] = \text{Exit}$$

$$\forall t \in \mathbb{N} : k < t < l \Rightarrow y[t] \neq \text{Exit} \lor p[t] \neq p[k]$$

72 implies 34.

Proof of 35: 31 implies

$$\text{Delayed}((\text{ReRpl} \times \{\text{Exit}\})\circledR(bp_j, r_j), op_j) \tag{73}$$

$$\forall k \in \text{dom}(\overline{ap_j}) : \tag{74}$$

$$\text{let } m = \text{CallNumb}(r_j|_k, \{\text{Exit}\}) \text{ in } \text{tm}(ap_j, k) > \text{tm}(ip_j, m)$$

51, 54, 55, 73, 74 imply

$$\forall l \in \text{dom}(i) : \tag{75}$$

$$\text{let } k = p[l]$$

$$w = \Pi_1.[(\text{RpEx} \times \{k\})\circledS(r|_l, p)]$$

$$m = \text{CallNumb}(w, \{\text{Exit}\})$$

$$\text{in } \text{tm}(ip_k, m) < t[l] \leq \text{tm}(op_k, m)$$

50, 75 imply 35.

Proof of 36: 28 implies

$$\#\overline{ap_j} = \#\overline{bp_j} \tag{76}$$

37, 38, 56, 57, 61, 76 imply

$$\#o = \#i \tag{77}$$

27 implies

$$\forall l \in \mathrm{dom}(o') : \tag{78}$$

$$\text{let } w = [\,\mathrm{VldWr}(\mathrm{Loc}(i'[l]))\mathbb{S}(i'|_l)\,]$$

$$\text{in SeqMcBehavior}(i'[l], o'[l], w)$$

We want to prove that

$$\forall k \in \mathrm{dom}(o) : \tag{79}$$

$$q[k] = \mathrm{Ok} \Rightarrow$$

$$\text{let } w = \Pi_1.[\,(\mathrm{VldWr}(\mathrm{Loc}(i[k])) \times \{\mathrm{Ok}, \mathrm{Pfail}\})\mathbb{S}(i|_k, q)\,]$$

$$\text{in SeqMcBehavior}(i[k], o[k], w)$$

$$q[k] \in \{\mathrm{Pfail}, \mathrm{Tfail}\} \Rightarrow o[k] = \mathrm{MemFail}$$

Let

$$k \in \mathrm{dom}(o) \tag{80}$$

$$l = p[k] \tag{81}$$

$$w = \Pi_1.[\,(\mathrm{RpExIns} \times \{l\})\mathbb{S}(y|_k, p)\,] \tag{82}$$

$$m = \mathrm{CallNumb}(w, \mathrm{ExIns}) \tag{83}$$

39, 40, 52, 53, 77 imply

$$\forall t \in \mathrm{dom}(o) : q[t] = \mathrm{Tfail} \Leftrightarrow y[t] = \mathrm{Ins} \tag{84}$$

There are three cases to consider.

Case 1: Assume

$$y[k] = \mathrm{Rep} \tag{85}$$

37 implies

$$i[k] = i'[k - \#(\{\mathrm{Ins}\}\mathbb{S}(y|_k))] \tag{86}$$

38, 57 imply

$$o[k] = o'[k - \#(\{\mathrm{Ins}\}\mathbb{S}(y|_k))] \tag{87}$$

53 implies

$$q[k] = \mathrm{Ok} \tag{88}$$

78, 84, 86, 87, 88 imply 79.

Case 2: Assume

$$y[k] = \mathrm{Ins} \tag{89}$$

52, 81, 82, 83, 84, 89 imply

$$q[k] = q_l[m] = \mathrm{Tfail} \tag{90}$$

28, 56, 90 imply 79.

Case 3: Assume

$$y[k] = \text{Exit} \tag{91}$$

52, 81, 82, 83, 84, 91 imply

$$(q[k] = q_l[m] = \text{Pfail}) \vee (q[k] = q_l[m] = \text{Ok}) \tag{92}$$

If the first disjunct holds, then 28, 56 imply 79. Assume

$$q[k] = q_l[m] = \text{Ok} \tag{93}$$

37, 91 imply

$$i[k] = i'[k - \#(\{\text{Ins}\}\text{\textcircled{S}}(y|_k))] \tag{94}$$

28, 38, 56, 91, 93 imply

$$o[k] = o'[k - \#(\{\text{Ins}\}\text{\textcircled{S}}(y|_k))] \tag{95}$$

78, 84, 93, 94, 95 imply 79.

6 Problem IV: The Lossy RPC Component

We now specify the *lossy* RPC component. We consider only the *sequential* case — in other words, a lossy RPC component with respect to one user. We refer to this specification as SeqLossyRPC. In the same way as we specified the RPC component by the conjunction of n SeqRPC specifications, we may specify the lossy RPC component by the conjunction of n SeqLossyRPC specifications. However, this is trivial and therefore left out.

6.1 The Sequential Lossy RPC Component

The specification of the sequential lossy RPC component is given below.

```
┌─SeqLossyRPC════════════════════════════ time_dependent ═══
│  in    r ∈ ReCall^∞, d ∈ PrRpl^∞
│  out   s ∈ ReRpl^∞, c ∈ PrCall^∞
├───────────────────────────────────────────────────────────
│  #d̄ = #c̄
│
│  Delayed(c, d)
│
│    ⇒
│
│  ∃ q ∈ OkFail^∞, s' ∈ ReRpl^∞ :
│
│    s = ((ReRpl ∪ {√}) \ {RPCFail})⊗s'
│
│    RPCBehavior(r̄, d̄, s̄', c̄, q)
│
│    RPCDelayed(r, d, s', c, q)
│
│    RPCBounded(r, d, s', c, q)
└───────────────────────────────────────────────────────────
```

As for the sequential RPC component specified in Sect. 4.2, we assume that exactly one reply is received on d for each call sent along c. Moreover, we assume that each reply is received with a delay of at least one time unit with respect to the transmission of the call. The commitment is split into four conjuncts. The second and third conjunct correspond to the two conjuncts in the commitment of SeqRPC with the exception that s' is substituted for s. This means that s' contains an RPCFail for each remote call that fails. The informal description of the lossy RPC component disallows the output of RPCFail exceptions, which is why the first conjunct in the commitment of SeqLossyRPC defines s to be equal to s' minus the occurrences of RPCFail. The fourth conjunct refers to an auxiliary function which is defined below.

RPCBounded(r, d, s', c, q) ————————————————————

$$\text{ReCall}^{\infty} \times \text{PrRpl}^{\infty} \times \text{ReRpl}^{\infty} \times \text{PrCall}^{\infty} \times \text{OkFail}^{\infty} \to \mathbb{B}$$

---

let

$\quad A = \text{VldReCall} \times \{\text{Ok}, \text{Pfail}\}$

$\quad B = (\text{ReCall} \times \text{OkFail}) \setminus A$

$\quad C = \{\text{BadCall}, \text{RPCFail}\} \times \{\text{Ok}, \text{Tfail}\}$

$\quad D = (\text{ReRpl} \setminus \{\text{BadCall}\}) \times \{\text{Ok}, \text{Pfail}\}$

in

$\quad \text{Bounded}(A \circledR(r, q), c, \delta)$

$\quad \text{Bounded}(B \circledR(r, q), C \circledR(s', q), \delta)$

$\quad \text{Bounded}(d, D \circledR(s', q), \delta)$

For any j RPCBounded compares what has been sent along the output streams s' and c until time $j + \delta$ with what has been received on the input streams r and d until time j. δ stands for the number of time units that corresponds to the upper bound on the response time imposed by the problem statement.

The first conjunct makes sure that if a remote call leads to a procedure call then this procedure call takes place within δ time units after the transmission of the remote call.

The second conjunct makes sure that if a remote call leads to a BadCall then this reply is output within δ time units of the transmission of the remote call.

The third conjunct makes sure that if any other value than BadCall is returned then this takes place within δ time units of the reply to the corresponding procedure call.

Note that the second and third conjuncts also impose response time constraints on the occurrences of RPCFail in s'. These constraints have no effect on the externally observable behavior of SeqLossyRPC. However, they simplify the proof in Sect. 7.3.

The auxiliary function Bounded is defined below.

$$\text{Bounded}(a, b, \delta)$$

$$\alpha^{\infty} \times \alpha^{\infty} \times \mathbb{N} \rightarrow \mathbb{B}$$

$$\forall j \in \mathbb{N} : \#(\overline{a\downarrow_j}) \leq \#(\overline{b\downarrow_{j+\delta}})$$

α is a type variable.

7 Problem V: Implementing the RPC Component

The next task is to implement the sequential RPC component with the sequential lossy RPC component. We first specify the required driver, which we refer to as the sequential RPC clerk. It is connected to the lossy RPC component in accordance with Fig. 4. In the following we assume that $\sigma = 2\delta + \epsilon$, where ϵ

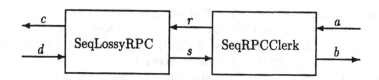

Fig. 4. Network Implementing the RPC Component.

is the number of time units corresponding to the upper bound on the response time of the environment assumed by the problem statement.

7.1 The Sequential RPC Clerk Component

The sequential RPC Clerk component is specified below.

$$\text{SeqRPCClerk} \qquad \qquad \text{time\_dependent}$$

in $a \in \text{ReCall}^{\infty}, s \in \text{ReRpl}^{\infty}$

out $b \in \text{ReRpl}^{\infty}, r \in \text{ReCall}^{\infty}$

RPCClerkBehavior(a, s, b, r)

RPCClerkDelayed(a, s, b, r)

The I/O-relation consists of two conjuncts captured by two auxiliary functions. The first one is defined below.

RPCClerkBehavior(a, s, b, r)

$\text{ReCall}^{\infty} \times \text{ReRpl}^{\infty} \times \text{ReRpl}^{\infty} \times \text{ReCall}^{\infty} \to \mathbb{B}$

$\overline{r} = \overline{a}$

$(\text{ReRpl} \setminus \{\text{RPCFail}\}) \text{\textcircled{S}} \overline{b} = \overline{s}$

$\#\overline{b} = \text{NbRp}(s, r)$

$\forall\, k \in \text{dom}(\overline{r}) :$

$\quad \text{let } m = \text{NbRp}(s\!\downarrow_{\text{tm}(r,k)}, r) + 1$

$\quad \text{in } s\!\downarrow_{\text{tm}(r,k)} \frown \sqrt{\sigma} \sqsubseteq s \Rightarrow \overline{b}[m] = \text{RPCFail}$

$\forall\, k, l \in \text{dom}(\overline{r}) : k < l \Rightarrow$

$\quad \text{tm}(r,l) - \text{tm}(r,k) > \sigma \vee \#\overline{s\!\downarrow_{\text{tm}(r,l)-1}} - \#\overline{s\!\downarrow_{\text{tm}(r,k)}} > 0$

There are five main conjuncts. The first requires that any message received on a is forwarded along r, and that no other message is sent along r.

The second conjunct requires that if the RPCFail exceptions are ignored then the output along b is exactly the input received on s.

The third conjunct requires that the number of messages in $\overline{b}$ is equal to the number of messages in $\overline{s}$ plus the number of *time-outs* — in other words, the number of messages in r for which no reply is received on s within σ time units.

The fourth conjunct requires that if a message is sent along r at some time k and no reply is received on s within the next σ time units then the mth message output along b is RPCFail, where $m - 1$ is the number of messages (time-outs included) received on s until time $\text{tm}(r,k)$.

The fifth conjunct requires that the component always waits for a reply to the previous call before it makes a new call. This means that the next call comes at least $\sigma + 1$ time units after the previous call or at least one time unit after the transmission of a reply to the previous call. The auxiliary function NbRp is defined below.

NbRp(s, r)

$\text{ReRpl}^{\omega} \times \text{ReCall}^{\infty} \to \mathbb{N}$

$\#\overline{s} + \#\{m \in \text{dom}(\overline{r}) \mid s\!\downarrow_{\text{tm}(r,m)} \frown \sqrt{\sigma} \sqsubseteq s\}$

It yields the number of replies in s including the time-outs with respect to r.

The second main conjunct of the I/O-relation of SeqRPCClerk refers to the auxiliary function defined below.

RPCClerkDelayed(a, s, b, r)

$\text{ReCall}^{\infty} \times \text{ReRpl}^{\infty} \times \text{ReRpl}^{\infty} \times \text{ReCall}^{\infty} \rightarrow \mathbb{B}$

$\text{Delayed}(a, r)$

$\forall j \in \mathbb{N} : \#(\overline{b{\downarrow}_{j+1}}) \leq \text{NbRp}(s{\downarrow}_j, r)$

The first conjunct makes sure that the messages received on a are forwarded along r with a delay of at least one time unit. The second conjunct imposes a similar requirement with respect to s and b. It looks a bit different since it not only considers the ordinary messages received on s, but also the time-outs with respect to r.

7.2 The Implementation

The network pictured in Fig. 4 is specified as follows.

SeqRPCImpl ================================ **time_dependent** ==

in	$a \in \text{ReCall}^{\infty}, d \in \text{PrRpl}^{\infty}$
out	$b \in \text{ReRpl}^{\infty}, c \in \text{PrCall}^{\infty}$
loc	$r \in \text{ReCall}^{\infty}, s \in \text{ReRpl}^{\infty}$

$\text{SeqLossyRPC}(r, d, s, c) \otimes \text{SeqRPCClerk}(a, s, b, r)$

7.3 Verification

In order to prove that SeqRPCImpl implements SeqRPC we need a more general concept of refinement — namely what we refer to as conditional refinement. Let S and S' be time-dependent specifications of the same syntactic interface, and let B be a formula whose free variables are either input or output streams according to the declarations in the syntactic interface. We define S' to be a *conditional refinement* of S modulo the condition B if

$$B \wedge R_{S'} \Rightarrow R_S$$

under the assumption that any free variable is typed in accordance with its declaration in the syntactic interface.

We now prove that SeqRPCImpl is a conditional refinement of SeqRPC modulo the *condition* $\text{Cond}(c, d)$ defined below.

$$\begin{array}{|l}
\underline{\quad \text{Cond}(c,d)\quad}\rule{5cm}{0.4pt} \\[4pt]
\text{PrCall}^{\infty} \times \text{PrRpl}^{\infty} \to \mathbb{B} \\[4pt]
\rule{2cm}{0.4pt} \\[4pt]
\text{Delayed}(c,d) \wedge \text{Bounded}(c,d,\epsilon)
\end{array}$$

Remember that for any specification S, we use R_S to denote its I/O-relation. If the I/O-relation has $\Rightarrow$ as its main operator, we use A_S to denote its antecedent (assumption) and C_S to denote its consequent (commitment). Although this is normally not pointed out explicitly, the validity of the many deductions below depends on the type definitions listed in Sect. 3.1, 4.1, and also the assumptions 1-7 listed in Sect. 3.1, 4.1, 5.1.

In the following we assume that

$$a \in \text{ReCall}^{\infty} \tag{96}$$

$$r \in \text{ReCall}^{\infty} \tag{97}$$

$$b \in \text{ReRpl}^{\infty} \tag{98}$$

$$s \in \text{ReRpl}^{\infty} \tag{99}$$

$$c \in \text{PrCall}^{\infty} \tag{100}$$

$$d \in \text{PrRpl}^{\infty} \tag{101}$$

We want to prove that

$$\text{Cond}(c,d) \wedge R_{\text{SeqLossyRPC}(r,d,s,c)} \wedge R_{\text{SeqRPCClerk}(a,s,b,r)} \tag{102}$$

$$\Rightarrow R_{\text{SeqRPC}(a,d,b,c)}$$

Since

$$\text{Cond}(c,d) \Rightarrow A_{\text{SeqLossyRPC}(r,d,s,c)} \wedge A_{\text{SeqRPC}(a,d,b,c)} \tag{103}$$

it follows that 102 holds if

$$\text{Cond}(c,d) \wedge C_{\text{SeqLossyRPC}(r,d,s,c)} \wedge R_{\text{SeqRPCClerk}(a,s,b,r)} \tag{104}$$

$$\Rightarrow C_{\text{SeqRPC}(a,d,b,c)}$$

It remains to prove 104. Let a, r, b, s, c, d be such that

$$\text{Cond}(c,d) \tag{105}$$

$$C_{\text{SeqLossyRPC}(r,d,s,c)} \tag{106}$$

$$R_{\text{SeqRPCClerk}(a,s,b,r)} \tag{107}$$

It must be shown that

$$C_{\text{SeqRPC}(a,d,b,c)} \tag{108}$$

106 implies there are $q \in \text{OkFail}^\infty$, $s' \in \text{ReRpl}^\infty$ such that

$$s = ((\text{ReRpl} \cup \{\surd\}) \setminus \{\text{RPCFail}\}) \text{\textcircled{S}} s' \tag{109}$$

$$\text{RPCBehavior}(\overline{r}, \overline{d}, \overline{s'}, \overline{c}, q) \tag{110}$$

$$\text{RPCDelayed}(r, d, s', c, q) \tag{111}$$

$$\text{RPCBounded}(r, d, s', c, q) \tag{112}$$

107 implies

$$\text{RPCClerkBehavior}(a, s, b, r) \tag{113}$$

$$\text{RPCClerkDelayed}(a, s, b, r) \tag{114}$$

108 follows if we can show that

$$\text{RPCBehavior}(\overline{a}, \overline{d}, \overline{b}, \overline{c}, q) \tag{115}$$

$$\text{RPCDelayed}(a, d, b, c, q) \tag{116}$$

We first prove the following two lemmas

$$\text{Delayed}(s', b) \tag{117}$$

$$\overline{s'} = \overline{b} \tag{118}$$

Then we use 117, 118 to deduce 115, 116.

Proof of 117: 111 implies

$$\text{Delayed}(r, s') \tag{119}$$

2, 105, 112 imply

$$\text{Bounded}(r, s', \sigma) \tag{120}$$

119, 120 imply

$$\forall j \in \mathbb{N} : \#(\overline{s'\downarrow_{j+1}}) \leq \#(\overline{r\downarrow_j}) \leq \#(\overline{s'\downarrow_{j+\sigma}}) \tag{121}$$

113 implies

$$\forall k, l \in \text{dom}(\overline{r}) : k < l \Rightarrow \tag{122}$$

$$\text{tm}(r, l) - \text{tm}(r, k) > \sigma \vee \#\overline{s\downarrow_{\text{tm}(r,l)-1}} - \#\overline{s\downarrow_{\text{tm}(r,k)}} > 0$$

109, 122 imply

$$\forall k, l \in \text{dom}(\overline{r}) : k < l \Rightarrow \tag{123}$$

$$\text{tm}(r, l) - \text{tm}(r, k) > \sigma \vee \#\overline{s'\downarrow_{\text{tm}(r,l)-1}} - \#\overline{s'\downarrow_{\text{tm}(r,k)}} > 0$$

121, 123 imply

$$\forall k, l \in \text{dom}(\overline{r}) : k < l \Rightarrow \#\overline{s'\downarrow_{\text{tm}(r,l)-1}} - \#\overline{s'\downarrow_{\text{tm}(r,k)}} > 0 \tag{124}$$

119, 120, 124 imply

$$\forall k, l \in \text{dom}(\overline{r}) : k < l \Rightarrow \tag{125}$$

$$\text{tm}(r, k) < \text{tm}(s', k) < \text{tm}(r, l) < \text{tm}(s', l)$$

109, 120, 125 imply

$$\forall j \in \mathbb{N} : \text{NbRp}(s{\downarrow_j}, r) \leq \#\overline{s'{\downarrow_j}} \tag{126}$$

114 implies

$$\forall j \in \mathbb{N} : \#(\overline{b{\downarrow_{j+1}}}) \leq \text{NbRp}(s{\downarrow_j}, r) \tag{127}$$

126, 127 imply 117.

Proof of 118: 113 implies

$$(\text{ReRpl} \setminus \{\text{RPCFail}\})\text{⑤}\overline{b} = \overline{s} \tag{128}$$

$$\#\overline{b} = \text{NbRp}(s, r) \tag{129}$$

$$\forall k \in \text{dom}(\overline{r}) : \tag{130}$$

$$\text{let } m = \text{NbRp}(s{\downarrow_{\text{tm}(r,k)}}, r) + 1$$

$$\text{in } s{\downarrow_{\text{tm}(r,k)}} \frown \sqrt{}^{\sigma} \sqsubseteq s \Rightarrow \overline{b}[m] = \text{RPCFail}$$

109, 128 imply

$$(\text{ReRpl} \setminus \{\text{RPCFail}\})\text{⑤}\overline{b} = (\text{ReRpl} \setminus \{\text{RPCFail}\})\text{⑤}\overline{s'} \tag{131}$$

109, 122, 125 imply

$$\forall j \in \text{dom}(\overline{s'}) : \overline{s'}[j] = \text{RPCFail} \Rightarrow s{\downarrow_{\text{tm}(r,j)}} \frown \sqrt{}^{\sigma} \sqsubseteq s \tag{132}$$

109, 122, 125, 130, 132 imply

$$\forall j \in \text{dom}(\overline{s'}) : \overline{s'}[j] = \text{RPCFail} \Rightarrow \overline{b}[j] = \text{RPCFail} \tag{133}$$

109, 129, 131, 133 imply 118.

Proof of 115: 113 implies

$$\overline{a} = \overline{r} \tag{134}$$

110, 118, 134 imply 115.

Proof of 116: 111 implies

$$\text{Delayed}((\text{VldReCall} \times \{\text{Ok}, \text{Pfail}\})\text{®}(r, q), c) \tag{135}$$

$$\text{Delayed}(r, s') \tag{136}$$

$$\text{Delayed}(d, ((\text{PrRpl} \setminus \{\text{BadCall}\}) \times \{\text{Ok}, \text{Pfail}\})\text{®}(s', q)) \tag{137}$$

113, 114 imply

$$\overline{a} = \overline{r} \tag{138}$$

$$\text{Delayed}(a, r) \tag{139}$$

135, 138, 139 imply

$$\text{Delayed}((\text{VldReCall} \times \{\text{Ok}, \text{Pfail}\}) \circledR (a, q), c) \tag{140}$$

117, 136, 139 imply

$$\text{Delayed}(a, b) \tag{141}$$

117, 118, 137 imply

$$\text{Delayed}(d, ((\text{PrRpl} \setminus \{\text{BadCall}\}) \times \{\text{Ok}, \text{Pfail}\}) \circledR (b, q)) \tag{142}$$

140, 141, 142 imply 116.

8 Conclusions

We have employed a specification and refinement technique based on *streams* to solve the RPC-memory specification problem. We have emphasized the use of *oracles* to capture time-independent nondeterministic behavior. We find oracles intuitive. Moreover, they allow us to deal with nondeterminism in a structured way. The commitments of our specifications are all written in the form

$\exists$ *Oracle_Decls* : *Oracle_Constraint* $\wedge$ *Behavior_Constraint*

Oracle_Decls is a list of oracle declarations. *Oracle_Constraint* is a formula imposing additional constraints on the oracles. *Oracle_Constraint* is typically used to impose fairness requirements or to make sure that the oracles satisfy certain compatibility conditions. *Behavior_Constraint* is formula which for each oracle interpretation such that *Oracle_Constraint* holds, determines the (time-independent) output history as a function of the input history. If the timing is ignored *Behavior_Constraint* can easily be replaced by a functional program viewing the oracles as additional input streams. Thus, with respect to the time-independent behavior, our specifications are quite close to what one might think of as "nondeterministic" functional programs.

We have carried out detailed proofs. They are all relatively straightforward. Our proofs are not formal. However, they seem easy to formalize. The main obstacle on the road to formalization is the definitions of the new oracles in Section 5.5. They must be restated in a constructive manner. This is not technically difficult, but nevertheless quite tedious.

The use of streams to model dataflow networks was first proposed in [Kah74]. Timed streams and relations on timed streams are also well-known from the literature [Par83], [Kok87]. The same holds for oracles [Kel78], [AL88] (called prophecy variables in the latter). The presented approach is based on [BS96] which can be seen as a complete rework/relational reformulation of [BDD+93]. There are also some obvious links to Z [Spi88].

9 Acknowledgements

The author has benefited from discussions with Manfred Broy on this and related topics. A very constructive referee report by Leslie Lamport led to many improvements and simplifications. A second anonymous referee report also provided some useful remarks. Øystein Haugen read a more recent version of the paper. His detailed comments were very helpful.

References

[AL88]   M. Abadi and L. Lamport. The existence of refinement mappings. Technical Report 29, Digital, SRC, Palo Alto, 1988.

[AL95]   M. Abadi and L. Lamport. Conjoining specifications. *ACM Transactions on Programming Languages and Systems*, 17:507–533, 1995.

[BDD⁺93] M. Broy, F. Dederichs, C. Dendorfer, M. Fuchs, T. F. Gritzner, and R. Weber. The design of distributed systems — an introduction to Focus (revised version). Technical Report SFB 342/2/92 A, Technische Universität München, 1993.

[BL]   M. Broy and L. Lamport. The rpc-memory specification problem. This volume.

[BS96]   M. Broy and K. Stølen. Focus — a method for the development of interactive systems. Book manuscript, June 1996.

[Kah74]   G. Kahn. The semantics of a simple language for parallel programming. In *Proc. Information Processing*, pages 471–475. North-Holland, 1974.

[Kel78]   R. M. Keller. Denotational models for parallel programs with indeterminate operators. In *Proc. Formal Description of Programming Concepts*, pages 337–366. North-Holland, 1978.

[Kok87]   J. N. Kok. A fully abstract semantics for data flow nets. In *Proc. PARLE, Lecture Notes in Computer Science 259*, pages 351–368. Springer, 1987.

[Par83]   D. Park. The "fairness" problem and nondeterministic computing networks. In *Proc. Foundations of Computer Science, Mathematical Centre Tracts 159*, pages 133–161. Mathematisch Centrum Amsterdam, 1983.

[Spi88]   J. M. Spivey. *Understanding Z, A Specification Language and its Formal Semantics*, volume 3 of *Cambridge Tracts in Theoretical Computer Science*. Cambridge University Press, 1988.

[Stø96a]   K. Stølen. Assumption/commitment rules for data-flow networks — with an emphasis on completeness. In *Proc. ESOP, Lecture Notes in Computer Science 1058*, pages 356–372. Springer, 1996.

[Stø96b]   K. Stølen. Refinement principles supporting the transition from asynchronous to synchronous communication. *Science of Computer Programming*, 26:255–272, 1996.

A   Specifying the Hand-Shake Protocol

As pointed out in the introduction to this paper, we have not specified the hand-shake protocol on which [BL] is based. The protocol has not been left out because it cannot be expressed in our formalism. In fact, as shown below, we can easily specify the hand-shake protocol. We have ignored the hand-shake protocol because our formalism is tailored towards asynchronous communication with *unbounded* buffering. Our approach is based on the idea that the use of unbounded buffering is helpful when a system is described and reasoned about during its design — helpful because it allows us to abstract from the synchronization protocols needed in system descriptions based on bounded buffering.

Of course, at some point in a system development boundedness constraints have to be introduced — after all, any real system is based on bounded resources. To show that our approach supports the introduction of hand-shake communication, we now use conditional refinement, as defined in Sect. 7.3, to refine McImpl into a specification SynMcImpl that differs from McImpl in only one respect: the hand-shake protocol is imposed. See [Stø96b] for a detailed discussion of refinement principles supporting the introduction of synchronization in a compositional manner. The new overall specification is given below.

SynMcImpl ══════════════════════════════ time_dependent ══

in $ip \in (\mathrm{Call}^{\infty})^n$

out $op \in (\mathrm{Rpl}^{\infty})^n$

loc $cp \in (\mathrm{Call}^{\infty})^n, dp \in (\mathrm{Rpl}^{\infty})^n, ap \in (\mathrm{ReCall}^{\infty})^n, bp \in (\mathrm{ReRpl}^{\infty})^n$

$\mathrm{SynRelMc}(cp, dp) \otimes \mathrm{SynRPC}(ap, dp, bp, cp) \otimes \mathrm{SynClerk}(ip, bp, op, ap)$

To simplify the specifications of the three components we introduce an auxiliary function HandShaked.

HandShaked(a, b, j) ──────────────────────────────

$(\alpha^{\infty})^n \times (\alpha^{\infty})^n \times \mathbb{N}_{\infty} \to \mathbb{B}$

$\forall k \in [1..n], l \in [1..j] : \#(\overline{a_k{\downarrow}_l}) \leq \#(\overline{b_k{\downarrow}_{l-1}}) + 1$

α is a type variable. HandShaked(a, b, ∞) holds if for any k, l the number of messages transmitted on the channel a_k until time l is maximum one greater than the number of messages transmitted on the channel b_k until time $l-1$. The component specification SynRelMc is adapted from RelMc as follows.

$=$SynRelMc$========================$ time_dependent $==$

in $cp \in (\mathrm{Call}^{\infty})^n$

out $dp \in (\mathrm{Rpl}^{\infty})^n$

$\forall j \in \mathbb{N}_{\infty} : \mathrm{HandShaked}(cp, dp, j) \Rightarrow$

    $\exists cp' \in (\mathrm{Call}^{\infty})^n, dp' \in (\mathrm{Rpl}^{\infty})^n :$

      $R_{\mathrm{RelMc}(cp', dp')}$

      $\forall k \in [1..n] : cp_k\!\downarrow_j \sqsubseteq cp'_k \wedge dp_k\!\downarrow_{j+1} \sqsubseteq dp'_k$

The component characterized by SynRelMc is required to behave in accordance with RelMc at least one time unit longer than its environment behaves in accordance with HandShaked. This is sufficient to ensure hand-shake behavior, since RelMc requires that a reply is never output before at least one time unit after the call is transmitted. Note the relationship to the interpretation of assumption/commitment specifications in [AL95] (see also [Stø96a]).

In exactly the same way as the specifications RPC and Clerk are defined as the conjunctions of n sub-specifications, we define SynRPC and SynClerk as the conjunctions of n SeqSynRPC and SeqSynClerk specifications, respectively. We give only the specifications of the sequential components. The following auxiliary function is useful.

$\_$RplDelayed(a, b, j) $_____$

$(\alpha^{\infty})^n \times (\alpha^{\infty})^n \times \mathbb{N}_{\infty} \to \mathbb{B}$

$\forall k \in [1..n] :$

    $\forall l \in [1..j] : \#(\overline{b_k\!\downarrow_l}) \leq \#(\overline{a_k\!\downarrow_{l-1}})$

    $j = \infty \Rightarrow \#\overline{b_k} = \#\overline{a_k}$

RplDelayed is used to capture that for any message sent on a exactly one reply is received on b with a delay of at least one time unit. The sequential synchronous RPC component is specified as follows.

SeqSynRPC ———————————————————————— time_dependent ———

in $a \in \mathrm{ReCall}^{\infty}, d \in \mathrm{PrRpl}^{\infty}$

out $b \in \mathrm{ReRpl}^{\infty}, c \in \mathrm{PrCall}^{\infty}$

$\forall j \in \mathbb{N}_{\infty} : \mathrm{HandShaked}(a, b, j) \wedge \mathrm{RplDelayed}(c, d, j) \Rightarrow$

$\quad \exists\, a' \in \mathrm{ReCall}^{\infty}, d' \in \mathrm{PrRpl}^{\infty}, b' \in \mathrm{ReRpl}^{\infty}, c' \in \mathrm{PrCall}^{\infty} :$

$\quad\quad A_{\mathrm{SeqRPC}(a',d',b',c')}$

$\quad\quad C_{\mathrm{SeqRPC}(a',d',b',c')}$

$\quad\quad a{\downarrow}_j \sqsubseteq a' \wedge d{\downarrow}_j \sqsubseteq d' \wedge b{\downarrow}_{j+1} \sqsubseteq b' \wedge c{\downarrow}_{j+1} \sqsubseteq c'$

Remember that for any specification S, whose I/O-relation has $\Rightarrow$ as its main operator, we use A_S and C_S to denote its antecedent (assumption) and consequent (commitment), respectively. SeqSynRPC requires the specified component to behave in accordance with the commitment of SeqRPC at least one time unit longer than the environment of SeqSynRPC behaves in accordance with the antecedent (environment assumption) of SeqSynRPC. The sequential synchronous clerk component is specified below.

SeqSynClerk ———————————————————————— time_dependent ———

in $i \in \mathrm{Call}^{\infty}, b \in \mathrm{ReRpl}^{\infty}$

out $o \in \mathrm{ReRpl}^{\infty}, a \in \mathrm{ReCall}^{\infty}$

$\forall j \in \mathbb{N}_{\infty} : \mathrm{HandShaked}(i, o, j) \wedge \mathrm{RplDelayed}(a, b, j) \Rightarrow$

$\quad \exists\, i' \in \mathrm{Call}^{\infty}, b' \in \mathrm{ReRpl}^{\infty}, o' \in \mathrm{ReRpl}^{\infty}, a' \in \mathrm{ReCall}^{\infty} :$

$\quad\quad A_{\mathrm{SeqClerk}(i',b',o',a')}$

$\quad\quad C_{\mathrm{SeqClerk}(i',b',o',a')}$

$\quad\quad \mathrm{Delayed}(\langle \mathrm{RPCFail}, \sqrt{}\rangle \frown b', \langle \sqrt{}\rangle \frown a')$

$\quad\quad i{\downarrow}_j \sqsubseteq i' \wedge b{\downarrow}_j \sqsubseteq b' \wedge o{\downarrow}_{j+1} \sqsubseteq o' \wedge a{\downarrow}_{j+1} \sqsubseteq a'$

This specification has exactly the same structure as SeqSynRPC with the exception that an additional causality constraint is introduced to make sure that the clerk never sends a new call along a before it receives a reply on b to its previous call. Note that we could have replaced RPCFail by any other type correct message (remember that $\sqrt{}$ is not a message).

We now prove that SynMcImpl is a refinement of McImpl under the condition that a user never makes another call before it has received a reply to its previous call. In the following we assume that

$$ip \in (\mathrm{Call}^{\infty})^n \tag{143}$$

$$cp \in (\mathrm{Call}^{\infty})^n \tag{144}$$

$$op \in (\mathrm{Rpl}^{\infty})^n \tag{145}$$

$$dp \in (\mathrm{Rpl}^{\infty})^n \tag{146}$$

$$ap \in (\mathrm{ReCall}^{\infty})^n \tag{147}$$

$$bp \in (\mathrm{ReRpl}^{\infty})^n \tag{148}$$

$$j \in [1..n] \tag{149}$$

It must be shown that

$$\mathrm{HandShaked}(ip, op, \infty) \wedge R_{\mathrm{SynMcImpl}(ip,op)} \Rightarrow R_{\mathrm{McImpl}(ip,op)} \tag{150}$$

We start by proving that the sub-specifications of SynMcImpl are conditional refinements of the corresponding sub-specifications of McImpl. More explicitly, conditional refinements in the following sense

$$\mathrm{HandShaked}(cp, dp, \infty) \wedge R_{\mathrm{SynRelMc}(cp,dp)} \Rightarrow R_{\mathrm{RelMc}(cp,dp)} \tag{151}$$

$$\mathrm{HandShaked}(ap_j, bp_j, \infty) \wedge R_{\mathrm{SeqSynRPC}(ap_j,dp_j,bp_j,cp_j)} \Rightarrow \tag{152}$$

$$R_{\mathrm{SeqRPC}(ap_j,dp_j,bp_j,cp_j)}$$

$$\mathrm{HandShaked}(ip_j, op_j, \infty) \wedge R_{\mathrm{SeqSynClerk}(ip_j,bp_j,op_j,ap_j)} \Rightarrow \tag{153}$$

$$R_{\mathrm{SeqClerk}(ip_j,bp_j,op_j,ap_j)}$$

151 holds trivially. Since

$$A_{\mathrm{SeqRPC}(ap_j,dp_j,bp_j,cp_j)} \Rightarrow \mathrm{RplDelayed}(cp_j, dp_j, \infty) \tag{154}$$

$$A_{\mathrm{SeqClerk}(ip_j,bp_j,op_j,ap_j)} \Rightarrow \mathrm{RplDelayed}(ap_j, bp_j, \infty) \tag{155}$$

it is also clear that 152, 153 hold. Let ip, op be such that

$$\mathrm{HandShaked}(ip, op, \infty) \tag{156}$$

$$R_{\mathrm{SynMcImpl}(ip,op)} \tag{157}$$

150 follows if we can show that

$$R_{\mathrm{McImpl}(ip,op)} \tag{158}$$

157 implies there are cp, dp, ap, bp such that

$$R_{\mathrm{SynRelMc}(cp,dp)} \tag{159}$$

$$R_{\mathrm{SynRPC}(ap,dp,bp,cp)} \tag{160}$$

$$R_{\mathrm{SynClerk}(ip,bp,op,ap)} \tag{161}$$

151, 152, 153, 156, 159, 160, 161 imply that 158 follows if we can show that

$$\text{HandShaked}(ap, bp, \infty) \wedge \text{HandShaked}(cp, dp, \infty) \tag{162}$$

For any $k \in \mathbb{N}$, let

$$I_k \stackrel{\text{def}}{=} \text{HandShaked}(ap, bp, k) \wedge \text{HandShaked}(cp, dp, k) \tag{163}$$

$$\text{RplDelayed}(ap, bp, k) \wedge \text{RplDelayed}(cp, dp, k)$$

163 implies

$$I_0 \tag{164}$$

156, 159, 160, 161, 163 imply

$$\forall k \in \mathbb{N} : I_k \Rightarrow I_{k+1} \tag{165}$$

164, 165 and induction on k imply

$$\forall k \in \mathbb{N} : I_k \tag{166}$$

163, 166 imply 162. This ends our proof.

In Sect. 5.5 we have shown that the composite specification McImpl(ip, op) is a refinement of UnrelMc(ip, op). Above we have shown that SynMcImpl(ip, op) is a conditional refinement of McImpl(ip, op) modulo HandShaked(ip, op, ∞). By the definitions of refinement it follows that SynMcImpl(ip, op) is a conditional refinement of UnrelMc(ip, op) modulo HandShaked(ip, op, ∞).

The RPC-Memory Specification Problem: UNITY + Refinement Calculus

Rob T. Udink* & Joost N. Kok

Department of Computer Science, Leiden University,
P.O. Box 9512, 2300 RA Leiden, The Netherlands.

Abstract. We use the ImpUNITY framework to solve the "RPC-Memory Specification problem" of the Dagstuhl Workshop on reactive systems. ImpUNITY supports the development of parallel and distributed programs from specification to implementation in a stepwise manner. It is an extension of UNITY, as introduced by Chandy and Misra, with features of the Action System formalism of Back and Kurki-Suonio. Due to this extension, the ImpUNITY framework is also suitable for the *implementation phase* of the development process. It supports local variables and (remote) procedure calls and it has a UNITY like temporal logic.

1 Introduction

The UNITY framework, as introduced by Chandy and Misra [CM88], supports the idea of stepwise refinement of specifications. The framework consists of a programming language and a programming logic. The logic is based on a small set of temporal properties for describing specifications. The UNITY approach is to refine specifications towards a specific architecture until a program can be derived easily. Case studies show that the method is useful for deriving parallel and distributed algorithms [CM88]. However, it is not always easy to deal with low-level implementation details at the level of specifications. In this stage of the development process, program refinement seems to be preferable to refinement of specifications. Program refinement consists of program transformations that preserve semantic properties of the programs. The standard UNITY framework does not support program refinement, but several proposals have been put forward [San90, Sin93] where refinement is defined as preservation of (specific) properties. However, these approaches do not support refinement of components of programs and the UNITY programming language does not does not support local variables and procedure calls.

The Action System framework [BKS83, Bac90] is a framework for refinement of parallel and distributed programs. It is based on Back's Refinement Calculus [Bac93], which was originally built for preservation of total correctness, i.e.,

---

* The work of Rob Udink was carried out at the Department of Computer Science, Utrecht University. It has been supported by the Foundation for Computer Science in the Netherlands SION under project 612-317-107. Rob Udink is currently working at Philips Research Laboratories, Eindhoven.

all pre- and postcondition pairs of programs. By modeling reactive systems as sequential programs and by using data refinement, the Refinement Calculus can also be used for the refinement of reactive systems [Bac90]. The programming language supports local variables and nondeterminism. Remote procedures can be added to split programs into modules [BS94]. Refinement corresponds to the reduction of possible behaviors (sequences of states) of a program and preserves all temporal properties. However, the framework does not support temporal reasoning about programs.

The ImpUNITY framework combines UNITY and Action Systems in such a way that it supports a modular way of program design [UK95, Udi95]. Like the UNITY framework it consists of a programming language and a programming logic. ImpUNITY programs are similar to Action Systems: a program can have local variables, statements in a program may be nondeterministic and may contain (remote) procedure calls. The notion of fairness of a program execution is taken from UNITY. The ImpUNITY logic is a generalization of the UNITY logic to support the extra features of ImpUNITY programs. It is an extension of the compositional logic presented in [UHK94] which, as a generalization of the logic of Sanders [San91], takes invariants of programs in a context into account. In this way, the union theorem of UNITY (giving a way to derive properties of a composed program from properties of its components) is still valid. Program refinement is defined as preservation of all properties in any context, which, by definition, results in a compositional notion of refinement. This notion is supported by a small set of transformation rules that are flexible enough to do interesting program refinements like the refinement of the memory component proposed in the "RPC-Memory Specification Problem". The main difference between our approach and most of the other approaches presented at the workshop is that our approach is transformational. Proving refinements of the memory component is done by deriving the implementation by several applications of the program transformation rules.

The paper is organized as follows. In section 2 we present the ImpUNITY programming language using a specification of the memory component as an example. Section 3 gives a brief overview of a part of the UNITY logic. We only present properties that are needed in section 4 for defining program refinement, and for the formulation of refinement rules. Section 5 deals with the RPC-Memory Specification Problem of the workshop. The last section gives some more detail about the refinements.

2 The ImpUNITY Programming Language

An ImpUNITY program is similar to a UNITY program. We introduce the ImpUNITY language by means of an example: the specification of the memory component is given in figure 1. A program consists of several sections. In comparison with UNITY some extra sections are added to support new features, like local variables and a procedure call mechanism. A program may contain several sections for the declaration of variables. In the example, we only use a

Program *Memory*
  local *slot*[*SlotLocs*] : *SlotType*
    | *mem*[*MemLocs*] : *MemVals*
  export
    proc *call*(*a* : *CallType*) =
        IsMemcall(*a.name, a.args*)
        → **if** ‖$_i$*slot*[*i*].*stat* = *FREE*
            →   *slot*[*i*] := (*CALL, a.proc, a.name, a.args, MemFailure*)
        if
  import proc *return*(*RetType*)
  init ⟨∀*i* : *i* ∈ *MemLocs* : *mem*[*i*] = *InitVal*⟩ ∧ ⟨∀*i* : *i* ∈ *Slot* : *slot*[*i*].*stat* = *FREE*⟩
  assign
    ⟨ ‖*s* : *s* ∈ *SlotLocs* :
      slot[*s*].*stat* = *CALL*
      → **if** *IsRead*(*slot*[*s*].*name, slot*[*s*].*args*) → *slot*[*s*].*ret* := *mem*[*slot*[*s*].*args*.1]
        | *IsWrite*(*slot*[*s*].*name, slot*[*s*].*args*) → *mem*[*slot*[*s*].*args*.1] := *slot*[*s*].*args*.2
                                ; *slot*[*s*].*ret* := *FixedVal*
        | *BadArgs*(*slot*[*s*].*name, slot*[*s*].*args*) → *slot*[*s*].*ret* := *BadArgs*
        | *true*   → *slot*[*s*].*ret* := *MemFailure*
      if
    ⟩
  | ⟨ ‖*s* : *s* ∈ *SlotLocs* :
      slot[*s*].*stat* = *CALL* → *return*((*slot*[*s*].*proc, slot*[*s*].*ret*))
                    ; *slot*[*s*].*stat* := *FREE*
    ⟩
end{*Memory*}

Fig. 1. The Memory Component

local-section: a section for declaring variables that cannot be read nor written by an environment. Variables in a *shared*-section can be read and written by both the program and its environment. The memory component has two local variables, *slot* for storing information about a procedure call, and *mem* for simulating the memory. The *import*-section is used for declaring procedures that are imported by the program. Definitions of these procedures must be provided by an environment. A procedure declaration consists of the name of the procedure and the type of its argument. For simplicity, we only consider procedures with one argument, but tuples can be used to pass more than one value. The memory component imports one procedure *return* which passes a parameter of the type *RetType* = *P* × *Value*, consisting of a process identity and a value. This procedure is called by the memory component to end a read or a write operation. The *export*-section of a program is used to define the procedures that are exported. These procedures can be called both by the environment and by the program itself. A procedure definition consists of a procedure declaration, where a name is given to the parameter, and a statement on the state space of the program extended with the parameter variable. The memory component exports the procedure *call* which is called by the environment to issue a memory operation. The argument of the call procedure is of type $CallType = P \times Names \times Args$, passing the identity of the calling process, the name of the operation and a list of arguments.

To perform the operations, the memory component has to administrate the calls that it has to perform. This is done in the array *slot*. Each member of *slot* is of type $SlotType = Status \times P \times Names \times Args \times Value$, and can store information about *one* call: the status of progress, the identity of the calling procedure, the name of the operation, the argument list and the value to return. The status field is about the progress in handling the call: *FREE* indicates that the slot is free and no call is stored, *CALL* indicates that the a call is stored but has not yet returned (later on we will refine this field). On a call, the procedure looks for a free slot, stores its information and changes the status to *CALL*.

Then the call will be handled by statements in the *assign*-section that are associated with that slot. In general, the *assign*-section consists of a finite set of statements on the program variables. Like UNITY, execution of a program consists of execution of its statements in the *assign*-section. In each step, an arbitrary statement from this section (or from the environment) is executed. The fairness of UNITY is assumed: each statement is executed infinitely often. This fairness principle guarantees that each call to the memory component is eventually returned: for each slot the corresponding return statement is eventually executed. However it also shows one of the drawbacks of the UNITY type of fairness: a UNITY program only contains a fixed and finite number of statements, and hence only a finite number of slots can be served. In the memory specification this means that at any moment in time only a finite number of calls can be accepted. If this number is exceeded (no slot is free at the moment *call* is called) then the calls are not answered.

Statements of ImpUNITY programs are interpreted as (weakest precondition) predicate transformers, and we use the Refinement Calculus of Back [Bac93] to reason about them. Unlike UNITY, we allow statements that are nondeterministic, but the nondeterminism can only be demonic. To denote statements we use the command language of the refinement calculus. In this paper we will (almost) only use the assign statement and the if-statement. The if-statement

$$
\begin{aligned}
&\text{if } p_1 \rightarrow S_1 \\
&\quad \| \; p_2 \rightarrow S_2 \\
&\quad \| \; \cdots \\
&\text{if}
\end{aligned}
$$

chooses nondeterministicly one of the branches which guard evaluates to *true*. If all guards are *false*, then the statement skips, that is, it does not change the state space. This is different from the standard if-statement that aborts if no guard is *true*. The if-statement if $p \rightarrow S$ if with only one branch is abbreviated by $p \rightarrow S$.

Statements may also contain procedure calls to procedures mentioned in the *export* and *import*-sections of the program. A call consists of the name of a procedure and an expression (a function on the state space) of the proper type. For a procedure

$$proc \ d(a : int) \ = \ S,$$

a call $d(e)$ is equivalent to the execution of the statement

$$[\textbf{var } a = e. \ S]$$

where a is a variable that is initialized with the parameter and is local to statement S. So if the procedure definition is known, a call to the procedure can be resolved by substituting the call by its corresponding statement. For an ImpUNITY program, this can be done for all calls to procedures defined in the *export*-section. Calls to procedures in the *import*-section can only be resolved by composing the program with an environment that exports the procedure. If a section contains more than one item then these items are separated by a ‖, and a UNITY way of quantification is used. The *assign*-section of the memory component consists of two statements for every slot. These statements handle calls (as stored in *slot*) to the memory component. The first statement performs the requested read or write operation on the memory and decides upon the value to return. The second statement issues the return.

Finally, the *initially*-section contains a state predicate giving the set of possible initial states for a program execution.

ImpUNITY programs are meant to be composed with an environment, i.e., other ImpUNITY programs. The environment should provide imported procedures and it can call exported procedures. Together with an environment, a program can form a closed system, and can then be seen as a standard UNITY program. Composition of two programs F and G is denoted by the union $F\|G$ and is constructed similar to the UNITY way of program union. The *local*, *external* and *assign*-sections of the union consist of the union of the corresponding sections of both components. This models parallelism by interleaving of actions. The *import*-section consists of all procedures that are called but not declared in the union, and the *initially*-section of the union is the conjunction of the *initially*-sections of its components.

3 The ImpUNITY Logic

For reasoning about UNITY programs and for the formulation of specifications, Chandy and Misra give a nice and simple (temporal) logic [CM88] based on three temporal properties: unless, ensures and leadsto ($\mapsto$). A modification of this logic for reasoning about closed systems was given by Sanders [San90]. We lift both logics to ImpUNITY programs.

UNITY properties are attached to an entire program and are defined in terms of the *assign*-section of the program. In contrast to UNITY, ImpUNITY program may contain procedure calls, and bodies of procedures calls can be unknown. However, we do know that a call $d(e)$ to a procedure of $import(F)$ does not change the local variables of F. This information can be used for the refinement of a procedure call. Let X be a set of variables, and $\downarrow_X$ the predicate transformer that can change the values of all variables outside X but does not change the values of variables in X. Then $\downarrow_\emptyset$ corresponds to quantification over the state space, and for the set Y of all local variables of F, $\downarrow_Y$ is the predicate transformer that may change the values of all global variables. By replacing procedure calls by $\downarrow_Y$ we can check the properties of programs as defined in the following definition. Since we introduce more logics later, we subscript the properties by CM.

Definition 1. (Chandy-Misra Logic) Let p, q be arbitrary state predicates and F an ImpUNITY program. Define the following properties of F by

1. $p \ unless_{CM} \ q \ in \ F \ = \ \langle \forall S : S \in F : \downarrow_\emptyset ((p \wedge \neg q) \Rightarrow S(p \vee q)) \rangle$.
2. $\quad p \ ensures_{CM} \ q \ in \ F$
   $= p \ unless_{CM} \ q \ in \ F \ \wedge \ \langle \exists S : S \in F : \downarrow_\emptyset ((p \wedge \neg q) \Rightarrow S(q)) \rangle$.
3. $\mapsto$ is the the smallest binary relation $Prop$ such that
   (a) $p \ Prop \ q \ in \ F \supseteq p \ ensures_{CM} \ q \ in \ F$,
   (b) $Prop$ is transitive,
   (c) for any index set W, if $\langle \forall m : m \in W : p_m \ Prop \ q \ in \ F \rangle$
       then $\langle \exists m : m \in W : p_m \rangle \ Prop \ q \ in \ F$.

Sanders [San91] gave a modification of the UNITY logic for reasoning about programs as closed systems. For closed systems, some states are not reachable by the program, and this can be coded into the properties by taking the invariants of the program into account. A characterisation of this logic is given in the following definition. We use the subscript S for properties in this logic.

Definition 2. For an ImpUNITY program F, and predicates p, q, properties of F are defined by

$$p \ unless_S \ q \ in \ F \ = \ \langle \exists r : invariant_{CM} \ r \ in \ F : (r \wedge p) \ unless_{CM} \ q \ in \ F \rangle,$$
$$p \ ensures_S \ q \ in \ F \ = \ \langle \exists r : invariant_{CM} \ r \ in \ F : (r \wedge p) \ ensures_{CM} \ q \ in \ F \rangle,$$
$$p \mapsto_S q \ in \ F \ = \ \langle \exists r : invariant_{CM} \ r \ in \ F : (r \wedge p) \mapsto_{CM} q \ in \ F \rangle.$$

Properties in this logic can be interpreted in terms of (stutter-free) execution sequences of a program [Pac92]:

1. $p \ unless_S \ q \ in \ F$ holds if and only if for every state in every execution sequence of F, if $p \wedge \neg q$ hold, then $p \vee q$ holds in the next state.
2. $p \mapsto_S q \ in \ F$ holds if and only if whenever p holds, q will hold later on in every execution sequence of F.

To reason about ImpUNITY programs in a compositional way, ImpUNITY supports a logic that is a generalisation of the logics above [UHK94]. Here we only define the *unless*$_*$ and *ensures*$_*$ property in this logic. These properties, which are subscripted by $*$, take local invariants into account. Local invariants are invariants that cannot be disturbed by an environment. We use these properties in the formulation of program transformation rules.

Definition 3. For an ImpUNITY program F with local variables Y, the local invariant of F is defined by

$$linvariant_* \ r \ \text{in} \ F \ = \ (\downarrow_Y (r) = r) \wedge invariant_{CM} \ r \ \text{in} \ F.$$

For predicates p, q, properties of F are defined by

$$p \ unless_* \ q \ \text{in} \ F \ = \ \langle \exists r : linvariant_{CM} \ r \ \text{in} \ F : (r \wedge p) \ unless_{CM} \ q \ \text{in} \ F \rangle,$$
$$p \ ensures_* \ q \ \text{in} \ F \ = \ \langle \exists r : linvariant_{CM} \ r \ \text{in} \ F : (r \wedge p) \ ensures_{CM} \ q \ \text{in} \ F \rangle.$$

4 Program Refinement

The original UNITY framework was developed for refinement of specifications, and a specification of a program is given as a set of properties. UNITY does not support refinement of programs, but a natural notion of program refinement is preservation of properties [Sin93, UK93, UHK94]. We adopt this notion with the modification that we take locality of variables into account and that we define a compositional notion of refinement. This results in the following notion of program refinement:

Definition 4. ImpUNITY program F is refined by ImpUNITY program G, denoted $F \sqsubseteq G$, iff for every ImpUNITY program H and all state predicates p, q,

$$(\downarrow_{\overline{Y}} p) \ unless_S \ (\downarrow_{\overline{Y}} q) \ \text{in} \ F \| H \Rightarrow (\downarrow_{\overline{Z}} p) \ unless_S \ (\downarrow_{\overline{Z}} q) \ \text{in} \ G \| H,$$
$$(\downarrow_{\overline{Y}} p) \mapsto_S (\downarrow_{\overline{Y}} q) \ \text{in} \ F \| H \ \ \Rightarrow (\downarrow_{\overline{Z}} p) \mapsto_S (\downarrow_{\overline{Z}} q) \ \text{in} \ G \| H,$$

where Y is the set of local variables of $F \| H$ and Z is the set of local variables of $G \| H$, and $\overline{Y}$ and $\overline{Z}$ are the complements of Y and Z in the set of all variables.

This definition states that program refinement preserves all properties that do not depend on local variables, in any context.

Often it is difficult and tedious to prove refinements using this definition. Therefore, we provide program transformation rules that respect this notion of refinement. Although this set is not complete, it is sufficient for the refinements in this paper.

The first refinement rule concerns data refinement, the modification of local data structures. This tool is well know in the refinement calculus as refinement via a command A and is defined by $S \leq_A T \ = \ A; S \leq T; A$. Here, $\leq$ is the refinement notion of the refinement calculus corresponds to reduction of non-determinism. It is formally defined by $S \leq_A T \ = \ \langle \forall p :: A; S(p) \Rightarrow T; A(p) \rangle$ where statements are seen as predicate transformers. For replacing variables in Y by variables in Z we use $Y \sim Z$ abstractions, i.e., terminating, disjunctive predicate transformers such that $A(p \wedge \downarrow_{\overline{Y/Z}} q) \ = \ A(p) \wedge \downarrow_{\overline{Y/Z}} q$ and $A(\downarrow_Y p) = \downarrow_Z (A(q))$. We want to refine statements that may contain calls to procedures of other components. So the definition of the procedure can be unknown. We do know however that an imported procedure does not refer to the local variables of the component. The following lemma can be used to refine these procedure calls.

Lemma 5. *Let f be a state transformer and let $\langle f \rangle$ the predicate transformer $\langle f \rangle(p) = p \circ f$. If $\langle f \rangle$ is a $Y \sim Z$ abstraction and d is a procedure not referring to variables in Y, Z,*

$$d(e) \leq_{\langle f \rangle} d(e \circ f).$$

Data refinement can be used for refinement of ImpUNITY programs by refining all statements of the *assign*-section and the procedure bodies. To preserve fairness properties, statements are refined independently.

Transformation 6 (Data refinement) *Let F, G be the following programs*

Program F	**Program G**
shared *shared*	**shared** *shared*
local *locF*	**local** *locG*
export	**export**
$\langle i : i \in E : exp_i(x_i : T_i) = dF_i \rangle$	$\langle i : i \in E : exp_i(x_i : T_i) = dG_i \rangle$
import *imp*	**import** *imp*
init *initF*	**init** *initG*
assign $\langle \| i : i \in Stats : statF_i \rangle$	**assign** $\langle \| i : i \in Stats : statG_i \rangle$
end$\{F\}$	$\| \, S$
	end$\{G\}$

and let A be a $locF \sim locG$ abstraction and let $\{r\}$ be a statement based on state predicate r $(wp(\{r\}, p) = p \wedge r)$ such that

- *linvariant, r in F,*
- *$(A; \{r\}(initF)) \Leftarrow initG$,*
- *$\{r\}; dF_i \leq_A dG_i$, for all $i \in E$,*
- *$\{r\}; statF_i \leq_A statG_i$, for all $i \in Stat$, and*
- *$\{r\}; ((\bigwedge_{i \in Stats} statF_i) \wedge skip) \leq_A S$.*

Then, F is refined by G.

A special case of this transformation rule $(A = skip)$ is that we can refine statements of the program using the standard refinement calculus. However we are not allowed to introduce angelic nondeterminism nor miraculous termination. In the rewriting of statements we can use local invariants.

The structure of the set of statements in the *assign*-section of a program determines the fairness properties of the program. The following rules can be used to change this structure without losing relevant fairness properties. The first rule gives a method for combining statements.

Transformation 7 (Combining statements) *Let F be an ImpUNITY program with statements $\langle \| j : j \in J : q_j \rightarrow S \rangle$. Replacement of these statements by $\langle \exists j : j \in J : q_j \rangle \rightarrow S$ is a correct refinement*

From this rule and the (simple) data refinement rule, we can derive that statements with disjoint guards can be replaced by a single if-statement. Under certain conditions, a statement can be split into more statements using the following rule.

Transformation 8 (Splitting a statement) *Let F be an ImpUNITY program with a statement $p \wedge \langle \exists j : j \in J : q_j \rangle \to S$. Replacement of this statement by $\langle [\![j : j \in J : (p \wedge q_j) \to S \rangle$ is a correct refinement if*

- *linvariant$_*$ $(p \Rightarrow \langle \exists j : j \in J : q_j \rangle)$, and*
- *q_j unless$_*$ $\neg p$ in F, for $j \in J$.*

The last rule gives a way to strengthen the guard of a statement, i.e., the domain on which the statement stutters.

Transformation 9 (Strengthening a guard) *Let F be an ImpUNITY program with a statement $p \to S$. Replacement of this statement by $(p \wedge q) \to S$ is a correct refinement if*

- *q unless$_*$ $\neg p$ in F', and*
- *p ensures$_*$ $(q \vee \neg p)$ in F',*

where F' is the new program.

For the rules above it follows that a guard of a statement can also be strengthened with a state predicate q' if a stronger state predicate q exists for which the conditions of the last rule hold.

5 The RPC-Memory Specification Problem

In this section, we give an overview of the ImpUNITY solution of the "RPC-Memory Specification Problem". We examine the problem of the specification of the memory component and the reliable memory component and prove that the latter is an implementation of the first. Then we specify the RPC component and prove that a memory component can be implemented using an RPC component, a reliable memory component and a so-called clerk component. We do not consider the implementation of the RPC component by a lossy RPC component since this step considers absolute time which is not considered in the ImpUNITY framework.

Problem 1: The Memory Component We already gave the ImpUNITY specification of the memory component in figure 1. This component accepts read and write calls from the environment, performs the proper action and issues a return. However, the memory component can fail, in which case it returns the value *Memfailure*. In case of a write operation, the memory might have written the memory several times.

The Reliable Memory component is similar to the memory component but it cannot fail, i.e., it does not return a *MemFailure*. This can be modeled by the program in figure 2.

The Reliable Memory component is a refinement of the memory component, by eliminating the failure behavior. This is done in two steps. First, the second statement of the (Reliable) Memory component performs the proper memory

Program *Reliable Memory*
  local *slot[SlotLocs]* : *SlotType*
    ❘ *mem[MemLocs]* : *MemVals*
  export
    proc *call*(*a* : *CallType*) =
      IsMemcall(*a.name, a.args*)
      → **if** ❘$_i$ *slot[i].stat* = *FREE*
          →   *slot[i]* := (*CALL, a.proc, a.name, a.args, MemFailure*)
        if
  import proc *return*(*RetType*)
  init ⟨∀*i* : *i* ∈ *MemLocs* : *mem[i]* = *InitVal*⟩ ∧ ⟨∀*i* : *i* ∈ *SlotLoc* : *slot[i].stat* = *FREE*⟩
  assign
    ⟨ ❘$_s$: *s* ∈ *SlotLocs* :
    slot[s].stat = *CALL*
      → **if** *IsRead*(*slot[s].name, slot[s].args*)   → *slot[s].ret* := *mem[slot[s].args.1]*
        ❘ *IsWrite*(*slot[s].name, slot[s].args*)   → *mem[slot[s].args.1]* := *slot[s].args.2*
                                 ; *slot[s].ret* := *FixedVal*
        ❘ *BadArgs*(*slot[s].name, slot[s].args*) → *slot[s].ret* := *BadArgs*
      if
    ⟩
  ❘ ⟨ ❘$_s$: *s* ∈ *SlotLocs* :
    slot[s].stat = *CALL* ∧ (*ret* ≠ *MemFailure*) → *return*((*slot[s].proc, slot[s].ret*))
                                      ; *slot[s].stat* := *FREE*
    ⟩
end{*Reliable Memory*}

Fig. 2. The Reliable Memory Component

operation and decides which value to return. The Memory component can choose between a normal and a failure behavior. This nondeterminism is reduced, by (a trivial data-) refinement in the Reliable Memory. Secondly, the guard of the second statement is strengthened to delay the return until a proper memory operation has taken place (and a non-*Memfailure* can be returned). This can only be done if *Memfailure* ∉ *MemVals*, because otherwise the condition for the strengthening of guards is not satisfied.

Problem 2: The RPC Component The RPC component is an interface component between two components, a sender and a receiver. It provides a procedure-calling interface to the sender. So the component exports a call procedure (*snd_call*) and imports a return procedure (*snd_return*) and uses the slot mechanism as described before. The status field has been extended with the following values: *CALLING* indicating that the call is currently being forwarded to another component (a call was issued but has not been returned yet) and *RETURN* indicating that the call is processed and a return must be issued. Furthermore it uses the procedure-calling interface of the receiver. Therefore it imports a call procedure (*rcv_call*) and exports a return procedure (*rcv_return*).

Program *RPC*
  local *slot[SlotLocs]* : *SlotType*
  export
    proc *snd_call(a : CallType)* =
      IsRpcCall(a.name)
      → **if** ‖$_i$ *slot[i].stat = FREE*
          →   *slot[i]* := *(CALL, a.comp, a.proc, a.name, a.args, RPCFailure)*
      if
  ‖ **proc** *rcv_return(a : RetType)* =
      if *true* → *slot[a.proc].ret* := *a.val*
              ; *slot.[a.proc].stat* := *RETURN*
      ‖ *true* → *slot[a.proc].ret* := *RPCFailure*
              ; *slot.[a.proc].stat* := *RETURN*
      if
  import proc *snd_return(RetType)*
    ‖ **proc** *rcv_call(CallType)*
  init ⟨∀i : i ∈ *SlotLoc* : *slot[i].stat = FREE*⟩
  assign
    ⟨ ‖*s* : *s* ∈ *SlotLocs* :
    if *slot[s].stat = CALL*
      →   **if** *GoodCall(slot[s].args)* → *slot[s].ret* := *CALLING*
                        ; *rcv_call(s, hd(args), tl(args))*
          ‖ *BadCall(slot[s].args)* → *slot[s].ret* := *BadCall*
                        ; *slot[s].stat* := *RETURN*
         ‖ *true*   → *slot[s].ret* := *RPCFailure*
                        ; *slot[s].stat* := *RETURN*
         if
    ‖ *slot[s].stat = RETURN*
      →   *snd_return((slot[s].proc, slot[s].ret))* ; *slot[s].stat* := *FREE*
    if
    ⟩
end{*RPC*}

Fig. 3. The Remote Procedure Call Component

The procedure *RemoteCall* is the only procedure that is served by the RPC component. The argument of this call must be a list of a procedure names and some more arguments. Let *Procs* be the set of names of procedures served by the component, and let *ArgNum* a function on *Procs* yielding the number of arguments of the procedure. Procedures in *Procs* with the proper number of arguments are relayed to the receiver. This is modeled by the program in figure 3.

Problem 3: The Implementation A Memory component is implemented by combining a RPC component with a (Reliable) Memory component. The RPC component and the Memory component are given above. The implementation *Imp* will be the union of both components and an interface component *Clerk*, where

Program *Clerk*
  local *slot*[*SlotLocs*] : *SlotType*
  export
    proc *call*(*a* : *CallType*) =
      IsMemcall(*a.name*, *a.args*)
      → **if** $\|_i$ *slot*[*i*] = *FREE*
          →   *slot*[*i*] := (*CALL*, *a.proc*, *a.name*, *a.args*, *MemFailure*)
       if
  $\|$ **proc** *rpc_return*(*a* : *RetType*) =
      if *slot*[*a.proc*].*stat* = *CALLING* → *slot*[*a.proc*].*ret* := *Map*(*a.val*)
                          ; *slot*[*a.proc*].*stat* := *CALLED*
      $\|$ *slot*[*a.proc*].*stat* = *CALLING* → *slot*[*a.proc*].*ret* := *Map*(*a.val*)
                          ; *slot*[*a.proc*].*stat* := *RETURN*
      $\|$ *slot*[*a.proc*].*stat* = *TERM*   → *slot*[*a.proc*].*ret* := *Map*(*a.val*)
                          ; *slot*[*a.proc*].*stat* := *RETURN*
      if
  import proc *return*(*RetType*)
      $\|$ **proc** *rpc_call*(*CallType*)
  init $\langle \forall i : i \in SlotLoc : slot[i].stat = FREE \rangle$
  assign
    $\langle \, \| s : s \in SlotLocs :$
    if *slot*[*s*].*stat* = *CALL*   → *slot*[*s*].*stat* := *CALLING*
                         ; *rpc_call*(*s*, *RemoteCall*, *name* : *args*)
    $\|$ *slot*[*s*].*stat* = *CALLED* → *slot*[*s*].*stat* := *CALLING*
                         ; *rpc_call*(*s*, *RemoteCall*, *name* : *args*)
    $\|$ *slot*[*s*].*stat* = *RETURN* → *return*((*slot*[*s*].*proc*, (*slot*[*s*].*ret*))
                         ; *slot*[*s*].*stat* := *FREE*
    if
    $\rangle$
  $\| \, \langle \| slot : slot \in SlotLocs :$
    if *slot*[*s*].*stat* = *CALLED* → *slot*[*s*].*stat* := *RETURN*
    $\|$ *slot*[*s*].*stat* = *CALLING* → *slot*[*s*].*stat* := *TERM*
    if
    $\rangle$
end{*Clerk*}

Fig. 4. The Clerk Component

some local variables and procedures are renamed. Here we only mention that
the *rcv_call* procedure of RPC is bound to the *call* procedure of *Memory*, and
the *return* procedure of Memory is bound to *rcv_return* of RPC.

    The component *Clerk* is an interface component that accepts memory calls
and relays them, at least once, via the RPC component to the Memory component. The Clerk component provides a procedure-calling interface to the environment. So, the component exports a call procedure (*call*), imports a return

procedure (*return*), and uses the slot mechanism in which the use of the status field has been extended with the following values: *CALLED* indicating that the call was relayed to another component at least once but may be relayed another time; here *TERM* s indicating that the call is currently being forwarded to another component and on a return from this component the call itself must be returned. The state *CALLED* is introduced to allow the relay of a call to the RPC more than once. The *RETURN* state indicates that a call has finished and should be returned. By allowing the *CALLED* state on return from a relay to the RPC, a new relay is possible. To prevent the clerk from relaying a call infinitely often, the last statement (which is eventually executed) decides not to relay a call anymore by changing the status to *TERM* if the call is currently forwarded, and *RETURN* otherwise. Furthermore it uses the procedure-calling interface of the RPC component. Therefore it imports a call procedure (*rpc_call*), which is bound to *snd_call* of RPC, and exports a return procedure (*rpc_return*) to which the *snd_return* procedure of RPC is bound.

The Clerk component is given in figure 4. There *Map* is the function that maps *RPCFailure* to *MemFailure* and is the identity on all other arguments.

To show that this is a proper implementation of the Memory component we have to prove the refinement

$$Mem \sqsubseteq Imp.$$

The complete proof is rather long but all steps are applications of the refinement rules we have given before. We will give some of the main steps in the proof in the next section.

5.1   Implementing the RPC Component

Our framework does not yet support real time. Therefore, we do not address the problem of implementing the RPC component by a lossy RPC component.

6   Refinement Steps for The Memory Component

The main goal of this section is to give some feeling for the amount of work in the refinement steps of the previous section.

The refinement of the Memory component is done in three steps. First we transform the Memory component into the interface component *Clerk* combined with a component called *RPCMem*. The latter is a kind of Memory component with an interface similar to the RPC component. In the second step, the *RPCMem* component is refined to a combination of a RPC component and the Memory component. Finally the Memory component is refined by the Reliable Memory component. Next we will discuss the first step in detail, and outline the second step.

If we extract the clerk component from the memory then we obtain the program in figure 5.

Program *RPCMem*
  local *Rpc[SlotLocs]* : *SlotType*
    | *mem[MemLocs]* : *MemVals*
  export
    proc *rpc_call(a : CallType)* =
      IsRpcCall(a.name)
        → **if** |$_i$ *Rpc[i].stat* = *FREE*
           → *Rpc[i]* := (*CALL, a.proc, a.name, a.args, RPCFailure*)
        if
  import proc *rpc_return(RetType)*
  init ⟨∀*i* : *i* ∈ *MemLocs* : *mem[i]* = *InitVal*⟩ ∧ ⟨∀*i* : *i* ∈ *SlotLoc* : *Rpc[i].stat* = *FREE*⟩
  assign
    ⟨ |*r* : *r* ∈ *SlotLocs* :
      if *Rpc[r].stat* = *CALL* → **if** *IsRead(hd(Rpc[r].args), tl(Rpc[r].args))*
                   → *Rpc[r].ret* := *mem[args.2]*
               | *IsWrite(hd(Rpc[r].args), tl(Rpc[r].args))*
                   → *Rpc[r].ret* := *FixedVal* ; *mem[args.2]* := *Rpc[r].args.3*
               | *BadArgs(hd(Rpc[r].args), tl(Rpc[r].args))*
                   → *Rpc[r].ret* := *BadArg*
               | *BadCall(hd(Rpc[r].args), tl(Rpc[r].args))*
                   → *Rpc[r].ret* := *BadCall*
               | *true*
                   → *Rpc[r].ret* := *MemFailure*
               | *true*
                   → *Rpc[r].ret* := *RPCFailure*
               if
  if
  ⟩
  | ⟨ |*r* : *r* ∈ *SlotLocs* :
    Rpc[r].stat = *CALL* → **if** *rpc_return(Rpc[r].proc, Rpc[r].ret)*; *Rpc[r].stat* := *FREE*
        if
  ⟩
end{*RPCMem*}

Fig. 5. RPCMemory

Formally, the Memory component is refined by the union of the interface component *Clerk* and the program *RPCMem*:

$$\text{Memory} \sqsubseteq hide_{\{rpc\_call, rpc\_return\}}(Clerk \| RPCMem)$$

Here $hide_{\{rpc\_call, rpc\_return\}}(\cdot)$ denotes that the procedures *rpc_call* and *rpc_return* are not exported.

The steps in the proof of this refinement are as follows. We start with the Memory component of figure 1. The first step is to split the status *CALL* into the possibilities of the clerk component *CALL, CALLING, TERM, CALLED* and *RETURN*. This is done by applying the data refinement rule with invariant *true* and the the following abstraction statement (*Slot'* is the slot structure in the next program):

$$Slot[i].stat := \begin{cases} FREE & \text{if } Slot'[i] = FREE \\ CALL & \text{otherwise.} \end{cases}$$

We add three extra statements that are refinements of the skip statement. The second and third statement correspond to the second statement of the *Clerk* component. The third statement corresponds to the last statement of the *Clerk* component. The first and fourth statement of the program will become part of the *RPCMem* component, and the fourth statement is a call to the *rpc_return* procedure of *Clerk*. This results in the program of figure 6.

Using data refinement the nondeterminism of the body of the call procedure is reduced. We strengthen the guard of the first statement using *false* $\Rightarrow$ $(Slot[s].stat = CALLING) \lor (Slot[s].stat = TERM)$, *false unless*$_*$ $(Slot[s].stat = FREE)$ and $\neg(Slot[s].stat = FREE)$ *ensures*$_*$ *false* $\lor (Slot[s].stat = FREE)$.

Then we strengthen the guard of the second statement. This is done in three steps. First, it is strengthened with $(Slot[s].stat = CALLING \lor Slot[s].stat = TERM \lor Slot[s].stat = CALLED \lor Slot[s].stat = RETURN)$ using the progress of the third statement:

$$\begin{pmatrix} Slot[s].stat = CALLING \\ \lor \\ Slot[s].stat = TERM \\ \lor \\ Slot[s].stat = CALLED \\ \lor \\ Slot[s].stat = RETURN \end{pmatrix} \text{ unless}_* \ Slot[s].stat = FREE$$

$$Slot[s].stat = CALL \text{ ensures}_* \begin{pmatrix} Slot[s].stat = CALLING \\ \lor \\ Slot[s].stat = TERM \\ \lor \\ Slot[s].stat = CALLED \\ \lor \\ Slot[s].stat = RETURN \\ \lor \\ Slot[s].stat = FREE \end{pmatrix}.$$

In a similar way the guard can be strengthened by $(Slot[s].stat = TERM \lor Slot[s].stat = RETURN)$ using the progress caused by the last statement. Finally the guard is strengthened with $Slot[s].stat = RETURN$ using the progress caused by the fourth statement. This results in the program of figure 7.

Then the second and third statement are combined in one if-statement. This can be done since the guards of both statements are disjoint. Now we have the structure of the *clerk* component: the last two statements are of the *clerk* component. The second statement corresponds to a call of the *rpc_return* procedure.

```
Program Memory
    local Slot[SlotLocs] : SlotType|mem[MemLocs] : MemVals
    export
      proc call(a : CallType) =
          IsMemcall(a.name, a.args)
          → if |ᵢ Slot[i].stat = FREE
              → if true → Slot[i] := (CALL, a.proc, a.name, a.args, MemFailure)
                  | true → Slot[i] := (CALLING, a.proc, a.name, a.args, MemFailure)
                  | true → Slot[i] := (TERM, a.proc, a.name, a.args, MemFailure)
                  | true → Slot[i] := (CALLED, a.proc, a.name, a.args, MemFailure)
                  | true → Slot[i] := (RETURN, a.proc, a.name, a.args, MemFailure)
                  if
            if
    import proc return(RetType)
    init ⟨∀i : i ∈ MemLocs : mem[i] = InitVal⟩ ∧ ⟨∀i : i ∈ SlotLoc : Slot[i].stat = FREE⟩
    assign
      ⟨ |s : s ∈ SlotLocs :
        if Slot[s].stat = CALL ∨ Slot[s].stat = CALLING ∨ Slot[s].stat = TERM∨
           Slot[s].stat = CALLED ∨ Slot[s].stat = RETURN
          → if IsRead(Slot[s].name, Slot[s].args)
              →   Slot[s].ret := mem[Slot[s].args.1]
              | IsWrite(Slot[s].name, Slot[s].args)
              →   Slot[s].ret := FixedVal ; mem[Slot[s].args.1] := Slot[s].args.2
              | BadArgs(Slot[s].name, Slot[s].args) → Slot[s].ret := BadArgs
              | true → Slot[s].ret := MemFailure
              if
        if
      )
    | ⟨ |s : s ∈ SlotLocs :
        if Slot[s].stat = CALL ∨ Slot[s].stat = CALLING ∨ Slot[s].stat = TERM∨
           Slot[s].stat = CALLED ∨ Slot[s].stat = RETURN
          →   return((Slot[s].proc, Slot[s].ret)) ; Slot[s].stat := FREE
        if
      )
    | ⟨ |s : s ∈ SlotLocs :
        if (Slot[s].stat = CALL ∨ Slot[s].stat = CALLED)
          →   Slot[s].stat := CALLING ; Slot[s].ret := MemFailure
        if
      )
    | ⟨ |s : s ∈ SlotLocs :
        if Slot[s].stat = CALLING → Slot[s].stat := CALLED
          | Slot[s].stat = CALLING → Slot[s].stat := RETURN
          | Slot[s].stat = TERM    → Slot[s].stat = RETURN
        if
      )
    | ⟨ |s : s ∈ SlotLocs :
        if Slot[s].stat = CALLED  → Slot[s].stat := RETURN
          | Slot[s].stat = CALLING → Slot[s].stat := TERM
        if
      )
end{Memory}
```

Fig. 6. Memory

```
Program Memory
   local Slot[SlotLocs] : SlotType
      | mem[MemLocs] : MemVals
   export
     proc call(a : CallType) =
         IsMemcall(a.name, a.args)
         → if |ᵢ Slot[i].stat = FREE
               →   Slot[i] := (CALL, a.proc, a.name, a.args, MemFailure)
            if
   import proc return(RetType)
   init ⟨∀i : i ∈ MemLocs : mem[i] = InitVal⟩ ∧ ⟨∀i : i ∈ SlotLoc : Slot[i].stat = FREE⟩
   assign
      ⟨ |s : s ∈ SlotLocs :
        Slot[s].stat = CALLING ∨ Slot[s].stat = TERM
        → if IsRead(Slot[s].name, Slot[s].args)
              →   Slot[s].ret := mem[Slot[s].args.1]
           | IsWrite(Slot[s].name, Slot[s].args)
              →   Slot[s].ret := FixedVal ; mem[Slot[s].args.1] := Slot[s].args.2
           | BadArgs(Slot[s].name, Slot[s].args)
              →   ret := BadArgs
           | true
              →   Slot[s].ret := MemFailure
           if

      )
   | ⟨ |s : s ∈ SlotLocs :
        if Slot[s].stat = RETURN
           →   return((Slot[s].proc, Slot[s].ret)) ; Slot[s].stat := FREE
        if

      )
   | ⟨ |s : s ∈ SlotLocs :
        if (Slot[s].stat = CALL ∨ Slot[s].stat = CALLED)
           →   Slot[s].stat := CALLING ; Slot[s].ret := MemFailure
        if

      )
   | ⟨ |s : s ∈ SlotLocs :
        if Slot[s].stat = CALLING → Slot[s].stat := CALLED
           | Slot[s].stat = CALLING → Slot[s].stat := RETURN
           | Slot[s].stat = TERM    → Slot[s].stat := RETURN
        if

      )
   | ⟨ |s : s ∈ SlotLocs :
        if Slot[s].stat = CALLED  → Slot[s].stat = RETURN
           | Slot[s].stat = CALLING → Slot[s].stat = TERM
        if

      )
end{Memory}
```

Fig. 7. Memory

The first two statements both use the slot structure of this component. We remove this dependency by introducing another slot structure. This is done by superposition (data refinement).

The first two statements of the program are split using

$$q_r = (Rpc[r].stat = CALL \land Rpc[r].proc = s)$$

$$linvariant_* \begin{pmatrix} Slot[s].stat = CALLING \\ \lor \\ Slot[s].stat = TERM \end{pmatrix} \Rightarrow \langle \exists r :: \begin{pmatrix} Rpc[r].stat = CALL \\ \land \\ Rpc[r].proc = s \end{pmatrix} \rangle$$

$$\begin{pmatrix} Rpc[r].stat = CALL \\ \land \\ Rpc[r].proc = s \end{pmatrix} unless_* \mathbf{in} \neg(\begin{pmatrix} Slot[s].stat = CALLING \\ \lor \\ Slot[s].stat = TERM \end{pmatrix})$$

Now we refine the first two (sets of) statements using ordinary refinement and determine the choice of the if-statements. Then we change the use of the return field of the *Slot* structure: we postpone the updates for these fields in case the status is *CALLING* or *TERM*. This is done by data refinement. Then we rewrite some statements using the local invariants

$$linvariant_* \begin{pmatrix} Rpc[r].stat = CALL \\ \land \\ Rpc[r].proc = s \end{pmatrix} \Rightarrow \begin{pmatrix} Slot[s].stat = CALLING \\ \lor \\ Slot[s].stat = TERM \end{pmatrix}$$

$$linvariant_* \begin{pmatrix} Rpc[r].stat = CALL \\ \land \\ Rpc[r].proc = s \end{pmatrix} \Rightarrow (Rpc[r].args = name : args).$$

We also introduce the local procedure *rpc_return*. Now we combine subsets of statements of the first and second set of statements of the program. Then we can extract the *clerk* component. We split the program in the *clerk* component and the rest of the program and hide the local procedures in the union.

This concludes the first part of the refinement.

For the second part we have to show that the RPCMem component can be implemented by the union of an RPC component and a Memory component:

$$RpcMem \sqsubseteq hide_{\{rcv\_call, rcv\_return\}}(RPC' \| Memory'),$$

where

$$RPC' = RPC[rpc\_call/snd\_call][rpc\_return/snd\_return][Rpc/Slot]$$
$$Memory' = Memory[rcv\_call/call][rcv\_return/return]$$

The goal is to transform the program *RpcMem* into a composition of an RPC and a Memory component. Therefore we introduce all the constructs of the RPC component and then remove the references to these items in the rest of the program. The proof is similar to the proof of first refinement, and therefore omitted.

7 Conclusions

In this paper, we gave a brief overview of the ImpUNITY framework and successfully applied it to solve the "Specification Problem". Programs in the ImpUNITY framework may have local variables and remote procedure calls. These features play an important role in this paper.

The specification of the memory component is given by a ImpUNITY program. This program was refined, using the ImpUNITY transformation rules, towards an implementation containing a remote procedure call component. Concluding, the ImpUNITY framework is able to treat the RPC-Memory Specification Problem in a satisfactory way.

Acknowledgement We would like to thank the referees of this paper. The referees' comments were very helpful.

References

[Bac90] R.J.R. Back. Refinement calculus, part II: Parallel and reactive programs. In J.W. de Bakker, W.-P. de Roever, and G. Rozenberg, editors, *Stepwise Refinement of Distributed Systems: Models, Formalisms, Correctness*, volume 430 of *Lecture Notes in Computer Science*, pages 42–66. Springer-Verlag, 1990.

[Bac93] R.J.R. Back. Refinement calculus, lattices and higher order logic. In M. Broy, editor, *Program Design Calculi*, volume 118 of *Nato ASI Series, Series F*, pages 53–72. Springer-Verlag, 1993.

[BKS83] R.-J.R. Back and R. Kurki-Suonio. Decentralization of process nets with centralized control. In *2nd ACM SIGACT-SIGOPS Symp. on Distributed Computing*, pages 131–142. ACM, 1983.

[BS94] R.J.R. Back and K. Sere. Action systems with synchronous communication. In E.-R. Olderog, editor, *Programming Concepts, Methods and Calculi*, volume A-56 of *IFIP Transactions*, pages 107–126. IFIP, Elsevier Science Publishers B.V. (North Holland), June 1994.

[CM88] K. Mani Chandy and Jayadev Misra. *Parallel Program Design – A Foundation*. Addison-Wesley Publishing Company, Inc., 1988.

[Pac92] Jan Pachl. A simple proof of a completeness result for *leads-to* in the UNITY logic. *Information Processing Letters*, 41:35–38, 1992.

[San90] Beverly A. Sanders. Stepwise refinement of mixed specifications of concurrent programs. In M. Broy and Jones C.B., editors, *Proceedings of the IFIP Working Conference on Programming and Methods*, pages 1–25. Elsevier Science Publishers B.V. (North Holland), May 1990.

[San91] Beverly A. Sanders. Eliminating the substitution axiom from UNITY logic. *Formal Aspects of Computing*, 3(2):189–205, 1991.

[Sin93] Ambuj K. Singh. Program refinement in fair transition systems. *Acta Informatica*, 30(6):503–535, 1993.

[Udi95] Rob Udink. *Program Refinement in UNITY-like Environments*. PhD thesis, Utrecht University, September 1995.

[UHK94] R.T. Udink, T. Herman, and J.N. Kok. Progress for local variables in UNITY. In E.-R. Olderog, editor, *Programming Concepts, Methods and Calculi*, volume A-56 of *IFIP Transactions*, pages 127–146. IFIP, Elseviers Science Publishers B.V. (North Holland), June 1994.

[UK93] R.T. Udink and J.N. Kok. Two fully abstract models for UNITY. In Eike Best, editor, *CONCUR'93, Proceedings of the 4th International Conference on Concurrency Theory*, volume 715 of *Lecture Notes in Computer Science*, pages 339–352. Springer-Verlag, August 1993.

[UK95] R.T. Udink and J.N. Kok. ImpUNITY: UNITY with procedures and local variables. In Bernhard Möller, editor, *Mathematics of Program Construction*, volume 947 of *Lecture Notes in Computer Science*, pages 452–472. Springer-Verlag, 1995.

List of Authors

Martín Abadi 21

Egidio Astesiano 67

Dieter Barnard 213

Eike Best 109

Johan Blom 161

Manfred Broy 1, 5, 183

Jorge Cuéllar 213

Reinhard Gotzhein 253

Jozef Hooman 275

Martin Huber 213

Hardi Hungar 305

Bengt Jonsson 161

Nils Klarlund 341

Joost N. Kok 521

Reino Kurki-Suonio 375

Leslie Lamport 1, 21

Kim G. Larsen 405

Stephan Merz 5, 21

Mogens Nielsen 341

Gianna Reggio 67

Judi Romijn 437

Katharina Spies 5

Bernhard Steffen 405

Ketil Stølen 477

Kim Sunesen 341

Rob T. Udink 521

Carsten Weise 405

Lecture Notes in Computer Science

For information about Vols. 1–1099

please contact your bookseller or Springer-Verlag

Vol. 1100: B. Pfitzmann, Digital Signature Schemes. XVI, 396 pages. 1996.

Vol. 1101: M. Wirsing, M. Nivat (Eds.), Algebraic Methodology and Software Technology. Proceedings, 1996. XII, 641 pages. 1996.

Vol. 1102: R. Alur, T.A. Henzinger (Eds.), Computer Aided Verification. Proceedings, 1996. XII, 472 pages. 1996.

Vol. 1103: H. Ganzinger (Ed.), Rewriting Techniques and Applications. Proceedings, 1996. XI, 437 pages. 1996.

Vol. 1104: M.A. McRobbie, J.K. Slaney (Eds.), Automated Deduction – CADE-13. Proceedings, 1996. XV, 764 pages. 1996. (Subseries LNAI).

Vol. 1105: T.I. Ören, G.J. Klir (Eds.), Computer Aided Systems Theory – CAST '94. Proceedings, 1994. IX, 439 pages. 1996.

Vol. 1106: M. Jampel, E. Freuder, M. Maher (Eds.), Over-Constrained Systems. X, 309 pages. 1996.

Vol. 1107: J.-P. Briot, J.-M. Geib, A. Yonezawa (Eds.), Object-Based Parallel and Distributed Computation. Proceedings, 1995. X, 349 pages. 1996.

Vol. 1108: A. Díaz de Ilarraza Sánchez, I. Fernández de Castro (Eds.), Computer Aided Learning and Instruction in Science and Engineering. Proceedings, 1996. XIV, 480 pages. 1996.

Vol. 1109: N. Koblitz (Ed.), Advances in Cryptology – Crypto '96. Proceedings, 1996. XII, 417 pages. 1996.

Vol. 1110: O. Danvy, R. Glück, P. Thiemann (Eds.), Partial Evaluation. Proceedings, 1996. XII, 514 pages. 1996.

Vol. 1111: J.J. Alferes, L. Moniz Pereira, Reasoning with Logic Programming. XXI, 326 pages. 1996. (Subseries LNAI).

Vol. 1112: C. von der Malsburg, W. von Seelen, J.C. Vorbrüggen, B. Sendhoff (Eds.), Artificial Neural Networks – ICANN 96. Proceedings, 1996. XXV, 922 pages. 1996.

Vol. 1113: W. Penczek, A. Szałas (Eds.), Mathematical Foundations of Computer Science 1996. Proceedings, 1996. X, 592 pages. 1996.

Vol. 1114: N. Foo, R. Goebel (Eds.), PRICAI'96: Topics in Artificial Intelligence. Proceedings, 1996. XXI, 658 pages. 1996. (Subseries LNAI).

Vol. 1115: P.W. Eklund, G. Ellis, G. Mann (Eds.), Conceptual Structures: Knowledge Representation as Interlingua. Proceedings, 1996. XIII, 321 pages. 1996. (Subseries LNAI).

Vol. 1116: J. Hall (Ed.), Management of Telecommunication Systems and Services. XXI, 229 pages. 1996.

Vol. 1117: A. Ferreira, J. Rolim, Y. Saad, T. Yang (Eds.), Parallel Algorithms for Irregularly Structured Problems. Proceedings, 1996. IX, 358 pages. 1996.

Vol. 1118: E.C. Freuder (Ed.), Principles and Practice of Constraint Programming — CP 96. Proceedings, 1996. XIX, 574 pages. 1996.

Vol. 1119: U. Montanari, V. Sassone (Eds.), CONCUR '96: Concurrency Theory. Proceedings, 1996. XII, 751 pages. 1996.

Vol. 1120: M. Deza. R. Euler, I. Manoussakis (Eds.), Combinatorics and Computer Science. Proceedings, 1995. IX, 415 pages. 1996.

Vol. 1121: P. Perner, P. Wang, A. Rosenfeld (Eds.), Advances in Structural and Syntactical Pattern Recognition. Proceedings, 1996. X, 393 pages. 1996.

Vol. 1122: H. Cohen (Ed.), Algorithmic Number Theory. Proceedings, 1996. IX, 405 pages. 1996.

Vol. 1123: L. Bougé, P. Fraigniaud, A. Mignotte, Y. Robert (Eds.), Euro-Par'96. Parallel Processing. Proceedings, 1996, Vol. I. XXXIII, 842 pages. 1996.

Vol. 1124: L. Bougé, P. Fraigniaud, A. Mignotte, Y. Robert (Eds.), Euro-Par'96. Parallel Processing. Proceedings, 1996, Vol. II. XXXIII, 926 pages. 1996.

Vol. 1125: J. von Wright, J. Grundy, J. Harrison (Eds.), Theorem Proving in Higher Order Logics. Proceedings, 1996. VIII, 447 pages. 1996.

Vol. 1126: J.J. Alferes, L. Moniz Pereira, E. Orlowska (Eds.), Logics in Artificial Intelligence. Proceedings, 1996. IX, 417 pages. 1996. (Subseries LNAI).

Vol. 1127: L. Böszörményi (Ed.), Parallel Computation. Proceedings, 1996. XI, 235 pages. 1996.

Vol. 1128: J. Calmet, C. Limongelli (Eds.), Design and Implementation of Symbolic Computation Systems. Proceedings, 1996. IX, 356 pages. 1996.

Vol. 1129: J. Launchbury, E. Meijer, T. Sheard (Eds.), Advanced Functional Programming. Proceedings, 1996. VII, 238 pages. 1996.

Vol. 1130: M. Haveraaen, O. Owe, O.-J. Dahl (Eds.), Recent Trends in Data Type Specification. Proceedings, 1995. VIII, 551 pages. 1996.

Vol. 1131: K.H. Höhne, R. Kikinis (Eds.), Visualization in Biomedical Computing. Proceedings, 1996. XII, 610 pages. 1996.

Vol. 1132: G.-R. Perrin, A. Darte (Eds.), The Data Parallel Programming Model. XV, 284 pages. 1996.

Vol. 1133: J.-Y. Chouinard, P. Fortier, T.A. Gulliver (Eds.), Information Theory and Applications II. Proceedings, 1995. XII, 309 pages. 1996.

Vol. 1134: R. Wagner, H. Thoma (Eds.), Database and Expert Systems Applications. Proceedings, 1996. XV, 921 pages. 1996.

Vol. 1135: B. Jonsson, J. Parrow (Eds.), Formal Techniques in Real-Time and Fault-Tolerant Systems. Proceedings, 1996. X, 479 pages. 1996.

Vol. 1136: J. Diaz, M. Serna (Eds.), Algorithms – ESA '96. Proceedings, 1996. XII, 566 pages. 1996.

Vol. 1137: G. Görz, S. Hölldobler (Eds.), KI-96: Advances in Artificial Intelligence. Proceedings, 1996. XI, 387 pages. 1996. (Subseries LNAI).

Vol. 1138: J. Calmet, J.A. Campbell, J. Pfalzgraf (Eds.), Artificial Intelligence and Symbolic Mathematical Computation. Proceedings, 1996. VIII, 381 pages. 1996.

Vol. 1139: M. Hanus, M. Rogriguez-Artalejo (Eds.), Algebraic and Logic Programming. Proceedings, 1996. VIII, 345 pages. 1996.

Vol. 1140: H. Kuchen, S. Doaitse Swierstra (Eds.), Programming Languages: Implementations, Logics, and Programs. Proceedings, 1996. XI, 479 pages. 1996.

Vol. 1141: H.-M. Voigt, W. Ebeling, I. Rechenberg, H.-P. Schwefel (Eds.), Parallel Problem Solving from Nature – PPSN IV. Proceedings, 1996. XVII, 1.050 pages. 1996.

Vol. 1142: R.W. Hartenstein, M. Glesner (Eds.), Field-Programmable Logic. Proceedings, 1996. X, 432 pages. 1996.

Vol. 1143: T.C. Fogarty (Ed.), Evolutionary Computing. Proceedings, 1996. VIII, 305 pages. 1996.

Vol. 1144: J. Ponce, A. Zisserman, M. Hebert (Eds.), Object Representation in Computer Vision. Proceedings, 1996. VIII, 403 pages. 1996.

Vol. 1145: R. Cousot, D.A. Schmidt (Eds.), Static Analysis. Proceedings, 1996. IX, 389 pages. 1996.

Vol. 1146: E. Bertino, H. Kurth, G. Martella, E. Montolivo (Eds.), Computer Security – ESORICS 96. Proceedings, 1996. X, 365 pages. 1996.

Vol. 1147: L. Miclet, C. de la Higuera (Eds.), Grammatical Inference: Learning Syntax from Sentences. Proceedings, 1996. VIII, 327 pages. 1996. (Subseries LNAI).

Vol. 1148: M.C. Lin, D. Manocha (Eds.), Applied Computational Geometry. Proceedings, 1996. VIII, 223 pages. 1996.

Vol. 1149: C. Montangero (Ed.), Software Process Technology. Proceedings, 1996. IX, 291 pages. 1996.

Vol. 1150: A. Hlawiczka, J.G. Silva, L. Simoncini (Eds.), Dependable Computing – EDCC-2. Proceedings, 1996. XVI, 440 pages. 1996.

Vol. 1151: Ö. Babaoğlu, K. Marzullo (Eds.), Distributed Algorithms. Proceedings, 1996. VIII, 381 pages. 1996.

Vol. 1152: T. Furuhashi, Y. Uchikawa (Eds.), Fuzzy Logic, Neural Networks, and Evolutionary Computation. Proceedings, 1995. VIII, 243 pages. 1996. (Subseries LNAI).

Vol. 1153: E. Burke, P. Ross (Eds.), Practice and Theory of Automated Timetabling. Proceedings, 1995. XIII, 381 pages. 1996.

Vol. 1154: D. Pedreschi, C. Zaniolo (Eds.), Logic in Databases. Proceedings, 1996. X, 497 pages. 1996.

Vol. 1155: J. Roberts, U. Mocci, J. Virtamo (Eds.), Broadbank Network Teletraffic. XXII, 584 pages. 1996.

Vol. 1156: A. Bode, J. Dongarra, T. Ludwig, V. Sunderam (Eds.), Parallel Virtual Machine – EuroPVM '96. Proceedings, 1996. XIV, 362 pages. 1996.

Vol. 1157: B. Thalheim (Ed.), Conceptual Modeling – ER '96. Proceedings, 1996. XII, 489 pages. 1996.

Vol. 1158: S. Berardi, M. Coppo (Eds.), Types for Proofs and Programs. Proceedings, 1995. X, 296 pages. 1996.

Vol. 1159: D.L. Borges, C.A.A. Kaestner (Eds.), Advances in Artificial Intelligence. Proceedings, 1996. XI, 243 pages. (Subseries LNAI).

Vol. 1160: S. Arikawa, A.K. Sharma (Eds.), Algorithmic Learning Theory. Proceedings, 1996. XVII, 337 pages. 1996. (Subseries LNAI).

Vol. 1161: O. Spaniol, C. Linnhoff-Popien, B. Meyer (Eds.), Trends in Distributed Systems. Proceedings, 1996. VIII, 289 pages. 1996.

Vol. 1162: D.G. Feitelson, L. Rudolph (Eds.), Job Scheduling Strategies for Parallel Processing. Proceedings, 1996. VIII, 291 pages. 1996.

Vol. 1163: K. Kim, T. Matsumoto (Eds.), Advances in Cryptology – ASIACRYPT '96. Proceedings, 1996. XII, 395 pages. 1996.

Vol. 1164: K. Berquist, A. Berquist (Eds.), Managing Information Highways. XIV, 417 pages. 1996.

Vol. 1165: J.-R. Abrial, E. Börger, H. Langmaack (Eds.), Formal Methods for Industrial Applications. VIII, 511 pages. 1996.

Vol. 1166: M. Srivas, A. Camilleri (Eds.), Formal Methods in Computer-Aided Design. Proceedings, 1996. IX, 470 pages. 1996.

Vol. 1167: I. Sommerville (Ed.), Software Configuration Management. VII, 291 pages. 1996.

Vol. 1168: I. Smith, B. Faltings (Eds.), Advances in Case-Based Reasoning. Proceedings, 1996. IX, 531 pages. 1996. (Subseries LNAI).

Vol. 1169: M. Broy, S. Merz, K. Spies (Eds.), Formal Systems Specification. XXIII, 541 pages. 1996.

Vol. 1170: M. Nagl (Ed.), Building Tightly Integrated Software Development Environments: The IPSEN Approach. IX, 709 pages. 1996.

Vol. 1171: A. Franz, Automatic Ambiguity Resolution in Natural Language Processing. XIX, 155 pages. 1996. (Subseries LNAI).

Vol. 1172: J. Pieprzyk, J. Seberry (Eds.), Information Security and Privacy. Proceedings, 1996. IX, 333 pages. 1996.

Vol. 1173: W. Rucklidge, Efficient Visual Recognition Using the Hausdorff Distance. XIII, 178 pages. 1996.

Vol. 1174: R. Anderson (Ed.), Information Hiding. Proceedings, 1996. VIII, 351 pages. 1996.

Vol. 1175: K.G. Jeffery, J. Král, M. Bartošek (Eds.), SOFSEM'96: Theory and Practice of Informatics. Proceedings, 1996. XII, 491 pages. 1996.

Vol. 1176: S. Miguet, A. Montanvert, S. Ubéda (Eds.), Discrete Geometry for Computer Imagery. Proceedings, 1996. XI, 349 pages. 1996.

Vol. 1177: J.P. Müller, The Design of Intelligent Agents. XV, 227 pages. 1996. (Subseries LNAI).